ALAN GREENSPAN

THE AGE OF TURBULENCE

ADVENTURES IN A NEW WORLD

THE PENGUIN PRESS | NEW YORK | 2007

THE PENGUIN PRESS
Published by the Penguin Group
Penguin Group (USA) Inc., 375 Hudson Street, New York, New York 10014, U.S.A. • Penguin Group
(Canada), 90 Eglinton Avenue East, Suite 700, Toronto, Ontario, Canada M4P 2Y3 (a division of Pearson
Penguin Canada Inc.) • Penguin Books Ltd, 80 Strand, London WC2R 0RL, England • Penguin Ireland,
25 St. Stephen's Green, Dublin 2, Ireland (a division of Penguin Books Ltd) • Penguin Books Australia
Ltd, 250 Camberwell Road, Camberwell, Victoria 3124, Australia (a division of Pearson Australia Group
Pty Ltd) • Penguin Books India Pvt Ltd, 11 Community Centre, Panchsheel Park, New Delhi–110 017,
India • Penguin Group (NZ), 67 Apollo Drive, Rosedale, North Shore 0745, Auckland, New Zealand
(a division of Pearson New Zealand Ltd.) • Penguin Books (South Africa) (Pty) Ltd,
24 Sturdee Avenue, Rosebank, Johannesburg 2196, South Africa

Penguin Books Ltd, Registered Offices:
80 Strand, London WC2R 0RL, England

First published in 2007 by The Penguin Press,
a member of Penguin Group (USA) Inc.

3   5   7   9   10   8   6   4   2

Library of Congress Cataloging-in-Publication Data
Greenspan, Alan, 1926–
The age of turbulence : adventures in a new world / by Alan Greenspan.
p.   cm.
Includes bibliographical references and index.
ISBN 978-1-59420-147-9
1. Greenspan, Alan, 1926–   2. Government economists—United States—Biography.
3. United States—Economic conditions—1945–   I. Title
HB119.G74A3 2007
332.1'1092—dc22
[B]
2007013169

Printed in the United States of America

Designed by Amanda Dewey

FOR MY BELOVED ANDREA

CONTENTS

The sun was breaking through the overcast as I arrived in Tokyo on a warm day in June 2007. I'd come to exchange insights with bankers, insurance executives, and financiers, several of whom I've known for years. In the meetings that followed, they expressed growing concern about the rapid aging of Japan's population and the sluggishness of its growth compared with the glory days of the 1970s and 1980s—worries compounded by the fact that other parts of East Asia, led by China, have been experiencing one of the most extraordinary economic booms in history.

I agree that Japan's challenges are significant. My views, however, are more nuanced and less gloomy than those of my hosts. Without question, gigantic changes are afoot. Japan and the rest of the developed world are in the process of ceding a significant part of their long-held economic hegemony to the high-growth economies of East Asia, especially China, Korea, Singapore, Hong Kong, Taiwan, Malaysia, and Thailand. Between 2000 and 2006, these economies significantly increased their share of world gross domestic product (GDP) and the World Bank projects that share to rise further by 2030.

As recently as 1997, much of this region was engulfed in a severe financial crisis, requiring a massive international bailout. How were these economies able to transform themselves in less than a decade from distressed borrowers into leading-edge dynamos? A first, crucial step was to jettison the fixed-rate currency regimes that, by shackling their economies to the U.S. dollar, gave rise to financial practices that almost did them in. The carry trade, as these ill-advised practices were known, entailed borrowing from industrialized nations at pegged exchange rates and in effect relending the money, unhedged, at what were then higher domestic interest rates. It was profitable for a while, but it ultimately led to cascading defaults that spread from East Asia to Russia and even threatened the United States.

I explore this crisis later in this book, including the question of why China, which was not yet fully engaged in international finance, was able to ride out the calamity unscathed. Today, China and the newly industrialized economies of East Asia exhibit real GDP annual growth rates ranging between 4 and 10 percent, far in excess of the growth rates of Japan and the developed economies of the West. Inflation rates are in the single digits, as are long-term interest rates.

How the export-growth model developed in Japan, embraced later by the "Asian Tigers" and still later by China, propelled East Asia to utterly unexpected levels of prosperity is a main theme of this book. Today Japan and China alone generate a fourth of the world saving that finances global investment. The newly industrialized economies of East Asia supply an additional 5 percent. I view the end of the cold war as the most significant *economic* event of recent history, because it unleashed the vast, educated, but low-wage workforce not only of Eastern Europe but also of much of what was then called the third world, especially China, to participate in the competitive world market. Communist China's subtle shift toward market capitalism accelerated after the fall of the Berlin Wall revealed central planning as a failed and unworkable economic system.

Foreign direct investment in China, encouraged by increasing protection of property rights, surged from $4 billion in 1991 to more than $70 billion a year by 2006. The application of the advanced technologies embodied in that imported capital drove Chinese growth, supported by an explosive increase in exports, to double-digit rates. Much of Japanese and other East Asian exports became reoriented—shipped to China for low-cost final fabrication before being launched anew into the markets of the developed world, especially the United States.

While this explosion of economic growth in the economies of East Asia has been a boon to global economic activity, it cannot be expected to continue indefinitely. First, technology borrowed from Japan and the West has enabled East Asian productivity levels to soar far beyond those of the developed world, which, being at the cutting edge of technology, can advance incrementally only with innovation. Current East Asian productivity growth levels ranging from 3½ to 9 percent will eventually have to slide back to no more than 3 percent annually, a number I identify in later chapters as the maximum that can be engendered by advances in human knowledge. That, however, may be many years in the future.

In the interim, East Asia is flying high. Even Japan, which accounts for the major share of total East Asian GDP by far, is beginning to shake off the fifteen years of stagnation that followed the collapse of its stock and real estate markets in 1990. Confronting a rapidly aging population, it is beginning to stir out of a virtual financial isolation that hit a peak in 2003, an aspect of which was the almost patriotic imperative felt by most Japanese to invest their ample savings in yen-denominated assets. This self-imposed reluctance to invest abroad led huge amounts of savings, especially from households, insurance companies, and pension funds, to be invested in Japanese government bonds (JGBs), either directly or indirectly through Japan's vast postal savings system. The flood of yen drove JGB ten-year maturity yields down to 0.5 percent, incomprehensibly low compared with ten-year U.S. treasuries, which yielded 3.6 percent at the time. Only 3 percent of JGBs were held outside of Japan (and then largely in international bond funds that required diversification), while more than a third of U.S. treasuries were held abroad. Low long-term rates enabled the Bank of Japan to hold short-term rates close to zero.

The spread between these suppressed yen-denominated interest rates and those in the rest of the world fostered another kind of carry trade. Instead of capitalizing on the higher yields abroad, the Japanese were indirectly lending yen at low interest rates to foreigners, enabling them to turn around and invest to their profit in higher-yielding assets, often securities with very little credit risk. The yield spreads became so large as to absorb much of the exchange rate risk. The Japanese, in effect, were subsidizing foreign investors. But since 2003, that has changed. Japanese investors, apparently fed up with low rates of return, have begun to look increasingly beyond their borders. The effect has been to remove much of Japan's "home bias." Net foreign acquisitions by Japanese investors rose from ¥3.4 trillion in the first quarter of 2003 to ¥6.7 trillion in the first quarter of 2007. Since 2003, as postal savings system deposits shrank by almost 20 percent, more than a third of the issuance of JGBs has had to be financed abroad. The withdrawal of domestic demand and the need to attract foreign demand for JGBs pressed the interest rates on ten-year JGBs up to 2 percent—still low, but a substantial increase. Japanese household purchases of shares in trusts invested substantially in foreign assets have soared.

As Japanese investors have become more active globally, Japanese banks have reasserted themselves as a global presence. And as real estate prices stabilized in 2006, Japanese banks returned to normal lending after years of inhibition and restraint. In short, Japan is gradually rejoining the club of "regular" economies as its deflation ebbs and its growth rate picks up.

Without question, Japan faces a daunting future characterized by a declining population and labor force, as I will discuss. Unless this is reversed by a surprising rise in the birth rate or a culture-clashing opening up of Japan to large-scale immigration, the country's international presence will likely fade as its share of global, and East Asian, GDP declines. All the same, however, Japan will remain wealthy, a formidable world force in both technology and finance. And the twenty-first century should be kind to all the economies of East Asia, as China, Korea, Singapore, Taiwan, and other stars emerge to claim their shares of prosperity and growth.

INTRODUCTION

On the afternoon of September 11, 2001, I was flying back to Washington on Swissair Flight 128, returning home from a routine international bankers' meeting in Switzerland. I'd been moving about the cabin when the chief of the security detail that escorted me on trips abroad, Bob Agnew, stopped me in the aisle. Bob is an ex–Secret Service man, friendly but not especially talkative. At that moment, he was looking grim. "Mr. Chairman," he said quietly, "the captain needs to see you up front. Two planes have flown into the World Trade Center." I must have had a quizzical look on my face because he added, "I'm not joking."

In the cockpit, the captain appeared quite nervous. He told us there had been a terrible attack against our country—several airliners had been hijacked and two flown into the World Trade Center and one into the Pentagon. Another plane was missing. That was all the information he had, he said in his slightly accented English. We were returning to Zurich, and he was not going to announce the reason to the other passengers.

"Do we have to go back?" I asked. "Can we land in Canada?" He said no, his orders were to head to Zurich.

I went back to my seat as the captain announced that air traffic control had directed us to Zurich. The phones on the seats immediately became jammed, and I couldn't get through to the ground. The Federal Reserve colleagues who had been with me in Switzerland that weekend were already on other flights. So with no way to know how events were developing, I had nothing to do but think for the next three and a half hours. I looked out the window, the work I'd brought along, the piles of memos and economic reports, forgotten in my bag. Were these attacks the beginning of some wider conspiracy?

My immediate concern was for my wife—Andrea is NBC's chief foreign affairs correspondent in Washington. She wasn't in New York, which was one big relief, and visiting the Pentagon hadn't been on her agenda that day. I assumed she would be at the NBC bureau in the middle of town, heavily involved in covering the news. So I wasn't deeply worried, I told myself . . . but what if she'd gone on a last-minute visit to some general in the Pentagon?

I worried about my colleagues at the Federal Reserve. Were they safe? And their families? The staff would be scrambling to respond to the crisis. This attack—the first on U.S. soil since Pearl Harbor—would throw the country into turmoil. The question I needed to focus on was whether the economy would be damaged.

The possible economic crises were all too evident. The worst, which I thought highly unlikely, would be a collapse of the financial system. The Federal Reserve is in charge of the electronic payment systems that transfer more than $4 trillion a day in money and securities between banks all over the country and much of the rest of the world.

We'd always thought that if you wanted to cripple the U.S. economy, you'd take out the payment systems. Banks would be forced to fall back on inefficient physical transfers of money. Businesses would resort to barter and IOUs; the level of economic activity across the country could drop like a rock.

During the cold war, as a precaution against nuclear attack, the Federal Reserve had built a large number of redundancies into the communication and computer facilities on which the money system relies. We have all sorts of safeguards so that, for example, the data of one Federal Reserve bank are backed up at another Federal Reserve bank hundreds of miles away or in some remote location. In the event of a nuclear attack, we'd be back up and running in all nonirradiated areas very quickly. This system was the one Roger Ferguson, the vice chairman of the Fed, would be calling on this day. I was confident that he and our colleagues would be taking the necessary steps to keep the world dollar system flowing.

Yet even as I thought about it, I doubted that physically disrupting the financial system was what the hijackers had in mind. Much more likely, this was meant to be a symbolic act of violence against capitalist America—like the bomb in the parking garage of the World Trade Center eight years earlier. What worried me was the fear such an attack would create—especially if there were additional attacks to come. In an economy as sophisticated as ours, people have to interact and exchange goods and services constantly, and the division of labor is so finely articulated that every household depends on commerce simply to survive. If people withdraw from everyday economic life—if investors dump their stocks, or businesspeople back away from trades, or citizens stay home for fear of going to malls and being exposed to suicide bombers—there's a snowball effect. It's the psychology that leads to panics and recessions. A shock like the one we'd just sustained could cause a massive withdrawal from, and major contraction in, economic activity. The misery could multiply.

Long before my flight touched down, I'd concluded that the world was about to change in ways that I could not yet define. The complacency we Americans had embraced for the decade following the end of the cold war had just been shattered.

We finally reached Zurich just after 8:30 p.m. local time—still early afternoon in the United States. Swiss banking officials met me as I got off the plane and rushed me to a private room in the departure lounge. They offered to show videos of the Twin Towers coming down and the fires at the Pentagon, but I declined. I'd worked in the neighborhood of the World Trade Center for much of my life and had friends and acquaintances there. I assumed the death tolls would be horrendous and would include people I knew. I didn't want to see the destruction. I just wanted a phone that worked.

I finally reached Andrea on her cell phone a few minutes before nine, and it was a great relief to hear her voice. Once we'd assured each other we were okay, she told me she had to rush: she was on the set, about to go on the air with an update of the day's events. I said, "Just tell me quickly what's happening there."

She was holding the cell phone to one ear while the special-events producer in New York was on her earpiece in the other ear, almost shouting, "Andrea, Tom Brokaw is coming to you! Are you ready?" All she had time to say was, "Listen up." With that, she put the open cell phone on her lap and addressed the cameras. I heard exactly what America was hearing at that point—that the missing United Flight 93 had crashed in Pennsylvania.

I was then able to get a call through to Roger Ferguson at the Fed. We ran through our crisis-management checklist, and just as I'd figured, he had things well in hand. Then, with all civilian air travel to the United States shut down, I contacted Andy Card, the White House chief of staff, to request transportation back to Washington. Finally I went back to the hotel, escorted by my security detail, to get some sleep and await instructions.

By daybreak I was airborne again, on the flight deck of a United States Air Force KC-10 tanker—it may have been the only aircraft available. The crew was used to flying refueling sorties over the North Atlantic. The mood in the cockpit was somber: "You'll never believe this," the captain said. "Listen." I put my ear to the headset but couldn't hear anything other than static. "Normally the North Atlantic is full of radio chatter," he explained. "This silence is eerie." Apparently nobody else was out there.

As we came down the eastern seaboard and entered prohibited U.S. airspace, we were met and escorted by a couple of F16 fighters. The captain got permission to fly over what had been the site of the Twin Towers at the southern tip of Manhattan, now a smoking ruin. For decades, my offices had never been more than a few blocks from there; during the late 1960s and early 1970s I had watched day by day as the Twin Towers went up. Now, from thirty-five thousand feet, their smoky wreckage was New York's most visible landmark.

I went straight to the Fed that afternoon, driven with a police escort through barricaded streets. Then we went to work.

For the most part, the electronic flows of funds were doing fine. But with civilian air traffic shut down, the transportation and clearing of good old-fashioned checks were being delayed. That was a technical problem—a substantial one, but one that the staff and the individual Federal Reserve banks were entirely capable of handling by temporarily extending additional credit to commercial banks.

I spent most of my time in the days that followed watching and listening for signs of a catastrophic economic slowdown. For seven months before 9/11, the economy had been in a very minor recession, still shaking off the effects of the dot-com crash of 2000. But things had started to turn around. We had rapidly been lowering interest rates, and the markets were beginning to stabilize. By late August public interest had shifted from the economy to Gary Condit, the California congressman whose less-than-forthcoming statements about a missing young woman dominated the nightly news. Andrea couldn't get on the air with anything of global significance, and I remember thinking how incredible that seemed—the world must be in pretty good shape if the TV news focused mainly on domestic scandal. Within the Fed, the biggest issue we faced was how far to lower interest rates.

After 9/11, the reports and statistics streaming in from the Federal Reserve banks told a very different story. The Federal Reserve System consists of twelve banks strategically situated around the country. Each one lends money to and regulates the banks in its region. The Federal Reserve banks also serve as a window on the American economy—officers and staff stay constantly in touch with bankers and businesspeople in their districts, and the information they glean about orders and sales beats official published data by as much as a month.

What they were telling us now was that all across the country people had stopped spending on everything except items bought in preparation for possible additional attacks: sales of groceries, security devices, bottled water, and insurance were up; the whole travel, entertainment, hotel, tourism, and convention business was down. We knew the shipping of fresh vegetables from the West Coast to the East Coast would be disrupted by the suspension of air freight, but we were somewhat surprised by how quickly many other businesses were hit. For example, the flow of auto parts from Windsor, Ontario, to Detroit's plants slowed to a crawl at the river crossings that join the two cities—a factor in the decision by Ford Motor to shut down temporarily five of its factories. Years earlier, many manufacturers had shifted to "just-in-time" production—instead of stockpiling parts and supplies at the plant, they relied on air freight to deliver critical components as they were needed. The shutdown of the airspace and the tightening of borders led to shortages, bottlenecks, and canceled shifts.

In the meantime, the U.S. government had gone into high gear. On Friday, September 14, Congress passed an initial emergency appropriation of $40 billion and authorized the president to use force against the "nations, organizations, or persons" who had attacked us. President Bush rallied the nation with what will likely go down as the most effective speech of his presidency. "America was targeted for attack because we're the brightest beacon for freedom and opportunity in the world," he said. "And no one will keep that light from shining." His approval ratings soared to 86 percent, and politics, if only for a short period, became bipartisan. Lots of ideas were being floated on Capitol Hill for helping the nation bounce back. There were plans that involved pumping funds into airlines, tourism, and recreation. There was a raft of proposals to extend tax breaks to businesses in order to encourage capital investment. Terrorism insurance was much discussed—how do you insure against such catastrophic events, and what role, if any, does the government have in that?

I thought it urgent to get commercial aircraft flying again, in order to abort all the negative ripple effects. (Congress quickly passed a $15 billion air transport rescue bill.) But beyond that, I paid less attention to most of these debates, because I was intent on getting the larger picture—which still wasn't clear to me. I was convinced that the answer would not lie in big, hasty, expensive gestures. It's typical that in times of great national urgency, every congressman feels he has to put out a bill; presidents feel the pressure to act too. Under those conditions you can get shortsighted, ineffective, often counterproductive policies, like the gasoline rationing that President Nixon imposed during the first OPEC oil shock in 1973. (That policy caused gas lines in some parts of the country that fall.) But with fourteen years under my belt as Fed chairman, I'd seen the economy pull through a lot of crises—including the largest one-day crash in the history of the stock market, which happened five weeks after I took the job. We'd survived the real-estate boom and bust of the 1980s, the savings and loan crisis, and the Asian financial upheavals, not to mention the recession of

1990. We'd enjoyed the longest stock-market boom in history and then weathered the ensuing dot-com crash. I was gradually coming to believe that the U.S. economy's greatest strength was its resiliency—its ability to absorb disruptions and recover, often in ways and at a pace you'd never be able to predict, much less dictate. Yet in this terrible circumstance, there was no way to know what would happen.

I thought the best strategy was to observe and wait until we understood better what the precise fallout from 9/11 would be. That is what I told the congressional leadership in a meeting in the House Speaker's office on the afternoon of September 19. Speaker Dennis Hastert, House minority leader Dick Gephardt, Senate majority leader Trent Lott, and Senate minority leader Tom Daschle, along with Bob Rubin, the former secretary of the treasury under President Clinton, and White House economic adviser Larry Lindsey, all met in a plain conference room attached to Hastert's office on the House side of the Capitol. The legislators wanted to hear assessments of the economic impact of the attacks from Lindsey, Rubin, and me. There was great seriousness to the ensuing discussion—no grandstanding. (I remember thinking, This is the way government should work.)

Lindsey put forward the idea that as the terrorists had dealt a blow to American confidence, the best way to counter it would be a tax cut. He and others argued for pumping about $100 billion into the economy as soon as possible. The number didn't alarm me—it was about 1 percent of the country's total annual output. But I told them we had no way of knowing yet whether $100 billion was too much or too little. Yes, the airlines and the tourism industries had been severely impacted, and the newspapers were full of stories about all sorts of layoffs. Yet on Monday, September 17, amazingly, the New York Stock Exchange had succeeded in reopening just three blocks from Ground Zero. It was an important step because it brought a sense of normalcy back to the system—a bright spot in the picture we were still piecing together at the Fed. At the same time, the check payment system was recovering, and the stock market hadn't crashed: prices had merely gone down and then stabilized, an indication that most companies were not in serious trouble. I told them the prudent course was to continue to work on options and meet back in two weeks, when we'd know more.

I delivered the same message the next morning to a public hearing of the Senate Banking Committee, counseling patience: "Nobody has the capacity to fathom fully how the tragedy of September 11 will play out. But in the weeks ahead, as the shock wears off, we should be able to better gauge how the ongoing dynamics of these events are shaping the immediate economic outlook." I also emphasized, "Over the past couple of decades, the American economy has become increasingly resilient to shocks. Deregulated financial markets, far more flexible labor markets, and, more recently, the major advances in information technology have enhanced our ability to absorb disruptions and recover."

In fact, I was putting a better face on the situation than I feared might be the case. Like most people in government, I fully expected more attacks. That feeling went mainly unspoken in public, but you could see it in the unanimity of the Senate votes: 98–0 for authorizing the use of force against terrorists, 100–0 for the aviation security bill. I was particularly concerned about a weapon of mass destruction, possibly a nuclear device stolen from the Soviet arsenal during the chaos of the collapse of the USSR. I also contemplated the contamination of our reservoirs. Yet on the record I took a less pessimistic stance because if I had fully expressed what I thought the probabilities were, I'd have scared the markets half to death. I realized I probably wasn't fooling anybody, though: people in the markets would hear me and say, "I sure hope he's right."

In late September, the first hard data came in. Typically, the earliest clear indicator of what's happening to the economy is the number of new claims for unemployment benefits, a statistic compiled each week by the Department of Labor. For the third week of the month, claims topped 450,000, about 13 percent above their level in late August. The figure confirmed the extent and seriousness of the hardships we'd been seeing in news reports about people who'd lost their jobs. I could imagine those thousands of hotel and resort workers and others now in limbo, not knowing how they would support themselves and their families. I was coming to the view that the economy was not going to bounce back quickly. The shock was severe enough that even a highly flexible economy would have difficulty dealing with it.

Like many other analysts, economists at the Fed were looking at all the proposed packages of spending and tax cuts, and the numbers associated with them. In each case, we tried to cut through the details to gauge the order of magnitude; interestingly, they all fell in the ballpark of $100 billion—Larry Lindsey's initial suggestion.

We reconvened in Hastert's conference room on Wednesday, October 3, to talk again about the economy. Another week had passed, and the number of initial jobless claims had gotten worse—an additional 517,000 people had applied for unemployment benefits. By now, my mind was made up. While I still expected more attacks, there was no way to know how devastating they might be or how to protect the economy in advance. I told the group that we should take steps to offset the damage we could measure, and that it was indeed time for a constrained stimulus. What seemed about right was a package of actions on the order of $100 billion—enough, but not so much that it would overstimulate the economy and cause interest rates to rise. The lawmakers seemed to agree.

I went home that night thinking that all I'd done was articulate and reinforce a consensus; the $100 billion figure had first come from Larry. So I was surprised to read the media's spin on the meeting, which made it sound almost as though I were running the entire show.* While it was gratifying to hear that Congress and the administration were listening to me, I found these press reports unsettling. I've never been entirely comfortable being cast as the person who calls the shots. From my earliest days, I had viewed myself as an expert behind the scenes, an implementer of orders rather than the leader. It took the stock-market crisis of 1987 to make me feel comfortable making critical policy decisions. But to this day, I feel ill at ease in the spotlight. Extrovert, I am not.

Of course, the irony was that in spite of my supposed persuasive power, in the weeks after 9/11 nothing worked out as I expected. Anticipating a second terrorist attack was probably one of the worst predictions I ever

---

*Time magazine, for example, opined on October 15, 2001, "Greenspan's shift provided the green light lawmakers had been waiting for. . . . The White House and leaders of both parties have agreed with Greenspan's assessment that new spending and tax cuts should total about 1% of the country's annual income, that it should make its effects felt quickly and that it should not threaten to balloon the deficit so much down the road that it immediately raises long-term interest rates."

made. And the "constrained stimulus" I had supposedly green-lighted didn't happen either. It bogged down in politics and stalled. The package that finally emerged in March 2002 not only was months too late but also had little to do with the general welfare—it was an embarrassing mess of pork-barrel projects.

Yet the economy righted itself. Industrial production, after just one more month of mild decline, bottomed out in November. By December the economy was growing again, and jobless claims dropped back and stabilized at their pre-9/11 level. The Fed did have a hand in that, but it was only by stepping up what we'd been doing before 9/11, cutting interest rates to make it easier for people to borrow and spend.

I didn't mind seeing my expectations upset, because the economy's remarkable response to the aftermath of 9/11 was proof of an enormously important fact: our economy had become highly resilient. What I'd said so optimistically to the Senate Banking Committee turned out to be true. After those first awful weeks, America's households and businesses recovered. What had generated such an unprecedented degree of economic flexibility? I asked myself.

Economists have been trying to answer questions like that since the days of Adam Smith. We think we have our hands full today trying to comprehend our globalized economy. But Smith had to invent economics almost from scratch as a way to reckon with the development of complex market economies in the eighteenth century. I'm hardly Adam Smith, but I've got the same inquisitiveness about understanding the broad forces that define our age.

This book is in part a detective story. After 9/11 I knew, if I needed further reinforcement, that we are living in a new world—the world of a global capitalist economy that is vastly more flexible, resilient, open, self-correcting, and fast-changing than it was even a quarter century earlier. It's a world that presents us with enormous new possibilities but also enormous new challenges. *The Age of Turbulence* is my attempt to understand the nature of this new world: how we got here, what we're living through, and what lies over the horizon, for good and for ill. Where possible, I convey my understanding in the context of my own experiences. I do this out of a sense of responsibility to the historical record, and so that readers will know where I'm coming from. The book is therefore divided into halves: the first half is my effort to retrace the arc of my learning curve, and the second half is a more objective effort to use this as the foundation on which to erect a conceptual framework for understanding the new global economy. Along the way I explore critical elements of this emerging global environment: the principles of governing it that arose out of the Enlightenment of the eighteenth century; the vast energy infrastructure that powers it; the global financial imbalances and dramatic shifts in world demographics that threaten it; and, despite its unquestioned success, the chronic concern over the justice of the distribution of its rewards. Finally, I bring together what we can reasonably conjecture about the makeup of the world economy in 2030.

I don't pretend to know all the answers. But from my vantage point at the Federal Reserve, I had privileged access to the best that had been thought and said on a wide range of subjects. I had access to the broad scope of academic literature that addressed many of the problems my Fed colleagues and I had to grapple with every day. Without the Fed staff, I could never have coped with the sheer volume of academic output, some exceptionally trenchant and some tedious. I had the privilege of calling one or more of the Federal Reserve Board's economic staff and asking about academic work of current or historical interest. I would shortly receive detailed evaluations of the pros and cons on virtually any subject, from the latest mathematical models developed to assess risk neutrality, to the emergence and impact of land-grant colleges in the American Midwest. So I have not been inhibited in reaching for some fairly sweeping hypotheses.

A number of global forces have gradually, sometimes almost clandestinely, altered the world as we know it. The most visible to most of us has been the increasing transformation of everyday life by cell phones, personal computers, e-mail, BlackBerries, and the Internet. The exploration after World War II of the electronic characteristics of silicon led to the development of the microprocessor, and when fiber optics combined with lasers and satellites revolutionized communications capacities, people from Pekin, Illinois, to Peking, China, saw their lives change. A large percentage of the world's population gained access to technologies that I, in setting out on my long career in 1948, could not have imagined, except in the context of science fiction. These new technologies not only opened up a whole new vista of low-cost communications but also facilitated major advances in finance that greatly enhanced our ability to direct scarce savings into productive capital investments, a critical enabler of rapidly expanding globalization and prosperity.

Tariff barriers declined in the years following World War II, a result of a general recognition that protectionism before the war had led to a spiraling down of trade—a reversal of the international division of labor which contributed to the virtual collapse of world economic activity. The postwar liberalization of trade helped open up new low-cost sources of supply; coupled with the development of new financial institutions and products (made possible in part by silicon-based technologies), it facilitated the forward thrust toward global market capitalism even during the years of the cold war. In the following quarter century, the embrace of free-market capitalism helped bring inflation to quiescence and interest rates to single digits globally.

The defining moment for the world's economies was the fall of the Berlin Wall in 1989, revealing a state of economic ruin behind the iron curtain far beyond the expectations of the most knowledgeable Western economists. Central planning was exposed as an unredeemable failure; coupled with and supported by the growing disillusionment over the interventionist economic policies of the Western democracies, market capitalism began quietly to displace those policies in much of the world. Central planning was no longer a subject for debate. There were no eulogies. Except in North Korea and Cuba, it was dropped from the world's economic agenda.

Not only did the economies of the former Soviet bloc, after some chaos, embrace the ways of market capitalism, but so did most of what we previously called the third world—countries that had been neutral in the cold war but had practiced central planning or had been so heavily regulated that it amounted to the same thing. Communist China, which had edged toward market capitalism as early as 1978, accelerated the movement of its vast, tightly regulated, then more-than-500-million-person workforce toward the Free Trade Zones of the Pearl River delta.

China's shift in protecting the property rights of foreigners, while subtle, was substantial enough to induce a veritable explosion in foreign direct investment (FDI) into China following 1991. From a level of $57 million

in 1980, FDI drifted upward, reaching $4 billion in 1991, and then acceler-
ated at a 21 percent annual rate, reaching $70 billion in 2006. The invest-
ment, joined with the abundance of low-cost labor, resulted in a potent
combination that exerted downward pressure on wages and prices throughout the developed world. Earlier, the much smaller so-called Asian Tigers,
especially South Korea, Hong Kong, Singapore, and Taiwan, had showed
the way by engaging developed-country technologies to bring their standard of living sharply higher through exports to the West.

The rate of economic growth of these and many other developing nations far outstripped the rate of growth elsewhere. The result has been the
shift of a significant share of the world's gross domestic product (GDP)
to the developing world, a trend with dramatic ripple effects. Developing
countries typically have much higher savings rates than do industrialized
nations—in part because developing nations' social safety nets are weaker,
so households naturally set aside more money for times of need and retirement. (Other factors also play a part. In the absence of well-established
consumer cultures, for example, households have less inclination to spend.)
The shift of shares of world GDP since 2001 from low-saving developed
countries to higher-saving developing countries has increased world saving
so much that the aggregate growth of savings worldwide has greatly exceeded planned investments. The market process that equalizes actual
global saving and investment, we have to assume, has driven real interest
rates (nominal interest rates adjusted for inflation expectations) markedly
lower. Or to put it another way, the supply of funds looking for a return on
investment has grown faster than investor demand.

The apparent excess in savings, combined with globalization,
technology-driven increases in productivity, and the shift of workforces
from centrally planned economies to competitive markets, has helped suppress interest rates both real and nominal and rates of inflation for all developed and virtually all developing nations. It is why annual inflation rates
almost everywhere (Venezuela, Zimbabwe, and Iran being notable exceptions) are currently in single digits—one of the few times, perhaps the only
time, this has happened since the abandonment of the gold standard and
the embrace of fiat, or paper, currencies in the 1930s. What is particularly
striking about this set of forces is that, largely serendipitously, they all came

together at the beginning of the twenty-first century. Central banks' monetary policy was not the primary cause of the persistent decline in inflation and long-term interest rates, but we central bankers chose to alter our policies to maximize the long-term benefits of these tectonic shifts in global finance. Yet for reasons I will outline later, none of these forces is likely to be permanent. Inflation in a fiat money world is difficult to suppress.

The decline of real (inflation-adjusted) long-term interest rates that has occurred in the past two decades has been associated with rising price-to-earnings ratios for stocks, real estate, and in fact all income-earning assets. The market value of assets worldwide between 1985 and 2006 as a consequence rose at a pace faster than that of nominal world GDP (the 2001–2002 period was the notable exception). This created a major increase in world liquidity. Stock and bond prices, homes, commercial real estate, paintings, and most everything else joined in the boom. Homeowners in many developed nations were able to dip into their growing home equity to finance purchases beyond what their incomes could finance. Increased household spending, especially in the United States, absorbed much of the surge of exports from the rapidly expanding developing world. As the *Economist* put it at year-end 2006, "having grown at an annual rate of 3.2% per head since 2000, the world economy is over halfway towards notching up its best decade ever. If it keeps going at this clip, it will beat both the supposedly idyllic 1950s and the 1960s. Market capitalism, the engine that runs most of the world economy, seems to be doing its job well." Such developments have been on the whole both sweeping and positive. The reinstatement of open markets and free trade during the past quarter century has elevated many hundreds of millions of the world population from poverty. Admittedly many others around the globe are still in need, but large segments of the developing world's population have come to experience a measure of affluence, long the monopoly of so-called developed countries.

If the story of the past quarter of a century has a one-line plot summary, it is the rediscovery of the power of market capitalism. After being forced into retreat by its failures of the 1930s and the subsequent expansion of state intervention through the 1960s, market capitalism slowly reemerged as a potent force, beginning in earnest in the 1970s, until it now pervades almost all of the world to a greater or lesser extent. The spreading of a commercial rule of law and especially the protection of the rights to property has fostered a worldwide entrepreneurial stirring. This in turn has led to the creation of institutions that now anonymously guide an ever-increasing share of human activity—an international version of Adam Smith's "invisible hand."

As a consequence, the control of governments over the daily lives of their citizens has lessened; the forces of the marketplace have gradually displaced some significant powers of the state. Much regulation promulgating limits to commercial life has been dismantled. Throughout the early post–World War II years, international capital flows were controlled and exchange rates were in the grip of finance ministers' discretion. Central planning was widespread in both the developing and the developed world, including remnants of the earlier dirigiste planning still prominent in Europe. It was taken as gospel that markets needed government guidance to function effectively.

At the meetings in the mid-1970s of the Economic Policy Committee of the Organization for Economic Cooperation and Development (OECD), made up of policymakers from twenty-four countries, only Hans Tietmeyer of West Germany and I were pressing for market-based policymaking. We were a very small minority on a very large committee. The views of John Maynard Keynes, the great British economist, had replaced those of Adam Smith and his classical economics when the Great Depression of the 1930s failed to follow Smith's model of the way economies were supposed to behave. Keynes offered a mathematically elegant solution to why the world economy had stagnated and how government deficit spending could bring prompt recovery. Keynesian interventionism was still the overwhelmingly dominant paradigm in the mid-1970s, though it was already on the cusp of decline. The consensus within the Economic Policy Committee was that letting the market set wages and prices was inadequate and unreliable and needed to be supplemented by "incomes policies." These differed from country to country, but generally set guidelines for wage negotiations between unions, which were very much more widespread and powerful than today, and management. Incomes policies fell short of all-out wage and price controls in that they were ostensibly voluntary. The guidelines, however, were generally backed up by the regulatory levers of government which were employed to "persuade" transgressors. When such policies failed, formal wage and price controls were often the response. President Nixon's ill-fated, though initially immensely popular, wage and price controls of 1971 were among the last vestiges of postwar general wage and price interventionism in the developed world.

In my early schooling, I had learned to appreciate the theoretical elegance of competitive markets. In the six decades since, I have learned to appreciate how theories work (and sometimes don't) in the real world. I have been particularly privileged to have interacted with all the key economic policymakers of the past generation, and to have had unparalleled access to information measuring world trends, both numerical and anecdotal. It was inevitable that I would generalize on my experiences. Doing so has led me to an even deeper appreciation of competitive free markets as a force for good. Indeed, short of a few ambiguous incidents, I can think of no circumstances where the expanded rule of law and enhanced property rights failed to increase material prosperity.

Nonetheless, there is persistent widespread questioning of the justice of how unfettered competition distributes its rewards. Throughout this book I point to the continued ambivalence of people to market forces. Competition is stressful because competitive markets create winners and losers. This book will try to examine the ramifications of the collision between a rapidly changing globalized economy and unwavering human nature. The economic success of the past quarter millennium is the outcome of this struggle; so is the anxiety that such rapid change has wrought.

We rarely look closely at that principal operating unit of economic activity: the human being. What are we? What is fixed in our nature and not subject to change—and how much discretion and free will do we have to act and learn? I have been struggling with this question since I first knew to ask it.

As I've traveled across the globe for nearly six decades, I have found that people exhibit remarkable similarities that by no stretch of the imagination can be construed as resulting from culture, history, language, or chance. All people appear motivated by an inbred striving for self-esteem that is in large part fostered by the approval of others. That striving determines much of what households spend their money on. It will also continue to induce people to work in plants and offices side by side, even though they will soon have the technical capability of contributing in isolation through cyberspace. People have an inbred need to interact with other people. It is essential if we are to receive their approval, which we all seek. The true hermit is a rare aberration. What contributes to self-esteem depends on the broad range of learned or consciously chosen values that people believe, correctly or mistakenly, enhance their lives. We cannot function without some set of values to guide the multitude of choices we make every day. The need for values is inbred. Their content is not. That need is driven by an innate moral sense in all of us, the basis upon which a majority have sought the guidance of the numerous religions that humans have embraced over the millennia. Part of that innate moral code is a sense of what is just and proper. We all have different views of what is just, but none can avoid the built-in necessity of making such judgments. This built-in necessity is the basis of the laws that govern every society. It is the basis on which we hold people responsible for their actions.

Economists cannot avoid being students of human nature, particularly of exuberance and fear. Exuberance is a celebration of life. We have to perceive life as enjoyable to seek to sustain it. Regrettably, a surge of exuberance sometimes also causes people to reach beyond the possible; when reality strikes home, exuberance turns to fear. Fear is an automatic response in all of us to threats to our deepest of all inbred propensities, our will to live. It is also the basis of many of our economic responses, the risk aversion that limits our willingness to invest and to trade, especially far from home, and that, in the extreme, induces us to disengage from markets, precipitating a severe falloff of economic activity.

A major aspect of human nature—the level of human intelligence— has a great deal to do with how successful we are in gaining the sustenance needed for survival. As I point out at the end of this book, in economies with cutting-edge technologies, people, on average, seem unable to increase their output per hour at better than 3 percent a year over a protracted period. That is apparently the maximum rate at which human innovation can move standards of living forward. We are apparently not smart enough to do better.

The new world in which we now live is giving many citizens much to fear, including the uprooting of many previously stable sources of identity and security. Where change is most rapid, widening disparities in the distribution of income are a key concern. It is indeed an age of turbulence, and it would be imprudent and immoral to minimize the human cost of its disruptions. In the face of the increasing integration of the global economy, the world's citizens face a profound choice: to embrace the worldwide benefits of open markets and open societies that pull people out of poverty and up the ladder of skills to better, more meaningful lives, while bearing in mind fundamental issues of justice; or to reject that opportunity and embrace nativism, tribalism, populism, indeed all of the "isms" into which communities retreat when their identities are under siege and they cannot perceive better options. There are enormous obstacles facing us in the decades ahead, and whether we surmount them is up to us. For Americans, opening our borders to the world's skilled workforce and education reform must be high on the policy agenda. So too must be finding a solution to our looming Medicare crisis. These are subjects to which I will return at the book's end. I conclude in the last chapter that despite the many shortcomings of human beings, it is no accident that we persevere and advance in the face of adversity. It is in our nature—a fact that has, over the decades, buoyed my optimism about our future.

CITY KID

If you go to the West Side of Manhattan and take the subway north, past Times Square, Central Park, and Harlem, you come to the neighborhood where I grew up. Washington Heights is almost at the opposite end of the island from Wall Street—and not far from the meadow where Peter Minuit is said to have bought Manhattan from the Indians for $24 (there's a commemorative rock there today).

The neighborhood was mostly low-rise brick apartment buildings filled with families of Jewish immigrants who had streamed in before the First World War, as well as some of Irish and German origin. Both sides of my family, the Greenspans and the Goldsmiths, arrived at the turn of the century, the Greenspans from Romania and the Goldsmiths from Hungary. Most families in the neighborhood, including ours, were lower middle class—unlike the utterly poverty-stricken Jews of the Lower East Side. Even during the worst years of the Depression, when I was in grade school, we had enough to eat; if any of our relatives experienced hardship I never knew it. I even got an allowance: 25 cents a week.

I was an only child, born in 1926, and my parents were soon divorced. They split up before I can remember. My father, Herbert, moved back to

Brooklyn, where he'd grown up. He lived with his parents until eventually he remarried. I remained with my mother, Rose, who raised me. Though she was only twenty-six and was very attractive, she took back her maiden name and never married again. She found a job as a saleslady at the Ludwig-Baumann furniture store in the Bronx and was able to hold it through the Depression. She was the one who made ends meet.

She was the youngest of five brothers and sisters, so we were part of a larger family. My cousins and uncles and aunts were always in and out of our lives, which made up somewhat for not having a father around, or siblings. For a time my mother and I lived with my grandparents, Nathan and Anna. The Goldsmiths were a lively, musical bunch. My uncle Murray was a pianist who could sight-read the most famously complex masterpieces. Changing his name to Mario Silva, he went into show business and cowrote a Broadway musical, *Song of Love*, about the composer Robert Schumann. Eventually he headed to Hollywood, where *Song of Love* was made into a movie starring Katharine Hepburn and Paul Henreid. At family gatherings every few months, my uncle would play and my mother would sing—she had a soulful contralto voice and liked to imitate Helen Morgan, a torch singer and Broadway actress famous for popularizing songs like "Can't Help Lovin' Dat Man." Otherwise my mother lived a quiet, family-centered life. She was optimistic and even-tempered, and not intellectual in the least. Her reading consisted of the *Daily News*, a tabloid; instead of bookshelves, our living room featured a piano, a baby grand.

My cousin Wesley, who is four years older than I, was the nearest I had to a brother. During the summer months of the early 1930s, his family would rent a house not far from the ocean in a neighborhood called Edgemere, way down in the southern reaches of Queens. Wesley and I would scour the beaches looking for coins. We were very successful at it. Even though it was the depths of the Great Depression, people could still be relied upon to take coins to the beach and lose them in the sand. The only obvious legacy of our hobby is my habit of walking with my head down; if anyone asks, I tell them, "I'm looking for money."

But not having a dad left a big hole in my life. Every month or so I'd take the subway and go visit him in Brooklyn. He worked on Wall Street as a broker, or in those days what they called a customer's man, for small firms you've never heard of. He was a slim, handsome guy who looked a little like Gene Kelly, and he presented himself well. Yet he never made very much money. He always seemed to feel awkward talking to me, and it made me feel awkward too. He was smart, though, and in 1935, when I was nine, he wrote a book called *Recovery Ahead!*, which he dedicated to me. It predicted that FDR's New Deal was going to bring back good times to the U.S. economy. He made a big deal of presenting a copy to me, with this inscription:

To my son Alan:

    May this my initial effort with constant thought of you branch out into an endless chain of similar efforts so that at your maturity you may look back and endeavor to interpret the reasoning behind these logical forecasts and begin a like work of your own. Your dad.

During my years as Fed chairman, I would show this to people from time to time. They all concluded that the ability to give inscrutable testimony before Congress must have been inherited. As a nine-year-old, however, I was totally mystified. I looked at the book, read a few pages, and put it aside.

My affinity for numbers probably did come from him. When I was very young, my mother used to trot me out in front of relatives and ask, "Alan, what's thirty-five plus ninety-two?" I'd announce the answer after adding in my head. Then she'd use bigger numbers, then switch to multiplication, and so on. Despite this early claim to fame, I was not a confident boy. While my mother could make herself the star of the family party, I was more inclined to sit in the corner.

At the age of nine, I became an avid baseball fan. The Polo Grounds were just a short walk away, and kids from the neighborhood could often get in free to watch the Giants play. My favorite team was the Yankees, however, and getting to Yankee Stadium involved a subway trip, so mainly I read about them in the newspapers. Although regular game radio broadcasts did not arrive in New York until 1939, the 1936 World Series was broadcast, and I developed my own technique of keeping box scores. I always used green paper, and recorded each game pitch by pitch, using an elaborate code I made up. My mind, which had been essentially empty to that point, filled with baseball statistics. To this day I can recite the lineup of Yankees starting players, complete with their positions and batting averages, for that World Series. (It was Joe DiMaggio's rookie season—he hit .323—and the Yanks beat the Giants four games to two.) I learned fractions doing batting averages: 3 for 11 was .273, 5 for 13 was .385, 7 for 22 was .318. I was never as good converting fractions above 4 for 10, since few batters hit over .400.

I wanted to be a ballplayer myself. I played on neighborhood teams, and I was pretty good—I'm a lefty, and I had the agility and reflexes to make a solid first baseman. By the time I was fourteen, one of the bigger guys, who was maybe eighteen, told me, "You keep going at the rate you're going, you could be in the major leagues someday." Needless to say, I was thrilled—but that is the very moment at which my progress stopped. I never fielded or hit as well after that season. I'd peaked at fourteen.

Besides baseball, I got into Morse code. In the late 1930s, cowboy movies were in vogue—we'd pay 25 cents to go to the local theater to see the latest adventure of Hopalong Cassidy. But the characters who really intrigued me were the telegraph operators. Not only did they have the power of instantaneous communication at their fingertips—at crucial moments in the plot, they could call for help or warn of an impending Indian attack, as long as the lines hadn't been cut—but also there was artistry involved. A skilled telegraph operator could communicate forty or fifty words per minute, and an equally skilled person at the other end not only would get the message but could tell just from the distinctive rhythm and sound of the code who was transmitting. "That's Joe's fist," he would say. My buddy Herbie Homes and I rigged up a battery and two key sets and practiced sending messages. We never got above tortoise speed, but just knowing the code gave me the thrill of that world. Much later in life, I was able to experience that same sense of awe at communicating across continents via satellite with my fellow central bankers.

Secretly I yearned for a way out of New York. At night sometimes I'd huddle at the radio, turning the dial, trying to pick up stations far away. From about age eleven, I built a collection of railroad timetables from all over the country. I'd spend hours memorizing the routes and the names of towns in the forty-eight states. Methodically I'd imagine taking a trip on, say, the Great Northern, crossing the vast plains of Minnesota, North Dakota, and Montana, stopping at places like Fargo and Minot and Havre, then heading onward across the Continental Divide.

When I was thirteen, my father unexpectedly invited me on a business trip to Chicago. We went to Penn Station and boarded the Broadway Limited, the Pennsylvania Railroad's flagship train, which headed down to Philadelphia before turning west. Then it carried us through Harrisburg and Altoona, and by the time we reached Pittsburgh it was night. In the dark we passed by huge steelmaking furnaces spewing flame and sparks—my first exposure to the industry that would become my specialty in later years. In Chicago I took pictures of landmarks like the Water Tower and Lake Shore Drive, and after we got home I developed them in my darkroom (photography was another of my hobbies). That trip helped solidify my dream of finding a more interesting life than being an average kid in Washington Heights. But I never discussed this with another soul. Though my mother knew I collected timetables, I'm certain she didn't realize what they meant to me. It was her world that I was escaping.

My other great passion was music. I took up the clarinet at age twelve after hearing my cousin Claire play, and practiced with total dedication, between three and six hours a day. Initially I focused on classical music, but quickly I expanded to jazz. A friend who had a phonograph invited me over and put on a record of Benny Goodman and his orchestra playing "Sing, Sing, Sing," and instantly I was hooked.

It was a thrilling time in music. Goodman and Artie Shaw and Fletcher Henderson had sparked a new era by combining 1920s dance music with elements of ragtime, black spirituals, blues, and European music to create the so-called big-band sound. It was so popular and influential that in 1938, Goodman and his orchestra were invited to play the first nonclassical concert at Carnegie Hall. I took up tenor sax in addition to clarinet—to my ear, sax was the most satisfying, jazziest element of the big-band sound.

One of my heroes was Glenn Miller, who gave the music a new, velvet dimension by grouping a clarinet with two alto and two tenor saxes in his band. In 1941, when I was fifteen, I took the subway to the Hotel Pennsylvania to hear his band play. I was able to maneuver myself right up next to the bandstand, just ten feet from Glenn Miller himself. The band started to play a dance arrangement of Tchaikovsky's Sixth Symphony. I piped up, "That's the *Pathétique!*" and Miller looked over at me and said, "That's terrific, kid."

George Washington High School, about a mile and a half from our apartment, was one of the city's largest and best public schools. When I started in the fall of 1940, it had room for three thousand students, including the night school, but many more of us attended. If you were from outside the neighborhood, you had to compete for admission, and the classes were fiercely competitive. Partly this was because of the Depression: many of us felt we weren't starting with any advantages, so it was imperative that we work hard.* There was also the added uncertainty of war. Although Pearl Harbor was still more than a year away, Nazi Germany had just conquered Western Europe. The radio was full of news of freighters on the Atlantic being sunk by U-boats, and crackly transmissions from Edward R. Murrow reported on London under siege by the Luftwaffe.

We were particularly conscious of the war because our classes had swelled with refugees—mainly Jews whose families had fled the Nazis a few years before. Henry Kissinger was a senior when I enrolled, though we were not to meet for three decades. I remember sitting in math class with John Kemeny, a Hungarian refugee who would one day become Albert Einstein's mathematical assistant and who would coinvent the BASIC computer language with Thomas Kurtz (and still later become president of Dartmouth College). John hadn't been in America long and spoke with a heavy accent, but he was brilliant at math. I wondered if this might be at least in part a result of superior schooling he'd received in Hungary. So I asked, "Is that because you're from Europe?" I hoped he'd say yes because that would mean his advantage wasn't innate and I could possibly catch him by studying hard. But the question just seemed to bemuse him. He shrugged and said, "Everybody is."

I worked hard at George Washington but did not get uniformly great grades. When I concentrated I was a good student, and I did really well in

---

*The same competition expressed itself on the playing field: GW was a force among the city schools in both baseball and football.

math. But I did just okay in courses that didn't interest me, because base-ball and music took up so much of my time. Music was becoming ever more central to my life. Playing was a source of cash—I joined dance bands and could make $10 a weekend by playing a couple of jobs.

I remember exactly where I was on the day the Japanese attacked Pearl Harbor: in my room practicing my clarinet. I'd turned on the radio to take a break, and there was the announcement. I didn't know where Pearl Harbor was—nobody did. I didn't immediately think, Oh, we're going to war. In-stead, I hoped this calamity would just go away. When you're a fifteen-year-old boy, you blank out a lot of things. You just focus on what you're doing.

Of course, the war was impossible to ignore. Rationing started that spring, and most of the kids were going straight into the service as soon as they graduated and turned eighteen. In the summer of 1942, I joined a six-piece band that went up to play the season at a resort hotel in the Catskills. There weren't many young people staying there—we were mostly playing for people our parents' age—and the mood was subdued. All spring we'd been rapidly losing the war in the Pacific, and even after the decisive U.S. victory in the Battle of Midway, the censorship was such that you couldn't really tell what was going on. But it rarely seemed good.

I graduated from GW in June 1943 and had no interest in college. I would turn eighteen in March 1944 and wanted to use the time before I was drafted for more musical training. So I kept playing in small bands and signed up for classes at Juilliard, the city's great private conservatory of music, where I studied clarinet, piano, and composition. If I had any plan for the future at all, it was the thought that maybe I could join an army band.

The draft board called me in that following spring. I took the long sub-way ride downtown for my physical, which was at a big induction center they'd set up at the old Custom House on Battery Park, a huge building with sculptures and murals and high echoing spaces where hundreds of men my age waited in lines. Everything went along routinely until I had my fluoroscopy—that's when they check your lungs for tuberculosis. A ser-geant called me out of the line and over to his desk. "We found a spot on your lung," he said. "We can't tell if it's active." With that, he handed me some papers and the address of a tuberculosis specialist; I was to go see him and report back. When I saw the specialist the next day, he was unable to make a definitive diagnosis. He said, "We're going to have to watch this for a year." I was classified unfit to serve.

I was distraught. Everybody was in the army; I was the odd man out, excluded. There was also the deeper fear that I had something serious. I had no symptoms, no difficulty breathing or anything like that—and as a clarinetist and sax player, I'd have noticed. But the shadow on the X-ray couldn't be denied. I remember sitting with a girlfriend later that week on a slope of grass looking out toward the George Washington Bridge and saying, "If I have tuberculosis, I guess my life is over."

It was my tenor-sax teacher, Bill Sheiner, who gave me a way out of this limbo. Bill was one of the legendary mentors of jazz musicians. His method was to organize small ensembles of four or five saxophones and a clarinet and have the students compose some of the music themselves. In our little ensemble, Sheiner had me sit next to a fifteen-year-old by the name of Stanley Getz. Jazz historians today rank Getz in a league with Miles Davis and John Coltrane; Sheiner's asking me to keep up with him was a little like asking a cocktail-lounge piano player to trade arpeggios with Mozart. Getz and I got along fine, but when he played, I'd just listen in awe. Sometimes, when confronted with a supremely talented individual, you can see the road to that level of ability, and hope that you might follow that road yourself; with other people, the talent has a more genetic source, and no amount of practice can help you match it. Stan Getz was in that second category; I knew intuitively that I could never learn to do what he did.

Nonetheless, I did become a much better sax player from those sessions, which testifies to Sheiner's shrewdness as a teacher. When I told him I'd been rejected for military service he just laughed. He said, "That means there's nothing to stop you from getting a job." And he told me there was a slot open in Henry Jerome's outfit.

The Henry Jerome orchestra was a fourteen-man ensemble that had become fairly prominent on the East Coast. When I auditioned and got invited to join, it marked a big change in my life. It was not quite like making the major leagues, more like AAA ball, but it was still a full-fledged professional job in which I paid union dues and made a pretty good income for those days. And since the band spent about half of its time in the city and half touring the eastern United States, it also got me away from New York City on my own for the first time.

It was by far the best band I'd ever played with. Henry Jerome was part of the avant-garde; his band later brought the bop sound of Charlie Parker and Dizzy Gillespie to conventional big-band fare by adding a lot of percussion and flash. And though the band never achieved lasting fame, a surprising number of my fellow musicians and our successors went on to memorable careers. Johnny Mandel, one of our trombonists, went to Hollywood and wrote "The Shadow of Your Smile" and the theme music for *M*A*S*H* and won an Academy Award and four Grammys. A drummer, Stan Levey, later played with Charlie Parker. Larry Rivers became a major pop artist. And my fellow sax player, Lenny Garment, became President Nixon's lawyer.

Our music was the style that crowds liked as the tide of the war turned in 1944. For the next sixteen months, we played famous venues like the Blue Room at the Hotel Lincoln in New York and Child's Paramount Restaurant on Times Square. We played dances at Virginia Beach outside Newport News, where the audience was mostly shipbuilders and navy families. We played theaters where sometimes we'd share the bill with vaudeville acts—kid dance teams that were warming up for a shot at Hollywood, and singers who'd been prominent in Al Jolson's prime and were still around. We spent the month of December 1944 headlining at the Roosevelt Hotel in New Orleans, which was the farthest I'd ever been from home. One night I was walking on a street near the river and looked up to see an oil tanker pass by. It always stayed with me how far below sea level New Orleans is. When the levees broke after Hurricane Katrina in 2005, that early experience helped me understand immediately the extent of the disaster.

During my time with the band, we followed a routine dictated by union rules: forty minutes on the bandstand and twenty minutes off. I loved the forty minutes on—the experience of playing in a good band is utterly different from what you hear simply standing in front. Voices and overtones come to you from all directions; you feel the rhythm section in your bones; and all the people in the band dynamically interact. Soloists are able to build on that foundation to express their view of the world. I idolized the great improvisers like Benny Goodman and Artie Shaw, but I rarely sought a soloist role. I was content being a sideman, playing notes written by someone else.

I was known as the band's intellectual. I got along well with the other musicians (I did their income taxes), but my style was different from theirs. Between sets, many of them would disappear into the so-called greenroom, which would quickly fill with the smell of tobacco and pot. I spent those twenty-minute breaks reading books. In the course of a night, I could get in maybe an hour of reading. The books I borrowed from the New York Public Library weren't necessarily what you'd expect to find a young sax player reading. Maybe it was because my father was on Wall Street, or maybe it was my affinity for numbers, but what aroused my curiosity was business and finance. One of the first books I read was about the British stock market—I was fascinated to discover that they used exotic terminology like "ordinary shares." I read *Reminiscences of a Stock Operator,* a book by Edwin Lefèvre about Jesse Livermore, a famous 1920s speculator whose nickname was the Boy Plunger of Wall Street. Legend had it that he made $100 million by short-selling on the eve of the 1929 crash. He got rich and went broke three times before finally committing suicide in 1940. He was a great student of human nature; Lefèvre's book is a font of investing wisdom, with Livermore sayings such as "Bulls and bears make money; but pigs get slaughtered."

I also read every book I could find about J. P. Morgan. He not only financed the formation of U.S. Steel, consolidated the railroads, and had a hand in assembling General Electric, but also was the main stabilizing force in the U.S. financial system before the creation of the Federal Reserve. I marveled at his wealth—in breaking up the Morgan trusts just before World War I, Congress heard testimony that Morgan controlled more than $20 billion. And I was even more impressed by Morgan's character: famously, J. P. Morgan's word was his bond, and in 1907 it was his personal influence on other bankers that helped stem a financial panic that could have thrown the country into a depression.*

---

*As a member of the JPMorgan board in 1977, I would sit in the same conference rooms at 23 Wall Street where much of the financial chaos of 1907 had been resolved. History overhung 23 Wall. I was sorry when JPMorgan sold it in 2003.

These stories spoke to me in much the same way railroad timetables had. Wall Street was an exciting place. It wasn't long before I decided, This is where I want to go next.

With the war nearing an end, the future was opening up. The GI Bill passed in 1944, and veterans were already coming home and going to school. I was beginning to believe I had a future: the tuberculosis doctor had been checking my lungs periodically and was increasingly certain that the spot, whatever it was, was dormant.

I wasn't confident that I would succeed in finance. When I enrolled in the School of Commerce, Accounts and Finance at New York University for the fall of 1945, after being out of school for a couple of years, I was apprehensive about how I'd do. So that summer, I got the textbooks for all my freshman courses and read them before I took my first class. It surprised me that I got two Bs and the rest As in my first semester, and then all As after that. I was a far better student in college than I had been at George Washington High.

The School of Commerce was the largest and possibly the least prestigious part of NYU—it had ten thousand students, and people thought of it more as a trade school than as a real college. (A dean once described it proudly as "a huge educational factory.") But to my mind that was unfair; I got a very good education. I was exposed to an interesting curriculum of liberal arts and, of course, accounting, basic economics, business management, and banking and finance. I felt a pull toward the subjects that involved logic and data, and I loaded up on courses in advanced math. Economics appealed to me right from the start: I was enthralled by supply and demand curves, the idea of market equilibrium, and the evolution of international trade.

Economics was a hot topic in those first years after World War II (probably the only discipline hotter was atomic physics). There were a couple of reasons for this: Everyone appreciated that the U.S. economy, under the direction of our government planners, had been the industrial engine behind the Allied victory. What's more, new economic institutions were being created and a new economic order was taking shape right before our eyes. The leaders of the Western world had gathered in July 1944 at Bretton Woods, New Hampshire, to set up the International Monetary Fund (IMF) and the

World Bank. This marked what Henry Morgenthau called "the end of economic nationalism"—the leaders agreed that if world prosperity was to be sustained, it had to be shared, and it was the responsibility of the industrial nations to ensure that barriers were lowered in trade and finance.

The theoretical basis for much of this was laid down by the great Cambridge economist John Maynard Keynes. His masterwork, *The General Theory of Employment, Interest and Money*, had provided the intellectual underpinning for Roosevelt's New Deal, and as students we all read it. In that book, Keynes created the discipline now known as macroeconomics. He argued that free markets, left to themselves, do not always deliver the optimal good to society, and that when employment stagnated, as it did disastrously in the Great Depression, government has to step in.

It would be hard to invent a figure better suited to fire youthful imaginations. A School of Commerce classmate of mine was Robert Kavesh, now a professor emeritus of economics at NYU, who not long ago told the BBC that economics students in the late 1940s were on a mission: "What really bound us together was the sense that economics was undergoing a transition and we were there at the frontier. Anyone who was studying economics at that time was determined that there would never be another major depression. The depression of the 1930s had led to World War Two, and so there we were imbued with the sense that we couldn't let this disaster occur again. It was hard to find anyone who was not strongly influenced by the Democratic Party and John Maynard Keynes and his idea about the very strong role that government could and should play in dominating economic affairs."

Though Bob and most of my classmates were ardent Keynesians, I wasn't. I'd read the *General Theory* twice—it is an extraordinary book. But Keynes's mathematical innovations and structural analyses were what fascinated me, not his ideas on economic policy. I still had the sideman psychology: I preferred to focus on technical challenges and did not have a macro view. Economic policy didn't interest me.

Bob and I both loved classical music. Between classes, we'd hang out in Washington Square Park watching the girls, and when things got slow, we'd hum Mozart piano concerti to each other and ask, "What number was that?" Though I no longer played professionally, music was still the center of my social life—I sang in the glee club, played clarinet in the orchestra, and cofounded a club called the Symphonic Society, which would gather once a week to listen to records or to talks by guests.

But my primary obsession was math. Professors like diligent students, and my eagerness to apply myself must have been obvious. My first paid job as an economist came during the summer of my junior year. My statistics professor, Geoffrey Moore, who later became commissioner of labor statistics under President Nixon, called me in and told me to go over to Brown Brothers Harriman and see a partner named J. Eugene Banks. Brown Brothers Harriman was among New York's oldest, largest, most prestigious investment banks—W. Averell Harriman, the legendary statesman, had been a general partner before going to work for FDR. Prescott Bush, father of George H. W. Bush and grandfather of George W. Bush, served there as a partner both before and after his tenure in the U.S. Senate. The firm was literally on Wall Street right near the stock exchange, and the morning I went to see Mr. Banks was the first time I'd ever set foot in such a place. Walking into those offices, with their gilded ceilings and rolltop desks and thick carpets, was like entering the inner sanctum of venerable wealth—it was an awesome feeling for a kid from Washington Heights.

Gene Banks was a slender, friendly, soft-spoken guy in his late thirties whose job was to track the economy for the firm. He explained matter-of-factly that he wanted a weekly seasonal adjustment for the U.S. Federal Reserve's statistical series on department-store sales—basically a more refined version of the monthly adjusted numbers the government was putting out. Today, in a very few minutes with just a few typed computer instructions, I could construct the set of data he required. But in 1947 such statistics had to be painstakingly built by layering sets of statistics on top of one another, using pencil and paper, slide rules, and desktop adding machines.

Banks didn't give detailed instructions, which was fine with me. I went to the School of Commerce library and looked at textbooks and articles in professional journals to find out how one would go about constructing a weekly seasonal adjustment. Then I assembled the component data and set to work, checking in with Banks only occasionally. The amount of hand calculation and hand chart-drawing required was enormous, but I kept at it for the next two months. Banks was very pleased with the result, and I learned a great deal, not only about how seasonal adjustments are supposed to work, but also about how to organize data to come to a conclusion.

Graduating the following spring was a formality. I'd already decided to stay at NYU and accepted a scholarship to study for a master's degree at night. But I still had to find a job to make ends meet. I had two offers: one from an ad agency and one from the National Industrial Conference Board, where one of my professors was chief economist. Even though the advertising job paid a lot better—$60 a week versus $45 a week—I opted for the Conference Board, figuring I'd learn more. The Conference Board was a private institute underwritten by major corporations. It had been founded in 1916 as an advocacy group, but in the 1920s its focus shifted to doing thorough, disciplined research, based on the theory that the availability of objective knowledge might help businessmen and union leaders find common ground. Its constituency included more than two hundred companies, including General Electric, International Harvester, Brown Brothers Harriman, and Youngstown Sheet & Tube. The board had long been the best private source of business research; for instance, its economists developed the consumer price index in 1913, and it was the first organization to study workplace safety and to look at women in the labor force. In some instances its information was better than the government's. During the Depression, the board had been the original source of data on the extent of unemployment.

When I arrived in 1948, it was a vibrant place, with a big floor of offices on Park Avenue near Grand Central Station. There were dozens of researchers seated in rows of desks and a bustling chart room where designers, perched on high stools at drafting tables, created elaborate presentations and charts. For me, the library was the big event. I discovered that the Conference Board had amassed a treasure trove of data on every major industry in America dating back half a century and more. There were also shelves upon shelves of books that explained how the industries actually operated. The collection covered the entire spectrum of the economy, from mining to retailing, textiles to steel, advertising to foreign trade. There was a hefty volume entitled *Cotton Counts Its Customers*, for example: an annual survey by the National Cotton Council that explained in great detail what was then the world's dominant cotton industry. It could tell you everything you wanted to know about types and grades of cotton, how they were used, and what counted as state of the art in equipment, processes, and production rates among the makers.

There was no room to work in the library's crowded stacks, so I would lug armloads of materials to my desk. Usually I'd have to blow the dust off the books. The chief economist would assign the research projects, and in just a few months people began to tab me as a guy who knew all the data. In a sense, that was true. It became my passion to master all of the knowledge on those shelves. I read about the robber barons; I spent hours over the census of population of 1890; I studied railroad freight-car loadings of that era, trends in short staple cotton prices for the decades after the Civil War, and myriad other details of the vast American economy. It wasn't drudgery—far from it. Instead of reading *Gone with the Wind*, I was happy to immerse myself in "Copper Ore Deposits in Chile."

Almost from the start, I began publishing articles in *Business Record*, the Conference Board's monthly journal. The first, about trends in small manufacturers' profits, was based on a brand-new statistical series from the Federal Trade Commission and the Securities and Exchange Commission. After wringing every detail from the data, I declared, with all the enthusiasm of youth, "Since small business may act as a barometer of cyclical movements, a survey of both the immediate and long-term trends in small corporate manufacturing is of particular interest."

Over the next few years, my work gained momentum. Somebody picked up on one of my articles and wrote about it in the *New York Times*, and even mentioned my name. I finished my master's degree at NYU and continued publishing in a steady stream—articles on housing starts, the new-car market, consumer credit, and other current subjects. I was gaining confidence in my ability to take in data and make them tell a story. And while I was far from comfortable trying to comprehend the economy as a whole—leave that to the Keynesians—I understood more and more about its parts and how they connected.

I first visited Levittown during the Christmas season of 1950. Of course, I'd read about the young couples leaving the city to start families and live the American dream of owning a house in the suburbs. The only places I'd ever lived had been apartments in Manhattan, and what astonished me about Levittown was the tranquillity. The houses were small, but each had a front and back yard with grass, the streets were wide, and there were no tall buildings. You could buy one of these houses for $8,000. It seemed like Nirvana.

I'd been invited to dinner by Tilford Gaines, a college friend who was now an assistant vice president of the Federal Reserve Bank of New York. He and his wife, Ruth, and their little daughter, Pam, had just moved out there. A colleague of his was also there, a twenty-three-year-old Princeton graduate who had just started work at the New York Fed—a six-foot seven-inch behemoth named Paul Volcker.

An image from that evening remains etched in my brain: we're sitting and joking in the cozy living room in front of the fire (the house had an actual working fireplace). Optimism was the dominant feeling, not just that night but for that period in general. America was riding high. The U.S. economy dominated the world—it didn't have any competition. American auto-assembly plants were the envy of every nation. (I'd driven out to Levittown in my new blue Plymouth, paid for out of my earnings from research.) Our textile and steel companies never worried about imports, as there weren't any to speak of. Coming out of World War II, our labor force had the best supervisors and the most highly skilled workers. And because of the GI Bill, the level of education was rising rapidly.

Yet that December, we were also just beginning to recognize a terrible new danger. Nuclear confrontation had seemed very abstract as a threat eighteen months before, when the Soviet Union had detonated its first atomic bomb. But as the cold war began to make itself felt at home, the peril seemed more concrete. Alger Hiss had been convicted of perjury in a spying scandal, and Joseph McCarthy had made his famous I-have-here-in-my-hand-a-list-of-two-hundred-and-five-known-Communists speech. U.S. forces had been fighting a "police action" in Korea. That had triggered a rush by the Pentagon to rebuild army divisions and fighter and bomber wings that had been drawn down after World War II. We all wondered where it would lead.

I had enrolled in a Ph.D. program at Columbia University that fall, juggling coursework with my Conference Board research. (Even then, you generally needed a Ph.D. if you wanted to advance as an economist.) My faculty adviser was Arthur Burns, who in addition to being a full professor was also a senior researcher at the National Bureau of Economic Research, then in New York. It remains the largest independent economics-research organization in America. Back then it was best known for having worked with the government in the 1930s to set up what are called the national income accounts—the mammoth accounting system that gave Washington its first accurate picture of the gross national product. When America mobilized for the war, the system helped planners set goals for military production and gauge how much rationing would be needed on the home front to support the war effort. The NBER is also the authority on the ups and downs of the business cycle; its analysts to this day determine the official beginning and ending dates of recessions.

Arthur Burns was an avuncular, pipe-smoking scholar. He had a profound impact on business-cycle research—his 1946 book, written with Wesley Clair Mitchell, was the seminal analysis of U.S. business cycles from 1854 to 1938. His devotion to empirical evidence and deductive logic put him at odds with the economics mainstream.

Burns loved to provoke disagreements among his graduate students. One day, in a class about inflation's corrosive effect on national wealth, he went around the room asking, "What causes inflation?" None of us could give him an answer. Professor Burns puffed on his pipe, then took it out of his mouth and declared, "Excess government spending causes inflation!"

It was a different mentor who enabled me to see that I might someday attempt to understand and forecast the economy as a whole. In 1951 I signed up for a course in mathematical statistics, a technical discipline based on the notion that the inner workings and interrelationships of a major economy can be investigated, measured, modeled, and analyzed mathematically. Today this discipline is called econometrics, but then the field was just an assemblage of general concepts, too new to have a textbook or even a name. The professor was Jacob Wolfowitz, whose son Paul I would come to know during his years in the George W. Bush administration and as president of the World Bank. Professor Wolfowitz would chalk the equations on the board and give them to us to study on mimeographed sheets. I immediately saw the power of these new tools: if the economy could be accurately modeled using empirical facts and math, then large-scale forecasts could be derived methodically, without the quasi-scientific intuition employed by so many economic forecasters. I imagined how that could be put to work. Most important, at age twenty-five I'd found a growing field in which I could excel.

In later years I developed some skill in building quite large econometric models, and came to a deeper appreciation of their uses and, especially, their limitations. Modern, dynamic economies do not stay still long enough to allow for an accurate reading of their underlying structures. Early portrait photographers required their subjects to freeze long enough to get a useful picture; if the subject moved, the photo would blur. So too with econometric models. Econometricians use ad hoc adjustments to the formal structure of their models to create reasonable forecasts. In the trade, it's called add-factoring a model's equations; the add-factors are often far more important to the forecast than the results of the equations themselves.

If models have so little predictive power, what use are they? The least-heralded advantage of formal models is simply that the exercise of using them ensures that basic rules of national accounting and economic consistency are being applied to a set of assumptions. And models certainly can help maximize the effectiveness of the few parcels of information that can be assumed with certainty. The more specific and data-rich the model, the more effective it will be. I have always argued that an up-to-date set of the most detailed estimates for the latest available quarter is far more useful for forecasting accuracy than a more sophisticated model structure.

At the same time, of course, the structure of a model is quite important to its success. You can't (or at least I can't) draw abstract models out of thin air. They have to be inferred from facts. Abstractions do not float around in my mind, untied to real-world observations. They need an anchor. This is why I strive to ferret out every conceivable observation or fact about a happening. The greater the detail, the more representative the abstract model is likely to be of the real world I seek to understand.

My early training was to immerse myself in extensive detail in the workings of some small part of the world and infer from that detail the way that segment of the world behaves. That is the process I have applied throughout my career. I experience deep nostalgia every time I thumb through articles I wrote back in my twenties. The substance is from a far simpler world, but the method of analysis is as current as any I would apply today.

THE MAKING OF
AN ECONOMIST

I often did my work with the radio on. Korea dominated the news in 1950 and 1951—our military was now fighting bloody battles against the Chinese, and President Truman dismissed General MacArthur for his public insistence that the United States should declare a full-scale war on China. At home, atomic-bomb testing moved from New Mexico to Nevada, and we had the Red Scare—the Rosenbergs were sentenced to the electric chair for spying. Amid all this turmoil, what captured my imagination was the dawning of the atomic age. Some of the scientific work done during World War II was just then being declassified, and on the side I began to read deeply in atomic physics. My first foray was a fat technical book called *Sourcebook on Atomic Energy*, a government-sponsored synthesis of available information on the subject that wasn't classified. From there I moved on to books on astronomy, physics more broadly, and the philosophy of science.

Like many scientifically minded people, I believed that atomic energy was the most important frontier we would unlock in our lifetimes. This was the other side of the fear we all felt of atomic war. The science was extremely seductive. The atom conferred a power on humankind that could open a whole new phase of endeavor. This, in turn, called for a new way of thought.

I discovered that some of the scientists in the Manhattan Project subscribed to a philosophy called logical positivism, a variation of empiricism. Pioneered by Ludwig Wittgenstein, it is a school of thought whose main tenet is that knowledge can only be gained from facts and numbers—it heavily emphasizes rigorous proof. There are no moral absolutes: values and ethics and the way people behave are reflections of culture and are not subject to logic. They vary so arbitrarily that they're outside the realm of serious thought.

The mathematician in me embraced this stark analytical credo. It seemed the exact philosophy for the age. The world would become a better place, I thought, if people focused exclusively on what was knowable and important, which was precisely logical positivism's aim.

By 1952 I was happily immersed in working toward an economics Ph.D. and was earning more than $6,000 a year. None of my friends or colleagues had much money, and this was more than I needed. My mother and I moved to the suburbs—not all the way to Levittown, but to a two-family house in Forest Hills, Queens, a leafy neighborhood within easy walking distance of the commuter train. At last, I'd found a way to escape the city's congestion. It was a big step up.

If someone had told me then that I was about to enter the most confused and tumultuous phase of my life, I would have been incredulous. Yet over the next two years, I would marry and separate, drop out of graduate school, quit my job to go into business for myself—and change my whole way of looking at the world.

The woman I married was Joan Mitchell, an art historian from Winnipeg, Manitoba, who had come to New York to study at NYU's Institute of Fine Arts. We met on a blind date—I walked into her apartment and she had one of my favorite recordings on. Classical music was a passion we shared. We dated for several months, got married in October 1952, and split up after about a year. Without going into detail, I will say I was the main problem. I had no real understanding of the commitment required for marriage. I'd made an intellectual choice, not an emotional one, telling my-self, "This woman is very intelligent. Very beautiful. I'll never do better." My mistake was all the more painful because Joan is an extraordinary person. Happily, we are friends to this day.

Joan was best friends with the wife of Nathaniel Branden, who was Ayn Rand's young collaborator and, years later, her lover. That's how Ayn Rand and I met. She was a Russian émigré whose novel *The Fountainhead* had been a bestselling phenomenon during the war. She had recently moved from Hollywood to New York and had developed a small, intense follow-ing. I'd read the novel and found it intriguing. It's the story of an architect named Howard Roark who heroically resists all pressure to compromise his vision—he even blows up a public-housing project when he finds out that the builder has altered his design—and ultimately prevails. Rand wrote the story to illustrate a philosophy she had come to, one that emphasized rea-son, individualism, and enlightened self-interest. Later she named it objec-tivism; today she would be called a libertarian.

Objectivism championed laissez-faire capitalism as the ideal form of social organization; not surprisingly, Ayn Rand abhorred Soviet communism, in which she had been schooled. She saw it as the embodiment of brutal collectivism. And at the height of Soviet power, she held that the system was so inherently corrupt that eventually it would collapse from within.

She and her circle called themselves the Collective, an inside joke be-cause collectivism was the polar opposite of their belief. They would meet at Rand's apartment on East Thirty-fourth Street at least once a week to discuss world events and argue into the early hours. The night Joan intro-duced me, the group was small, maybe seven or eight people seated in the austere living room: Rand; her painter husband, Frank O'Connor; the Bran-dens; and a few others. Ayn Rand was quite plain to look at—short, in her late forties. Her face was dramatic, almost severe, with a wide mouth, broad brow, and great dark intelligent eyes—she kept her dark hair in a pageboy that emphasized them. She had a pronounced Russian accent even though she'd been in the United States for twenty-five years. She was unrelentingly analytical, ready to dissect any idea to its fundamentals, and had no interest in small talk. Yet despite this apparent ferocity, I noticed an openness in the way she approached conversation. She seemed ready to consider any idea from any person, and engage it strictly on the merits.

After listening for a few evenings, I showed my logical-positivist colors. I don't recall the topic being discussed, but something prompted me to postulate that there are no moral absolutes. Ayn Rand pounced. "How can that be?" she asked.

"Because to be truly rational, you can't hold a conviction without significant empirical evidence," I explained.

"How can that be?" she asked again. "Don't *you* exist?"

"I . . . can't be sure," I admitted.

"Would you be willing to say you *don't* exist?"

"I might. . . ."

"And by the way, who is making that statement?"

Maybe you had to be there—or, more to the point, maybe you had to be a twenty-six-year-old math junkie—but this exchange really shook me. I saw she was quite effectively demonstrating the self-contradictory nature of my position.

But there was much more to it than that. I prided myself on my reasoning ability, and thought I could beat anybody in an intellectual debate. Talking to Ayn Rand was like starting a game of chess thinking I was good, and suddenly finding myself in checkmate. It dawned on me that a lot of what I'd decided was true was probably just plain wrong. Of course, I was too stubborn and embarrassed to concede immediately; instead, I clammed up.

Rand came away from that evening with a nickname for me. She dubbed me "the Undertaker," partly because my manner was so serious and partly because I always wore a dark suit and tie. Over the next few weeks, I later learned, she would ask people, "Well, has the Undertaker decided he exists yet?"

At least my work at the Conference Board was going well. I was deep into my most ambitious project, an analysis of the Pentagon's buildup of jet fighters, bombers, and other new aircraft in the face of Korea and the cold war. It was going to require a lot of detective work. As soon as the Korean War began, the Defense Department classified its procurement plans. While the aircraft manufacturers knew their order books, military secrecy was keeping Wall Street and the rest of American industry in the dark. Yet, the economic impact was too big to ignore: after the post–World War II lull, military spending had by the 1953 fiscal year zoomed back up to nearly 14 percent of GDP (it was 4 percent in 2006). That was upsetting the markets for raw materials and equipment, not to mention those for skilled machinists and engineers, and it was putting a massive question mark over the business outlook. Most affected by the push to build airplanes were the makers of aluminum, copper, and steel, all of which were classified as controlled materials essential to the war effort.

I already knew a lot about the metals markets, so I volunteered to analyze the buildup, and my bosses agreed. I began with the public record, which was of almost no help: Congressional hearings on military production schedules were conducted in secret session, and the published transcripts were filled with redactions. The number and types of new planes were left blank; the number of aircraft per squadron, the number of squadrons per wing, the number of aircraft held in reserve, and the number of noncombat losses by type—all were blacked out. Then I decided to look at the congressional hearings of the late 1940s, which I suspected would have much of the information I'd need. Secrecy hadn't been an issue then. The Pentagon still was in the process of phasing down, and the top brass would appear before the subcommittee on military appropriations and explain in full detail how everything was then being calculated. The military would certainly be doing it the same way in 1950 as they did in 1949.

I took that information as my base. Now I needed to assemble all the publicly available facts. I hunted through technical and engineering manuals, organizational charts, the massive statistical tables of the federal budget, and the complex language of the materials orders put out by the Pentagon. Gradually all the data began to fit. For instance, I knew the weights of particular aircraft and could surmise the proportions of aluminum, copper, and other materials that went into each type. With all that in hand, I could estimate demand.

My research appeared in two long *Business Record* articles in the spring of 1952 entitled "The Economics of Air Power." Afterward I heard indirectly that some of the Pentagon's planners had been surprised by how closely the analysis matched their classified numbers. More important to me, however, was that my audience snapped up the information. I got requests from member companies to provide additional details of my calculations.

Around this time I started getting freelance research assignments from a fellow Conference Board analyst named Sanford Parker. Sandy, as everyone called him, was a short, disheveled whirlwind, about ten years older than I, who had made a name for himself writing weekly commentary in *BusinessWeek* starting in 1939. Now that he worked for the Conference Board, he would moonlight by writing economics articles for *Fortune*. When he offered to farm out some of the analytical work to me, I jumped at the chance.

Commissioning Sandy was *Fortune*'s way of capitalizing on what the editors believed was a nascent trend. Although the business world was not very intellectual, it seemed as though industrialists and financial people were starting to take an interest in what economics could tell them. (John Kenneth Galbraith was on the staff in the late 1940s, but I doubt he helped shape this awareness.) Sandy was a real authority, and he had skills I didn't have. For one thing, he knew how to write clearly in short, declarative sentences. He tried to teach me to do the same and almost succeeded; it was a skill I had to unlearn as chairman of the Fed. *Fortune*'s editors liked him because he could write with conviction about the economy as a whole, and because he was creative—he'd often come up with surprising approaches for spotting and analyzing trends.

As I worked with Sandy, I began to see that his authoritativeness derived largely from the fact that he simply knew more about the economy than anyone else. My knowledge was not as extensive as his, yet the gap wasn't wide. I was learning every day by doing work I loved—if I kept at it, I thought, I could catch up.

In late 1950, Sandy left the Conference Board to become *Fortune*'s first chief economist. I'd hoped to land a job in the department he was building, but instead *Fortune* offered a freelance assignment to work with Sandy and other writers in preparing a major series of articles called "The Changing American Market." (It ultimately appeared in twelve parts over a span of two years.) Having this new source of income made me feel that I could afford to take some risks.

I'd been getting calls from an investment adviser named William Wallace Townsend, who was the senior partner of a Wall Street firm called Townsend Skinner, one of the smallest members of the Conference Board. He'd been reading my work and we'd discussed it a bit on the phone. In early 1953, he called and said, "Why don't you come down and join me at the Bankers' Club for lunch?" I agreed.

I took the subway downtown. The Bankers' Club occupied three floors at the top of a financial-district landmark called the Equitable Building, with the reception area on the club's first floor and a library and dining room above. There were beautiful views out the window, and heavy rugs and furnishings and draperies. From our phone conversations, I'd figured Townsend to be about forty; he'd thought the same about me. But when I stepped out of the elevator and asked someone to point him out, Bill turned out to be more like sixty-five. I went over and introduced myself, and we both burst out laughing. We hit it off instantly.

Bill had been born in 1888 in upstate New York, and had had a series of impressive ups and downs. He'd made a couple of million dollars on Wall Street in the 1920s as an expert in corporate bonds; he'd written the Independent Bankers' Association book on bond salesmanship. Then he'd lost everything in the 1929 stock-market crash. In the thirties he'd bootstrapped his way back up by founding a small firm that put together statistical indexes for stock- and bond-market forecasting.

When we met, Townsend was also writing something called the *Savings and Loan Letter*, a technical report that thrift institutions subscribed to. His partner had been Richard Dana Skinner, a scion of a New England family and a great-great-grandson of Richard Henry Dana Jr., author of *Two Years Before the Mast*. The firm had many famous clients, such as Donald Douglas, the aviation pioneer who founded Douglas Aircraft, and former president Herbert Hoover, who now lived at the Waldorf Towers and whom Bill periodically visited. However, Skinner had died some years before, and now Townsend's son-in-law, who also worked at the firm, had been offered a job as fiscal agent of the Federal Home Loan Bank system. That, explained Townsend, was what had brought us to this lunch. "I'd like you to join me," he said.

Changing jobs was a remarkably easy decision. Besides the *Fortune* work, I had a steady stream of freelance research projects, and new clients were always calling. I had no real obligations—Joan and I had already decided to separate, and within a few months I would be moving back to Manhattan and would rent an apartment on Thirty-fifth Street.

Townsend-Greenspan opened for business in September 1953. (We were officially incorporated in 1954.) Our offices were on Broadway, a little south of the New York Stock Exchange. The space was nondescript, with just an office for Bill and one for me and a common area where two research assistants and a secretary sat.

Bill and I operated on separate tracks. Bill continued to put out his letter and to work with his investment-advisory clients. My first accounts were people who knew me from the Conference Board. The Wellington Fund, predecessor to the Vanguard Group, was the first to sign on. Republic Steel, America's third-largest steelmaker, was next, and within two years, ten more steel companies followed, including U.S. Steel, Armco, Jones & Laughlin, Allegheny-Ludlum, Inland, and Kaiser. For Townsend-Greenspan, this was the best possible advertisement. Steel was the symbol of American strength, and if you ran your finger down the Fortune 500 list, which appeared for the first time in 1955, those names were right near the top. We gradually added a whole range of clients—Alcoa, Reliance Electric, Burlington Industries, Mellon National Bank, Mobil Oil, Tenneco, and many more.

A casualty was my Ph.D.—I was just too busy to get it done. Several times each month I'd have to hop on a plane to call on clients in Pittsburgh or Chicago or Cleveland; the rest of the time, I was racing to create reports. I was torn because I liked the topic I'd chosen for my dissertation: the spending and saving patterns of American households. But taking the oral exams and completing the dissertation would require at least six solid months, and to do that, I'd have to scale back my business. I convinced myself I wouldn't lose anything by dropping out, because I'd continue to read and study economics in my work. But every couple of months, I'd run into Professor Burns. He'd always say, "When are you going to get back to work?" I always felt a pang. (Much later, in the 1970s, I did return to graduate school, at NYU, and completed my Ph.D.)

The key to Townsend-Greenspan's appeal was our ability to translate economic analysis into a form business leaders could apply in making decisions. Say the economy was entering a period of growth. The typical industrial CEO was most likely a salesman or an engineer or a general manager who had worked his way up in the company. Knowing what the gross national product (GNP) was going to do wasn't useful to him. But if you talked to the CEO of an automobile-parts manufacturing company and could tell him that "assemblies for Chevrolet over the next six months are going to be different from what General Motors has announced," that was something he could understand and act on.

Today's supply chains are so totally integrated that information between suppliers and manufacturers flows freely—it's how modern just-in-time manufacturing works. But back then, the relationship between manufacturers and suppliers was more like a poker game. If you were a purchasing manager at an appliance manufacturer looking to buy steel sheet to make refrigerators, telling the steelmaker's salesman how much sheet you already had in inventory would only weaken your bargaining position.

The lack of such information left the steel company flying partially blind in planning its production. Moreover, many of our steel clients' customers knew only their part of the market. The steel outlook could be radically affected by a shift in demand for passenger cars, or skyscraper construction, or oil-drilling pipe, or even tin cans. And that demand, in the short run, was a reflection of the demand for inventories as well as steel to be consumed.

A forecast system is only as good as the accuracy of its historical database from which future turns in a cycle can be projected. I'd take into account historical levels of car and truck output, aircraft assemblies, and more. Data on steel shipments by product and consuming industry I'd get from the American Iron and Steel Institute each month, and data on exports (the United States was heavily exporting steel in those days) and imports (almost none) from the Department of Commerce. Combining shipments of domestically produced steel products with imports and exports gave me the tonnage of each product's receipts by consuming industry. The next challenge was to figure how much of each historical quarter's steel receipts the buyers had consumed, and how much had been added to or subtracted from the buyers' inventory. For that I went back to World War II and Korean War data: the government had declassified masses of statistics on the metals industries from the War Production Board, which had been in charge of Uncle Sam's industrial rationing system. Each industry that consumed steel—autos, machinery, construction, oil drilling—had a unique inventory cycle, and all of them were documented there.

Further analyzed, those figures, combined with my newly acquired macroeconomic forecasting capabilities (thanks to Sandy Parker), enabled us to project the level of aggregate steel-industry product shipments. Over time, we were also able to track individual steel company market shares—which meant a producer could make informed decisions, given the outlook for shipments, as to where to shift its resources in the coming quarters to maximize its profit.

By 1957 I'd worked with the steel companies for several years. Late that year, I flew to Cleveland to make a presentation to the executive committee of Republic Steel, whose CEO was Tom Patten. My system indicated that inventories were building rapidly and that the industry's production rate was therefore well above the rate at which steel was being consumed. Production was going to have to come way down just to stop the accumulation. And it wasn't just the steel industry that was facing a big problem. "Nineteen fifty-eight is going to be an awful year," I told them. Patten took issue with that: "Well, the order books are pretty good," he said. Republic Steel stuck to its production schedule.

About three months later, demand for steel plunged. It was the onset of the 1958 recession, which turned out to be the sharpest business downturn since the war. When I was next in Cleveland, Patten generously acknowledged in front of the executive committee, "Well, you got it right, my friend."

Predicting the economic downturn that became the 1958 recession was my first forecast of the economy as a whole. Spending as much time studying the steel industry as I did put me in an excellent position to see the downturn coming. Steel was a much more central force in the American economy then—the economy's strength was much more in durable goods, most of which are made of steel. I could extrapolate the wider consequences of steel's weakening, and warn other, nonsteel clients as well.

Still, while calling the 1958 recession benefited our reputation, it wasn't successful macroeconomic forecasting per se that our clients found most useful. Our work was an analytical evaluation of the forces making the *current* economy do what it was doing. Forecasting is simply a projection of how current imbalances will ultimately resolve. Our service was to deepen our clients' understanding of the exact nature of the relationships between forces; what they did with that information was up to them. CEOs of large corporations are not going to take the word of a thirty-year-old kid as to where the economy is going. But they might very well listen to what he thinks are the various balances here and there, especially if they can check this input against their own knowledge. I'd try to talk on their terms: not "What's the GNP doing?" but "What is the demand for machine tools six months out?" or "What is the likelihood of the markup changing between broad-woven fabrics on the one hand and the market for men's suits on the other?" I would define what was going on in general terms and then translate that into the implications for individual businesses. That was my value-added, and we prospered.

Working with heavy industry gave me a profound appreciation of the central dynamic of capitalism. "Creative destruction" is an idea that was articulated by the Harvard economist Joseph Schumpeter in 1942. Like many powerful ideas, his is simple: A market economy will incessantly revitalize itself from within by scrapping old and failing businesses and then reallocating resources to newer, more productive ones. I read Schumpeter in my twenties and always thought he was right, and I've watched the process at work through my entire career.

The telegraph was a perfect illustration. By the time my friend Herbie and I had set out as kids to learn Morse code in the late 1930s, the telegraph industry was at its peak. Starting in the heyday of those quick-fingered operators in the 1850s and 1860s, it had transformed the entire American economy. By the late 1930s, well over half a million telegrams were being sent per day, and the Western Union messenger boy was as familiar a sight as the FedEx person is now. Telegrams tied together cities and towns across America, compressing the amount of time it took businesses and people to communicate, and connected U.S. industrial and financial markets to the rest of the world. They were the way all important or urgent family and business news arrived.

Yet despite this enormous success, the industry was on the verge of disappearing. Those lightning-fast telegraph operators I'd idolized were already long gone. Teletypewriters had replaced the old single-key transmission equipment, and Western Union operators now were essentially typists who relayed your message in English, not Morse. Learning Morse code had literally become child's play.

Now telephones were the new growth business—they would displace the telegraph as the best tool for remote communication. By the late 1950s at Townsend-Greenspan, Bill Townsend might send a telegram to an old client once in a while, but the telegraph no longer played any major role in the firm. We used phones to maintain contact with clients between visits: they were efficient, cost-effective, and therefore productive. I always felt wistful about the artistry lost when the new technology put the Morse code experts out of business. (Then again, it was they who had displaced the Pony Express.)

I saw this pattern of progress and obsolescence repeat over and over. During my consulting days, I had a ringside seat at the demise of the tin can. The 1950s was the era of tuna casseroles and tinned soup; cooking dinner for your family from canned and packaged food was a hallmark of the suburban lifestyle, and a can opener was an essential tool in the modern kitchen. Food manufacturers loved the tin can: it offered a way to pack vegetables, meats, and beverages that allowed shipping over long distances and then stocking over long periods. The old-fashioned grocery store, where a clerk measured out the food a customer wanted to buy, never stood a chance. It was replaced by self-service supermarkets that were more efficient and offered lower prices.

Those tin cans of the fifties weren't literally made of tin, but rather tin-plated steel, and the steelmakers I consulted for at Townsend-Greenspan sold a lot of it. In 1959, it accounted for five million tons, or about 8 percent of the steel industry's entire output. At that point, the industry was hurting. A bitter nationwide strike had brought production to a standstill for nearly four months, during which, for the first time, Big Steel found itself facing major competition from rivals in Germany and Japan.

The aluminum industry was hurting too—the recession was squeezing the profits of the three big producers, Alcoa, Reynolds, and Kaiser. Five million tons a year was a lot of can sheet, and the market seemed too good an opportunity to pass up. Aluminum cans, which were just then being developed, were lighter and simpler in construction than steel cans—they required two pieces of metal rather than three. Aluminum was also easier to print on with colorful labeling. In the late 1950s it was already being used to make the ends of containers for frozen juice concentrate. Then Coors Brewing Company attracted a cult following by selling beer in seven-ounce aluminum cans, instead of conventional twelve-ounce steel cans. The smaller amount just seemed to add to the appeal, though the truth was that no one had yet figured out how to manufacture full-size aluminum beer cans. But by the early 1960s, the can makers had solved that puzzle.

The innovation that had the biggest impact was the pop-top, introduced in 1963. It eliminated the need for "church key" can openers—and pop-tops could be made only of aluminum. The biggest aluminum producer, Alcoa, was my client; its CEO was looking for ways to diversify beyond basic aluminum into new and profitable areas, much as Reynolds had done by pioneering household aluminum foil. His executive vice president was a zealot for cans: "Beer cans are the future of Alcoa!" he would say. And when pop-tops came along, he and the CEO put their weight behind the idea.

The first major brewery to sell beer in pop-top cans was Schlitz. Others quickly jumped on board and by the end of 1963, 40 percent of all U.S. beer cans had aluminum pop-tops. The soft drink giants came next: Coca-Cola and Pepsi both shifted to all-aluminum cans in 1967. The steel beverage can went the way of the telegraph key, and money followed the innovation. The shift to aluminum cans helped lift Alcoa's profits in the fall of 1966 to the highest level for any quarter in its seventy-eight-year history. And in the hot stock market of the late sixties, investors flocked to aluminum stocks.

For the steelmakers, losing the market for beer and soda cans was just one step in a harrowing long-term decline. Until then, the United States hadn't imported much steel, because the conventional wisdom was that foreign steel was not up to American quality standards. But as the 1959 strike stretched into its second and then its third month, automakers and other big customers had to search elsewhere. They discovered that some of the steel coming in from Europe and Japan was first-rate, and that much of it was cheaper. By the end of the 1960s, steel had lost its status as the icon of American business, and the glamour had shifted to high-growth companies like IBM. What Schumpeter called "the perennial gale of creative destruction" was starting to hit Big Steel.

Though my work at Townsend-Greenspan was in demand, I was careful not to expand too fast. I focused instead on keeping our profit margin high—on the order of 40 percent—and never becoming so dependent on any single client or group that losing the account would jeopardize the business. Bill Townsend completely agreed with this approach. He continued to be the best partner I could imagine. Though I had him for only five years—he died of a heart attack in 1958—we grew extraordinarily close. He was like the ultimate benevolent dad. He insisted on dividing our profits equitably—by the end I was taking home a considerably greater share. There was never any feeling of jealousy or competitiveness. After his death, I bought out the stock from his children, but I asked their permission to keep his name on the door. That felt right to me.

Ayn Rand became a stabilizing force in my life. It hadn't taken long for us to have a meeting of the minds—mostly my mind meeting hers—and in the fifties and early sixties I became a regular at the weekly gatherings at her apartment. She was a wholly original thinker, sharply analytical, strong-willed, highly principled, and very insistent on rationality as the highest value. In that regard, our values were congruent—we agreed on the importance of mathematics and intellectual rigor.

But she had gone far beyond that, thinking more broadly than I had ever dared. She was a devoted Aristotelian—the central idea being that there exists an objective reality that is separate from consciousness and capable of being known. Thus she called her philosophy objectivism. And she applied key tenets of Aristotelian ethics—namely, that individuals have innate nobility and that the highest duty of every individual is to flourish by realizing that potential. Exploring ideas with her was a remarkable course in logic and epistemology. I was able to keep up with her most of the time.

Rand's Collective became my first social circle outside the university and the economics profession. I engaged in the all-night debates and wrote spirited commentary for her newsletter with the fervor of a young acolyte drawn to a whole new set of ideas. Like any new convert, I tended to frame the concepts in their starkest, simplest terms. Most everyone sees the simple outline of an idea before complexity and qualification set in. If we didn't, there would be nothing to qualify, nothing to learn. It was only as contradictions inherent in my new notions began to emerge that the fervor receded.

One contradiction I found particularly enlightening. According to objectivist precepts, taxation was immoral because it allowed for government appropriation of private property by force. Yet if taxation was wrong, how could you reliably finance the essential functions of government, including the protection of individuals' rights through police power? The Randian answer, that those who rationally saw the need for government would contribute voluntarily, was inadequate. People have free will; suppose they refused?

I still found the broader philosophy of unfettered market competition compelling, as I do to this day, but I reluctantly began to realize that if there were qualifications to my intellectual edifice, I couldn't argue that others should readily accept it. By the time I joined Richard Nixon's campaign for the presidency in 1968, I had long since decided to engage in efforts to advance free-market capitalism as an insider, rather than as a critical pamphleteer. When I agreed to accept the nomination as chairman of the president's Council of Economic Advisors, I knew I would have to pledge to uphold not only the Constitution but also the laws of the land, many of which I thought were wrong. The existence of a democratic society governed by the rule of law implies a lack of unanimity on almost every aspect of the public agenda. Compromise on public issues is the price of civilization, not an abrogation of principle.

It did not go without notice that Ayn Rand stood beside me as I took the oath of office in the presence of President Ford in the Oval Office. Ayn Rand and I remained close until she died in 1982, and I'm grateful for the influence she had on my life. I was intellectually limited until I met her. All of my work had been empirical and numbers-based, never values-oriented. I was a talented technician, but that was all. My logical positivism had discounted history and literature—if you'd asked me whether Chaucer was worth reading, I'd have said, "Don't bother." Rand persuaded me to look at human beings, their values, how they work, what they do and why they do it, and how they think and why they think. This broadened my horizons far beyond the models of economics I'd learned. I began to study how societies form and how cultures behave, and to realize that economics and forecasting depend on such knowledge—different cultures grow and create material wealth in profoundly different ways. All of this started for me with Ayn Rand. She introduced me to a vast realm from which I'd shut myself off.

THREE

ECONOMICS
MEETS POLITICS

Economic forecasting took Washington by storm in the 1960s. It started when Walter Heller, a witty, erudite professor from Minnesota who was chairman of the Council of Economic Advisors, told President Kennedy that a tax cut would stimulate economic growth. Kennedy resisted the idea—after all, he had come into office calling for self-sacrifice by the American people. Also, under the circumstances, a tax cut would mean a major change in fiscal policy, because the government was already in deficit. The economy back then was governed by the model of household finance—you were supposed to balance your budget and make ends meet. One year, President Eisenhower actually apologized to the American people for running a $3 billion deficit.

But after the Cuban missile crisis, with the 1964 election already on the horizon, the economy was growing too sluggishly, and Kennedy finally let himself be persuaded. The $10 billion tax cut he proposed to Congress in January 1963 was dramatic—it is to this day the biggest tax cut since World War II, adjusting for the size of the economy, and almost as big as all three of George W. Bush's tax cuts combined.

Lyndon Johnson signed the tax cut into law soon after Kennedy's death. To everybody's delight, it had the effect that the Council of Economic Advisors had promised: by 1965 the economy was thriving. Its annual growth rate was more than 6 percent, right in line with Walter Heller's econometric forecast.

The economists were jubilant. They thought they'd at last solved the riddle of forecasting, and they weren't shy about congratulating themselves: "A new era for economic policy is at hand," the CEA's Annual Report in January 1965 declared. "Tools of economic policy are becoming more refined, more effective, and increasingly freed from inhibitions imposed by traditions, misunderstanding, and doctrinaire polemics." It said that economic policymakers should no longer just respond passively to events but should "foresee and shape future developments." The stock market boomed, and at the end of the year *Time* magazine put John Maynard Keynes on the cover (even though he'd been dead since 1946), declaring, "We are all Keynesians now."[*]

I could scarcely believe it. I'd never been confident in making macroeconomic forecasts, and while Townsend-Greenspan did provide them to clients, they weren't central to our business. I had to admire what Heller had pulled off. But I also remember sitting in my office at 80 Pine Street with its view of the Brooklyn Bridge and thinking, Boy, I'm glad I don't have Walter Heller's job. I knew that macroeconomic forecasts are far more art than science.

Those rosy economic results deteriorated as the Johnson administration began pumping vast sums of money into the Vietnam War and Great Society programs. Beyond the necessities of day-to-day operations at Townsend-Greenspan, I took a deep interest in governmental fiscal policy and often wrote newspaper op-eds and articles for economics journals that were critical of the administration. The economics of the Vietnam War in particular fascinated me because of my earlier work on Korean War spending. When my old colleague Sandy Parker, who was still chief economist at

---

[*]Richard Nixon picked up this line and used it as president in 1971 in defense of his administration's fiscal deficits and economic interventionism.

Fortune magazine, asked in early 1966 for Townsend-Greenspan to help examine the cost of the war, I readily agreed.

Something in President Johnson's accounting didn't add up. The administration's estimates of war costs seemed low, based on what was becoming known about the growth of the U.S. deployment—General William Westmoreland was reportedly asking behind closed doors for an increase to four hundred thousand troops. I pulled apart the president's budget proposal to Congress for the fiscal year starting July 1, 1966, and by applying what I knew about the patterns and practices of Pentagon spending, I determined that the budget lowballed the likely cost of the war for that year by at least 50 percent—$11 billion or more. (The budget also assumed, in a revealing footnote looking toward 1967, that combat operations would end on June 30 of that year, so no costly replacements of planes or other equipment lost would be needed after that.)

Fortune broke the story in an April 1966 piece entitled "The Vietnam War: A Cost Accounting." The article concluded bluntly: "The budget barely begins to suggest the level of Vietnam War spending that lies ahead." Coming from a respected business publication, it added fire to the growing debate about whether LBJ and his administration were hiding the cost of the war.*

Apart from being suspicious about the war's economics, however, I was pretty much out of step with the times. When people think of the sixties, they think of civil rights marches, antiwar demonstrations, and sex, drugs, and rock and roll—a culture dramatically and flamboyantly in upheaval. But I was on the other side of the generation gap. I'd turned forty in 1966, which meant I'd become an adult in the 1950s, when you wore a jacket and a tie and smoked a pipe (with tobacco in it). I was still listening to Mozart and Brahms, and to Benny Goodman and Glenn Miller. Popular music became almost wholly alien to me with the arrival of Elvis—to my ears, it was on the edge of noise. I thought the Beatles were reasonably good musicians; they could sing well and had engaging personalities—and compared with some of what soon followed, their music was almost classical. The culture

---

*President Johnson played loose with the numbers from the start. The historian and former LBJ consultant Eric Goldman, for example, described in a 1969 memoir how Johnson misled reporters about his first budget to "heighten the impression of devotion to economy and skill in achieving it."

of the sixties was alien to me because I thought it anti-intellectual. I had a deep conservatism and a belief in civility. So I didn't relate to flower power. I had the freedom not to participate, and I didn't.

My involvement in public life started in 1967 with Nixon's campaign for president. I'd been writing an economics textbook on the side with a Columbia University finance professor named Martin Anderson. Marty had made a reputation for himself in conservative circles with a book called *The Federal Bulldozer*, a critique of urban renewal that had caught Nixon's eye. Our plan had been to collaborate on a textbook describing a laissez-faire capitalist system; with some sense of irony, we'd decided that Marty, the academic, would write the chapters about business, and I, the business consultant, would write the chapters about theory. But we hadn't gotten very far when Nixon asked Marty to join his presidential campaign as his chief domestic policy adviser.

As soon as he joined the campaign, Marty asked if I could help their little crew develop policy and write speeches. The senior staff at that point consisted of just four people besides Marty: Pat Buchanan, who was chief of staff, William Safire, Ray Price, and Leonard Garment. Len was the only one I knew, although I had seen him only rarely since we'd played together in the Henry Jerome orchestra more than twenty years earlier. Now he was a partner at Nixon's law firm in New York, Nixon Mudge Rose Guthrie Alexander & Mitchell. The six of us went out for lunch and talked about what I could do for the campaign. They liked some of my ideas, and finally Buchanan suggested that before we went further, I should come talk to the candidate.

A couple of days later I went to meet Nixon at his office. It intrigued me that he was back in the political game. Like everybody, I remembered his farewell gibe at reporters after losing the California gubernatorial race in 1962, in which he thought the press had been against him: "You won't have Nixon to kick around anymore, because, gentlemen, this is my last press conference." Nixon's office at Nixon Mudge Rose was chock-full of memorabilia and autographed photos—I had the sense that here was a once-important figure who had been pushed off into a little room with a lot of memories. But Nixon was very elegantly dressed, and he didn't just look the part of the successful senior New York lawyer, he acted it too.

Without wasting time on chitchat, he drew me out with thoughtful questions about economics and policy. When he set forth his ideas, he did so in perfectly turned sentences and paragraphs. I was very impressed. Later in the campaign, I'd sometimes have to brief Nixon on an issue before he met with the media, and he'd go into that same intense, factually oriented lawyer mode. He could listen for five minutes on a subject he couldn't possibly know much about—a breaking news event, for instance—then get out there and sound as knowledgeable as a professor. I would say that he and Bill Clinton were by far the smartest presidents I've worked with.

The Nixon for President committee had offices at Park Avenue and Fifty-seventh Street in the old American Bible Society Building. I initially worked a couple of afternoons a week, increasing to four, five, or even more as the campaign geared up. They appointed me "economic and domestic policy adviser," but I was always strictly a volunteer. I worked very closely with Marty, who'd taken a leave from Columbia and who was on the campaign plane full-time. Part of my job was to coordinate responses on any issue that came up: we'd scramble to assemble the necessary research and fax it to Nixon and the campaign team overnight. He wanted to come across as informed, and I helped organize task forces on economic issues. The main objective of these task forces was to bring people into his camp. There were almost twice as many registered Democrats as Republicans in America,* and Nixon needed to include everyone he could. Each task force would get together, the members would tell Nixon what they thought, and everybody would smile and shake hands and take pictures. But the work I enjoyed most, and my most original contribution, was integrating state and local polls. During the election campaign of 2004, politicians could go on the Internet and each day get an up-to-date electoral count based on polls within the fifty states. That technology wasn't there in 1968, but I built something as close to it as you could get. I took all the state polls we could find, related them to past voting patterns and trends, and extrapolated for states that did not have polls—all to project the popular vote and the electoral vote.

---

*The distribution of voters, according to the Center for the Study of the American Electorate, was seventeen million registered Democrats versus nine million registered Republicans.

In late July 1968, just a week before the Republican convention, Nixon assembled the senior staff at Gurney's Inn, a beach resort in Montauk on the far eastern tip of Long Island. About fifteen people were present—all the senior staff including the handful I'd started with many months before. Nixon already knew he had enough votes for the nomination, and this was meant to be a working session to frame the issues he wanted to hit in his acceptance speech. When we sat down at the conference table, though, for some reason he was angry. Instead of the policy discussion I was expecting, he launched into a fulmination about how the Democrats were the enemy. He didn't raise his voice, but his speech was so intense and so laced with profanity that it would have made Tony Soprano blush. I was stunned: this was not the man I'd been dealing with. I had no inkling then that I was observing an important part of the Nixon personality. I couldn't understand how a single human being could have such different sides. After a while he subsided and the meeting went on, but I never looked at him the same way after that. It so disturbed me that after the election, when I was invited to join the White House staff, I said, "No, I much prefer to go back to my job."

Nixon's profane side became public five years later with the release of the Watergate tapes, of course. In them, he comes across as an extremely smart man who is sadly paranoid, misanthropic, and cynical. A member of the Clinton administration once was accusing Nixon of anti-Semitism, and I said, "You don't understand. He wasn't exclusively anti-Semitic. He was anti-Semitic, anti-Italian, anti-Greek, anti-Slovak. I don't know anybody he was pro. He hated everybody. He would say awful things about Henry Kissinger, yet he appointed him secretary of state." When Nixon left office, I was relieved. You didn't know what he might do, and the president of the United States has so much power that it's scary—it's very hard for a military officer sworn to uphold the Constitution to say, "Mr. President, I'm not going to do that."

Of course, Nixon was the extreme. But I came to see that people who are on the top of the political heap are really different. Jerry Ford was as close to normal as you get in a president, but he never was elected. There's a constitutional amendment that I've been pushing for years without success. It says, "Anyone willing to do what is required to become president of the United States is thereby barred from taking that office." I'm only half joking.

Even though I did not take a permanent job in the administration, Washington became an important part of my life. I worked as interim budget director before the inauguration, helping plan Nixon's first federal budget. I served on task forces and commissions—most important, the President's Commission on an All-Volunteer Armed Force, which Martin Anderson masterminded and which paved the way in Congress for the abolition of the draft.* And with friends and professional acquaintances manning many of the government's key economic and domestic policy posts, I found myself spending more and more time inside the Beltway.

The economy was behaving erratically as business grappled with the effects of Vietnam and domestic unrest. A 10 percent surcharge on the federal income tax, belatedly clamped on under President Johnson and kept in place by Nixon to help pay for the war, wasn't having a healthy effect. In 1970 we slid into a recession that pushed unemployment up to 6 percent—about five million people were out of work.

At the same time, inflation seemed to be taking on a life of its own. Instead of dropping, as all the forecasting models said it should, it was running at an annual rate of about 5.7 percent—low compared with what came later, but disturbingly high by the standard of the day. Under the prevailing Keynesian view of the economy, unemployment and inflation are like kids on a seesaw: when one goes up, the other goes down. To oversimplify, it was argued that the more people there are out of work, the less upward pressure there is on wages and prices. Conversely, when unemployment falls and the labor market gets tight, wage and price increases are likely.

But the Keynesian economic models failed to account for the possibility that unemployment and inflation could climb in tandem. This phenomenon, which came to be called stagflation, put policymakers at a loss. The forecasting tools that had made government economists seem so prescient

---

*Though Anderson assembled the commission, he did not serve on it. It was chaired by Thomas S. Gates Jr., who had served as secretary of defense under Eisenhower.

a decade before were in reality not good enough to let the government fine-tune the economy. (A poll a few years later showed that the public now rated economists' forecasting ability on a par with that of astrologers. This made me wonder what astrologers had done wrong.)

The political pressure on the administration to address these problems became intense. Arthur Okun, who'd been chairman of the Council of Economic Advisors under Johnson and who was known for his wry sense of humor, invented a "discomfort index" to describe the dilemma. It was simply the sum of the unemployment rate and the inflation rate. The discomfort index now stood at 10.6 percent, and since 1965 it had gone nowhere but up.*

I watched as my friends in Washington lurched from one remedy to another. To counter the recession and the chilling effect of the income-tax surcharge, the Fed cut interest rates and pumped money into the economy. This helped get GNP growing again but further fueled inflation. Meanwhile, among some of President Nixon's men, a movement was building for measures that were anathema to us free-market economists who had helped Nixon get elected: wage and price controls. Even my old friend and mentor Arthur Burns, whom Nixon appointed Fed chairman in 1970, began talking about something similar—incomes policies. I was stunned by Arthur's reversal—I chalked it up to political exigency combined with whatever alarming developments in the economy he must be seeing from his new vantage. Clearly the Fed was worried. (In retrospect, I suspect Burns was trying to preempt formal wage and price controls.) Finally, on Sunday, August 15, 1971, my phone rang at home—it was Herb Stein, who was then a member of Nixon's Council of Economic Advisors. "I'm calling from Camp David," he said. "The president wanted me to tell you he'll be speaking to the nation and he'll be announcing wage and price controls." That evening is memorable to me for two reasons: First, Nixon preempted *Bonanza*, America's favorite TV western and a show I loved to watch, to

---

*The discomfort index was later renamed the misery index and went on to figure in at least two presidential campaigns. Jimmy Carter used it to criticize President Ford in 1976, and Ronald Reagan used it to criticize President Carter in 1980.

announce his policy; and second, I reached for something on the floor and threw my back out. I had to go to bed for six weeks. To this day, I like to believe that it was wage and price controls that did me in.

I was glad that I wasn't in the government. Burns and his wife were living at the Watergate apartment complex, and sometimes I'd visit their home for dinner. Arthur would muse about the White House's latest initiative and say, "Oh my goodness, what are they thinking of doing now?" After Nixon imposed wage and price controls, I'd fly down to meet with Don Rumsfeld, who was head of the Economic Stabilization Program, the bureaucracy created to administer them. He also ran the Cost of Living Council, where Dick Cheney was his deputy. They asked for my advice because I knew a great deal about how particular industries worked. But all I could do for them was indicate what type of problem would be created by each type of price freeze. What they were running into was the problem of central planning in a market economy—the market will always undermine any attempt at control. One week the problem was textiles. Because of the political power of the farmers, the administration could not put price caps on raw cotton. So the cotton price was going up. But the government did freeze the price of greige goods—unbleached, undyed woven cloth that is the first stage in textile production (greige is pronounced "gray"). So the greige-goods manufacturers were squeezed—their costs were going up but they couldn't raise prices—and companies were abandoning that part of the business. All of a sudden, the fabric finishers and clothing manufacturers were complaining that there weren't enough greige goods. Rumsfeld asked me, "What do I do?" And I said, "Simple—raise the price." Situations like this came up week after week, and after a couple of years the whole system fell apart. Much later Nixon said wage and price controls had been his worst policy. But the sad thing was that he knew they were a bad idea all along. It was pure political expediency: a lot of businessmen had said they wanted to freeze wages, and a lot of consumers liked the idea of freezing prices, so he decided he had to do it.

The Arab oil embargo of October 1973 only made inflation and unemployment worse—not to mention hurting America's confidence and self-esteem. The consumer price index ballooned: the year 1974 gave rise to the expression "double-digit inflation" as the rate went up to a shocking

11 percent. Unemployment was still at 5.6 percent, the stock market was in a steep decline, the economy was about to sink into the worst recession since the 1930s, and the Watergate scandal cast a pall over everything.

In the middle of all this depressing news, Treasury Secretary Bill Simon called to ask if I would take over as chairman of the Council of Economic Advisors. Herb Stein, by then CEA chairman, was getting ready to leave. CEA chairman is one of the three top posts for an economist in Washington, the others being treasury secretary and chairman of the Fed. In most circumstances, I would have said yes in a heartbeat. But I didn't agree with many of the president's policies, and hence felt that I would not be able to function effectively. I told Simon I was honored and that I'd be happy to suggest other candidates, but my answer was no. He called a second time a week or so later, and I said, "Bill, I appreciate it, but I really mean it." "Well, would you at least go talk to Al Haig?" Haig was President Nixon's chief of staff. I agreed, and a day later Haig asked if I'd come to see him at Key Biscayne, Florida, where the president liked to spend time. Haig really put on the White House show of interest, sending a military executive jet, complete with a steward, to shuttle me down to Key Biscayne. When I arrived, Haig and I had a long talk. I told him, "You're making a mistake. If I come in as chairman and the administration starts implementing policies I can't agree with, I'd have to resign. You don't need that." Wage and price controls had mostly been lifted by this time, but there was a lot of pressure from Congress to reimpose them because of inflation. I told him I would have to resign if that happened. Haig said, "That's not the direction we're heading. You won't feel the need to resign." As I got ready to leave, he asked, "Do you want to see him?" He meant Nixon. I said, "I don't see any reason." The truth was that I still felt very uncomfortable with the man. I wasn't sure about the job offer, either, and I felt the hardest thing in the world would be to say no to the president of the United States.

I'd barely returned to my office in New York when the phone rang again. This time it was Arthur Burns. He asked me to come to see him in Washington, which I did. That was my mistake. My old mentor puffed on his pipe and played on my guilt. Referring to the Watergate scandal, he said, "This government is paralyzed. But there's still an economy out there and we still have to make economic policy. You owe it to your country to serve." Besides, he pointed out, I'd been building Townsend-Greenspan for twenty years; wasn't it time to see if the company could fend for itself? By the end of the conversation I was persuaded that maybe I could do something useful in Washington. But I told myself I'd take an apartment on a month-to-month lease, and figuratively, at least, keep a suitcase packed by the door.

If Nixon hadn't been in such trouble, I doubt I'd have taken the job. I viewed it almost as a caretaker position, to help hold things together. I expected to be there a relatively short time. If Nixon had somehow continued in office through the end of his term, I would probably not have stayed more than a year. But events took a radically different turn. My Senate confirmation hearing was on the afternoon of Thursday, August 8, 1974; that very evening, Nixon went on TV to announce his resignation.

I'd met Vice President Ford only once, for an hour-long conversation about the economy a few weeks before. But we'd gotten along well, and on the urging of Don Rumsfeld, who headed his transition team, he reaffirmed Nixon's appointment of me.

The Council of Economic Advisors is essentially a small consulting firm with a single client: the president of the United States. It has rooms in the Old Executive Office Building, across the street from the White House, and consists of three council members and a small staff of economists, mostly professors on one- or two-year leave from their universities. Under Nixon, the CEA had become quite political, with Herb Stein frequently speaking on the president's behalf. Though Herb was an effective chairman, it is very difficult to be both an adviser and a spokesman (normally it is the treasury secretary who is the economic spokesman for the administration), and I wanted to return the council to its advisory role. After discussing this briefly with the other council members, William Fellner and Gary Seevers, I canceled the regular monthly press briefings. I decided I would make as few speeches as possible and as few congressional contacts as necessary; of course, I'd have to give testimony when called upon.

As chairman I was an unusual choice, because I didn't yet have a Ph.D. and because I looked at the economy differently from most academicians. At Townsend-Greenspan, we had computers and state-of-the-art econometric models that any professor would recognize, but our focus was always industry-level analysis, not macrovariables such as unemployment and federal deficits.

Ford and Nixon were as different as day and night. Ford was a secure man, with fewer psychological hang-ups than almost anyone I'd ever met. You never got strange vibes from him, never any sense of hidden motives. If he was angry, he'd be angry for an objective reason. But that was rare—he was exceptionally even-tempered. In 1975, just after the fall of Saigon, the Khmer Rouge in Cambodia seized the *Mayaguez*, a U.S.-flagged container ship in a shipping lane off their coast. I was sitting next to Ford in an economics meeting when Brent Scowcroft, the deputy director of the National Security Council, came in and put a note in front of him. The president opened it up. He read it. This was the first Ford had learned of the incident. He turned to Scowcroft and said, "Okay, provided that we do not shoot first." Then he turned back to the meeting and continued the discussion. I never read the note, but it was clear that the president had just authorized the military to shoot back if necessary against the Khmer Rouge forces.

He always understood what he knew and what he didn't know. He didn't think he was intellectually superior to Henry Kissinger or that he knew more about foreign policy, but he wasn't intimidated. Ford was secure in himself—probably one of those rare people who would actually score normal in psychological tests.

Though he wasn't terribly articulate on the subject of economics, I found that President Ford had a sophisticated and consistent outlook on economic policy. Years on the House Appropriations Committee had taught him everything there is to know about the federal budget, and his budgets as president were truly his own. More important, he believed in restraint in federal spending, a balanced budget, and stable long-term growth.

Ford's top priority was to develop a solution to inflation, which in his first address to Congress he identified as public enemy number one. With the dollar losing more than 10 percent of its purchasing power that year, inflation had everybody spooked. People cut back on spending because they worried about making ends meet. In businesses, inflation creates uncertainty and risk, which makes planning more difficult and discourages managers from hiring, or building factories, or indeed doing any kind of investing for growth. That's what happened in 1974—capital spending essentially froze, making the recession far more severe.

I agreed with the president's priorities, but I was horrified to learn how his White House staff planned to tackle the issue. My first experience of policymaking in the Roosevelt Room of the White House almost sent me racing back to New York. It was a senior staff meeting at which the speechwriting department unveiled a campaign called Whip Inflation Now. WIN, as they wanted it to be known ("Get it?" one asked), was a vast program that would involve a national voluntary price freeze, a summit conference in Washington in October to discuss inflation with preliminary task forces and minisummits all over the country, and many other features. The speechwriters had ordered up millions of Whip Inflation Now buttons, samples of which they handed out to us in the room. It was surreal. I was the only economist present, and I said to myself, This is unbelievable stupidity. What am I doing here?

Because I was new, I wasn't sure of the protocol. I didn't think I should just say what I thought. So I zeroed in on things that made no economic sense. I pointed out, "You can't ask small-business owners to voluntarily forgo price increases. These people operate on thin margins, and they can't prevent their suppliers from raising prices." Over the next few days, I succeeded in getting them to water down a few of the provisions, but Whip Inflation Now went forward with great fanfare that fall. It was a low point of economic policymaking. It made me glad I'd canceled the CEA's press briefings, because I was never called upon in public to defend Whip Inflation Now. By the end of the year it was totally eclipsed by the worsening recession.

The main economic policy group at the White House met each workday at 8:30 a.m., and since the economy was at center stage politically, everybody wanted to participate. The group included five or six cabinet officers, the director of the budget, the so-called energy czar, and more. On key issues Arthur Burns would sit in to advise. Many days there would be twenty-five people in the room. This was a good forum in which to air issues, but not a place to make the real decisions. The inner circle of economic advisers was much smaller: Treasury Secretary Simon, Budget Director Roy Ash (later his successor, Jim Lynn), Arthur Burns, and me.

At first it seemed as though all any of us did was bring the president bad news. In late September, unemployment suddenly ticked up. Soon orders, production, and employment all started to fall. By Thanksgiving I was telling the president, "There's a possibility that we may have very severe problems going into next spring." On Christmas Eve, the policy group wrote a memorandum warning him to expect more unemployment and the deepest recession since World War II. It was not a nice present.

Worse, we had to tell him we didn't know how bad the recession would be. Recessions are like hurricanes—they range from ordinary to catastrophic. The ordinary ones are part of the business cycle: they happen when business inventories exceed demand, and companies cut production sharply until the excess inventory gets sold. The Category 5 kind happens when demand itself collapses—when consumers stop spending and businesses stop investing. As we talked through the possibilities, President Ford worried that America would find itself trapped in a vicious circle of falling demand, layoffs, and gloom. Since none of the forecasting models could deal with the circumstances we were facing, we were flying blind. All we could tell him was that this might be an inventory-based recession, aggravated by the oil shock and inflation—maybe a Category 2 or 3. Or it might be a Category 5.

The president had to make a choice. With the discomfort index nearing 20 percent, there was tremendous political pressure from Congress to slash taxes or massively pump up government spending. That was the way to deal with a Category 5. It could revive growth in the short term, though it risked pushing inflation even higher, with potentially disastrous long-term effects. On the other hand, if we were facing only an inventory recession, the optimum response—economically, not politically—was to do as little as possible; if we could keep our hand off the panic button, the economy would correct itself.

Ford was not a man given to panic. In early January 1975, he instructed us to develop the mildest possible plan. It ended up including steps to ease the energy crisis, restraints on federal budget growth, and a onetime income-tax rebate to give families a boost. The rebate was the brainchild of Andrew Brimmer, a private-sector economist who'd served in the LBJ years as the first African American governor of the Federal Reserve Board. A few days before presenting the plan to the public, President Ford quizzed me closely on whether a $16 billion tax rebate would hurt our prospects for long-term growth. Economically speaking, the rebate was a prudent response, I told him, and explained, "As long as it's a one-shot deal and doesn't become permanent, it's not going to do much harm."

I was a little startled when he answered, "If that's what you think should be done, then I'll propose it." Of course, he was also consulting with advisers more senior than I. But I thought, This is interesting. The president of the United States is taking my advice. I felt a big sense of responsibility—and gratification. Ford didn't owe me anything, politically or otherwise. Here was proof that ideas and facts did matter.

His restrained program made good economic sense. It jibed with my own decision-making philosophy. In reviewing a policy, I always asked my-self the question, What are the costs to the economy if we are wrong? If there is no downside risk, you can try any policy you want. If the cost of failure is potentially very large, you should avoid the policy even if the probability of success is better than fifty-fifty, because you cannot accept the cost of failure. All the same, the choice President Ford made took a lot of political courage. He was well aware that his program would be de-nounced as inadequate—and that it might, if it proved too mild, prolong the economic slide.

I decided the CEA had to treat this as an emergency. The president needed to know whether we were facing a temporary inventory shock or a major meltdown of demand. The only surefire economic measure of that was the gross national product, a comprehensive description of the econ-omy that the Bureau of Economic Analysis derived from a vast agglomera-tion of statistics. Unfortunately, the BEA produced the GNP only once per quarter—well after the fact. And you can't drive using a rearview mirror.

My idea was to rig up an emergency set of headlights: a weekly version of the GNP that would enable us to monitor the recession in real time. I believed this was possible because at Townsend-Greenspan we'd developed a monthly GNP. It appealed to clients who had to make decisions and did not want to wait for the official quarterly figures to be announced. So the analytical foundation was there; creating a weekly measure would mostly mean more work. Some crucial statistics, such as retail sales and new unemployment-insurance claims, were already available on a weekly basis, so those were easy. Other key data, such as auto sales or statistics on orders and shipments of durable goods (factory gear, computers, and so on), were normally reported every ten days or once a month. Inventory data too were monthly, with the further complication that the surveys were often inaccurate and subject to large revisions.

A way to fill these giant information gaps was to get on the phone. I'd built a large network of clients and contacts over the years in companies, trade associations, universities, and regulatory agencies, and many of these people responded generously when we called to ask for help. Companies shared confidential information about their order books and hiring plans; business leaders and experts guided us with their own observations and insights. We were able to build a clearer picture of inventories, for example, by combining this anecdotal information with sensitive measures of raw-materials prices, imports and exports, delivery schedules, and more.

The evidence we pulled together was still fragmentary—nowhere near the standard that the Bureau of Economic Analysis used in calculating GNP for public dissemination. But it fit our special needs. When the BEA economists and statisticians learned what we were trying to do, they pitched in and helped us structure our analysis. After two or three weeks of burning the midnight oil—our small staff was also busy preparing its annual assessment of the economy, which is published in early February—the weekly GNP system was up and running. Finally I was able to start going to President Ford with up-to-date facts instead of guesstimates.

The policy issues came into much sharper focus after that. Each week, at the regular cabinet meeting, I would update the picture of the recession. As we looked at the ten-day auto sales figures, the weekly retail sales, the data on housing permits and starts, detailed reports coming out of the unemployment-insurance system, and so on, we became convinced that this was the milder kind of storm. Consumers, it turned out, were still buying at a healthy rate despite all they'd been through. What was more, inventories were being liquidated at a very rapid clip, a pace that could not continue for long, or business would soon run out of inventories. This meant production soon had to rise to close the gap with consumption.

Thus I was able to tell the president and the cabinet that the recession was bottoming out. I said, with what for me was certainty: "I can't give you the exact date, but unless there is a collapse in consumer markets or housing, it's got to happen that way." Week after week, the data were unequivocal—it turned out to be one of those rare, fortunate occasions in economics when the facts are clear and you can know for sure what is going on. So when the time came in March 1975 for me to testify in Congress, I had the strong conviction necessary to be able to say that America was moving toward a recovery "on schedule." I testified that we faced another bad quarter and that unemployment could hit 9 percent, and yet it was now possible to be "marginally optimistic." And I warned against panicky spending increases or tax cuts that would overstimulate the economy and trigger another inflationary spiral.

The political storm surrounding the president's economic plan that spring was something to behold. There was tremendous fear in Congress. I used to joke that I had to put on my bulletproof vest and armor when I'd go up to the Hill to testify. *Newsweek* put my picture on the cover in February 1975 under the headline "How Far Is Down?" Congressman Henry Reuss thought Ford, like Herbert Hoover in 1930, would let us slide into a depression, and was quoted saying, "The President is getting the same kind of economic advice that Herbert Hoover was given." When I appeared before the Senate Budget Committee, the chairman, Ed Muskie, asserted that the administration was doing "too little, too late." Congressmen were putting forward proposals to stimulate the economy that would have pushed the deficit to $80 billion and beyond, a horrendous figure at that time. George Meany, the president of the AFL-CIO, was even more vociferous. "America is in the worst economic emergency since the Great Depression," he testified. "The situation is frightening now and it is growing more ominous by the day. This is not just another recession, for it has no parallel in the five recessions in the post–World War II period. America is far beyond the point where the situation can correct itself. Massive government action is needed." Meany wanted the government to run a $100 billion deficit, including massive tax cuts for low- and middle-income families, to stimulate growth.

One thing that surprised everyone was the lack of public protest. Coming off a decade of civil rights and anti–Vietnam War marches, anyone who could have foreseen 9 percent unemployment would have expected massive demonstrations and barricades in the streets, not just in the United States but also in Europe and Japan, where the economic problems were equally severe. Yet that didn't happen. Perhaps the world was simply exhausted by the oil shock and the decade that had led up to it. But the era of protest was over. America was going through this period with what seemed like a new sense of cohesion.

President Ford held off the pressure, and his economic program eventually made it into law (Congress did raise the tax rebate by almost 50 percent, to about $125 per average household). More important, the recovery began when we promised the public it would, in mid-1975. GNP growth rocketed—by October the economy was expanding at the highest rate in twenty-five years. Inflation and unemployment began slowly to abate. As is so often the case, the political hyperbole not only ceased virtually overnight, but also the frightening predictions were quickly forgotten. In July, the crisis having passed, we retired our emergency weekly GNP monitoring program, much to the relief of the CEA staff.

Deregulation was the Ford administration's great unsung achievement. It's difficult to imagine how straitjacketed American business was then. Airlines, trucking, railroads, buses, pipelines, telephones, television, stockbrokers, financial markets, savings banks, utilities—all operated under heavy regulation. Operations were monitored down to the tiniest detail. My favorite description of this was by Alfred Kahn, a wisecracking economist from Cornell University whom Jimmy Carter made head of the Civil Aeronautics Board and who became known as the Father of Airline Deregulation. Speaking in 1978 on the need for change, Fred couldn't resist riffing on the thousands of picayune decisions he and the board were called upon to make: "May an air taxi acquire a fifty-seat plane? May a supplemental carrier carry horses from Florida to somewhere in the Northeast? Should we let a scheduled carrier pick up stranded charter customers and carry them on seats that would otherwise be empty, at charter rates? ... May a carrier introduce a special fare for skiers but refund the cost of their ticket if there is no snow? May the employees of two financially affiliated airlines wear similar-looking uniforms?" Then he looked at the congressmen and said, "Is it any wonder that I ask myself every day: Is this action necessary? Is this what my mother raised me to do?"

President Ford launched his campaign to eliminate such folly in a speech in Chicago in August 1975. He promised a business audience that he would "take the shackles off American businessmen" and "get the federal government as far out of your business, out of your lives, out of your pocketbooks, and out of your hair as I possibly can." The choice of Chicago seemed fitting: deregulation's economic rationale came primarily from Milton Friedman and the other mavericks of the so-called Chicago school. These economists had built a large, impressive body of work around the theory that markets and prices, not central planners, were the best allocators of society's resources. The Keynesian presumption that had held sway in Washington since the Kennedy administration was that the economy could be actively managed; the Chicago economists argued that government should intervene less, not more, because scientific regulation was a myth. Now, after years of stagflation and with the failure of wage and price controls fresh in people's minds, politicians on both sides were ready to agree that micromanagement by government had gone too far. It was time to do less.

In fact, a remarkable consensus on economic policy emerged in Washington—a convergence of attitudes between the liberal left and the conservative right. Suddenly everybody was looking to restrain inflation, cut deficit spending, reduce regulation, and encourage investment. Ford's deregulation campaign initially targeted railroads, trucking, and airlines. And despite massive opposition by companies and unions, within a few years Congress deregulated all three.

It's hard to overemphasize how important Ford's deregulation was. True, most of the benefits took years to unfold—rail freight rates, for example, hardly budged at first. Yet deregulation set the stage for an enormous wave of creative destruction in the 1980s: the breakup of AT&T and other dinosaurs, the birth of new industries such as personal computing and overnight shipping, the mergers-and-acquisitions boom on Wall Street, and the remaking of companies would be the hallmarks of the Reagan era. And, we would ultimately find, deregulation also greatly increased the economy's flexibility and resilience.

Jerry Ford and I grew very close. He was consistent in his view that what the economy most needed was a return of confidence and cool. This meant staying away from the aggressive interventionism that started under Kennedy, and from the abrupt, politically reactive policymaking that made the nation so panicky and uncertain under Nixon. Ford wanted to slow the pace of policy action, simmer down the deficit and inflation and unemployment, and eventually achieve a stable, balanced, steadily growing economy. Since these were very much my views too, it became easy for the CEA to function. We didn't have to keep checking to find out what he thought. We could boil down a problem to a set of options, and then I could pick up the phone and say, "We've got this issue. Here are the choices. How would you like to proceed: one, two, three, or four?" We could have a three-minute conversation and I'd come away with very clear instructions on what he wanted to do.

Being at the center of things was admittedly fun. In January 1976, I was helping Jim Lynn draft the economics section of the president's State of the Union speech. Things were changing very rapidly and we were rewriting up to the last minute. One night we were working late at the White House making revisions, a tedious chore because there were no word processors. And Jim said, "I wonder how I'll feel after I leave. Maybe I'll be outside this building with my nose pressed against the glass, wondering what all these powerful people are doing." We burst out laughing. Sure, we were working with scissors and tape and Wite-Out—but we were writing the State of the Union address.

The White House was also great for my tennis game. I hadn't played since I was a teenager, but after the weather warmed up and the crisis cooled down, I started again from scratch on the White House tennis court. The court is outdoors, near the southwest gate, and its great advantage is that it's thoroughly concealed by fences. My opponent was Frank Zarb, the energy czar, who hadn't played tennis in a long time either. So we were very fortunate no one could see.

I was back and forth to New York every Saturday or Sunday—I'd water the plants in my apartment and spend time with my mother. These trips did not involve business: to satisfy conflict-of-interest rules, I'd removed myself entirely from the operations of Townsend-Greenspan and put my ownership into a blind trust. The company was in the hands of my vice presidents, Kathy Eichoff, Bess Kaplan, and Lucille Wu, and former vice president Judith Mackey, who had come back temporarily to help out. Townsend-Greenspan was unusual for an economics firm in that the men worked for the women (we had about twenty-five employees in all). My hiring of women economists was not motivated by women's liberation. It just made great business sense. I valued men and women equally, and found that because other employers did not, good women economists were less expensive than men. Hiring women did two things: it gave Townsend-Greenspan higher-quality work for the same money, and it marginally raised the market value of women.

I always brought along some CEA work on the weekends. During the week, I generally worked ten- to twelve-hour days. I followed a very satisfying routine, starting with a long, hot bath at dawn. This habit began after I'd thrown out my back in 1971. As part of the rehab process, my orthopedist had recommended soaking in a hot bath for an hour each morning. I found I liked it. It was an ideal environment for work. I could read, I could write, and it was perfectly private. I could get white noise by turning on the exhaust fan. My back eventually healed, but by then the bath was an activity of choice.

I'd be out the door by 7:30 a.m., and my apartment at the Watergate was close enough to the Old Executive Office Building for me to walk to work on occasion. The streets around the White House were much more placid than they'd been in the Nixon administration, when during visits to the city I'd often had to thread my way through protesters. My routine was much like that of anybody immersed in public life. The White House staff met at 8:00, and the Economic Policy Board at 8:30, and the day would go on from there. I'd usually work until 7:00, with breaks for tennis or occasionally golf. The president would periodically invite me to play golf with him at Burning Tree, a suburban Washington country club that became notorious for excluding women. Today, no president could do that, but few people complained in the early 1970s. I'd go to dinner or to a concert, often sitting in the president's box, or make an appearance at a reception. I took no real days off, but I didn't mind. I was doing what I loved.

The economic recovery greatly boosted Ford's chances of getting elected in 1976. Given the public's sour memories of Watergate, the pardon of Nixon, inflation, and OPEC, many pundits started out saying it was virtually impossible for Ford or any Republican to win. Before the summer's party conventions, polls had him trailing by more than 30 percentage points. But Ford's prudence and evenhandedness—and his results—were winning respect, and that gap soon narrowed.

I'd have been interested in a job in his new administration—in spite of my early skepticism about working in government, I'd become convinced that it was sometimes possible to do good in Washington. I would have loved a chance to serve as treasury secretary. But when asked early on if I wanted to be in his campaign, I said I did not. I thought it inappropriate for a CEA chairman. Certain officers of the government—the secretary of state, the attorney general, and the CEA chairman—should not, I felt, be involved in electoral politics, because they run institutions that are supposed to generate information of a bipartisan nature. The president thought I'd made the right call.

Nevertheless, as Ford got ready to square off against Jimmy Carter, I inadvertently supplied the buzzword that was used against the president throughout the campaign. The central economic debate of Campaign '76 was whether the recovery had collapsed. After growing extremely rapidly through the first quarter of the year—at a tigerlike annual rate of 9.3 percent—the economy had abruptly cooled, to a growth rate of less than 2 percent by summer. From an economist's standpoint, this was not a cause for concern. Because a modern economy involves so many moving parts, it rarely accelerates or decelerates smoothly, and in this case all the other major indicators—inflation, unemployment, and so on—looked fine.

I laid this out in a cabinet meeting in August, using charts to demonstrate how this recovery mirrored past ones. "The pattern is advance and pause, advance and pause," I told them. "We are in one of those pause periods. But the basic recovery is solidly in place with no evidence of underlying deterioration." Those remarks, relayed by press secretary Ron Nessen to the media, turned out to be red meat for the president's critics. To them, "pause" was an administration euphemism for "we failed."

Suddenly the debate of early 1975 reignited, and Ford was again under tremendous pressure—from Congress and even his own campaign team—to abandon his commitment to a long-term, sustainable recovery and pull out the stops on economic stimulus. In the presidential debate that October, columnist Joseph Kraft asked bluntly: "Mr. President, the country is now in something that your advisers call an economic pause. I think to most Americans that sounds like an antiseptic term for low growth, unemployment, standstill at a high, high level, decline in take-home pay, lower factory earnings, more layoffs. Isn't that a really rotten record and doesn't your administration bear most of the blame for it?" Ford stoically defended his achievement, and history proved him right: economic growth went on to accelerate for another full year. But by the time this became apparent, Election Day had come and gone, and Ford had lost narrowly to Jimmy Carter, by little more than 1.5 million votes. Years afterward Henry Kissinger used to tease me, "You were right about the pause. It's just too bad it happened to coincide with a presidential election."

On January 20, 1977, Jimmy Carter was inaugurated as the thirty-ninth president of the United States. As he stood in front of the Capitol and took the oath of office, I was on the noon shuttle on my way back to New York.

FOUR

PRIVATE CITIZEN

It's never easy being on the losing side. Still, I found plenty of reasons to be glad to come home to New York. The services of Townsend-Greenspan were more in demand than ever. All kinds of doors opened to me, and I accepted as many interesting commitments as the calendar would allow. I rejoined *Time* magazine's Board of Economists and the Brookings Panel on Economic Activity, with people like Walter Heller, Martin Feldstein, George Perry, and Arthur Okun. I stepped up my speechmaking, appearing two or three times a month before companies, management groups, and associations, mostly to talk about their businesses and the economic outlook.

I also found myself in demand as a corporate director, joining the boards of Alcoa, Mobil, JPMorgan, General Foods, Capital Cities/ABC, and more. People serve on Fortune 500 boards for lots of reasons, but the primary reason for me was that being a director gave me a chance to learn the economic workings of things that are familiar but that I've never fully understood. Like Cool Whip and Post Toasties: until I became a director at General Foods, I never knew how the processed-food business worked. Townsend-Greenspan had done a lot of analysis of wheat, corn, and soybeans, but never of the foods you see in commercials and on supermarket shelves. For instance, General Foods owned Maxwell House, a dominant brand of coffee in those days before people were mesmerized by Starbucks. I was amazed to learn (though it made sense once I thought about it) that the main competitors for Maxwell House were not only other coffees but also soda and beer—the marketers were competing for a share of the nation's stomach capacity. General Foods also made me feel close to business history—the company still bore the stamp of its founder, the heiress Marjorie Merriweather Post. She'd been only twenty-seven when her father died and left her in charge of the family business, the Postum Cereal Company; with the second of her four husbands, the Wall Street financier E. F. Hutton, she built Postum into General Foods. She'd died just a few years before I joined the board, but their only child, the actress Dina Merrill, was a real presence at the company.

After all the years I'd spent studying business economics, it was still hard to fathom how big some of these companies were. Mobil, which in 1977 had $26 billion in sales and ranked number five on the Fortune 500, was operating everywhere—in the North Sea, in the Middle East, in Australia, in Nigeria. I gave a toast at my first dinner with the other directors that included a joke only an economist could appreciate: "I feel right at home here. Mobil is on the same order of magnitude as the U.S. government— the number 0.1 on a financial statement means $100 million."

Among all the boards I joined, JPMorgan's was the one that I found most engaging. It was the holding company for Morgan Guaranty, arguably then the world's premier bank. The board was a roll call of America's business elite: Frank Cary of IBM, Walter Fallon of Eastman Kodak, John Dorrance of Campbell's Soup, Lewis Foy of Bethlehem Steel—and me. We would meet at 23 Wall Street, which J. P. Morgan himself had built in the era when he reigned over American finance. On the fortresslike facade, you could still see the pockmarks from the terrorist bombing of 1920, when in the middle of a busy day a horse-drawn wagon of dynamite and shrapnel was set off in front of the bank, killing and injuring dozens of people. The bombing was attributed to anarchists but was never solved. Inside, the company had preserved the decor, with its high ceilings and rolltop desks.

The first time I sat in that boardroom I felt a little intimidated. There was a portrait of J. P. Morgan on the wall above the board table, and where I happened to be seated, when I raised my head, he was looking right at me.

You might have expected the people running Morgan to be loaded with pedigrees and manners. Instead, the business was a meritocracy. A good example was Dennis Weatherstone, who rose to CEO in the 1980s. Dennis never went to university; he started right out of a polytechnic school as a trader in Morgan's London branch. His success was hardly a result of social connections, because he didn't have any.

Being on the Morgan board was a wonderful opportunity to learn the inner workings of international finance. It puzzled me, for example, that month after month the bank consistently showed a profit on currency trading. I knew that because of the efficiency of foreign-exchange markets, forecasting exchange rates for major currencies is as accurate as forecasting the outcome of the flip of a coin. Finally I confronted the management: "Look, gentlemen, all the studies I'm aware of say you can't make profits consistently in foreign exchange."

"That's true," they explained. "But it's not forecasting that makes us money. We're market makers; we collect on the spread between the bid and the ask, no matter which way rates move." Like eBay today, they were taking a small cut on every transaction in which they served as middleman—and they were doing it on a vast scale.

One of the people on JPMorgan's international advisory council was a Saudi billionaire named Suleiman Olayan. He was an entrepreneur a few years older than I who'd gotten his start driving trucks for the Arabian-American Oil Company (Aramco) in the 1940s. Pretty soon he'd spun that off into a business that sold water, among other things, to the drillers, and provided other services. From there he diversified into construction and manufacturing; he was also the man who had introduced insurance into the kingdom.

He was already enormously wealthy when Saudi Arabia nationalized Aramco and took control of its own oil. And with the rise of OPEC, he'd developed a taste for American banks. He'd bought 1 percent of the stock not only in JPMorgan, but also in Chase Manhattan, Mellon, Bankers Trust, and four or five other big names. I got a kick out of him and his wife, Mary, an American who'd been working for Aramco when they met. Olayan was even more of a sponge for information than I—he was forever asking me questions about different aspects of the American economy.

I never asked him about it, but later it occurred to me that being on the Morgan council may have given him a better feel for the flows of petrodollars. A major business for U.S. banks in those days was taking in vast deposits of profits from Saudi Arabia and other OPEC nations and looking for places, mainly in Latin America, to lend the money out. OPEC didn't want to take on the risks of investing its surplus. The banks, to their eventual sorrow, did.

Returning to New York from the Ford administration, I continued dating Barbara Walters, whom I had met in 1975 while I was in Washington, at a tea dance given by Vice President Nelson Rockefeller. The following spring, I'd helped her think through a difficult and very high-profile career decision: whether to leave NBC's *Today* show, where she had worked for twelve years, rising to become a hugely popular cohost, and join ABC News, where she would be TV's first evening news anchorwoman. To entice her, ABC was offering a record-breaking salary of $1 million a year; and as everyone knows, she finally opted to make the move.

I'm not threatened by a powerful woman; in fact, I'm now married to one. The most boring activity I could imagine was going out with a vacuous date—something I learned the hard way over my years as a bachelor.

Before getting to know Barbara, a typical evening for me would be a professional dinner with other economists. Barbara, however, interacted constantly with news, sports, media, and entertainment personalities, interviewing a tremendous range of people, from Judy Garland to Mamie Eisenhower, from Richard Nixon to Anwar Sadat. She also had show-business roots. Her father, Lou, had been a big-time nightclub owner and Broadway producer—his Latin Quarter clubs in Manhattan and Miami Beach were the 1950s equivalent of the Stork Club of the 1930s, or more to the point by this time, the disco era's Studio 54.

During the several years we dated and afterward (we remain good friends), I escorted Barbara to lots of parties where I met people I otherwise would never have encountered. I usually thought the food was good but the conversation dull. Of course, they probably thought the same about me. Business economists are not exactly party animals.

Even so, I did build up a wonderful circle of friends. Barbara threw me a fiftieth-birthday party at her house. The guests were the people I'd come to think of as my New York friends: Henry and Nancy Kissinger, Oscar and Annette de la Renta, Felix and Liz Rohatyn, Brooke Astor (I knew her as a kid of seventy-five), Joe and Estée Lauder, Henry and Louise Grunwald, "Punch" and Carol Sulzberger, and David Rockefeller. I'm still friends with many of these people today, more than thirty years later.

Barbara's social network extended to Hollywood, of course. Business would take me to Los Angeles five or six times a year, where I'd play golf at the Hillcrest Country Club—the place where Jack Benny, Groucho Marx, Henny Youngman, and other comedians used to have a roundtable every day at lunch. (Ronald Reagan was also a Hillcrest member.) I learned a bit about the media industry doing work for the William Morris Agency, which was a Townsend-Greenspan client, and from spending time with the legendary producer Lew Wasserman. And I'd tag along with Barbara to parties in Beverly Hills, where I felt totally out of place. I'll never forget the moment when Sue Mengers came up to me at a party she was throwing for Jack Nicholson and gave me a hug. She was by far the most powerful agent in Hollywood, representing stars like Barbra Streisand, Steve McQueen, Gene Hackman, and Michael Caine. "I know you don't remember me," she began. Then she explained how when I was fifteen and she was thirteen, we used to hang out with other Washington Heights kids on the wall of Riverside Park. "You never noticed me, but I always looked up to you," she said. I was as speechless as I probably would have been at age fifteen.

Diverting as all this was, I still kept an eye on Washington. Jimmy Carter had no use for me—we met on only a couple of occasions and never hit it off. (Of course, I'd been part of the Ford administration, and he'd defeated Ford.) But from the sidelines in New York, I saw much going on in government to cheer about. Many of the moves that the administration and Congress made were the very ones I'd have pushed for, had I been there.

Most important, the Carter administration carried on the deregulation initiative that had begun under Jerry Ford. The airline-deregulation bill, promoted by Teddy Kennedy, passed in 1978. (Kennedy's right-hand man on this project was Stephen Breyer, who was on leave from Harvard Law School and who later became a justice of the Supreme Court and a good friend.) After that, Congress moved methodically to deregulate telecommunications and a half dozen other industries. Deregulation had a lasting effect not just on the economy but also on the Democratic Party, ending its domination by labor and opening it to business. But as important as these changes were, President Carter got little credit for them, mainly because of his style. Unlike Reagan, who knew how to present economic renewal stirringly, Carter came across as hesitant and dispirited: he made change seem like something you did because you had no choice.

The economy did not work in Carter's favor. For a year or so, his administration enjoyed the benefits of the recovery that had started under Ford. Then growth slowed and inflation resumed a steady and ominous rise. It cast a continuing pall of uncertainty on wage negotiations and investment decisions. It affected the rest of the world too, because other countries depended on the stability of the dollar, and the dollar was weakening. Throughout 1978 inflation ratcheted up—from 6.8 percent at the beginning of the year to 7.4 percent in June to 9 percent by Christmas. Then in January 1979 Islamic fundamentalists overthrew the shah of Iran, and the second oil crisis began. As gas lines formed that summer owing to gasoline price controls, the economy started to spiral toward another recession and inflation crossed again into the double-digit range, hitting 12 percent by fall.

It's not that Carter didn't try. His administration proposed no fewer than seven economic programs. But none was strong enough to contain what was fast becoming a crisis. From talking to my friends and professional contacts in the administration, I thought I understood their problem. Carter felt compelled to be all things to all people. So he'd propose new social programs while simultaneously trying to reduce the deficit, lower unemployment, and cut inflation. Among all those largely incompatible goals, controlling inflation was the one most fundamental to long-term prosperity. Under Carter it never got the priority it deserved. That was the analysis I gave to the *New York Times* in early 1980. I contrasted Carter's position with that of President Ford: "Our general policy was that until we beat inflation into the ground, we weren't doing anything else."

The Federal Reserve—by law independent of the White House—only seemed to mirror Carter's indecisiveness. My old mentor Arthur Burns and his successor, Bill Miller, kept trying to find a middle ground on monetary policy that would accommodate conflicting economic needs. They didn't want to make credit so easy as to further fuel inflation, but they didn't want to make it so tight as to choke the economy into another recession. From what I could see, that middle ground they were looking for didn't exist.

But I was in the minority. To most people, the peril to the economy wasn't clear. There was a widespread feeling in Washington that since you couldn't bring down inflation without causing more unemployment, it wasn't worth the cost.

Some on the right and on the left even began to argue that inflation as high as, say, 6 percent a year might be fine to live with—like Brazil, we could index wages to take it into account. (As any good economist could have predicted, Brazil later wound up with 5,000 percent inflation and a total economic collapse.) This complacency even extended to Wall Street. You could see it most clearly in the bond market, which, while it gets far fewer headlines than its noisy cousin the stock market, is even larger.* The interest rates on ten-year treasury notes, one of the best indicators of investors' long-term inflation expectations, climbed fairly steadily into the summer of 1979 but only modestly above where they were in 1975. This implied that investors were still betting that the American economy was inflation-resistant—and that the problem would somehow just go away.

The gas lines are what jolted everybody awake. The coming to power of Iran's ayatollahs and the subsequent Iran-Iraq War cut oil production by millions of barrels a day, and the resulting shortages at the pump had a scary cascading effect. The cuts drove up oil prices enough to boost inflation still more, and the high prices further increased instability by putting

---

*According to the Securities Industry and Financial Markets Association, the U.S. bond market in 1980 had a total value of $2.24 trillion, versus $1.45 trillion for the stock market. At the end of 2006, those figures were $27.4 trillion and $21.6 trillion, respectively.

the banks in the position of having to recycle even more petrodollars. The jump in inflation finally forced President Carter's hand. In July 1979, he shook up his cabinet and at the same time named Paul Volcker to replace Bill Miller as chairman of the Fed. In the years since I'd met Paul as a freshly minted Princeton graduate, he'd risen to become president of the New York Fed, the most important bank in the Federal Reserve System. Later it emerged that until Carter appointed him, the president didn't even know who Volcker was; David Rockefeller and Wall Street banker Robert Roosa had urged him on the president as the necessary choice to reassure the financial world. Volcker captured the dark mood when he said at his swearing-in, "We are face to face with economic difficulties really unique to our experience. We have lost that euphoria that we had 15 years ago, that we knew all the answers to managing the economy."

Volcker and I were not personal friends. At six foot seven, with an ever-present cigar, he made a vivid impression, but in conversation I always found him quite introverted and withdrawn. He didn't play tennis or golf—instead, he liked to go off by himself and fly-fish. He was a bit of a mystery to me. Of course, knowing how to play one's cards close to the vest is a strength in a central banker, and underneath that eccentric exterior Paul clearly had tremendous force of character. Having been a civil servant most of his career, he didn't have much money. He kept his family at their house in suburban New York for the entire time he was Fed chairman. All he had in Washington was a tiny apartment—he invited me over once in the early 1980s to talk about the Mexican debt crisis, and the place was filled with piles of old newspapers and all the other clutter of a bachelor apartment.

From the moment he was sworn in, Volcker knew that his job was, as he later said, to "slay the inflationary dragon." He did not get much time to prepare. He'd been Fed chairman barely two months when a crisis erupted: investors all over the world started dumping long-term bonds. The interest rate on ten-year treasury notes leaped to nearly 11 percent on October 23. Suddenly investors began to picture an oil-induced inflationary spiral leading to breakdowns in trade, a global recession, or even worse. All this started to happen while Volcker was at an IMF meeting in Belgrade, where he had gone to make a speech. He cut his trip short—much as I would do years later on Black Monday, 1987, when the stock market crashed—and rushed back to convene an emergency Saturday-morning meeting of the Federal Open Market Committee.

What he masterminded that Saturday was arguably the most important change in economic policy in fifty years. The committee decided on his urging that it would no longer try to fine-tune the economy by focusing on short-term interest rates; instead it would clamp down on the amount of money available to the economy.

The money supply, then measured by a statistic called M1, consists mostly of currency in circulation and demand deposits, such as checking accounts. When money expands faster than the totality of goods and services produced—in other words, when too many dollars chase too few goods—everybody's money tends to be worth less; that is, prices rise. The Fed could indirectly control the money supply by controlling the monetary base, mainly currency and bank reserves. Monetarists like the legendary Milton Friedman had long argued that until you contained the money supply, you hadn't tamed inflation. But the medicine required to do this was thought to be extremely harsh. No one knew how tight a rein on the monetary base would be required, or how high the associated rise in short-term interest rates would have to be, before inflation was choked off. It would almost certainly mean more unemployment, probably a deep recession, and possibly a major outbreak of social unrest. President Carter backed Volcker in the spring of 1980, declaring inflation to be the nation's number one problem. That prompted Senator Ted Kennedy, then running against Carter for president, to complain that the administration wasn't paying enough attention to the poor or to tax cuts. By October, with the election drawing near, Carter himself had begun to hedge. He too started talking about tax cuts and criticized the Fed for putting too many eggs in the basket of strict monetary policy.

Doing what Volcker did took exceptional courage—I thought so at the time and believed it even more strongly after I became chairman myself. Though he and I rarely discussed his experience of those events, I can imagine how tough it was for him to push America into the brutal recession of the early 1980s.

The consequences of his policy were even more severe than Volcker had expected. In April 1980, interest rates on Main Street USA climbed to more than 20 percent. Cars went unsold, houses went unbuilt, and millions of people lost their jobs—unemployment rose to near 9 percent in mid-1980, on its way to near 11 percent by late 1982. Early in 1980, letters from people who'd been put out of work flooded Volcker's office. Builders sent him and other officials cut-up two-by-fours to symbolize the houses they were unable to build. Car dealers sent keys to represent cars they hadn't sold. But by the middle of the year, after peaking at nearly 15 percent, inflation began gradually to decline. Long-term interest rates inched down too. Still, it would take three years before inflation was fully in check. The economic misery, coupled with the Iranian hostage crisis, cost Jimmy Carter the 1980 election.

Coming out of the Ford years I was the ex officio senior Republican economist—the last who'd held high-level public office. So it was natural for me to get involved in Ronald Reagan's campaign. It made no difference that Ford and Reagan had competed four years earlier for the 1976 Republican nomination. My old friend and ally Martin Anderson joined the Reagan team—Marty had spent the post-Nixon years as a fellow at the Hoover Institution—and I resumed my old campaign role too. Marty was chief domestic policy adviser, a full-time position on the campaign plane, and I was an unpaid part-time consultant to the staff, much the same relationship I'd had to the Nixon campaign in 1968.

I worked mainly from New York, but on occasion I'd fly out to spend a few days with the campaign. It was on one such trip, in late August, that I clumsily made what was probably my most important contribution to the election of Ronald Reagan. He had by this time already received the Republican nomination, and had been stepping up his criticism of the Carter administration. Speaking at a Teamsters lunch in Ohio, he declared that working people's lives had been shattered by "a new depression—the Carter depression." This, of course, was technically incorrect—I'd written much of that speech, and the wording had been "one of the major economic contractions in the last fifty years." Reagan had changed it on the fly. Marty Anderson and I took pains to explain to reporters that afternoon that the governor had misspoken. He had really meant to say "a severe recession."

Reagan thanked us for setting things straight. But he also stuck to his guns. When Democrats started challenging him on his mistake, he told reporters, "As far as I am concerned, the line between recession and depression cannot be measured in the strict economists' terms, but must be measured in human terms. When our working people—including those who are unemployed—must endure the worst misery since the 1930s, then I think we ought to recognize that they consider it a depression." I was impressed at how he'd been able to turn a mistake to his political advantage.

I assumed this would be the end of the matter, but apparently the episode touched off an association in Reagan's memory. The following week he added a new punch line to his stump speech. He started telling the crowds that the president was hiding behind a dictionary. "If it's a definition he wants, I'll give him one," Reagan would continue. "A recession is when your neighbor loses his job. A depression is when you lose yours. And recovery is when Jimmy Carter loses his!"

The crowds loved it, and it became one of his most oft-quoted lines. You had to hand it to Reagan. Even though President Carter wasn't actually the one who'd corrected his economics and even though the first two clauses of the punch line were an old joke by Harry Truman, Reagan had spun the episode into a funny and powerful campaign story.

What attracted me to Reagan was the clarity of his conservatism. There was another line he often used on the stump: "Government exists to protect us from each other. Where government has gone beyond its limits is in deciding to protect us from ourselves." A man who talks in such terms is clear on what he believes. Very rarely in those days would you find conservatives who didn't fudge on social issues. But Reagan's kind of conservatism was to say that tough love is good for the individual and good for society. That proposition starts with a judgment about human nature. If it's accurate, then it implies much less government support for the downtrodden. Yet mainstream Republicans were conflicted about thinking or talking in such terms, because they seemed contrary to Judeo-Christian values. Not Reagan. Like Milton Friedman and other early libertarians, he never gave the impression he was trying to be on both sides of the issue. It's not that there wasn't sympathy for people who, through no fault of their own, find themselves in dire straits; nor would you find any less personal willingness than among liberals personally to assist the downtrodden. But that wasn't government's role, according to Reagan. Tough love, in the long run, is love.

A little later in the campaign, they put me on the plane with Reagan for a cross-country flight. I was given a very specific task. The presidential debates were approaching, and the governor's top aides were concerned about criticism that Reagan sometimes seemed oblivious of facts. Martin Anderson asked if I would use a cross-country flight to brief the candidate thoroughly—not just on the economy, but on all the significant domestic issues. "He knows you were a good adviser to Ford," Marty told me. "He'll listen to you." When I agreed, Marty pulled out a briefing book and handed it to me. It was a binder labeled Domestic Policy that must have been half an inch thick. He said, "Just make sure you get through every topic."

I studied up on the material, and later that day, when we got on the flight, Reagan's staffers sat me at a table facing the governor, with Marty by his side. I noticed that they'd helpfully provided copies of the binder, one for each of us. But Reagan was in an expansive mood, and by the time the plane took off, he was asking friendly questions about Milton Friedman and other people we knew in common. The conversation blossomed from there. I think I heard more clever stories during that flight than in any other five-hour period in my life. Marty kept shooting me glances, but I couldn't get Reagan to open the briefing book. I tried a few times to steer the conversation that way and then gave up. After we landed, I said, "Thank you, Governor. That was a very enjoyable trip." And Reagan said, "Oh, I know Marty doesn't like the fact that I didn't crack a book."

His temperament fascinated me. He brought a sunniness and benevolence to the presidency that never wavered, even when he had to deal with a dysfunctional economy and the global danger of nuclear war. Stored in his head must have been four hundred stories and one-liners; while most of them were humorous, he was able to tap them instantly to communicate politics or policy. It was an odd form of intelligence, and he used it to transform the country's self-image. Under Reagan, Americans went from believing they were a former great power to regaining their self-confidence.

His stories sometimes had an edge. He told one on the airplane that seemed particularly meant for me. It started with Leonid Brezhnev on the reviewing stand at Lenin's Tomb, surrounded by underlings, watching the

May Day parade. The Soviet Union's full military might is there on display. First come battalions of elite troops, impressive soldiers, all six foot two, marching in absolute lockstep. Right behind them are phalanxes of state-of-the-art artillery and tanks. Then come the nuclear missiles—it's an awesome show of strength. But after the missiles comes a straggle of six or seven civilians, unkempt, shabbily dressed, utterly out of place. An aide rushes up to Brezhnev and begs forgiveness. "Comrade Secretary, my apologies, I do not know who these people are or how they've come into our parade."

"Do not be concerned, Comrade," replies Brezhnev. "I am responsible for them. They are our economists, and you have no idea how much damage they can do."

Behind the humor was Reagan's long-held distrust of economists who promoted what he saw as destructive government interference in the marketplace. He was, of course, at root devoted to free markets. He wanted to open up the action in the economy. Though his grasp of economics wasn't very deep or sophisticated, he understood the tendency of free markets to self-correct, and the fundamental wealth-creating power of capitalism. He trusted Adam Smith's invisible hand to both encourage innovation and produce outcomes that he generally perceived as fair. That's why it sometimes made sense to leave the briefing book closed. Reagan's emphasis on the big picture helped him defeat a president who seemed compelled to micromanage.*

My involvement with the campaign made me a bit player in Reagan's choice of a running mate, a drama that unfolded at the Republican convention in late July. By then, Reagan had the nomination locked up, but the race against President Carter looked close. Polls showed that the choice of a running mate could be crucial. In particular, a ticket of Ronald Reagan and Jerry Ford would pick up 2 or 3 percentage points, enough to win.

I learned this in the midst of the convention, which that year was in Detroit. Reagan had a suite on the sixty-ninth floor of the Renaissance

---

*Years later, I learned that Reagan always worried about being "overbriefed" by his advisers; in the 1984 campaign, he blamed overbriefing for his poor performance against Mondale in the first televised debate.

Center Plaza Hotel, and on Tuesday of convention week he called Henry Kissinger and me to his room and asked if we would feel out the former president. He and Ford had been political rivals for years, but they had buried the hatchet several weeks before, when Reagan had gone to visit Ford in Palm Springs. Evidently the governor had broached the idea of a joint ticket then; and while Ford had said no, he'd also made it clear to Reagan that he wanted to help defeat Jimmy Carter. Reagan told us he had raised the possibility of the vice presidency again with Ford earlier that day and now he was pulling us in because we'd been among Ford's closest advisers (Kissinger of course had been his secretary of state).

Ford was staying in a suite just one floor above Reagan's, and Henry and I called and asked if we could stop by. We met with him and talked briefly that night. The following afternoon we came back so Henry could present a set of talking points about the vice presidency written by Reagan's counselor Ed Meese and others in the Reagan camp. Because a former president had never served as vice president, they were envisioning an expanded role that would make the job attractive and appropriate for Ford. In their proposal, Ford would be the head of the president's executive office, with power over national security, the federal budget, and more. In effect, while Reagan would be America's chief executive officer, Ford would be its chief operating officer.

Personally I hoped Ford would accept; I felt the nation needed his skills. But while he clearly felt the pull both of duty and of the limelight, Ford was skeptical that a "super vice presidency" would actually work. For one thing, it raised constitutional questions—the role was clearly beyond what the Founders had envisioned. For another thing, he doubted that any president could or should accept a dilution of power in carrying out his oath of office. Also he was ambivalent about going back to Washington. "I've been out of office four years, and I'm having a wonderful life in Palm Springs," he said. Yet he really wanted to help unseat Carter, who he thought was a weak president. There was lots of back-and-forth between the two camps, and toward the end of the day Ford told us, "The answer now is still no, but I'll consider it."

Rumors of a Reagan-Ford "dream ticket" meanwhile were sweeping the convention floor. When Ford made a previously scheduled appearance on the *CBS Evening News*, Walter Cronkite asked pointedly about the possibility of a "co-presidency." Ford answered with his typical forthrightness. He would never come back as a "figurehead vice president," he said. "I have to go there with the belief that I will play a meaningful role across the board in the basic and the crucial and the important decisions."

Reportedly this infuriated Reagan, who was watching. He couldn't believe Ford would discuss their private negotiation on national TV. But by then I think both men were concluding that to redefine the vice president's role was too important and complex a task to be accomplished on the fly. Henry, in full shuttle-diplomacy mode, was hoping to continue the discussions Thursday, but Reagan and Ford both knew that prolonging the uncertainty would hurt Reagan's image. So Ford made his decision. He went down to Reagan's suite around ten o'clock and told the governor he could help the ticket more by campaigning as an ex-president on Reagan's behalf than as his running mate. "He was a gentleman," Reagan said afterward. "I feel we're friends now." He quickly selected George H. W. Bush as his vice presidential candidate and made the announcement that very night.

I didn't expect a role in the new administration and was not sure I wanted one. Coming into the White House, Reagan had more talented and experienced people than places to put them. That was either a problem or an opportunity, depending on what you did about it. Anderson, who'd been named assistant to the president for domestic policy development, likes to joke that he went to Reagan and Meese, who headed the transition, and said, "We've got these incredible people, but if we don't use 'em pretty soon, they'll attack us." Instead of dissolving the team that had helped him win, Reagan instituted an advisory group called the Economic Policy Board. George Shultz chaired it, and it included Milton Friedman, Arthur Burns, Bill Simon, me, and several other prominent economists.

One of the first cabinet-level officers to be appointed was David Stockman, the director of the budget. Reagan had campaigned on lowering taxes, building up the military, and cutting down the size of government. The strategy before the inauguration was to give Stockman a head start on the budget, so tough cuts could be presented to incoming cabinet members as a fait accompli. Stockman was a brilliant, hungry thirty-four-year-old congressman from rural Michigan who relished being the point man for what came to be called the Reagan Revolution. In speeches Reagan had compared downsizing the government to applying fatherly discipline: "You know, we can lecture our children about extravagance until we run out of breath. Or we can cure their extravagance by simply reducing their allowance." In Stockman's version this philosophy had a fiercer name: it was called "starving the beast."

I worked closely with Stockman during the transition as he fashioned a budget that was tough as nails. And I was there the day shortly before the inauguration when he presented it to Reagan. The president said, "Just tell me, David. Do we treat everyone the same? You have to cut everybody equally nastily." Stockman assured him he had, and Reagan gave his okay.

The Economic Policy Board found itself called into action more quickly than anyone expected. The cornerstone of the Reagan tax cuts was a bill that had been proposed by Congressman Jack Kemp and Senator William Roth. It called for a dramatic three-year, 30 percent rollback of taxes on both businesses and individuals, and was designed to jolt the economy out of its slump, which was now entering its second year. I believed that if spending was restrained as much as Reagan proposed, and as long as the Federal Reserve continued to enforce strict control of the money supply, the plan was credible, though it would be a hard sell. That was the consensus of the rest of the economic board as well.

But Stockman and Don Regan, the incoming treasury secretary, were having doubts. They were leery of the growing federal deficit, already more than $50 billion a year, and they began quietly telling the president he ought to hold off on any tax cuts. Instead, they wanted him to try getting Congress to cut spending first, then see whether the resulting savings would allow for tax reductions.

Whenever this talk of postponement would get intense, George Shultz would summon the economics advisory board to Washington. This happened five or six times during Reagan's first year. We'd meet in the Roosevelt Room from 9:00 a.m. to 11:00 a.m. and compare our assessments of the economic outlook. Promptly at 11:00, the door would open, and in would come Reagan. Our group reported directly to him. And we'd tell him, "Under no circumstances should you delay the tax cut." He'd smile and joke; Shultz and Friedman and others were old friends of his. Regan and Stockman, who were permitted to attend the meetings but were not allowed to take seats at the conference table or to vote, would sit along the wall and smolder. Presently the session would end and Reagan would leave, fortified in his resolve to press for his tax cuts. Ultimately, of course, Congress approved a version of his economic plan. But since Congress shied away from the necessary restraints on spending, the deficit remained a huge and growing problem.

I played a small role in another presidential decision that first year: not to meddle with the Fed. Reagan was being urged to do so by many people in both parties, including some of his top aides. With double-digit interest rates now entering their third year, people wanted the Fed to expand money supply growth. Not that Reagan could command the chairman of the Fed to do this. But, the theory went, if he were to criticize the Fed publicly, Volcker might feel obliged to ease up.

Whenever the question arose, I would tell the president, "Don't pressure the Fed." For one thing, Volcker's policy seemed right—inflation did seem to be slowly coming under control. For another thing, open disagreement between the White House and the Fed could only shake investors' confidence, slowing the recovery.

Volcker didn't make things easy for the new president. The two men had never met, and a few weeks after taking office, Reagan wanted to get acquainted. In order to avoid the appearance of summoning the Fed chairman to the White House, he asked if he could come see Volcker at the Fed—only to have Volcker send back word that such a visit would be "inappropriate." I was perplexed: I did not see how a visit by the president could compromise the Fed's independence.

Nevertheless, Reagan persisted, and finally Volcker allowed that he would be willing to meet at the Treasury Department. The president's opening line at their lunch in Don Regan's office became part of the Reagan legend. He said mildly to Volcker, "I'm curious. People are asking why we need a Fed at all." I am told Volcker's jaw dropped; he had to regroup before coming back with a persuasive defense of the institution. This evidently satisfied Reagan, who went back to being his amiable self. He had communicated that the Federal Reserve Act was subject to change. The two men cooperated quietly from then on. Reagan gave Volcker the political cover he needed; no matter how much people complained, the president made it his practice never to criticize the Fed. And though Volcker was a Democrat, when his term ended in 1983, Reagan reappointed him.

In late 1981, Reagan asked me to take the lead in dealing with a colossal headache that had been building for years: Social Security was running out of money. During the Nixon administration, when the program had seemed flush with reserves, Congress had taken the fateful step of indexing benefits to inflation. As inflation soared through the 1970s, so did the cost-of-living increases in people's Social Security checks. The system was in such financial straits that an added $200 billion was going to be needed as early as 1983 to keep the program afloat. The long-term prospects looked even worse.

Reagan had shied away from talking in any detail about Social Security during his campaign—when the question came up, he'd pledged simply to preserve the system. And no wonder. Social Security is truly the third rail of American politics. There was nothing more explosive than Social Security reform: everybody knew that no matter how you dressed it up, any solution was in the end going to involve either raising taxes or cutting benefits for a huge and powerful bloc of voters, or both.

Yet the problem was serious, and leaders in both parties understood that something needed to be done—either that, or face the likelihood of not being able to mail checks to thirty-six million senior citizens and disabled Americans. We were getting down to the wire. Reagan's opening gambit, in his first budget, was to propose a $2.3 billion reduction in Social Security outlays. That raised such a storm of protest that he was forced to back down. Three months later he came back harder, with a reform proposal that would cut $46 billion in benefits over five years. But it was clear that a bipartisan compromise was the only hope. Thus the Greenspan Commission was born.

Most commissions, of course, don't do anything. But Jim Baker, the architect of this one, believed passionately that government could be made to work. The commission he built was a virtuoso demonstration of how to get things done in Washington. It was a bipartisan group, with five members chosen by the White House, five by the Senate majority leader, and five by the Speaker of the House. Virtually every commissioner was an all-star in his or her field. There were congressional heavy hitters like Bob Dole, the chairman of the Senate Finance Committee; Pat Moynihan, the brilliant maverick senator from New York; and Claude Pepper, the outspoken eighty-one-year-old congressman from Florida who was a senior citizens' icon. Lane Kirkland, the head of the AFL-CIO, was a member and became a close friend; so was Alexander Trowbridge, the head of the National Association of Manufacturers. House Speaker Tip O'Neill appointed the top Democrat—Bob Ball, who had run the Social Security Administration for LBJ. And the president appointed me as chairman.

I won't go into the intricacies of demographics and finance we mastered, or the policy debates and hearings that ate up more than a year. I ran the commission in the spirit that Jim Baker had envisioned, aiming for an effective bipartisan compromise. We took four key steps to make the whole thing work, which I'll mention because I've used variations of them ever since.

The first was to limit the problem. In this case, it meant not taking up the issue of the future funding of Medicare—while technically part of Social Security, Medicare was a far more complex problem, and trying to solve both could mean we would do neither.

The second was to get everyone to agree on the problem's numerical dimensions. As Pat Moynihan later put it, "You're entitled to your own opinion, but you're not entitled to your own facts." When it was clear that a long-term shortfall was real, commission members lost their ability to demagogue. They had to support cuts in benefits and/or support a rise in revenues. Reverting to the cop-out of financing Social Security from the federal government's "general revenues" was adamantly ruled out early by Pepper, who worried it would cause Social Security to become a welfare program.

The third smart tactic came from Baker. If we wanted a compromise to succeed, he argued, we had to bring everybody along. So we made a point of keeping both Reagan and O'Neill in the loop as we worked. It became Bob Ball's job to inform O'Neill, and my job and Baker's to inform the president.

Our fourth move was to agree among the commissioners that once a compromise was reached, we would stand firm against any amendments being imposed by either party. I later told reporters, "If you take pieces out of the package, you will lose the consensus, and the whole agreement starts to unravel." We published our report in January 1983; when it was finally time to present the reform proposals to Congress, Ball and I resolved to testify side by side. Whenever a Republican asked a question, I would answer it. And whenever a Democrat asked a question, he would answer it. Which is just what we tried to do, though the senators didn't entirely cooperate.

Diverse as our commission was, we found ways to agree. What brought together men like Claude Pepper and the head of the manufacturers was the care we took to spread the burden. The Social Security Amendments, which Reagan ultimately signed into law in 1983, involved pain for everyone. Employers had to absorb further increases in the payroll tax; employees faced higher taxes too and in some cases saw the date when they could anticipate receiving benefits pushed further into the future; retirees had to accept postponement of cost-of-living increases, and wealthier retirees began having their benefits taxed. But by doing all this, we succeeded in funding Social Security over the seventy-five-year planning period that is conventional for social insurance programs. Moynihan, with his usual eloquence, declared: "I have the strongest feeling that we all have won. What we have won is a resolution of the terrible fear in this country, that the Social Security system was, like a chain letter, something of a fraud."

As all this was still unfolding in 1983, I was in my office one day in New York poring over demographic projections when the telephone rang. It was Andrea Mitchell, a reporter for NBC. "I've got some questions about the president's budget proposals," she said. She explained that she'd been trying to figure out whether the Reagan administration's latest fiscal-policy assumptions were credible, and that David Gergen, the assistant to the White House communications chief, had suggested my name. She told me

Gergen had said, "If you really want to know about the economy, why don't you call Alan Greenspan? He knows more than anybody."

"I'll bet you say that to all the economists," I replied, "but sure, let's talk." I'd noticed Andrea on NBC newscasts. She was a White House correspondent. I thought she was very articulate and that her voice had the nicest authoritative resonance. Also, I'd noted, she was a very good-looking woman.

We talked that day and a few more times, and soon I became a regular source. Over the next two years, Andrea would phone whenever she had a big economics story in the works. I liked the way she handled the material on TV; even when the issues were too complex to present in their full technical detail, she would find the crux of the story. And she was accurate with the facts.

In 1984 Andrea asked if I'd come with her to the White House Correspondents' Dinner, where reporters invite their sources. I had to tell her that I'd already agreed to go with Barbara Walters. But I added, "Do you ever get to New York? Maybe we could have dinner."

It took another eight months before we could connect—it was an election year, and Andrea was extremely busy through November, when Reagan defeated Mondale in a landslide. Finally when the holidays arrived, we scheduled a date, and I made a reservation at Le Périgord, my favorite restaurant in New York, for December 28. It was a snowy night and Andrea rushed in late, looking very beautiful if a bit disheveled after a day of reporting the news and trying to hail cabs in the snow.

That night I discovered she was a former musician like me; she'd played violin in the Westchester Symphony. We loved the same music—her record collection was similar to mine. She liked baseball. But mainly we shared an intense interest in current affairs—strategic, political, military, diplomatic. There was no shortage of things to talk about.

It might not be everybody's idea of first-date conversation, but at the restaurant we ended up discussing monopolies. I told her I'd written an essay on the subject and invited her back to my apartment to read it. She teases me about that now, saying, "What, you didn't have any etchings?" But we did go to my apartment and I showed her this essay I'd written on antitrust for Ayn Rand. She read it and we discussed it. To this day, Andrea claims I was giving her a test. But it wasn't that; I was doing everything I could think of to keep her around.

For much of Reagan's second term, Andrea was my main reason to go to Washington. I stayed in touch with people in the government, but my focus was almost entirely in the business and economics world of New York. As business economics matured as a profession, I'd gotten deeply involved in its organizations. I'd served as president of the National Association of Business Economists and as chairman of the Conference of Business Economists, and was slated to become chairman of the Economic Club of New York, the financial and business world's equivalent of the Council on Foreign Relations.

Townsend-Greenspan itself had changed. Large economics firms with names like DRI and Wharton Econometrics had grown up to supply much of the basic data needed by business planners. Computer modeling had become much more widespread, and many corporations had economists of their own. I'd experimented with diversifying into investment and pension-fund consulting, but while those ventures made money, they weren't as lucrative as corporate consulting. Also, more projects meant more employees, which meant more of my time had to be spent managing the business.

Ultimately I concluded that the best course was to focus exclusively on what I did best: solve interesting analytical puzzles for sophisticated clients who needed answers and could pay high-end fees. So in the second half of the Reagan administration I planned to scale back Townsend-Greenspan. But before I could implement those plans, in March 1987, I received a phone call from Jim Baker. Baker was by this time treasury secretary—after an intense four years as White House chief of staff, he'd made an unusual job swap, trading posts in 1985 with Don Regan. Jim and I had been friends since the Ford days, and I'd helped him prepare for his Senate confirmation hearing the spring he took over at Treasury. He had his assistant call to ask if I could come to Washington for a meeting at his house. This struck me as odd—why not meet at his office? But I agreed.

The next morning a Washington driver delivered me to Baker's nice old Georgian colonial on an elegant stretch of Foxhall Road. I was surprised to find waiting for me not only Jim but also Howard Baker, President Reagan's current chief of staff. Howard got right to the point. "Paul Volcker may be leaving this summer when his term runs out," he began. "We're not in a position to offer you the job, but we'd like to know—if it were to be offered, would you accept?"

I was briefly at a loss for words. Until a few years before, I'd never thought of myself as a potential Fed chairman. In 1983, as Volcker's first term was ending, I'd been startled when one of the Wall Street firms conducted a straw poll of who might replace Volcker if he were to leave and my name turned up on top of the list.

As close as I was to Arthur Burns, the Fed had always been a black box to me. Having watched him struggle, I did not feel equipped to do the job; setting interest rates for an entire economy seemed to involve so much more than I knew. The job seemed amorphous, the type of task in which it is very easy to be wrong even if you have virtually full knowledge. Forecasting a complex economy such as ours is not a ninety-ten proposition. You're very fortunate if you can do sixty-forty. All the same, the challenge was too great to turn down. I told the Bakers that if the job were offered, I would accept.

I had plenty of time to get cold feet. Over the next two months, Jim Baker would phone to say things like "It's still under discussion" or "Volcker is thinking about whether he wants to stay." I felt alternately fascinated by the possibility and a little unsettled. It wasn't until just before Memorial Day that Baker phoned and said, "Paul has decided to leave." He asked if I was still interested and I said yes. He said, "You'll be getting a call from the president in a few days."

Two days later I was at my orthopedist's office and the nurse came in to say the White House was on the line. It had taken the call a few minutes to get through because the receptionist had thought it was a prank. They let me use the doctor's private office to take the call. I picked up the phone and heard that familiar, easy voice. Ronald Reagan said, "Alan, I want you to be my chairman of the Federal Reserve Board."

I told him I would be honored to do so. Then we chatted a bit. I thanked him and hung up.

As I stepped back into the hall, the nurse seemed very concerned. "Are you all right?" she asked. "You look like you've gotten bad news."

FIVE

BLACK MONDAY

I'd scrutinized the economy every working day for decades and had visited the Fed scores of times. Nevertheless, when I was appointed chairman, I knew I'd have a lot to learn. That was reinforced the minute I walked in the door. The first person to greet me was Dennis Buckley, a security agent who would stay with me throughout my tenure. He addressed me as "Mr. Chairman."

Without thinking, I said, "Don't be silly. Everybody calls me Alan."

He gently explained that calling the chairman by his first name was just not the way things were done at the Fed.

So Alan became Mr. Chairman.

The staff, I next learned, had prepared a series of intensive tutorials diplomatically labeled "one-person seminars," in which I was the student. This meant that for the next ten days, senior people from the professional staff gathered in the Board's fourth-floor conference room and taught me my job. I learned about sections of the Federal Reserve Act I never knew existed—and for which I was now responsible. The staff taught me arcana about banking regulation that, having been a director of both JPMorgan and Bowery Savings, I was amazed I'd never encountered. Of course, the

Fed had experts in every dimension of domestic and international economics as well as the capability to call in data from everywhere—privileged access that I was eager to explore.

Though I'd been a corporate director, the Board of Governors of the Federal Reserve System, as it is formally known, was an order of magnitude larger than anything I'd ever run—today the Federal Reserve Board staff includes some two thousand employees and has an annual budget of nearly $300 million. Fortunately, running it wasn't my job—the long-standing practice is to designate one of the other Board members as the administrative governor to oversee day-to-day operations. There is also a staff director for management who acts as a chief of staff. This way, only issues that are out of the ordinary or that might spark public or congressional interest are brought to the chairman, such as the massive challenge of upgrading the international payments system for the turn of the millennium. Otherwise he is free to concentrate on the economy—just what I was eager to do.

The Fed chairman has less unilateral power than the title might suggest. By statute I controlled only the agenda for the Board of Governors meetings—the Board decided all other matters by majority rule, and the chairman was just one vote among seven. Also, I was not automatically the chairman of the Federal Open Market Committee, the powerful group that controls the federal funds rate, the primary lever of U.S. monetary policy.* The FOMC is made up of the seven Board governors and the presidents of the twelve regional Federal Reserve banks (only five can vote at any one time), and it too makes decisions by majority rule. While the Board chairman is traditionally the chair of the FOMC, he or she must be elected each year by the members, and they are free to choose someone else. I expected precedent to prevail. But I was always aware that a revolt of the six other governors could remove all of my authority, except writing the Board agendas.

---

*When the FOMC changes this rate, the committee directs the Fed's so-called open market desk in New York to either buy or sell treasury securities—often billions of dollars' worth in a day. Selling by the Fed acts as a brake, withdrawing from the economy the money received in the transaction and pushing short-term interest rates higher, while buying does the reverse. Today the fed funds rate that the FOMC is seeking is publicly announced, but in those days it wasn't. So Wall Street firms would assign "Fed watchers" to divine changes in monetary policy from the actions of our traders or changes in our weekly reported balance sheet.

I quickly got hold of Don Kohn, the FOMC secretary, and had him walk me through the protocols of a meeting. (Don, who would prove to be the most effective policy adviser in the Fed system during my eighteen years, is now vice chairman of the Board.) The FOMC held its meetings in secret, so I had no idea what the standard agenda or timetable was, who spoke first, who deferred to whom, how to conduct a vote, and so on. The committee also had its own lingo that I needed to get comfortable with. For example, when the FOMC wanted to authorize the chairman to notch up the fed funds rate if necessary before the next regular meeting, it did not say, "You may raise interest rates if you decide you have to"; instead it voted to give an "asymmetric directive toward tightening."* I was scheduled to run one of those meetings the following week, on August 18, so I was a highly motivated student. Andrea still jokes about my coming over to her house that weekend to curl up with *Robert's Rules of Order.*

I felt a real need to hit the ground running because I knew the Fed would soon face big decisions. The Reagan-era expansion was well into its fourth year, and while the economy was thriving, it was also showing clear signs of instability. Since the beginning of the year, when the Dow Jones Industrial Average had risen through 2,000 for the first time, the stock market had run up more than 40 percent—now it stood at more than 2,700 and Wall Street was in a speculative froth. Something similar was happening in commercial real estate.

The economic indicators, meanwhile, were far from encouraging. Huge government deficits under Reagan had caused the national debt to the public to almost triple, from just over $700 billion at the start of his presidency to more than $2 trillion at the end of fiscal year 1988. The dollar was falling, and people were worried about America losing its competitive edge—the media were full of alarmist talk about the growing "Japanese threat." Consumer prices, which had gone up just 1.9 percent in 1986, were rising at nearly double that rate in my first days in office. Though 3.6 percent inflation was far milder than the double-digit nightmare people remembered from the 1970s, once inflation begins, it usually grows. We were in danger

---

*For the record, even as I learned "Fedspeak," I would joke to the staff, "Whatever happened to the English language?"

of forfeiting the victory that had been gained at such great misery and cost under Paul Volcker.

These were vast economic issues, of course, far beyond the power of the Fed alone to resolve. Yet the worst course would be to sit idly by. I thought a rate increase would be prudent, but the Fed hadn't raised interest rates for three years. Hiking them now would be a big deal. Any time the Fed changes direction, it can rattle the markets. The risk in clamping down during a stock-market surge is especially acute—it can pop the bubble of investor confidence, and if that scares people enough, can trigger a severe economic contraction.

Though I was friendly with many of the committee members, I knew better than to think that a chairman who had been around for a week could walk into a meeting and shape a consensus on such a risky decision. So I did not propose a rate increase; I simply listened to what the others had to say. The eighteen committee members* were all seasoned central bankers and economists, and as we went around the table comparing assessments of the economy, it was apparent that they, too, were concerned. Gerry Corrigan, the gruff president of the New York Fed, said we ought to raise rates; Bob Parry, the Fed president from San Francisco, reported that his district was seeing good growth, high optimism, and full employment—all reasons to be leery of inflation; Si Keehn from Chicago agreed, reporting that the Midwest's factories were running near full capacity and that even the farm outlook had improved; Tom Melzer of the St. Louis Fed told of how even the shoe factories in that district were operating at 100 percent; Bob Forrestal from Atlanta described how his staff had been surprised at the strength of employment figures even in chronically depressed sections of the South. I think everyone walked away persuaded that the Fed would have to raise rates soon.

The next opportunity to do so was two weeks later, on September 4, at a meeting of the Board of Governors. The Board controls the other main lever of monetary policy, the "discount rate" at which the Federal Reserve lends to depository institutions. This rate generally moves in lockstep with the rate on fed funds. Prior to the scheduled Board meeting, I spent a few

---

*There was one vacancy on the Federal Reserve Board.

days working my way up and down the corridor seeking out the governors in their offices, building consensus. The meeting, when it came, moved quickly to a vote—the rate increase, from 5.5 percent to 6 percent, was approved by the governors unanimously.

To subdue inflationary pressures, we were trying to slow the economy by making money more expensive to borrow. There's no way to predict how severely the markets will respond to such a move, especially when investors are gripped with speculative fervor. I couldn't help but remember accounts I'd read of the physicists at Alamogordo the first time they detonated an atom bomb: Would the bomb fizzle? Would it work the way they hoped? Or would the chain reaction somehow go out of control and set the earth's atmosphere on fire? After the meeting ended, I had to fly to New York; from there I was scheduled to leave that weekend for Switzerland, where I was attending my first meeting of the central bankers of the ten leading industrialized nations. The Fed's hope was that the key markets—stocks, futures, currency, bonds—would take the change in stride, maybe with stocks cooling off slightly and the dollar strengthening. I kept calling back to the office to check how the markets were responding.

The sky did not catch fire that day. Stocks dipped, banks upped their prime lending rates in line with our move, and the financial world, as we'd hoped, noted that the Fed had begun acting to quell inflation. Perhaps the most dramatic impact was reflected in a *New York Times* headline a few days later: "Wall Street's Sharpest Rise: Anxiety." I was finally allowing myself to breathe a sigh of relief when a message reached me from Paul Volcker. He knew exactly what I'd been going through. "Congratulations," it read. "You are now a central banker."

I did not for a minute think we were out of the woods. Signs of trouble in the economy continued to mount. Slowing growth and a further weakening of the dollar put Wall Street on edge, as investors and institutions began confronting the likelihood that billions of dollars in speculative bets would never pay off. In early October, that fear turned to near panic. The stock market skidded, by 6 percent the first week, then another 12 percent the second week. The worst loss was on Friday, October 16, when the Dow Jones average dropped by 108 points. Since the end of September nearly half a trillion dollars of paper wealth had evaporated in the stock market alone—not to mention the losses in currency and other markets. The decline was so stunning that *Time* magazine devoted two full pages to the stock market that week under the headline "Wall Street's October Massacre."

I knew that from a historical perspective this "correction" was not nearly the most severe. The market slump in 1970 had been proportionally twice as large, and the Great Depression had wiped out fully 80 percent of the market's value. But given how poorly the week had ended, everyone was worried about what might happen when the markets opened again on Monday.

I was supposed to fly on Monday afternoon to Dallas, where on Tuesday I was to speak at the American Bankers' Association convention—my first major speech as chairman. Monday morning I conferred with the Board of Governors, and we agreed that I should make the trip, lest it seem that the Fed was in a panic. The market that morning opened weakly, and by the time I had to leave it looked awful—down by more than 200 points. There was no telephone on the airplane. So the first thing I did when I arrived was to ask one of the people who greeted me from the Federal Reserve Bank of Dallas, "How did the stock market finally go?"

He said, "It was down five oh eight."

Usually when someone says "five oh eight," he means 5.08. So the market had dropped only 5 points. "Great," I said, "what a terrific rally." But as I said it, I saw that the expression on his face was not shared relief. In fact, the market had crashed by 508 points—a 22.5 percent drop, the biggest one-day loss in history, bigger even than the one on the day that started the Great Depression, Black Friday 1929.

I went straight to the hotel, where I stayed on the phone into the night. Manley Johnson, the vice chairman of the Fed's Board, had set up a crisis desk in my office in Washington, and we held a series of calls and teleconferences to map out plans. Gerry Corrigan filled me in on conversations he'd had in New York with Wall Street executives and officials at the stock exchange; Si Keehn had talked to the heads of the Chicago commodities futures exchanges and trading firms; Bob Parry in San Francisco reported what he was hearing from the chiefs of the savings and loan industry, who were mainly based on the West Coast.

The Fed's job during a stock-market panic is to ward off financial paralysis—a chaotic state in which businesses and banks stop making the payments they owe each other and the economy grinds to a halt. To the senior people on the phone with me that night, the urgency and gravity of the situation was apparent—even if the markets got no worse, the system would be reeling for weeks. We started exploring ways we might have to supply liquidity if major institutions ran short of cash. Not all of our younger people understood the seriousness of the crisis, however. As we discussed what public statement the Fed should make, one of them suggested, "Maybe we're overreacting. Why not wait a few days and see what happens?"

Though I was new at this job, I'd been a student of financial history for too long to think that made any sense. It was the one moment I spoke sharply to anybody that night. "We don't need to wait to see what happens," I told him. "We *know* what's going to happen." Then I backed up a little and explained. "You know what people say about getting shot? You feel like you've been punched, but the trauma is such that you don't feel the pain right away? In twenty-four or forty-eight hours, we're going to be feeling a lot of pain."

As the discussion ended, it was clear that the next day would be full of major decisions. Gerry Corrigan made a point of telling me solemnly, "Alan, you're it. The whole thing is on your shoulders." Gerry is a tough character and I couldn't tell whether he meant this as encouragement or as a challenge for the new chairman. I merely said, "Thank you, Dr. Corrigan."

I was not inclined to panic, because I understood the nature of the problems we would face. Still, when I hung up the phone around midnight, I wondered if I'd be able to sleep. That would be the real test. "Now we're going to see what you're made of," I told myself. I went to bed, and, I'm proud to say, I slept for a good five hours.

Early the next morning, as we were honing the language of the Fed's public statement, the hotel operator interrupted with a call from the White House. It was Howard Baker, President Reagan's chief of staff. Having known Howard a long time, I acted as though nothing unusual were going on. "Good morning, Senator," I said. "What can I do for you?" "*Help!*" he said in mock plaintiveness. "Where are you?"

"In Dallas," I said. "Is something bothering you?" Handling the administration's response to a Wall Street crisis is normally the job of the treasury secretary. But Jim Baker was in Europe trying to make his way back, and Howard didn't want to deal with this one on his own. I agreed to cancel my speech and return to Washington—I'd been inclined to do so anyway, because in light of the 508-point market drop, going back seemed the best way to assure the bankers that the Fed was taking matters seriously. Baker sent a military executive jet to pick me up.

The markets that morning gyrated wildly—Manley Johnson sat in our makeshift operations center giving me the play-by-play while I was airborne. After I got in a car at Andrews Air Force Base, he told me the New York Stock Exchange had called to notify us it was planning to shut down in one hour—trading on key stocks had stalled for lack of buyers. "That'll blow it for everybody," I said. "If they close, we've got a real catastrophe on our hands." Shutting down a market during a crash only compounds investors' pain. As scary as their losses on paper may seem, as long as the market stays open investors always know that they can get out. But take away the exit and you exacerbate the fear. To restore trading afterward is extraordinarily hard—because no one knows what prices should be, no one wants to be the first to bid. The resuscitation process can take many days, and the risk is that in the meantime the entire financial system will stall, and the economy will suffer a crippling shock. There wouldn't have been much we could do to stop the executives at the exchange, but the marketplace saved us by itself. Within those sixty minutes enough buyers materialized that the NYSE decided to shelve its plan.

The next thirty-six hours were intense. I joked that I felt like a seven-armed paperhanger, going from one phone to another, talking to the stock exchange, the Chicago futures exchanges, and the various Federal Reserve presidents. My most harrowing conversations were with financiers and bankers I'd known for years, major players from very large companies around the country, whose voices were tightened by fear. These were men who had built up wealth and social status over long careers and now found themselves looking into the abyss. Your judgment is less than perfect when you're scared. "Calm down," I kept telling them, "it's containable." And I would remind them to look beyond the emergency to where their long-term business interest might lie.

The Fed attacked the crisis on two fronts. Our first challenge was Wall

Street: we had to persuade giant trading firms and investment banks, many of which were reeling from losses, not to pull back from doing business. Our public statement early that morning had been painstakingly worded to hint that the Fed would provide a safety net for banks, in the expectation that they, in turn, would help support other financial companies. It was as short and concise as the Gettysburg Address, I thought, although possibly not as stirring: "The Federal Reserve, consistent with its responsibilities as the nation's central bank, affirmed today its readiness to serve as a source of liquidity to support the economic and financial system." But as long as the markets continued to function, we had no wish to prop up companies with cash.

Gerry Corrigan was the hero in this effort. It was his job as head of the New York Fed to convince the players on Wall Street to keep lending and trading—to stay in the game. A Jesuit-educated protégé of Volcker's, he'd been a central banker for his entire career; there was no one more streetwise or better suited to be the Fed's chief enforcer. Gerry had the dominant personality necessary to jawbone financiers, yet he understood that even in a crisis, the Fed must exercise restraint. Simply ordering a bank to make a loan, say, would be an abuse of government power and would damage the functioning of the market. Instead, the gist of Gerry's message to the banker had to be: "We're not telling you to lend; all we ask is that you consider the overall interests of your business. Just remember that people have long memories, and if you shut off credit to a customer just because you're a little nervous about him, but with no concrete reason, he's going to remember that." That week Corrigan had dozens of conversations along these lines, and though I never knew the details, some of those phone calls must have been very tough. I'm sure he bit off a few earlobes.

As all this was going on, we were careful to keep supplying liquidity to the system. The FOMC ordered the traders at the New York Fed to buy billions of dollars of treasury securities on the open market. This had the effect of putting more money into circulation and lowering short-term rates. Though we'd been tightening interest rates before the crash, we were now easing them to help keep the economy moving.

Despite our best efforts, there were a half dozen near disasters, mostly involving the payment system. A lot of transactions during the business day on Wall Street aren't made simultaneously: companies will do business with one another's customers, for instance, and then settle up at day's end. On Wednesday morning Goldman Sachs was scheduled to make a $700 million payment to Continental Illinois Bank in Chicago, but initially withheld payment pending receipt of expected funds from other sources. Then Goldman thought better of it, and made the payment. Had Goldman withheld such a large sum, it would have set off a cascade of defaults across the market. Subsequently, a senior Goldman official confided to me that had the firm anticipated the difficulties of the ensuing weeks, it would not have paid. And in future such crises, he suspected, Goldman would have second thoughts about making such unrequited payments.

We also went to work on the political front. I spent an hour Tuesday at the Treasury Department as soon as Jim Baker returned (he'd been able to catch the Concorde). We huddled in his office with Howard Baker and other officials. President Reagan's initial reaction to Wall Street's calamity on Monday had been to speak optimistically about the economy. "Steady as she goes," he'd said, later adding, "I don't think anyone should panic, because all the economic indicators are solid." This was meant to be reassuring, but in the light of events sounded disturbingly like Herbert Hoover declaring after Black Friday that the economy was "sound and prosperous." Tuesday afternoon we met with Reagan at the White House to suggest he try a different tack. The most constructive response, Jim Baker and I argued, would be to offer to cooperate with Congress on cutting the deficit, since that was one of the long-term economic risks upsetting Wall Street. Even though Reagan had been at loggerheads with the Democratic majority, he agreed that this made sense. That afternoon he told reporters that he would consider any budget proposal Congress put forward, short of cutting Social Security. Though this overture never led to anything, it did help calm the markets.

We manned the operations center around the clock. We tracked markets in Japan and Europe; early each morning we'd collect stock quotes on U.S. companies trading on European bourses and synthesize our own Dow Jones Industrial Average to get a preview of what the New York markets were likely to do when they opened. It took well over a week for all the crises to play out, though most of them were hidden from public view. Days after the crash, for example, the Chicago options market nearly collapsed when its biggest trading firm ran short of cash. The Chicago Fed helped engineer a solution to that one. Gradually, though, prices in the various markets stabilized, and by the start of November the members of the crisis management team returned to their regular work.

Contrary to everyone's fears, the economy held firm, actually growing at a 2 percent annual rate in the first quarter of 1988 and at an accelerated 5 percent rate in the second quarter. By early 1988 the Dow had stabilized at around 2,000, back where it had been at the beginning of 1987, and stocks resumed a much more modest, and more sustainable, upward path. Economic growth entered its fifth consecutive year. This was no consolation to the speculators who had lost their shirts, or to the scores of small brokerage houses that failed, but ordinary people hadn't been hurt.

In retrospect, it was an early manifestation of the economic resilience that would figure so prominently in the coming years.

The Federal Reserve and the White House are not automatically allies. In giving the Fed its modern mandate in 1935, Congress took great care to shield it from the influence of the political process. While the governors are all appointed by the president, their positions are semipermanent—Board members serve terms of fourteen years, longer than any appointees except the justices of the Supreme Court. The chairmanship itself is a four-year appointment, but the chairman can do little without the votes of the other Board members. And while the Fed must report twice a year to Congress, it controls its own purse strings by funding itself with interest income from the treasury securities and other assets it holds. All this frees the Fed to focus on its statutory mission: putting in place the monetary conditions needed for maximum sustainable long-term growth and employment. In the view of the Federal Reserve and most economists, a necessary condition for maximum sustainable economic growth is stable prices. In practice, this means Federal Reserve policies that contain inflationary pressures beyond the current election cycle.

No wonder politicians often find the Fed a hindrance. Their better selves may want to focus on America's long-term prosperity, but they are far more subject to constituents' immediate demands. That's inevitably reflected in their economic policy preferences. If the economy is expanding, they want it to expand faster; if they see an interest rate, they want it to be lower—and the Fed's monetary discipline interferes. As William McChesney Martin Jr., a legendary chairman in the 1950s and 1960s, is alleged to have put it, the Fed's role is to order "the punch bowl removed just when the party was really warming up."

You could hear that frustration in the voice of Vice President George Herbert Walker Bush in spring 1988 as he campaigned for the Republican presidential nomination. He told reporters that he had "a word of caution" for the Fed: "I wouldn't want to see them step over some [line] that would ratchet down, tighten down on the economic growth."

In fact, tightening was just what we were doing. Once it became clear that the stock-market crash had not seriously damaged the economy, the FOMC had started inching up the fed funds rate in March. We'd done so because again signs were accumulating that inflation pressures were rising and the long Reagan-era boom had maxed out: factories were full, and joblessness was at its lowest level in eight years. This tightening proceeded into the summer, and by August it was necessary to raise the discount rate too.

Since the discount rate, unlike the fed funds rate, was publicly announced, raising it was much more politically explosive—Fed officials called such a move "ringing the gong." The timing for the Bush campaign could not have been worse. Bush wanted to piggyback on Reagan's success, and he was trailing the Democratic contender, Michael Dukakis, by as much as 17 points in the polls. The vice president's campaign staff was hypersensitive to any news that might point to a slowing economy or otherwise dim the luster of the administration. So when we voted to raise the rate just a few days before the Republican convention, we understood that people were going to be upset.

I'm a believer in delivering bad news in person, privately, and in advance—especially in Washington, where officials hate to be blindsided and need time to decide what they want to say publicly. I don't enjoy doing it, but there's no alternative if you want to have a relationship thereafter. So as soon as we voted, I left the office and drove over to the Treasury Department to see Jim Baker. He had just announced he was leaving his job as secretary of the treasury to become chief of staff of the Bush campaign. Jim was an old friend, and as treasury secretary, he needed to be told.

As we sat down in his office, I caught his eye and said, "I'm sure you're not going to be happy about this, but after a long discussion of all the factors"—I listed a few—"we arrived at a decision to raise the discount rate. It's going to be announced in an hour." The increase, I added, was not the usual one-quarter of a percentage point, but twice that, from 6 percent to 6.5 percent.

Baker sat back in his chair and jabbed his fist into his stomach. "You've hit me right here," he growled.

"I'm sorry, Jim," I said.

Then he cut loose and lambasted me and the Fed for not being responsive to the real needs of the country, and expressed whatever other angry thoughts came into his head. Having been friends for a while, I knew this tirade was just an act. So after a minute, when he paused for air, I smiled at him. Then he laughed. "I know you had to do it," he said. A few days later, he publicly endorsed the rate increase as essential for the long-term stability of the system. "In the medium and long term it will be a very good thing for the economy," he added.

W hen George Bush won that fall, I hoped the Fed and his administration would get along. Everybody knew that whoever came in after Reagan would face big economic challenges: not just an eventual downturn in the business cycle, but whopping deficits and the rapidly mounting national debt. I thought Bush had upped the ante substantially when he'd declared in his acceptance speech at the Republican convention: "Read my lips: no new taxes." It was a memorable line, but at some point he was going to have to tackle the deficit—and he'd tied one hand behind his back.

People were surprised by the thoroughness with which the new administration replaced Reagan appointees. My friend Martin Anderson, who had long since shifted out of Washington back to the Hoover Institution in California, joked that Bush fired more Republicans than Dukakis would have. But I told him it didn't bother me. It was a new president's prerogative, and the moves did not affect the Fed. Besides, the senior economic team coming in—Treasury Secretary Nicholas Brady, Budget Director Richard Darman, CEA chairman Michael Boskin, and others—were longtime professional acquaintances and friends of mine. (Jim Baker, of course, moved up to become secretary of state.)

My main concern, shared by many senior people within the Fed, was that the new administration attack the deficit right away, while the economy was still strong enough to absorb the shock of cuts in federal spending. Big deficits have an insidious effect. When the government overspends, it must borrow to balance its books. It borrows by selling treasury securities, which siphons away capital that could otherwise be invested in the private economy. Our deficits had been running so high—well over $150 billion a year on average for five years—that we were undermining the economy. I highlighted this problem just after the election, testifying before the National Economic Commission, a bipartisan group Reagan had set up in the wake of the 1987 crash. The deficit was no longer a mañana problem, I told them: "The long run is rapidly becoming the short run. If we do not act promptly, the effects will be increasingly felt and with some immediacy." Unsurprisingly, because of Bush's no-new-taxes pledge, the commission ended in a stalemate, with the Republicans arguing that spending should be cut and the Democrats arguing to raise taxes, and it never had any effect.

I quickly found myself in the same public conflict with President Bush that we'd had during the campaign. In January, I testified to the House Banking Committee that inflation risks were still high enough that Fed policy would be to "err more on the side of restrictiveness rather than stimulus." The next day with reporters, the president challenged this approach. "I do not want to see us move so strongly against inflation that we impede growth," he said. Normally such differences would get aired and resolved behind the scenes. I'd been looking toward building the same collaborative relationship with the White House that I'd seen during the Ford administration and that I knew had existed at times between Reagan and Paul Volcker. It was not to be. Great things happened on George Bush's watch: the fall of the Berlin Wall, the end of the cold war, a clear victory in the Persian Gulf, and the negotiation of the NAFTA agreement to free North American trade. But the economy was his Achilles' heel, and as a result we ended up with a terrible relationship.

He faced a worsening trade deficit and the politically damaging phenomenon of factories moving overseas. The pressure to cut the federal deficit finally forced him, in July 1990, to accept a budget compromise in which he broke his no-new-taxes pledge. Just days later came Iraq's invasion of Kuwait. The ensuing Gulf War proved to be great for his approval ratings. But the crisis also threw the economy into the recession we'd been worried about, as oil prices rose and uncertainty hurt consumer confidence. Worse still, the recovery, which began in early 1991, was unusually slow and anemic. Most of these events were beyond anyone's control, but they still made "the economy, stupid" an effective way for Bill Clinton to beat Bush in the 1992 election, despite the fact that the economy during that year had grown by 4.1 percent.

Two factors greatly complicated the economic picture. The first was the collapse of America's thrift industry, which put a big, unexpected drain on the federal budget. Savings and loans, which had been instituted in their modern form to finance the building of the suburbs after World War II, had been failing in waves for a decade. The inflation of the seventies—compounded by mismanaged deregulation and, ultimately, fraud—did hundreds of them in. As originally conceived, an S&L was a simple mortgage machine, not much different from the Bailey Building and Loan run by Jimmy Stewart in *It's a Wonderful Life*. Typically, customers would deposit money in passbook savings accounts, which paid only 3 percent interest but were federally insured; then the S&L would lend out those funds in the form of thirty-year mortgages at 6 percent interest. As a result, S&Ls for decades were dependable moneymakers—and the thrift industry grew huge, with more than 3,600 institutions and $1.5 trillion in assets by 1987.

But inflation spelled doom for this tidy state of affairs. It drove both short-term and long-term interest rates sharply higher, putting the S&Ls in a terrible squeeze. For the typical S&L, the cost of deposits soared immediately, but because the mortgage portfolios turned over only slowly, revenues lagged. Soon many S&Ls were in the red, and by 1989 the great majority were technically insolvent: if they'd sold all their loans, they wouldn't have had enough money to pay off all their depositors.

Congress tried repeatedly to prop up the industry but mainly succeeded in making the problem worse. Just in time for the building boom of the Reagan era, it increased the level of taxpayer-funded deposit insurance (from $40,000 to $100,000 per account) and relaxed the restrictions on the kinds of loans S&Ls could make. Before long, emboldened S&L executives were financing skyscrapers and resorts and thousands of other projects that in many cases they barely understood, and they were often losing their shirts.

Others took advantage of the loosened rules to commit fraud—most notoriously Charles Keating, a West Coast entrepreneur who was ultimately sent to prison for racketeering and fraud for having misled investors through sham real estate transactions and the sale of worthless junk bonds. Salesmen at Keating's Lincoln Savings were also said to have talked unsophisticated people into shifting their savings from passbook accounts into risky, uninsured ventures controlled by him. When the business collapsed, cleaning up the mess cost taxpayers $3.4 billion, and as many as twenty-five thousand bond buyers lost an estimated $250 million. The revelation in 1990 that Keating and other S&L executives were major contributors to Senate campaigns made for a full-blown Washington drama.

I had a complicated involvement in this mess not only because of my job but also because of a study I'd done while still a private consultant. Years before, at Townsend-Greenspan, a major law firm representing Keating had hired me to evaluate whether Lincoln was financially healthy enough to be allowed to invest directly in real estate. I'd concluded that with its then highly liquid balance sheet, it could do so safely. This was before Keating undertook dangerous increases in the leveraging of his balance sheet and long before he was exposed as a scoundrel. To this day I don't know whether he'd started committing crimes by the time I began my research. My report surfaced when the Senate Ethics Committee opened hearings into Keating's connections to five senators, who came to be known as the Keating Five. John McCain, one of those being investigated, testified that my assessment had helped reassure him about Keating. I told the *New York Times* that I was embarrassed by my failure to foresee what the company would do, and added, "I was wrong about Lincoln."

The incident was doubly painful for me because it caused trouble for Andrea. By this time she had become her network's chief congressional correspondent, and she was covering the Keating scandal. Andrea had always taken extreme care to keep what she called a firewall between my work and hers as our relationship deepened. For example, she never attended any of my congressional testimonies; she strove to avoid even the appearance of a conflict of interest. The Keating hearings put this to the test. Reluctantly, Andrea decided to take herself off the story while the news media explored my connection to the case.

No one knew how much the final cleanup of the thrift industry would cost taxpayers—the estimates were in the hundreds of billions of dollars. As the work proceeded, the drain on the Treasury was perceptible, worsening the fiscal challenge for President Bush. The job of trying to recoup some of the losses fell to the Resolution Trust Corporation, which Congress had created in 1989 to sell off the assets of the ruined companies. I was on its oversight board, which was chaired by Treasury Secretary Brady and included Jack Kemp, then the secretary of housing and urban development; real estate developer Robert Larson; and former Fed governor Philip Jackson. The RTC had a professional staff, but for me by early 1991 being on the oversight board was almost like having a second job. I spent large amounts of time poring over detailed documents and attending meetings. The vast numbers of uninhabited properties we managed were deteriorating rapidly from lack of maintenance, and unless we moved quickly to get rid of them, we would end up with one huge write-off. Moreover, we would probably have been saddled with a bill to tear a lot of them down. I kept adding up the cost in my mind. It was not a pretty thought.

S&L mortgages that were still paying interest had sold off readily in the market. But now the RTC had gotten down to the assets nobody seemed to want: half-built malls in the desert, marinas, golf courses, tacky new condo complexes in overbuilt residential markets, repossessed half-empty office buildings, uranium mines. The scope of the problem beggared the imagination: Bill Seidman, who chaired both the RTC and the Federal Deposit Insurance Corporation, calculated that if the RTC sold off $1 million of assets a day, it would need three hundred years to sell them all. Clearly, we needed a different approach.

I'm not sure who came up with the creative sales idea. As we finally presented it, the plan was to group the properties into $1 billion blocks. For the first package, which we offered at auction, we especially solicited the bids of a few dozen qualified buyers, mostly businesses with track records of turning around sick properties. "Qualified" doesn't necessarily mean "savory"—the groups we approached included so-called vulture funds and speculators whose reputations could have used a face-lift.

Only a few bids materialized, and the package went for a comparative song—just over $500 million. What's more, the winning bidder had to make a down payment of only a fraction of the price, and then pay installments based on how much cash the properties generated. The deal looked like a giveaway, and as we'd expected, public watchdogs and Congress were outraged. But there's nothing like a bargain to stimulate demand. Large numbers of greedy investors rushed to get in on the action, the prices of the remaining blocks of property soared, and within a few months the RTC's shelves were stripped bare. By the time it disbanded in 1995, the RTC had liquidated 744 S&Ls—more than a quarter of the industry. But thanks in part to the asset sales, the total bill to taxpayers was $87 billion, far less than originally feared.

Commercial banks also were in serious trouble. This was an even bigger headache than the S&Ls because banks represent a far larger and more important sector of the economy. The late 1980s was their worst period since the Depression; hundreds of small and medium-size banks failed, and giants like Citibank and Chase Manhattan were in distress. Their problem, as with the S&Ls, was too much speculative lending: in the early eighties, the major banks had gambled on Latin American debt, and then, as those loans went bad, like amateur gamblers trying to get square they'd bet even more by leading the whole industry into a binge of commercial real estate lending.

The inevitable collapse of the real estate boom really shook the banks. Uncertainty about the value of the real estate collateral securing their loans made bankers unsure how much capital they actually had—leaving many of them paralyzed, frightened, and reluctant to lend further. Big businesses were able to tap other sources of funds, such as innovative debt markets that had sprung up on Wall Street—a phenomenon that helped keep the 1990 recession shallow. But small and midsize manufacturers and merchants all over America were finding it hard to get even routine business loans approved. And that, in turn, made the recession unusually difficult to snap out of.

Nothing we did at the Fed seemed to work. We'd begun easing interest rates well before the recession hit, but the economy had stopped responding. Even though we lowered the fed funds rate no fewer than twenty-three times in the three-year period between July 1989 and July 1992, the recovery was one of the most sluggish on record. "The U.S. economy is best described as moving forward, but in the teeth of a fifty-mile-an-hour headwind" was how I explained the situation to an audience of worried New England businessmen in October 1991. I couldn't be very encouraging, because I didn't know when the credit crunch would end.

I would see President Bush every six or seven weeks, usually in the context of a meeting with others but sometimes one-on-one. We had known each other since the Ford years. He'd even had me over to Langley for lunch when he was director of Central Intelligence in 1976. During the early months of the 1980 campaign, he often called me on economic policy issues. While Bush was vice president, I would join him every so often at the White House. He was intelligent and in person we always got along well. I was particularly taken with his wife, Barbara, a spunky and formidable presence. But during his presidency, he was far less focused on the economy than on foreign affairs.

Though his father had worked on Wall Street and he'd majored in economics at Yale, he had never experienced the markets firsthand. He didn't think of interest rates as being set mainly by market forces; he seemed to believe that they were matters of preference. It was not a thoughtful view. He preferred to delegate economic policy to his top aides. This meant that I dealt mainly with Nick Brady, Dick Darman, and Mike Boskin.

Darman, the budget director, was in many ways similar to David Stockman—a major-league policy intellectual and a believer in sound fiscal management. Unlike Stockman, though, Dick was often less than direct with people and was more driven by political expediency. Over time I learned to keep my distance.

Darman wrote years later that behind closed doors at the White House, he'd strenuously opposed keeping the no-new-taxes pledge. Instead he tried to persuade the president to attack the deficit early on, when they might have put the issue quickly behind them. But the president wasn't convinced. As 1989 progressed, the White House found itself at loggerheads with the Democratic Congress. So much debt continued to hang over the budget that when the recession came, the administration didn't have the fiscal flexibility to address it.

Before long, the administration began blaming its troubles on the Fed. Supposedly we were choking the economy by keeping the money supply too tight. I got my first taste of this in August 1989, while Andrea and I were visiting Senator John Heinz and his wife, Teresa, at their Nantucket summerhouse. We put on the Sunday morning talk shows and there was Dick Darman on *Meet the Press*. I was only half paying attention when I heard him say, "It's important to not merely Chairman Greenspan but the other members of the Board and the FOMC . . . that they be more attentive to the need to avoid tipping this economy into recession. I'm not sure they're quite there yet." I nearly spilled my coffee. "What!" I said. Listening to his argument, I thought it made no economic sense. But then I realized it didn't have to: it was political rhetoric.

Treasury Secretary Brady didn't like the Fed either. He and the president were friends and had a lot in common—both were wealthy, Yale-educated patricians and members of Skull and Bones. Nick had spent more than three decades on Wall Street, rising to become chairman of a major investment house. He brought with him to Washington a depth of real-world trading experience and the habit of command.

Throughout the Bush administration, Nick and I cooperated on many major issues—we traveled to Moscow in 1991 and worked closely and effectively on complex matters of bank regulation and foreign exchange. Not only did he and I work together, but he even invited me down to Augusta National to play golf, and Andrea and I socialized with him and his wife, Kitty.

But he reinforced President Bush's instrumental view of monetary policy. To Nick, slashing short-term interest rates seemed a no-risk proposition: if the Fed flooded the economy with money, the economy would grow faster. We would have to stay on the lookout for a flare-up of inflation, of course, but if that happened, the Fed could rein it back in. If I had done what they wanted, I'd have pushed for faster, steeper cuts, and no doubt have had my head handed to me by the market—deservedly.

The treasury secretary, however, was not receptive to debate. Like many traders, he'd had great success going by his gut; in matters like exchange rate policy, I found his sense of the markets quite acute. But he was not a conceptualizer, and was not inclined to take the long-term view. Nick and I would meet for a working breakfast once a week, and whenever the subject of monetary policy came up, we would simply go round and round.

This impasse made coping with the deficit and the recession doubly difficult, because it meant the administration was always looking for a quid pro quo from the Fed. When the 1990 budget bill was on the table—and President Bush finally faced the necessity of breaking his no-new-taxes pledge—Nick asked me for a commitment that if the budget went through, the Fed would lower interest rates.

In fact, the budget package impressed me. It included a couple of Darman innovations that I thought were very promising, such as a "pay-go" rule that any new spending program had to have some offsetting source of funding, either a new tax or a budget cut ("pay-go" was Washington shorthand for "pay as you go"). The proposed budget did not cut the deficit as deeply as it might have, but the consensus at the Fed, with which I agreed, was that it was a big step in the right direction. In a congressional hearing in October when the budget was finally up for approval, I pronounced the plan "credible"—which might sound like faint praise, but it was enough to make the stock market jump, as traders bet that the Fed would instantly cut interest rates. Of course, we had no such intention: before easing credit, we needed to see first whether the budget cuts actually became law, and most important, whether they had any real economic effect.

So I was always very careful in what I privately told Nick. I said, "A sound budget will bring long-term rates down because inflation expectations will fall. Monetary policy, appropriately, should respond to that by lowering short-term rates." This was standard Fed policy, but it frustrated Nick because it was not the promise he was looking for.

When the recession hit that fall, the friction only got worse. "There has been too much pessimism," President Bush declared in his 1991 State of the Union address. "Sound banks should be making sound loans now, and interest rates should be lower, now." The Fed, of course, had been lowering rates for over a year, but the White House wanted more, faster cuts.

I still have a letter Nick sent me during that time. He'd taken the extraordinary step of inviting eight prominent economists from industry and academia to the White House for lunch with the president. At the lunch, each economist was asked whether the Fed ought to further cut short-term rates. Put on the spot in front of the president, Nick wrote, "every single one replied that it would do no harm"—and virtually all felt it would help. "Alan, in my travels you stand alone in your view," the letter continued, complaining bluntly of "lack of forceful leadership by the Fed."

In the event, the administration's bark was worse than its bite. As my term as Fed chairman ended in the summer of 1991, there was a behind-the-scenes meeting in which the treasury secretary was fishing for a commitment to further relax monetary policy in exchange for a second term. Nick later claimed I had made such a deal. In fact there was no way I could commit to that, even if I had wanted to (and even though I privately thought our rate decreases might continue). Nonetheless, President Bush reappointed me. I think he concluded I was his least worst choice: the Fed itself by all accounts was functioning well, there was no other candidate whom Wall Street seemed to prefer, and a change would have roiled the markets.

The impasse on monetary policy made it hard for Nick and me to remain friends; though we continued to cooperate professionally, he canceled our weekly breakfasts, and our socializing came to an end. With the election year nearing, the administration decided to change its approach to the Fed and its pigheaded chairman. The "Greenspan account," as they called it in the White House, shifted to CEA chairman Mike Boskin and the president himself.

The recovery was in fact finally picking up steam as the campaign season began. By July I felt confident enough to declare that the fifty-mile-per-hour headwinds had partially abated. Later analysis showed that by spring GDP (which in 1990 replaced GNP as the standard measure of aggregate output) was growing at a healthy 4 percent annual rate. But that was hard to discern at the time, and the president, understandably, was concerned that the growth be as robust and obvious as possible.

I met with the president only a handful of times that year. He was always extremely cordial. "I don't want to bash the Fed," he'd say. He'd probe and raise substantive questions based on what he'd been hearing from his business contacts. He'd ask things like, "People are saying restrictions on bank reserves are part of the problem; how should I be looking at this?" These were not questions Reagan would have raised—he had no patience for discussing economic policy—and I was delighted that Bush wanted to know. I felt a lot more comfortable dealing with him than I did with Brady because the discussion was never adversarial. But when we talked about interest rates, I was never able to convince him that lowering rates further and faster almost certainly wouldn't have speeded the recovery and would have increased the risk of inflation.

The fact was, the economy was recovering, just not in time to save the election. The deficit probably hurt Bush worse than anything else. Although the belated budget cuts and the tax hikes of 1990 had put the country on a somewhat better fiscal footing, the recession cut so deeply into federal revenues that the deficit temporarily mushroomed. It hit $290 billion in the last year of Bush's term. Ross Perot was able to hammer at that in the campaign and succeeded in dividing the Republican vote enough to sink Bush.

I was saddened years later when I discovered that President Bush blamed me for his loss. "I reappointed him and he disappointed me," he told a television interviewer in 1998. It's not in my nature to be suspicious. I realized only in retrospect the extent to which Brady and Darman had convinced the president that the Fed was sabotaging him. His bitterness surprised me; I did not feel the same way about him. His loss in the election reminded me of how voters in Britain had ousted Winston Churchill immediately after the Second World War. As best I could judge, Bush had done an exemplary job on the most important issues confronting the United States, our confrontation with the Soviet Union and the crisis in the Middle East. If a president can earn reelection, he did. But then, so did Winston Churchill.

SIX

THE FALL OF
THE WALL

It was October 10, 1989. Jack Matlock, the U.S. ambassador to the Soviet Union, was introducing me to an audience of Soviet economists and bankers at Spaso House, the ambassador's official residence in Moscow. My assignment was to explain capitalist finance.

Of course, I had no notion that in a month the Berlin Wall would be torn down, or that in a little more than two years the Soviet Union would be no more. Nor did I know that I would, in the years following the Eastern bloc's collapse, become witness to a very rare event: the emergence of competitive market economies from the ashes of centrally planned ones. In the process, the demise of central planning exposed the almost unimaginable extent of the rot that had accumulated over decades.

But the biggest surprise that awaited me was an extraordinary tutorial on the roots of market capitalism. This is the system with which, of course, I am most familiar, but my understanding of its foundations was wholly abstract. I was reared in a sophisticated market economy with its many supporting laws, institutions, and conventions long since in place and mature. The evolution I was about to observe in Russia had occurred in Western economies scores of years before I was born. As Russia struggled to recover from the crash of all the institutions related to the old Soviet Union, I felt like a neurologist who learns by observing how a patient functions when a part of the brain has been impaired. Watching markets try to work in the absence of the protection of property rights or a tradition of trust was a wholly new experience for me.

But that was all ahead of me as I looked out at the hundred or so people assembled before me at Spaso House and wondered, What are they thinking? How can I reach them? They were all products of Soviet schools, I assumed, and deeply indoctrinated with Marxism. What did they know of capitalist institutions or market competition? Whenever I addressed a Western audience, I could judge its interests and level of knowledge and pitch my remarks accordingly. But at Spaso House, I had to guess.

The lecture I had prepared was a dry, diffuse presentation on banks in market economies. It delved into such topics as the value of financial intermediation, various types of risk commercial banks face, the pluses and minuses of regulation, and the duties of central banks. The talk was very slow going, especially as I had to pause paragraph by paragraph for the translator to render my words into Russian.

Yet the audience was quite attentive—people stayed alert throughout, and several seemed to be taking detailed notes. Hands went up when I finally reached the end and Ambassador Matlock opened the floor for questions. To my surprise and pleasure, the ensuing half hour of discussion made it obvious that some people got what I was talking about. The questions they asked revealed an understanding of capitalism that startled me in its sophistication.*

I'd been invited by Leonid Abalkin, the deputy prime minister in charge of reform. I'd expected our meeting that week to be largely ceremonial, but it turned out to be anything but. An academic economist in his late fifties

---

*How did these people know so much? In 1991 I finally asked Grigory Yavlinsky, one of Gorbachev's top reformers. He laughed and explained, "We all had access to books on econometrics in the university libraries. The Party ruled that because these were mathematical works, they were purely technical, devoid of ideological content." Of course, the ideology of capitalism was embodied in many of the equations—econometric models revolve around the driving forces of consumer choice and market competition. Thus, Yavlinsky said, Soviet economists had become quite knowledgeable about how markets worked.

who was one of Gorbachev's kitchen cabinet of reformers, Abalkin had built a reputation for political flexibility and grace. His long face made him look as if he was carrying a lot of stress, and there were plenty of reasons for that to be the case. Winter was setting in, there were reports of looming electricity and food shortages, Gorbachev was talking publicly about the risk of anarchy, and the prime minister had just asked the parliament for emergency powers to ban strikes. Perestroika, Gorbachev's ambitious four-year-old economic reform initiative, was in danger of collapse. I sensed that Abalkin had his work cut out for him because his boss understood so little of the mechanics of markets.

Abalkin asked my opinion of a proposal being touted by the Soviet state planners. It was an inflation-fighting program that revolved around indexation—tying wages to prices—as a way to reassure the population that the purchasing power of their wages wouldn't be destroyed. I told him briefly about the U.S. government's ongoing struggle to foot the bill for having indexed Social Security benefits, and volunteered my strongly held view that indexing is only a palliative that, in the longer run, is likely to cause even more serious problems. Abalkin didn't seem surprised. He said he thought that the transition from bureaucratic central planning to the private market, which he called "the most democratic form of regulating economic activity," would take many years.

Fed chairmen had ventured behind the iron curtain before—both Arthur Burns and William Miller had come to Moscow during the period of détente in the 1970s—but I knew they'd never had a conversation like this one. In those years, there had been little to discuss: the ideological and political divide between the centrally planned economies of the Soviet bloc and the market economies of the West was simply too vast. Yet the late 1980s had brought astonishing changes, most obviously in East Germany and other satellites, but also in the Soviet Union itself. Just that spring, Poland had held its first free elections, and the ensuing events had amazed the world. First the Solidarity union won decisively against the Communist Party, and then, instead of sending in the Red Army to reassert control, Gorbachev declared that the USSR accepted the outcome of a free election. More recently East Germany had started to dissolve—tens of thousands of its people took advantage of the state's weakening hold to emigrate illegally to the West. And just days before I arrived in Moscow, Hungary's Communist Party renounced Marxism in favor of democratic socialism.

The Soviet Union itself was obviously in crisis. The collapse of oil prices a few years before had eliminated its only real source of growth, and now there was nothing to offset the stagnation and corruption that had become epidemic during the Brezhnev era. Compounding this was the cold war, whose pressure was greatly increased by America's huge arms buildup under President Reagan. Not only was the Soviet Union's grip on its satellites slipping, but also it was having trouble feeding its population: only by importing millions of tons of grain from the West was it able to keep bread on the shelves. Inflation, Abalkin's immediate concern, was indeed out of control—I'd seen with my own eyes long lines outside jewelry stores, where customers desperate to convert rubles into goods with lasting value reportedly were being restricted to one purchase per visit.

Gorbachev, of course, was moving as rapidly as he could to liberalize the system and reverse the decay. The general secretary of the Communist Party of the Soviet Union struck me as an extraordinarily intelligent and open man, but he was of two minds. Intelligence and openness were his problems, in a way. They made it impossible for him to ignore the contradictions and lies the system presented him with day in and day out. Though he'd grown up under Stalin and Khrushchev, he could see that his country was stagnating and why, which unraveled his indoctrination.

The big mystery to me was why Yuri Andropov, the hard-liner who preceded Gorbachev, had brought him forward. Gorbachev didn't bring down the Soviet Union purposely, yet he did not raise his hand to prevent its dissolution. Unlike his predecessors, he did not send troops into East Germany or Poland when they moved toward democracy. And Gorbachev was calling for his country to become a major player in world trade; without question he understood this was implicitly procapitalist, even if he didn't understand the mechanics of stock markets or other Western economic systems.

My visit dovetailed with Washington's growing effort to encourage reform-minded Soviets under Gorbachev's openness policy, glasnost. As soon as the KGB allowed people to attend evening gatherings, for instance, the U.S. embassy instituted a series of seminars at which historians, economists, and scientists could attend lectures by their Western counterparts on previously forbidden subjects such as black markets, ecological problems in the southern republics, and the history of the Stalin era.

A large part of my itinerary consisted of meetings with high officials. Each surprised me in some way. While I'd studied free-market economics for much of my life, encountering the alternative and seeing it in crisis forced me to think more deeply than I ever had before about the fundamentals of capitalism and how it differed from a centrally planned system. My first inkling of this difference had come during the drive into Moscow from the airport. In a field beside the roadway, I'd spotted a 1920s steam tractor, a clattering, unwieldy machine with great metal wheels. "Why do you suppose they still use that?" I asked the security man who was with me in the car. "I don't know," he said. "Because it still works?" Like the 1957 Chevrolets on the streets of Havana, it embodied a key difference between a centrally planned society and a capitalist one: here there was no creative destruction, no impetus to build better tools.

No wonder centrally planned economic systems have great difficulty in raising standards of living and creating wealth. Production and distribution are determined by specific instructions from the planning agencies to the factories, indicating from whom and in what quantities they should receive raw materials and services, what they should produce, and to whom they should distribute their output. The workforce is assumed to be fully employed, and wages are predetermined. Missing is the ultimate consumer, who in a centrally planned economy is assumed to passively accept the goods planning agencies order produced. Even in the USSR, consumers didn't behave that way. Without an effective market to coordinate supply with consumer demand, the consequences are typically huge surpluses of goods that no one wants, and huge shortages of products that people do want but that are not produced in adequate quantities. The shortages lead to rationing, or to its famous Moscow equivalent—the endless waiting in line at stores. (Soviet reformer Yegor Gaidar, reflecting on the power of being a dispenser of scarce goods, later said, "To be a seller in a department store was the same as being a millionaire in Silicon Valley. It was status, it was influence, it was respect.")

The Soviets had staked their entire nation on the premise that central planning, rather than open competition and free markets, is the way to achieve the common good. Contemplating this made me eager to meet Stepan Sitaryan, the right-hand man of the chief of Gosplan, the state planning committee. The Soviet Union had a bureaucracy for everything, and the key ones had names beginning with *gos*, or state. Gosnab allocated raw materials and supplies to industry, Gostrud set wages and work rules, Goskomtsen set prices. At the pinnacle sat Gosplan—which, as one analyst memorably put it, dictated "the type, quantity, and price of every commodity produced at every single factory and plant across 11 time zones." Gosplan's vast empire included military factories, which had access to the best labor and the best materials and were universally regarded as the USSR's finest.* In total, Western analysts estimated, the agency controlled between 60 percent and 80 percent of the nation's GDP. And Sitaryan and his boss, Yuri Maslyukov, were the officials at the controls.

A diminutive man with a white pompadour and a good command of English, Sitaryan turned me over to a senior Gosplan aide who trotted out elaborate input-output matrices, the mathematics of which would have dazzled even Wassily Leontief, the Russian-born Harvard economist who pioneered them. Leontief's notion was that you could precisely characterize any economy by mapping the flow of materials and labor through it. Done thoroughly, your model would be the ideal instrument panel. Theoretically it would let you anticipate every impact on every segment of the economy from the change of one output, such as the production of tractors—or, more to the point in the Reagan era, a major increase in military production to respond to the U.S. arms buildup for the "Star Wars" missile defense. But Western economists generally considered input-output matrices to be of limited use because they failed to capture the dynamism of an economy—in the real world, the relationships between inputs and outputs almost invariably shift faster than they can be estimated.

Gosplan's input-output model had been elaborated to Ptolemaic perfection. But judging by the top aide's remarks, I couldn't see that any of the

---

*Indeed, the USSR's supposedly passive consumers flocked whenever possible to acquire the superior household goods produced by military factories. These consumers were as sophisticated as any in the West.

limitations had been solved. So I asked how the model took into account dynamic change. He just shrugged and changed the subject. Our meeting obliged him to keep up the pretext that planners can set production schedules and manage a vast economy more efficiently than free markets can do. I suspected that the aide didn't actually believe that, but I couldn't tell whether what he really felt was cynicism or doubt.

One might think that smart planning authorities should have been able to adjust to their models' shortcomings. People like Sitaryan are smart, and they tried. But they took too much on themselves. Without the immediate signals of price changes that make capitalist markets work, how was anyone to know how much of each product to manufacture? Without the help of a market pricing mechanism, Soviet economic planning had no effective feedback to guide it. Just as important, the planners did not have the signals of finance to adjust the allocation of savings to real productive investments that accommodated the population's shifting needs and tastes.

Years before becoming Fed chairman, I'd actually tried picturing myself in the central planner's job. From 1983 to 1985, I served under Reagan on the President's Foreign Intelligence Advisory Board (PFIAB), where I was asked to review U.S. assessments of the Soviet ability to absorb the strain of accelerated armament. The stakes were enormous: The president's Star Wars strategy rested on the assumption that the Soviet economy was no match for ours. Ramp up the arms race, the thinking went, and the Soviets would collapse trying to keep up, or they'd ask to negotiate; in either case, we'd hold out our hands and the cold war would end.

The assignment was clearly too important to turn down, but it daunted me. It would be a Herculean task to learn the ins and outs of a production and distribution system so different from ours. Once I dug into the project, though, it took me only a week to conclude that it was impossible: there was no reliable way to assess their economy. Gosplan's data were rotten— Soviet managers up and down the line had every incentive to exaggerate their factories' output and pad their payrolls. Worse, there were large internal inconsistencies in their data that I couldn't reconcile and I suspected neither could Gosplan. I reported to the PFIAB and the president that I couldn't forecast whether the challenge from Star Wars would overload the Soviet economy—and I was fairly certain the Soviets couldn't either.

As it turned out, of course, the Soviets didn't try to match Star Wars—Gorbachev came to power and launched his reforms instead.

I mentioned none of this to the Gosplan officials. But I was glad I wasn't in Sitaryan's shoes—the Fed's job was challenging, but Gosplan's was surreal.

Meeting with the head of the Soviet central bank, Viktor Gerashchenko, was much less fraught. Officially he was my counterpart, but in a planned economy, in which the state decides who gets funds and who does not, banking plays a much smaller role than in the West: Gosbank was little more than a paymaster and record keeper. If a borrower fell behind in payments on a loan or went into default, so what? Loans were essentially transfers among entities all owned by the state. Bankers did not need to worry about credit standards, or interest rate risks, or market value changes—the financial signals that determine who gets credit, and who does not, and hence who produces what, and sells to whom, in a market economy. All the topics I'd talked about the previous evening were simply not part of Gosbank's world.

Gerashchenko was forthcoming and friendly—he insisted we call each other Viktor and Alan. He spoke excellent English, having spent several years running a Soviet-owned bank in London, and he understood what Western banking was about. Like many people, he made believe that the Soviet Union was not that far behind the United States. He sought me out, and sought out other bankers in the West, because he wanted to be part of the prestigious central banking establishment. To me he seemed totally benign, and we had a pleasant talk.

Just four weeks later, on November 9, 1989, the Berlin Wall came down. I was in Texas on Fed business, but like everybody else that night I was glued to the TV. The event itself was remarkable, but even more amazing to me in the following days was the economic ruin the fall of the wall exposed. One of the most fateful debates of the twentieth century had been the question of how much government control is best for the common good. After World War II, the European democracies all moved toward socialism, and the balance was tilted toward central government control even in America—the entire war effort by American industry had been effectively centrally planned.

That was the economic backdrop of the cold war. In essence, it turned out to be a contest not just between ideologies but between two great theories of economic organization: free-market economies versus centrally planned ones. And for the past forty years, they'd seemed almost evenly matched. There was a general belief that even though the Soviet Union and its allies were laggards economically, they were catching up to the wasteful market economies of the West.

Controlled experiments almost never happen in economics. But you could not have created a better one than East and West Germany, even if you'd done it in a lab. Both countries started with the same culture, the same language, the same history, and the same value systems. Then for forty years they competed on opposite sides of a line, with very little commerce between them. The major difference subject to test was their political and economic systems: market capitalism versus central planning.

Many thought it was a close race. West Germany, of course, was the scene of the postwar economic miracle, rising from war's ashes to become Europe's most prosperous democracy. East Germany, meanwhile, became the powerhouse of the Eastern bloc; it was not only the Soviet Union's biggest trading partner but also a country whose standard of living was seen to be only modestly short of West Germany's.

I'd compared the East and West German economies as part of my work for the PFIAB. Experts had estimated that East German GDP per capita was 75 percent to 85 percent of West Germany's. I thought this couldn't be right—all you had to do was look at the crumbling apartment buildings on the other side of the Berlin Wall to conclude that productivity levels and standards of living there fell far short of those in the vibrant West. The irony was that East Germany's GDP estimates did not seem out of line. The narrow spread between West and East German standards of living appeared the result of West Germany's understating its progress. Each country, for example, counted the number of cars it produced. But West German statistics did not fully capture the quality difference between a 1950 Mercedes, say, and one assembled in 1988. Meanwhile, the design of the Trabant, the boxy, pollution-belching East German sedan, hadn't changed in thirty years. So the quality-adjusted production gap between the two economies was almost certainly greater than generally thought.

The fall of the wall exposed a degree of economic decay so devastating that it astonished even the skeptics. The East German workforce, it turned out, had little more than one-third the productivity of its western counterpart, nothing like 75 percent to 85 percent. The same applied to the population's standard of living. East German factories produced such shoddy goods, and East German services were so carelessly managed, that modernizing was going to cost hundreds of billions of dollars. At least 40 percent of East German businesses were judged so hopelessly obsolete that they would have to close; most of the rest would need years of propping up to be able to compete. Millions of people were losing their jobs. Those people would need retraining and new work, or else they were likely to join the throngs migrating west. The extent of the devastation behind the iron curtain had been a very well kept secret, but now the secret was out.

At least East Germans could look to the West Germans for help. The other nations of the Soviet bloc all were suffering the same blight or worse, yet they had to fend for themselves. Poland's great reformer, Leszek Balcerowicz, was taking a page from the book of another great economic reformer, Ludwig Erhard. The economics director of West Germany under the Allied occupation in 1948, Erhard sparked the revival of the devastated economy by abruptly declaring the end of price and production controls. Erhard arguably overstepped his authority doing this, but he made the announcement on a weekend, and prices had completely changed by the time the occupation administration could react. The gambit worked. To the amazement of critics, West Germany's stores, which had been gripped by chronic shortages of food and merchandise, quickly flooded with goods, and its notorious black markets dried up. At first prices were exorbitant, but they declined as additional supply overwhelmed demand.

A Western-educated economics professor from central Poland, Balcerowicz followed Erhard's example to propose what he called a market revolution. Everybody else called it shock therapy. When Solidarity won the Polish election in August 1989, the economy was on the verge of collapse.

There were food shortages in the stores, hyperinflation was destroying the value of people's money, and the government was bankrupt and couldn't pay its debts. At Balcerowicz's urging, the new government designated January 1, 1990, as the day of the "big bang," when virtually all price controls would cease. I met him for the first time at an international banking meeting in Basel, Switzerland, a few weeks before the event, and he astonished me by saying he did not know whether the strategy would work. But, he said, "you cannot reform by small steps." He was convinced that in a society where the government had dictated every aspect of buying and selling for four decades, there was no such thing as a smooth transition from central planning to competitive markets. Drastic action was required to spur people to start making their own decisions and, as he put it, to be convinced that change was inevitable.

His big bang, predictably, brought tremendous upheaval. Just as had happened in Erhard's Germany, prices initially leaped up—the zloty lost almost half its purchasing power in the first two weeks. But more goods appeared in the stores, and gradually prices evened out. Balcerowicz had people constantly checking the shops, and as he later recalled, "It was a very important day when they said, 'The price of eggs is falling.'" There was no more eloquent sign that the shift to a free market had begun to work.

Poland's success encouraged Czechoslovakia to try an even bolder reform. Václav Klaus, the economics minister, wanted to turn state-owned enterprises over to the private sector. Instead of trying to auction them off to investor groups—no one in Czechoslovakia had much ready cash—he proposed to distribute ownership to the entire population in the form of vouchers. Each citizen would receive an equal allotment of vouchers, which could be traded or sold or exchanged for stock in a state-owned enterprise. In this way, Klaus wanted not only to bring about "the radical transformation of property rights" but also to lay the groundwork for a stock market.

Klaus talked about this and many other ambitious plans in a lunchtime presentation at a Fed conference at Jackson Hole, Wyoming, in August 1990. A square-built man with a brushy mustache, he was fierce about the urgency of reform. "Losing time means losing everything," he told us. "We have to act rapidly because gradual reform provides a convenient excuse to the vested interests, to monopolists of all kinds, to all beneficiaries of paternalistic socialism, to change nothing at all." This sounded so fiery and un-compromising that when we opened the floor for questions, I brought up the impact of the reforms on people's jobs. "Are you contemplating provid-ing some kind of social safety net for the unemployed?" I asked. Klaus cut me short. "In your country you can afford such luxuries," he said. "To suc-ceed we need a clean break with the past. The competitive market is the way to produce wealth, and that's where we're going to focus." He and I became good friends, but this was the first time in my life that I had ever been rebuked for not sufficiently appreciating the power of free markets. It was a singular experience for an admirer of Ayn Rand.

As the Eastern European countries raced ahead with reform, the insta-bility in Moscow only seemed to worsen. It was hard from the West even to determine what was going on. Just a week after being elected presi-dent of the Russian Republic in June 1991, Boris Yeltsin visited New York and spoke at the New York Fed. Yeltsin had gotten his start as a construc-tion industry boss and had been Moscow's mayor in the 1980s; then he'd quit the Communist Party to take up the cause of radical reform. His election with a nationwide majority of 60 percent was a crushing defeat for Com-munism. Though he was subordinate to Gorbachev, his popularity coupled with his impetuousness made him a magnet for attention—like Khrushchev in an earlier era, he seemed to personify his country's unnerving contradic-tions. His first trip to the United States in 1989 had been a disaster—people remembered mostly the news reports of his behaving erratically and get-ting drunk on Jack Daniel's.

Gerald Corrigan, the president of the New York Fed, had taken the lead in encouraging Wall Street to connect with the Soviet reformers, some-thing the Bush administration wanted to see happen. So when Yeltsin came to town, the New York Fed invited him to speak at a dinner of some fifty bankers, financiers, and corporate chiefs. Yeltsin arrived with a large entou-rage, and Corrigan and I talked with him briefly before he was introduced to the assembled dinner guests. The Yeltsin we met that night was no drunken buffoon; he seemed smart and determined. At the podium, he spoke cogently on reform for twenty minutes without notes and then answered detailed, specific questions from the audience without calling on his advisers for help.

It was increasingly unclear whether Gorbachev, or anyone, could end the Communist regime without causing a complete collapse into violence. After Gorbachev dissolved the Warsaw Pact in June and launched his plan to reconstitute the USSR as a voluntary confederation of democratic states, the resistance facing him became brutally apparent. In August a coup attempt by Stalinist hard-liners almost brought him down—to many it was only the inspired theatrics of Yeltsin, who climbed on a tank outside the Soviet parliament, that enabled Gorbachev to survive.

The West started looking for ways to help. That was the reason Treasury Secretary Nick Brady and I led a team to Moscow in September to meet with Gorbachev and confer with his economic advisers. Our ostensible mission was to assess what reforms were needed for the Soviet Union to join the International Monetary Fund, but mainly we wanted to see for ourselves what was going on.

From the perspective of the Fed and the Western world, in purely economic terms the Soviet Union was not much of a concern. Its economy wasn't that large; of course there were no reliable statistics, but experts estimated its GDP to be about the same size as the United Kingdom's, or about one-sixth the size of all Europe's. The iron curtain had kept it so isolated that its share of world trade was small. So was the amount of debt it owed Western nations, which might be subject to default if the government collapsed. But none of this took into account nuclear warheads. We were all acutely aware of the danger a Soviet collapse could pose to the world's stability and safety.

For that reason alone, we were horrified by the picture that emerged during our stay.

It was clear that the government was falling apart. The institutions of central planning were all beginning to fail, and the well-being of the population was threatened. Eduard Shevardnadze, who was then foreign minister, told us of unrest in the Soviet republics along Russia's border—he said the lives of the twenty-five million ethnic Russians living in those regions could be in jeopardy. Worse, he said, was the risk that Russia and Ukraine, which both held weapons from the Soviet nuclear arsenal, might end up at odds.

The economic data, which were fragmentary at best, were equally alarming. Inflation was out of control, with prices going up by anywhere from 3 percent to 7 percent a week. This was because all of the central mechanisms of production and distribution were breaking down, and more and more money was chasing fewer and fewer goods. In an effort to keep things moving at all, the government was flooding the economy with cash. A Gorbachev aide told me, "The printing presses can't keep up. We are printing rubles twenty-four hours a day."

Over all this hung the shadow of not being able to put food on the shelves. There had been times in the past when the output of Ukraine had made it famous as the breadbasket of the world. But while harvests were still relatively bountiful, some of the crops had rotted in the fields because there was no way to collect and distribute the produce and grain. Soviet grain purchases from abroad were up to forty million tons a year. Bread shortages were a sore point in the national memory—it was the Bread Riots of 1917, when the old women of St. Petersburg rose up in rebellion, that helped bring about the fall of the czar.

A separate conversation gave me a glimpse of how brittle this economy was and how difficult it would be to change. Boris Nemtsov, a reformist economist, confided, "Let me tell you about military cities," and rattled off names I'd never heard of. Across the nation, Nemtsov explained, were at least twenty cities, each of two million people or more, that had been built around military plants. They were isolated and specialized and had no reason to exist other than to serve the Soviet military. His point was clear: ending the cold war, and shifting to a market economy, would leave entire cities and millions of workers with little to do and no ready way to adapt. The rigidity built into the Soviet economic system was far more extreme than any we'd ever encountered in the West. Among the many worries was that, in order to survive, these military workers, who included world-class scientists and engineers and technicians, would eventually have to sell their skills to rogue states.

There were more briefings, but the message was the same. When we met with President Gorbachev, and he repeated his goal of making the nation "a major trading force in the world," I admired his courage. But in the margin of my notepad I jotted down, "USSR is a Greek tragedy waiting to happen."

Grigory Yavlinsky, chief economist for Gorbachev's Council of Ministers, led a delegation in October 1991 to Thailand, where the World Bank and International Monetary Fund were holding their annual meeting. This was a truly historic moment: the first time Soviet officials had ever sat down with the key economic policymakers of the capitalist world.

The Soviet Union had already been granted provisional status—formally giving it access to IMF and World Bank advice, but not to loans. Yavlinsky and his team came to argue that the confederation of remaining Soviet republics ought to be accorded full membership. The question of massive Western loans was not immediately on the table—the Soviets insisted they could manage the transition to a market economy themselves, and none of the G7 nations was offering.

The discussions lasted two full days, and if I had to pick a word to describe what the Western central bankers and finance ministers felt, it would be "impotence." We knew that what was left of the Soviet Union was crumbling; we knew the armed forces hadn't been paid and that a collapse of the military could pose a serious threat to world peace. We had grave concerns about what would happen to the nuclear weapons. The deterioration was internal and political. All the IMF could do was talk about money, and money wasn't the problem. We ended up doing what organizations usually do under such circumstances: we delegated a committee for further study and discussion (in this instance, the deputy finance ministers of the G7 were to go to Moscow in a few weeks for consultations). So it was up to the Soviet reformers. The challenges they faced were more difficult than those that had confronted their counterparts in Eastern Europe. The Polish and Czech leaders had been able to draw on the goodwill of the population—as trying as the economic circumstances may have been, their nations were being liberated from Moscow's grasp. But many Soviet citizens had prided themselves on their country's superpower status and had sacrificed much to help achieve it. For them, the upheavals meant nothing but sorrow—a great loss of national prestige. Humiliation made the reformers' tasks much harder.

What's more, too many years had gone by in the Soviet Union since 1917—scarcely anyone alive even remembered private property, or had firsthand business experience or training. There were no accountants, auditors, financial analysts, marketers, or commercial lawyers, even among retirees. In Eastern Europe, where Communism had reigned for forty years instead of eighty, free markets could be restored; in the Soviet Union, they had to be resurrected from the dead.

Gorbachev did not stay in power long enough to oversee the market reforms; he resigned in December 1991 as the Soviet Union formally broke up and was replaced by a loose economic confederation of former Soviet republics. "End of the Soviet Union; Gorbachev, Last Soviet Leader, Resigns; U.S. Recognizes Republics' Independence" read the headline of the *New York Times* on December 26—I looked at it and felt regret that Ayn Rand hadn't lived to see it. She and Ronald Reagan had been among the few who had predicted decades before that the USSR would ultimately collapse from within.

The man Boris Yeltsin chose to launch economic reforms in Russia was Yegor Gaidar. In the 1980s when he and other young economists had dreamed of creating a market economy in the Soviet Union, they'd imagined an organized, methodical transition. But now, amid growing chaos, there was no time for that—unless the government could jump-start the markets, people might starve. So in January 1992, Gaidar, as Russia's acting prime minister, turned to the scheme that had worked in Poland: abruptly ending price controls.

Shock therapy jolted the Russians much more than it had the Poles. The size of the country, the system's rigidity, the fact that the state had dictated prices for people's entire lives—it all worked against them now. Inflation rose so fast that people's wages, when they could collect them, became worthless, and their meager savings were wiped out. The ruble lost three quarters of its value in four months. Goods remained in scarce supply in the stores, and the black market flourished.

Then, in October, Yeltsin and his economists unleashed the second massive reform: they issued vouchers to 144 million citizens and started privatizing state-owned enterprises and real estate on a massive scale. This reform, too, was far less effective than in Eastern Europe. Millions of people ended up with stock in businesses or owning their apartments, which was the goal, but millions more were bilked out of their vouchers. Entire industries ended up in the hands of a small number of opportunists who came to be known as the oligarchs. Like Jay Gould and some of the railroad tycoons in nineteenth-century America who built vast fortunes in part by manipulating government land grants, the oligarchs constituted an entirely new wealthy class and compounded the political chaos.

I was fascinated to see these events unfold. Economists have had considerable experience observing how market economies convert to centrally planned ones—indeed, the shift toward Communism in the East and socialism in the West was the dominant economic trend of the twentieth century. Yet until recent years we have had little exposure to movement in the opposite direction. Until the wall fell and the need to develop market economies out of the rubble of Eastern Europe's central-planning regimes became apparent, few economists had been thinking about the institutional foundations that free markets need. Now, unintentionally, the Soviets were performing an experiment for us. And some of the lessons were startling.

The collapse of central planning did not automatically establish capitalism, contrary to the rosy predictions of many conservative-leaning politicians. Western markets have a vast underpinning of culture and infrastructure that has evolved over generations: laws, conventions, behaviors, and business professions and practices for which there was no need in a centrally planned state.

Forced to make the shift overnight, the Soviets achieved not a free-market system but a black-market one. Black markets, with their unregulated prices and open competition, seemingly replicate what goes on in a market economy. But only in part. They are not supported by the rule of law. There is no right to own and dispose of property backed up by the enforcement power of the state. There are no laws of contract or bankruptcy, and no opportunity to take disputes to court for resolution. The linchpin of a free-market economy, property rights, is missing.

The result is that black markets bring few of the benefits to society of legally sanctioned trade. Knowing that the government will protect one's property encourages citizens to take business risks, a prerequisite of wealth creation and economic growth. Few will risk their capital if the rewards are going to be subject to arbitrary seizure by the government or mobsters.

By the mid-1990s, that was the picture across much of Russia. For generations of people who had been brought up on the Marxist notion that private property is theft, the shift to a market economy already challenged their sense of right and wrong.* The rise of the oligarchs further undermined popular support. From the start, law enforcement in defense of private ownership was extremely uneven. Private security forces to a large extent took over the job, sometimes warring with each other and further aggravating the sense of chaos.

It wasn't at all clear that the Yeltsin government itself understood how a market economy's legal system must work. In 1998, for instance, an influential Russian academic told the *Washington Post:* "The state thinks . . . private capital should be defended by those who have it. . . . It's a completely conscious policy of the law enforcement authorities to remove themselves from defending private capital." To me this suggested a basic ignorance of the need to embody property rights in the judicial system. The use of rival private police forces is not the rule of law; it is the rule of fear and force.

Trust in the word of others, especially strangers, was another element conspicuously lacking in the new Russia. We hardly ever think about this facet of market capitalism, yet it is crucial. Despite each person's right in the West to file a lawsuit to address a perceived grievance, if more than a small fraction of contracts were adjudicated, our courts would be swamped to the point of paralysis. In a free society, the vast majority of transactions are thus, of necessity, voluntary. Voluntary exchange, in turn, presupposes

---

*Marx was hardly the first to condemn private ownership; the notion that private property is sinful, along with profit making and lending at interest, has deep roots in Christianity, Islam, and other religions. Only with the Enlightenment did countervailing principles emerge to provide a moral basis for ownership and profit. John Locke, the great seventeenth-century British philosopher, wrote of the "natural right" of every individual to "life, liberty and estate." Such thinking profoundly influenced America's Founding Fathers and helped foster free-market capitalism in the United States.

trust. I have always been impressed that in Western financial markets, transactions involving hundreds of millions of dollars often are simply oral agreements that get confirmed in writing only at a later date, and at times after much price movement. But trust has to be earned; reputation is often the most valuable asset a business has.

The fall of the Soviet Union concluded a vast experiment: the long-standing debate about the virtues of economies organized around free markets and those governed by centrally planned socialism is essentially at an end. To be sure, there are still a few who support old-fashioned socialism. But what the vast majority of the remaining socialists now advocate is a highly diluted form, often called market socialism.

I am not alleging that the world is about to embrace market capitalism as the only relevant form of economic and social organization. Vast numbers of people still consider capitalism with its emphasis on materialism degrading. And one can seek material well-being and yet view competitive markets as subject to excessive manipulation by advertisers and marketers who trivialize life by promoting superficial and ephemeral values. Some governments, such as that of China, even now attempt to override the evident preferences of their citizens by limiting their access to foreign media, which they fear will undermine their culture. Finally, there remains a latent protectionism, in the United States and elsewhere, which could emerge as a potent force against international trade and finance and the free-market capitalism they support, particularly if today's high-tech world economy should falter. Nonetheless, the verdict on central planning has been rendered, and it is unequivocally negative.

A DEMOCRAT'S AGENDA

On the evening of February 17, 1993, I found myself in the uncomfortable glare of the TV lights at a joint session of Congress, sitting between Hillary Clinton and Tipper Gore. The front row of the gallery was not exactly where I'd expected to be for President Clinton's first major congressional address. I had assumed that my invitation to sit with the First Lady was a matter of courtesy and that I'd be at the back of the box with White House aides. I guess it was nice to know that the Federal Reserve was considered a valuable national asset after the somewhat less than favorable embrace we'd gotten from President Bush, but obviously I'd been positioned up front for a political purpose. Mrs. Clinton was wearing a bright red suit, and as the president spoke, the cameras focused on us again and again.

Afterward it turned out that not everyone had been pleased to see me there, on the grounds that it might compromise the independence of the Fed. I had no intention of doing that, of course. But I was intent on building a working relationship with this president, who seemed seriously fiscally responsible.

I'd met Clinton in early December, when he was president-elect. He hadn't moved to Washington yet, so seeing him meant flying out to Little Rock, Arkansas. He and his transition team had set up shop there in the governor's mansion, which turned out to be a big redbrick building with white pillars set on acres of flat lawn and gardens near the center of town.

As I was ushered into an anteroom, I wasn't sure what to expect. One thing I'd heard, though, was that he always ran late, so I'd brought along some economic reports to read and busied myself for twenty minutes or so until he appeared. "Mr. Chairman," he said, striding toward me smiling and reaching to shake hands. I could see why he was reputed to be a great retail politician. He made me believe he really had been looking forward to seeing me.

Clinton had outlined a broad, ambitious economic agenda during his campaign. He wanted to cut taxes on the middle class, halve the federal deficit, stimulate job growth, increase U.S. competitiveness through new education and training programs, invest in the nation's infrastructure, and more. I had seen, and been part of, too many presidential campaigns. Candidates promised something for everybody. But I wondered what Clinton's real priorities were. He must have been reading my mind; one of the first things he said was: "We need to set our economic priorities, and I'm interested in your outlook on the economy."

From the Fed's perspective, if he wanted to address the economy's long-term health, the deficit was by far the most pressing concern. I'd made that argument at the start of Bush's term, and now the problem was four years worse. The national debt held by the public had risen to $3 trillion, causing interest payments to become the third-largest federal expense after Social Security and defense. So when Clinton asked for my economic assessment, I was ready with a pitch.

Short-term interest rates were rock-bottom low—we'd cut them to 3 percent—and the economy was gradually shaking off the effects of the credit crunch and growing at a fairly reasonable pace, I told him. More than a million net new jobs had been created since the beginning of 1991. But long-term interest rates were still stubbornly high. They were acting as a brake on economic activity by driving up the costs of home mortgages and bond issuance. They reflected an expectation of ongoing inflation for which investors had come to require an extra margin of interest to offset the added uncertainty and risk.

Improve investors' expectations, I told Clinton, and long-term rates could fall, galvanizing the demand for new homes and the appliances, furnishings, and the gamut of consumer items associated with home ownership. Stock values, too, would rise, as bonds became less attractive and investors shifted into equities. Businesses would expand, creating jobs. All told, the latter part of the 1990s could look awfully good. I was not oblivious of the fact that 1996 would be a presidential election year. The path to a beneficent future, I told the president-elect, was lowering the long-term trajectory of federal budget deficits.

To my delight, Clinton seemed fully engaged. He seemed to pick up on my sense of urgency about the deficit, and asked a lot of smart questions that politicians usually don't ask. Our meeting, which had been scheduled for an hour, turned into a lively discussion that went on for almost three. We touched on a whole range of topics beyond economics—Somalia and Bosnia and Russian history, job-training programs, education—and he asked for my assessment of world leaders whom he hadn't yet had a chance to meet. After a while, aides brought in lunch.

So saxophone wasn't the only thing we had in common. Here was a fellow information hound, and like me, Clinton clearly enjoyed exploring ideas. I walked away impressed, yet not entirely sure what I thought. Clearly, for sheer intelligence, Bill Clinton was on a par with Richard Nixon, who, despite his obvious flaws, was the smartest president I'd met to that point. And either Clinton shared many of my views on the way the economic system was evolving and on what should be done, or he was the cleverest chameleon I'd ever encountered. I mulled all this on the airplane on my way home. After I got back to Washington, I told a friend, "I don't know that I'd have changed my vote, but I'm reassured."

That feeling was reinforced a week later when Clinton announced as his senior economic team a number of familiar faces. As treasury secretary he'd picked Lloyd Bentsen, the chairman of the Senate Finance Committee, with Roger Altman, a very smart Wall Street investment banker, as his deputy. As budget director he chose Leon Panetta, a California congressman who chaired the House Budget Committee, with economist Alice Rivlin as his deputy. She was the only economist on the team, and her credentials were impressive: she'd been the founding director of the Congressional Budget Office and had been an early recipient of one of the MacArthur Foundation's genius grants. Just as interesting was Clinton's choice of Robert Rubin, the cochairman of Goldman Sachs, to run a new White House council on economic policy. As the *New York Times* explained it, Rubin was to act as the economic equivalent of a national security adviser: his job would be to elicit economic ideas from Treasury, State, the budget office, the CEA, and other departments, and weave them into policy options for the president. What jumped out at me was that Clinton was taking a page from John F. Kennedy's book. All of Clinton's economic-policy appointees were fiscally conservative centrists like Doug Dillon, the Republican banker whom Kennedy picked as treasury secretary. Choosing them made Bill Clinton seem about as far from the classic tax-and-spend liberal as you could get and still be a Democrat.

L ike every new administration, the Clinton White House had to scramble to pull together its first budget, due for submission to Congress by early February. The president by all accounts did not have an easy time dealing with the recommendations of his economic team. The full extent of the fiscal problems confronting them was only now becoming clear: in December the Office of Management and Budget offered a revised analysis projecting that the government was headed toward a $360 billion deficit in 1997—some $50 billion higher than its previous estimate. This made it clear that to come anywhere near his goal of halving the deficit, Clinton would have to abandon or postpone other cherished plans, such as the middle-class tax cut and the "investments" in training and jobs.

I kept tabs on the budget-making process mainly through Lloyd Bentsen. The new treasury secretary had first caught my attention in the 1976 primaries—Jimmy Carter ultimately beat him for the Democratic nomination, but I thought Bentsen had looked like a president and acted like one. Courtly, gray-haired, and sophisticated, he was a former World War II B-24 bomber pilot who'd served four terms in the Senate, where he had a well-earned reputation for good judgment and for quietly getting things done. Andrea and I had known Bentsen and his impressive wife, B.A., socially for some time. I was not surprised to find him a pleasure to work with, even when we disagreed.

Bentsen and the others on the economic team were careful to acknowledge the Fed's boundaries. In fact, their decision not to comment publicly on monetary policy was a big break from the past, and helped us and them by bolstering our independence. When he and Panetta came to brief me in mid-January on the evolving budget plan, they avoided asking for an endorsement or even an opinion. I simply indicated that I understood, and we left it at that. In fact, I thought the plan noninflationary and testified to that effect in Congress in late January.

Bentsen asked me to weigh in with the president just once—the day after I'd first testified in favor of their overall approach. (I had steered clear of commenting on the details of Clinton's program.) As the team crunched the numbers and the budget took shape, Clinton found himself faced with a choice that was increasingly stark. Either he could opt for a package of spending programs that would fulfill some of his campaign promises, or he could opt for a deficit-cutting plan, whose success would depend on impressing the financial markets and that would pay off chiefly in the longer term. There was no in-between—we couldn't afford both. This dilemma had opened a rift in the White House staff, some of whom privately ridiculed the deficit-cutting approach as a sellout to Wall Street. That's why Bentsen asked me to the White House—to reemphasize the urgency of budget reform.

We met the president in the Oval Office on the morning of January 28; Bob Rubin joined us. Clinton was all business, so I got straight to the point. I focused on the danger of not confronting the deficit right away, playing out for him how, in that instance, the decade was apt to unfold. Because of the end of the cold war, I told him, "defense spending will come down over the next few years and that will mask a lot of problems. But by 1996 or 1997, the deficits will be hard for the public to ignore. You can see it in the data." And I outlined for him how the mandated outlays for Social Security and other social benefits were scheduled to increase, which would cause deficit gaps to open further. "So the debt rises markedly into the twenty-first century, and the interest on the debt rises, threatening a spiral of rising deficits. Unless it's aborted, that could lead to a financial crisis," I said. As we finished, Clinton, unsurprisingly, looked grim.

Though I hadn't put it in so many words, the hard truth was that Reagan had borrowed from Clinton, and Clinton was having to pay it back. There was no reason to feel sorry for Clinton—these very problems were what had enabled him to defeat George Bush. But I was impressed that he did not seem to be trying to fudge reality to the extent politicians ordinarily do. He was forcing himself to live in the real world on the economic outlook and monetary policy. His subsequent decision to go ahead and fight for the deficit cuts was an act of political courage. It would have been very easy to go the other way. Not many people would have been the wiser for a year or two or even three.

I took one other step to help the deficit hawks—I advised Bentsen on how deeply I thought the deficit would have to be cut in order to convince Wall Street and thereby bring down long-term interest rates. "Not less than $130 billion a year by 1997" was his shorthand description of what I said. Actually the advice I gave him was more complex. I sketched out a range of possibilities, with a probability attached to each—all the while carefully emphasizing that the substance and credibility of the program would be more important than the numbers. But I understood when he finally said, "You know I can't work with something this complicated." The figure he extracted made its way to the president and had a powerful effect. Within the White House, $130 billion became known as the "magic number" that the deficit cuts had to hit.

The budget was major news when it finally appeared. "Clinton Plan to Remake the Economy Seeks to Tax Energy and Big Incomes" was the banner headline of the *New York Times* the morning after Clinton's speech. "Ambitious Program Aims at a 4-Year Deficit Cut of $500 Billion." *USA Today* declared "A Battle Launched" and described Clinton's proposals as "a five-year package of pain." The media coverage focused mainly on whom the cuts would hit (every constituency except poor households—the plan put burdens on the rich, the middle class, retirees, and business). Interestingly, the public reaction was initially favorable: polls showed Americans unexpectedly receptive to the idea of making a sacrifice to put the nation's house in order.

Most new presidents get a honeymoon from Congress, but Clinton got a trench war. Despite the budget plan's initial popularity, a majority of congresspeople hated it—not surprisingly, since it aimed at abstract, distant goals and offered no new highway projects, weapons programs, or other lucrative goodies to bring home to constituents. I think Clinton was jolted by the degree of resistance. Republicans rejected the budget outright and many Democrats rebelled, and the debates dragged on well into the spring. Even though Democrats held a 258–177 majority in the House, there was serious question whether the budget would pass—and its prospects in the Senate looked even worse. The conflict extended to within the White House, where key people were still pushing for an agenda less compatible with Wall Street. One was Clinton adviser James Carville, who famously wisecracked, "I used to think if there was reincarnation, I wanted to come back as the president or the pope or a .400 baseball hitter. But now I want to come back as the bond market. You can intimidate everybody." The discord, which was widely reported in the media, made Clinton look weak, and his initial popularity melted away. By late spring his approval rating sank to an abysmal 28 percent.

The president was in a funk when I saw him again on June 9. The House had finally passed his budget two weeks earlier—by a single vote. And the fight had only begun in the Senate. I'd gotten a call from David Gergen, Clinton's counselor. "He's distressed," he said, and asked if I could come buck the president up. I'd known Gergen for twenty years, as an adviser to Nixon, Ford, and Reagan. Clinton had recruited him partly because he was a balanced, nonneurotic Washington pro, and partly because he was Republican—the president was hoping to solidify his image as a centrist.

When I went to the Oval Office that morning, you could see that people were under strain. Word had it that they'd been working pretty much around the clock, even Bentsen, who was seventy-two. (Andrea confirmed this; she was now NBC's chief White House correspondent.) They'd been going back and forth with Congress, trying to get the numbers to work, and

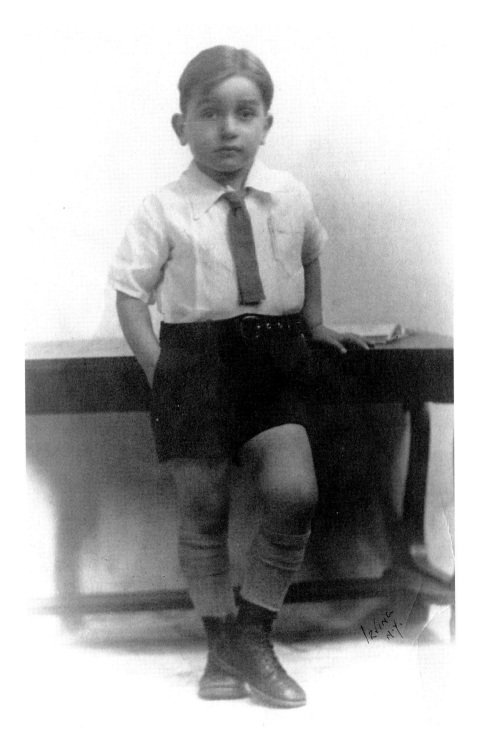

Age five, Washington Heights, New York City, 1931.
The collection of Alan Greenspan

With three cousins on the Greenspan side, circa 1934 (I'm on the left).
The collection of Alan Greenspan

Sixteen years old, Lake Hiawatha, New Jersey.
The collection of Alan Greenspan

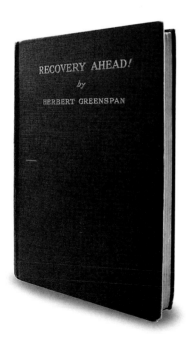

RECOVERY AHEAD!
by
HERBERT GREENSPAN

My father, who sold stocks on Wall Street, left my mother when I was two. When I was nine, he gave me a copy of his book, *Recovery Ahead!*, which confidently predicted the end of the Depression and included this affectionate, if somewhat mystifying, inscription: "To my son Alan: May this my initial effort with constant thought of you branch out into an endless chain of similar efforts so that at your maturity you may look back and endeavor to interpret the reasoning behind these logical forecasts and begin a like work of your own."
Photograph by Darren Haggar

After a year at the Juilliard School, I toured the country as a sideman with the Henry Jerome dance band, playing saxophone and clarinet (I'm sitting at far left). I also did tax returns for the band members. *Courtesy of Henry Jerome Music*

With my mother, Rose Goldsmith, a brave and lively woman who gave me my love of music. *The collection of Alan Greenspan*

By 1950, I was earning enough as an economist to think about leaving New York City for the suburbs, which I did just over a year later. *The collection of Alan Greenspan*

Of all my teachers, Arthur Burns and Ayn Rand had the greatest impact on my life. An economist who did groundbreaking work on business cycles, Burns was my faculty adviser and mentor during my first year of graduate school at Columbia, and years later persuaded me to finish my Ph.D. He served before me as head of the Council of Economic Advisors and chairman of the Federal Reserve Board. Ayn Rand expanded my intellectual horizons, challenging me to look beyond economics to understand the behavior of individuals and societies.

LEFT: *Bettmann/Corbis*; RIGHT: The New York Times/*Getty Images*

Adam Smith's Enlightenment ideas of individual initiative and the power of markets came back from near eclipse in the 1930s to their current dominance of the global economy. Smith *(above left)* remains among my deepest intellectual influences. I was also influenced by the thinking of John Locke *(above right)*, the great British moral philosopher who articulated fundamental notions of life, liberty, and property, and Joseph Schumpeter, the twentieth-century economist whose concept of creative destruction gets to the heart of the role of technological change in a modern capitalist society.

At my firm, Townsend-Greenspan, I focused on heavy industry—textiles, mining, railroads, and especially steel. Studying steel put me in an excellent position to warn of the recession of 1958—my first forecast of the U.S. economy as a whole.

Walter Daran/Time Life Pictures/Getty Images

When I took my first Washington job in 1974, I left Townsend-Greenspan in the hands of vice presidents *(from left)* Kathy Eichoff, Lucille Wu, and Bess Kaplan *(seated)*. Former vice president Judith Mackey *(right)* came back temporarily to help out. The predominance of women made Townsend-Greenspan unusual in the economics world.
The New York Times/*Redux*

My involvement in public life started with Richard Nixon's campaign for the presidency in 1967. I was an unpaid member of the campaign staff. Though I was impressed by Nixon's intelligence, he had a dark side that troubled me, and I decided against joining the administration. Seated to my left at this July 1974 meeting is Hewlett-Packard cofounder David Packard, who served as deputy secretary of defense from 1969 to 1971. *Bettmann/Corbis*

My mother congratulates me after I was sworn in as chairman of the Council of Economic Advisors, while President Ford looks on. With the nation reeling from Watergate, high oil prices, and inflation, it was a challenging moment to take a government job. *Bettmann/Corbis*

At this April 1975 meeting in the Oval Office to discuss economic policy, Secretary of State Henry Kissinger had just interupted with news of the U.S. evacuation of Saigon. *Left to right*: President Ford, Deputy Chief of Staff Dick Cheney, me, Chief of Staff Donald Rumsfeld, Vice President Nelson Rockefeller, and Kissinger. *David Hume Kennerly/The Gerald R. Ford Presidential Library/Getty Images*

The White House senior staff often gathered in the chief of staff's office to watch the evening news and chew over the day's events. I would add my two cents from the carpet, where I'd stretch out to ease my aching back. *David Hume Kennerly/The Gerald R. Ford Presidential Library/Getty Images*

Working at Camp David, *left to right:* Secretary of the Treasury Bill Simon, Press Secretary Ron Nessen, President Ford, Dick Cheney, Donald Rumsfeld, and me. *David Hume Kennerly/The Gerald R. Ford Presidential Library/Getty Images*

With President Ford in Palm Springs, 1980. Contrary to his reputation for being physically clumsy, he was a formidable golfer and a former All-American football player. *Photograph by Neil Leifer*

During the presidential campaign of 1980, my mission on this cross-country flight with Ronald Reagan was to brief him on a long list of domestic issues. Adviser Martin Anderson, in the foreground, put me up to it. "He'll listen to you," he said. But I couldn't get Reagan to stop telling stories. *Michael Evans photograph, courtesy of the Ronald Reagan Presidential Foundation*

At the Republican convention that July, Henry Kissinger and I tried to persuade former president Ford to become Reagan's running mate. Polls showed that Reagan and Ford would be a "dream ticket," but after a suspenseful twenty-four hours, the negotiations fell apart and the vice presidential nomination went to George H. W. Bush.

David Hume Kennerly/Getty Images

Social Security developed financial trouble in the late 1970s and early 1980s, and both Republicans and Democrats knew that it had to be fixed. Reagan's reform commission, which I ran, achieved a compromise. Joining Reagan in the Rose Garden in April 1983 as he signed it into law were leaders from both parties, including Senator Bob Dole (to my left in the photo), Congressman Claude Pepper (partially obscured), and House Speaker Tip O'Neill (joking with the president). The caricature below appeared that year in the financial press.

ABOVE: *AP Images/Barry Thumma;* BELOW: *David Levine*

The New York Times reprint reads:

STOCKS PLUNGE 508 POINTS, A DROP OF 22.6%; 604 MILLION VOLUME NEARLY DOUBLES RECORD

On June 2, 1987, President Reagan announced that he would nominate me to succeed Paul Volcker as chairman of the Fed. Chief of Staff Jim Baker *(right)* had quietly sounded me out about the job months before. A scant ten weeks after my swearing-in came my baptism by fire: the stock market crash of October 19, 1987.

ABOVE: *Courtesy of the Ronald Reagan Library*; LEFT: *Copyright © 1987 by the New York Times Co. Reprinted with permission.*

History took an astonishing turn when the Berlin Wall fell in November 1989. But even more amazing to me in the following days was the economic ruin exposed by the fall of the wall. By the time Soviet premier Mikhail Gorbachev made his third visit to the United States during the following spring, the Soviet Union itself had begun to disintegrate. He is shown below with President George H. W. Bush and me in a receiving line at a state dinner in Washington on May 31, 1990.

LEFT: *AP Images/John Gaps III;* BELOW: *Courtesy of the George Bush Presidential Library*

The strain between President George H. W. Bush and the Federal Reserve Board was evident in this July 1991 meeting in the Oval Office. He made no secret of his view that the Fed hadn't eased interest rates sufficiently. He reappointed me as chairman that year but later blamed me for his loss of the presidential election of 1992. *Courtesy of the George Bush Presidential Library*

The Federal Open Market Committee, the Fed's most powerful and sensitive decision-making group, in session in June 2003. It meets eight times a year.
Federal Reserve photo—Britt Leckman

I had access to an increasingly broad range of information in my Fed office, as technology revolutionized economic analysis at the Board.
Photograph by Diana Walker

I made it a point to reserve time each day
for quiet study and reflection.
Photograph by Linda L. Creighton

doubtless felt as if they were up against an impossible problem. The president himself seemed subdued. It wasn't hard to imagine why. He was spending his political capital, yet the budget for which he'd sacrificed so much was in peril.

I encouraged him as best I could. I told him that his plan was our best chance in forty years to get stable long-term growth. I tried to get him to see that the strategy was on track, was working—long-term rates were already trending down, I showed him. The very fact that he'd come out and recognized that the deficit had to be addressed was a very important plus. But I also warned that it wouldn't be easy. Indeed, Clinton had to fight, arm-twist, and horse-trade for another two months to push his budget through the Senate. As in the House, it passed by a single vote—this time a tiebreaker by Vice President Gore.

Clinton impressed me again that fall by fighting for the ratification of NAFTA. The treaty, negotiated under President Bush, was designed primarily to phase out tariffs and other trade barriers between Mexico and the United States, though it also included Canada. Labor unions hated it, and so did most Democrats, as well as some conservatives; few Congress watchers thought it had a prayer. But Clinton argued, in effect, that you cannot stop the world from turning; like it or not, America was increasingly part of the international economy, and NAFTA embodied the belief that trade and competition create prosperity, and you need free markets to do that. He and the White House staff went all out, and after a two-month struggle they got the treaty approved.

All this convinced me that our new president was a risk taker who was not content with the status quo. Again he'd shown a preference for dealing in facts. And on free trade, the fact was this: The distinction between domestic competition and cross-border competition has no economic meaning. If you're in a Dubuque, Iowa, plant, it makes no difference whether you're competing with someone in Santa Fe or across the border. With the geopolitical pressure of the cold war now removed, the United States had a historic opportunity to knit the international economy more closely together. Clinton was often criticized for inconsistency and for a tendency to take all sides in a debate, but that was never true about his economic policy.

A consistent, disciplined focus on long-term economic growth became a hallmark of his presidency.

The Fed was having its own difficulties with Congress that year, and for some of the same reasons. Our fiercest critic was Congressman Henry B. Gonzalez of Texas, the chairman of the House Banking Committee. A hot-tempered populist from San Antonio, Gonzalez was famous for socking in the eye a constituent at a restaurant who called him a Communist. At various times in Congress, Gonzalez had called for the impeachment of Reagan, Bush, and Paul Volcker. He was deeply distrustful of what he labeled "the tremendous power of the Fed"—I think he simply assumed that the Board was a cabal of Republican appointees who were running monetary policy more for the benefit of Wall Street than the workingman. In the fall of 1993, Gonzalez really turned up the heat.

The Fed has always rubbed Congress the wrong way, and it probably always will, even though Congress created it. There's inherent conflict between the Fed's statutory long-term focus and the short-term needs of most politicians with constituents to please.

This friction often surfaced in oversight hearings. The Fed was obligated to render a biannual report on its monetary-policy decisions and the economic outlook. At times these hearings sparked substantive discussions of major issues. But just as often they were a theater in which I was a prop—the audience was the voters back home. During the Bush administration, Senate Banking Committee chairman Alfonse D'Amato of New York rarely missed a chance to bash the Fed. "People are going to starve out there, and you are going to be worried about inflation," he'd tell me. That sort of remark I always let slide. But when he or anyone would assert that interest rates were too high, I would answer and explain why we'd done what we'd done. (I took care, naturally, to couch any discussion of possible future moves in Fedspeak to keep from roiling the markets.)

Gonzalez went on a crusade to make the Fed more accountable, zeroing in on what he saw as our excessive secrecy. He wanted the Federal Open Market Committee, in particular, to conduct its affairs in public, and even open its deliberations to live TV coverage. At one point he dragged eighteen members of the FOMC to Capitol Hill to testify under oath and denounced the long-standing FOMC practice of never publicly announcing policy moves or rate changes. The only public record of each meeting was a brief set of minutes published six weeks after the fact—for the financial markets, a virtual eternity. As a consequence, any signals coming from the Fed's open-market operations, or public statements by Fed officials, were subject to avid scrutiny by Wall Street.

For its part, the Federal Reserve, in the interest of economic stability, had long sought to foster highly liquid debt markets through the use of what we called constructive ambiguity. The idea was that markets uncertain as to the direction of interest rates would create a desired large buffer of both bids and offers. By the early 1990s, however, markets were becoming sufficiently broad and liquid without this support from the Fed. Moreover, the advantage of market participants being able to anticipate the Federal Reserve's future moves was seen as stabilizing the debt markets. We had begun a path toward greater transparency in our deliberations and operations, but far short of the policy Henry Gonzalez would have liked us to pursue.

I was opposed to the idea of throwing these meetings open. The FOMC was our primary decision-making body. If its discussions were made public, with the details of who said what to whom, the meetings would become a series of bland, written presentations. The advantages to policy formulation of unfettered debate would be lost.

My effort to convey this argument in the hearings, however, did not go well. As Gonzalez bored in on the question of what records we kept, I found myself in an extremely awkward position. In 1976, during the Ford administration, Arthur Burns had directed the staff to audiotape FOMC meetings to assist in the writing of the minutes. This practice continued, and I knew about it, but I'd always assumed the tapes were erased once the minutes were done. In preparing for the Banking Committee testimony, I learned that this wasn't exactly the case: although the tapes indeed were routinely erased, the staff kept copies of the complete unedited transcripts in a locked file cabinet down the hall from my office. When I revealed the transcripts' existence, Gonzalez pounced. Now more convinced than ever that we were conspiring to hide embarrassing secrets, he threatened to subpoena the records.

Gonzalez was especially suspicious of two conference calls the FOMC had conducted in preparing for the hearings. We did not want to release these tapes, for fear of creating a precedent. After a bit of negotiation, we agreed to let lawyers for the committee—one Democrat and one Republican—come to the Fed and listen.

The Watergate tapes had been a lot more exciting, they quickly discovered. After listening patiently for the better part of two hours to the FOMC's deliberations, the Democrat left without a word, and the Republican remarked that the tape ought to be used to teach students in high school civics classes how government meetings should work.*

All the same, my colleagues were upset—mainly with Gonzalez, but they probably weren't too happy with me either. For one thing, most of them hadn't even known our meetings were being taped. And the thought that any remarks they now made might be published immediately if Gonzalez got his way put a chill in the air. The next time the FOMC met, on November 16, people were clearly less willing to kick around ideas. "You could notice a difference, and not for the better," a governor told a *Washington Post* reporter.

After thorough discussion, the Board decided to resist, in court if necessary, any subpoena or demand that might hamper the effectiveness of the institution. But the controversy also accelerated our recent deliberations about transparency. Eventually we decided that the FOMC would announce its moves immediately after each meeting and that the complete transcript would be published after a five-year lag. (People joked that this was the Fed equivalent of glasnost.) We did these things knowing that published transcripts made our meetings longer and a little less creative. In the event, the sky did not fall. Not only did the changes make the process more transparent but they also gave us new ways to communicate with the markets.

I was grateful that President Clinton kept his distance from this whole

---

*Congressman Gonzalez was quoted in the *New York Times* (November 16, 1993) complaining that the tapes included "disparaging remarks about one distinguished member of the House Banking Committee and Banking Committee members in general."

teapot tempest. "Does anybody in his right mind think we would do anything to change the independence of the Fed?" was all he would say afterward, adding, "I have no criticism of the Federal Reserve since I've been President."

In the midst of such Washington melodramas, it was sometimes easy to forget that there was a real world out there in which real things were happening. That summer, flooding from the Mississippi and Missouri rivers paralyzed nine midwestern states. NASA astronauts went into orbit to repair the Hubble Space Telescope. There was a failed coup against Boris Yeltsin, and Nelson Mandela won the Nobel Peace Prize. There were disconcerting outbreaks of violence in the United States: the bombing of the World Trade Center, the siege at Waco, and the killing and maiming of scientists and professors by the Unabomber. In corporate America, something called business-process reengineering became the latest management fad, and Lou Gerstner began an effort to turn around IBM. Most important from the Fed's standpoint, the economy seemed finally to have shaken off its early-1990s woes. Business investment, housing, and consumer spending all rose sharply, and unemployment fell. By the end of 1993, not only had real GDP grown 8.5 percent since the 1991 recession, but it was expanding at a 5.5 percent annual rate.

All of which led the Fed to decide that it was time to tighten. On February 4, 1994, the FOMC voted to hike the fed funds interest rate by one-quarter of a percentage point, to 3.25 percent. This was the first rate hike in five years, and we imposed it for two reasons. First, the post-1980s credit crunch had finally ended—consumers were getting the mortgages they needed and businesses were getting loans. For many months, while credit was tight, we'd kept the fed funds rate exceptionally low, at 3 percent. (In fact, if you allowed for inflation, which was also nearly at a 3 percent annual rate, the rate on fed funds was next to nothing in real terms.) Now that the financial system had recovered, it was time to end this "overly accommodative stance," as we called it.

The second reason was the business cycle itself. The economy was in a growth phase, but we wanted the inevitable downturn, when it came, to be less of a roller-coaster ride—a moderate slowing instead of a sickening plunge into recession. The Fed had long tried to get ahead of the curve by tightening rates at the first sign of inflation, before the economy had a chance to seriously overheat. But raising rates in this way had never averted a recession. This time, we opted to take advantage of the relative economic tranquillity to try a more radical approach: moving gently and preemptively, before inflation even appeared. It was a matter of psychology, I explained to the Congress that February. Based on what we'd learned in recent years about inflation expectations, I said, "if the Federal Reserve waits until actual inflation worsens before taking countermeasures, it would have waited too long. Modest corrective steps would no longer be enough to contain the emerging economic imbalances. . . . Instead more wrenching measures would be needed, with unavoidable adverse side effects on near-term economic activity."

Because so much time had passed since our last rate increase, I worried that the news would rattle the markets. So with the FOMC's consent, I hinted strongly in advance that a policy shift was imminent. "Short-term interest rates are abnormally low," I told Congress in late January. "At some point, absent an unexpected and prolonged weakening of economic activity, we will need to move them." (This may sound overly subtle to the reader, but on the scale of Fed public statements in advance of a policy move, it was like banging a pot.) I also visited the White House to give the president and his advisers a heads-up. "We haven't made a final decision," I told them, "but the choices are, we sit and wait and then likely we'll have to raise rates more. Or we could take some small increases now." Clinton responded, "Obviously I would prefer low rates," but he said he understood.

The rest of the world, by contrast, seemed to turn a deaf ear. The markets did nothing to discount a rate hike (typically, in advance of an expected increase, short-term interest rates would edge up and stocks would edge down). So when we actually made the move, it was a jolt. In keeping with our new openness, we decided at the February 4 FOMC meeting to announce the rate hike as soon as we adjourned. By day's end, the Dow Jones Industrial Average had plunged 96 points—almost 2.5 percent. Some politicians reacted vehemently. Senator Paul Sarbanes of Maryland, a frequent Fed critic, compared us to "a bomber coming along and striking a farmhouse . . . because you think that the villain inflation is inside . . . when in fact what's inside . . . is a happy family appreciating the restoration of economic growth."

To me such reactions merely showed how attached Americans were becoming to low, stable interest rates. Behind the closed doors of the Fed, several of the bank presidents had pushed for twice as large an increase. Fearing a panicky market reaction to too sharp a rise, I had urged my colleagues to keep this initial move small.

We continued to apply the brakes throughout 1994, until by year end the fed funds rate stood at 5.5 percent. Even so, the economy had a very good year: it grew a robust 4 percent, it added 3.5 million new jobs, productivity increased, and business profits rose. Equally important, inflation did not increase at all—for the first time since the 1960s, it had been under a 3 percent annual rate for three years running. Low to stable prices were becoming a reality and an expectation—so much so that in late 1994, when I spoke to the Business Council, an association made up of the heads of major companies, a few of the CEOs were complaining that it was hard to make price increases stick. I was unsympathetic. "What do you mean, you're having problems?" I asked. "Profit margins are going up. Stop complaining."

For decades, analysts had wondered whether the dynamics of the business cycle ruled out the possibility of a "soft landing" for the economy—a cyclical slowdown without the job losses and uncertainty of a recession. The term "soft landing" actually came from the 1970s space race, when the United States and the Soviet Union were competing to land unmanned probes on Venus and Mars. Some of those spacecraft made successful soft landings, but the economy never had; in fact, the expression wasn't even used at the Fed. But in 1995, a soft landing was exactly what took place. Economic growth slowed throughout the year, to an annualized rate of less than 1 percent in the fourth quarter, when our metaphoric spacecraft gently touched down.

In 1996, the economy picked back up again. By November, when President Clinton would win reelection, activity was expanding at a solid 4 percent rate. The media celebrated a soft landing long before I was willing to; even in December 1996 I was still cautioning colleagues, "We haven't fully completed the process. Six months from now we could run into a recession." But in hindsight the soft landing of 1995 was one of the Fed's proudest accomplishments during my tenure.

All of this lay hidden in the future, of course, as the FOMC was tightening rates. Knowing when to start tightening, and by how much, and most important, when to stop was a fascinating and sometimes nerve-racking intellectual challenge, especially because no one had tried it this way before. It didn't feel like "Oh, let's execute a soft landing"; it felt more like "Let's jump out of this sixty-story building and try to land on our feet." The toughest call for some committee members was the rate hike that proved to be the last—a 0.5 percent increase on February 1, 1995. "I fear that if we act today, our move may be the one we turn out to regret," said Janet Yellen, a governor who would later become chairman of Clinton's Council of Economic Advisors. She was the most vocal advocate for shifting to a stance of wait and see. The increase, which we went on to adopt unanimously that day, brought the fed funds rate all the way to 6 percent—double where it had stood when we'd started less than a year before. Everyone on the FOMC knew the risks. Had we turned the screw one time too many? Or not enough? We were groping through a fog. The FOMC has always recognized that in a tightening cycle, if we stop too soon, inflationary pressures will resurge and make it very difficult to contain them again. We therefore always tend to take out the insurance of an additional fed funds increase, fully expecting that it may not be necessary. Ending the course of monetary antibiotics too soon risks the reemergence of the infection of inflation.

For President Clinton, meanwhile, 1994 had been a miserable year. It was marked by the collapse of his health care initiative, followed by the stunning loss of both the House and the Senate in the midterm elections. The Republicans won on the basis of Newt Gingrich's and Dick Armey's "Contract with America," an anti-big-government plan that promised tax cuts, welfare reform, and a balanced budget.

Within weeks Clinton was put to the test again. In late December, Mexico revealed that it was on the brink of financial collapse. Its problem was billions of dollars of short-term debt, borrowed when the economy was thriving. Lately that growth had slowed, and as the economy weakened, the peso had to be devalued, making the borrowed dollars increasingly expensive to repay. By the time Mexico's leaders asked for help, government finances were in a downward spiral, with $25 billion coming due in less than a year and only $6 billion in dollar reserves, which were dwindling fast.

None of us had forgotten the Latin American debt crisis of 1982, when an $80 billion default by Mexico had triggered a cascade of emergency refinancings in Brazil, Venezuela, Argentina, and other countries. That episode nearly toppled several giant U.S. banks, and had set back economic development in Latin America by a decade. The crisis of late 1994 was smaller. Yet the risk was hard to overstate. It, too, could spread to other nations, and because of the growing integration of world financial markets and trade, it threatened not just Latin America but other parts of the developing world. What's more, as NAFTA demonstrated, the United States and Mexico were increasingly interdependent. If Mexico's economy were to collapse, the flow of immigrants to the United States would redouble and the economy of the Southwest would be clobbered.

The crisis hit just as Andrea and I were leaving on a post-Christmas getaway to New York. I'd booked us into the Stanhope, an elegant Fifth Avenue hotel directly across from Central Park and the Metropolitan Museum of Art. We'd been looking forward to a few days of concerts, shopping, and just wandering around in the relative anonymity of the city where we'd met. Ten years had passed since the snowy evening of our first date for dinner at Le Périgord on East Fifty-second Street, and while this wasn't a formal anniversary, we always liked to make it back to the city and the site of that first date between Christmas and New Year's.

As soon as we arrived, though, the phone began to ring—it was my office at the Fed. Bob Rubin, now the treasury secretary designee, urgently needed to talk about the peso. Bob was slated to take over officially from Lloyd Bentsen, who was retiring, right after New Year's Day, but for all intents and purposes he was already on the job. I'm sure he'd been hoping for an easier transition than this. Instead he was facing a baptism by fire.

Andrea realized instantly what the phone call meant. On any foreign financial crisis affecting the United States, the Treasury Department takes the lead but the Fed always gets involved. "So much for romance," she sighed. She understood me and my job too well after all these years—I was grateful for her generosity and patience. So as the Mexico crisis unfolded, she went shopping and visited friends, and I spent the entire stay in our hotel room on the phone.

In the following weeks, the administration huddled with Mexican officials, the International Monetary Fund, and other institutions. The IMF was prepared to offer Mexico what help it could, but it lacked the funds to make a decisive difference. Behind the scenes I argued, as did Bob Rubin and his top deputy, Larry Summers, and others, that U.S. intervention should be massive and fast. To forestall a collapse, Mexico needed sufficient funding to persuade investors not to dump pesos or demand immediate repayment of their loans. This was based on the same principle of market psychology as piling currency in a bank's window to stop a run on the bank—something U.S. banks used to do during crises in the nineteenth century.

In Congress, remarkably, leaders from both parties were in accord; potential chaos in a nation of eighty million people with whom we shared a two-thousand-mile border was too serious to ignore. On January 15, President Clinton; Newt Gingrich, the new House Speaker; and Bob Dole, the new Senate majority leader, jointly put forward a $40 billion package of loan guarantees for congressional approval.

As dramatic as that gesture was, within days it became clear that politically the bailout didn't have a prayer. Americans have always resisted the idea that a foreign country's money problems can have major consequences for the United States. Mexico's crisis, coming so soon after NAFTA, aggravated this isolationist impulse. Everyone who'd fought NAFTA—labor, consumer, and environmental activists, and the Republican right—rose up again to oppose the rescue. Gene Sperling, one of Clinton's top economic advisers, summed up the political dilemma: "How do you deal with a problem that to the public doesn't seem important, that seems like giving money away, that seems like bailing out people who made dumb investments?"

When the $40 billion proposal was rolled out, Newt Gingrich asked me if I would call Rush Limbaugh and explain why it was in America's best interest to intervene. "I don't know Rush Limbaugh," I said. "Do you really think calling him will make a difference?" "He'll listen to you," Gingrich told me. The ultracombative radio host was a force among conservatives. Some of the freshman congressmen had actually taken to calling themselves the Dittohead Caucus, using the favorite nickname of fans of his show. Needless to say, Limbaugh was having a field day trashing the thought of giving Mexico a hand. I was still dubious, but it impressed me that the new House Speaker was willing to support a Democratic president on a clearly unpopular issue. So reluctantly, I picked up the phone.

Limbaugh seemed even less comfortable than I. He listened politely as I laid out my arguments, and thanked me for taking the time. This surprised me—I'd expected Rush Limbaugh to be more confrontational.

The situation couldn't wait for Congress to come around. In late January, with Mexico teetering on the brink, the administration took matters into its own hands. Bob Rubin turned to a solution that had been proposed and dismissed early on: tapping an emergency Treasury fund that had been created under FDR to protect the value of the dollar. Rubin felt great trepidation about risking tens of billions of taxpayers' dollars. And even though the congressional leaders promised to acquiesce, there was the risk of appearing to circumvent the will of the people: a major poll showed voters opposed helping Mexico by a stunning margin of 79 percent to 18 percent.

I pitched in to help work out the details of the plan. Rubin and Summers presented it to President Clinton on the night of January 31. The surprise was still in Bob's voice when he phoned afterward to report the result. Clinton had said simply, "Look, this is something we have to do," Rubin told me, adding, "He didn't hesitate at all."

That decision broke the logjam. The International Monetary Fund and other international bodies more than matched some $20 billion of guarantees from the Treasury to offer Mexico a package totaling, with all its components, $50 billion, mostly in the form of short-term loans. These weren't giveaways, as opponents had claimed; in fact, the terms were so stiff that Mexico ended up using only a fraction of the credit. The minute that confidence in the peso was restored, it paid the money back—the United States actually profited $500 million on the deal.

It was a sweet victory for the new treasury secretary and his team. And the experience formed a lasting bond between Rubin, Summers, and me. In the countless hours we spent analyzing the issues, brainstorming and testing ideas, meeting with our foreign counterparts, and testifying before Congress, we became economic foxhole buddies. I felt a mutual trust with Rubin that only deepened as time passed. It would never enter my mind that he would do something contrary to what he said he would do without informing me in advance. I hope it was the same way with him. Even though we came from opposing parties, there was a sense that we were working for the same firm. We agreed on many basic issues and neither of us liked confrontation for confrontation's sake, which made it easy to communicate and spark off each other's ideas.

Summers, of course, had started as the economics wunderkind. The son of Ph.D. economists and the nephew of two Nobel laureates in economics, he was one of the youngest professors ever to get tenure at Harvard. Before joining the administration, he'd been chief economist of the World Bank. He was an expert in public finance, development economics, and other fields. What I liked best was that he was a technician and a conceptualizer like me, with a passion for grounding theory in empirical fact. He was also steeped in economic history, which he used as a reality check. He worried, for example, that the president was getting carried away with the promise of information technology—as though the United States had never gone through periods of rapid technological progress before. "Too yippity about productivity" was how Larry once described Clinton's techno-enthusiasm. I disagreed, and we had debates about the Internet's potential, with Bob taking it all in. Larry could be shrewd too: it was his idea to put such a high interest rate on the Mexico loans that the Mexicans felt compelled to pay us back early.

Rubin and Summers and I met confidentially over breakfast each week for the next four and a half years, and we would phone and drop by one another's offices frequently in between. (Larry and I continued the practice after Bob returned to Wall Street in mid-1999 and Larry became treasury secretary.) We'd gather at 8:30 a.m. in Bob's office or mine, have breakfast brought in, and then sit for an hour or two, pooling information, crunching numbers, strategizing, and brewing ideas.

I always came out of these breakfasts smarter than when I arrived. They were the best forum I could imagine for puzzling out the so-called New Economy. The dual forces of information technology and globalization were beginning to take hold, and as President Clinton later put it, "the rulebooks were out of date." Democrats joyfully labeled the constellation of economic policies "Rubinomics." Looking back in 2003, a *New York Times* reviewer of Bob's memoir called Rubinomics "the essence of the Clinton presidency." He defined it as "soaring prices for stocks, real estate, and other assets, low inflation, declining unemployment, increasing productivity, a strong dollar, low tariffs, the willingness to serve as global crisis manager, and most of all, a huge projected federal budget surplus." I wish I could say that it was all the result of conscious, effective policy coming out of our weekly breakfasts. Some of it surely was. But mostly it reflected the onset of a new phase of globalization and the economic fallout from the demise of the Soviet Union, issues I will address in later chapters.

I saw President Clinton only infrequently. Because Bob and I worked together so well, there was rarely any need for me to attend an economic policy meeting in the Oval Office except in moments of crisis—such as when a budget standoff between Clinton and Congress forced a shutdown of the government in 1995.

I did eventually hear that the president had been sore at me and the Fed for much of 1994, while we were hiking interest rates. "I thought the economy had not picked up enough to warrant it," he explained to me years later. But he never challenged the Fed in public. And by mid-1995, Clinton and I had settled into an easy, impromptu relationship. At a White House dinner or reception, he'd pull me aside to see what was on my mind or to try out an idea. I didn't share his baby-boom upbringing or his love of rock and roll. Probably he found me dry—not the kind of buddy he liked to smoke cigars and watch football with. But we both read books and were curious and thoughtful about the world, and we got along. Clinton publicly called us the economic odd couple.

I never ceased to be surprised by his fascination with economic detail:

the effect of Canadian lumber on housing prices and inflation, the trend toward just-in-time manufacturing. He had an eye for the big picture too, like the historic connection between income inequality and economic change. He believed dot-com millionaires were an inevitable by-product of progress. "Whenever you shift to a new economic paradigm, there's more inequality," he'd say. "There was more when we moved from farm to factory. Vast fortunes were made by those who financed the Industrial Revolution and those who built the railroads." Now we were shifting into the digital age, so we had dot-com millionaires. Change was a good thing, Clinton said—but he wanted ways to get more of that new wealth into the hands of the middle class.

Politics being what they are, I never thought Clinton would reappoint me as chairman when my term ended in March 1996. He was a Democrat and no doubt he would want one of his own. But by the end of 1995, my prospects had changed. American business was doing exceptionally well— profits at large companies were up 18 percent and the stock market had had its best growth in twenty years. Fiscal and monetary policy were both working, with the 1996 deficit projected to shrink to less than $110 billion, and inflation still below 3 percent. GDP growth was starting to revive without a recession. The relationship between the Fed and the Treasury had never been better. As New Year's came and went, the press began speculating that the president might ask me to stay. In January, Bob Rubin and I went to a G7 meeting in Paris. During a pause in the proceedings, we wandered off to the side. I could tell that Bob had something on his mind. I can still picture the scene: we were standing in front of a floor-to-ceiling plate-glass window with a panoramic view of the city. "You'll be getting a call from the president when we get back to Washington," he said. He didn't come right out and tell me, but I knew from his body language that the news must be good.

President Clinton set a little challenge for me and for the two Fed officials he appointed at the same time: Alice Rivlin, who was to be Fed vice chairman, and Laurence Meyer, a highly regarded economics forecaster, who would become a Fed governor. "There is now a debate, a serious debate in this country, about whether there is a maximum growth rate we can have over any period of years without inflation," the president told report-ers. It wasn't hard to read between the lines. With the economy entering its sixth year of expansion, and with the soft landing looking real, he was ask-ing for faster growth, higher wages, and new jobs. He wanted to see what this rocket could do.

IRRATIONAL
EXUBERANCE

ugust 9, 1995, will go down in history as the day the dot-com boom was born. What set it off was the initial public offering of Netscape, a tiny, two-year-old software maker in Silicon Valley that had almost no revenues and not a penny of profits. Netscape was actually giving most of its products away. Yet its browser software had fueled an explosion in Internet use, helping turn what had started as a U.S.-government-funded online sandbox for scientists and engineers into the digital thoroughfare for the world. The day Netscape stock began to trade, it rocketed from $28 a share to $71, astonishing investors from Silicon Valley to Wall Street.

The Internet gold rush was on. More and more start-ups went public to fantastic valuations. Netscape stock continued to climb; by November the company had a higher market capitalization than Delta Airlines, and Netscape chairman Jim Clark became the first Internet billionaire. High-tech excitement brought extra sizzle that year to what was already a hot market for stocks: the Dow Jones Industrial Average broke 4,000, then 5,000, ending 1995 up by well over 30 percent. The technology-heavy NASDAQ, where the new stocks were listed, finished even better, with a gain of more than

40 percent in its composite index. And the market growth roared unabated into 1996.

We generally did not talk about the stock market very much at the Fed. In a typical FOMC meeting, in fact, the word "stock" was used more often in reference to capital stock—machine tools, rail cars, and, lately, computers and telecom gear—than in reference to equity shares. As far as the tech boom was concerned, our focus was more on the people who make the chips, write the software, build the networks, and integrate information technology into factories and offices and entertainment. Yet we were all aware of a "wealth effect": investors, feeling flush because of gains in their portfolios, borrowed more and spent more freely on houses and cars and consumer goods. More important, I thought, was the impact of rising equity values on business outlays on plant and equipment. Ever since I'd delivered a paper entitled "Stock Prices and Capital Evaluation" at an obscure session of the annual meeting of the American Statistical Association in December 1959, I had been intrigued by the impact of stock prices on capital investment and hence on the level of economic activity.* I showed that the ratio of stock prices to the price of newly produced plant and equipment correlated with new orders for machinery. The reasoning was clear to real estate developers, who work by a similar principle: If the market value of office buildings in a certain location exceeds the cost of building one from scratch, new buildings will sprout up. If, on the other hand, the market values fall below the cost of constructing a building, new construction will stop.

It appeared to me that the correlation between stock prices and new machinery orders was telling a similar story: when corporate management saw higher market values on capital equipment than the cost of purchase, such spending would rise, and the reverse was also true. I was disappointed when that simple ratio failed to work as well in forecasting during the 1960s as it had in earlier years. But that was, and is, a common complaint of econometricians. Today's version of that relationship is converted to its equivalent implicit rates of return on newly contemplated capital invest-

*This paper, which appeared in the American Statistical Association's *Proceedings of the Business and Economic Statistics Section 1959*, later formed part of my doctoral thesis.

ment. It still doesn't work as well in forecasting as I always thought it should, but the notion was a backdrop to my thoughts at a December 1995 FOMC meeting.

Mike Prell, the Fed's top domestic economist, argued that the wealth effect might boost consumer expenditures by $50 billion in the coming year, causing GDP growth to accelerate. Governor Larry Lindsey, who would go on to become President George W. Bush's chief economic adviser, thought this was implausible. Most stocks were held in pension funds and 401(k)s, he argued, making it hard for consumers to lay hands on their gains. And most individuals who owned large stock portfolios were already very well off, not the types to indulge automatically in spending sprees. I wasn't sure I agreed with him on that point, but the issue was new; none of us knew what to expect.

The morning's discussion also revealed how clueless we were about the growing strength of the bull market. Janet Yellen predicted that any effect of the stock boom would surely dissipate soon. "It will be gone by the end of 1996," she said. I was concerned that the stock boom could set the stage for a crash. "The real danger is that we are at the edge of a bond and stock bubble," I said. Yet the market did not seem as superheated as it had seemed in 1987. I speculated that we probably were close to "at least some temporary peak in stock prices, if for no other reason than that markets do not go straight up indefinitely."

That statement did not turn out to be my most prescient. But then, the stock market wasn't my main concern that day. I had a different agenda. I was determined to start people thinking about the big picture of technological change. In studying what was going on in the economy, I'd become persuaded that we were on the verge of a historic shift; the soaring stock prices were just a sign of it.

The meeting was scheduled to wrap up with a proposal to continue easing the fed funds rate, and a vote. But before we got to that, I told the committee, I wanted to step back. For months, I reminded them, we'd been seeing evidence of the economic impacts of accelerating technological change. I told them: "I want to raise a broad hypothesis about where the economy is going over the longer term, and what the underlying forces are."

My idea was that as the world absorbed information technology and learned to put it to work, we had entered what would prove to be a protracted period of lower inflation, lower interest rates, increased productivity, and full employment. "I've been looking at business cycles since the late 1940s," I said. "There has been nothing like this." The depth and persistence of such technological changes, I noted, "appear only once every fifty or one hundred years."

To suggest the global scale of the change, I alluded to a new phenomenon: inflation seemed to be ebbing all over the world. My point was that monetary policy might now be operating at the edge of knowledge where, at least for a while, time-honored rules of thumb might not apply.

This was all pretty speculative, especially for a working session of the FOMC. No one at the table said much in response, though a few of the bank presidents mildly agreed. Most committee members seemed relieved to return to the familiar ground of deciding whether to lower the fed funds rate by 0.25 percent—we voted to do so. But before we did, one of our most thoughtful members couldn't resist teasing me. "I hope you will allow me to agree with the reasons you've given for lowering the rate," he said, "without signing on to your brave-new-world scenario, which I am not quite ready to do."

Actually that was fine. I didn't expect the committee to agree with me—yet. Nor was I asking them to do anything. Just ponder.

The fast-paced high-tech boom is what finally gave broad currency to Schumpeter's idea of creative destruction. It became a dot-com buzz phrase—indeed, once you accelerate to Internet speed, creative destruction is hard to overlook. In Silicon Valley, companies were continually remaking themselves and new businesses were constantly flaring up and flaming out. The reigning powers of technology—giants like AT&T, Hewlett-Packard, and IBM—had to scramble to catch up with the trend, and not all succeeded. Bill Gates, the world's biggest billionaire, issued an all points bulletin to Microsoft employees comparing the rise of the Internet to the advent of the PC—upon which, of course, the company's great success was based.

The memo was entitled "The Internet Tidal Wave." They had better pay attention to this latest upheaval, he warned; adapt to it, or die.

Though it wasn't obvious, the revolution in information technology had been forty years in the making. It began after World War II with the development of the transistor, which provoked a surge of innovation. The computer, satellites, the microprocessor, and the joining of laser and fiber-optic technologies for communications all helped set the stage for the Internet's seemingly sudden and rapid emergence.

Business now had an enormous capacity to gather and disseminate information. This accelerated the creative-destruction process as capital shifted from stagnant or mediocre companies and industries to those at the cutting edge. Silicon Valley venture capital firms with names like Kleiner Perkins and Sequoia and investment banks like Hambrecht & Quist suddenly achieved great wealth and prominence by facilitating this money shift. But the financing actually involved, and continues to involve, all of Wall Street.

To take a more recent example, compare Google and General Motors. In November 2005, GM announced plans to terminate up to thirty thousand employees and close twelve plants by 2008. If you looked at the company's flows of cash, you could see GM was directing billions of dollars it historically might have used to create products or build factories into funds to cover future pensions and health benefits for workers and retirees. These funds, in turn, were investing the capital where returns were most promising—in areas like high tech. At the same time Google, of course, was growing at a tremendous rate. The company's capital expenditures increased nearly threefold in 2005 to more than $800 million. And in the expectation that the growth would continue, investors bid up the total market value of Google stock to eleven times that of GM's. In fact, the General Motors pension fund owned Google shares—a textbook example of capital shifting as a result of creative destruction.

Why should information technology have such a vast transforming effect? Much of corporate activity is directed at reducing uncertainty. For most of the twentieth century, corporate leaders lacked timely knowledge of customers' needs. This has always been costly to the bottom line. Decisions were made based on information that was days or even weeks old.

Most companies hedged: they maintained extra inventory and backup teams of employees ready to respond to the unanticipated and the misjudged. This insurance usually worked, but its price was always high. Standby inventories and workers are all costs, and standby "work" hours produce no output. They produce no revenue or added productivity. The real-time information supplied by the newer technologies has markedly reduced the uncertainties associated with day-to-day business. Real-time communication between the retail checkout counter and the factory floor and between shippers and truckers hauling freight has led to shorter delivery times and fewer hours of work required to provide everything from books to factory gear, from stock quotes to software. Information technology has released much of the extra inventory and the ranks of backup workers to productive and profitable uses.

Also new for the consumer was the convenience of being able to call up information online, track packages in shipment, and order virtually anything for delivery overnight. Overall, the tech boom also had a major positive effect on employment. Many more jobs were being created than were being lost. Indeed, our unemployment rates fell, from over 6 percent in 1994 to less than 4 percent in 2000, and in the process the economy spawned sixteen million new jobs. Yet, much as happened with the nineteenth-century telegraph operators I'd idealized in my youth, technology began in a major way to upend white-collar occupations. Suddenly millions of Americans found themselves exposed to the dark side of creative destruction. Secretarial and clerical functions got absorbed into computer software, as did drafting jobs in architecture and in automotive and industrial design. Job insecurity, historically a problem mainly of blue-collar workers, became an issue starting in the 1990s for more highly educated, affluent people. This came through dramatically in survey data: In 1991, at the bottom of the business cycle, a survey of employees of large corporations showed 25 percent were afraid of being laid off. In 1995 and 1996, despite a sharp intervening decline in the unemployment rate, 46 percent were afraid. That trend, of course, put job worries squarely in the public eye.

Important, but not as obvious, was the increase in job mobility. Today Americans change employers on a truly stupendous scale. Out of nearly 150 million people employed in the workforce, 1 million leave their jobs each week. Some 600,000 quit voluntarily, while roughly 400,000 get laid off, often when their companies are acquired or downsized. At the same time, a million workers are hired or return from layoffs each week as new industries expand and new companies come onstream.

The swifter the spread of technological innovation, and the broader its impact, the more we economists had to scramble to figure out which fundamentals had changed and which hadn't. Experts in the mid-1990s spent endless hours debating the so-called natural level of unemployment, for instance (technically, the Non-Accelerating Inflation Rate of Unemployment, or NAIRU for short). This is a neo-Keynesian concept that was used in the early 1990s to argue that if unemployment fell below 6.5 percent, then workers' wage demands would accelerate, causing inflation to heat up.

So as unemployment trended down, to 6 percent in 1994, 5.6 percent in 1995, on its way to 4 percent and lower, many economists contended that the Fed should put the brakes on growth. I argued against this way of thinking within the Fed and in public testimony. The "natural rate," while unambiguous in a model, and useful for historical analyses, has always proved elusive when estimated in real time. The number was continually revised and did not offer a stable platform for inflation forecasting or monetary policy, in my judgment. No matter what was supposed to happen, during the first half of the 1990s wage rate growth held to a low and narrow range, and there was no sign of mounting inflation. Ultimately it was the conventional wisdom itself that gave way—economists began revising the natural level of unemployment downward.

Years later, Gene Sperling told a story of how this controversy played out in the Oval Office. In 1995 President Clinton's top economic advisers—Sperling, Bob Rubin, and Laura Tyson—worried that the president was getting carried away with his hopes for the high-tech boom. So they enlisted Larry Summers to administer a reality check. As I knew from our lively breakfast debates, Larry was a technology skeptic. And he normally weighed in with the president only on international issues, so Clinton would realize this was an unusual event.

The economists trooped into the Oval Office, and Summers did a short presentation on why tightness in the labor market meant growth would have to slow. Then the others chimed in. Clinton listened for a while, then finally interrupted. "You're wrong," he said. "I understand the theory, but with the Internet, with technology, I can feel the change. I can see growth everywhere." The fact was, Clinton wasn't relying solely on instinct. He'd been out talking to CEOs and entrepreneurs, as he always did. Politicians never want to believe that there are limits to growth, of course. But at that moment the president probably had a better hands-on feel for the economy than his economists.

Both the economy and the stock market continued to boom. Output as measured by GDP grew at a superhot rate of over 6 percent in the spring of 1996—calling into question another chunk of conventional wisdom, namely that 2.5 percent was the maximum growth the U.S. economy could healthily sustain. We were doing a lot of rethinking at the Fed. It's easy to forget the speed with which innovations like the Internet and e-mail went from exotic to ubiquitous. *Something* extraordinary was happening, and the challenge in trying to figure it out as it was happening, in real time, was considerable.

By the time I convened the FOMC on September 24, 1996, eight months and seven meetings had passed since we'd last lowered the interest rate. Many committee members were now leaning the other way, toward an increase so as to preempt inflation. They wanted to take away the punch bowl again. Corporate profits were very strong, unemployment had dropped to well under 5.5 percent, and one big factor had changed: wages were finally rising. Under boom conditions like these, inflation was the obvious risk. If companies were having to pay more to keep or attract workers, they might soon pass along that added cost by raising prices. The textbook strategy would be to tighten rates, thereby slowing economic growth and nipping inflation in the bud.

But what if this wasn't a normal business cycle? What if the technology revolution had, temporarily at least, increased the economy's ability to expand? If that was the case, raising interest rates would be a mistake.

I was always wary of inflation, of course. Yet I felt certain that the risk was much lower than many of my colleagues thought. This time, it wasn't a case of upsetting conventional wisdom. I didn't think the textbooks were wrong; I thought our numbers were. I'd zeroed in on what I believed to be the primary riddle of the technology boom: the question of productivity.

The data we were getting from the Commerce and Labor departments showed that productivity (measured as output per hour worked) was virtually flat in spite of the long-running trend toward computerization. I could not imagine how that could be. Year in and year out, business had been pouring vast amounts of money into desktop computers, servers, networks, software, and other high-tech gear. I had worked with a sufficient number of plant managers on capital investment projects over the years to know how such purchasing decisions were made. They would order expensive equipment only if they believed the investment would expand their production capacity, or enable their employees to produce more per hour. If the equipment failed to do at least one of these, the managers would stop buying. Yet they'd kept pumping money into high tech. This became evident as early as 1993 when new orders for high-tech capital began to accelerate after a protracted period of sluggish growth. The surge continued into 1994, suggesting that the early profit experience with the new equipment had been positive.

There were other, even more persuasive indications that the official productivity figures were awry. Most companies were reporting rising operating profit margins. Yet few had raised prices. That meant that their costs per unit of output were contained or even falling. Most consolidated costs (that is, for business considered as a whole) are labor costs. So if labor costs per unit of output were flat or declining, and the rate of growth of average hourly labor compensation was rising, it was an arithmetical certainty that if these data were accurate, the growth of output per hour must be on the rise; productivity was truly accelerating. And if so, then rising inflation would be unlikely.

Even though I was sure my analysis was right, I knew better than to try to convince my colleagues on the basis of back-of-the-envelope figuring. I needed something more persuasive. With a few weeks to go before the September 24, 1996, meeting, I asked the Fed staff to pull apart the federal productivity statistics and study the underlying data, industry by industry, for dozens of industries. I had been bothered by an apparent discrepancy between the Bureau of Labor Statistics data on output per hour for all nonfarm industries and a separate estimate for corporations. Matching the two implied that there was no productivity growth in noncorporate America, an unlikely conclusion.

When I asked for the detailed industry breakdown, typically the staff would joke that the chairman wanted "embellishments and enhancements." This time they said it was more like I was asking them to undertake the Manhattan Project. Nevertheless, they burrowed into the data and rendered their report just in time for the FOMC meeting.

On that Tuesday, opinion in the committee was divided. Half a dozen members wanted to raise rates right away—as Tom Melzer, the hawkish president of the Federal Reserve Bank of St. Louis, put it, "to take out an insurance policy" against inflation. Others were on the fence. Alice Rivlin, who was now in her third month as vice chairman of the Board of Governors, sized up the situation in her usual droll manner: "The worried faces around this table, I think we should remind ourselves, are worrying about the best set of problems we could think of having. Central bankers all around the world would wish for this set of statistics." While she agreed that we were in an inflationary "danger zone," she also pointed out that "we have not seen higher inflation yet."

When it was my turn to speak, I came on strong using the staff's report. It seemed that the government had been underestimating productivity growth for years. It had not, for example, found *any* efficiency gains in the service economy—in fact, the government's calculations made it appear that productivity there was *shrinking.* Every committee member knew that was absurd on its face: law firms, business services, medical practices, and social service organizations had been automating and streamlining themselves along with the manufacturing sector and the rest of the economy.

No one could convincingly explain why the statistics were off, I said.* But I was reasonably confident that the risk of inflation was too weak to warrant a rate hike. My recommendation was that we simply watch and wait.

This argument didn't convince everyone—indeed, we are still debating the nature and extent of information technology's impact on productivity. But it cast enough reasonable doubt that the committee voted 11 to 1 to keep the rate where it was, at 5.25 percent.

---

*Some argued that service purchases by goods manufacturers were being mispriced in the calculations and that the growth of total output per hour was correct, but goods production and output per hour were being overestimated at the expense of service output and productivity growth. While technically possible, this explanation seemed very unlikely.

We did not find it necessary to raise rates for another six months—and then only to 5.5 percent, and for a different reason. GDP continued to grow at a solid pace, unemployment shrank, and inflation stayed in check, for another four years. By not being too quick to raise rates, we helped clear the way for the postwar period's longest economic boom. This was a classic example of why you can't just decide monetary policy based on an econometric model. As Joseph Schumpeter might have pointed out, models are subject to creative destruction too.

Even rising productivity could not explain the looniness of stock prices. On October 14, 1996, the Dow Jones Industrial Average vaulted past 6,000—a milestone achieved, declared a front-page story in USA Today, "on the opening day of the seventh year of the most consistent bull market in history." Papers all across the country put the news on the front page too. The New York Times noted that more and more Americans were shifting their retirement savings into stocks, reflecting "a widespread belief that the stock market is the only place to make long-term investments."

America was turning into a shareholders' nation. If you compared the total value of stock holdings with the size of the economy, the market's significance was increasing at a rapid rate: at $9.5 trillion, it now was 120 percent as large as GDP. That was up from 60 percent in 1990, a ratio topped only by Japan at the height of its 1980s bubble.

I had ongoing conversations with Bob Rubin on the subject. We were both somewhat concerned. We'd now seen the Dow break through three "millennium marks"—4,000, 5,000, and 6,000—in just over a year and a half. Though economic growth was strong, we worried that investors were getting carried away. Stock prices were beginning to embody expectations so exorbitant that they could never be met.

A stock-market boom, of course, is an economic plus—it predisposes businesses to expand, makes consumers feel flush, and helps the economy to grow. Even a crash is not automatically bad—the crash of 1987, hair-raising though we'd felt it to be, had very few lingering negative effects. Only when a collapsing market might threaten to hamstring the real economy is there cause for people like the treasury secretary and the chairman of the Fed to worry.

We'd seen that sort of disaster happen in Japan, where the economy was still crippled from a stock and real estate collapse in 1990. While neither Bob nor I thought the United States had yet reached the bubble stage, we couldn't help but notice that more and more households and businesses were exposing themselves to equity risks. So over breakfast we often discussed what we should do in the event of a bubble.

Bob thought that a federal financial official should never talk about the stock market in public. An inveterate maker of lists, he offered three reasons noted subsequently in his memoirs. "First, there's no way to know for certain when a market is overvalued or undervalued," he said. "Second, you can't fight market forces, so talking about it won't do any good. And third, anything you say is likely to backfire and hurt your credibility. People will realize you don't know any more than anybody else."

I had to admit that all of those things were true. But I still didn't agree that raising the issue in public was necessarily a bad idea. The growing importance of the stock market was impossible to deny. How could you talk about the economy without mentioning the eight-hundred-pound gorilla? While the Fed had no explicit mandate to focus on the stock market, the effects of the run-up in prices seemed to me a legitimate concern. In quelling inflation, we had established that price stability is central to long-term economic growth. (In fact, one major factor causing stock prices to rise was investors' growing confidence that stability would continue.)

Yet the concept of price stability wasn't as self-evident as it seemed. There were probably ten different statistical series on prices you could look at. For most economists, price stability referred to product prices—the cost of a pair of socks or a quart of milk. But what about the prices of income-earning assets, like stocks or real estate? What if those prices were to inflate and become unstable? Shouldn't we worry about the price stability of nest eggs and not just the eggs you buy at the grocery store? It wasn't that I wanted to stand up and shout, "The stock market is overvalued and it will lead to no good." I didn't believe that. But I thought it important to put the issue on the table.

The concept of irrational exuberance came to me in the bathtub one morning as I was writing a speech. To this day, the bathtub is where I get many of my best ideas. My assistants have gotten used to typing from drafts scrawled on damp yellow pads—a chore that got much easier once we found a kind of pen whose ink doesn't run. Immersed in my bath, I'm as happy as Archimedes as I contemplate the world.

After the Dow had broken 6,000, in mid-October 1996, I'd begun looking for an opportunity to speak up about asset values. I decided that the American Enterprise Institute's annual dinner on December 5, where I'd agreed to give the keynote address, would be perfect. It's a major black-tie affair that attracts more than a thousand people, including many Washington public policy experts, and it comes early enough in the holiday season to count as a serious event.

To put the stock-market question in proper perspective, I thought I should embed it in a capsule history of U.S. central banking. I reached all the way back to Alexander Hamilton and William Jennings Bryan and worked my way up to the present and the future. (A more general audience might have been put off by the wonkiness of this approach, but it was about the right speed for the American Enterprise Institute crowd.)

I wrote the speech so that the issue of asset values accounted for only a dozen sentences toward the end, and I carefully hedged what I had to say in my usual Fedspeak. Yet when I showed the text to Alice Rivlin on the day of the speech, "irrational exuberance" jumped right out at her. "Are you sure you want to say this?" she asked.

On the podium that night, I delivered the key passage, watching carefully to see how people would react. "As we move into the twenty-first century," I said, referring to the Fed,

the Congress willing, we will remain as the guardian of the purchasing power of the dollar. But one factor that will continue to complicate that task is the increasing difficulty of pinning down the notion of what constitutes a stable general price level. . . .

Where do we draw the line on what prices matter? Certainly prices of goods and services now being produced—our basic measure of inflation—matter. But what about futures prices? Or more

importantly, prices of claims on future goods and services, like equities, real estate, or other earning assets? Is stability of these prices
essential to the stability of the economy?

Clearly, sustained low inflation implies less uncertainty about
the future, and lower risk premiums imply higher prices of stocks
and other earning assets. We can see that in the inverse relationship exhibited by price/earnings ratios and the rate of inflation in
the past.

But how do we know when irrational exuberance has unduly
escalated asset values, which then become subject to unexpected
and prolonged contractions, as they have in Japan over the past decade? And how do we factor that assessment into monetary policy?
We as central bankers need not be concerned if a collapsing financial
asset bubble does not threaten to impair the real economy, its production, jobs, and price stability. Indeed, the sharp stock market
break of 1987 had few negative consequences for the economy. But
we should not underestimate, or become complacent about, the
complexity of the interactions of asset markets and the economy.

Admittedly, this was not Shakespeare. It was pretty hard to process, especially if you'd had a drink or two during the cocktail hour and were hungry for dinner to be served. When I came back to the table, I whispered to
Andrea and the others seated there, "What part of that do you think will
make news?" No one guessed. But I'd seen people in the audience sit up
and take notice, and as the evening ended, the buzz began. "Fed Chairman
Pops the Big Question: Is the Market Too High?" wrote the *Wall Street Journal* the next day; "Irrational Exuberance Denounced," said the *Philadelphia
Inquirer*; "A Buried Message Loudly Heard," said the *New York Times*. "Irrational exuberance" was on its way to becoming a catchphrase of the boom.

But the stock market did not slow down—which only reinforced my
concern. It's true that my remarks initially caused a sell-off around the
world, partly on the suspicion that the Fed would immediately raise rates.
Stock prices fell first in Japan's markets, where it was already morning when
I spoke, then hours later as the markets opened in Europe, and finally in
New York the following day. On the New York Stock Exchange, the Dow

dropped almost 150 points at the opening bell. But by afternoon the U.S. markets had bounced back, and after one more trading day they had regained all the lost ground. America's stock markets ended the year up by well over 20 percent.

And the bull charged on. The Dow Jones Industrial Average was already nearing 7,000 when the FOMC convened for the first time in 1997, on February 4. By then I knew from private conversations with many of the governors and bank presidents that the committee shared my worry that the development of a stock bubble might cause inflationary instability. Apart from the run-up in the stock market, the economy was as robust as it had been six months before, when I'd resisted the idea of tightening rates. But my concern about a bubble had changed my mind. I told the committee we might need an interest rate increase to try to rein in the bull. "We have to start thinking about some form of preemptive move," I said, "and how to communicate that."

I was choosing my words very carefully because we were on the record and we were playing with political dynamite. The Fed has no explicit mandate under the law to try to contain a stock-market bubble. Indirectly we had the authority to do so, if we believed stock prices were creating inflationary pressures. But in this instance, that would have been a very hard case to make because the economy was performing so well.

The Fed does not operate in a vacuum. If we raised rates and gave as a reason that we wanted to rein in the stock market, it would have provoked a political firestorm. We'd have been accused of hurting the little investor, sabotaging people's retirements. I could imagine the grilling I'd get in the next congressional oversight hearing.

All the same, we agreed that trying to avoid a bubble was consistent with our mission, and that it was our duty to take the chance. I mused aloud in our meeting that day, "We need above all to make certain that we keep inflation low, risk premiums low, the cost of capital low. . . . If we are talking about long-term equilibrium, high market values are better than low market values. What we are trying to avoid is bubbles that break, volatility, and the like." With the committee's consent, I hinted at an impending rate hike in my public remarks over the next several weeks. This was to keep from shocking the markets with an abrupt move. Then we met again on March 25 and raised short-term rates by 0.25 percent, to 5.5 percent. I wrote the FOMC's statement announcing the decision myself. It talked purely in terms of the Fed's wish to address underlying economic forces that threatened to create inflation, and did not say a word about asset values or stocks. As I described the rate increase shortly afterward in a speech, "We took a small step to increase the odds that the good performance of the economy can continue."

In late March and early April of 1997, right after our meeting, the Dow dipped by some 7 percent. This represented a loss of almost 500 points, to some minds a delayed reaction to our rate hike. But within a few weeks, the momentum shifted and the market came roaring back. It recouped all of its losses and gained 10 percent more, so that by mid-June, it was nearing 7,800. In effect, investors were teaching the Fed a lesson. Bob Rubin was right: you can't tell when a market is overvalued, and you can't fight market forces.

As the boom went on—for three more years, it turned out, greatly increasing the nation's paper wealth—we continued to wrestle with big questions of productivity and price stability and other aspects of what people had come to call the New Economy. We looked for other ways to deal with the risk of a bubble. But we did not raise rates any further, and we never tried to rein in stock prices again.

Andrea and I expressed some exuberance of our own by finally getting married that spring. She always jokes that it took me three tries to propose to her, because I kept popping the question in Fedspeak, but that is not true. Actually I proposed five times—she missed a couple. On Christmas Day 1996, though, the message finally got through and she said yes. In April 1997 Supreme Court justice Ruth Bader Ginsburg married us in a simple, beautiful ceremony at one of our favorite places, the Inn at Little Washington in the Virginia countryside.

Typically, we put off having a honeymoon: too much was happening in Andrea's professional world and mine. But friends kept urging us to go, and recommended Venice. Finally I studied my calendar and suggested adding a honeymoon to the tail end of an international monetary conference meeting in Interlaken, Switzerland, in June, two months after our wedding.

At the monetary conference, German chancellor Helmut Kohl gave a predictably dry luncheon speech. Central-bank independence and the revaluation of Germany's gold reserves were the topics. Afterward Andrea and I avoided flocks of reporters who wanted comments about the U.S. economic outlook and the prospects for the continuation of the Internet boom on the stock market. Even though they knew it was my policy not to give interviews, some asked Andrea to serve as a go-between, figuring that as a fellow journalist she might be willing to help. All Andrea wanted to do was go to the spa. By the time we left Interlaken she had jokingly declared our trip so far "the least romantic honeymoon in history."

And then we arrived in Venice. As necessary as creative destruction is for material standards of living to improve, it's no coincidence that some of the world's most cherished places are those that have changed the least over the centuries. I'd never visited the city, and like so many travelers before me, I was enchanted. Our notion had been to wander and do things completely spontaneously. And while that doesn't really happen when you are traveling with a security detail, we came close. We ate at open-air cafés, went shopping, and toured churches and the old Jewish ghetto.

For centuries, the Venetian city-state was the center of world trade, linking Western Europe with the Byzantine Empire and the rest of the known world. After the Renaissance, trade routes shifted to the Atlantic, and Venice declined as a sea power. Yet throughout the 1700s, it remained Europe's most graceful city, a center of literature, architecture, and art. "What news on the Rialto?" the famous line from *The Merchant of Venice* referring to the commercial heart of the city, still strikes a vibrant cosmopolitan note.

Today the Rialto district looks much as it did when traders unloaded silks and spices from the Orient. The same is true of the city's splendidly painted Renaissance palaces, St. Mark's Square, and dozens of other sights. Except for the motorized launches—the vaporetti—you could just as readily be in the seventeenth or eighteenth century.

As we strolled along one of the canals, my inner economist finally got the better of me. I asked Andrea, "What is the value-added produced in this city?"

"You're asking the wrong question," she replied, and burst out laughing.

"But this entire city is a museum. Just think of what goes into keeping it up."

Andrea stopped and looked at me. "You should be looking at how beautiful it is."

Of course my wife was right. But the conversation helped crystallize something that had been in the back of my mind for months.

Venice, I realized, is the antithesis of creative destruction. It exists to conserve and appreciate a past, not create a future. But that, I realized, is exactly the point. The city caters to a deep human need for stability and permanence as well as beauty and romance. Venice's popularity represents one pole of a conflict in human nature: the struggle between the desire to increase material well-being and the desire to ward off change and its attendant stress.

America's material standard of living continues to improve, yet the dynamism of that same economy puts hundreds of thousands of people per week involuntarily out of work. It's no surprise that demands for protection against the forces of market competition are on the rise—as well as nostalgia for a slower and simpler time. Nothing is more stressful for people than the perennial gale of creative destruction. Silicon Valley is without question an exciting place to work, but its allure as a honeymoon destination has, I would guess, thus far gone largely unrecognized.

The following evening in Venice, Andrea and I went to hear a Vivaldi cello concerto, played on baroque instruments. His melodies filled the air around us, a thrilling complement to the somber majesty of the ancient church with its shadows and curves and thick stones that seemed to breathe the damp of the canals. I've heard Vivaldi played better, but never have I enjoyed it so much.

MILLENNIUM FEVER

In the late nineties, the economy was so strong that I used to get up in the morning, look in the mirror, and say to myself, "Remember, this is temporary. This is not the way the world is supposed to work."

I loved watching the economy flourish, as well as the strange new challenges this prosperity brought on. The emergence of a federal budget surplus, for example. This wondrous happening first occurred in 1998. It came after a run of five years during which the federal deficit dwindled steadily from the fiscal year 1992 peak of almost $300 billion. The surplus derived from factors we thought we understood: fiscal conservatism and economic growth. But the scale of the change was far beyond that. No one at the Fed or elsewhere anticipated the emergence in fiscal year 2000 of the largest surplus (relative to GDP) since 1948.

History told us booms like this couldn't and wouldn't last forever. Yet this one was lasting longer than I'd believed it could. Throughout the late nineties the economy grew at a better than 4 percent annual rate. That translated to $400 billion or so of prosperity—equal in size to the entire economy of the former Soviet Union—being added to the U.S. economy *each year.*

Virtually every household benefited. Gene Sperling, the Clinton economic adviser, liked to call attention to the breadth of the social effects: between 1993 and 2000, the typical American family had a real gain in annual income of $8,000.

This economic growth boosted the national psyche, changing the way we saw ourselves in the world. Throughout the 1980s and well into the early 1990s, Americans had gone through a period of being fearful and depressed. People worried we were losing ground to Germany, the newly unifying Europe, and Japan. As Larry Summers later described it, these economic rivals "were more investment oriented, more manufacturing oriented, had fewer lawyers, more scientists, more discipline than we."

In the eighties, Japan's giant *zaibatsu*, or conglomerates, had seemed to pose a particular threat: they had usurped America in steel and in factory equipment, put our automakers on the defensive, and so completely overwhelmed us in consumer electronics that even the TVs we depended on for news bore Sony, Panasonic, and Hitachi brands. Not since Sputnik had America felt itself to be at such a scary disadvantage. Even the end of the cold war didn't lift the gloom—our vast military power suddenly felt irrelevant, and international status was now defined by economic prowess.

Then the technology boom came along and changed everything. It made America's freewheeling, entrepreneurial, so-what-if-you-fail business culture the envy of the world. U.S. information technology swept the global market, as did innovations ranging from Starbucks lattes to credit derivatives. Students gravitated from other countries to American universities. The changes the United States had undertaken to modernize its economy—two decades of often painful deregulation and downsizing and the lowering of barriers to trade—all now paid off. While both Europe and Japan slid into economic doldrums, America was on the rise.

The federal budget surplus was an amazing development. "We all need to go back to the drawing board on forecasting taxes," a senior official of the New York Fed told the FOMC in May 1997, after a report that the Treasury's receipts for the year were running $50 billion ahead of projections. Economists at the Office of Management and Budget, the Congressional Budget Office, and the Fed were all at sea. Even though the economy was on a roll, it wasn't enough to account for this big a surge in tax receipts. We suspected we might be seeing a stock-market effect, and I encouraged the Fed staff to accelerate its work estimating the boost to household taxable income from the exercise of stock-option grants and realized capital gains. Stock options, of course, had become the primary lure used by tech companies to attract and keep employees—they were even being handed out to secretaries and clerks. It was very difficult to measure accurately this new source of wealth. Years later, this hypothesis was proved correct, but at the time all our economists could do was to confirm that it might be the case. The federal deficit for 1997 shrank to just $22 billion—statistically insignificant in the context of a $1.6 trillion federal budget and a $10 trillion GDP.

Almost overnight, the administration found itself facing a budget surplus that was expanding as fast as the deficit had dwindled. President Clinton had no sooner started talking about the possibility of actually being able to balance the federal budget in 1998 than his policymakers had to scramble to plan what to do with the surplus. And while this was a happy problem to have, success, like everything else in budgetary matters, must be managed. This is particularly so in Washington, where if politicians discover $1 billion they will instantly come up with at least $20 billion worth of ways to spend it. And the surplus looked to be truly epic: the Congressional Budget Office projection in 1998 was for it to total $660 billion over ten years.*

As soon as the news was announced, both parties claimed credit. "Republican fiscal policy, emphasizing controlled spending, less government, and tax relief, has moved the nation from deficit to surplus in just three years," declared a GOP leader, Congressman John Boehner of Ohio. President Clinton, for his part, formally announced the surplus at a special White House ceremony where Democratic leaders were present but Republicans were banned. Not a single Republican had voted for his milestone deficit-reduction budget in 1993, the president reminded the audience, adding that if they had, "they would have been eligible to be here today."

Predictably, dissension about what to do with the extra revenue was intense. Liberal Democrats wanted to devote the money to social programs

---

*The $660 billion figure from the Congressional Budget Office was the sum of projections from 1999 to 2008. Meanwhile, the White House envisioned surpluses in the next decade to total $1.1 trillion. The discrepancy reflected in part the fact that CBO projections are based on current law, while administration projections assume that the administration's policies will be enacted.

they said had been shortchanged for years; conservative Republicans proposed to "give back" the surplus in the form of tax cuts. Bill Archer, a Republican from Texas and a good friend who was chairman of the House Ways and Means Committee, won the prize for the most amusing statement of the debate. "Because of record-high taxation," he declared, tongue in cheek, "the surplus is raging out of control."

Fiscal conservatives like Bob Rubin and me, meanwhile, believed that neither tax cuts nor new spending was the right way to go. We thought the surplus should be used to pay down the national debt to the public. It now totaled $3.7 trillion, the accumulated consequence of a quarter century of deficit spending (the last year the budget had been in surplus was 1969).

My longtime involvement in Social Security reform had made me all too aware that, in the not-too-far-off future, Social Security and Medicare would face demands in the trillions of dollars as the baby-boom generation aged. There was no practical way to pay those obligations in advance. The most effective policy would be to pay down the debt, creating in the process additional savings, which in turn could increase the nation's productive capacity and federal revenues at existing tax rates by the time the boomers hit retirement age.

Debt repayment had one other advantage: it was the simplest option. So long as Congress does not pass legislation appropriating the money for some other use, any surplus revenues that flow into government coffers automatically pay down the debt. If only Congress could keep its hands out of the cash box. Or, as I suggested more diplomatically to the Senate Budget Committee, the accumulated national debt was so massive that the government could happily whittle away at it for years. "It will not harm the economy in any way of which I am aware to allow the surpluses to run for quite a long period of time before you touch them," I said. "If the surpluses are evolving, let's not look at them as though they are a threat to the economy. They are surely not."* Yet, compared with tax cuts or spending in-

---

*It had not yet entered my mind that surpluses could become so large as to reduce the debt level to zero and eventually could require the federal government to accumulate private assets. That prospect would confront me in 2001.

creases, debt repayment was admittedly an ugly-duckling policy. I wondered whether Clinton would be able to stick with the fiscal conservatism that had marked his first term, even if he wanted to.

I played no role in finding the answer, but I had to admire the one Clinton and his policymakers came up with. They lit on a politically irrefutable argument to take the money off the table: tying the budget surplus to Social Security. He delivered his pitch as part of the 1998 State of the Union address:

> What should we do with this projected surplus? I have a simple four-word answer: Save Social Security first. Tonight, I propose that we reserve 100% of the surplus—that's every penny of any surplus—until we have taken all the necessary measures to strengthen the Social Security system for the 21st century.

The crux of Clinton's "necessary measures," it quickly emerged, was to set aside the lion's share of any surplus to pay down the debt. I was impressed that Clinton had preempted much of the debate that would have arisen had he focused on debt reduction pure and simple. "I'm amazed," I told Gene Sperling. "You've found a way to make debt reduction politically attractive."

As the budget surpluses mounted over the next few years—all the way from $70 billion in 1998 to $124 billion in 1999 and to $237 billion in 2000—I watched Congress grab again and again for the money. In the summer of 1999, the Republicans put forward a plan to cut taxes by almost $800 billion over ten years, and the Senate Banking Committee summoned me to testify whether the plan made long-term economic sense. I had to tell them it did not, or at least not yet. "We probably would be better off holding off on a tax cut," I said, "largely because of the fact that it is apparent that the surpluses are doing a great deal of positive good to the economy." I had two other arguments, I added. First, while projections of the surplus over the next decade were now up to $3 trillion, uncertainty about the economy put those big numbers in doubt. "They could just as rapidly go in the other direction," I said. Second, given how strong the economy already was, the stimulus of a major tax cut might cause it to overheat. On the other hand, I said, I saw "no problem" in delaying such a cut.

These observations made a few headlines but did not dissuade Congress from proceeding with the bill. It passed a week later—only to be vetoed by the president. "At a time when America is moving in the right direction, this bill would turn us back to the failed policies of the past," he said as he signed the veto in the Rose Garden.

President Clinton's old-fashioned attitude toward debt might have had a more lasting effect on the nation's priorities. Instead, his influence was diluted by the uproar about Monica Lewinsky, whose name surfaced in news reports just days before he unveiled his approach for the surplus. As the scandal unfolded and details of their alleged encounters appeared in the press, I was incredulous. "There is no way these stories could be correct," I told my friends. "I've been in the area of the White House between the Oval Office and the private dining room. There are staff people and Secret Service in and out all the time. No way." Later, when it came out that the accounts were true, I wondered how the president could take such a risk. It seemed so alien to the Bill Clinton I knew, and made me feel disappointed and sad. And it had a devastating effect—you could see it, for example, in a pair of headlines that appeared side by side on CNN's Web site: "Lewinsky Set to Provide Handwriting, Fingerprint Samples" and "Clinton Announces $39 Billion Projected Budget Surplus."

While America was booming, the rest of the world shook. In the wake of the end of the cold war and the demise of much central planning, developing nations were seeking ways to attract direct foreign investment by further securing property rights and opening up larger sectors of their economies. But as part of those initiatives, an unsettling pattern started to emerge: U.S. investors, rich with capital gains from the U.S. boom, would crowd into unfamiliar emerging markets in search of diversification. Big banks would come, too, seeking higher returns on loans than they could get in the United States, where interest rates had now reached near-historic lows. To attract such capital and promote trade, some developing nations tied their currency to the dollar at a fixed exchange rate. In that way, U.S. and foreign investors could consider themselves protected from exchange-rate risk at least for a while. The borrowers of the dollars, meanwhile, would convert them into the domestic currency and lend the money within the developing country at the prevailing high interest rates. By doing so, they were gambling that when the loan was repaid, they'd be able to convert the money back into dollars at the fixed exchange rate and repay their own dollar borrowings with no exchange-rate loss. When shrewd market players who didn't believe in the tooth fairy realized that the developing countries could maintain the fixed-exchange-rate regime only so long, and they started to sell the domestic currencies for dollars, the game was up. Central banks trying to hold their dollar exchange rate fixed rapidly ran out of their reserves of dollars.

This sequence of events led to the so-called Asian contagion, a series of financial crises that began with the collapse of the Thai baht and Malaysian ringgit in the summer of 1997 and grew into a threat to the world economy. Almost immediately, Thailand and Malaysia plunged into recession. The economies of Hong Kong, the Philippines, and Singapore were hard-hit too. In Indonesia, a nation of two hundred million people, the rupiah imploded, the stock market collapsed, and the ensuing economic disarray led to food riots, widespread misery, and eventually the fall of President Suharto.

Just as during Mexico's crisis two years before, the International Monetary Fund moved in with financial support. Bob Rubin, Larry Summers, and the Treasury Department again spearheaded the U.S. response; the Fed again played largely an advisory role. I got more deeply involved only in November, when a senior official at the Bank of Japan called the Fed to warn that South Korea would be the next to go. "The dam is bursting" is how the official put it, explaining that Japanese banks had lost confidence in Korea and were about to stop renewing tens of billions of dollars in loans.

This was a shock. A symbol of Asia's remarkable growth, South Korea was now the world's eleventh-largest economy, twice the size of Russia. Korea was so successful that it was no longer even considered a developing nation—the World Bank officially listed it as part of the first world. And while market watchers knew that there had been problems recently, the economy by all indications was still growing solidly and fast. Korea's central bank was also sitting on $25 billion in dollar reserves—ample protection against the Asian contagion, or so we thought.

What we didn't know, but soon discovered, was that the government had played games with those reserves. It had quietly sold or lent most of the dollars to South Korean commercial banks, which in turn had used them to shore up bad loans. So when Charlie Siegman, one of our top international economists, phoned a Korean central banker on Thanksgiving weekend and asked, "Why don't you release more of your reserves?" the banker answered, "We don't have any." What they'd published as reserves had already been spoken for.

This mess took weeks to unwind. Rubin's task forces worked virtually around the clock, and the IMF assembled a financial-support package of $55 billion—its largest financial rescue ever. The deal required the cooperation of Kim Dae Jung, Korea's newly elected president, whose first major decision was to commit to stringent economic reforms. Part of the challenge for the Treasury and the Fed, meanwhile, was to talk scores of the world's largest banks into not calling in their Korea loans. All these initiatives came to a head at the same time, prompting Bob to say in retrospect, "We must have set some kind of record for disturbing the slumber of finance ministers and central bankers all over the world."

There was always the chance that a rescue this large would set a bad precedent: how many more times would investors pour money into willing but shaky economies, figuring that if they got into big enough trouble, the IMF would bail them out? This was a version of what the insurance industry calls the "moral hazard" of protecting individuals from risk. The bigger the safety net, the theory goes, the greater the recklessness with which people, businesses, or governments will tend to behave.

Yet the consequences of allowing South Korea to default would have been worse, possibly far worse. A default by a nation of Korea's size would almost certainly have destabilized global markets. Major banks in Japan and elsewhere would likely have failed, sending additional tremors through the system. Shell-shocked investors would have withdrawn not just from East Asia but from Latin America and other emerging regions, causing development to stall. Credit would very likely have become much tighter in the industrialized nations as well. And that is leaving aside the military risk unique to South Korea's situation. For their handling of that crisis alone, Bob Rubin and Larry Summers belong in the finance ministers' hall of fame.

In the United States, things were still booming, as the Internet wove itself into people's lifestyles. The computer in the household was becoming as essential as the phone, the refrigerator, and the TV. It became a way to get news: in summer 1997, millions had gone online to view dazzling photos from *Pathfinder*, the first U.S. probe to set down successfully on Mars in twenty years. And it became a way to shop: in 1998 "e-commerce" arrived in a big way, with people flocking to Web sites like Amazon and eToys and eBay, especially during the holiday season.

But the Asian contagion wasn't finished with us yet. The grim scenario we'd imagined in the Korean crisis came perilously close to being realized eight months later: in August 1998, Russia defaulted on a vast dollar debt.

Like the crises in Asia, Russia's resulted from the toxic interaction of overeager investing by foreigners and irresponsible management at home. The precipitating factor was a drop in the price of oil, which eventually hit $11 a barrel, the lowest level in twenty-five years, as the economic impact of the Asian crises sapped worldwide demand. Since oil was a major Russian export, this meant big trouble for the Kremlin: suddenly Russia could no longer afford to pay the interest on its debts.

I'd last visited Moscow seven years before, on the eve of the Soviet Union's dissolution, and still remembered the high hopes of the economic reformers and the gray desolation on the streets. Conditions, if anything, were now worse. In the vacuum left by the collapse of central planning, Boris Yeltsin's economists had tried and failed to foster reliable markets to supply food, clothing, and other essentials. Families and businesses got by largely off the books, with the result that the government could not even collect the taxes it needed to provide basic services or pay its debts. Oligarchs had come to control large shares of the nation's resources and wealth, and inflation periodically ran rampant, amplifying the misery of tens of millions of Russians on limited incomes. The government had singularly failed to establish, or even to comprehend the need for, property rights and the rule of law.

As the crisis unfolded, the IMF again stood ready with financial aid—it announced a $23 billion support package in July. But as soon as Russia received the first payments, its parliament made clear that it had no intention of accepting the usual IMF conditions of better fiscal management and economic reform. This defiance prompted the IMF to conclude that sending the rest of the aid would be throwing good money after bad: it would only postpone, and probably worsen, the inevitable default. By mid-August, the Russian central bank had burned through more than half of its foreign-exchange reserves. Frenzied last-minute diplomacy failed, and on August 26 the central bank withdrew support for the ruble. The exchange rate fell 38 percent overnight. The IMF package was withdrawn.

The default, when it came, stunned investors and banks that had poured money into Russia in spite of the obvious risks. Many operated on the assumption that the West would always bail out the fallen superpower—if for no other reason, the saying went, than that Russia was "too nuclear to fail." Those investors bet wrong. The United States and its allies had worked quietly and effectively to help Yeltsin's government keep its warheads under lock and key; it turned out that the Russians were much better at controlling an arsenal than at managing an economy. So after careful deliberation, President Clinton and other leaders judged that the IMF's withdrawal would not increase the nuclear risk, and approved its decision to pull the plug. We all held our breath.

Sure enough, the shock wave from Russia's default hit Wall Street much harder than the Asian crises had. In the last four trading days of August alone, the Dow lost more than 1,000 points, or 12 percent of its value. The bond markets reacted even more strongly, as investors fled to the safety of treasuries. Banks, too, pulled back from new lending and raised interest rates on commercial loans.

Lurking behind all these expressions of uncertainty was the growing fear that after seven spectacular years, the U.S. economic boom was coming to an end. That fear, it turned out, was premature. Once we coped with the Russian crisis, the boom would continue for another two years, until late 2000, when the business cycle finally turned. But I could see the dangers, and I felt we needed to address them.

In early September I had a long-planned date to speak to an audience of business scholars at the University of California at Berkeley. I'd intended to talk about technology and the economy, touching on productivity, innovation, virtuous cycles, and the like. But as the date drew near, I decided I couldn't limit my focus to the domestic economy. Not after what had just happened in Russia. America's problem was not that the U.S. economy had run out of steam. It was that the imbalances caused by the technology revolution and rapidly globalizing markets were straining the world's financial systems.

In my talk, I noted the impact of the turmoil abroad. Up to now, I said, all it had done was hold down prices and slow demand for U.S. products. But I warned that as dislocations abroad mounted, feeding back on our financial markets, these effects would likely intensify. That dimmed the economic outlook.

"It is just not credible that the United States can remain an oasis of prosperity unaffected by a world that is experiencing greatly increased stress," I said. We could never gain the full benefits of the technology revolution unless the rest of the world shared in the growth. The standard of living in every nation we did business with had to be a matter of concern. For many in the audience who'd been riding the wave of the high-tech revolution, this probably came as news.

I don't think my "oasis of prosperity" remark made much of an impact that day. But the idea was meant to have a long fuse. I wasn't talking about the next six months or the next year. America's isolationism runs so deep that people still haven't let it go. There's always a presumption that since America is better, we should go it alone.

I told the Berkeley audience that the Russian crisis had prompted a major rethinking at the Fed. We'd been so focused on domestic inflation that we hadn't paid enough attention to the warning signs of a possible international financial breakdown. This was the part of the speech the media picked up: Wall Street read my message loud and clear that the FOMC was poised to lower interest rates.

The threat of a worldwide recession seemed increasingly real to me. And I was convinced that the Fed did not have the power to cope alone. The financial pressures we faced were on a global scale, and the effort to contain them would have to be global too. Bob Rubin shared this view. Behind the scenes, he and I began contacting the finance ministers and central bankers of the G7 nations to try to coordinate a policy response. We argued, quietly but urgently, for the need to increase liquidity and ease interest rates throughout the developed world.

Some of our counterparts proved very difficult to convince. But at last, as the markets in Europe closed on September 14, the G7 issued a carefully written statement. "The balance of risks in the world economy has shifted," it declared. It went on to detail how G7 policy would shift too, from single-mindedly battling inflation toward also fostering growth. As Rubin noted eloquently in his memoir, as bland as those ten words may have seemed, they marked a major change in the global financial picture: "Every war has its weapons, and when you're dealing with volatile financial markets and jittery investors, the subtleties of a carefully crafted communiqué, signed by the top financial authorities in the world's seven largest industrialized countries, can make a crucial difference."

None of this did much at first to ease the sense of impending doom. Brazil became the latest victim of the malaise, and Rubin and Summers spent most of September working with the IMF to craft a rescue. Meanwhile Bill McDonough, the head of the New York Fed, took on the challenge of coping with the implosion of one of Wall Street's largest and most successful hedge funds, Long-Term Capital Management.

Hollywood could not have scripted a more dramatic financial train wreck. Despite its boring name, LTCM was a proud, high-visibility, high-prestige operation in Greenwich, Connecticut, that earned spectacular returns investing a $125 billion portfolio for wealthy clients. Among its principals were two Nobel-laureate economists, Myron Scholes and Robert Merton, whose state-of-the-art mathematical models were at the heart of the firm's money machine. LTCM specialized in risky, lucrative arbitrage deals in U.S., Japanese, and European bonds, leveraging its bets with more than $120 billion borrowed from banks. It also carried some $1.25 trillion in financial derivatives, exotic contracts that were only partly reflected on its balance sheet. Some of these were speculative investments, and some were engineered to hedge, or insure, LTCM's portfolio against every imaginable risk. (Even after the smoke cleared, no one ever knew for sure how highly leveraged LTCM was when things started to go wrong. The best estimates were that it had invested well over $35 for every $1 it actually owned.)

The Russian default turned out to be the iceberg for this financial *Titanic*. That development contorted the markets in a way even the Nobel winners had never imagined. LTCM's fortunes reversed so abruptly that its elaborate safeguards never had a chance to work. Practically overnight, its stunned founders watched the nearly $5 billion in capital they'd built up drain away.

The New York Fed, whose job is to help maintain order in Wall Street's markets, tracked LTCM's death spiral. Ordinarily a business that makes a fatal blunder ought to be left to fail. But the markets were already spooked and skittish; Bill McDonough worried that if a company of LTCM's size had to dump its assets on the market, prices could collapse. That would set off a chain reaction that would bankrupt other firms. So when he called to say he'd decided to intervene, I wasn't happy with the idea, but I couldn't disagree.

The story of how he godfathered LTCM's bailout by its creditors has been told so many times that it is part of Wall Street lore. He literally gathered top officials of sixteen of the world's most powerful banks and investment houses in a room; suggested strongly that if they fully comprehended the losses they would face in a forced fire sale of LTCM's assets, they would work it out; and left. After days of increasingly tense negotiations, the bankers came up with an infusion of $3.5 billion for LTCM. That bought the firm the time it needed to dissolve in an orderly way.

No taxpayer money was spent (except perhaps for some sandwiches and coffee), but the Fed's intervention touched a populist raw nerve. "Seeing a Fund as Too Big to Fail, New York Fed Assists Its Bailout," trumpeted the *New York Times* on its front page. A few days later, on October 1, McDonough and I were called before the House Banking Committee to explain why, as *USA Today* put it, "a private firm designed for millionaires [should] be saved by a plan that was brokered and supported by a federal government organization." The criticism came from both sides of the aisle.

Congressman Michael Castle, a Delaware Republican, half jokingly said that his mutual funds and real estate investments weren't doing so well, but "no one is helping me out." And Congressman Bruce Vento, a Democrat from Minnesota, complained that we were shielding rich people from the harsh effects of market forces that often caused misery for the little guy: "There seem to be two rules," he said, "one for Main Street and another one for Wall Street."

But telling the banks involved with LTCM that they might save themselves money if they facilitated an orderly liquidation of the fund was by no stretch of the imagination a bailout. By facing the harsh reality and acting in their self-interest, they saved themselves and, I suspect, millions of their fellow citizens on both Main Street and Wall Street a lot of money.

I was tracking the signs of trouble in the financial world with mounting concern for how all this might damage the economy. At a speaking engagement on October 7, after thirty-year treasury bonds hit their lowest interest rates in thirty years, I threw away my prepared remarks and told an audience of economists, "I've been watching the U.S. markets for fifty years and I have never seen anything like this." Specifically, I said, investors in the bond market were behaving irrationally—paying substantially extra for the newest, most liquid treasury bonds, even though slightly older but less liquid ones were equally safe. This rush to liquidity was unprecedented, I noted, and reflected not judgment but panic. "They basically are saying, 'I want out. I don't want to know anything about whether an investment is risky or not. I can't stand the pain. I just want out.'" The economists knew precisely what I was getting at. Panic in a market is like liquid nitrogen—it can quickly cause a devastating freeze. And indeed, the Fed's research was already showing that banks were increasingly hesitant to lend.

It took no argument at all to get the FOMC to lower interest rates. We did so three times in rapid succession, between September 29 and November 17. Other European and Asian central banks, honoring their new G7 commitment, also eased their rates. Gradually, as we'd hoped, the medicine took hold. The world's markets calmed down, and a year and a half after the Asian crises began, Bob Rubin was finally able to take an uninterrupted family vacation.

The way the Fed responded to the Russian crisis reflected a gradually evolving departure from the policymaking textbook. Instead of putting all our energy into achieving the single best forecast and then betting everything on that, we based our policy response on a range of possible scenarios. When Russia defaulted, the Fed's mathematical models showed that it was highly likely that the U.S. economy would continue expanding at a healthy pace in spite of Russia's problems and with no action by the Fed. Yet we opted to ease interest rates all the same because of a small but real risk that the default might disrupt global financial markets enough to severely affect the United States. That was a new kind of trade-off for us: we judged this unlikely but potentially greatly destabilizing event to be a greater threat to economic prosperity than the higher inflation that easier money might cause. I suspect there had been many such decisions in the Fed's past, but the underlying decision-making process had never been made systematic or explicit.

Weighing costs and benefits systematically in this way gradually came to dominate our policymaking approach. I liked it because it generalized from a number of ad hoc decisions we'd made in years past. It let us reach beyond econometric models to factor in broader, though less mathematically precise, hypotheses about how the world works. Importantly, it also opened the door to the lessons of history: for example, by letting us explore how the railroad boom of the 1870s might hold clues to behavior in the markets during the Internet craze.

Some economists still argue that such an approach to policy is too undisciplined—overly complex, seemingly discretionary, difficult to explain. They want the Fed to set interest rates according to formal benchmarks and rules. We should manage the economy, say, to achieve an optimal level of employment, or by "targeting" a set rate of inflation. I agree that sensible policies can be made only with the help of rigorous analytic structures. But too often we have to deal with incomplete and faulty data, unreasoning human fear, and inadequate legal clarity. As elegant as modern-day econometrics has become, it is not up to the task of delivering policy prescriptions. The world economy has become too complex and interlinked. Our policymaking process must evolve in response to that complexity.

I suppose we might have guessed that the last year of the millennium would be the wildest, giddiest boom year of all. Euphoria swept the U.S. markets in 1999, partly because the East Asian crises hadn't done us in. If we'd made it through those, the thinking went, then the future was bright for as far as the eye could see.

What made this optimism so infectious was that it had a basis in fact. Driven by technological innovation and helped by strong consumer demand and other factors, the economy was booming right along. Yet while the opportunities were real, the degree of hype was surreal. You couldn't open the paper or read a magazine without encountering stories of the latest high-tech zillionaires. The head of a major consulting company made headlines when he quit to start Webvan, a company meant to deliver groceries ordered over the Internet. It raised $375 million in its initial public offering. Some London fashionistas I'd never heard of founded something called Boo.com, an apparel Web site that raised $135 million with a scheme to become the leading global seller of trendy sportswear. Everybody, it seemed, had an uncle or a neighbor who'd made big gains on Internet stock. The Fed, where people are constrained by conflict-of-interest rules from financial speculation, was probably one of the few places in America where you could ride an elevator without overhearing stock tips. (Like scores of other Internet start-ups, Webvan and Boo.com flamed out—in 2001 and 2000, respectively.)

The Internet boom became part of TV news, not just on the networks (of which I am a faithful viewer, because of Andrea) but also on CNBC and other upstart cable channels that catered to businesspeople and investors. On Super Bowl Sunday of 2000, half the thirty-second ad slots were bought by seventeen Internet start-ups for $2.2 million each—the Pets.com sock puppet appeared alongside Budweiser's Clydesdales and Dorothy from *The Wizard of Oz* (in a FedEx spot).

In pop culture, I was right up there with the sock puppets. CNBC invented a gimmick called the "briefcase indicator" in which cameras would follow me on the mornings of FOMC meetings as I arrived at the Fed. If my briefcase was thin, the theory went, then my mind was untroubled and the economy was well. But if it was stuffed full, it meant I'd been burning the midnight oil and a rate hike loomed. (For the record, the briefcase indicator was not accurate. The fatness of my briefcase was solely a function of whether I had packed my lunch.)

People would stop me on the street and thank me for their 401(k); I'd be cordial in response, though I admit I occasionally felt tempted to say, "Madam, I had nothing to do with your 401(k)." It's a very uncomfortable feeling to be complimented for something you didn't do. Andrea, who was by turns exasperated and amused, kept a box filled with "Greenspan-alia"—cartoons and postcards and clippings that were especially strange, not to mention Alan Greenspan T-shirts and even a doll.

Undoubtedly I could have avoided some of this—it would have been easy to duck the cameras, for example, by driving into the Fed's garage. But I was in the habit of walking those last several blocks to the office, and once they started doing the briefcase indicator, I didn't want to give the impression I was hiding. Besides, it wasn't mean-spirited—why be a killjoy?

The briefcase indicator was not a good way to convey monetary policy, however. Often, the ideas we needed to present were subtle and had to be thought through, making them poor fodder for sound bites as well. If sound bites had been our only contact with the media, I'd have been extremely concerned. But the Fed got a great deal of expert coverage. While it was my practice to avoid on-the-record interviews, my door was open to serious reporters. When someone called with questions for an important story, I'd often take the time to meet on background and talk through the ideas. (This practice helped print journalists more than it did TV people, Andrea was quick to point out, but I couldn't do anything about that.)

In the midst of all this craziness there was still real work to do. In the fall, Larry Summers and I had to settle a major turf war between the Treasury and the Fed. What had set it off was a push by Congress to overhaul the laws governing America's financial industries—banks, insurance companies, investment houses, real estate companies, and the like. Years in the making, the Financial Services Modernization Act finally did away with the Glass-Steagall Act, the Depression-era law that limited the ability of banks, investment firms, and insurance companies to enter one another's markets.

Banks and other companies were eager to diversify—they wanted to be able, for instance, to offer customers one-stop shopping for financial services. They argued that they were losing ground to foreign competitors, especially European and Japanese "universal banks," that operated under no such restrictions. I agreed that liberalization in these markets was long overdue. The Treasury through the Office of the Comptroller of the Currency was responsible for the supervision of all nationally chartered banks. The Fed oversaw bank holding companies and state-chartered institutions that chose to be regulated by the Fed. The version of the reform bill that had been passed by the Senate assigned responsibility mostly to the Fed; the House version favored the Treasury. After endless efforts to reconcile the two versions, Congress threw up its hands and gave our institutions until October 14 to settle it ourselves. So the Fed and Treasury staffs began to negotiate.

This wasn't quite the OK Corral, but there was plenty of friction. The Treasury and the comptroller's staff felt that all the regulatory authority should belong to them, and the Fed staff felt the same. Working day and night they were able to solve a number of issues, but by October 14 they'd fought to a standstill on others—they had a whole list of irreconcilable differences. I suspected tempers were running high.

As it happened, October 14 was the day slated for Larry and me to have our weekly breakfast. We looked at each other and said, "We have to settle this thing." That afternoon I went over to his office and we shut the door.

He and I are a lot alike: we both like to argue from basic principles and from evidence. I'm sorry we didn't have a tape recorder running, because this was a textbook case of policymaking by rational compromise. We sat and argued point by point. Periodically I'd say, "Your argument sounds more credible than mine," and the Treasury Department would carry that point. On other issues, Larry would accept the Fed's argument. After an hour or two, we'd divided the pie. Treasury and the Fed came together on a single bill, and up it went that day to Capitol Hill, where it passed. Historians view the Financial Services Modernization Act as a milestone of business legislation, and I'll always remember it as an unsung moment of policymaking for which there ought to be a little song.

The boom rose to a crescendo late in the year, with the NASDAQ stock-market index at the end of December having nearly doubled in twelve months (the Dow rose 20 percent). Most people who'd invested in stocks were feeling flush, and with good reason.

This presented the Fed with a fascinating puzzle:

How do you draw the line between a healthy, exciting economic boom and a wanton, speculative stock-market bubble driven by the less savory aspects of human nature? As I pointed out drily to the House Banking Committee, the question is all the more complicated because the two can coexist: "The interpretation that we are currently enjoying productivity acceleration does not ensure that equity prices are not overextended." An example that intrigued me was the epic, multibillion-dollar competition involving Qwest, Global Crossing, MCI, Level 3, and other telecom companies. Like the railroad entrepreneurs of the nineteenth century, they were racing to expand the Internet by laying thousands of miles of fiber-optic cable. (The link to the railroads is not merely metaphorical—Qwest, for one, actually built fiber-optic networks using old railroad rights-of-way.) There was nothing wrong with this—demand for bandwidth was increasing exponentially—except that each competitor was laying enough cable to accommodate 100 percent of the projected overall demand. So while something of great value was being built, it seemed clear that most of the competitors would lose, the value of their stock would plunge, and billions of dollars of their shareholders' capital would evaporate.

I'd given a lot of thought to whether we were experiencing a stock-market bubble, and if we were, what to do about it. If the market were to fall 30 percent or 40 percent in a short time, I reasoned, I'd be willing to stipulate that, yes, there had been a bubble. But this implied that if I wanted to identify a bubble, I had to confidently predict that the market was going to drop by 30 percent or 40 percent in a short time. That was a tough position to take.

Even if the Fed were to decide there was a stock bubble and we wanted to let the air out of it, would we be able to? I wondered. We had tried and failed. In early 1994, the FOMC began a 3-percentage-point tightening that lasted a year. We did it to address a concern that inflationary pressures were building. But I could not fail to notice that as we tightened, the nascent stock-market advance that had carried through most of 1993 went flat. Then, when our tightening episode came to an end in February 1995, stock prices resumed their rise. We tightened again in 1997 only to see stock prices again resume their rise after the rate move. We seemed in effect to be ratcheting up the long-term price trend. If Fed tightening could not knock stock prices down by weakening the economy and profits, owning stocks became a seemingly ever less risky activity. Our modest forays therefore had only set the stage for further increases in stock prices.

A giant rate hike would be a different story. I had no doubt that by abruptly raising interest rates by, say, 10 percentage points, we could explode any bubble overnight. But we would do so by devastating the economy, wiping out the very growth we sought to protect. We'd be killing the patient to cure the disease. I was reasonably certain that seeking to defuse a mounting bubble with incremental tightening, as many had recommended, would be counterproductive. Unless the tightening broke the back of the economic boom and with it profits, an incremental tightening would, in my experience, reinforce the perceived power of the boom. Modest tightening was more likely to raise stock prices than to lower them.

After thinking a great deal about this, I decided that the best the Fed could do would be to stay with our central goal of stabilizing product and services prices. By doing that job well, we would gain the power and flexibility needed to limit economic damage if there was a crash. That became the consensus within the FOMC. In the event of a major market decline, we agreed, our policy would be to move aggressively, lowering rates and flooding the system with liquidity to mitigate the economic fallout. But the idea of addressing the stock-market boom directly and preemptively seemed out of our reach.

A few eyebrows were raised when I presented this back-to-basics philosophy to Congress in 1999. I said I was still worried that stock prices might be too high, but that the Fed would not second-guess "hundreds of thousands of informed investors." Instead, the Fed would position itself to protect the economy in the event of a crash. "While bubbles that burst are scarcely benign, the consequences need not be catastrophic for the economy," I told the legislators.

Reflecting on this, the *New York Times* editorialized: "That sounds markedly different from the old Greenspan, who 30 months ago warned investors against 'irrational exuberance.'" Despite the article's tone—you could almost hear the *harrumph*—the editor's impression was correct. I'd come to realize we'd never be able to identify irrational exuberance with certainty, much less act on it, until after the fact. The politicians to whom I explained this did not mind; on the contrary, they were relieved that the Fed seemed disinclined to try to end the party.

Ironically, very soon afterward, we ended up tightening interest rates all the same. Between mid-1999 and mid-2000, we raised the fed funds rate in steps from 4.75 percent to 6.5 percent. We did so first to take back the liquidity we'd added to the system to safeguard it during the international financial crisis. Then we took back a little more to build "a bit of insurance," as Bill McDonough put it, against the tightness of the U.S. labor market and the possible overheating of the economy. In other words, we were positioning ourselves to try for another soft landing when the business cycle ultimately turned. But stock prices were largely undeterred—they didn't peak until March 2000, and even then the bulk of the market moved sideways for several months more.

Those challenges lay in the future as the world paused to ring in the New Year on December 31, 1999. The hottest ticket in Washington was the dinner at 1600 Pennsylvania Avenue, and Andrea and I were invited—along with Muhammad Ali, Sophia Loren, Robert De Niro, Itzhak Perlman, Maya Lin, Jack Nicholson, Arthur Schlesinger Jr., Bono, Sid Caesar, Bill Russell, and scores more. To celebrate the new millennium, the Clintons were planning a huge extravaganza: a dusk-to-dawn affair starting with a black-tie dinner for 360 at the White House, then a nationally televised entertainment spectacle at the Lincoln Memorial produced by my friends George Stevens Jr. and Quincy Jones. "American Creators" was the theme. Then, after midnight and fireworks, it would be back to the White House for breakfast and dancing till dawn.

I already had an inkling about what the new millennium held in store for me: I'd received word from John Podesta, the White House chief of staff, that President Clinton wanted to reappoint me for a fourth term. I'd said yes. To be involved in the analysis of the world's most vibrant economy, then be able to apply that analysis to decisions and have feedback from the real world—I couldn't think of anything I'd rather do than serve as Fed chairman. I was seventy-three, true, but I saw no diminution of my creativity, or of my ability to handle mathematical relationships, or of my appetite for work—changes that would have made me hang up my spurs. In his book *Maestro*, about me, Bob Woodward wrote that being reappointed put me in "a state of sober rapture"; I have to admit, I was having fun.

All this added a happy glow to the holiday season, though the announcement of my reappointment hadn't yet been made, and Andrea and I had to keep it to ourselves. She'd bought a dress for the White House occasion—a cut-velvet burgundy and black Badgley Mischka—and looked ravishing, even though she'd been working at her usual intense pace and had the flu.

The Millennium Dinner filled both the East Room and the State Dining Room, which, as a reporter gushed the next day, "were transformed into a fantasy of white and silver, with white orchids and roses set atop silver velvet tablecloths." I don't have much of an eye for such things. But as we nibbled beluga caviar and sipped champagne, what did strike me was that both host and hostess seemed genuinely pleased—he rounding out his second term as president, she preparing to launch her political career with a run for the U.S. Senate. The president toasted the guests: "I cannot help but think how different America is, how different history is, and how much better, because those of you in this room and those you represent were able to imagine, to invent, to aspire." After seven years in the White House—after the trials of Bosnia, the sleaze of Monicagate, and a historic economic and financial boom—this was the Clintons' Camelot moment.

The dinner broke up a little after nine, and the crowd moved to the buses that were to take us to the Lincoln Memorial. But Andrea and I peeled off. We had another millennium gathering to attend—at the Fed, where a sizable team was poised to work through the night to monitor the transition of the nation's financial systems.

The Fed had devoted years of effort to ensure that the turn of the millennium would not be a disaster. The threat was from obsolete software—the Y2K bug, it was called—embedded in computers all over the world. In order to save precious computer storage capacity, programmers in decades past had routinely used only two digits instead of four to represent the year, so for example "1974" would show up simply as "74." As I wrote programs using punchcards in the 1970s (I'd used this technique myself, writing programs on punchcards at Townsend-Greenspan. It had never entered my mind that such programs, extensively patched, might still be in use at the end of the century, and I never bothered to document the work.) There was understandably widespread concern that the shift from 1999 to 2000 might cause such software to go haywire. This potential glitch was often devilishly hard to detect and costly to fix. But in Y2K doomsday scenarios, the consequences of failing to do so were dire: vital civilian and military networks would crash, causing electricity to go out, phones to fail, credit cards to stop working, airplanes to collide, and worse. To prevent chaos from breaking out in the financial system, Fed governor Mike Kelley had spearheaded a massive two-and-a-half-year drive to modernize the computers of America's banks and of the Fed itself. The Fed had worked hard to mobilize other central banks around the world to do the same.

Tonight we were to learn whether all those precautions had paid off. Mike and his team had sacrificed their holiday to man a command post on the terrace level of the Fed's William McChesney Martin Building, where they'd fitted out a big room near the cafeteria with phones and screens and televisions and workspaces for about a hundred people. The kitchen was open; there was no champagne but plenty of nonalcoholic sparkling cider. When Andrea and I stopped in, the team had already been there all day, watching celebration after celebration on TV as the millennium made its way around the globe. First the New Year had come to Australia, then Japan, then the rest of Asia, then Europe. In each of those places, the TV coverage would show the fireworks, of course, but what Mike and his team were really watching was the city lights in the background to see if they were still on.

I felt out of place walking into this scene in black tie; most everybody else had on a red T-shirt bearing a patch emblazoned with an eagle on a red, white, and blue shield and the words "Federal Reserve Board" and "Y2K." Mike, who had been keeping me up-to-date, said things were still going remarkably well. Britain had just entered the twenty-first century apparently without problems. We were now in the hiatus as midnight crossed the Atlantic. The United States would be the last major economy to go, which added to the suspense, because after all our poking and prodding of other nations, it would have been an embarrassment to have our systems fail. But we were extremely well prepared: the U.S. financial industry had spent many billions of dollars replacing and updating old systems and programs; crisis-management teams stood ready in every Federal Reserve district and in every major bank. The FOMC had released billions of dollars of liquidity into the financial system, using options and other innovative techniques. And in the event America's credit card system or ATM networks broke down, the Fed had even positioned stockpiles of extra cash at ninety locations around the United States. Having had a hand in creating the problem, there was no way I could have shown up at the office on January 3 without having visited the troops in the trenches on the eve of potential catastrophe.*

From there, Andrea and I headed home. It was only 10:30, but we felt strangely as though we'd already seen the new millennium come and go. By the time midnight finally reached Washington—and began to cross the United States without incident—we were tucked snugly in bed.

---

*We didn't know it then, but the huge investments directed at clarifying and rationalizing all the undocumented pre-Y2K programs greatly enhanced the flexibility and resilience of America's business and government infrastructure. There were no more undocumented "black boxes" to try to puzzle out when something went wrong. I suspect a good part of the surge in productivity in the years immediately following was owed to those precautionary Y2K investments.

DOWNTURN

My first meeting with President-elect Bush took place on December 18, 2000, less than a week after the Supreme Court decision that enabled him to claim his election victory. We met at the Madison, the hotel about five blocks from the White House, where he and his team had set up shop. This was his first trip to Washington as president-elect; we'd met a few times over the years but had spoken at length only once before, on the dais at a banquet that spring.

The breakfast at the Madison included Vice President–elect Cheney; Bush's chief of staff, Andy Card; and a couple of aides. The situation had a familiar feel: I'd briefed five previous incoming presidents on the state of the economy, including, of course, the president-elect's father.

In this instance, I was obliged to report that the short-term outlook was not good. For the first time in years, we seemed to be faced with the real possibility of recession.

The deflation of the tech-stock bubble had been the great financial drama of the preceding months. The NASDAQ lost a stunning 50 percent of its value between March and year-end. The broader markets declined far less—the S&P 500 was down by 14 percent, and the Dow by 3 percent. But while the total losses were small in comparison with the paper wealth that the bull market had created, these were significant declines, and the Wall Street outlook remained gloomy, putting a damper on public confidence.

Of greater concern was the overall state of the economy. For much of the year, we'd appeared to be entering a mild cyclical slowdown; this was to be expected as businesses and consumers adjusted to the effects of so many boom years, so much technological change, and the deflation of the bubble in stocks. Indeed, to foster this adjustment process, the Fed had tightened interest rates in a series of steps from July 1999 to June 2000. We were hoping we might achieve another soft landing.

But in the past couple of weeks, I said, the numbers had slipped badly. There had been production slowdowns among automakers and other manufacturers, lowered estimates of corporate profits, swelling inventories in many industries, a marked rise in initial unemployment claims, and a weakening of consumer confidence. Energy was putting a drag on the economy too: oil had spiked up to more than $30 a barrel earlier in the year, and natural gas prices were up. Then there was the anecdotal evidence. Wal-Mart had told the Fed that it was cutting back its expectations for holiday sales, and FedEx reported to us that shipments were below predictions. You can't judge the health of the economy by the length of the lines to visit Santa at Macy's, but it was mid-December and anyone who had gone Christmas shopping knew that the stores were eerily quiet.

Despite all this, I told the president-elect, the economy's long-term potential remained strong. Inflation was low and stable, long-term interest rates were trending down, and productivity was still on the rise. And of course the federal government was running a surplus for the fourth straight year. The latest forecast for the 2001 fiscal year, which had just begun in October, had the surplus at nearly $270 billion.

As breakfast ended, Bush asked me aside for a private word. "I want you to know," he said, "that I have full confidence in the Federal Reserve and we will not be second-guessing your decisions." I thanked him. We chatted a bit more. Then it was time for him to leave for meetings on Capitol Hill.

There were cameras and reporters waiting as we walked out of the hotel.

I assumed that the president-elect would just go up to the microphones, but instead he put his arm around my shoulders and brought me along. An Associated Press photo from that morning shows me smiling broadly, as if I'd just gotten good news. Indeed I had. He'd zeroed in on the issue of most pressing importance to the Fed: our autonomy. I wasn't yet sure what to think about George W. Bush, but I felt inclined to believe him when he said we weren't going to have fights about monetary policy.

I felt relieved that the election crisis had been resolved. In unprecedented circumstances, after thirty-six days of hanging chads, recounts, lawsuits, and bitter allegations of vote tampering and fraud that in other countries would have caused rioting in the streets, we'd at least achieved a civil conclusion. Though I'm a lifelong libertarian Republican, I have close friends on both sides of the political aisle, and I thought I understood the Democrats' dismay at seeing George W. Bush take the White House. But it is worth focusing on how rare it is in world politics for a bitter political brawl to end up with the opposing candidates wishing each other well. Al Gore's concession speech ending the presidential race was the most gracious I'd ever heard. "Almost a century and a half ago," he said, "Senator Stephen Douglas told Abraham Lincoln, who had just defeated him for the Presidency: 'Partisan feeling must yield to patriotism. I'm with you, Mr. President, and God bless you.' Well, in that same spirit, I say to President-elect Bush that what remains of partisan rancor must now be put aside, and may God bless his stewardship of this country."

While I did not know where George W. Bush would lead us, I had confidence in the team that was taking shape. People wisecracked that America was witnessing the second coming of the Ford administration, but what was just a witticism to them meant a great deal to me. I'd started my public service in the Ford White House, and looked back to those years as something special. Gerald Ford was a very decent man, thrust into a presidency that he had never sought and that he probably would never have been able to win on his own. As he showed in his race against Jimmy Carter in 1976, he was not very good at the bare-knuckle politicking of a presidential campaign; his dream had been to serve as Speaker of the House of Representatives. Yet in the turmoil of a president resigning in disgrace, he'd proclaimed, "Our long national nightmare is over," and gathered around him as talented a group of people to run government as I have ever witnessed.

And now, in December 2000, George W. Bush was staffing the core of his government with Ford administration stalwarts, a lot older and far more experienced. The new secretary of defense, Donald Rumsfeld, had been Ford's first White House chief of staff. Under Ford, Rumsfeld had proved exceptionally effective. Called back by the president from his assignment as ambassador to NATO, he had quickly organized the Ford White House and ruled over it with great skill until Ford appointed him to his first turn as secretary of defense in 1975. After he returned to the private sector, Rumsfeld took the reins of a faltering G. D. Searle, a worldwide pharmaceutical company. I was brought on as the company's outside economic consultant and was fascinated to see this former U.S. Navy flight instructor, congressman, and government official fit so easily into the business world.

Another stalwart from the Ford administration was the new secretary of the treasury, my friend Paul O'Neill. Paul had impressed everybody as Gerald Ford's deputy director of the Office of Management and Budget. His had been a midlevel job, yet we'd pulled Paul in for all the important meetings because he was one of the few with full command of the details of the budget. Leaving the government to join the business world, he'd risen to become CEO of Alcoa—I was on the board of directors that hired him. In twelve years in that job, he'd been a great success. But he was ready to retire from the company, and I was enthusiastic to learn he was at the top of the list for treasury secretary. Dick Cheney called to tell me that Paul had met with President-elect Bush and was feeling torn. "He's got two pages of pros and cons," Cheney said. "Can you talk to him?"

I was delighted to pick up the phone. Using the same words with Paul that Arthur Burns had spoken to me in the waning days of the Nixon administration, I said, "We really need you down here." That argument had helped persuade me to leave New York and go to work in government for the first time, and it worked on Paul too. I thought his presence would be an important plus for the new administration. Would the president's programs and budgets foster the American economy's long-term prospects? What would be the caliber of his economic advisers and staff? On those counts, it seemed to me that making Paul the man who signed the dollar bills was a major step in the right direction.

There was another consideration, partly professional and partly personal. President Clinton had reappointed me early in 2000, so I had before me at least three more years as chairman. The Fed and the Treasury Department had made great music together throughout most of the 1990s. (Granted, there had been the occasional discord over turf.) We'd managed economic policy through the longest boom in modern U.S. history, improvised effectively in times of crisis, and helped the White House work down the horrendous federal deficits of the 1980s. My collaboration with Clinton's three treasury secretaries, Lloyd Bentsen, Bob Rubin, and Larry Summers, had contributed to that success, and we considered one another friends for life. I wanted to build an equally fruitful dynamic with the incoming administration—for both the Fed's sake and my own. So I was gratified when Paul finally said yes.

The most important returning Ford veteran, of course, was the vice president–elect. Dick Cheney had succeeded Rumsfeld, his mentor, as White House chief of staff, becoming at age thirty-four the youngest person ever to hold that post. With his combination of intensity and sometimes sphinxlike calm, he'd shown extraordinary skill in the job. The camaraderie we built in those years following Watergate had not waned. I would see him at Ford reunions and at other gatherings during his years as a congressman, and I was delighted when the first President Bush appointed him secretary of defense in 1989. There is little overlap between the duties of the secretary of defense and the chairman of the Federal Reserve, yet we'd kept in touch.

So now he was vice president–elect. I knew that many commentators believed he would be much more than vice president; because Cheney was so much more experienced in national and global affairs than George W. Bush, they thought he would become de facto head of government. I did not believe that—from my brief acquaintance with the president-elect, it was my impression that he was his own man.

In the weeks following the election, Cheney sought my input, as I'm sure he sought the input of other old friends. He and his wife, Lynne, hadn't yet moved to the vice presidential residence at the Naval Observatory, so on Sunday afternoons I'd drive to their home in the Washington suburb of McLean, Virginia, where he and I would sit at the kitchen table or settle down in the den.

The tone of our friendship shifted with his new position: I no longer called him Dick, but rather "Mr. Vice President," and while he hadn't asked for this new formality, he acquiesced. Our talks were mainly about the challenges facing the United States. Often we went into very specific detail. A key topic was energy. The recent oil-price spike had been a reminder that even in the twenty-first century, supplies of basic industrial-age resources remained a major strategic concern. Indeed, Cheney's first major focus in office was to convene a task force on energy policy. So I gave him my analysis of oil's role in the economy and of how the international oil and natural gas markets were evolving; we discussed nuclear power, liquefied natural gas, and other alternatives.

The greatest economic challenge on the domestic front, I argued, was the aging of thirty million baby boomers. Their retirement was no longer on the distant horizon, the way it had been when I'd become involved in Social Security reform under Reagan. The oldest boomers were set to turn sixty in six years, and the financial demands on the system would become extremely heavy in the decades beginning in 2010. Social Security and Medicare would need major revision to stay solvent and effective over that long term.

Dick made it clear that domestic economic policy was not going to be his bailiwick. All the same, he was curious about my ideas; he listened closely and often took notes that I assumed he might pass along.

During those last days of December and first days of January, I indulged in a bit of fantasy, envisioning this as the government that might have existed had Gerald Ford garnered the extra 1 percent of the vote he'd needed to edge past Jimmy Carter into a second term. What was more, for the first time since 1952, the Republican Party had ended up with not just the White House but both houses of Congress. (The Senate was actually split 50–50 between Republicans and Democrats, but as Senate president, Cheney would hold the tie-breaking vote.) I thought we had a golden opportunity to advance the ideals of effective, fiscally conservative government and free markets. Reagan had brought conservatism back to the White

House in 1980; Newt Gingrich had brought it back to Congress in 1994. But no one had put it together the way this new administration now had a chance to do.

I looked forward to at least four years of working collegially with many of government's best and brightest, men with whom I had shared many memorable experiences. And on a personal basis, that is how it worked out. But on policy matters, I was soon to see my old friends veer off in unexpected directions. People's ideas—and sometimes their ideals—change over the years. I was a different person than I had been when first exposed to the glitter of the White House a quarter of a century before. So were my old friends: not in personality or character, but in opinions about how the world works and, therefore, what is important.

In the weeks before the inauguration, the FOMC was scrambling to make sense of a complicated picture: the sudden slowdown of our $10-trillion-a-year economy and the practical implications for the Fed of the huge ongoing government surpluses. When the FOMC convened the day after my meeting with the president-elect, the downturn was at the top of the agenda.

Recessions are tricky to forecast because they are driven in part by nonrational behavior. Sentiment about the economic outlook usually does not shift smoothly from optimism to neutrality to gloom; it's like the bursting of a dam, in which a flood backs up until cracks appear and the dam is breached. The resulting torrent carries with it whatever shreds of confidence there were, and what remains is fear. We seemed to be confronting just such a breach. As Bob McTeer, the head of the Federal Reserve Bank of Dallas, put it: "The R word is now used openly just about everywhere."

We decided that unless conditions improved over the next two or three weeks, interest rates would have to come down. For now, our position would be simply to express concern. As our public statement put it: "The Committee will continue to monitor closely the evolving economic situation. . . . The risks are weighted mainly toward conditions that may generate economic weakness in the foreseeable future." Or as one committee member wryly translated, "We are not yet panicking."

Within two weeks, it was plain that the downtrend was not leveling off. On January 3, the first business day of the New Year, we convened again via conference call and cut the fed funds rate by half a percentage point, to 6 percent. The media took this move as a surprise, even though we'd hinted at it before Christmas, but that was fine: the Fed was responding to the markets and the economy.

In fact, we thought that this cut might be the first of many that would be necessary to stabilize the economy. I told the committee that it seemed to me any subsequent cuts might have to be made more quickly than usual. The same technology that was boosting productivity growth also might be speeding up the process of cyclical adjustment. A just-in-time economy demanded just-in-time monetary policy. Indeed, that would become our rationale as we cut the fed funds rate by another half percentage point before January was out, and again in March, April, May, and June, bringing it all the way down to 3.75 percent.

The other issue looming large for the FOMC was the disappearance of the national debt. Strange as it may seem in hindsight, in January 2001 the possibility was real. Nearly a decade of rising productivity growth and budget discipline had put the U.S. government in a position to generate surpluses "as far as the eye could see," to borrow the phrase coined by President Reagan's budget director David Stockman in projecting deficits nearly two decades earlier. Even allowing for the recession that might now be setting in, the nonpartisan Congressional Budget Office was getting ready to raise its projection of the surplus to a stunning $5.6 trillion over ten years. This was $3 trillion higher than the CBO had forecast in 1999, and $1 trillion more than it had predicted just the previous July.

I'd always had doubts that budget surpluses could persist. Given the inherent tendency of politicians to err on the side of spending, I found it difficult to imagine Congress ever accumulating anything but deficits. My skepticism that surpluses were here to stay had been why, a year and a half before, I'd urged Congress to hold off on the nearly $800 billion ten-year tax cut that President Clinton ultimately vetoed.

Yet I had to acknowledge that the general consensus among economists and statisticians I respected—not just at the CBO but also at the Office of Management and Budget, at the Treasury, and at the Fed—was that under current policy, surpluses would continue to build. It seemed that the surge in productivity growth unleashed by the technology revolution was upsetting the old assumptions. As the evidence for this ongoing surplus mounted, I felt an odd sense of loss. The economic model I carried around in my head seemed obsolete. Congress was in fact not spending money faster than the Treasury was taking it in. Had human nature changed? For months I'd been wrestling with the idea that it might be possible—it was a question of do you believe your crazy old theories or your lying eyes?

My colleagues at the FOMC seemed a bit disoriented too. In our late-January meeting, we spent hours trying to imagine how the Fed would operate in a brave new world of minimal federal debt. Of course, shedding the debt burden would be a happy development for our country, but it would nevertheless pose a big dilemma for the Fed. Our primary lever of monetary policy was buying and selling treasury securities—Uncle Sam's IOUs. But as the debt was paid down, those securities would grow scarce, leaving the Fed in need of a new set of assets to effect monetary policy. For nearly a year, senior Fed economists and traders had been exploring the issue of what other assets we might buy and sell.

A result was a dense 380-page study that plopped on our desks in January. The good news was that we weren't going out of business; the bad news was that nothing could really match the treasuries market in size, liquidity, and freedom from risk. To conduct monetary policy, the report concluded, the Fed would have to learn to manage a complex portfolio of municipal bonds, bonds issued by foreign governments, mortgage-backed securities, auctioned discount-window credits, and other debt instruments. It was a daunting prospect. "I feel kind of like Alice in Wonderland," Cathy Minehan, the president of the Federal Reserve Bank of Boston, had said when the issue first came up, and we all knew what she meant. The very fact of the discussion showed how profoundly and rapidly we thought the economic landscape might change.

The surplus was also what had Paul O'Neill and me excited as we met during January to swap budget ideas. We both knew, of course, that the CBO's figure of $5.6 trillion over ten years needed to be unpacked.

About $3.1 trillion would be untouchable money—reserved for Social Security and Medicare. That left a prospective $2.5 trillion in usable funds. A major tax cut, of course, had been the centerpiece of George Bush's presidential campaign. He'd set himself apart from his father by vowing early on, "This is not only 'No new taxes.' This is 'Tax cuts, so help me God.'" Cutting taxes was the highest, best use of the surplus, Bush asserted, rejecting Al Gore's position that equally important priorities should be to pay down debt and create social programs. As Bush put it in the first debate: "My opponent thinks the surplus is the government's money. That's not what I think. I think it's the hardworking people of America's money." Taking a page out of Reagan's book, he was proposing a sweeping $1.6 trillion cut, phased in over ten years across all tax brackets. Gore had campaigned on a $700 billion tax reduction.

In the context of a major ongoing surplus, a tax cut of some sort was a sensible idea, O'Neill and I agreed. As he pointed out, taxes now accounted for more than 20 percent of GDP versus a historic average of 18 percent. But there were competing uses for the surplus to consider. Paying down government debt, most importantly—Al Gore had that right. Federal debt to the public, as it is technically called, now stood at $3.4 trillion; more than $2.5 trillion of this was considered "reducible," or readily paid off (irreducible debt includes savings bonds and other securities that investors would decline to sell).

Another major item on our wish list was Social Security and Medicare reform. I'd long hoped to see Social Security transformed into a system of private accounts; to launch such a change while meeting the obligations already on the books for today's workers and retirees would probably require $1 trillion of additional funds as a down payment. And the nation hadn't even begun to reckon with the ballooning costs of Medicare. We'd taken that issue off the table when I'd run the Social Security reform commission for President Reagan almost twenty years before, but with the aging of the baby boomers, the challenge was becoming urgent. I pointed out that the statisticians were counting an awful lot of unhatched chickens by forecasting surpluses ten years ahead. What would happen if those surpluses failed to materialize?

O'Neill took as dim a view of deficits as I did. His answer was "triggers"—provisions added to any new spending and tax legislation that would put off or reduce the cuts if the surplus disappeared. Some sort of capping mechanism might work, I agreed. One of the most important achievements of Congress and the last two administrations had been to make budget balancing the law of the land. The government now operated under so-called pay-go rules, whereby if you added a program you had to come up with a source of funds for it, either by raising taxes or cutting other spending. "We are not going back into the red," I declared.

E vents in January moved very quickly indeed. The preparations for a new administration and a new Congress are always hectic, and that year they were doubly so—because of the prolonged dispute over the outcome of the presidential race, Bush and his transition team had just six weeks instead of the usual ten to gear up for inauguration day.

Taxes were, as expected, the front-burner issue. In a private conversation in mid-January, Cheney told O'Neill and me that, after the disputed election, Bush felt that a clean victory on his tax cut was crucial. This echoed the uncompromising note I'd heard Cheney strike in a Sunday-morning TV interview a few weeks before: "As President-elect Bush has made very clear, he ran on a particular platform that was very carefully developed; it's his program and it's his agenda and we have no intention at all of backing off of it."

Having been around Washington a long time, I thought I recognized a familiar pattern. Campaign promises are the starting point of every new presidency. Each administration, as it takes office, puts out budget proposals and other plans identical to those in the campaign. The problem with turning such promises into policy, however, is that platforms are written for political perception, not optimal effect. The campaign agenda is a hastily constructed road map based on conditions at the time; by definition, it cannot be a fully vetted policy for operating government. Invariably other forces in government—in Congress and the executive branch—act as a reality check, testing and tempering the plans. I knew this from experience; I'd worked for Nixon in his campaign of 1968 and for Reagan in 1980, and in no instance had the policy mix or forecast survived the early weeks of a new administration.

I did not foresee how different the Bush White House would be. Their stance was "This is what we promised; this is what we'll deliver," and they meant it quite literally. Little value was placed on rigorous economic policy debate or the weighing of long-term consequences. As the president himself put it to O'Neill a couple of months later, in rejecting a suggestion on how the administration's plan for Social Security reform might be improved: "I didn't go with that approach in the campaign." My friend soon found himself the odd man out; much to my disappointment, economic policymaking in the Bush administration remained firmly in the hands of White House staff.

The surplus was the first issue the Senate Budget Committee took up when the new Congress convened. That is how I found myself sitting under the bright lights of a hearing room on the morning of Thursday, January 25, about to touch off a political furor.

The key questions, as committee chairman Pete Domenici noted in welcoming me, were whether the projected long-term surplus would be transitory or permanent, and, if it did continue to rise, "What do we do about it?" My response in previous years had always been simply "Pay off the debt." But now the projected surpluses were so large that debt repayment would be completed within a very few years. Yet the surplus would continue. The CBO statisticians now envisioned the surpluses under current policy at $281 billion in 2001, $313 billion in 2002, $359 billion in 2003, and so on. Assuming no major shift in fiscal policy, the CBO expected the reducible debt to be fully paid off by 2006; any surpluses thereafter would have to be held in some form of nonfederal assets. In 2006 the surplus would break $500 billion. Thereafter, more than a half trillion extra dollars would flow into Uncle Sam's coffers each year.

As I contemplated this prospect, I felt a bit stunned: $500 billion is an almost unimaginable accumulation, roughly equivalent to the combined assets of America's five largest pension funds, piling up *each year.* What would the Treasury do with all that money? Where would it invest?

The only private markets large enough to absorb such sums are in stocks, bonds, and real estate, in the United States and abroad. I found myself picturing American government officials becoming the world's largest investors. I'd encountered this prospect once before and found the idea truly scary. Two years earlier, President Clinton had proposed investing $700 billion of Social Security funds in the stock market. To prevent political meddling with investment decisions, he suggested creating a privately managed mechanism to oversee the funds. But with such financial leverage at the government's disposal, I could readily envision the abuses that might occur under a Richard Nixon or a Lyndon Johnson. As I told the House Ways and Means Committee, I didn't believe it was "politically feasible to insulate such huge funds from government direction." To my relief, Clinton dropped the idea soon after. Yet now it would very likely arise again.

Taking all this into account, I came to a stark realization: chronic surpluses could be almost as destabilizing as chronic deficits. Paying off the debt was not enough. I decided to propose a way for Uncle Sam to pay off his debts while leaving little or no additional surplus to invest once the debt reached zero. Spending would have to be raised or taxes cut, and to me the preferable course seemed clear. I have always worried that once spending is notched up, it is difficult to rein in. The same is less true about tax cuts.* Moreover, lowering taxes eases the burden on private business, potentially raising the tax base. We could, alternatively, wait a couple of years and then, if the surpluses continued, reduce taxes sharply to eliminate them. But there was no way to know whether that would be a prudent option at the time; if inflation was pressing, tax cuts would end up stimulating an already overheated economy. The only course that did appeal to me was to act now to put fiscal policy on what I called a "glide path" to a balanced budget. This would involve phasing out the surpluses over the next several years, through a combination of tax cuts and Social Security reform.

Two pieces of tax-cut legislation were already on the table. On the first day of the new Congress, Senators Phil Gramm and Zell Miller had introduced a bill embodying the $1.6 trillion plan from Bush's campaign, and Senate minority leader Tom Daschle had introduced a more modest $700 billion plan. Either tax cut would serve my objective of scaling down the surplus while leaving enough money for Social Security reform.

---

*There is no upper limit to spending, but tax revenues cannot go below zero.

Of course, I still had the fear in the back of my mind that Congress and the White House might again go overboard on spending, or that revenues would unexpectedly flag, either of which would cause deficits to come back with a vengeance. So in writing my testimony, I was careful to include Paul O'Neill's notion of making the tax cuts conditional. I asked Congress to consider "provisions that limit surplus-reducing actions if specified targets for the budget surplus and federal debt were not satisfied." If chronic surpluses did not develop as forecast, then the tax cuts or newly enacted spending increases should be curtailed.

I could not shake a conviction of many decades that the biases in our political system favor deficits. So I made sure to end the statement on a strong note of caution: "With today's euphoria surrounding the surpluses," I wrote, "it is not difficult to imagine the hard-earned fiscal restraint developed in recent years rapidly dissipating. We need to resist those policies that could readily resurrect the deficits of the past and the fiscal imbalances that followed in their wake."

My office provided the Budget Committee leaders with a copy of my remarks a day in advance, as we often did with complex testimony that had no direct bearing on the financial markets. I was surprised on Wednesday afternoon to get a call from the committee's ranking Democrat, Kent Conrad of North Dakota. He asked if I could stop by his office to talk. A former tax commissioner, Conrad had been in the Senate as long as I'd been chairman, and had a reputation as a fiscal conservative. After thanking me for taking the time to see him, the senator went straight to the point. "You're going to create a feeding frenzy," he said. "Why are you backing the Bush tax cut?" He predicted that my testimony would not only ensure the passage of the White House proposals but also encourage Congress to jettison the fragile consensus on fiscal discipline it had built up over the years.

"That is not what I'm saying at all," I told him, pointing out that my testimony endorsed a tax cut of some kind to remove the surplus, but not necessarily the president's. My ultimate goals were still debt reduction and zero deficits. I went over my assessment of how dramatically the outlook on the surplus had changed, explaining how productivity growth, according to virtually all analysts, seemed on a permanently higher path—or on a higher path at least for the years immediately ahead. That had fundamentally altered the outlook for revenues. Finally, I agreed that it remained crucial to emphasize fiscal restraint, and volunteered to expand on the need for a safety mechanism like O'Neill's triggers if the senator would ask me about it during the Q&A.

When I left, I could see that Senator Conrad wasn't entirely satisfied with this response, but I didn't buy the idea that Congress would act on my say-so. Politicians had never hesitated to discount or ignore my recommendations in the past as it served their convenience. I do not recall my turning the tide when I advocated cuts in Social Security benefits. I had no intention of taking sides on whose tax cut was better; as I would tell Senator Domenici the following morning at the hearing when he asked me to endorse the Bush plan, that was a fundamentally political question. I was an analyst, not a politician; the job would be no fun if I had to worry about the political implications of everything I said. I was offering what I thought was a novel insight and hoped my testimony would add an important dimension to the debate.

I went back to the Fed and hadn't been at my desk for even an hour when Bob Rubin phoned. "Kent Conrad called me," he said. "He said I needed to talk to you before you testify." Bob hadn't read my statement but Conrad had filled him in, and he told me he shared some of the senator's concerns. With a big tax cut, said Bob, "the risk is, you lose the political mind-set of fiscal discipline."

He and I had labored for years to promote that consensus, so I asked if he knew that I was still presenting debt reduction as the ultimate goal. "I understand that," he said. Then what was the problem? I asked. "Bob, where in my testimony do you disagree?"

There was silence. Finally he replied, "The issue isn't so much what you're saying. It's how it's going to be perceived."

"I can't be in charge of people's perceptions," I responded wearily. "I don't function that way. I can't function that way."

It turned out that Conrad and Rubin were right. The tax-cut testimony proved to be politically explosive. The hubbub began even before I reached Capitol Hill: copies of my statement had leaked, and *USA Today* that morning ran a front-page headline: "Greenspan to Back Tax Cuts." Both Conrad and Domenici were quoted in the accompanying story, with Domenici confirming that I was about to change my position on tax cuts "because the surplus is so big."

The hearing room itself was as full as I'd ever seen it, with twenty senators and their staffs, a wall of cameras, and a substantial crowd. Reading my statement took nearly half an hour, and afterward I wasn't sure what to expect. Senator Conrad started by thanking me for what he declared was a "very balanced" approach—a gracious thing to say, I thought, as I hadn't changed a word after the previous day's conversation.

Then he asked, "As I hear you testifying, you're proposing that we don't abandon fiscal discipline?"

"Absolutely, Senator," I answered, dancing the little pas de deux I'd suggested the previous day. I amplified on my views about the continued need for debt reduction and fiscal restraint.

Then it was the other senators' turn, and for the two hours that followed, the questioning split sharply along party lines. While both sides had been proposing a tax cut, the Republicans were clearly the ones thrilled to hear me bless the idea. "I think we pretty well know where we're going," said Phil Gramm of Texas. "The sooner we write the budget the better, and get on with it!" The Democrats, in their comments, mostly voiced dismay. "You're going to start a stampede," said Fritz Hollings of South Carolina. Paul Sarbanes of Maryland chimed in, "It wouldn't be far off the mark for the press to carry the story, 'Greenspan Takes the Lid Off of Punch Bowl.'" The most vivid complaint was from the longest-serving senator in American history, Bob Byrd. In his West Virginia drawl, he began, "Now, I'm a Baptist. We have a hymnal. We have a song in our hymnal, 'The Anchor Holds.' And I've looked at you through this economic expansion period, and I've considered you to be a great portion of the anchor. I have listened to you over the past several years, that we need to pay down the debt, that is the basic need. I believe that you were right then and I am somewhat stunned by the fact that the anchor seems to be wavering today."

Remarks like that are the kind people remember. As the hearing ended, I was optimistic that the ideas I'd set forth—the risks of excessive surpluses, the glide-path proposal, the notion of a trigger—would in the long run get attention as the legislative process proceeded. But for the moment, I resigned myself to the idea that my testimony would be politically framed. I later told my wife, "I am shocked, shocked, that there is politics on Capitol Hill."

The White House was quick to signal its pleasure—President Bush himself met with reporters that evening to call my testimony "measured and just right." The major newspapers, too, saw the testimony as political. "Tax cuts are inevitable and it makes sense for Mr. Greenspan to avoid disagreeing with the new administration at this early stage," wrote the *Financial Times*. The *New York Times* reported that I was helping the White House in much the same way as I had supported President Clinton's deficit-cutting initiative when he first took office in 1993: "Just as his hedged backing of Mr. Clinton's plan provided invaluable political cover . . . as [the Democrats] voted to raise taxes, his guarded endorsement of a tax cut today gave new impetus to the effort by Republicans to push through the biggest tax cut since the Reagan administration."

Reading these comments, I saw that while politics had not been my intent, I'd misjudged the emotions of the moment. We had just gone through a constitutional crisis over an election—which, I realized in hindsight, is not the best time to try to put across a nuanced position based on economic analysis. Yet I'd have given the same testimony if Al Gore had been president.

I did what I could to keep the concept of triggers in play during the weeks that followed. In congressional hearings in February and March, I repeatedly drew attention to the tentativeness of all forecasts, and continued to bang the drum for installing safeguards. "It is crucial that we develop budgetary strategies that deal with any disappointments that could occur," I told a House committee on March 2.

A few days later a small bipartisan group of Senate fiscal conservatives called a press conference and declared that triggers were the way to go. I'd met with and encouraged this group, five Republicans and six Democrats led by Olympia Snowe of Maine.

But triggers, it turned out, never stood much of a chance. Neither side's leadership liked the idea. On the day of my testimony, when reporters asked White House spokesman Ari Fleischer about adding antideficit safeguards to the president's tax cut, he answered flatly, "We need to make it the *permanent* law of the land." Soon after, *Time* magazine quoted chief political adviser Karl Rove calling the trigger concept "dead on arrival with this President." And when President Bush formally unveiled his 2002 budget plan in February, it incorporated the $1.6 trillion tax cut just as he had proposed it during the campaign. The Democratic leadership rejected the trigger concept as well. "You don't need a trigger if you limit the size of a tax cut," said Senate minority leader Daschle. In early March, the Republican House leadership decisively blocked a trigger amendment from reaching the floor, and the House passed the Bush tax cut virtually unchanged. When the debate shifted to the Senate, triggers never drew any additional support.

In the end, Bush had his victory. At $1.35 trillion, the tax cut that ultimately took shape was smaller than he had wanted, about halfway between the Republican and Democratic plans. But it was structured à la Bush as an across-the-board cut. The legislation embodied only one major feature that had not been part of the original plan: a taxpayer rebate designed to give back nearly $40 billion of the 2001 surplus. It mandated that each working household was to receive up to $600, depending on how much income tax it had paid the year before. Congress approved the "Bush rebate," as it came to be called, as a short-term stimulus aimed at jolting the economy from its stupor. "American taxpayers will have more money in their pockets," the president declared, "and the economy will receive a well-deserved shot in the arm."

He signed the tax cut into law on June 7—record time for a major budget initiative. I was willing to be optimistic about the legislation's effect. It would work down the surpluses before they became dangerous. And though the tax cut had not been designed as a short-term stimulus—the economy hadn't needed one when Bush's people conceived it during the campaign—it could prove serendipitously to have that effect. The timing was now right.

My regret that the legislation had passed without triggers, however, was soon to become a lot more intense. Within weeks, it turned out that I'd been wrong to abandon my skepticism about the ongoing surplus. Those rosy ten-year forecasts were in fact utterly mistaken.

Even before the Bush rebate checks were in the mail, suddenly and inexplicably, federal revenues plunged. The flow of personal income tax payments to the Treasury, as seasonally adjusted by the Department of Commerce, started to come up billions of dollars short. The vaunted surplus, still going strong when Bush signed the tax cut in June and forecast to continue for many years, was effectively wiped out overnight. Starting that July, red ink was back to stay.

Our best statisticians got blindsided by this change; it took budget experts many months, tabulating tens of millions of tax returns, to piece together what went wrong. The revenue shortfall was evidently a reflection of the stock market's broad, ongoing decline. (Between January and September 2001, the S&P 500 lost more than 20 percent of its value.) This caused a sharp fall in taxes on capital gains and the exercise of stock options—a decline far more abrupt than the experts had forecast. Just as the bull market of the tech boom had generated the surplus, the post-dot-com bear market took it away.

How could the forecasts have been so colossally wrong? The mildness of the economic downturn had fooled the tax statisticians into expecting a gentler drop in receipts. But by 2002, the extent of the collapse was evident in the numbers. In January 2001, the CBO had estimated total receipts at $2.236 trillion for fiscal year 2002. By August 2002, that figure had shrunk to $1.860 trillion—a $376 billion downward revision in eighteen months. Of that money, $75 billion reflected the Bush tax cut and $125 billion the weakening of economic activity. The other $176 billion, a startlingly large sum, reflected what budgeters call technical changes—code language for items that cannot be explained by what is going on in the economy or on Capitol Hill, such as blown estimates of taxes from capital gains.

That September, Bob Woodward came to my office to interview me on the state of the economy. He was preparing a new chapter for the paperback edition of *Maestro*, his bestseller about me and the Fed. I told him I was puzzled by the course the 2001 recession was taking—it was like nothing I'd ever seen. Following December's sharp break in confidence and the significant decline in stock prices through the summer, I'd steeled myself for a marked downturn in GDP. Industrial production was off 5 percent during the year. GDP, however, held steady. Instead of being in a deep valley, we were on a plateau. (Indeed, it would turn out that the economy actually eked out a slight expansion for the year.)

The shallowness of the recession looked to be a consequence of global economic forces that had driven long-term interest rates lower and ignited a sharp rise in home prices in many parts of the world. In the United States, homes had increased in value so much that households, feeling flush, seemed more willing to spend. That, coupled with underlying productivity growth, appeared to have endowed the American economy with a whole new degree of buoyancy.

So, said Woodward, trying to sum up, "maybe the story of the economy this year is the disaster averted rather than the downturns."

"It's too soon to tell," I answered. "Until the whole thing settles down into a boring pattern, you can't know."

The conversation was not much different from a dozen other background sessions I'd held with reporters in the course of the summer—except for the timing. It was Thursday, September 6, just before I was to leave for an international bankers' meeting in Switzerland. The date on the airplane ticket for my return was Tuesday, September 11.

ELEVEN

THE NATION CHALLENGED

For a full year and a half after September 11, 2001, we were in limbo. The economy managed to expand, but its growth was uncertain and weak. Businesses and investors felt besieged. The immediate crises of the first few months—the hunt for al Qaeda suspects, the anthrax attacks, the Afghanistan war—gave way to the low-grade strain of coping with domestic security's anxieties and costs. Enron's bankruptcy in December 2001 compounded the uncertainty and gloom; it touched off a wave of accounting scandals and bankruptcies exposing the infectious greed and malfeasance that had been the dark side of the great economic boom.

At times there seemed no end to disturbing news: the controversy over campaign finance, the sniper killings in Washington, D.C., the terrorist bombing of a nightclub district in Bali. In summer 2002, telecom giant WorldCom collapsed in a cloud of accounting fraud—at $107 billion in assets, it was the biggest bankruptcy in history.

Then came SARS, the lethal flulike contagion that began in China and for weeks disrupted business travel and trade. During that period, of course, the administration was stepping up its attacks on Saddam Hussein, and in

March and April 2003 the invasion of Iraq and Saddam's overthrow dominated the headlines.

Behind everything loomed the expectation of continued terrorist attacks on U.S. soil. In official Washington, especially, it was hard to shake the feeling of imminent threat: new traffic barriers, checkpoints, surveillance cameras, and heavily armed guards were everywhere. For me, there was no more strolling a couple of blocks on the way to work, past TV cameras for the briefcase indicator; each morning I was driven into the Fed's heavily guarded underground garage. Visitors to the Fed, though still allowed to park there, would have to wait as a dog sniffed the car for explosives—the dog would actually get into the trunk.

There was no bigger question in Washington than, Why no second attack? If al Qaeda's intent was to disrupt the U.S. economy, as bin Laden had declared, the attacks had to continue. Our society was open, our borders were porous, and our ability to detect weapons and bombs was weak. I asked this question of a lot of people at the highest levels of government, and no one seemed to have a convincing response.

The expectation of additional terrorism affected virtually everything the government did. And, inevitably, the defensive bubble we'd created to protect our institutions influenced every decision. In 2002, the new homeland security program was prepared to significantly curtail individual freedoms by such measures as tightening identification requirements, stepping up identity checks, restricting travel, and limiting privacy.* The leaders of both parties were on board. But when no further attacks came, the politicians gradually reverted to their pre-9/11 positions on civil liberties, some more quickly than others. It is interesting to hypothesize how the United States would look today if there had been a second, third, and fourth attack. Could our culture stand it? Would we be able to maintain a viable economy as the Israelis have, and as Londoners did during the decades of bombings by the Irish Republican Army? I had great confidence that we could . . . but there is always that doubt.

---

*The Homeland Security Act itself was less draconian, but did curtail civil liberties by making it easier for the government to deny Freedom of Information Act requests, by imposing criminal penalties on officials who disclosed "critical infrastructure information" obtained from private companies, and by developing a program that would monitor citizens' everyday lives.

The Fed's response to all this uncertainty was to maintain our program of aggressively lowering short-term interest rates. This extended a series of seven cuts we'd already made in early 2001 to mitigate the impact of the dot-com bust and the general stock-market decline. After the September 11 attacks, we cut the fed funds rate four times more, and then once again at the height of the corporate scandals in 2002. By October of that year, the fed funds rate stood at 1.25 percent, a figure most of us would have considered unfathomably low a decade before. (Indeed, rates had not been so low since the days of Dwight Eisenhower.) As officials whose entire careers had been devoted to fighting inflation, we found the experience of making such cuts decidedly strange. Yet, the economy was clearly in the grip of disinflation, in which market forces combine to hold down wages and prices and cause inflation expectations, and hence long-term interest rates, to recede.

So inflation, for the moment at least, was not a problem. Between 2000 and 2003, long-term interest rates continued to decline—the rate on ten-year treasuries dropped from nearly 7 percent to less than 3.5 percent. It was clear that the ultimate explanation extended far beyond American shores, because long-term interest rates around the world also were trending down. Globalization was exerting a disinflationary impact.

We put that broader issue aside to wrestle with the immediate challenge facing the Fed, a weakened economy. The FOMC's working assumption was that rising prices did not pose an imminent threat and that gave us the flexibility to lower short-term rates.

By 2003, however, the economic funk and disinflation had gone on so long that the Fed had to consider a more exotic peril: a declining price level, deflation. This was the possibility that the U.S. economy might be entering a crippling spiral like the one we'd seen paralyze Japan for thirteen years. I found it to be a very unsettling issue. In modern economies, whose chronic headache is inflation, deflation is a rare disease. After all, the United States was no longer on a gold standard. I couldn't conceive of deflation occurring under a fiat money standard. I'd always assumed that if deflation seemed imminent, we could start up the printing presses and create as many dollars as would be necessary to stop a deflationary spiral. Now I was not so sure. Japan had figuratively opened its money taps, driven interest rates to zero, and run a large budget deficit, yet its price level had continued to fall. The Japanese seemed unable to break the grip of deflation and must have been quite fearful that they were in the type of downward spiral that nobody had witnessed since the 1930s.

Deflation became the focus of increasing concern within the Fed. While the economy eked out 1.6 percent real GDP growth during 2002, it clearly was being constrained. Even powerful companies like Aetna and SBC Communications were showing weak profits, laying people off, and reporting difficulty making price increases stick. Unemployment had risen from 4 percent at the end of 2000 to 6 percent.

At the FOMC meeting in late June, where we voted to reduce interest rates still further, to 1 percent, deflation was Topic A. We agreed on the reduction despite our consensus that the economy probably did not need yet another rate cut. The stock market had finally begun to revive, and our forecasts called for much stronger GDP growth in the year's second half. Yet we went ahead on the basis of a balancing of risk. We wanted to shut down the possibility of corrosive deflation; we were willing to chance that by cutting rates we might foster a bubble, an inflationary boom of some sort, which we would subsequently have to address. I was pleased at the way we'd weighed the contending factors. Time would tell if it was the right decision, but it was a decision done right.

Consumer spending carried the economy through the post-9/11 malaise, and what carried consumer spending was housing. In many parts of the United States, residential real estate, energized by the fall in mortgage interest rates, began to see values surge. The market prices of existing homes rose 7.5 percent a year in 2000, 2001, and 2002, more than double the rate of just a few years before. Not only did construction of new houses rise to record levels, but also historic numbers of existing houses changed hands. This boom provided a big lift in morale—even if your house was not for sale, you could look down the block and see other people's homes going for what seemed like astonishing prices, which meant your house was worth more too.

By early 2003, thirty-year mortgages were below 6 percent, the lowest they'd been since the sixties. Adjustable-rate mortgages cost even less. This spurred the turnover of houses that drove prices higher. Since 1994, the proportion of American householders who became homeowners had accelerated. By 2006, nearly 69 percent of households owned their own home, up from 64 percent in 1994 and 44 percent in 1940. The gains were especially dramatic among Hispanics and blacks, as increasing affluence as well as government encouragement of subprime mortgage programs enabled many members of minority groups to become first-time home buyers. This expansion of ownership gave more people a stake in the future of our country and boded well for the cohesion of the nation, I thought. Home ownership resonates as deeply today as it did a century ago. Even in a digital age, brick and mortar (or plywood and Sheetrock) are what stabilize us and make us feel at home.

Capital gains, especially gains realized in cash, began burning holes in people's pockets. Soon statisticians could see a bulge in consumer spending that matched the surge in capital gains. Some analysts estimated that 3 percent to 5 percent of the increase in housing wealth showed up annually in the demand for all manner of goods and services, from cars and refrigerators to vacations and entertainment. And, of course, people poured money into home modernization and expansion, further fueling the boom. This pickup in outlays was virtually all funded through increases in home mortgage debt, which financial institutions made particularly easy to tap.* The net effect was characterized neatly by economics columnist Robert Samuelson, who wrote in *Newsweek* on December 30, 2002: "The housing boom saved the economy. . . . Fed up with the stock market, Americans went on a real-estate orgy. We traded up, tore down and added on."

Booms, of course, beget bubbles, as the owners of dot-com stocks had painfully learned. Were we setting ourselves up for a harrowing real estate crash? That concern started to surface in hot markets like San Diego and New York, where prices in 2002 jumped by 22 percent and 19 percent, respectively, and where some investors now began viewing houses and condos as the latest way to get rich quick. The Fed tracked such developments closely. As the boom rolled on, the evidence of speculation became hard to miss. The market for single-family homes in the United States had always been

---

*When a home changed hands, the buyer almost invariably took out a mortgage that exceeded the unpaid balance on the seller's outstanding mortgage. The net increase of debt on the house went as cash to the seller. Such home equity extraction tends to track, but is not exactly equal to, the realized capital gain on the sale.

predominately for home ownership, with the proportion of purchases for investment or speculation rarely more than 10 percent.* But by 2005, investors accounted for 28 percent of homes bought, according to the National Association of Realtors. They became a force in the market, driving up turnover of existing homes by almost one-third. By then, the TV news was carrying reports of "flippers"—speculators in places like Las Vegas and Miami. They would use easy credit to load up on five or six new condos, aiming to sell them at a large profit even before the apartments were built. Such dramas remained strictly regional, however. I would tell audiences that we were facing not a bubble but a froth—lots of small, local bubbles that never grew to a scale that could threaten the health of the overall economy.

Whether a bubble or a froth, the party was winding down by late 2005, when first-time buyers began to find prices increasingly out of reach. Higher prices required larger mortgages, which began to claim a burdensome share of monthly income. The heady days when buyers paid above offering prices to bid away a house were over. Sellers' offering prices held up, but buyers pulled their bids. Sales volumes accordingly fell sharply for both new and existing homes. The boom was over.

It had been part of a historic international trend. Mortgage interest rates had fallen not just in the United States but also in Great Britain, Australia, and many other countries that have viable mortgage markets. In response, home prices worldwide had soared. The *Economist*, which tracks home prices in twenty countries, has estimated that between 2000 and 2005 the market value of residential property in developed nations rose from $40 trillion to more than $70 trillion. The largest share of that increase—$8 trillion—occurred in U.S. single-family homes. But the experience of other economies was suggestive because their booms began—and ended—a year or two ahead of ours. In Australia and Britain, demand began to cool in 2004 for the same reasons it later cooled in the United States: first-time buyers got priced out of the market, and speculative investors

---

*Such purchases are largely made by people who purchase and rent out dwellings. Often, such an individual is the owner of a condominium or of a two-family attached house, one unit of which is rented out.

drew back. Importantly, as the boom ended in those countries, prices leveled out or declined slightly, but at this writing have not crashed.

Because of the housing boom and the accompanying explosion in new mortgage products, the typical American household ended up with a more valuable home and better access to the wealth it represented. Its mortgage is bigger too, of course, but since the debt carries a lower interest rate, the drain on income from debt service as a share of homeowner income did not change much between 2000 and 2005.

The post-9/11 recovery had a dark side, however. It was marred by a disturbing shift in the concentration of income. For the past four years, gains in the average hourly salaries of supervisory workers have significantly outstripped gains in the average hourly earnings of production and non-supervisory workers. (For many households, the lag in real incomes was offset by capital gains on their homes, even though the bulk of the capital gains went to households in the upper-middle and upper income groups.)

You could see the income divergence reflected in the polls even as economic growth returned. By 2004, real GDP was expanding at a healthy 3.9 percent a year, unemployment declined, and aggregate wages and salaries weren't doing all that badly either. Yet most of the rise in average incomes was owing to disproportionate gains among the highly skilled. There are a lot more workers who earn at the median income, and they have not been doing all that well. Thus, it is no surprise that researchers who telephoned a thousand households found that 60 percent thought the economy was awful, while only 40 percent thought it was just fine. Two-tier economies are common in developing countries, but not since the 1920s have Americans experienced such inequality of income. It used to be that when the aggregate numbers were good, the polls would be positive as well.

More recently, the unwinding of the housing boom has hurt some groups. It did not create great difficulties for the great mass of homeowners who had built up substantial equity in their houses as prices rose. But many low-income families who took advantage of subprime mortgage offerings to become first-time homeowners joined the boom too late to enjoy its benefits. Without an equity buffer to fall back on, they are having difficulty making their monthly payments, and increasing numbers are facing fore-closure. Of the nearly $3 trillion of home mortgage originations in 2006, a fifth were subprime and another fifth were so-called Alt-A mortgages. The latter are mortgages taken out by people with good credit histories, but whose monthly payments are often interest-only, and whose documenta-tion with respect to the borrower's income and other characteristics is in-adequate. Poor performance of this two-fifths of originations has induced a significant tightening of credit availability, with a noticeable impact on home sales. I was aware that the loosening of mortgage credit terms for subprime borrowers increased financial risk, and that subsidized home ownership initiatives distort market outcomes. But I believed then, as now, that the benefits of broadened home ownership are worth the risk. Protec-tion of property rights, so critical to a market economy, requires a critical mass of owners to sustain political support.

A s much as the economy's overall resilience heartened me, I was dis-tressed by the performance of the government. Red ink flooded back in 2002: we ran a deficit of $158 billion, a deterioration of more than a quarter trillion dollars from the $127 billion surplus of 2001.

President Bush continued to direct his administration toward fulfilling the promises he had made during the 2000 presidential campaign: cutting taxes, strengthening national defense, and adding prescription drug benefits to Medicare. These goals had not been unrealistic in the light of large and projected surpluses. But the surpluses were gone six to nine months after George W. Bush took office. And in the revised world of growing deficits, the goals were no longer entirely appropriate. He continued to pursue his presidential campaign promises nonetheless.

Most troubling to me was the readiness of both Congress and the ad-ministration to abandon fiscal discipline. Four years of surplus had made thrift an increasingly scarce commodity on Capitol Hill. Surpluses are irre-sistible to officials who thrive on the political "free lunch." I cannot count how many letters I received from Capitol Hill in the 1990s outlining one scheme or another to spend more or tax less, with the pay-go requirement satisfied by some sleight-of-hand financing obscurity, the purpose of which was to hide the cost of the scheme. In the Congress, double-entry bookkeeping had become a lost art.

It finally dropped the pretense. During the final year of the Clinton administration, Congress had ignored its self-imposed discretionary spending caps to legislate an estimated $1 trillion of additional spending over ten years. Without this spending, the record $237 billion surplus in 2000 would have been even larger. Then with George Bush came the tax cuts, unmatched by decreased spending, and, in the wake of September 11, still *more* openhanded spending.

Laws passed after 9/11 included needed increases for defense and homeland security, of course. But our national emergency fiscal measures also seemed to whet Congress's appetite for "pork"—spending programs for constituents. An early example was a $60 billion transportation bill that passed almost unanimously in December 2001. It allocated large sums to expand airline security and imposed a tax on plane tickets to partly offset the cost—sensible moves, arguably. Yet it also included more than $400 million of pure pork—highway funding taken out of the states' control and earmarked by legislators for pet road projects back home.

I was even more offended by the farm bill the following May. It was a budget-busting six-year, $250 billion handout that reversed hard-fought earlier initiatives to scale back agricultural subsidies and open up farm trade to market forces. The new package greatly increased subsidies on cotton and grain, and heaped new subsidies on everything from sugar to chickpeas. The chairman of the House Agriculture Committee, Texas Republican Larry Combest, pushed for the bill, as did midwestern Democrats, like Senate leader Daschle of South Dakota.

There is a remedy for legislative excess: it's called a presidential veto. In conversations behind the scenes with senior economic officials, I made no secret of my view that President Bush ought to reject a few bills. It would send a message to Congress that it did not have carte blanche on spending. But the answer I received from a senior White House official was that the president didn't want to challenge House Speaker Dennis Hastert. "He thinks he can control him better by not antagonizing him," the official said.

And indeed, not exercising veto power became a hallmark of the Bush presidency: for nearly six years in the White House, he did not throw out a single bill. This was without modern historical precedent. Johnson, Nixon, Carter, Reagan, George H. W. Bush, Clinton—all had vetoed dozens of bills. And Jerry Ford had vetoed everything in sight—more than sixty bills in less than three years. This enabled him, even though faced with large Democratic majorities in both houses of Congress, to assert a great deal of power and steer the lawmakers in directions he thought important. To my mind, Bush's collaborate-don't-confront approach was a major mistake—it cost the nation a check-and-balance mechanism essential to fiscal discipline.

Budget discipline in Washington gave up the ghost on September 30, 2002. That was the day Congress allowed America's primary antideficit law to expire. The Budget Enforcement Act of 1990 had been a monument to congressional self-restraint. Enacted with bipartisan support under the first President Bush, the law had played an important role in bringing the federal deficit under control, thereby helping to set the stage for the 1990s boom. In it, Congress imposed on itself strict discretionary caps and pay-go rules that required new spending increases or tax cuts to be offset elsewhere in the budget. Violating these provisions would automatically trigger heavy penalties, such as across-the-board reductions in social programs and defense—cuts any politician would take pains to avoid.

But the Budget Enforcement Act never envisioned years of surplus (ironically, its goal had been to achieve a balanced budget by 2002). And in the late-1990s rush to spend, Congress seized on technicalities to flout its rules. As a longtime House staffer put it, "We were required to be 'deficit-neutral'—but there were no deficits!" Yet now, with the safeguards due to expire, deficits were flooding back.

In mid-September I made the most strenuous plea I could for Congress to retain this first line of defense. "The budget enforcement rules are set to expire," I told the House Budget Committee. "Failing to preserve them would be a grave mistake. For without clear direction and constructive goals, the inbuilt political bias in favor of budget deficits likely will again become entrenched. . . . If we do not preserve the budget rules and reaffirm our commitment to fiscal responsibility, years of hard effort will be squandered." The worst consequences would not be immediate, I acknowledged, but they would be severe. I warned, "History suggests that an abandonment of fiscal discipline will eventually push up interest rates, crowd out capital spending, lower productivity growth, and force harder choices upon us in the future."

My statement had circulated in advance. It was obviously not a message the committee members wanted to hear. Of the forty-one members of the committee, only about half showed up. I watched the congresspeople's reactions as I read a passage invoking the historic bipartisan consensus that had given birth to the Budget Enforcement Act. Mostly I was met with blank stares. Worse, the question-and-answer session made it plain that few, if any, of the legislators had any interest in perpetuating spending constraints. Instead of addressing my proposal and the larger economic danger to which it pointed, the questioners simply changed the subject. The discussion focused almost entirely on tax cuts, present and future, pro and con. And that was what dominated the sparse news reports of my testimony the following day.

In the Senate, Pete Domenici, Phil Gramm, Kent Conrad, Don Nickles, and other fiscal conservatives worked to retain the budget-balancing mechanisms. But the political will wasn't there. All they managed was to put through a six-month extension of a procedural rule that made it slightly harder to pass legislation increasing the deficit. But without the Budget Enforcement Act's mandatory penalties, the rule had no teeth. The budget discipline that had served us so well was effectively dead.

After the Republicans scored a sweeping victory in the November 2002 midterm elections, the situation got worse. Glenn Hubbard, the chairman of the Council of Economic Advisors, argued in a December speech that it made little difference to the overall economy whether the budget was balanced or not. "One can hope that the discussion will move away" from the idea that higher deficits would push up long-term interest rates and chill growth, he said. "That's Rubinomics, and we think it's completely wrong." Leaving aside this gibe at the Democrats, what Hubbard said was accurate in a short-term context. Securities markets have become so efficient that current interest rates move only when new information brings changes in expectations of future budget deficits and Treasury debt. Incremental, immediate changes in the supply of U.S. Treasury obligations are generally quite small relative to the global supply of comparably safe long-term debt instruments. Small changes in relative prices (that is, interest rates) can induce investors to replace considerable quantities of Treasury debt with equal amounts of high-quality corporate debt or foreign government obligations. The converse is also true: such changes in debt or, by extension, deficits are associated with surprisingly small changes in interest rates. The size and efficiency of the global market for bonds competitive with U.S. treasuries obscure the underlying long-term relationship between federal deficits, debt, and interest rates.

Sometimes when an issue is complex, it is a useful exercise to take it to an extreme. If it were true that deficits did not matter and tax cuts unmatched by spending cuts were good public policy, then why not just eliminate *all* taxes? Congress could borrow as much as it wanted and spend as freely as it liked, all without fear that the government's rapidly accumulating ocean of debt would erode economic growth. Yet as we have seen time after time in developing countries, unbridled government borrowing and spending produce hyperinflation and economic devastation.

So deficits *must* matter. The crucial question for policymakers is not, Do they hurt growth? but How much do they hurt growth? In fact Hubbard, whose econometric models show only a small impact on interest rates from changes in Treasury debt outstanding, nonetheless recently wrote, "Our findings should not be construed as implying that deficits don't matter. Substantially larger, persistent, and unsustainable levels of government debt can eventually put increasing strains on the available domestic and foreign sources of loanable funds. . . . In the United States at the present time, unfunded implicit obligations associated with the Social Security and Medicare programs are particularly of concern." But the subtleties of the economic debate got lost in the political realities. Congress and the president viewed budgetary restraint as inhibiting the legislation they wanted. "Deficits don't matter," to my chagrin, became part of Republicans' rhetoric.

It was a struggle for me to accept that this had become the dominant ethos and economic policy of the Republican Party. But I'd had a preview of it many years before, in the 1970s, over lunch with Jack Kemp, then a young congressman from upstate New York. He complained that Democrats were always buying votes by boosting spending all over the place. And eventually the resulting deficits would land in the lap of a Republican administration to solve. "Why can't *we* be a little irresponsible ourselves?" he asked, startling me. "Why can't we cut taxes and give away the goodies before they can?" And indeed, that's what was happening now. My sensibilities as a libertarian Republican were offended.

In late December 2002 and early January, I took the unusual step of pushing senior economic officials in the White House to adopt a more rational approach. I can't say my protests had much substantive effect, but the White House must have realized that "deficits don't matter" sounded extreme, because it adjusted its language by the time President Bush presented his 2004 budget plan. "My administration firmly believes in controlling the deficit and reducing it as the economy strengthens and our national security interests are met," he declared to Congress on February 3, 2003. He went on to argue that deficits for the moment were inevitable because of the need for new tax cuts to stimulate growth and the need for new spending to fund the war against terror. The next day John Snow, who had recently succeeded Paul O'Neill as Treasury chief, struck a similar note. "Deficits matter," he told the House Ways and Means Committee, but the ones projected in the president's new budget were both "manageable" and "unavoidable."

The new budget to me was a little more discouraging. Outlays totaled more than $2.2 trillion, and the bottom line was a projected deficit of more than $300 billion in both 2003 and 2004, and another $200 billion (using rather rosy assumptions, I thought) in 2005. The proposal, predictably, provided for substantial spending jumps for homeland security and defense. Yet it did not include funding for the looming war in Iraq. (If that occurred, the administration would have to seek a special appropriation, which would push the deficit still higher.)

The budget's centerpiece was a second major round of tax cuts, which President Bush had initially proposed a few weeks before. Of these, the most costly was the partial elimination of the double taxation of dividends. For years, I have advocated the full elimination of the double taxation of corporate dividends as an incentive to capital investment. The new plan also accelerated Bush's across-the-board income tax reductions so that they would take effect right away, and made permanent the repeal of the estate tax. Bottom line, the tax package was projected to add $670 billion (or more than $1 trillion, if the cuts were made permanent) over ten years to the $1.35 trillion cost of Bush's first round of tax relief.

Mitch Daniels, the director of the Office of Management and Budget, was quick to point out that a $300 billion budget deficit was the equivalent of only 2.7 percent of GDP, relatively modest by historical standards. True, but my main concern was the failure to address the longer-term path of promised benefits that are going to leave a very large hole in future budgets. We should be preparing ourselves for the retirement of the baby boomers with balanced budgets or surpluses for the difficult years ahead.*

There was talk that additional tax cuts would revitalize economic growth. But in the Fed's analysis, the lingering lethargy reflected anxiety and uncertainty about war, not a need for more stimulus. Iraq dominated the news. On February 5, Colin Powell had given his United Nations speech accusing Iraq of hiding weapons of mass destruction; ten days later there were antiwar marches in cities around the world. Until the situation in Iraq was resolved, there was no way to know whether more tax cuts made sense. I told the Senate Banking Committee on February 11, "I am one of the few people who still are not as yet convinced that stimulus is a desirable policy at this particular point."

Far more urgent than tax cuts, I said, was the need to address the threat posed by the soaring new deficits. Bring back statutory spending caps and pay-go rules, I urged the senators. "I am concerned that, should the enforcement mechanism governing the budget process not be restored, the resulting lack of clear direction and constructive goals would allow . . . budget deficits to again become entrenched." That, in turn, would beget problems no amount of stimulus would solve. The supply-side argument that faster economic growth would make deficits easier to contain was doubtless true,

---

*Surpluses no longer pose the threat of an accumulation of private assets that they did in 2001. The level of debt is now substantially higher than contemplated in 2001.

I said. Except in the unlikely event that a tax cut is wholly saved, the part that is spent raises GDP and the tax base and hence tax receipts. Thus, the gross tax cut is larger than the loss in receipts. But there is still a loss. Given the size of the shortfalls we faced, I warned, "Economic growth cannot be safely counted upon to eliminate deficits and the difficult choices that will be required to restore fiscal discipline."

The fact that I was openly challenging the administration's plan caused a stir. "No, Mr. President: Greenspan Delivers a Stern Rebuke on Rising Deficits" was a headline the next morning in the *Financial Times*. But the headlines in U.S. papers showed that I had failed to shift the debate to where it belonged. I was trying to get people to see the need for fiscal restraint, encompassing not just taxes but more important, spending. Yet all anyone focused on was taxes. The *Washington Post* wrote, "Greenspan Says Tax Cuts Are Premature; War Fears Blamed for Stagnation." "Greenspan Advises Putting Tax Cuts on Hold," said *USA Today*. Nor did anyone in the congressional leadership take up the cause of budgetary controls.

The tax-cuts issue briefly became a media circus. That week, more than 450 economists, including ten Nobel laureates, published a letter arguing that the tax cuts proposed by Bush would drive up the deficits without much helping the economy; the White House countered with a letter, signed by 250 economists, supporting its plan. I knew many of the names— the 450 were mainly Keynesians and the 250 were mainly supply-siders. The entire debate shed less light than heat, and was quickly eclipsed by the war in Iraq. By May, when Congress gave the president the tax cut he wanted and he signed it into law, the need for budgetary discipline was nowhere on the priority list. I knew how Cassandra must have felt.

During the Bush administration, particularly after 9/11, I spent more time at the White House than ever before in my Fed career. At least once a week, I'd make the short walk from my office to the elevator that took me to the Fed garage for the half-mile drive to the southwest gate. These trips sometimes involved routine meetings with National Economic Council chief Steve Friedman, his successor Al Hubbard, or other senior economic officials. Periodically I would visit with Dick Cheney, Condo-

leezza Rice, Andy Card, or any of a number of other officials. And sometimes, of course, I'd be there to see the president.

I was back to being a consultant. The agendas of these meetings covered
international economics, the global dynamics of energy and oil, the future
of Social Security, deregulation, accounting fraud, problems with Fannie
Mae and Freddie Mac, and, when appropriate, monetary policy. Many of
the ideas I worked hardest to convey appear in the chapters that follow.

The Bush administration turned out to be very different from the reincarnation of the Ford administration that I had imagined. Now, the political operation was far more dominant. As Fed chairman I was an independent
force, and I'd been around for quite a long while, but I certainly did not
qualify as part of the inner circle, nor did I want to be.

It quickly became clear that there was no room in the administration
for an outspoken deficit hawk like Paul O'Neill. Initiatives he and I spent
many hours planning—the transition to Social Security private accounts,
for example, and a strict new law to govern CEO accountability—got no
better reception than the triggers we'd advocated during the first round of
tax cuts. Paul's outspokenness put him at odds with the administration,
which emphasized loyalty and staying on message. Paul spent much of his
two years as treasury secretary feuding with the Bush economists, especially Larry Lindsey, the primary architect of the tax cuts. After the 2002
election, the White House obtained both men's resignations. It replaced
Paul with another former CEO, John Snow, who had headed the giant railroad company CSX. John proved to be a better administrator than Paul
and a smoother, much more effective spokesman for economic policy, which
was all that the White House wanted its treasury secretary to be.

The president and I continued to relate much as we had that first
morning at the Madison Hotel. Several times each year, he would invite me
to lunch in his private dining room, usually with Vice President Cheney,
Andy Card, and one of the economic advisers. In these meetings, as in the
first, I would do most of the talking, about global economic trends and
problems. I talked so much that I don't recall ever having time to eat. I
would end up grabbing a bite back at my office.

For the five years we overlapped, President Bush honored his commitment to the autonomy of the Fed. Of course, during most of that time we

kept short-term interest rates extremely low, so there wasn't much to complain about. Yet even in 2004, after economic growth returned and the FOMC began ratcheting up rates, the White House did not comment. Meanwhile the president remained tolerant of, if not receptive to, my criticism of his fiscal policy. Barely a month after I countered his argument for the urgency of another tax cut, for instance, he announced he intended to nominate me for a fifth term as chairman. This caught me by surprise; my fourth term wasn't even due to expire for another year.

The administration also took the Fed's advice on policies we thought were essential for the health of the financial markets. Most important was the effort that began in 2003 to curb excesses at Fannie Mae and Freddie Mac, the companies chartered by Congress to help underwrite home mortgages. They are granted a de facto subsidy by financial markets in the form of interest rates with very low credit-risk premiums on their debt—the markets presume Uncle Sam will bail them out in the event of default. Fannie and Freddie had been using this subsidy to pad their profits and grow. But their dealings had begun to distort and endanger the markets and seemed likely to become a bigger and bigger problem. The companies employed skillful lobbyists and had powerful advocates in Congress. President Bush had very little to gain politically by supporting a crackdown. Yet he backed the Fed through a two-year struggle that resulted in crucial reforms.

My biggest frustration remained the president's unwillingness to wield his veto against out-of-control spending. Not long ago I had occasion to assess the change in fiscal status of the United States since January 2001, when the administration took office. I compared the budget outlook through September 2006, under the then current policy (existing law and budget conventions) as estimated by the Congressional Budget Office, with the actual outcomes through 2006. Debt to the public outstanding projected for the end of September 2006 was $1.2 trillion. The actual outcome was $4.8 trillion. That is a rather large miss. To be sure, a significant part of the shortfall in receipts owed to the CBO's failure to judge adequately the looming shortfall in capital gains and other taxes related to the stock-market decline. But by 2002, that was already known to the administration and the Congress— and they altered their policy approach very little.

The rest of the shortfall owes to policy: tax cuts and spending increases. The costs of the Iraq war and antiterrorism measures do not explain the gap. Appropriations for both totaled $120 billion in fiscal year 2006, the Congressional Budget Office estimated. This is a large sum, but in a $13 trillion economy, it's readily absorbable. Federal outlays on national defense, which in fiscal 2000 hit a sixty-year low of 3 percent of GDP, jumped back to around 4 percent in 2004 and have since flattened out—they were 4.1 percent in 2006. (By comparison, national defense spending at the height of the Vietnam War absorbed 9.5 percent of GDP, and during the Korean War, more than 14 percent.)

But spending in the civilian sector, so-called nondefense discretionary outlays, has soared past the projections made in the surplus-rich days of the new millennium. Most dispiriting to me was the enactment in late 2003 of the prescription drug act. Instead of incorporating much-needed Medicare reforms, it was estimated to add more than $500 billion over ten years to the system's vast and intractable costs. While it allowed the president to check off another of his campaign promises, it provided no way to come up with the needed funds.

This wasn't an isolated event. As the administration and Congress set a course toward a federal deficit of more than $400 billion in 2004, Republicans actually tried to rationalize the abandonment of the libertarian small-government ideal. "It turned out the American people did not want a major reduction of government," wrote Congressman John Boehner of Ohio in a position paper just after the drug bill passed. Boehner had been an architect of the Republican takeover of the House nine years before, but now the party was facing "new political realities," he said. Rather than shrinking the size of government, the best that could be hoped for was slowing its growth. "Republicans have accepted such realities as the burdens of majority governance," he wrote. Bigger but more efficient government should be the new goal, he and other party leaders argued. They achieved the former, but not the latter.

The reality was even uglier. For many party leaders, altering the electoral process to create a permanent Republican-led government became a major goal. House Speaker Hastert and House majority leader Tom DeLay seemed readily inclined to loosen the federal purse strings any time it might help add a few more seats to the Republican majority. The Senate leadership proved only somewhat better. Majority leader Bill Frist, an exceptionally intelligent physician who favored fiscal discipline, lacked the force of personality to do the necessary head-knocking. Conservatives like Phil Gramm, John McCain, Chuck Hagel, and John Sununu usually found their warnings unheard.

Congress was too busy feeding at the trough. The abuse of "earmarks" became extreme, as politicians exercised this power to direct government spending to particular projects, leading to lobbying and corruption scandals in 2005. The Pork Barrel Reduction Act, introduced afterward by a bipartisan group led by McCain, observed that earmarks in congressional appropriations had proliferated from 3,023 in 1996, at the end of Clinton's first term, to nearly 16,000 in 2005, the start of Bush's second. The total dollar amount of the pork was harder to gauge—some earmarks are legitimate—but by any definition, it was in the tens of billions of dollars. Admittedly, such sums are a very small percentage of the $2 trillion-plus federal budget, but that is not the point. Earmarks are the canaries in the coal mine when it comes to the collapse of fiscal discipline. And the canaries looked sick.

After the Republicans lost control of Congress in the November 2006 election, former House Republican majority leader Dick Armey published a perceptive op-ed piece in the *Wall Street Journal*. Its headline was "End of the Revolution," and it harked back to the 1994 Republican takeover of Congress:

> Our primary question in those early years was: *How do we reform government and return money and power back to the American people?* Eventually, the policy innovators and the "Spirit of '94" were largely replaced by political bureaucrats driven by a narrow vision. Their question became: *How do we hold on to political power?* The aberrant behavior and scandals that ended up defining the Republican majority in 2006 were a direct consequence of this shift.

Armey had it exactly right. The Republicans in Congress lost their way. They swapped principle for power. They ended up with neither. They deserved to lose.

Tears welled in my eyes as I observed the throngs of Americans standing in silent tribute to Gerald R. Ford in the waning days of 2006. They lined the streets as a motorcade delivered the body of the thirty-eighth president of the United States from Andrews Air Force Base to the Capitol, where it would lie in state. At ninety-three, he had been our longest-living president. It was remarkable to see Washington, D.C., so torn with partisan strife and harboring a dysfunctional government, universally embrace this symbol of bipartisan camaraderie of a distant era. It was a tribute to this genial soul, but also evidence of Americans' thirst for the civility in politics that Ford represented and that had long since departed.

Ford was beaten by Jimmy Carter in the presidential election of 1976, and it was symbolic that Carter delivered one of the eulogies as Ford was put to rest in Grand Rapids, Michigan, mourned by the people whom he had represented in the Congress for a quarter century. What cost Ford the 1976 election was the presidential pardon he had granted Richard Nixon. That decision had created a firestorm among the Democrats, who wanted Nixon held accountable for his malfeasance in office. Yet as the years passed, many prominent Democrats came to believe that Ford's pardon had been essential to getting the trauma of Watergate behind us. Senator Ted Kennedy called it "an extraordinary act of courage."*

As I looked out the window of my car in the procession on that sunny day, only yards from the hearse carrying Ford's casket (I was an honorary pallbearer), I couldn't help but wonder what had happened to American politics since Jerry Ford would battle Tip O'Neill, then Speaker of a Democratic Congress, from 9 a.m. to 5 p.m., but still invite his longtime friend for evening cocktails at the White House.

I joined the Ford administration in August 1974, with the trauma of Watergate still gripping Washington. Yet partisan fervor was largely set aside as the sun went down. The dinners I attended (a Washington political

---

*Senator Kennedy made this statement on May 21, 2001, as Ford was awarded the John F. Kennedy Profile in Courage Award by the Kennedy Library in Boston.

ritual) were invariably bipartisan. Senators and representatives from both parties would mix with administration stalwarts, the media, and the city's social power brokers. During 2005, my last full year in government, the ritual dinners were still there, but they had become intensely partisan. On many occasions, I was the only Republican present. And at "Republican dinners" I attended, there were few, if any, Democrats. The annual black-tie events sponsored mainly by the media—the Gridiron and other correspondents' dinners—were as bipartisan as they'd been in my Ford years. But the camaraderie at those events was forced and synthetic.

There is considerable academic analysis but little agreement about the causes of partisan frictions. There is even an intriguing thesis that the halcyon days of bipartisan camaraderie in the 1950s and 1960s were the historical aberration, and today's frictions are not much out of line with history. From my narrower perch, where I watched Nixon's "Southern strategy" successfully evolve in his 1968 campaign, it seemed that the roots of our political dysfunction trace back to a shift in southern conservative congressional representation from Democratic to Republican control following the Civil Rights Act of 1964. Democrats greatly outnumbered Republicans in the 1960s, and for almost all of the years since the New Deal they had controlled the Congress and the White House. With a lock on the South, southern Democrats built up important seniority in the Congress and had been dominant as committee chairmen since the presidency of Franklin D. Roosevelt. The uneasy coalition of northern liberals and southern conservatives had yet to fragment over civil rights and fiscal policy.

Legend has it that Lyndon Johnson declared of the Democratic Party when signing the Civil Rights Act, "We have lost the South for a generation." If he said it, he was prophetic. Southern Democratic senators led by Richard B. Russell of Georgia felt betrayed by their leader from Texas. The Democrats' senatorial representation from the states of the Deep South declined from seventeen of eighteen in 1964 to four of eighteen in the Congress elected in 2004. The Democrats' share in the House declined commensurately. With the movement of northern industry to the South, a trend that began after World War II, the lock the Democrats had on southern politics was bound to change. There is little doubt, however, that the

Civil Rights Act accelerated the process. I am saddened that from a Republican perspective, a good outcome was achieved for the wrong reasons.

The four congressional caucuses, two in each body, have shifted dramatically over the years. Each caucus, two Republican, two Democratic, used to comprise liberals, moderates, and conservatives. To be sure, the proportions differed by party, but there was rarely enough cohesion to produce overwhelming majorities for any piece of legislation in any of the four caucuses. Votes on legislation typically would be Democrats 60 percent for, 40 percent against, and Republicans 40 percent for, 60 percent against, or vice versa.

Today's congressional caucuses, reflecting the reorientation of party affiliations in the South, have become either predominantly liberal (the Democrats) or conservative (the Republicans). Accordingly, legislation that used to split party votes 60 percent to 40 percent is now more likely to be 95 percent to 5 percent. Legislation has consequently become highly partisan.

One could argue that over our long history there's never been any love lost between liberals and conservatives. But people did not run under the banner of a "Conservative Party" or a "Liberal Party." The mechanisms of governing—committee assignments and leadership posts—were Democratic or Republican, and party power held sway. The eventual dominance of Republicans in southern state politics brought the two major parties to numerical parity but, in the process, induced an ideological divide between conservative Republicans and liberal Democrats. It has left a vast untended center from which a viable, well-financed independent presidential candidate could conceivably emerge in 2008 or, if not then, in 2012.

The political chasm has gone beyond the titillation of political pundits. Governance has become dangerously dysfunctional. The media and the large crowds paying extraordinary tribute to Gerald Ford were also mourning the demise of collegial politics. Americans had voted the Republicans out of congressional leadership less than two months earlier. I don't think the Democrats won. It was the Republicans who lost. The Democrats came to power in the Congress because they were the only party left standing.

I often wonder if a ticket of a Republican for president and a Democrat for vice president, or the reverse, would attract the vast untended center. Perhaps this issue wouldn't matter if the world were at peace. With the increasing prominence of the "invisible hand" of globalization effectively overseeing the billions of daily economic decisions, who the leaders are would be less important. But that has not been the case since 9/11. Who holds the reins of government matters.

THE UNIVERSALS OF ECONOMIC GROWTH

As chairman of the Fed, I often found that dealing with the urgent issues confronting U.S. economic policy required exploring the many ways human nature and market forces interact. I've told the story in the preceding chapters of how I came to understand the workings of the economic world—a sixty-year learning process. In the chapters that follow, I will set forth some of the conclusions I've reached; I'll try to convey my understanding of the forces that bind together the world economy and drive its evolution, as well as the forces that threaten to pull it apart.

I identified early in my professional career competition as the primary driver of economic growth and standards of living in the United States. In moving to a global context decades later, I was required to alter my perspective very little. When I was nominated in 1987 by President Reagan to chair the Federal Reserve Board, numerous commentators expressed concern about my lack of international economic experience. For good reason. In running the domestically oriented Townsend-Greenspan, I had little exposure to the international economy aside from the economics of international oil. My stint at the Council of Economic Advisors in the mid-

1970s did expose me to the successes and travails of Europe, and to some extent those of emerging Asia. But it was not until I arrived at the Federal Reserve in August 1987 that I immersed myself in the details of the rest of the world and the forces that drove it. Latin America's periodic crises during the 1980s and 1990s, the collapse of the Soviet Union and its economy, Mexico's near default in 1995, and the scary financial crises that spread across emerging markets, culminating in Russia's default in 1998, dramatically rearranged my priorities and focus. My first tutor at the Federal Reserve was the head of its Division of International Finance, Ted Truman. A distant relative of President Harry Truman, he had earned a Ph.D. from Yale, where he taught for several years before joining the Fed's staff. I absorbed a great deal from Ted, but after a long, distinguished Federal Reserve career, in 1998 Truman was appointed assistant secretary of the treasury for international affairs. His replacement, Karen Johnson, with a doctorate from MIT, continued my education.

During my Fed years, I interacted with experts on virtually every international economic issue imaginable, from the opaque budget accounting rules governing our financial contributions to the IMF to the economics of China's Pearl River delta. I also had to continually recalibrate my views of how the U.S. economy worked in the context of ever-expanding globalization. Overseeing my schooling on the U.S. economy in addition to Don Kohn was David Stockton, the Fed's chief economist since 2000 and a Fed staffer since 1981. He never sought nor received the press that Fed governors get, but when the governors gave speeches, it was his forecast of the U.S. economy that Fed watchers were getting. We governors learned to see him as the indispensable, behind-the-scenes staffer.*

Long before Adam Smith wrote his 1776 masterpiece, *An Inquiry into the Nature and Causes of the Wealth of Nations*, people were arguing over the shortest, straightest path to prosperity. Truly it is an argument without end. But even so, the data point to three important characteristics influencing global growth: (1) the extent of competition domestically, and,

---

*David is so low-key that it wasn't until after we'd worked together closely for years that I learned that his distant forebear, Richard Stockton, was a signer of the Declaration of Independence.

especially for developing nations, the extent of a country's openness to trade and its integration with the rest of the world; (2) the quality of a country's institutions that make an economy work; and (3) the success of its policymakers in implementing the measures necessary for macroeconomic stability.

But while there appears to be a general consensus that these three conditions are essential to prosperity, I suspect that if economic-development experts were polled, many would offer them in different orders of importance and probably also highlight different aspects of each one. My experience leads me to consider state-enforced property rights as the key growth-enhancing institution. For if those rights were not enforced, open trade and the huge benefits of competition and comparative advantage would be seriously and dramatically impeded.

People generally do not exert the effort to accumulate the capital necessary for economic growth unless they can own it. Ownership, of course, can be quite conditional. Do I own a parcel of land outright, or are there so many easements that it is of very little value to me? Or, most important, if governments at their discretion can seize my property, how valuable are my property rights? Under constant fear of expropriation, what effort will I put forward to improve my property? And what price can I set for it if I choose to sell it?

It has been startling to see over the years what even a little private ownership will do. When China granted highly diluted rights of ownership to the rural residents who tilled vast community-owned agricultural plots, yield per acre and rural standards of living rose measurably. It was an unrelentingly embarrassing stain on the Soviet Union's central planning that a very substantial percentage of its crops came from "privately owned" plots that covered only a small fraction of tilled land.

As living requires physical property—food, clothing, homes—people need the legal protection to own and dispose of such property without the threat of arbitrary confiscation by the state or mobs in the street. To be sure, people have to and do survive in totalitarian societies. But theirs is a lesser existence. John Locke, the seventeenth-century British philosopher whose contributions to the Enlightenment evoked a set of principles that profoundly influenced the notions of the Founding Fathers of the United

States, wrote in 1690 that man "hath by nature a power" to preserve "his life, liberty and estate, against the injuries and attempts of other men."*

Regrettably, the notion of rights to capital and other income-earning assets remains conflicted, especially in societies that still believe that profit seeking is not quite moral. A key purpose of property rights, after all, is to protect assets in order to use them to profit. Such rights are not supportable in a society that holds any significant remnant of the Marxist view of property as "theft." That notion rests on the presumption that wealth created under a division of labor is produced jointly, and hence is owned collectively. Any rights inhering in an individual therefore must be "stolen" from society as a whole. Such a view, of course, predates Marx and has deep roots in many religions.

The presumption of individual property ownership and the legality of its transfer must be deeply embedded in the culture of a society for free-market economies to function effectively. In the West, the moral validity of property rights is accepted, or at least acquiesced in, by virtually the whole of the population. Attitudes toward property ownership are passed from one generation to the next through family values and education. These attitudes derive from the deepest values governing social interaction that people hold. Hence, the transition from the so-called collective rights of socialist economies to the individual property rights of market economies can be expected to be slow. Altering what a nation teaches its children is difficult and cannot be accomplished overnight.

Clearly, not all democracies protect the private right of property with the same fervor. Indeed, they vary widely. India, the largest democracy in the world, has so much regulation of business activity that it significantly weakens the right to freely use and dispose of individual property, an essential measure of the degree of property-rights protection. Nor is it the

---

*Locke's assertion, in his *Second Treatise of Civil Government*, is worth citing in full: "Man being born, as has been proved, with a title to perfect freedom, and an uncontrouled enjoyment of all the rights and privileges of the law of nature, equally with any other man, or number of men in the world, hath by nature a power, not only to preserve his property, that is, his life, liberty and estate, against the injuries and attempts of other men; but to judge of, and punish the breaches of that law in others, as he is persuaded the offence deserves, even with death itself, in crimes where the heinousness of the fact, in his opinion, requires it" (chapter 7, section 87).

case that all societies with firmly protected property rights bend invariably to the majority will of the populace on all public issues. Certainly in its earlier years Hong Kong did not have a democratic process but a "list of rights" protected by British common law. Singapore, from a similar heritage, protects property and contract rights, the crucial pillars of market efficiency, but lacks other characteristics of Western democracies with which we are familiar. Nonetheless, democracies with a free press and protection of minority rights are the most effective form of government that safeguards property rights, largely because such democracies rarely allow discontent to rise to a point that leads to explosive changes in economic regimes. Authoritarian capitalism, on the other hand, is inherently unstable because it forces aggrieved citizens to seek redress outside the law. That risk is capitalized in higher financing costs.

While the debate over property rights and democracy will doubtless persist, I was taken with an observation made by Amartya Sen, the Nobel Prize winner in economics: "In the terrible history of famines in the world, no substantial famine has ever occurred in any independent and democratic country with a relatively free press. We cannot find exceptions to this rule, no matter where we look." With the media in authoritarian regimes tending toward self-censorship, market-interventionist policies—the most prevalent cause of disrupted distribution of food—go unreported and uncorrected until too late.

The importance of property rights is a larger issue than that of creating incentives to invest by established business or even incentives for inventors tinkering in a garage. Hernando de Soto, the Peruvian economist, came to the Federal Reserve in January 2003 to brief me on a seemingly radical idea to elevate the standard of living of a significant segment of the world's impoverished. One of the aspects of my job was meeting with foreign visitors who passed through my office when they were in town. These opportunities were a valuable source of information for me and the Fed staff members who often sat in on the meetings. De Soto's reputation, at least as best I could judge it, was of a well-intentioned but misguided idealist, or somewhat less flatteringly, a Don Quixote attacking windmills. His simple notion was that most poverty-stricken squatters had effective use of property—homes or land—but suffered from the lack of legal title that would enable them to sell the property for cash or use it as collateral for a loan from a bank or other financial institution. If a clear, legal title to the property could be established, large amounts of wealth would be unlocked. I thought it a novel idea worth considering; certainly other theories of development had little to show for themselves, despite the vast sums of official foreign aid spent on them since World War II.

In any event, I was sufficiently intrigued to meet with de Soto. His calculations suggested untapped property values exceeding $9 trillion worldwide. If even remotely accurate, it would be a notable addition to the value of legally protected property. He had been meeting with politicians in many developing countries to try to bring legal clarity to much of the poverty-stricken world's de facto land ownership. De Soto was optimistic, but I did not believe he was likely to make as much progress as he hoped.

After he departed, I wondered: Is it possible that he is onto something that we have somehow missed? It was evident to me that he would have difficulty persuading often corrupt politicians to cede the rights to what amounted to de facto, if not de jure, state property. There were two seemingly insurmountable barriers to de Soto's goals. First, a significant number of developing-world politicians believe in some form of collective ownership, even if they shy away from the notion that property is theft. Perhaps more relevant, granting legal authority to sell or collateralize squatters' land would empower a significant segment of a society, with a comparable dilution of politicians' power. Legalization would remove the latent power to confiscate at will large segments of squatters' land. However, recent incidents in China suggest how politically destabilizing that can be. In the endeavor to modernize, many provincial and local Chinese authorities in their version of creative destruction periodically confiscate peasants' land for development. Riots have been widespread. Granting clear legal ownership rights to peasants for the land they till would go a very long way toward putting an end to such discontent.* Though the means to get there may not be altogether clear, Hernando de Soto's goal is a very appealing one.

Protection of property has always been a moving target as the law continually tries to keep up with the nature of economic change. Even in the

---

*"Recognition" of property rights by China's National Congress of the People in March 2007 shied away from granting unequivocal rights to rural land.

United States, where property rights are broadly protected, the claims of property owners in New London, Connecticut, whose land was taken over by city government in 2005 for commercial redevelopment, were brought to the U.S. Supreme Court. The Court's ruling in favor of city government provoked loud outcries in the Congress. So it's not surprising that different cultures have different views as to whether and to what extent property should be protected. This issue is becoming pronounced as property is becoming increasingly intellectual. I explore that thicket in chapter 25.

While the rule of law and property rights appear to me to be the most prominent institutional pillars of economic growth and prosperity, other factors are also clearly essential.

Historically, societies that seek high levels of instant gratification and are willing to borrow against future incomes to achieve it have more often than not suffered inflation and stagnation. The economies of such societies tend to run larger government budget deficits financed with fiat money from a printing press. Eventually, the ensuing inflation leads to recession, or worse, often because central banks are forced to clamp down. Then the process starts all over again. Many countries in Latin America have been particularly prone to this "populist" malady, as I discuss in chapter 17. I regret that the United States may not be wholly immune to it.

A rarely discussed, but important, macroeconomic determinant of economic success is the extent of an economy's flexibility and hence its resilience to shocks. The bounceback of the U.S. economy following 9/11 is testament to the importance of flexibility, as I've pointed out. Moreover, flexibility and the extent of property rights are related. To obtain flexibility, the competitive marketplace must be free to adjust, which means market participants must be free to allocate property as they see fit. Restrictions on pricing, borrowing, affiliations, and market practice more generally have slowed growth. Its obverse, deregulation, is increasingly associated with "reform." (As recently as the 1960s, "reform" was associated with regulation of business. Ideas govern policy.)

Another important requirement for the proper functioning of market capitalism is also not often, if ever, covered in lists of factors contributing to economic growth and standards of living: trust in the word of others. Where the rule of law prevails, despite everyone's right to legal redress of a perceived grievance, if there is more than a small fraction of outstanding contracts that require adjudication, court systems would be overwhelmed, as would society's ability to be governed by the rule of law.

This implies that in a free society governed by the rights and responsibilities of its citizens, the vast majority of transactions must be voluntary, which, of necessity, presupposes trust in the word of those with whom we do business—in almost all cases, strangers. It is remarkable that, as I noted in an earlier chapter, large numbers of contracts, especially in financial markets, are initially oral, confirmed by a written document only at a later time, even after much price movement. It is remarkable how much trust we have in the pharmacist who fills the prescription ordered by our physician. Or the trust we grant to automakers that their motor vehicles will run as certified. We are not fools. We bank on the self-interest of our counterparties in trade. Just contemplate how little business would get done if that were not the prevailing culture in which we lived. The division of labor so essential to our standard of living would not exist.

As I noted earlier, material well-being—that is, wealth creation—requires people to take risks. We can't be sure our actions to acquire food, clothing, and shelter, for example, will succeed. But the greater our trust in the people with whom we trade, the greater the accumulation of wealth. In a market system based on trust, reputation will have a significant economic value. Reputation, capitalized formally as "goodwill" on business balance sheets or otherwise, is an important contributor to the market value of a company.

Reputation and the trust it fosters have always appeared to me to be the core required attributes of market capitalism. Laws at best can prescribe only a small fraction of the day-by-day activities in the marketplace. When trust is lost, a nation's ability to transact business is palpably undermined. In the marketplace, uncertainties created by not always truthful counterparties raise credit risk and thereby increase real interest rates.

As a bank regulator for more than eighteen years, I came to recognize that government regulation cannot substitute for individual integrity. In fact, any form of government guarantees of credit lessens the need of financial counterparties to earn a reputation for honest dealings. It is conceivable, of course, that government guarantees are superior to an individual's reputation. But guarantees—even the most widely praised, such as deposit insurance—have costly consequences. I concluded, and I suspect most regulators agree, that the first and most effective line of defense against fraud and insolvency is counterparties' surveillance. For example, JPMorgan thoroughly scrutinizes the balance sheet of Merrill Lynch before it lends. It does not look to the Securities and Exchange Commission to verify Merrill's solvency.

While banking and medicine may be the most visible exemplars of the market value of reputation, it is pervasive throughout all professions. When I was a child, jokes about the scruples of used-car salesmen were widespread, but in truth a flagrantly unscrupulous used-car salesman is one who will be out of business before long. These days, almost every professional field is constrained by *some* regulatory framework, so it's harder than it once was to isolate the reputation effect, but a sector in which one can is e-commerce. Alibris, for example, is a Web site that acts as a broker between sellers and buyers of used books. If you were eager to buy an early edition of Adam Smith's *The Wealth of Nations*, you might search on Alibris for the names of booksellers around the country who had copies for sale. Customers are given the opportunity to rate the reliability of booksellers from whom they've purchased at least one book, and those ratings no doubt play an important role in the decision as to which of several booksellers to use. This form of public feedback is a powerful incentive to booksellers to be honest about the condition of their wares, and to fulfill orders fully and promptly. But no one is immune to customer skepticism: as Fed chairman, I was queried by fellow central bankers with large holdings of U.S. dollars about whether dollars were safe investments.

More surprising than any list of key factors for growth and improved standards of living is what would *not* be on such a list. How is it possible that a superabundance of natural resources—oil, gas, copper, iron ore—would not significantly add to a nation's production and wealth? Paradoxically, most analysts conclude that, particularly in developing countries, natural-resource bonanzas tend to reduce rather than enhance living standards.

The danger takes the form of an economic affliction nicknamed "Dutch disease." (The *Economist* coined the term in the 1970s to describe the travails of manufacturers in the Netherlands after the discovery there of natural gas.) Dutch disease strikes when foreign demand for an export drives up the exchange value of the exporting country's currency. This increase in the currency's value makes the nation's other export products less competitive. Analysts often cite this pattern as a reason why relatively resource-poor Hong Kong, Japan, and Western Europe have thrived while oil-rich Nigeria and others have not.*

"Ten years from now, twenty years from now, you will see: Oil will bring us ruin," is how former Venezuelan oil minister and OPEC cofounder Juan Pablo Pérez Alfonso put it in the 1970s. He correctly foresaw the inability of virtually all OPEC nations to use their riches to diversify significantly beyond petroleum and related products. Besides distorting the value of the currency, natural-resource wealth often has crippling social effects. Easy, unearned wealth tends to dampen productivity, it turns out. Some Gulf oil states have extended so many amenities to their citizens that those without an inbred will to work don't. Mundane tasks fall to immigrants and guest workers who gladly collect what is to them a good wage. There are political effects too: a ruling clique can use part of the resource revenue to placate the population and keep people from marching against the regime.

No wonder tiny São Tomé and Príncipe off the west coast of Africa, upon the discovery in its territorial waters of significant reservoirs of crude oil, had a mixed reaction about exploiting them. President Fradique de Menezes remarked in 2003: "I have promised my people that we will avoid what some call 'the Dutch disease,' or 'the crude awakening' or 'the curse of oil.' Statistics show that resource-rich developing countries perform markedly worse in terms of GDP development than resource-poor coun-

---

*In the Dutch case, heavy foreign demand for the gas led to large purchases of guilders, which drove up the value of the Dutch currency relative to the dollar, the deutsche mark, and all other major currencies. This meant that Dutch exports of anything other than natural gas were put at a competitive disadvantage in world markets. Producers of export goods paid wages and other costs in guilders, which with their higher foreign-exchange value meant higher costs denominated in dollars and other currencies. To sell competitively in foreign markets, Dutch nongas exporters would receive fewer guilders for their wares and would have to live with lower profit margins, or—more likely—raise prices in dollars and sell less. The condition became known as the Dutch disease even though the Netherlands handled the problem without major disruption.

tries. Their social indicators are also below average. In São Tomé and Príncipe we are determined to avoid this paradox of plenty."

Dutch disease primarily afflicts developing countries because they are ill-prepared to fend it off. At the same time, the scale of the challenge tends to be greater: since nature distributes its treasures without regard to the size or sophistication of national economies, resource bonanzas are more apt to dwarf the GDP of a developing country than that of a developed one. In general, it appears that if a country is "developed" before the discovery of a natural-resource bonanza, it is immune to any long-lasting pernicious effect. Nevertheless, Dutch disease can strike anywhere. Great Britain went through an apparent bout of it in the early 1980s, following the development of North Sea oil. As Britain changed from a net importer of oil to a net exporter, the dollar-sterling exchange rate rose and the prices of British export goods temporarily became increasingly uncompetitive. Norway, with a population of less than five million, had to take dramatic action to insulate its small economy from the North Sea oil bonanza. The country created a large stabilization fund that reduced pressure on the krone's exchange rate after it spiked in the late 1970s. And in the wake of the collapse of Communism, Russia is struggling with a mild form of Dutch disease today.

Over the past thirty-five years, as many countries have labored to liberalize their economies and improve the quality of their policies, global per capita income has risen steadily. This has especially been the case in countries that previously were fully or partially centrally planned and that, since the fall of the Berlin Wall, have embraced some form of market capitalism. I recognize that poverty rates are notoriously hard to quantify, but according to the World Bank, the number of people living on less than $1 per day, a commonly used extreme-poverty threshold, has fallen dramatically from 1,247 million in 1990 to 986 million in 2004. In addition, since 1970, the infant mortality rate has declined by more than half, school enrollment rates have risen steadily, and literacy rates are up.*

---

*Figures on world poverty rates are from the World Bank and a 2002 study by Columbia University economist Xavier Sala-i-Martin. The $1-per-day threshold is measured in 1985 dollars on a purchasing power parity basis. Economists use purchasing power parity as an alternative to market exchange rates when gauging and comparing outputs and incomes across

While, from a global perspective, wealth and the overall quality of life have risen, that success has not been uniform across regions or countries. The economies of East Asia are often-cited success stories. Some, including China, Malaysia, South Korea, and Thailand, stand out not only as growing very strongly but also as having seen the greatest declines in poverty rates. Moreover, Asia was not alone. Per capita incomes in Latin America also expanded during the period, and poverty rates fell, although progress was somewhat slower. But, sadly, levels of per capita income in many countries in sub-Saharan Africa have fallen.

It is striking to me that our ideas about the efficacy of market competition have remained essentially unchanged since the eighteenth-century Enlightenment, when they first emerged, to a remarkable extent, largely from the mind of one man, Adam Smith. With the demise of central planning at the end of the twentieth century, the forces of capitalism have had free rein, prodded by ever-expanding globalization. No doubt economists' views of what works to enhance material well-being will continue to evolve over time. Still, in a sense, the history of market competition and the capitalism it represents is the story of the ebb and flow of Smith's ideas. Accordingly, the story of his work and its reception repays special attention. It also serves to pave the way for my next chapter, which addresses the great "problem" inherent in capitalism: that creative destruction is often, and by a great many, viewed simply as destruction. The history of Smith's ideas is the history of attitudes toward the social dislocation capitalism brings and its potential remedies.

Born in Kirkcaldy, Scotland, in 1723, Smith lived in an era influenced by the ideas and events of the Reformation. For the first time in the history of Western civilization, individuals began to view themselves as able to act independently of ecclesiastic and state restraint. Modern notions of political and economic freedom gained currency. Those ideas taken together were the beginnings of the Age of Enlightenment, especially in France, Scotland, and

---

countries. It is a useful if inexact way to measure the standard of living of residents of an economy, in part because it takes into account "nontradable" goods and services—for example, a man's haircut. The World Bank bases PPP on the 1985 prices of basic goods and services in local currencies, adjusting for inflation. It uses purchasing power parity in its calculations of world poverty rates at $1 and $2 a day.

England. Suddenly, there was a vision of a society in which individuals guided by reason were at liberty to choose their destinies. What we now know as the rule of law—specifically, the protection of the rights of individuals and their property—became firmly established, encouraging people to produce, trade, and innovate. Market forces began eroding the rigid customs that had lingered from feudal and medieval times.

At the same time, the nascent Industrial Revolution was causing turmoil and dislocation. Factories and railroads reconfigured the English landscape, farmlands were converted to sheep meadows to supply a new, booming textile industry, and enormous numbers of peasants were uprooted. The new industrialist class came into conflict with the aristocracy, whose wealth was based on inherited estates. The protectionist thinking known as mercantilism, which served the interests of landowners and colonialists, began losing its hold over commerce and trade.

Amid these complex and bewildering circumstances, Adam Smith identified a set of principles that brought conceptual clarity to the seeming chaos of economic activity. Smith framed a global view of how market economies, just then emerging, worked. He offered the first comprehensive examination of why some countries are able to achieve high standards of living while others make little progress.

Smith started out as a lecturer in Edinburgh; he soon moved to Glasgow, where he had first attended university, as a professor. One of his areas of expertise was what he called "the progress of opulence" in society (as a profession, economics didn't yet even have a name). Over the years Smith's fascination with market behavior intensified, and after a lucrative two-year sojourn in France as tutor of a young Scottish lord, he came home to his birthplace in Kirkcaldy in 1766 and devoted himself full-time to his magnum opus.

The book he produced ten years later, which came to be known simply as *The Wealth of Nations*, is one of the great achievements in intellectual history. In effect, Smith tried to answer what is probably the most important macroeconomic question: What makes an economy grow? In *The Wealth of Nations*, he accurately identified capital accumulation, free trade, an appropriate—but circumscribed—role for government, and the rule of law as keys to national prosperity. Most important, he was the first to emphasize personal initiative: "The natural effort of every individual to better his own condition, when suffered to exert itself with freedom and security is so powerful a principle, that it is alone, and without any assistance . . . capable of carrying on the society to wealth and prosperity." He concluded that to enhance the wealth of a nation, every man, consistent with the law, should be "free to pursue his own interest his own way." Competition was a key factor because it motivated each person to become more productive, often through specialization and division of labor. And the greater the productivity, the greater the prosperity.

This led Smith to his most famous turn of phrase: individuals who compete for private gain, he wrote, act as if "led by an invisible hand" to promote the public good. The metaphor of the invisible hand, of course, captured the world's imagination—possibly because it seems to impute a godlike benevolence and omniscience to the market, whose workings are in reality as impersonal as natural selection, which Darwin came along and described more than half a century later. The expression "invisible hand" does not seem to have been very important to Smith; in all his writings, he used it only three times. The effect it describes, however, is something he discerns at every level of society, from the great flows of goods and commodities between nations to everyday neighborhood transactions: "It is not from the benevolence of the butcher, the brewer, or the baker, that we expect our dinner, but from their regard to their own interest."

Smith's insight into the importance of self-interest was all the more revolutionary in that, throughout history in many cultures, acting in one's self-interest—indeed, seeking to accumulate wealth—had been perceived as unseemly and even illegal. Yet in Smith's view, if government simply provides stability and freedom and otherwise stays out of the way, personal initiative will see to the common good. Or as he put it in a 1755 lecture: "Little else is requisite to carry a state to the highest degree of opulence from the lowest barbarism but peace, easy taxes and a tolerable administration of justice: all the rest being brought about by the natural course of things."

Smith succeeded in drawing broad inferences about the nature of commercial organization and institutions based on remarkably little empirical evidence—unlike economists today, he didn't have access to reams of government and industrial data. Yet over time, the numbers would bear him out. Throughout much of the civilized world, free-market activity first created levels of sustenance adequate to enable the population to grow and later—much later—created enough prosperity to foster a general rise in living standards and an increase in life expectancy. The latter developments opened the possibility for individuals in developed countries to establish long-term personal goals. Such a luxury had been remote to all but a sliver of earlier generations.

Capitalism also made change a way of life. For most of recorded history, people lived in societies that were static and predictable. A young twelfth-century peasant could look forward to tilling the same plot of his landlord's soil until disease, famine, natural disaster, or violence ended his life. And that end often came quickly. Life expectancy at birth was, on average, twenty-five years, about the same as it had been for the previous millennium. Moreover, the peasant could expect that his children and their children would till the same plot. Perhaps such a rigidly programmed life conferred the sense of security that comes from utter predictability, but it left little to individual enterprise.

To be sure, improved agricultural techniques and the expansion of trade beyond the largely self-sufficient feudal manor increased the division of labor, raised living standards, and allowed populations to expand in the sixteenth and seventeenth centuries. But the pace of growth was glacial. In the seventeenth century, the great mass of people still were engaged in the same productive practices as their forebears many generations earlier.

Smith held that working smarter, not merely harder, was the way to wealth. In the opening paragraphs of *The Wealth of Nations*, he underscored the crucial role played by the expansion of labor productivity. An essential determinant of a nation's standard of living, he said, was "the skill, dexterity, and judgment with which labor is generally applied." This flew in the face of earlier theories, such as the mercantilist precept that a nation's wealth was measured in troves of gold bullion, or the Physiocrat tenet that value derived from the land. "Whatever be the soil, climate, or extent of territory of any particular nation," Smith wrote, "the abundance or scantiness of its annual supply" must depend upon "the productive powers of labor." Two centuries of economic thought later, little has been added to those insights.

With the help of Smith and his immediate successors, mercantilism was gradually dismantled and economic freedom spread widely. In Britain, this process reached its finale with the 1846 repeal of the Corn Laws, a set of tariffs that for many years had blocked imports of grain, keeping grain prices and therefore landowners' rents artificially high—and elevating, of course, the price paid by industrial wage earners for a loaf of bread. The acceptance of Smith's economics was, by then, prompting the reorganization of commercial life in much of the "civilized" world.

Yet Smith's reputation and influence eroded as industrialization spread. He was no hero to many who struggled during the nineteenth and twentieth centuries against what they saw as the barbarism and injustice that accompanied laissez-faire market economies. Robert Owen, a successful British factory owner, believed that laissez-faire capitalism by its very nature could lead only to poverty and disease. He founded the utopian movement, which advocated, in Owen's phrase, "villages of cooperation." In 1826, his adherents set up New Harmony, Indiana. Ironically, strife among the residents brought New Harmony to collapse within two years. But Owen's charisma continued to draw large followings among those struggling to eke out a living in appalling working environments.

Karl Marx was dismissive of Owen and his utopians but was no devotee of Smith's. While Smith's intellectual rigor attracted him—in Marx's view, Smith and other so-called classical economists had accurately described the origins and workings of capitalism—Marx thought Smith had missed the main point, that capitalism was but a step. Marx saw it as a historical stage in an inevitable progression to the revolution of the proletariat and the triumph of communism. His followers eventually took a substantial segment of the world's population out of capitalism's way—for a while.

Unlike Marx, the Fabian socialists of the late nineteenth century were not looking for revolution. The group named itself after the ancient Roman general Fabius, who held off Hannibal's invading army with a military strategy of attrition rather than all-out confrontation. Similarly, the Fabians aimed not to destroy capitalism but to constrain it. Government, they believed, should actively safeguard public welfare from the harsh competitiveness of the marketplace. They advocated protectionism in trade and the nationalization of land, and counted among their ranks such luminaries as George Bernard Shaw, H. G. Wells, and Bertrand Russell.

The Fabians laid the groundwork for modern social democracy, and their influence on the world would end up being at least as powerful as that of Marx. While capitalism succeeded brilliantly in delivering higher and higher standards of living for workers throughout the nineteenth and twentieth centuries, it was the tempering effect of Fabian socialism that many argued would make market economies politically palatable and keep communism from spreading. Fabians took part in founding Britain's Labour Party. They also had a profound influence on British colonies as the colonies gained independence: in India in 1947, Jawaharlal Nehru drew on Fabian principles to set economic policy for one-fifth of the world's population.

When I first read Adam Smith after World War II, regard for his theories was at a low ebb. And for much of the cold war, economies on both sides of the iron curtain remained either heavily regulated or centrally planned. "Laissez-faire" was practically a term of opprobrium; the most prominent advocates of free-market capitalism were iconoclasts like Ayn Rand and Milton Friedman. The pendulum of economic thinking began to swing in Smith's favor in the late sixties, just as I began my public career. The comeback has been long and slow, particularly in his native land. A U.S. economist looking for Smith's grave in an Edinburgh churchyard in 2000 reported having to clear away beer cans and debris to read the worn inscription on the stone:

HERE ARE DEPOSITED THE REMAINS OF ADAM SMITH.
AUTHOR OF THE THEORY OF MORAL SENTIMENTS
AND WEALTH OF NATIONS.

Yet Scotland, too, has come around to according Smith the kind of honor he deserves. The way to the grave is now marked by a newly installed stone that quotes from *The Wealth of Nations*, and a college near Kirkcaldy has been renamed after Smith. A ten-foot-tall bronze statue of him is planned for Edinburgh's Royal Mile. Appropriately, it is being paid for with private funding. And, on a personal note, in late 2004 I was delighted to accept a request from my good friend Gordon Brown, Britain's longtime chancellor of the exchequer and now prime minister, to deliver the first Adam Smith Memorial Lecture in Kirkcaldy. That a leader of Britain's Labour Party, whose roots in Fabian socialism are such a far cry from the tenets espoused by Smith, would sponsor such an occasion is indeed a measure of change. As I will discuss, Britain has endeavored to join some of the tenets of the Fabians with market capitalism—a pattern that repeats itself to a greater or lesser extent throughout the trading world.

THIRTEEN

THE MODES OF CAPITALISM

A mid the remarks of the speakers in the large, crowded meeting room at IMF headquarters, I could hear the chanting and shouts of the antiglobalization dissidents on the street. It was April 2000, and somewhere between ten thousand and thirty thousand students, church group members, unionists, and environmentalists had converged on Washington to protest the spring meeting of the World Bank and the International Monetary Fund. While we finance ministers and central bankers in the room couldn't make out the words of the chants, it wasn't hard to understand the gist. They were protesting what they viewed as the depredations of increased global trade, particularly the oppression and exploitation of the poor in developing countries. I was, and am, saddened by such events, since were the protesters to succeed in destroying global trade, those most harmed would be hundreds of millions of the world's poor, the very people in whose name the protesters had chosen to speak.

While central planning may no longer be a credible form of economic organization, it is clear that the intellectual battle for its rival—free-market capitalism and globalization—is far from won. For twelve generations, capitalism has achieved one advance after another, as standards and quality of living have risen at an unprecedented rate over large parts of the globe. Poverty has been dramatically reduced and life expectancy has more than doubled. The rise in material well-being—a tenfold increase in real per capita income over two centuries—has enabled the earth to support a six-fold increase in population. Yet, for many, capitalism still seems difficult to accept, much less fully embrace.

The problem is that the dynamic that defines capitalism, that of unforgiving market competition, clashes with the human desire for stability and certainty. Even more important, a large segment of society feels a growing sense of injustice about the allocation of capitalism's rewards. Competition, capitalism's greatest force, creates anxiety in all of us. One major source of it is the chronic fear of job loss. Another, more deeply felt angst stems from competition's perpetual disturbance of the status quo and style of living, good or bad, from which most people derive comfort. I am sure the American steel manufacturers I advised in the 1950s would have been quite happy if Japanese steelmakers hadn't improved their quality and productivity so markedly. Conversely, I doubt that IBM was thrilled to see computerized word processors upstage the venerable Selectric typewriter.

Capitalism creates a tug-of-war within each of us. We are alternately the aggressive entrepreneur and the couch potato, who subliminally prefers the lessened competitive stress of an economy where all participants have equal incomes. While competition is essential to economic progress, I can't say I always personally enjoy the process. I never thought kindly of rival firms seeking to lure clients from Townsend-Greenspan. But to compete, I had to improve. I had to offer a better service. I had to become more productive. In the end, of course, I was better off for it. So were my clients, and I suspect so were my competitors as well. Down deep that is probably the message of capitalism: "creative destruction"—the scrapping of old technologies and old ways of doing things for the new—is the only way to increase productivity and therefore the only way to raise average living standards on a sustained basis. Finding gold or oil or other natural wealth, history tells us, does not do that.

There is no denying capitalism's record. Market economies have succeeded over the centuries by thoroughly weeding out the inefficient and poorly equipped, and by granting rewards to those who anticipate consumer demand and meet it with the most efficient use of labor and capital resources. Newer technologies increasingly drive this unforgiving capitalist process on a global scale. To the extent that governments "protect" portions of their populations from what they perceive as harsh competitive pressures, they achieve a lower overall material standard of living for their people.

Regrettably, economic growth cannot produce lasting contentment or happiness. Were that the case, the tenfold increase in world real per capita GDP over the past two centuries would have fostered a euphoric rise in human contentment. The evidence suggests that rising incomes do raise happiness, but only up to a point and only for a time. Beyond the point at which basic needs are met, happiness is a relative state that, over the long run, is largely detached from economic growth. The evidence shows it is determined mainly by how we view our lives and accomplishments relative to those of our peers. As prosperity spreads, or perhaps even as a result of its spread, many people fear competition and change that threaten their sense of status, which is critical to their self-esteem. Happiness depends far more on how people's incomes compare with those of their perceived peers, or even those of their role models, than on how they are doing in any absolute material sense. When graduate students at Harvard were asked a while back whether they would be happier with $50,000 a year if their peers earned half that, or $100,000 if their peers earned double that, the majority chose the lower salary. When I first saw the story, I chuckled and started to brush it off. But it struck a chord that unearthed a long-dormant memory of a fascinating 1947 study by Dorothy Brady and Rose Friedman.

Brady and Friedman presented data showing that the share of income that an American family spent on consumer goods and services was largely determined not by the level of family income but by its level relative to the nation's average family income. Thus, their study suggests that a family with the nation's average income in 2000 would be expected to spend the same proportion of its income as a family with average family income in 1900, even though in inflation-adjusted terms the 1900 income was only a small fraction of that of 2000. I reproduced and updated their calculations and confirmed their conclusion.* Consumer behavior has not changed much over the last century and a quarter.

The data made clear that how much people spent or saved was determined not by the level of their real purchasing power, but by their pecking order on the income scale, their income relative to that of others.† What is all the more remarkable about this finding is that it held even in the latter part of the nineteenth century, when households spent much more of their income on food than they did in 2004.‡

None of this would have surprised Thorstein Veblen, the American economist who in his book *The Theory of the Leisure Class*, written in 1899, famously gave the world the expression "conspicuous consumption." He noted that an individual's purchase of goods and services is tied to what used to be called "keeping up with the Joneses." If Katie had an iPod, Lisa had to have one too. I always thought Veblen carried his analysis to an extreme, but there is little doubt that he identified a very important element of the way people behave. As the data show, we are all competitively sensitive to what our peers earn and spend. They may be friends, but they are also seen as rivals in the pecking order. Individuals are demonstrably happier and less stressed as their incomes rise with a rising national economy, and rich people, surveys show, are generally happier than those lower down the income scale. But human psychology being what it is, the initial eupho-

---

*Sample surveys of U.S. consumer income and outlays have been published periodically by the U.S. Department of Labor and its predecessors since 1888. I collected data from seven surveys from 1888 to 2004. The raw survey data appeared to have no consistent pattern until I exhibited each income bracket's ratio of spending to income against each particular year's average family income. Then, as in Brady and Friedman, for all seven surveys, the ratio of spending to income for those households with a third of the nation's average income concentrates around 1.3 (their spending exceeds income by 30 percent). The spending/income ratio then falls eventually to about 0.8 at double the average income level.

†An alternate way to reach the same conclusion is to observe that there is no discernible long-term trend in the nation's household saving rate. Yet all surveys show the saving rate is higher for upper-income households than for lower-income households. For both statements to be true (and if the distribution of incomes does not veer outside its historical range), households at any given dollar income level must be saving less as the aggregate incomes rise with time. The extent of the downward creep in saving must be directly related to the growth rate of average household income.

‡Food, of course, is a very useful proxy for the subsistence level, which shouldn't be tied to where a family stood in the income pecking order.

ria of a higher standard of living soon wears off as the newly affluent adjust to their better status in life. The new level is quickly perceived as "normal." Any gain in human contentment is transitory.*

People's conflicted reactions to capitalism have spawned a variety of modes of capitalist practice in the postwar years, from highly regulated to lightly constrained. While each individual has an opinion, there is a visible tendency for much of a society to coalesce around a common point of view, which often differs measurably from the choices of other societies. This, I sense, results from the need of people to belong to groups defined by religion, culture, and history, which, in turn, is fostered by an innate need of people for leaders: of the family, the tribe, the village, the nation. It is a universal trait that probably reflects the imperative for people to make choices to govern their day-by-day behavior. Most people, much of the time, feel inadequate to the task and seek guidance from religious direction, the recommendations of family members, and the pronouncements of presidents. Almost all human organizations reflect this need for hierarchy. The shared views of any society, in practice, are views embraced by its leadership.

If happiness were tied solely to material well-being, I suspect, all forms of capitalism would converge to the American model, which has been the most dynamic and productive. But it is also the one that creates the most stress, especially in the job market. As noted in chapter 8, some four hundred thousand people in the United States lose their jobs every *week*, and another six hundred thousand change or leave jobs voluntarily. Average job tenure for Americans is 6.6 years, well short of the 10.6 years for Germans and 12.2 years for Japanese. Market-based societies, which today means virtually all, have had to choose where on the spectrum they wish to reside between two extremes that could be symbolized by two points on the map: frenetic but highly productive Silicon Valley at the one end and unchanging Venice at the other.

For each society, the choice, in effect the trade-off between material

---

*Fortunately, this psychology also works in reverse. Sharp financial adversity brings deep depression. But people not otherwise psychologically incapacitated rebound with time. Their smile returns.

wealth and lack of stress, appears to rest on its history and the culture it has spawned. By culture, I mean the shared values of members of a society that are inculcated at an early age and that pervade all aspects of living.

Some aspects of a nation's culture end up visibly affecting the GDP. Positive attitudes toward business success, for example, a deeply cultural response, have in the course of generations been an important springboard to material well-being. Clearly, a society with such attitudes will give enterprises far greater freedom to compete than a society that perceives competitive business as unethical or unsettling. In my experience, even many of those who acknowledge the advantages to material well-being of competitive capitalism are conflicted for two somewhat related reasons. First, competition and risk taking cause stress, which most people wish to avoid; second, many feel deep-seated ambivalence toward the accumulation of wealth. On the one hand, wealth is a much-sought-after means of flaunting status (Veblen would understand). But that view is opposed by the well-nurtured belief best captured by the biblical injunction "it is easier for a camel to go through the eye of a needle than for a rich man to enter the kingdom of God." The ambivalence toward accumulation of material wealth has a long cultural history that pervades society to this day. It has had a profound influence on the development of the welfare state and the social safety net that is at its core. It is argued that unconstrained risk taking increases the concentration of income and wealth. The purpose of the welfare state is to lessen that income and wealth concentration, which it does largely through legislation that, via regulation, constrains risk taking and, via taxation, reduces the pecuniary rewards that may result from taking risks.

Although the roots of socialism are secular, its political thrust parallels many religious prescriptions for a civil society, seeking to assuage the anguish of the poor. The pursuit of wealth has been deemed unethical, if not immoral, since long before the emergence of the welfare state.

This antimaterialist ethic has always been a low-intensity suppressant to the acceptance of dynamic competition and the unfettered institutions of capitalism. Many of the business titans of nineteenth-century American industry were conflicted about the morality of holding on to material gains from their ventures and gave away much of their wealth. To this day, a residue of guilt about wealth accumulation exists under the surface of our market culture, but the degree of ambivalence toward wealth accumulation and attitudes toward risk taking differ widely across the globe. Take the United States and France, for example, both of whose most fundamental values are rooted in the Enlightenment. A recent poll shows that 71 percent of Americans agree that the free-market system is the best economic system available. Only 36 percent of the French agree. Another poll indicates that three-fourths of young French men and women aspire to a job in government. Few young Americans express that preference.

Such numbers speak to a remarkable difference in risk tolerance. The French are far less inclined to suffer the competitive pressures of a free market and overwhelmingly seek the security of a government job, despite the widespread evidence that risk taking is essential for economic growth. I can't say the greater the risk taking, the greater the rate of growth. Obviously, reckless gambling rarely pays off in the end. The risk taking I have in mind is the rationally calculated kind of most business judgments. It has to be the case that restraint on freedom of action, the essence of government regulation of business, or heavy taxation of successful ventures must suppress the willingness of market participants to act. To me, the degree of willingness to take risks is, in the end, the major defining characteristic that separates countries into the various modes of capitalism. Whether different degrees of risk aversion stem from an ethical antipathy toward wealth accumulation or the stress of competitive battle does not affect the consequences. They are both captured in the choice of legal inhibitions imposed on competition that dilute laissez-faire capitalism, an important purpose of the welfare state.

But there are other, less fundamental suppressants of competitive behavior as well. Most politically prominent is the inclination of many societies to protect "national treasures" from the winds of creative destruction, or worse, foreign ownership. That is a dangerous restraint on international competition and another issue that differentiates one culture from another. In 2006, for example, French officials blocked an Italian firm's attempt to buy Suez Company, a large Paris-based utility manager, by promoting the merger of Suez and Gaz de France. Both Spain and Italy have made similarly protectionist moves.

The United States is scarcely innocent of such behavior. For example, in June 2005, China National Offshore Oil Corporation (CNOOC), a sub-sidiary of China's third-largest oil company, made a bid to buy Unocal, an American oil company, for $18.5 billion in cash. This topped an earlier $16.5 billion cash-and-stock offer from Chevron. Chevron cried foul, say-ing the bid represented unfair competition from a government-controlled company. U.S. lawmakers complained that "China's governmental pursuit of world energy resources" represented a strategic threat. By August politi-cal opposition rose to such a pitch that CNOOC withdrew its bid, saying the controversy had produced "a level of uncertainty that presents an unac-ceptable risk." Chevron got the deal, at the expense of a valuable U.S. asset: our reputation for nondiscriminatory international fair dealing, particularly our pledge to treat foreign corporations the same as domestic ones for reg-ulatory purposes.

Just three months later, an Arab corporation named Dubai Ports World bought a company that managed container terminals on the U.S. East and Gulf coasts. The deal touched off more protest in Congress, as legislators from both parties claimed that Arab management of U.S. ports would un-dermine antiterrorism efforts and hurt national security. Finally, in March 2006, under pressure, Dubai Ports World announced it would transfer man-agement of the ports to an unnamed U.S. company. It had never been shown that there was any meaningful threat to U.S. national security.

More broadly, a nation's depth of reverence for tradition and its efforts, however misguided, to protect it are rooted in the need of people to have an immutable environment, one to which they have become accustomed and that brings them joy and pride.

Although I am a strong advocate of "in with the new, out with the old," I am not an advocate of tearing down the U.S. Capitol and replacing it with a more modern, efficient office building. However, no matter what one's depth of feeling is on such issues, to the extent that creative destruc-tion is restrained to preserve icons, some improvement in material stan-dards of living is forgone.

Of course, there are other disturbing and counterproductive examples of government intervention in a country's competitive markets. When a government's leaders routinely seek out private-sector individuals or busi-nesses and, in exchange for political support, bestow favors on them, the society is said to be in the grip of "crony capitalism." Particularly appalling was Indonesia under Suharto in the last third of the twentieth century, Russia immediately following the collapse of the Soviet Union, and Mexico during its many years under the PRI (the Institutional Revolutionary Party). The favors generally take the form of monopoly access to certain markets, preferred access to sales of government assets, or special access to those in political power. Such actions distort the effective use of capital, and, accordingly, lower standards of living.

Then there is the broader issue of corruption of which crony capitalism is but a part. In general, corruption tends to exist whenever governments have favors to extend, or something to sell. If there were unobstructed, free flow of goods and people across national boundaries, customs and immigration officials, for example, would have nothing to sell. Indeed, their jobs would not exist. This was largely the case in the United States before World War I. It is difficult for a twenty-first-century American to comprehend the extent to which government was separated from business in those early years. The little corruption that existed drew large newspaper headlines. There were questionable transactions relating to the construction of canals in the early 1800s. Similarly, the building of the transcontinental railroad, with its huge land-grant subsidies, engendered much duplicitous activity, leading to the Union Pacific–Crédit Mobilier scandal of 1872. As infrequent as they were, such scandals are what people remember of that period.

Despite the heavy involvement of government in business since the 1930s, a number of countries have achieved high ratings for staying free of corruption, even though their civil servants have potentially sellable discretion in fulfilling their regulatory roles. Particularly impressive have been Finland, Sweden, Denmark, Iceland, Switzerland, New Zealand, and Singapore. Culture obviously also plays a role in a society's level of corruption. My longtime good friend Jim Wolfensohn, as president of the World Bank from 1995 to 2005, fashioned the bank's policies to constrain corruption in the developing world. I always thought this was a critical contribution to world development.

There is no direct measure of the impact of cultural mores on economic activity. But a joint venture of the Heritage Foundation and the *Wall*

Street Journal has in recent years combined statistics from the IMF, the Economist Intelligence Unit, and the World Bank to calculate the Index of Economic Freedom for 161 countries. The index combines, among other considerations, the estimated strength and enforcement of property rights, the ease of starting and closing a business, the stability of the currency, the state of labor practices, openness to investment and international trade, freedom from corruption, and the share of the nation's output appropriated for public purposes. There is, of course, a good deal of subjectivity in placing numbers on such qualitative attributes. But, as best I can judge, their evaluations drawn from the data do seem to square with my more casual observations.

The index for 2007 lists the United States as the most "free" of the larger economies; ironically Hong Kong, now a part of undemocratic China, is also at the top of the list. It is perhaps not a coincidence that the top seven economies (Hong Kong, Singapore, Australia, the United States, the United Kingdom, New Zealand, and Ireland) all have roots in Britain—the home of Adam Smith and the British Enlightenment. But Britishness obviously does not convey a permanent imprint. Zimbabwe, a former British colony (as Southern Rhodesia), ranks almost dead last.

The greater the economic freedom, the greater the scope for business risk and its reward, profit, and thus the greater the inclination to take risk. Societies that comprise risk takers form governments whose rules foster economically productive risk taking: property rights, open trade, and open opportunities. They have laws that offer few regulatory benefits that government officials can sell or exchange for cash or political favors. The index measures a country's degree of *conscious* effort to restrict competitive markets. The rankings are thus not necessarily a measure of economic "success," as each nation, over the long run through its policies and laws, chooses the degree of economic freedom it wants.* For example, Germany, which ranks number nineteen overall, has opted to maintain a large welfare state that requires a substantial diversion of economic output. Also, German labor markets are quite restrictive; discharging employees is very expensive. Yet

---

*In some instances, however, political impediments have prevented governments from creating or abolishing institutions to better reflect the cultural choices of their constituents.

I was sandwiched between Hillary Clinton and Tipper Gore as President Bill Clinton presented his deficit-cutting package to a joint session of Congress on February 17, 1993. While the political theater of the seating made me slightly uncomfortable, I enjoyed the company, and more important, I applauded the president's focus on deficit reduction. *Luke Frazza/AFP/Getty Images*

I found President Clinton refreshingly
engaged in economic issues.

ABOVE: *Ron Sachs/CNP/Corbis;* BELOW: *Official White House Photograph*

Andrea and I got married at the Inn at
Little Washington in Virginia on April 6, 1997.
Courtesy of Denis Reggie

Across the net from Treasury Secretary Lloyd Bentsen at the Senate tennis court, 1994. Lloyd, a good friend, played an underappreciated role in launching Clinton's successful economic policies. *Courtesy of the U.S. Department of the Treasury*

As America's economy became more and more integrated with the world's during my tenure as Fed chairman, I became increasingly involved in aid for other countries in economic crisis. Magazine cover hyperbole aside, Treasury Secretary Robert Rubin, Deputy Treasury Secretary Lawrence Summers, and I had an unusually fruitful and harmonious working relationship; I greatly respect them both.
Time *Magazine/Time Life Pictures/ Getty Images*

At the height of the dot-com boom, CNBC invented a gimmick called the briefcase indicator, in which cameras would follow me on the mornings of FOMC meetings as I arrived at the Fed. If my briefcase was thin, one theory went, then my mind was untroubled and the economy was well. But if it was stuffed full, a rate hike loomed. *Courtesy of CNBC*

Andrea and I checked in on the Fed's Y2K crisis management team on our way home from the Clinton White House's "Millennium Dinner" on New Year's Eve, December 31, 1999. *Courtesy of Howard Amer*

Testifying on the U.S. economy before the Joint Economic Committee of Congress, April 21, 2004. The admonition "First, do no harm" applies to Fed chairmen speaking in public as well as to physicians.

Photograph by David Burnett/Contact Press Images

President-elect George W. Bush and I faced the media after our first meeting, on December 18, 2000, at Washington's Madison Hotel.
Cynthia Johnson/Time Life Pictures/Getty Images

I was sworn in as Fed chairman for the fifth and final time on June 19, 2004, by Vice President Cheney at Gerald Ford's Colorado home.
Official White House Photo/David Bohrer

The world's top finance ministers *(back row)* and central bankers *(front row)* gathered in Washington, D.C., for a G7 meeting of economic policymakers. Among the finance ministers are France's now-president Nicolas Sarkozy *(second from left)* and Great Britain's now–prime minister Gordon Brown *(back row, far right)*. *Courtesy of Banca d'Italia*

A band of protesters hoped to disrupt the World Bank/IMF annual meeting in Washington on April 17, 2000. Ironically, the intensity of such public protests has increased almost in lockstep with the diminution of the power of nation-states, separately or in coordination, to bend global market forces to their will. *AP Images/Khue Bui*

During an engaging trip to Great Britain in September 2002, I had the honor of being knighted by Queen Elizabeth II and dedicating the new Treasury Building. In 2005, I received an honorary degree from the University of Edinburgh in the presence of my friend, then–chancellor of the exchequer Gordon Brown.

ABOVE: *AP Images/David Cheskin*; BELOW: *Christopher Furlong/Getty Images*

I was struck by how quickly the Chinese leadership acquired a relatively sophisticated understanding of the workings of market economies, given the distance it had to travel. Here I am meeting with Chinese president Jiang Zemin in the Great Hall of the People in Beijing. Chinese finance minister Jin Renqing is to the right. *The collection of Alan Greenspan*

Chinese premier Zhu Rongji ranks with Mikhail Gorbachev in his impact on world economic events. In the course of meetings over many years, he and I became good friends. Bob Rubin and I saw him during his visit to Washington, D.C., in 1999, when he urged President Clinton and Congress to back China's accession to the World Trade Organization. *Epix/Getty Images*

Taking in Tiananmen Square from a balcony near the spot where Mao declared the creation of the People's Republic of China. *The collection of Alan Greenspan*

I talked to middle-school students in Washington, D.C., about the importance of staying in school, as part of a financial education program in June 2003. The solution to some of our gravest problems lies in reforming the way we educate our children. *AP Images/Susan Walsh*

Attending funeral services for President Ford in the Rotunda of the U.S. Capitol, December 30, 2006. To my left in front are Henry Kissinger, Brent Scowcroft, and Bob Dole. I was struck by the public outpouring of grief at Ford's death and couldn't help but perceive it as in part also a lament for a less bitterly partisan time in American political life. *Mark Wilson/Getty Images*

At Ben Bernanke's swearing-in as the fourteenth chairman of the Federal Reserve on February 6, 2006. I was very comfortable leaving the post in the hands of such an experienced successor. *Jim Young/Reuters/Corbis*

With Roger Ferguson, my close associate and the vice chairman of the Fed for eight and a half critical years, from 1997 to 2006. *Photograph by Diana Walker*

"HI, IT'S AL ... DOWN AT GREENSPAN'S GARAGE ... LOOK, THIS TUNE-UP
IS TAKING LONGER THAN I THOUGHT ..."

*"And please let Alan Greenspan accept the things he
cannot change, give him the courage to change the things
he can and the wisdom to know the difference."*

Caricature comes with the territory.

THE TEMPTATION OF ALAN GREENSPAN

ALAN GREENSPAN IN RETIREMENT

Sweet harmony.

Photograph by Harry Benson

at the same time, Germany ranks among the highest in terms of the freedom of its people to open and close businesses, property-rights protection, and the overall rule of law. France (number forty-five) and Italy (number sixty) have profiles that are similarly mixed.

The ultimate test of the usefulness of such a scoring process is whether it correlates with economic performance. And it does. The correlation coefficient of 157 countries between their "Economic Freedom Score" and the log of their per capita incomes is 0.65, impressive for such a motley body of data.*

Thus, we are left with a critical question: Granted that open competitive markets foster economic growth, is there an optimum trade-off between economic performance and the competitive stress it imposes on the one hand, and the civility that, for example, the continental Europeans and many others espouse? Many Europeans contemptuously brand America's economic regime "cowboy capitalism." Highly competitive free markets are viewed as obsessively materialistic and largely lacking in meaningful cultural values. This marked difference between the United States and continental Europe on support for competitive markets was captured most clearly for me several years ago in a soliloquy attributed to former conservative French prime minister Édouard Balladur. He asked, "What is the market? It is the law of the jungle, the law of nature. And what is civilization? It is the struggle against nature." While acknowledging the ability of competition to promote growth, many such observers nonetheless remain concerned that economic actors, to achieve that growth, are required to behave in a manner governed by the law of the jungle. These observers then choose lesser growth for more civility, or at least they think so.

But *is* there a simple trade-off between civil conduct, as defined by those who find raw competitive behavior deplorable, and the quality of material life most nonetheless seek? It is not obvious from a longer-term perspective that such a trade-off exists in any meaningful sense. During the past century, for example, competitive-market-driven economic growth in the United States created resources far in excess of those required to main-

---

*In calculating the index, all ten elements are given equal weight. Allowing the weights to change on the basis of time-series correlations would increase the degree of correlation.

tain subsistence. That surplus, even in the most aggressively competitive economies, has been in large measure employed to improve the quality of life along many dimensions. To cite a short list: (1) greater longevity, owing first to the widespread development of clean, potable water and later to rapid advances in medical technology; (2) a universal system of education that enabled greatly increased social mobility; (3) vastly improved conditions of work; and (4) the ability to enhance our environment by setting aside natural resources in national parks rather than having to employ them to sustain a minimum level of subsistence.* At a fundamental level, Americans have used the substantial increases in wealth generated by our market-driven economy to purchase what many would view as greater civility.

Clearly, not all activities undertaken in markets are civil. Many, though legal, are decidedly unsavory. Violation of law and breaches of trust do undermine the efficiency of markets. But the discipline of the marketplace in the United States, for one, is sufficiently rooted in a rule of law to limit these aberrations. It is instructive that despite the egregious breaches of trust by some of America's business and financial leaders in recent decades, productivity growth, an important metric of corporate efficiency, between 1995 and 2002 accelerated. I will have more to say on corporate governance in chapter 23.

What can history tell us about the stability of economic cultures over the generations? What does it suggest about culture's impact on future outcomes? Today, America's culture is much changed from what it was at our founding, though it remains rooted in the values of our Founding Fathers. As unfettered as today's American capitalism may appear, it is a pale image of the capitalism of our earlier years. We probably came as close as we will ever come to pure capitalism in the decades before our Civil War. Following a largely, but not wholly, laissez-faire policy toward business and business practice, the federal government provided little or no safety net for aspiring capitalists in the race for wealth creation. If you failed, as many did, you were expected to pick yourself up and start from scratch, often in the rapidly growing settlements of America's frontier. Decades later Herbert Spen-

---

*The tragedy of the denuding of Brazil's Amazon rain forests is that the inhabitants of the region need to cut down trees to survive.

cer, a follower of Charles Darwin, coined the phrase "survival of the fittest," a philosophy of competition that captured much of the prevailing ethos of early America. FDR's New Deal was still a century in the future.

In my early twenties, I was drawn to this image of a rough-and-tumble capitalist society based, I fantasized, largely on merit. I did not dwell on the glaring constitutional contradiction of slavery and its treatment of people as property. Notwithstanding some restraint on business practices passed into law under populist prodding in the late nineteenth century, the U.S. economy through the 1920s retained much of the laissez-faire glow of early-nineteenth-century America.

To be sure, the years of the New Deal produced a vast constraining web of new government regulations on previously unfettered competition, much of which remains in place to this day. Some of the rougher edges of creative destruction were legislated away. Congress enacted the Employment Act of 1946, which formalized many of the ad hoc initiatives of the 1930s. It committed the U.S. government to organize its policies to ensure employment for "those able and willing to seek work." This was scarcely a Marxist rallying cry, but it was a distinct change from the role of government in economic affairs that had existed before Roosevelt's New Deal. It established the Council of Economic Advisors, which I was to chair twenty-eight years later. The new commitment to a permanent presence of government in economic affairs distinctly downgraded the role of markets.

Nonetheless, assisted by the wave of deregulation since the mid-1970s, today's U.S. economy remains the most competitive large economy in the world, and American culture still exhibits much of the risk taking and taste for adventure of the country's earlier years. More than a century after Frederick Jackson Turner declared in 1893 that the frontier was closed, Americans reveled in stories of the exploits of the free-spirited cowboys who, following the Civil War, manned the cattle drives up the Chisholm Trail from Texas to the rail depots of Kansas.

The cultural changes in America are noticeable, to be sure, but rather narrow in the context of more than two millennia of recorded human history characterized by tectonic changes in institutions. Moreover, I believe the United States is sufficiently culturally stable to expect little change over the next generation or two. I say this even though ongoing immigration from Latin America will alter the cultural composition of our society. But these are people who have chosen to *leave* their home countries, a seeming rejection of much of the populist culture that has so inhibited Latin American economic growth. That was also the case with the open immigration at the turn of the last century. Those immigrants were successfully absorbed in our nation's "melting pot."

In the less pressing period after World War II, but before globalization took hold, governments were able to construct social safety nets and engage in other policies to shelter citizens from the gale of creative destruction. In the United States, major expansions of Social Security, unemployment insurance, worker-safety legislation, and, of course, Medicare headed a much longer list. Most industrialized nations did likewise. The share of U.S. GDP accounted for by government social benefits rose from 3.4 percent in 1947 to 8.1 percent in 1975 (and has since drifted higher). Even though such safety-net initiatives were often recognized as adding substantial costs to labor and product markets, thereby reducing their flexibility, policymakers did not judge them as meaningful impediments to economic growth. Pent-up demand from the Depression and World War II drove world GDP forward.

In economies not broadly subject to international trade, competition was not as punishing to the less efficient as it is today, and there is clearly a significant segment of society that looks back at such circumstances with nostalgia. In today's global competitive markets, maintaining the kind of safety net that evolved in an earlier day is proving increasingly problematic, notably in most continental European countries, where high unemployment appears chronic. Governments of all persuasions may still choose to help people acquire the skills they need to utilize new technologies. And they generally try to support the incomes of those who have been less able to adapt. But technology and international competition are extracting a high price for the more intrusive forms of intervention that impair market incentives to work, save, invest, and innovate. In India, for example, direct foreign investment inflows are clearly being inhibited by a still oppressive degree of regulation.

The European governments that emerged out of World War II, reflecting their collectivist bias, legislated far larger safety nets than did the U.S.

government, and as a consequence, European economies are structurally more rigid even today. As I noted in an earlier chapter, when I started as an economist just after World War II, confidence in capitalism was at its lowest ebb since its beginnings in the eighteenth century. In academia, capitalism was considered passé. Most of Europe was enthralled with one or more of the various forms of socialism. Socialists and Communists had a significant presence in European parliaments. In 1945, Communists garnered a fourth of the French vote. Britain moved dramatically toward a planned economy under its postwar Labour government, and it was hardly alone. West Germany under Allied occupation was heavily regulated at first. Largely because of a misreading of Soviet economic strength, central planning, even in a somewhat diluted form, had a wide hold on European economic thinking.

After the war, Europe and Japan were in ruins, of course, and even in America few people were confidently predicting economic growth. In fact, the memories of the 1930s were so vivid that people feared the Depression would pick up where it had left off. In Britain, the birthplace of capitalism, the fears for the postwar economic world were so deep that their revered wartime leader, Winston Churchill, was judged not sufficiently focused on domestic economic needs and was unceremoniously voted out of office as he was meeting at Potsdam with Truman and Stalin. The newly installed Labour government nationalized a significant segment of British industry. In Germany, the social welfare system initiated under Bismarck in the 1880s was expanded.

Conventional wisdom credits the Marshall Plan for Europe's recovery. I do not doubt that the Marshall Plan helped, but it was too small to account for the remarkable dynamics of the postwar recovery. I would regard the freeing of product and financial markets in 1948 by West German economics director Ludwig Erhard as by far the more important spur to the postwar recovery of Western Europe. West Germany, of course, was to become the region's dominant economic power.

As the years went by, a growing disillusionment with the rigidity and the results of government economic planning set in, and all European economies moved toward market capitalism, if on different time frames and to different degrees. For the most part, while acknowledging the downside of creative destruction, advocates of markets convinced their populations of capitalism's benefits, thereby gaining electoral dominance. Because of deeply different cultures, however, each nation practiced its own nuanced version.

Britain was driven off its socialist track in part by periodic foreign-exchange crises that forced fallbacks to more competitive markets. Margaret Thatcher jolted Britain toward a capitalist paradigm. I first encountered Thatcher at a September 1975 British Embassy function in Washington, shortly after she became the Conservative Party's leader. And an encounter it was. Seated next to her at dinner, I was prepared for a dull evening with a politician. "Tell me, Chairman Greenspan," she asked, "why is it that we in Britain cannot calculate M3?" I awoke. M3 is an arcane measure of money supply embraced by followers of Milton Friedman. We spent the evening discussing market economics and the problems confronting the British economy. I repeated a concern I had expressed to President Ford the previous April: "The British economy appears to be at the point where they must accelerate the amount of governmental fiscal stimulus just to stand still. This is clearly a very dangerous situation."

My favorable initial impressions of Thatcher were reinforced after she became prime minister. Elected to that office in 1979, she confronted Britain's sclerotic economy head-on. Her seminal battle was with the miners who struck in March 1984 following Thatcher's announcement of the closing of some unprofitable government-owned coal mines. A strike by the mine workers' union in 1973 had been instrumental in bringing down Edward Heath's government. But Thatcher's strategy of building up large stockpiles of coal in advance of her closure announcement insulated the country from the power outages that had given the union its bargaining strength in the past. Outmaneuvered, the militant workers capitulated after a year and returned to work.

Thatcher's embrace of market capitalism gained the grudging acceptance of the British electorate. She was reelected in 1983 and 1987, and became the longest continuously serving prime minister since 1827. Her spectacular run was finally undermined not by the general British electorate but by a revolt within the Conservative Party. She was forced to step down in late 1990. Thatcher remained bitter toward those who removed her from power. The insult still rankled in September 1992 when, shortly after Britain's humiliating forced withdrawal from the European Community's Exchange Rate Mechanism, I was at a dinner with her and her husband, Denis Thatcher. Denis, filled with hopes of a restoration, told the story of a London taxi driver's remark following the financial debacle: "Governor, I expect to see you back at Number Ten within the month." It was not to be.

The Conservative Party under Prime Minister John Major was still in power two years later when the premature death of John Smith vaulted his deputies, Gordon Brown and Tony Blair, to the leadership of the Labour Party. Shortly after, in the fall of 1994, Brown and Blair trekked into my office at the Federal Reserve. As we exchanged greetings, it appeared to me that Brown was the senior person. Blair stayed in the background while Brown did most of the talking about a "new" Labour. Gone were the socialist tenets of postwar Labour leaders like Michael Foot and Arthur Scargill, the fiery leader of the miners' union. Brown espoused globalization and free markets and did not seem interested in reversing much of what Thatcher had changed in Britain. The fact that he and Blair had arrived on the doorstep of a renowned defender of capitalism (namely, me) solidified my impressions.

In office from 1997 forward, Tony Blair and Gordon Brown, heads of a rejuvenated and far more centrist Labour Party, accepted Thatcher's profoundly important structural changes to British product and labor markets. In fact Brown, the chancellor of the exchequer for a record number of years, appeared to revel in Britain's remarkable surge of economic flexibility. (Brown encouraged my proselytizing to our G7 colleagues about the importance of flexibility to economic stability.) What socialism was left in twenty-first-century Britain was much reduced. Fabian socialism was still reflected in Britain's social safety net but, from my perspective, in its most diluted form. Britain's success with the free-market thrust of Thatcher and "New Labour" suggests that their GDP-enhancing reforms are likely to persevere through the next generation.

Britain's evolution from the ossified economy of the years immediately following World War II to one of the most open economies in the world is reflected in the intellectual journey of Gordon Brown, who described his education in an e-mail to me in 2007: "I came to economics principally through the concern about social justice my father taught me. As the early Fabian socialists did, I felt it was a failure of economics, so the answer was Keynesian—more demand, at least making jobs possible. In the eighties, I saw that we needed a more flexible economy to create jobs. My understanding of an inclusive globalization is that we must combine stability, free trade, open markets, and flexibility with investment in equipping people for jobs of the future, principally through education. I hope in Britain we have prepared ourselves best for the global economic challenge, buttressing our policies for stability with a commitment to free trade, not protectionism; the most open competition policy in the world; flexible markets; and substantially increased investment in people through education and related measures."

The level of economic activity required to restore the war-destroyed German economic infrastructure and to catch up with the technologies developed during the war propelled German GDP growth. Almost wholly unanticipated, the German "economic miracle" carried the Federal Republic to the status of world economic power barely four decades later. West German growth averaged an amazing 6 percent annually between 1950 and 1973. The average rate of unemployment stayed minimal through the 1960s, an outcome inconceivable in the Depression years preceding the war. When I started making forecasts in the late 1950s for the U.S. economy as a whole, I viewed Europe as a group of markets to which we exported, financed with U.S. aid, not economies with which we competed. A few decades later, Europe had become a formidable competitive force.

The postwar structure of American industry and commerce reflected the historical antipathy to bigness that emerged from a society of small farms (in part a result of nineteenth-century western land grants for homesteading) and small businesses. Bank charters were rarely issued to corporate businesses. A government-owned corporation in competition with the private sector was unusual. The populist assault on bigness engaged the large business "trusts" and culminated in the landmark Supreme Court decision dissolving the Standard Oil Trust in 1911.

With this anti-bigness tradition, the United States differed from Germany, and from Europe generally. Postwar European economies embraced much government ownership of business and, by statute, encouraged large industrywide unions and wage negotiation at a national level. In Germany, labor representation on supervisory boards became mandatory. Large businesses and large unions controlled the economy. Large so-called universal banks were encouraged to invest in, and lend to, major corporate enterprises. This ethos of bigness had its roots in late-nineteenth-century economic cartelization that was fostered in part by the needs of the military.

In the decades immediately following World War II, creative destruction in Europe was largely "creative." Most of the "destruction" of what would have been obsolescent facilities after the war had been done by the bombing during it. The stress of the capitalist process and the need for an economic safety net through the 1970s were minimal. German business expanded rapidly, even in the face of formidable regulatory and cultural constraints.

By the late 1970s, however, the German economic miracle was fading. West Germany had largely worked through the backlog of reconstruction demand that so buoyed its economy. Demand was easing off and economic growth slowed. Creative destruction—the need for painful economic changes and redeployment of economic resources—largely dormant since the war, reemerged. Much of the economic infrastructure that had been put in place in the 1950s was edging toward obsolescence. Companies and their employees began to feel the strain.

The labor laws enacted to protect jobs shortly after the war had little bite in a period of unexpectedly huge demand for labor. In the years of rapid economic growth employers were under pressure to *hire* enough workers to meet burgeoning demand. They rarely considered the new statutory costs of discharging workers since the chances of incurring them seemed remote. Now the balance was changing as the postwar rebuilding approached completion. The cost of firing workers soon made employers reluctant to hire. In West Germany, the unemployment rate soared from a low of 0.4 percent in 1970 to nearly 7 percent by 1985 and over 9 percent in 2005. A global cyclical upturn fostered German export-led growth that brought the unemployment rate down to 6.4 percent by the spring of 2007. The longer-term structural problems, however—high unemployment and shortfalls in productivity—have yet to be adequately addressed. The costs of discharging workers have been a major deterrent to hiring.

More generally, the OECD identifies high business taxes on employee compensation and generous unemployment benefits as also contributing to a level of unemployment in Western Europe that significantly exceeds that of the United States. According to the IMF, labor productivity in the EU-15* in 2005 was only 83 percent of that of the United States, down from over 90 percent in 1995. Currently, no member's labor productivity level exceeds that of the United States. The IMF attributes the growing shortfall relative to the United States "to the slower take-up of new technologies, particularly rapid advances in information and communications technology (ICT)," owing to lagging ICT investment in finance and retail and wholesale trade. The IMF suggests that this implies a need for Europe to reduce its barriers to competition.

The crowning blow to West Germany's earlier economic growth performance was the fateful decision that as part of the unification of East and West Germany, East German mark–denominated assets and liabilities would be converted into West German deutsche marks on a one-to-one basis. As the levels of East German productivity prior to unification were discovered to have been far below those of West Germany, it was feared that East German industry would be wholly uncompetitive and would collapse into bankruptcy. But failure to convert one to one would have caused a massive stampede of the productive workforce from East to West, then-chancellor Helmut Kohl argued, probably correctly. Either way, East German industry would have to be subsidized by the Federal Republic to survive. In addition, the East gained access to the generous West German social safety net, which has since required a transfer of about 4 percent or more of German GDP to support retirees and the unemployed in the East.

As standards of living in East Germany eventually caught up to those in the West, Chancellor Kohl concluded that the economic difficulties would be resolved and the drain on West German taxpayers would come to an end. Kohl thought the adjustment might take five to ten years. Karl Otto Pöhl, the very effective president of the Deutsche Bundesbank, West Germany's central bank, told me and others in the days leading up to unifi-

---

*European Union member countries prior to the expansion of 2004.

cation that he feared the consequences to Germany would be severe. His judgment proved prescient.

The French are somewhat special in that their sense of civility and history very consciously guides their economy. Most French reject market competition, the very basis on which capitalist economies function. It is viewed as uncivil, or the "law of the jungle," in the words of Balladur. Yet they protect the institutions of capitalism—the rule of law and especially property rights—as well as any other developed nation.

The intellectual conflict plays out in the day-by-day functioning of the economy. The French publicly eschew the economic liberalism of open markets and globalization. In 2005, then-president Jacques Chirac boldly stated that "ultra-liberalism is as great a menace as communism in its day." Yet France has a whole host of world-class companies that compete very effectively on the world scene (and gain four-fifths of their profits from abroad). France, with Germany, led the way into the European Union's economic free-trading zone, which celebrated its fiftieth anniversary in March 2007. (To be sure, the motives were less economic and more a step toward political integration of the Continent, which had seen the devastation of two world wars in a third of a century.) Nonetheless, the failure of a new European constitution to be approved in a referendum in France (and elsewhere) has stayed the process of integration.

Although union representation in the French private sector is relatively low, national collective-bargaining agreements bind all employees whether unionized or not. Unions therefore wield considerable power in the marketplace, and especially in government. In France as in Germany, regulations fostered by unions to protect jobs by making it costly to discharge employees have curbed hiring, with the effect that unemployment has been significantly higher than in economies where the cost of discharging workers is low, as in the United States.

The loading-up of employment costs on business (especially retirement costs) periodically induces French governments in desperation to initiate modest reforms, only to be thwarted by opposition marches on the Champs-Élysées, a tactic that has brought many a French government to grief.

It is difficult not to be gloomy about France's economic prospects. In world rankings of income per capita, France has fallen from eleventh in 1980 to eighteenth in 2005, according to IMF data. The unemployment rate in the early 1970s averaged 2.5 percent. Since the late 1980s, it has ranged between 8 percent and 12 percent.* Yet the French people's sense of freedom and nationalism is so pervasive that when pushed to the edge, they seem to regroup and productively engage the global community. I suspect there will be more of the same now that Nicolas Sarkozy has been elected president. From my perspective, he offers hope. To be sure, in public he has been staunchly protectionist. But in my conversations with him as finance minister in 2004, he exhibited admiration for the United States' economic model of flexibility. World-competitive markets will drive him in that direction in any event. Culture and economic well-being are destined to clash.

Italy harbors many of the same problems as France and in many respects has the same outlook. Rome has been at the center of civilization for more than two millennia. Like France, Italy has had its ups and its downs, but it struggles forward. Adopting the euro in 1999 immediately gained Italy the economic power of a strong currency (the lira had to decline in value continually to maintain Italy's global competitiveness), lower interest rates, and low inflation. But its culture of fiscal extravagance did not abate with its new currency. Without the safety valve of periodic depreciations, the Italian economy has lagged. Talk of Italy's returning to the lira (and devaluations) is mostly talk. The problem of how and when Italy could be converted back to the lira is hugely formidable and extremely costly. Looking into that abyss and not liking what is there will eventually force Italian governments to engage in the reform whose need is obvious to both Italians and their global partners.

But history and a culture of civility will not in themselves sustain the economy of the euro area, or the European Union more generally. The European leaders' March 2000 meeting in Lisbon recognized that the European economic model was in need of a competitive fix. They launched what came to be known as the Lisbon Agenda, which set a fully innovative and competitive Europe as a ten-year goal. To date, progress has fallen far

---

*In April 2007, the rate was 8.2 percent.

short of that laudable goal. Some catch-up is required. In the last year or so, Europe has exhibited signs of cyclical growth driven by a booming world economy. But for reasons I outline in chapter 25, the pace of world growth will slow, and unless they are addressed, the euro area's culture-driven structural economic problems will remain.*

Japan is probably the most culturally uniform society of the major industrial powers. Its immigration laws generally discourage anyone of other than Japanese origin, and it encourages conformity. It is a very civil society, which eschews creative destruction. The Japanese frown upon the large turnover of jobs and the frequent discharging of workers associated with the elimination or evolution of obsolescent companies. Nonetheless, from the end of World War II to 1989, Japan succeeded in developing one of the world's most successful capitalist economies. Postwar rebuilding absorbed all of the labor force—very few employees were discharged and Japan became famous for its embrace of lifetime employment. Similarly, poorly run companies were bailed out by rising demand. By 1989, the value world investors placed on the land on which the Imperial Palace resides was said to be equal to the value of all the real estate in California. I remember thinking at the time how bizarre these values were.

Japan in recent years has had to struggle back from the stock-market and real estate crash of 1990. Japanese banks became heavily invested in loans backed by real estate as collateral, as real estate prices soared. When the turn came and prices cascaded downward, the collateral became inadequate. But instead of calling the loans, as most Western banks would do, the bankers refrained. It took years and many government bailouts before real estate prices stabilized and the banking system returned to normal lending, with realistic estimates of bad loans and, hence, capital.

I concluded from this and other historical episodes that Japan behaved differently from other capitalist countries. My epiphany was to realize how humiliating "loss of face" is to the Japanese. In January 2000, I met with Kiichi Miyazawa, the Japanese finance minister and former prime minis-

---

*Parts of the euro area, however, have already undertaken considerable reform. Ireland and the Netherlands particularly have developed programs that lowered the rate of unemployment. And Germany's incomplete labor reforms of earlier in the decade may be having a greater impact than previously contemplated.

ter, in his offices in Tokyo. After our customary exchange of pleasantries (his English is fluent), I launched into a detailed analysis of the deteriorating Japanese banking system. I had had many such conversations with Miyazawa, a very effective policymaker. I now told the story of how in the United States we'd set up the Resolution Trust Corporation to liquidate the assets of our approximately 750 failed savings-and-loan associations, and how, as soon as most of the seemingly unsellable real estate had been cleared off the shelves, the real estate market had revived and the new, smaller savings-and-loan industry had begun to prosper. I suggested that the U.S. government strategy of (1) bankrupting a large part of our failed thrift industry, (2) placing its assets in a liquidation vehicle, and (3) unloading the assets at large discounts in a manner that would reliquefy the real estate market fit the Japanese situation rather closely.

After listening patiently to my lecture, Miyazawa smiled gently as he said, "Alan, you have analyzed our banking problems quite perceptively. As to your solution, that is not the Japanese way." Throwing delinquent debtors into bankruptcy and liquidating their bank collateral was to be avoided, as was firing people. The Japanese hewed to a code of civility that made inducing a loss of face virtually unthinkable.

There is no doubt in my mind today, as then, that an RTC-like strategy invoked during the period of Japanese economic stagnation, from 1990 to 2005, would have shortened the period of adjustment and returned Japan to a normally functioning economy years sooner. Throughout most of those years, forecasters, myself included, were continually projecting a recovery. But it never seemed to happen. What was the invisible economic force holding Japan back? My conversation with Miyazawa supplied it. The missing force was not economic; it was cultural. The Japanese had purposely accepted hugely expensive economic stagnation to avoid a massive loss of face for many companies and individuals. I cannot imagine U.S. economic policy following such a track.

Strangely, the same sense of collective solidarity is likely to rescue the Japanese economy from the retirement financing requirements that will confront virtually all large developed countries in the years ahead. I recently asked a high Japanese official how his nation would handle what appears to be a level of commitments to future Japanese retirees that the government may not be able to deliver. He responded that the benefits would be cut and that doing so would not be a problem—the Japanese would see the changes as in the national interest, and that would be enough. I cannot imagine the U.S. Congress or American voters behaving so reasonably.

Continental Europe was able to rebuild its war-torn economies at a capitalist pace despite the regulatory inhibitions imposed by the democratic socialist culture that was pervasive at the end of the war. Just as the exceptional demand to rebuild the Continent never placed a large call on the safety net of the welfare state, the similar rapid growth of Japan in the first three decades after the war never required significant discharging of workers or banks' throwing defaulting debtors into bankruptcy. "Face" was never in jeopardy.

As Europe's growth rate slowed in the 1980s, welfare-state costs rose, reinforcing the slowdown. Similarly in Japan, when the real estate price bubble burst, the refusal of banks to foreclose on borrowers compounded the economic problem. With the real estate market at a virtual standstill, banks could not make realistic estimates of the value of the collateral that supported their assets, and hence could not judge whether they themselves were still solvent. Caution accordingly dictated that bank lending to new customers be constrained, and, since banks dominated Japan's financial system, the financial intermediation so vital to any large developed economy virtually dried up. Deflationary forces took hold. It was not until the long decline in real estate prices bottomed out in 2006 that reasonable judgments of bank solvency were possible. Only then were new loans forthcoming, producing a marked resurgence of economic activity.

While I have spent much of this chapter tracing the impact of economic forces on the larger economies, much the same set of forces is at play, for example, in Canada, Scandinavia, and the Benelux countries. I have not given Canada, our major trading partner, with which we share the world's longest undefended border, the coverage it deserves, because many Canadian economic, political, and cultural trends are mirrored in those of Britain and the United States, which are already prominent in this book.

Australia and New Zealand are particularly interesting in how they developed after adopting market-opening reforms and gradually increasing ties with Asia, especially China. Indeed, Australia and New Zealand are two of the seemingly endless examples from the last quarter century of how opening up an otherwise ossified economy to competition paid off in large gains in standards of living. Australian Labour prime minister Bob Hawke, in the 1980s, confronted with an economy held in check by competition-stifling regulation, embarked on a series of significant but painful reforms, especially in labor markets. Tariffs were reduced markedly, and the exchange rate was allowed to float. These reforms sparked an amazing economic turnaround. The economic revival that began in 1991 persevered through 2006 without recession, increasing real per capita income by more than 40 percent. New Zealand, goaded by Finance Minister Roger Douglas, engaged in similar reforms in the mid-1980s with the same impressive results.

Australia has always fascinated me as a microcosm of the United States in many ways. It is a land with vast open spaces, similar in many respects to the American West. The trek of early Australian explorers reaching out over their huge, virtually uninhabited continent is reminiscent of Lewis and Clark's exploration of America's Northwest. From a dumping ground for British felons in the late eighteenth century, Australian society morphed to a level of culture whose poster image is the Sydney Opera House. I know I can't generalize on the basis of a few years of observations, but I nonetheless found myself during my tenure at the Fed looking to Australia as a leading indicator of many aspects of U.S. economic performance. For example, the recent housing boom developed and ended in Australia a year or two ahead of the United States. I continually monitor Australia's current account deficit, which has persisted far longer (since 1974) than that of the United States with no evident significant macroeconomic impact other than large, increasing foreign ownership of Australian corporate assets.

The strong ties that developed between Australia and the United States during the harrowing early years of World War II persist to this day. Australia, now with a vibrant market economy, has an unusually prominent footprint in the United States considering its size (a population of 21 million) and its distance (7,500 miles from Sydney to Los Angeles). I have always been impressed by the depth of economic talent in so small a country. I found Ian McFarlane, the longtime governor of the Reserve Bank of Australia (Australia's central bank), unusually perceptive on global issues, as is

Peter Costello, the Australian treasurer (that is, its finance minister). Prime Minister John Howard impressed me with his deep interest in the role of technology in American productivity growth. Whereas most heads of government steer clear of such detail, he sought me out on such issues during numerous visits to the United States between 1997 and 2005. He needed no prodding from me on monetary policy. His government in 1996 had granted full independence to the Reserve Bank of Australia.

This chapter has dealt with the emergence of the various modes of capitalist practice in developed market economies. But there remain three important nations that cannot quite be seen as a simple trade-off of unfettered competition versus restraints from a social safety net: China, Russia, and India. They all follow market rules to a point, but with significant deviations that are not easy to categorize or forecast. China is becoming increasingly capitalistic, with only partial formal rules on property ownership. Russia has rules, but political convenience dictates the extent to which they are enforced. And India has legal property rights that are so qualified by specific regulations, often discretionarily enforced, that they are not as binding as they need to be to attract foreign direct investment. These countries comprise two-fifths of the world's population, but less than a fourth of world GDP. How their politics, cultures, and economies evolve over the next quarter century will leave a very large imprint on the economic future of the globe.

FOURTEEN

THE CHOICES THAT AWAIT CHINA

On my last visit to China as Fed chairman in October 2005, Zhu Rongji, China's retired premier, and his wife, Lao An, hosted a small farewell dinner at Beijing's elegant Diaoyutai State Guest House, where the Chinese leadership entertains visiting dignitaries. Zhu and I had a chance to talk during a formal tea before the dinner, and the manner in which he spoke raised serious doubts in my mind as to whether he was truly retired, as the official press so consistently maintained. He was wholly absorbed by and informed about the key issues between our nations and was as insightful and incisive as he had ever been in our eleven-year friendship.

As we compared views on China's exchange rate and America's trade imbalances, I marveled at his detailed knowledge of China's economic shortfalls and the needed remedies. I was struck again by the level of sophistication he brought to such matters, unusual even among world leaders. Over the years we had explored many issues: how China could disentangle its social safety net from the disintegrating state-run enterprises on which it depended, the optimum form of bank supervision, the need for the then-nascent Chinese stock market to be left alone to develop, and more.

I had grown quite fond of Zhu and was saddened to realize that we were unlikely to meet again. We'd become friends when he was vice premier and head of China's central bank, and I had followed his career closely. He was the intellectual heir of Deng Xiaoping, the great economic reformer who had brought China from the age of the bicycle to the age of the motor vehicle and all that that implies. Unlike Deng, who had a broad political base, Zhu was a technician; his influence, as best I can judge, rested on deep support from Jiang Zemin, China's president from 1993 to 2003 and Party leader from 1989 to 2002. It was Zhu who had brought to realization many of the sweeping institutional reforms that Deng had initiated.

As much pragmatist as Marxist, Deng had set in motion China's transformation from a walled-off centrally planned agrarian economy into a formidable presence on the economic scene. The nation's march to the market began in 1978, when, because of a severe drought, authorities were forced to ease tight administrative controls that had long governed individual farmers' plots. Under new rules, the farmers were allowed to keep a significant part of their produce to consume or sell. The results were startling. Agricultural output rose dramatically, encouraging further deregulation and the development of farm markets. After decades of stagnation, agricultural productivity blossomed.

Success on the farm encouraged the spread of reform to industry. Again, a modest easing of constraints produced greater-than-anticipated growth, giving impetus to the arguments of reformers who wished to move more quickly toward a competitive-market template. No advocates ever dared call the new model "capitalism." They used euphemisms like "market socialism" or, in the famous phrase of Deng, "socialism with Chinese characteristics."

China's leaders were far too perceptive not to see the contradictions and limitations of socialist economics and the evidence of capitalist success. Indeed, why else would they have embarked on so ambitious an enterprise so alien to the traditions of the Communist Party? As China was inexorably drawn further and further down the road toward capitalism, economic progress became so compelling that the ideological debate of earlier years seemed to have passed into history.

I first set foot in China in 1994, long after the reforms had begun. I've been back several times. Like all visitors, I've been impressed and often amazed by the changes from visit to visit. The Chinese economy, measured by purchasing power parity, has become the second largest behind that of the United States. China has also emerged as the world's largest consumer of commodities generally, the second-largest consumer of oil, and the largest steel producer, and has evolved from the bicycle economy of the 1980s into a country that produced more than seven million motor vehicles in 2006, with planned facilities to reach far beyond that. Skyscrapers are sprouting up in fields that for millennia went unchanged from harvest to harvest. The drab universal dress code of generations of Chinese has yielded to a riotous spectrum of color. And as incomes rise with prosperity, a shopping culture is emerging. Today advertising, once unknown, is one of China's most rapidly growing industries, and international retailing giants like Wal-Mart, Carrefour, and B&Q are vying with the newly innovative Chinese shopkeeper.

In a land not far removed in time from the collective farm, loosely articulated urban property rights appear to be enforced; otherwise, foreign investment in real estate, factories, and securities would long since have dried up. Investors behave as though they expect to get returns on their investments and return of principal. And they have.* Chinese citizens have been granted the right to own and sell homes, creating a major opportunity to accumulate capital. Hernando de Soto, I assume, is pleased. And in March 2007, the National People's Congress passed a more comprehensive right of ownership that grants the same legal protection of property that is granted to the state. But the right to own property still falls far short of the status of property rights in developed countries. Property rights require not only a statute but an administrative and judicial system that enforces the law. In this regard, China lags. An impartial judiciary is still a goal on the Chinese horizon. There are breaches, especially in intellectual property rights: complaints by foreign joint-venture investors are rife that technology

---

*Certainly the dramatic decontrol of prices for a large segment of the retail market encouraged foreign investment. By 1991, almost 70 percent of retail prices were market oriented—almost double the percentage in 1987, when the early evidence appeared that central planning behind the iron curtain was faltering. In the late 1980s, the import tax on parts and components for building export goods eased significantly, increasing the profitability of exports.

brought to a new plant turns up duplicated in a plant wholly owned by Chinese in direct competition.

An important casualty of China's growing affluence is the nation's commitment to its Communist revolutionary roots. In the myriad meetings I had with Chinese economic and financial officials, I do not recall ever hearing uttered the words "Communism" or "Marx." Of course, I was dealing largely with "liberals." I did participate in one ideological exchange—in 1994, when I "debated" free-market capitalism with Li Peng, a fervent Marxist and Zhu's predecessor as premier. He was quite knowledgeable about U.S. economic practice, and a formidable debater. Right from the start, it was clear that I wasn't facing Marxist dialectic of the type I'd had to deal with in college. Li listened intently to my carefully reasoned position on why China should open its markets faster. He responded by asking how, if the United States was so devoted to unregulated markets, I could account for Nixon's wage and price controls in 1971. I was delighted that he knew to ask. Not only was he connected to the real world, but also, for a reputed hard-liner, he sounded almost reasonable. I acknowledged that price controls had been a bad policy and that their only saving grace had been to reaffirm that such controls don't work. I added that we had not been tempted since. I didn't expect to change his mind, however. We were both in the sad state of government officials who engage in debate, yet even when proved wrong lack the authority to acknowledge error. No matter how hard I tried to convince him, or he me, neither of us could publicly veer from his government's declared policies.

I have not spoken with Li Peng for years and can only wonder what he must have thought when, in 2001, China joined the World Trade Organization, the bastion of free competitive trade. I had been a staunch supporter of legislation creating permanent normal trade relations with China, believing that its full acceptance into the world trade system would benefit Chinese citizens, who would see their standards of living rise, and U.S. businesses and farmers, who would find a more welcoming and as yet untapped market. In May 2000, at President Clinton's request, I spoke at the White House of my hopes of bringing China fully into the global marketplace, arguing that such a move would foster individual rights and strengthen the rule of law. I told reporters: "History has demonstrated that implicit in any removal of power from central planners and broadening of market mechanisms as would occur under WTO is a more general spread of rights to individuals." (Underscoring the reason for my presence, Clinton added mischievously, "We all know that when Chairman Greenspan talks, the world listens. I just hope that Congress is listening today.")

China's involvement in the institutions of global finance brought other benefits. Chinese central bankers now play a key role in the Bank for International Settlements (BIS) in Switzerland, an institution long associated with capitalist international finance. Zhou Xiaochuan, who was named China's central bank governor in 2002, was particularly welcome at regular BIS meetings of central bankers from major developing countries. In addition to fluency in English and international finance, Zhou brought a candid appraisal of what was happening in China that few of us could replicate from other sources. He would often detail the way the Chinese financial markets were evolving, and give me a new perspective. In 2006, after leaving the Fed, I served with Zhou on a committee to examine financing issues related to the International Monetary Fund. He and his colleagues, just a few years removed from isolated central planning, have become major players in operating the global financial system.

Significantly, China is also absorbing much Western culture. HSBC, one of the leading international banks, has for the past two years sponsored a multimillion-dollar golf tournament in Shanghai. Golf courses have been popping up across China, and the surprise is not that they have but that nobody seems to have thought it unusual.* Few sports are as symbolically capitalist as golf. The Soviet Union had professional tennis players, but no golfers.

I am told there are actually more Western classical symphony orchestras in China than in the United States. And I was taken aback when President Jiang Zemin told me that his favorite composer was Franz Schubert. This is a very far cry from the culture that greeted President Nixon on his visit to China in 1972.

---

*Tiger Woods came in second in both Shanghai tournaments. However, golf has lately been a source of controversy at some Chinese universities, where students have protested administration efforts to build golf "training courses" on which to teach the sport. Nonetheless, another international golf tournament, on China's Hainan Island, was staged in March 2007.

I have always been of the opinion that Mikhail Gorbachev's glasnost and perestroika were the proximate cause of the Soviet Union's demise. They exposed the Soviet people to "liberal" values that Stalin and most of his successors had long suppressed. After the Pandora's box was opened, given the way ideas spread, the demise of collectivism in the USSR and its satellites was just a matter of time. Efforts by the Chinese Communist Politburo to control information on the Internet suggest to me that they have drawn the same conclusion and do not wish to see history repeat itself.

In 1994, standing near the spot in Tiananmen Square where, in 1949, Mao Zedong declared the establishment of the People's Republic of China, I could only marvel at how difficult the Chinese transition to modernity has been—and yet, in recent years, how successful. Here, where a freedom-suppressing student massacre had occurred five years earlier, I also found myself wondering how after generations of Marxist indoctrination a society of 1.3 billion could turn abruptly and abandon the values inculcated during the impressionable years of childhood. Perhaps, despite China's dramatic progress, those values are more persistent than they seem. Although change is everywhere, Chairman Mao's face still adorns China's currency, a hint that the pull of tradition remains strong.

The Communist Party came to power through revolution, and has from its beginnings sought political legitimacy as the purveyor of a philosophy that was just and that offered material well-being for the whole of the population. Material well-being, however, is only part of what human beings strive for, and it alone cannot sustain an authoritarian regime. The cheer of new affluence rapidly fades and, with time, becomes the base from which additional, even higher, expectations evolve. In the last quarter century, it has been the rapid increases in standards of living that have gained the support of the people.

At any rate, it was just a matter of time before the inherent contradictions of Communist ideology became manifest. The specters of Marx and Mao, lying quiescent during the years of accelerating affluence, stirred in 2006 in the person of Liu Guoguang, a retired octogenarian Marxist economist who derailed a proposed constitutional amendment to clarify and expand property rights. He held up the ideological banner of the Communist state and, by attracting unexpected support, prevailed in the National People's Congress. The ground had been prepared by fiery remarks by Gong Xiantian, a professor at Beijing University Law School, which had been circulated on the Internet. In response to the criticism from the Marxist left, President Hu Jintao stated that China must "unshakably persist with economic reform." It remains to be seen whether this ideological eruption is the last gasp of an aging generation or a more fundamental undermining of China's road to capitalism. Encouraging, as I noted, was the passage of the amendment with only minor changes by the National People's Congress meeting in March 2007.

For the past generation, the Chinese leadership has been quite inventive in avoiding what virtually everyone has concluded: despite his brilliance, Karl Marx was wrong in his analysis of the way people can organize to successfully create value. To Marx, state ownership of the means of production was the essential fixture in a society's ability to produce wealth and justice. The right to virtually all property in Marx's society was thus to rest with the state, in trust for the people. Property rights granted to individuals were instruments of exploitation and could come only at the expense of the "collective," that is, society as a whole. He argued for the collectivization of the division of labor. All working together for a single goal would be far more productive than markets collating the disparate choices of individuals. Do human beings optimize their potential in a collectivized society? The ultimate arbiter of all such paradigms is reality. Does it work as proposed? Marx's economic model in practice—in the USSR and elsewhere—could not produce wealth or justice, as is now generally recognized. The rationale for collective ownership failed.

Socialists in the West, adjusting to the failure of Marxist economics, have redefined socialism to no longer require that all the means of production be owned by the state. Some simply advocate government regulation rather than state ownership to foster societal well-being.

Deng Xiaoping, confronting Marx's fall from favor, bypassed Communist ideology and rested Party legitimacy on its ability to meet the material needs of over a billion people. He set in motion a process that led to an unprecedented near-eightfold increase in real per capita GDP, a fall in infant mortality, and greater life expectancy. But as many in the Party leadership feared, replacement of government controls by market pricing began to weaken political control by the Party.

I saw how that worked in a visit to Shanghai in 1994. A senior official told the story of how five years earlier he had been assigned to oversee the produce depot. He had to be present every morning at five o'clock to allocate farm products coming into Shanghai, he told me. His job was to dictate who got what. Though he didn't elaborate on how he made those decisions, clearly he held considerable sway—I could imagine the favors he must have been offered by distributors eager to cultivate his goodwill. All the same, he said, he'd been delighted when the depot was converted to an open market, with the distributors bidding for produce. Now, instead of one guy deciding who got the bamboo shoots and at what price, buyers and sellers bargained until they agreed. The market set the price, and the produce was allocated according to demand and supply—a clear illustration of the fundamental difference between a command economy and a market economy. Because of this change, the official confided merrily, his life had become a lot easier. "Now I don't have to get up at four a.m. I can sleep in and let the market do my job for me."

I said to myself, "Can he conceivably understand what he just said?" As markets take over, Communist Party control shrinks. The Communist system is a pyramid in which power flows from the top. The general secretary enables, say, ten people who report to him to have discretionary powers. Each of them, in turn, grants discretionary power to much larger numbers directly below them. The handoff proceeds and expands as it works its way down to the bottom of the pyramid. The system holds together because each official is beholden to the person directly above him. This is the source of political power. This is how the Party governs. However, if market pricing is substituted for any level of the pyramid, political control is lost. You cannot have both market pricing and political control. One precludes the other. This is already causing a serious strain within the power structure of the Party.

To date, Party elders appear to have finessed this fundamental dilemma. Nonetheless, growing affluence is gradually freeing the Chinese peasant from the soil and subsistence, affording him or her the luxury of being able to protest perceived injustices. I cannot believe that the Party is unaware that affluence and recent education initiatives are moving China toward a far less authoritarian regime. Today, President Hu appears to wield less political power than did Jiang Zemin, and he less than Deng Xiaoping. And Deng far less than Mao. At the end of this road of ever-lessening power is the democratic welfare state of Western Europe. Along that way are the many hurdles that still separate China from "developed economy" status, Deng's avowed goal. Many of the huge challenges China's reformers face are well known: the reactionary old guard; the vast rural population that is to date barely sharing in the boom and is with modest exceptions forbidden to migrate to cities; the huge remaining chunks of the Soviet-style command economy, including still-bloated, inefficient state-owned enterprises; the largely struggling banking system that serves those enterprises; the lack of modern financial and accounting expertise; corruption, the almost necessary by-product of any pyramidal power structure based on discretion; and finally, lack of political freedom, which may not be needed for markets to function in the short run, but is an important safety valve for public distress about injustice and inequity. In addition, the Chinese leadership has to deal with widespread envy of the newly affluent and popular outrage at industrial pollution. Any of these factors could spark a conflagration. Despite having opened significant parts of its economy to market forces, China is still dominated by administrative controls, the remnants of central planning. As a consequence, the economy remains rigid and I fear would not be able to absorb debilitating shocks as the United States did following 9/11.

The depth of China's remaining problems can best be seen in the difficulty the leadership has had dismantling the remaining central-planning controls. After the initial burst of decontrol-engendered affluence that followed Deng's reform of the 1980s, further progress was inhibited for years. The primary culprits were China's misdirected foreign-exchange-rate regime and the laws that severely inhibit citizens' freedom to migrate between rural and urban locales, or between towns and cities. A major, though incomplete, dismantling of these two significant aspects of central planning was required to keep China on the heightened-growth path that it had experienced over the previous decade.

The first focus was the exchange-rate regime of China's currency, the renminbi, or RMB for short. No, the exchange rate was not too low, as most complain today; in the early 1980s it was too high. Central planners had fixed the RMB at an unrealistic rate in the face of a much lower rate that prevailed on the black market. International trade at the official rate in the early 1980s was understandably slow. Chinese exporters whose costs were in RMB had to charge noncompetitively high prices in dollars to recoup. As the contrast with the newly deregulated and thriving domestic trade became obvious, monetary authorities progressively devalued the RMB. But the process took them fourteen years. By 1994 it was fully freed for trade transactions, and the black market in RMB disappeared. The RMB went from under two to more than eight per dollar.

After an initial lag, Chinese exports exploded, rising from $18 billion in 1980 to $970 billion in 2006, an annual growth rate of nearly 17 percent. Well in excess of half of Chinese exports are fabricated from imported materials, and those exports are moving to ever-higher-valued products, as evidenced by the rise in average export prices that exceed price indexes based on a fixed basket of goods.* What is not clear, however, is how much of the rise in average prices merely reflects a higher quality of intermediate products imported for assembly in final export products.

This is important, because the greater the extent to which Chinese exports are becoming high tech, the greater China's competitive impact on the developed world. China may be moving up on the technology ladder. It is exporting far more sophisticated products than it did a decade ago. But is it the Chinese who are creating the higher level of sophistication? Or is China merely assembling more sophisticated products produced by others? The *Economist*, reflecting in part the views of Nicholas Lardy of the Peterson Institute of International Economics, commented in the spring of 2007 that "China's export model . . . consists in big measure of renting out cheap labour and land to foreigners. Even China's most successful domestic computer firm . . . contracts its production out to Taiwanese companies." I assume, however, that it is only a matter of time before China accounts for

---

*The U.S. Department of Commerce, for example, calculates fixed-weight prices of goods imported from China. In 2005, the United States accounted for 21 percent of total Chinese exports.

an increasing proportion of the value of its exports. I expect the Chinese to gradually replace their imported materials with high-value-added domestically produced components.

The rising path of exports paralleled the epochal shift of rural workers to the cities. The rural population peaked in 1995 at nearly 860 million. Eleven years later it was down to 737 million. That shift was not only the result of people moving to cities and some definitional changes but also the result of rural land being urbanized as new manufacturing enclaves began to sprout up, mainly in the Pearl River delta contiguous to vibrant Hong Kong. In the 1970s this fertile area was home to sleepy farms and villages, but in the last fifteen years pioneering foreign investors from Hong Kong and elsewhere have stoked the region's growth. The delta now produces everything from toys to textiles, most of it manufactured for export. Hong Kong's example and assistance in the development of the Pearl River delta's economy has been striking.

When China reestablished its sovereignty over Hong Kong in 1997, I did not hold much hope for the survival of Hong Kong capitalism. The notion that China would honor its pledge that Hong Kong would remain a bastion of capitalism for fifty years seemed to me rather naive. Capitalism and Communism side by side under the same sovereign authority was just not credible. But the decade of Deng's "One Country, Two Systems" has turned out quite differently than I feared. China, instead of replacing Hong Kong's culture and economy with its Communist imprint, has found itself increasingly influenced by the culture and economic rules of Hong Kong.

The 1.4 percent annual average net shift of rural to urban population over the last decade has measurably increased China's productivity: the capital stock in urban areas is significantly more sophisticated than that in rural China. That spread has created an urban output per hour more than three times that of rural China. Special Economic Zones (SEZs) inaugurated in 1980, which focused on manufacturing exports in facilities financed by foreign capital, have proved highly successful. Privatization of some state-owned enterprises (SOEs) has made significant progress, and other SOEs are undergoing major restructuring. As a consequence, employment in these organizations has fallen sharply, an indication that creative destruction is moving at a reasonably good clip.

Restructuring a number of SOEs and privatizing most of the remainder has required moving the social insurance and welfare obligations of the SOEs to other government entities or private financing. The SOEs would obviously not be able to compete if they had to carry the full cost of the social safety net on their books. Padding SOE employment rolls as an indirect form of unemployment insurance is fading. At one of those traditional tea servings in the Great Hall of the People, Chinese president Jiang Zemin in 1997 described to me how he had run a large state-owned steel complex. He was proud that with significantly fewer workers he had succeeded in producing as much steel as a rival SOE in northeast China.

It is a matter of conjecture whether the rural migration to the cities would have been even faster were it not for long-standing restrictions on internal migration. Such restrictions in their current form date back to 1958. Everyone from birth is required to live in the geographic area of his or her mother. Official permission to move is granted to only a small fraction of the population. Such enforced immobility satisfies the need of central planners to have the pieces of the economy stay in place to promote the outcome of the central plan, though political control is also certainly an objective. The restrictions on migration also effectively limit people's choice of occupation.

I cannot imagine how people can thrive in such an environment, though I suppose it's an improvement from the nightmare of the Cultural Revolution. The current leadership's ongoing efforts to ease these restrictions are important and welcome. But fear of a mass exodus from farms to cities and the unrest that could follow has inhibited change in this, as in so many aspects of Chinese life.

However, bottling up the frustrations imposed on the average person in rural areas, where the majority of the population still resides, is a recipe for insurrection. As the rapidly growing economy frees large numbers of Chinese to reach beyond the pursuit of mere subsistence, they have the leeway to contemplate perceived injustices, real or imagined. China does not have the safety valve of democracy to diffuse such unrest. Aggrieved people who do not have the option to vote officials out of office tend to rebel.

The hyperinflation in China in the late 1940s is often cited as a cause of the uprisings that brought the Communists to power in 1949, a lesson they learned well. So it is understandable that the Communists' greatest economic fear is an inflation that destabilizes society. As John Maynard Keynes noted in 1919: "Lenin was certainly right. There is no subtler, no surer means of overturning the existing basis of society than to debauch the currency. The process engages all the hidden forces of economic law on the side of destruction, and does it in a manner which not one man in a million is able to diagnose."

Chinese leaders harbor a deep-seated apprehension that unless inflation is contained, the economy will sputter, inducing a rise in unemployment in urban areas, sparking unrest. They see a stable exchange rate as necessary to avoid dreaded labor-market instability. They are mistaken. The current policy of suppressing the exchange rate risks a far greater disruption. As Chinese real per capita GDP has grown faster than that of the country's trading partners, the result largely of technology "borrowed" from developed economies, international competition has tended to elevate the demand for China's currency.* To offset this demand and hold the RMB relatively stable from 2002 to 2007 has required cumulative purchases with RMB by Chinese monetary authorities well in excess of $1 trillion.† To sop up, or sterilize, the excess cash that the central bank has created by purchasing foreign assets, the Chinese central bank has issued vast quantities of RMB-denominated debt. But it has not been enough. Money supply, as a consequence, has been growing at a rate disturbingly in excess of the growth in nominal GDP. That is tinder for inflation.

A different problem, but equally troubling to Chinese leaders, is the rapid increase in the concentration of income. Starting from very little con-

---

*The demand for the products of low-cost-labor countries increases the demand for the currency of the producing country relative to all other countries. The value of the currency with increased demand will rise relative to that of the others. And that rise will tend to continue until the value of wages adjusted by the exchange rate (and productivity differentials) rises to the level of that of other competing countries.

†The Chinese political imperative to resist a rise in the value of the RMB has caused great consternation among U.S. and other politicians; they believe, erroneously, that the suppression of the RMB is the major cause of U.S. imports and hence of manufacturing job losses. A rise in the RMB would likely decrease the trade deficit with China but not the overall deficit of the United States. American importers would merely turn to other low-cost-labor countries to replace no longer competitive Chinese exports. (China's $1 trillion of purchases since 2001 include U.S. dollars and other currencies converted to dollars.)

centration in the 1980s, when everyone was uniformly poor, the emergence of a society in which income disparity is judged by the World Bank to be greater than that in both the United States and Russia is truly astounding. Another headache is the Chinese banking system, which to this day remains a long way from being effectively reformed. Yet stock prices of Chinese banks soared through 2006 and into 2007. The state-controlled Industrial and Commercial Bank of China raised $22 billion in 2006, the largest-ever initial public offering. Other state-controlled banks had large IPOs and overseas listing of shares as well. But much of the rush into Chinese state-controlled institutions reflects investors' presumption that the Chinese government is in effect guaranteeing the liabilities of these banks. It has already recapitalized the banks with $60 billion from China's huge foreign-exchange reserves and in the process removed many of the banks' bad loans. Chinese banks have historically financed a lot of politically useful investment, but much of it is obviously serving no useful economic purpose.

Moreover, the still inchoate banking system does not afford the degree of flexibility needed for economic adjustment. Market-based economies are continuously slipping out of balance, but market-driven changes in interest rates and exchange rates, along with product and asset price adjustments, quickly rebalance them. The Chinese government does not allow interest rates to float with supply and demand but changes them administratively along with changes in reserve requirements of the banks—but only after the evidence of economic imbalance is unambiguous. That is invariably too late, and a good deal of the time the resulting moves are insufficient or even counterproductive. Monetary officials give administrative guidance to banks on loan growth when they perceive growth to be too large, but again belatedly. These initiatives rarely properly address financial imbalances. Ironically, the disconnect between finance in China and the rest of the world insulated China from the financial crisis that spread around the globe in 1997–98.

China is in dire need of financial expertise. No wonder, because people with such expertise had little role to play under central planning. Neither did business marketers, accountants, risk managers, or other experts so essential to the day-to-day workings of a market economy. These skills have entered the Chinese education curriculum in recent years, but it will take time before the economy, especially the banking sector, becomes adequately staffed. In December 2003, Liu Mingkang, the new chairman of the China Banking Regulatory Commission, visited the Federal Reserve Board. He acknowledged that Chinese banks lacked the professional expertise to judge what enabled a loan to be repaid. Liu indicated that increasing the foreign bank presence could help. I suggested that what China really needed was people who had worked in a market economy and had the sharp eyes and competitive judgment of able loan officers in the West. Much progress has been made since, but much needs to be done.

Because finance has little role to play in central planning, Chinese banks have not been banks as we know them in the West. Responding to political directives, state-owned banks in years past transferred funds to pay for state-initiated commitments. There were no bank loan officers to make loans that would be expected to be repaid, just transfer agents. Bad debts in national income accounting are part of the reconciliation between GDP, the presumed market value of production, and employee compensation and profits, the claims to that production. To the extent that there are a lot of bum investments, part of the measured GDP is waste and of no value. Chinese bad-debt levels raise the same questions about what the published Chinese GDP numbers mean. However, I should point out that even investments that turn out not to have any continuing value nonetheless consume raw materials. Accordingly, the published levels of Chinese GDP are probably reasonably useful in evaluating the resources needed for its production—that is, as a measure of the value of needed input.

Even after adjusting for the questionable quality of some of China's data, the results of the reforms that commenced in the late 1970s remain truly remarkable. One needs only to observe the vast changes in Beijing, Shanghai, and Shenzhen, and the lesser but still real changes in the rest of the country, to conclude that China is anything but a Potemkin village.

In my experience, it has been the technocrats in the Chinese government—mostly in the central bank, the finance ministry, and, surprisingly, the regulatory agencies—who have pressed for market initiatives. Most of them, however, serve only in advisory capacities. The key policy decisions are made by the State Council and the Politburo, and it is to their credit that they have largely embraced market-friendly advice. A remaining critical hurdle, and one that threatens Communist Party rule at its core, is its ideological challenge. Deng Xiaoping's goal of raising China to the status of "intermediate developed country" by midcentury requires additional reinforcement of property rights, even in the face of resistance from old-guard Marxists.

There has been progress on rights to urban property. Rights to land in the countryside, where 737 million Chinese reside, is another matter. Granting property rights to farmland is too unambiguous a break with Communist traditions to be countenanced easily. Farmers can lease land and sell products in open markets, but they have no legal rights to the land they till, and so cannot buy or sell it or use it as collateral for loans. In recent decades, as urbanization has encroached on rural China, local authorities have seized enormous expanses, granting as compensation only a small fraction of what the land would be worth as part of an urban enclave. Such seizures have been one of the main contributors to recent rising levels of protests and unrest. A top Chinese police official reported that the number of public protests nationwide rose to seventy-four thousand in 2004 from ten thousand a decade earlier. Estimates for 2006 were somewhat lower. Granting legal title to peasant land could, with the stroke of a pen, substantially narrow the wealth gap between urban and rural residents.

While economic supremacy is at the heart of Party initiatives, the leadership has other agendas, not the least of which is the status of Taiwan. Many, perhaps most, of the leaders know that a military confrontation would spook foreign capital investment and gravely damage the nation's aspiration to build a world-class economy.

In sum, the Communist Party leadership is confronted with very difficult choices. The track it is currently on will ultimately lead the Party to abandon its philosophical roots and more officially embrace some form of market capitalism. Does it then morph into a democratic socialist party, as has occurred in many states of the former Soviet bloc? Does it acquiesce in the political pluralism that is a likely consequence, thereby threatening the Party's hegemony? Or does the Party abandon reform and revert to an orthodox regime of central planning and authoritarianism, which would almost surely undermine the prosperity on which the leadership depends for legitimacy?

I have no doubt that the Communist Party of China can maintain an authoritarian, quasi-capitalist, relatively prosperous regime for a time. But without the political safety valve of the democratic process, I doubt the long-term success of such a regime. How those choices evolve will have profound implications not only for China but also for the world at large, an issue to which I will return.

FIFTEEN

THE TIGERS AND THE ELEPHANT

Before China reinvented itself as East Asia's eight-hundred-pound economic gorilla, the nations nicknamed the "Asian Tigers" tested and perfected the economic model China has chosen to pursue. China's export-led explosion in economic growth has clearly followed the earlier path of these Tigers—particularly Hong Kong, Taiwan, Korea, and Singapore. Their model is simple and effective. The developing nation opens up part or all of its economy to foreign investment to employ a low-wage, but often educated, workforce. Sometimes it is politically easier to set up designated geographic areas such as China's Special Economic Zones to welcome foreign investment and its technology. Critical to this model is that investors receive assurances that, if successful, they will be able to reap the rewards. This requires that property rights be respected by the developing country.

Given the devastation of Asia in World War II and the wars in Korea and Vietnam, economic advance started from a very low base. Per capita GDP of much of East Asia was not far above levels of subsistence. Major progress was possible merely by bringing together protected investment capital and low-cost labor. These were not free-market economies at the beginning. Forms of central planning and government ownership were widespread. Korea, mimicking Japan, granted favored positions to large business conglomerates (*chaebol*). Taiwan had significant government-owned companies and, like the other Tigers, heavy trade protection of domestic industry.

Most had charismatic but autocratic leaders. Singapore's Lee Kuan Yew sparked the emergence of a small but world-class city; other autocrats, like General Suharto, who ruled over Indonesia's system of crony capitalism, were arguably less successful. Malaysia's prime minister Mahathir Mohamad, still harboring resentments of his country's colonial past, was a very forceful nationalist leader.

I have met, but cannot say I have gotten to know, many of these leaders. Over the years, I have had the most contact with Lee Kuan Yew, most recently in 2006, and have always found him impressive, even though we do not always see eye to eye. I met him first when he was George Shultz's guest at the famous (or infamous, depending on your perspective) Bohemian Grove, a male-only bonding retreat among the redwoods of California. (*Time* magazine once sent a woman disguised as a man to report on the club's clandestine doings.)

When I visited Dr. Mahathir at Blair House (Washington's official guest house for heads of state and other visiting dignitaries) in May 2002, I found him less fiery than I had expected. In fact, he appeared both thoughtful and interesting so long as I put out of mind his jailing of Anwar Ibrahim, Malaysia's finance minister and Mahathir's presumed political heir apparent. Anwar was widely respected by those of us in leadership roles in international finance. I suspect U.S. vice president Al Gore spoke for most of us when, in 2000, he denounced "the show trial . . . [that] mocked international standards of justice." At our most partisan, I cannot imagine such political hardball being played in the United States.

When G7 finance ministers and central bank governors visited Thailand in 1991 and were given a tour of the ornate palace, I kept looking for traces of Anna Leonowens, the legendary nineteenth-century British schoolmarm who was recruited to tutor the children of the king of the nation then known as Siam. One of his descendants, King Bhumibol Adulyadej, has now reigned for more than sixty years. I am particularly fascinated by the role the monarchy plays in Thailand. King Bhumibol has murky legal authority but is revered and apparently wields considerable moral authority. When a political deadlock led to a military coup d'état in September 2006, the king smoothed the transition of government by appearing on television next to the coup leader, army commander Sonthi Boonyaratglin.

The leaders of these authoritarian governments all had initial success reviving their prostrate economies. The heavily subsidized and protected industries of East Asia produced rising exports and improved standards of living for their people into the 1970s. Despite the massive waste and inefficiencies of planned or quasi-planned economies, many did achieve progress. But the rigidities of economies jacketed by heavy intervention can carry progress just so far. So to avoid stalling out, the Tigers of East Asia lowered their barriers to foreign trade and, by the 1980s, were largely off the competition-stifling subsidies to which much of the Asian economy, excluding its export industries, was still addicted.

Export producers continued to compete effectively in international markets, as productivity-enhancing technologies (borrowed from developed countries) coupled with low wages created high rates of return. Export-oriented companies in turn were required to raise wages to attract the workforce they needed to fill their rapidly rising new orders, and domestic industries, in response, had to bid their wages higher to hold on to workers. Workers' standards of living in East Asia, as a consequence, moved markedly higher.

The Tigers, in addition to exporting to developed countries by the 1980s, were soon trading with one another. Concentration on ever-narrower (specialized) tasks almost always enhances competency and output per worker. This is especially the case when competitors are contiguous and transportation costs are accordingly low. The Tigers, confronting tighter labor markets and rising wages, have been losing their early competitive advantage in labor-intensive goods to lower-cost competitors in Asia, Latin America, and most recently, Eastern Europe. Fortunately, education was an early priority in the Tigers' drive toward competitiveness. East Asia has thus been able to move toward more complex products: semiconductors, computers, and the wide array of high-technology goods that yield high value-added in the international marketplace. Capital and more sophisticated labor forces have vaulted a number of Tigers to developed-economy incomes and status.

But are those gains at the expense of the rest of the world, particularly, as is alleged, the United States and Europe? The answer is no. Trade expansion is not a zero-sum game. In fact, global exports and imports have been rising significantly faster than world GDP for more than half a century. This occurred in the case of the Tigers because high tariffs and numerous other barriers to trade induced wide and persistent differences between costs, especially labor costs, of manufacturing. As barriers came down in the wake of global trade negotiations and major improvements in transport and communications technologies, manufacturing shifted to East Asia and Latin America, raising their real incomes. At the same time, the United States and other developed countries increasingly specialized in conceptual products and intellectual services that are valued highly in the marketplace. In the United States, for example, value-added in finance and insurance rose from 3.0 percent of GDP in 1953 to 7.8 percent in 2006, while in manufacturing it fell significantly over the same years. In chapter 25, I'll address the causes and implications to the United States of this dramatic shift.

Production shifts, such as the transfer of some U.S. textiles and apparel manufacturing abroad, have freed resources to engage in the output of products and services world consumers value more highly. The net result has been increased real incomes, on average, for both U.S. workers and, for example, those in East Asia. The "net," of course, obscures the trauma of job loss suffered by American textile and apparel workers.

The economies of East Asia have come a long way from their humble roots of a half century ago. But can they continue to advance, especially at the pace of recent years? Will the region's progress again be curtailed by a financial crisis, such as the one that was so devastating in 1997? Such a crisis is unlikely, at least in a similar form. Since 1997, the Asian Tigers have dramatically remedied their shortfall of foreign-exchange reserves. More important, they have unlocked their exchange rates from the dollar, which has eliminated much of the short-horizon "carry-trade" investments whose unwinding, in the context of inadequate reserves, set off the crisis.* Thus, unexpected economic shocks should be more easily absorbed than a decade ago.

But can trade and standards of living continue to increase indefinitely? Yes. That is the gift of competitive free markets and the irreversible accumulation of technology. The volume of cross-border trade has few national limits.† Luxembourg's exports, for example, were 177 percent of GDP in 2006, and its imports, 149 percent. Nonetheless, after the major opening up of world markets, especially following the demise of the Soviet Union, many barriers and inefficiencies have already been removed. In a sense, most of the low-hanging fruit of trade openings has already been picked. Certainly the inability to complete the Doha round of trade negotiations in 2006 should give us all pause regarding the future pace of global enhancement of the world's living standards. The rate of decline in trade barriers is almost surely going to slow as we reach the point of intractable political resistance to further lowering. This suggests that the growth of export-oriented economies, such as those of East Asia, is not likely to be as rapid as that of the last six decades.

Eventually, the convergence, or at least the reduction, of risk-adjusted spreads of costs among competitors of internationally traded goods—manufactures and commodities—will diminish the effectiveness of export-oriented growth strategies. And while service-export-oriented growth policies are very visible—for example, India exporting call-center and computer services to the United States, the process known in the United States as outsourcing—such markets are still very small.

One impediment to ever-rising export shares of China and the Tigers is their rising costs of production. In one of the great ironies of the postwar years, Vietnam is now being sought as the next production platform for expanding market-based—read capitalist—trade. Under the U.S.-Vietnam Bilateral Trade Agreement of 2001, Vietnamese exports to the United

---

*With fixed exchange rates against the dollar, U.S. dollars were borrowed to finance investment in higher-yielding loans to East Asian borrowers. With exchange rates floating, the perceived risk of such transactions rose sharply.

†For any country, exports less imports cannot be greater than GDP less inventory change, and for the world as a whole, exports equal imports. But there is no limit to gross flows.

States increased eightfold, from $1.1 billion in 2001 to $9.3 billion in 2006. U.S. exports to Vietnam more than doubled.

U.S. history after World War II chronicles two military defeats in our war to contain Communism. The first was the rapid retreat of U.S. forces in the face of masses of Chinese military crossing the Yalu River into North Korea in the winter of 1950; the second, our humiliation in abandoning South Vietnam in 1975. We may have lost the battles, but not the war. Both Communist China and Communist Vietnam have been struggling to loosen their central-planning straitjackets for the economic freedom of capitalism, while trying not to say out loud what they are doing. In 2006, America's Merrill Lynch, following Citigroup a year earlier, obtained the right to buy, sell, and market Vietnamese shares on Ho Chi Minh City's fledgling stock exchange. When Bill Gates, the world's richest capitalist, visited Hanoi, he was greeted by Vietnam's top Communist Party leaders and mobbed in admiration. Will miracles never cease? Ideas do matter. Indeed America's capitalistic ideas appeared mightier than our sword.

Perhaps more than any of the other major countries addressed in this book, India symbolizes most powerfully both the productiveness of market capitalism and the stagnation of socialism. India is fast becoming two entities: a rising kernel of world-class modernity within a historic culture that has been for the most part stagnating for generations.

This kernel of modernity appears to have largely leapfrogged the twentieth-century labor-intensive manufacturing-for-export model embraced by China and the rest of East Asia. India has focused instead on twenty-first-century high-tech global services, the most rapidly growing segment of world economic activity. The spark of modernity has triggered advances in the whole Indian service sector, including trade, tourism, and tourism-related construction. The pickup in real GDP growth from 3.5 percent between 1950 and 1980 to 9 percent in 2006 has been truly remarkable. These advances have elevated more than 250 million people out of the extreme subsistence poverty incomes of less than $1 per day.

Yet India's per capita GDP, which was at parity with China's in the early 1990s, is now only two-fifths that of China. In fact, at $730 per person, it is below the per capita GDP of Côte d'Ivoire and Lesotho. The reason for India's failure to follow China off the lower rungs of developing nations over the past fifteen years is an idea.

When Britain declared Indian independence in 1947, it withdrew all aspects of British governing, but left behind a concept that captivated India's elite: Fabian socialism. Jawaharlal Nehru, a disciple of the revered Mahatma Gandhi and Indian prime minister for sixteen years following independence, was firmly attracted by the rationality of the Fabians, and he perceived market competition as economically destructive. Because of him, socialism has retained a firm grip on Indian economic policy long after it was abandoned by Britain.

Nehru was entranced by central planning as the rational extension of human beings acting in concert to produce material well-being for the many rather than the few. As prime minister, he initially focused on state ownership of strategic industries, mainly electric power and heavy industry, while imposing significant controls on all else, administered by a cadre of knowledgeable, ostensibly benevolent government officials.

Soon these ubiquitous controls, the "license raj" as they came to be called, had infiltrated virtually all Indian economic activity. You needed a license, permit, or stamp for seemingly every conceivable economic action. Thus constrained, India settled into a placid rate of growth that came to be known derisively as the "Hindu 3 percent." The bureaucracy did not know what to do. Its "scientific" system was supposed to elevate growth. It didn't. Yet to abolish controls would be to abandon the egalitarian principles of Fabian socialism.

Since the plethora of licenses, permits, and stamps didn't seem to help the economy (in fact, they were stifling it), what decisions the bureaucracy made on granting permits soon lost all higher purpose and became arbitrary. But as I noted in describing the Chinese Communist Party's pyramid of authority, discretion is power. Even the most principled Indian civil servants were reluctant to cede it, and the less principled had something to sell. No wonder India was (and is) rated poorly in every measure of corruption.

Thus, a bureaucracy encompassing most every segment of the Indian economy was in firm control and ceded power only reluctantly. That reluctance was reinforced and supported by India's powerful and entrenched labor unions, and particularly by the communist parties that have always been prominent in Indian politics. Socialism not only is a form of economic organization but also, because of its fundamental premise of collective ownership, has profoundly important cultural implications, most of which have been embraced by a majority of Indians.

India is impressively the world's largest democracy. Democracy elects people who represent the population, and in India's case it, as it should, has continued to favor significantly those who believe in the collective principles of socialism. The notion that government intellectuals, driven by the good of society overall, can far better determine the appropriate allocation of resources than can "erratic" free-market forces dies hard in India.

In June 1991, an old-line functionary, P. V. Narasimha Rao of the leftist Congress Party, became prime minister. The economy was teetering on the edge of collapse, reflecting more than four decades of de facto central planning. Now, as it was becoming evident that India was suffering from the same failed paradigm that had blighted Eastern Europe, a major change was in the offing. To everyone's surprise, Rao broke with long-standing tradition and, as a balance-of-payments crisis loomed, moved to eliminate aspects of the deadening hand of controls. He appointed Manmohan Singh finance minister.

Singh, a market-oriented economist, was able to tear a modest hole in the regimented economy—he initiated liberalizing steps in a wide range of areas—and demonstrated once again that a little economic freedom and competition can exert extraordinary leverage on economic growth. The anti-capitalist voices were temporarily stilled by the gravity of the crisis, which created a window of opportunity for deregulation. Market capitalism was able to gain a foothold and demonstrate its effectiveness.

Much of recent global economic history is the story of the centrally planned states of Eastern Europe and China adopting market competition and being rewarded with a rapid increase in economic growth. India's is not quite that story. To be sure, Singh introduced much reform, but in many critical areas he was constrained by the enduring socialist inclinations of his governmental coalition. Even today, firms with more than one hundred employees with few exceptions cannot fire anyone without government permission.

The reforms initiated by Singh in 1991 are still unfolding. Somewhat lowered tariff barriers have freed entrepreneurs to participate in international competitive markets.* Both exports and imports of goods have risen sharply relative to nominal GDP, and net software exports went up from $5.8 billion in 2001 to $22.3 billion in 2006. Of course, Indian exporters still have to contend with red tape at home, but for them property-rights protection and price and cost determination are now largely beyond the bureaucracy's reach.†

The liberalizations of Singh, combined with the fall in global communications costs, educated Indians' English-language skills, and low wages, propelled India into the forefront of internationally outsourced business services: call centers, software engineering, insurance claim processing, mortgage lending, accounting, X-ray scan evaluations, and an ever-widening spread of Internet-based services. Indian software engineers helped the world rise to the Y2K challenge.

The image of India as a major provider of outsourcing was particularly evident to Americans, who exaggeratedly viewed India as cutting a wide swath through skilled U.S. white-collar jobs. But India's competitive incursion has been modest to small, especially in proportion to its workforce of nearly 450 million.

Total employment in India's information technology industry is currently about 1.5 million, five times its level of 1999. Almost all the increase is export related. Another 3 million jobs have apparently been created in telecommunications, power, and construction as a consequence of the IT surge. Directly and indirectly, that's barely 1 percent of total employment in India. And that's the problem.

The IT industry and other services isolated in the major cities of Bangalore, Delhi, and Mumbai have vaulted over the twentieth century into the twenty-first. But as a government official complained to a BBC inter-

---

*Nonetheless, India's tariffs are still double the average levels for Southeast Asian countries, increasing the costs of materials consumed in production for export. India still comprises only 2.5 percent of global trade in goods and services. China accounts for 10.5 percent.

†Property rights in India are significantly undermined by the cost of enforcing a contract. According to the World Bank, it takes 425 to 1,165 days (depending on the state) to enforce a contract in Indian courts. Nine-tenths of land in India is subject to disputes over ownership.

viewer in early 2007, "Go out beyond the glitter of some of the cities and you are back in the nineteenth century." For India to become the major player in the international arena that it aspires to be, it will need to build factories that entice a very large part of its agricultural workers to urban enclaves to produce labor-intensive exports, the time-honored path of the successful Asian Tigers and China.

Manufacturing in India, however, even high-tech, has been hobbled for decades by job-destroying labor laws, a decrepit infrastructure that cannot provide reliable electric power,* and roads and rails that inhibit movement of manufactured parts and finished products between plants and markets. Owing to costly labor laws that apply to establishments of ten or more employees, more than 40 percent of employment in all manufacturing takes place in firms employing five to nine workers. This compares with only 4 percent in Korea. Productivity in these small Indian firms is 20 percent or less of that of large firms; the small firms evidently can't create the economies of scale available to the larger firms. If mass manufacturing is ever to close the gap in standards of living between India and China, the rival to which it is so often compared, India will need to encourage agricultural labor to migrate to the manufacturing sector in the cities. And to encourage workers tied to the land to leave, manufacturing will have to become globally competitive. That will require a major scrapping of the remaining parts of the license raj. In play is the fate of the three-fifths of the Indian workforce who toil inefficiently on farms. They need a dramatic change for the better.

Rural India is mired in a level of poverty as bleak as anywhere in the world outside of sub-Saharan Africa. Here is where a high concentration of India's illiterate (two-fifths of the adult population) and most of the more than 250 million Indians who live on less than $1 a day reside. Half of India's homes have no electricity. Productivity on farms is only one-fourth of what it is in nonfarm areas. Rice yields are half of what they are in Vietnam and a third of what they are in China. India's cotton's comparative yields are even worse. Wheat yields, which so benefited from the enhanced seed of the green revolution of the 1970s, are still only three-fourths of China's.

---

*Many business establishments have installed their own small generators to ensure power.

Only in tea is India more productive than its Asian competitors. Moreover, Indian road transport linking farms and cities is so inadequate that output of perishable crops is largely restricted to on-farm consumption; a third of crops is reported to rot en route to market.

Growth of agricultural productivity has slowed since the 1980s. Although weather has been partly to blame, a highly subsidized government-directed agriculture that prevents market forces from adjusting acreage usage is the main culprit. The government in recent years has expended more than 4 percent of GDP on subsidies, mainly on food and fertilizer, while state subsidization of power and irrigation has added measurably more. If farmworkers are encouraged to migrate to the more productive cities, as has happened in China, a level of agricultural output that feeds 1.1 billion people must be maintained. India's ability to expand food imports is limited. Farm productivity growth is thus the only viable way to maintain food availability as manufacturing draws workers from rural India. Market competition in agriculture is badly needed.

Martin Feldstein, the eminent Harvard economist, in a somewhat different context, stressed an irony that is applicable to India's farm policy dilemma in an essay in the *Wall Street Journal* (February 16, 2006): "Cellphone service is widely available [in India] at low cost because it was regarded as a luxury and therefore left to the market, while electricity is hard to obtain because it has been regarded as a necessity and therefore managed by the government."

Regrettably, the dismantling of large farm subsidies seems no more likely in Delhi than it does in Paris or Washington. Long-term subsidies are capitalized in the value of the land. The net beneficiaries of subsidies are always those who own land when the subsidies are created. Future owners pay for the expected continued subsidy flow in an elevated purchase price of the land. They are not, in principle, net beneficiaries. To increase taxes on farmlands—which, in effect, is what an uncompensated reduction in subsidies does—is not taken lightly by farm owners. Some progress in trimming these subsidies has been accomplished on the edges, but a frontal assault will be difficult considering the leanings of the Congress Party and its twenty-three coalition partners, including the Communists. Prime Minister Singh is a highly reputable reform-oriented economist, but he does not have the authoritarian clout that enabled Deng Xiaoping to start China's agricultural reform in 1978. Indian democracy is up to this task. It needs only to focus on the urgent needs of India's population. A very large dose of deregulation and competition can spread India's IT revolution to the rest of the country.*

India's rapidly growing IT sector is largely the result of homegrown software programmers and engineers. While Indian entrepreneurs are doing exceptionally well in high-tech service, they are doing less well with high-tech hardware, which suffers many of the shortcomings of Indian manufacturing overall.

The manufacturing-for-export model that India urgently needs to embrace has an impressive record of success elsewhere in Asia. It is a model that employs in mass urban manufacturing centers low-wage rural workers with some education. A critical ingredient has been foreign direct investment (FDI) embodying advanced technologies and attracted by laws (often newly drawn) protecting property rights. With the demise of central planning, this model has spread across the developing world, especially China.

But clearly the license raj has discouraged foreign direct investment. India received $7 billion in FDI in 2005, a sum dwarfed by China's $72 billion. India's cumulative stock of FDI at 6 percent of GDP at the end of 2005 compares with 9 percent for Pakistan, 14 percent for China, and 61 percent for Vietnam. The reason FDI has lagged badly in India is perhaps no better illustrated than by India's unwillingness to fully embrace market forces. That is all too evident in India's often statist response to economic problems. Faced with rising food inflation in early 2007, the response was not to allow rising prices to prompt an increase in supply, but to ban wheat exports for the rest of the year and suspend futures trading to "curb speculation"—the very market forces that the Indian economy needs to break the stranglehold of bureaucracy.

---

*Growth in India's industrial production has accelerated since 2004, but the nation still lags behind China's growth in services and especially industrial production.

SIXTEEN

RUSSIA'S SHARP ELBOWS

To say I was startled doesn't do the moment justice. Vladimir Putin's chief economic adviser, Andrei Illarionov, approached me after a U.S.-Russia bilateral meeting at the International Monetary Fund in October 2004 and asked, "The next time you are in Moscow, would you be willing to meet with me and some of my friends to discuss Ayn Rand?" For Rand, the uncompromising defender of laissez-faire capitalism and fiery foe of Communism, to have penetrated the cloistered enclave of Russian intellectual leadership was to me mind-boggling. Putin certainly must have been familiar with Illarionov's staunch defense of free competitive markets when he hired him. Was Illarionov thus a window into the policy inclinations of Putin? Was the culture under which all Russians were raised being shed that quickly? It seemed incredible that Putin, this former member of the KGB, could have developed so un-Soviet a perspective in so short a time.

The reality, obviously, is far more complex. When Putin was appointed acting president by Boris Yeltsin at the end of 1999, he capped an astonishing rise through the ranks that had started only four years earlier when he began working in Moscow as a presidential adviser. He was named deputy head of presidential administration in 1997 and came to the attention of the world in 1998 when, as head of the Federal Security Service, he ordered Russian troops into Chechnya. His presidency was embraced by reformers, who felt confident he would promote continued evolution to a market economy. From the start, Putin expressed support for such reforms, although he argued that they must work in concert with "Russia's realities," including the tradition of a paternalistic state.

Within two years, Putin, along with Illarionov, pushed through the Duma an aggressive agenda of tax reform, deregulation, and some privatization of land, with the clear goal of steering Russia into the global economy.

But after this promising embrace of capitalism, Putin began to backtrack toward authoritarianism. Apparently, he feared that Russia would become subject to market forces over which he had no control. In particular, the oligarchs—business opportunists who had laid claim to much of Russia's productive wealth through special loans-for-shares deals with the Kremlin during the 1990s—were seen as using their riches to subvert his regime. As a consequence, starting in 2003, a different economic strategy began to emerge. Through selective enforcement of new and existing laws, Putin wrenched control of myriad energy assets back into the Kremlin's orbit. The key driver of Russian economic growth—oil and gas—is becoming increasingly nationalized in Russian government-owned or government-controlled monopolies like Gazprom, which dominates natural gas, and Rosneft, which dominates oil. Mikhail Khodorkovsky, the founder of Yukos Oil, was jailed and stripped of his assets, which Rosneft then swallowed.

I do not pretend to know whether Khodorkovsky was guilty of the crimes with which he was charged. But the stark shift from the Kremlin's earlier market liberalism clearly disillusioned Illarionov, and he was soon publicly criticizing his boss. He openly called the retroactive tax claim on Yukos's assets and the scarcely hidden financial manipulations in favor of Rosneft the "swindle of the year."

Given Putin's KGB roots and his upbringing in a collectivized society, it is unlikely that he has a deep understanding of how free markets work. But his choice of Illarionov as chief economic adviser had to mean he had been attracted by the evident successes of capitalism in fostering high standards of living. Ultimately, however, Putin may have found himself more threatened by the seeming anarchy of Yeltsin's capitalism than inspired by the stabilizing force of Adam Smith's invisible hand. Then again, I doubt that Adam Smith was the primary issue on Putin's mind. His seizure of Russia's oil and gas wealth, and his ham-handed cutoff of natural gas to Ukraine and Western Europe for two days in January 2006 were most likely aimed at restoring Russia's international relevance.

What is remarkable in all this is that it took so long for Illarionov to be demoted. Eventually he was relieved of his role as presidential representative to the G8 heads of government, and in 2005 he resigned, stating that Russia was no longer a free country. But Illarionov's extended Kremlin tenure may reflect a grudging attraction by Putin to the capitalist paradigm. Putin's ambivalence about retreating fully from Yeltsin's democracy surfaced in a revealing exchange with former Soviet leader Mikhail Gorbachev, who described it in a 2006 radio interview. Gorbachev quoted President Putin as saying that "the influence of mafia groups and other such elements is so strong that elections become buyer-seller situations." This was bad, Gorbachev said Putin told him, "because you can't have democracy and fight crime and corruption if criminal elements are able to infiltrate the ranks of the government in such a way."*

Is Putin a man who would be drawn to democracy if crime and corruption were largely eliminated, or is he just an effective debater on the side of authoritarianism? Gorbachev seems to believe the former. Certainly a significant part of the Russian economy under Putin continues to throw off

---

*In the same March 1, 2006, interview, Gorbachev said, "As a country in transition, it is inevitable that some freedoms are impinged on and that some mistakes are made. But I am convinced that our president is not trying to install any sort of authoritarian rule." Ironically, he made these remarks on Radio Free Europe, the American broadcasting system created to counter Soviet propaganda. He added in an August 18, 2006, interview, also on Radio Free Europe: "There are frequent accusations that democracy is being suppressed and that freedom of the press is being stifled. The truth is, most Russians disagree with this viewpoint. We find ourselves at a difficult historical juncture. Our transition to democracy has not been a smooth one. . . . When Putin first came to power, I think his first priority was keeping the country from falling apart, and this required certain measures that wouldn't exactly be referred to as textbook democracy. Yes, there are certain worrying antidemocratic tendencies. . . . However, I would not dramatize the situation."

the shackles of Soviet central planning, an indication of an acceptance of greater freedoms.*

Putin behaves as though he believes free markets are fine for most of Russia's economy. But he likely also believes that de facto state control of major energy assets would prevent continued exploitation of Russia's economic crown jewels by the oligarchs. Those crown jewels, of course, have become immensely more valuable as oil and gas prices have risen to several times their 1998 levels.

No longer bolstered by the Soviet Union's cold war military prestige, Russia at the beginning of the twenty-first century found itself relegated to being a distinctly lesser player on the world scene. Ukraine, Georgia, and other former Soviet republics had drifted out of Russia's orbit and control. To address that, Putin may be strategically employing an asset that in many ways is more potent than the Red Army: a huge presence in world energy markets. The USSR's military was restrained by potential U.S. counteraction. But Russia does not see itself threatened with massive retaliation should it use natural gas as an economic or political weapon. Because Russia is a critical supplier of gas to Western Europe (and to so-called near-abroads like Ukraine), its market power is largely uncontested. In addition, Russia has also become a major player in the world crude oil market, although its leverage there is weaker than in the market for natural gas because oil cannot be monopolized as easily.

I suspect Putin was puzzled by the West's reaction to his management of the negotiation over Gazprom's request for higher prices for natural gas in Ukraine—he was roundly denounced for Soviet-style bullying when his intervention resulted in a brief shutoff of supplies. But, he must have wondered, aren't capitalists supposed to charge what the market will bear and not hesitate to exploit economic advantage for profit? Besides, he was merely removing the subsidy Ukraine had been getting from Russia for years—the related shortfall in delivery of gas to Western Europe was inadvertent. Wouldn't nineteenth-century America's Vanderbilt or Carnegie

---

*A glaring exception is Russia's natural-gas monopoly: Gazprom, created in 1992. Its pricing and its rationing of supplies are reminiscent of Soviet central-planning opaqueness and inefficiencies. Its huge pipeline infrastructure, as a consequence, is not fully maintained and is aging.

have behaved this way? I think not. True capitalists protecting their long-term profitability would have sought a gradual adjustment in the name of good customer relations and maximum *long-term* profitability. While it appears that, since the gas shutdown, Ukraine has become more accepting of Russian near-abroad policies, the incident has prompted customers in Western Europe to seek alternatives to Russian gas, especially liquefied natural gas and other piped sources. That will not serve Russia's long-term interests.

But in the short run, Putin's gas and oil policy has succeeded impressively. Less than two decades after its fall as the leader of the Soviet behemoth, Russia has regained a full measure of global attention. And while Putin has gradually dismantled significant parts of the democracy that evolved under Yeltsin, I'd like to believe that, as Mikhail Gorbachev said in August 2006, "Russia has changed to such an extent that going back now is impossible."

There is no denying that Putin has selectively encouraged market openings and has initiated significant improvements in the rule of law. He has supported drastic revisions of the remnants of the collectivized Soviet legal system. The role of judges and the Russian courts, which were notoriously corrupt, has been redefined to reduce opportunities for bribery and the political manipulation of verdicts. For instance, laws promulgated in 2001 removed many economically meaningless requirements for businesses to obtain licenses, inspections, and product certifications—red tape that had been an open-ended invitation for official corruption. (Low-wage bureaucratic jobs were thus in great demand.) Property rights have been extended in recent years, though struggles over rights to buy and sell farmland reflect much the same Communist ideological hangover that exists in China. Except to challenge the power of the Kremlin, the Russian people are free—to travel, to congregate, and to engage in all the trappings of democratic societies.

The Russian economy is today best described as a market economy backed by a still-imperfect rule of law. A significant segment of the nation's most valued assets is in the hands of the state or of Kremlin allies. Political control has been reinforced through control of the major media operations, with most of the remainder "encouraged" to censor themselves. Putin and his policies remain immensely popular. Objections from the Russian public are few; apparently the chaos of Yeltsin's democracy—including financial defaults that savaged people's savings—left a residue of profound discomfort. A poll in 2006 reported that almost half of the Russian people value material well-being over freedom and human rights: democracy and freedom of speech are not high priorities. Given a choice between the democratic freedoms and economic instability of the Yeltsin years and the stability and authoritarianism that have emerged under Putin, for now most Russians prefer Putin.

This saddens me, but I am not surprised. Perhaps we in the West were too sanguine in expecting a radical reversal in people who for more than seven decades had been indoctrinated in collectivism. As Gorbachev once wrote in the *Financial Times* (July 12, 2006): "The economies of the major western countries took many decades, indeed centuries, to develop and mature. Russia is still less than 20 years on from a totalitarian state based on central planning, and our path to reform requires a little longer, even for us." But history suggests that just as Russians rebelled against the chaos of the 1990s, so too will they tire of restrictions on political freedom. Human nature in this regard is highly predictable. A reaction is not a question of whether, but when.

Since its collapse into bankruptcy in 1998, Russia's economy has recovered beyond most every analyst's expectations. Real per capita GDP has moved well above the precrisis level. The unemployment rate, hovering around 13 percent in 1998, declined to less than 7 percent by early 2007. The inflation rate has fallen to single digits from a twelve-month peak of 127 percent in July 1999, and Russia's foreign-exchange holdings rose from $8 billion at the end of 1999 to nearly $300 billion by 2007. The government's foreign debt has been paid down substantially.

Most of the credit for this sterling economic performance, of course, goes to the dramatic surge in the prices of oil and natural gas. Growth in the value of oil and gas exports accounted for a fifth of the growth in nominal GDP between 1998 and 2006. However, few natural-resource bonanzas arrive without a Faustian bargain. Russia's economic policymakers are confronted with a daunting dilemma: a faster rise in the ruble exchange rate will foster the spread of Dutch disease, but foreign-asset purchases to slow the rising foreign-exchange value of the ruble may uncork inflation, depending on the mechanism used. Either would undo much of the economic progress Russia has made since the dissolution of the Soviet Union.

Dutch disease symptoms are already evident. As oil and gas exports surged, the value of the ruble rose and the value of Russian noncommodity exports lagged. Between 1998 and 2006, the value of the ruble relative to the currencies of Russia's trading partners doubled, after adjusting for their relative inflation rates. The impact was predictable: exports excluding oil and gas went up only half as fast in real terms as oil and gas exports.

Fully cognizant of the danger they face—and having watched Dutch disease cripple the economies of many OPEC oil producers—the Russians are in a battle to counter its effects. The standard treatment for Dutch disease is to buy foreign currencies with the country's domestic currency and thereby attempt to fight the market-driven rise in the country's exchange rate. The hope is to avoid, or at least mitigate, the negative competitive effects of the higher exchange rate on domestically produced goods. In the case of Russia, the central bank uses rubles in vast quantities to buy dollars or euros.

But this increases the monetary base, the raw material of money-supply creation, and risks inflation. Between 1998 and the end of 2006, the money supply—currency plus bank deposits—rose at a 45 percent annual rate. Unit money supply—that is, money supply divided by output—rose at a 35 percent annual rate.* That even the relatively high Russian inflation rate of almost 10 percent a year has been running far short of the rate of increase in unit money supply is doubtless puzzling and worrying to Russian monetary authorities who fear a resurgence of inflation.

Of course, the Central Bank of Russia, like all central banks, has the ability to destroy as well as create money. It docs so by selling ruble-denominated debt to the public and then extinguishing the proceeds. But the CBR is limited by the lack of a broad ruble debt market and of a sophis-

---

*Over the long run, the general price level tends to track unit money supply, since prices are defined in terms of money—for example, $4 per bushel of wheat. In simple terms, the more money outstanding to purchase the flow of produced goods and services, the higher the average price.

ticated banking system to facilitate debt sales, a heritage of these institutions' lowly status in the USSR. Without ready means of sopping up and destroying the excess rubles created by CBR purchases of dollars and other foreign currency, Russia would soon have to curtail its foreign-currency purchases and allow the ruble to rise faster—triggering a Dutch disease relapse.

Finance Minister Alexei Kudrin and his colleagues addressed this challenge starting in 2004. They have been designating a long-term nominal oil price, which, when exceeded, triggers the diversion of oil-related revenue from the Russian budget into a special fund administered by the Ministry of Finance. This so-called stabilization fund can be invested only in designated foreign assets (largely foreign-government debt). Purchasing foreign assets directly with the budgeted "excess" oil revenues denominated in foreign currencies avoids increasing the monetary base and hence reduces the potential for inflation. By the spring of 2007, the fund had exceeded $117 billion, 97 percent of which was in foreign currencies (almost all in U.S. dollars and euros, roughly equally divided). For Russia's politicians, the downside of the stabilization fund is that it puts out of reach a great deal of cash. While it is true that government spending has risen significantly with the explosion of oil- and gas-related revenues, Kudrin has succeeded, so far, in fending off pressure to feast on the oil bonanza. I had many occasions to meet with Kudrin when he appeared as a guest at G7 meetings of finance ministers and central bankers. He is very able, but I fear he is facing an uphill battle. It is unclear to me how much sway he has with Putin, other than on technical financial issues.

Russia is still a developing nation whose oil and gas resources dominate its GDP. According to the World Bank, Russia's per capita gross national income in 2005 was below that of Mexico and about the same as Malaysia's. The ability to handle the stress of Dutch disease is obviously affected by the severity of the virus relative to the overall size of an economy.

Yet why should Russia care if it has created an economy beholden to oil and gas? It is using some of its export revenues to import high-quality consumer goods from the rest of the world. Does it matter if those goods are produced at home or abroad? Indeed, it would not matter at all if oil and gas value-added continued to grow as a consequence of ever-increasing output and/or ever-increasing prices. But oil and gas output is ultimately constrained by geology, and prices go down as well as up. Production from oil and especially natural gas reservoirs decays at a rate that requires a never-ending stream of new wells to keep production constant, not to mention rising. Without endless price increases, flat oil and gas output implies stagnant value-added per worker. Oil and gas investment has slowed in recent years; a stagnant standard of living could result. To be sure, to counter that risk, the Russian government is using some of its oil and gas revenues to directly or indirectly finance acquisition of nonenergy productive assets. The list is long—steel, aluminum, manganese, titanium, tankers, and aircraft. But these are largely technologies originally developed a century earlier. Moreover, these industries are poised to serve as "national champions" rather than profit-maximizing organizations. A Russian presence at the cutting edge of twenty-first-century technologies has yet to be felt, although President Putin and his advisers announced ambitious plans in 2005 for special, albeit state-controlled, technology zones.

The sharp fall in the value of the ruble following Russia's collapse into bankruptcy in 1998 forced the conversion of a grossly uncompetitive economy built up under generations of central planning into a marginally competitive one. With output per hour so low across Russia's vast territorial expanse, continuous shedding of grossly overmanned factories brought many industries to the margin of international competitiveness. Russia's substantial pent-up demand for consumer goods, combined with the possibilities of large foreign investment, would no doubt have propelled consumer goods output, if only investors had been able to count on ownership rights.*

Despite defined codes, property rights in Russia remain tenuous. In recent years the Duma has promulgated major pieces of legislation to support the rule of law. And the formal legal structure that rules today's Russia is a marked improvement over the black-market economy of the early 1990s. It is one thing, however, to change the law; it is quite another to enforce the new rules. Putin used selective enforcement of new or existing

---

*A markedly "overvalued" ruble, of course, would doubtless inhibit such investments.

statutes to take government control of energy assets. This selective enforcement, rather than any shortage of new rules, is the problem. There is little difference in legal certainty between a nation whose laws inhibit individual rights to property and one in which full legal rights are selectively enforced according to political priority. A right selectively enforced is not a right.

Civilized societies have built up a vast set of cultural imperatives and conventions governing people's interactions with one another and the state. Very few are written down, and most of us are not fully aware of the extent to which societal forces, religion, and education direct even the minutest of our choices day by day. To be sure, our legal system is also based on these values, but of necessity in only general terms.

Thus, a nation such as Russia may rewrite its legal code, but to reorder the cultural code is a task that will span years, if not generations. Consistent with Gorbachev's reports of his discussions with Putin, this may explain, but scarcely sanctions, the authoritarian thrust of recent Russian politics. In Russia if the "system" is not working, you tighten the political reins by eliminating political pluralism and the messy democratic process that drives it. Stability and political calm are highly valued over the seeming chaos of highly competitive markets for goods and services or the democratic battles for political power.

Capitalism, the engine of material well-being, thrives best with competitive politics. Authoritarian rule does not offer the necessary safety valve that in a capitalist society makes it possible to resolve disputes peacefully. The global economy—which must move forward if the world's standards of living are to continue to rise and poverty to retreat—requires capitalism's safety valve: democracy.

Russia is destined to play a role in the further evolution of global capitalism. Whether that role will be limited by a slow-growing domestic economy sapped by Dutch disease, and a suboptimal allocation of capital resources so typical of authoritarian regimes, will be determined over the next couple of decades. Certainly, to date, Russia appears to have weathered the Dutch disease more like a developed nation than like a developing one. So I would never count Russia out. As a graduate student, I was always impressed by the significant proportion of major mathematical insights footnoted with Russian names. Such a culture, I thought at the time, deserved a far more sophisticated economy than the Soviets were able to produce. Modern Russia has another shot at economic eminence. Much depends on whom Putin anoints as his successor. With its energy and military assets, Russia will be a major player on the world scene for decades ahead. Yet it is far too soon to conclude what type of player it will be.

SEVENTEEN

LATIN AMERICA AND POPULISM

Pedro Malan, the finance minister of Brazil, sat across the table from me at a December 1999 meeting in Berlin. He was typical of the many highly competent Latin American economic policymakers who attended that first meeting of the Group of Twenty, an organization of finance ministers and central bank governors that had been put together after several tumultuous years in global finance. While we already knew one another, establishment of the group was seen as a way to help make sure that emerging-market countries were fully involved in discussions of global economic developments.*

As central banker in 1994, Malan, under the leadership of Brazilian president Fernando Henrique Cardoso, was one of the architects of the Plano Real, which successfully brought the nation's roaring inflation to a halt after it had surged more than 5,000 percent during the twelve months between mid-1993 and mid-1994. I greatly admired Pedro. But I couldn't

---

*The G20 finance ministers and central bankers include the monetary authorities of the G7 nations (Canada, France, Germany, Italy, Japan, the United Kingdom, the United States), twelve other countries (Argentina, Australia, Brazil, China, India, Indonesia, Mexico, Russia, Saudi Arabia, South Africa, South Korea, Turkey), and the European Union.

let go of a nagging question about the country: How could an economy be so mismanaged as to require so drastic a reform? Even Cardoso himself now says, "When the job fell to me, who in their right mind would have wanted to be president of Brazil?"

More broadly, how did Latin America bolt from one economic crisis to another, and from civilian to military rule and back, in the 1970s, 1980s, and 1990s? The simple answer is that, with too few exceptions, Latin America had not been able to wean itself from the economic populism that had figuratively disarmed a whole continent in its competition with the rest of the world. I was particularly distressed by evidence that despite the indisputably bad economic outcomes of populist policies undertaken by almost all Latin American governments at one time or another since the end of World War II, these results had not seemed to dampen the impulse to resort to economic populism.

Clearly, the twentieth century was not kind to the United States' southern neighbors. According to the eminent economic historian Angus Maddison, Argentina began the century with a real per capita GDP greater than that of Germany and almost three-fourths that of the United States. By the end of the century, however, Argentine per capita GDP had declined to half or less of those of Germany and the United States. Mexico's, during the century, fell from one-third to one-fourth of U.S. per capita GDP.* The economic pull of its northern neighbor was not enough to avert the slide. During the twentieth century, the standards of living of the United States, Western Europe, and Asia each rose almost a third faster than those of Latin America. Only Africa and Eastern Europe did as poorly.

The dictionary defines "populism" as a political philosophy that supports the rights and power of the people, usually in opposition to a privileged elite. I see *economic* populism as a response by an impoverished populace to a failing society, one characterized by an economic elite who are perceived as oppressors. Under economic populism, the government accedes to the demands of the people, with little regard for either individual rights or the economic realities of how the wealth of a nation is increased or even sustained. In other words, the adverse economic consequences of the policies

---

*These per capita GDPs are all reported in real terms.

are ignored, willfully or inadvertently. Populism is most evident, as one would expect, in economies with high levels of income inequality, such as in Latin America. Indeed, inequality in all Latin American economies is among the highest in the world, far greater than in any industrial country and, notably, higher than that of any of the economies of East Asia.

The roots of Latin American inequality lie deep in the European colonization that, from the sixteenth through the nineteenth centuries, exploited slaves and indigenous populations. Its remnants today are to be seen, according to the World Bank, in large racial disparities in income. As a result, Latin America was fertile ground for the emergence of economic populism in the twentieth century. Grinding poverty exists side by side with economic affluence. The economic elites are invariably accused of using the power of government to pad their own money belts.

The United States is mistakenly perceived to this day to be a prime cause of economic misery south of its border. For decades, Latin politicians have railed against American corporate capitalism and "Yankee imperialism." Particularly nettlesome to Latins has been a century of U.S. economic and military dominance and the use of "gunboat diplomacy" to assert American property rights. President Theodore Roosevelt in 1903 went a step further, abetting a revolt that detached Panama from Colombia, after Colombia refused permission for the United States to build a canal through Panama. It is no wonder that Pancho Villa became a hero to Mexicans. Villa had been terrorizing American settlements on the border, and an extended U.S. military incursion into Mexico in 1916 (led by General John Pershing) failed to apprehend him.

The broader Latin response was best captured by Lázaro Cárdenas's act of defiant anti-Americanism that propelled him to become possibly the most popular Mexican president in the twentieth century. In 1938, he expropriated all foreign-owned oil properties, mainly those of Standard Oil of New Jersey and Royal Dutch Shell. His action had dire long-term consequences for Mexico.* Yet Cárdenas is remembered as a hero, and the family

---

*Petróleos Mexicanos (PEMEX), the government-owned oil monopoly successor to those foreign firms, is faltering. Unless the company obtains heretofore prohibited foreign assistance in deepwater drilling, its aged reserves will decline.

name, almost alone, fell just short of electing his son Cuauhtémoc to the presidency of Mexico in 1988.

Since the end of World War II, indeed going back to Franklin Roosevelt's Good Neighbor Policy, American foreign policy has made attempts to improve our negative image. Moreover, most objective analysts, I suspect, would credit postwar U.S. investment as an overall contributor to Latin America's prosperity. But history hangs heavy in the region. The beliefs that pass from one generation to another, a society's culture, change very slowly. Many twenty-first-century Latin Americans, in my experience, continue to rail against the United States. Venezuela's Hugo Chávez in particular has worked assiduously to fan anti-American feelings.

Economic populism seeks reform, not revolution. Its practitioners are clear about the specific grievances to be addressed, but its prescriptions are vague. Unlike capitalism or socialism, economic populism does not bring with it a formalized analysis of the conditions necessary for the creation of wealth and rising standards of living. It is far from cerebral. It is more a shout of pain. Populist leaders offer unequivocal promises to remedy perceived injustices. Redistribution of land and the prosecution of a corrupt elite who are allegedly stealing from the impoverished are common cure-alls; the leaders promise land, housing, and food for everyone. "Justice" is also coveted and is generally redistributional. In all of its various forms, of course, economic populism stands in opposition to free-market capitalism. But this stance is fundamentally wrong, and is based on a misconception of capitalism. I and many others, both inside and outside the region, would argue that economic populists have a better chance of achieving their goals through more capitalism, not less. Where there has been success—where living standards for the majority have increased—more open markets and increased private ownership have played a crucial part.

The best evidence that populism is primarily an emotional response and not one based on ideas is that populism does not seem to recede in the face of repeated failures. Brazil, Argentina, Chile, and Peru have had multiple episodes of failed populist policies since the end of World War II. Yet new generations of leaders seemingly have not learned from history and continue to reach for populism's simplistic solutions. Arguably, in the process, they have made matters worse.

I regret populist movements' disregard of previous economic failure in their struggle to articulate an answer to their current distress, but I am not surprised by it or by their rejection of free-market capitalism. In fact, I confess, with no small sense of irony, that I have always been puzzled by the willingness of large and often poorly educated populations and their governmental representatives to adhere to the rules of market capitalism. Market capitalism is a broad abstraction that doesn't always conform to untutored views of the way economies work. I presume markets are accepted because of their long history of creating wealth. Nonetheless, as people often complain to me: "I don't know how it works, and it always seems to teeter on the edge of chaos." That is not an altogether illogical feeling, but, as is taught in Economics 101, when a market economy periodically veers off a seemingly stable path, competitive responses act to rebalance it. Since millions of transactions are involved in the rebalancing, the process is very difficult to grasp. The abstractions of the classroom can only hint at the dynamics that, for example, enabled the U.S. economy to stabilize and grow after the September 11 attacks.

Economic populism imagines a more straightforward world, in which a conceptual framework seems a distraction from evident and pressing need. Its principles are simple. If there is unemployment, then the government should hire the unemployed. If money is tight and interest rates as a consequence are high, the government should put a cap on rates or print more money. If imported goods are threatening jobs, stop the imports. Why are such responses any less reasonable than supposing that if you want a car to start, you turn the ignition key?

The answer is that in economies where millions of people work and trade every day, individual markets are so intertwined that if you cap an imbalance, you inadvertently trigger a series of other imbalances. If you put a price ceiling on gasoline, shortages emerge and long lines at filling stations develop, as became all too apparent to Americans in 1974. The beauty of a market system is that when it is functioning well, as it does almost all the time, it tends to create its own balance. The populist view is equivalent to single-entry bookkeeping. It scores only credits, such as the immediate benefits of lower gasoline prices. Economists, I trust, practice double-entry bookkeeping.

Burdened by its dearth of meaningful economic policy specifics, populism, to attract a following, has to claim a moral justification. Accordingly, populist leaders must be charismatic and exhibit a take-charge aura, even an authoritarian competence. Many, perhaps most, such leaders have come out of the military. They do not effectively argue for the conceptual superiority of populism over free markets. They do not embrace Marx's intellectual formalism. Their economic message is simple rhetoric spiced with words like "exploitation," "justice," and "land reform," not "GDP" or "productivity."

To peasants tilling the soil of others, redistribution of land is a cherished goal. Populist leaders never address the potential downside, which can be devastating. Robert Mugabe, president of Zimbabwe since 1987, promised and delivered to his followers the confiscated land of white settlers. But the new owners were not prepared for management of the land. Food production collapsed, necessitating large-scale importation. Taxable income fell sharply, requiring Mugabe to resort to printing money to finance his government. Hyperinflation, at this writing, is unraveling Zimbabwe's social compact. One of Africa's historically most successful economies is being destroyed.

Hugo Chávez, who became Venezuela's president in 1999, is following Mugabe's example. He is ravishing and politicizing Venezuela's once-proud oil industry—the second largest in the world a half century ago. The level of essential oil-field maintenance declined sharply when he replaced most of the government-owned oil company's nonpolitical technicians with cronies of his regime. That caused a permanent loss of several hundred thousand barrels a day of productive capacity. Venezuelan crude oil output dropped from an average of 3.2 million barrels a day in 2000 to 2.4 million barrels a day during the spring of 2007.

Yet fortune has smiled on Chávez. His policies would have bankrupted most any other nation. But since he became president, world oil demand has engendered a near quadrupling of crude oil prices and has, at least for now, bailed him out. Counting its heavy crude oil, Venezuela may well have one of the largest petroleum reserves in the world. But oil in the ground is no more valuable than when it lay dormant for millennia unless you can create an economy to extract it.*

---

*That happened to Venezuela in 1914, the year Royal Dutch Shell brought the technology needed to develop its riches.

A significant dilemma plagues Chávez in his political stance. Two-thirds of his country's oil revenue comes from oil shipped to the United States. It would be quite costly to Venezuela to wean itself from its major customer, because it largely produces a heavy sour crude that requires the capability of U.S. refineries. Diverting oil to Asia would be possible but very costly. Higher prices, of course, would give Chávez room to absorb the extra costs. But by ratcheting up his buying of influence abroad and political support at home, he is gradually, but inexorably, tying his political future to the price of oil. He needs ever-higher prices to prevail. Fortune may not smile on him forever.

The world should be relieved that not all charismatic populists behave like Chávez and Mugabe when gaining office. Luiz Inácio Lula da Silva, a Brazilian populist with a large following, was elected president in 2002. In anticipation of his victory, Brazilian stock markets fell, inflation expectations rose, and much intended foreign investment was withdrawn. But to the surprise of most, myself included, he has largely followed the sensible policies embodied in the Plano Real, which Cardoso, his predecessor, had introduced in taming Brazil's hyperinflation of the early 1990s.

Economic populism makes large promises without considering how to finance them. Too often, delivering on the promises results in a fiscal revenue shortage and makes it impossible to borrow from the private sector or foreign investors. This almost always leads to desperate reliance on the central bank to serve as paymaster. Requiring a central bank to print money to increase government's purchasing power invariably ignites a hyperinflationary firestorm. The result through history has been toppled governments and severe threats to societal stability. This pattern characterized Brazil's inflation episode of 1994, Argentina's of 1989, Mexico's of the mid-1980s, and Chile's of the mid-1970s. The effects on their societies were devastating. As the well-regarded international economists Rudiger Dornbusch and Sebastian Edwards established, "at the end of every populist experiment, real wages are lower than they were at the beginning." Hyperinflation pops up periodically in developing nations—in fact it is one of their defining tendencies.

Can Latin America turn its back on economic populism? Over the past two decades, despite repeated failures of macroeconomic policy, or perhaps because of them, the major countries in the region have nurtured a coterie of economic technicians who certainly have the credentials to lead Latin America in a new direction. The list is studded with policymakers of exceptional talent, most of whom I have had the privilege of working with during some very difficult times in recent decades: Pedro Aspe, Guillermo Ortiz, José Ángel Gurría, and Francisco Gil Díaz in Mexico; Pedro Malan and Arminio Fraga Neto in Brazil; Domingo Cavallo in Argentina; and others. Most hold advanced degrees in economics from prestigious American universities. Some even went on to become heads of state—Ernesto Zedillo in Mexico and Fernando Henrique Cardoso in Brazil. Most instituted productive market-freeing reforms and policies in the face of deep populist resistance, policies that enhanced their economies. Latin America would be in far worse shape without these able practitioners, in my judgment. But the deep divide between the worldview of most of these policymakers and the societies they serve, which remain prone to economic populism, is stubbornly persistent.

Latin America's tenuous hold on economic stability was brought into sharp focus in 2006 by the presidential election in Mexico, which has the region's second-largest economy. Despite much success since the foreign-exchange crisis of late 1994 brought Mexico to the edge of default, a firebrand populist—Andrés Manuel López Obrador—came within a hairbreadth of being elected president. Whether he would, in office, be more Lula than Chávez, I cannot guess.

Can a society with deep economic populist roots change quickly? Individuals can and have. But can a developed economy's market structure—its laws, its practices, its culture—be imposed on a society bred on ancient antagonisms? Brazil's Plano Real suggests the possibilities.

Since stabilizing in 1994, Brazil's inflation has been contained, except for a transitory price surge during its 40 percent exchange-rate devaluation in late 2002. Its economy has performed well and standards of living have risen. To be sure, the failure of the devaluation to spark more than a short-term eruption of inflation may be tied more to global disinflationary forces than to domestic policy, but the Brazilian economy seems to be working for the Brazilian people.

The experience of Argentina, on the other hand, is more sobering. Its economy collapsed in 2002, as the decade-long constitutionally mandated one-to-one link of the Argentine peso to the U.S. dollar broke, with vast disruption to employment and standards of living. The story of the debacle is instructive as to how far reform-minded policymakers can go without the implicit support of the population for the necessary fundamental policies. A society's drive to meet current needs, for example, cannot be thwarted by the imposition of a financial straitjacket. The society must experience progress and trust its leaders before it is willing to invest for the longer term. This change of culture typically takes a very long time.

Argentina was, in most respects, a European culture prior to World War I. A succession of failed economic programs, and periods racked with inflation, created economic instability. Argentina lost ground in international economic comparisons, especially during the autocratic regime of Juan Perón. Its culture was gradually, but significantly, changing. Even the post-Perón regime of the well-intentioned Raúl Alfonsín failed to stem the explosive inflation and stagnation of the heavily regulated Argentine economy.

Finally, in 1991, the situation became so desperate that the newly elected president, Carlos Menem, who ironically ran under the banner of Perón, turned to his able finance minister, Domingo Cavallo, for help. With President Menem's backing, Cavallo tied the Argentine peso one-to-one to the American dollar. This extremely risky strategy could have blown apart within hours of implementation. But the boldness of the move and the seeming credibility of the commitment galvanized world financial markets. Argentine interest rates dropped sharply, inflation fell from 20,000 percent year over year in March 1990 to a single-digit annual inflation rate by late 1991. I was amazed and hopeful.

As a result, the Argentine government was in a position to raise large quantities of dollars in the international markets at interest rates only moderately higher than those required of the U.S. Treasury. The reform views of Cavallo sounded far more sensible to me than the uninformed rhetoric coming at the time from many Argentine legislators and provincial governors. Their views were too reminiscent of the fiscal irresponsibility of earlier decades. I recall looking across the table at Cavallo at another G20 meeting and wondering whether he was aware that the lending backstop to the peso would remain a source of support only if it was not used in excess.

Maintaining that large dollar buffer would likely have enabled the currency peg to hold indefinitely. However, the political system of Argentina could not resist using the abundance of seemingly costless dollars in attempts to accommodate constituents' demands.

Gradually but inexorably, the buffer of dollar-borrowing capacity was drawn down. Dollars often were borrowed to sell for pesos in a futile effort to support the peso-dollar parity. The bottom of the barrel was reached at the end of 2001. Protecting its remaining reserve of dollars, the central bank withdrew its one-for-one offer of dollars for pesos in international markets. As a result, on January 7, 2002, the peso collapsed. By mid-2002, it took more than three pesos to buy one dollar.

A massive default of Argentine debt induced an initial period of soaring inflation and interest rates, but much to my surprise, financial calm was restored relatively quickly. The sharp decline in the peso spurred export sales and economic activity. Inflation was far less a problem than past such episodes would have suggested. A decade from now, I suspect, economic historians will conclude that it was the disinflationary forces of globalization that eased the adjustment.

What I found unusual about this episode was not that Argentine leaders in 2001 were unable to marshal the fiscal restraint required to hold the peso-dollar link, but that they had been able for a while to persuade their population to maintain the degree of restraint that a pegged peso required. It was clearly a policy aimed at inducing a seminal shift in cultural values that would restore the international stature Argentina had enjoyed in the years immediately preceding World War I. But cultural inertia proved, as it had many times before, too formidable a barrier.

It's not that developed countries, such as the United States, have not had flirtations with economic populism. However, in my view, it is unlikely that populist leaders could change the U.S. Constitution or culture to wreak the devastation of a Perón or a Mugabe. William Jennings Bryan, with his stirring "Cross of Gold" speech at the 1896 Democratic convention, was, to me, the most effective voice of economic populism in U.S. history. ("You shall not press down upon the brow of labor this crown of thorns," he declared. "You shall not crucify mankind upon a cross of gold.") Yet I doubt that America would have changed much had he become president.

I would say the same about Huey Long of Louisiana, whose "share the wealth" rhetoric in the 1930s won him a governorship and a seat in the U.S. Senate. His eye was on the White House when he was assassinated in 1935. Populism, however, is clearly not in the genes. His son Russell, whom I knew quite well as the longtime chairman of the Senate Finance Committee, was a staunch supporter of capitalism and business tax breaks.

There have, of course, been numerous episodes of populist *policy*, but not governments, throughout American history, from the free-silver movement of the late nineteenth century to much New Deal legislation. The most recent was Richard Nixon's ill-fated wage-price freeze of August 1971. But President Nixon's and earlier populist policy episodes were aberrations in the economic progress of the United States. Populist policies and governments in Latin America have been endemic and hence much more consequential.

Economic populism is presumed to be an extension of democracy to economics. It is not. Small-*d* democrats support a form of government in which the majority rules on all public issues, but never in contravention of the basic rights of individuals. In such societies, the rights of minorities are protected from the majority. We have chosen to grant to the majority the right to determine all public policy issues that do not infringe on individual rights.*

Democracy is a messy process, and it certainly is not always the most efficient form of government. Yet I agree with Winston Churchill's quip: "Democracy is the worst form of government except for all those other forms that have been tried from time to time." For better or worse, we have no choice but to assume that people acting freely will ultimately make the right decisions on how to govern themselves. If the majority makes the wrong decisions, there will be adverse consequences—even, in the end, civil chaos.

Populism tied to individual rights is what most people call liberal democracy. "Economic populism" as used by most economists, however, refers implicitly to a democracy in which the "individual rights" qualifier is largely

---

*We may require supermajorities to implement certain laws. For example, in the United States, only a supermajority may override a presidential veto—but it was majorities in the assemblies of the thirteen original states that ratified the Constitution, choosing to be governed in that manner.

missing. Unqualified democracy, where 51 percent of the people can *legally* do away with the rights of the remaining 49 percent, leads to tyranny.* The term then becomes pejorative when applied to the likes of Perón, who to most historians is largely responsible for Argentina's long economic decline after World War II. Argentina is still laboring under that legacy.

The battle for capitalism is never won. Latin America demonstrates this perhaps more clearly than any other region. Income concentration and a landed gentry with roots in sixteenth-century Spanish and Portuguese conquests still foster deep and festering resentments. Capitalism in Latin America is still a struggle at best.

---

*Many of our Founding Fathers feared that American majority rule without the first ten amendments to the Constitution of the United States of America—our Bill of Rights—would be tyranny.

CURRENT ACCOUNTS AND DEBT

Consumer short-term debt ... is approaching a historical turning point. . . . It must soon adjust itself to the nation's capacity for going in hock, which is not limitless," declared *Fortune* in March 1956. A month later the magazine added, "The same general observations apply to mortgage debt—but with double force." Chief economist Sandy Parker and coauthor Gil Burck arrived at those dour conclusions after poring over detailed data on the money owed by U.S. households. (The data had been assembled by me, working as a *Fortune* consultant.) Their concern was hardly unique—many economists and policymakers were worried that the ratio of household debt to household income had risen to a point where the American family was in danger of delinquency and default. But the fears turned out to be misplaced, because assets and household net worth were rising more rapidly than we knew.

Today, nearly fifty years later, the ratio of household debt to income is still rising, and critics are still wringing their hands. In fact, I do not recall a decade free of surges in angst about the mounting debt of households and businesses. Such fears ignore a fundamental fact of modern life: in a market economy, rising debt goes hand in hand with progress. To put it more formally, debt will almost always rise relative to incomes so long as we have an ever-increasing division of labor and specialization of tasks, increasing productivity, and a consequent rise in *both* assets and liabilities as a percentage of income. Thus, a rising ratio of debt to income for households, or of total nonfinancial debt to GDP, is not in itself a measure of stress.*

This lesson is worth bearing in mind as we turn to a similar concern: the rise of America's trade deficit and the broader current account deficit. America's current account deficit has climbed steeply in recent years, from zero in 1991 to 6.5 percent of GDP by 2006. At the same time, it has gone from being an arcane footnote in academic journals to headline status across the globe. It has been on the agenda of virtually every international economic gathering I've attended in recent years. It is the focus of a world-wide fear that America's external imbalance—the dramatic gap between what the nation imports and what it exports—will precipitate both a collapse of the U.S. dollar's foreign-exchange value and a world financial crisis. A sliding dollar could become a central focus of policymakers' fears about the sustainability of globalization, the creator of much of the world's increased prosperity over the past decades.

The concerns about the U.S. external deficit are not groundless. It is certain that at some point foreign investors will not want to increase further the proportion of U.S. assets in their portfolios. That is the financing counterpart to the payments deficit. At that point, the U.S. imbalance must narrow, with the dollar likely having to decline in order to stimulate U.S. exports and dampen U.S. imports. Moreover, sudden reversals of foreign investor sentiment cannot be entirely ruled out, with the concomitant risk of rapid declines in the dollar's foreign-exchange value. However, it is easy to exaggerate the likelihood of a dollar collapse. Ongoing developments in the world economy have enabled the scale of sustainable financial surpluses and deficits—including those involving cross-border flows—to increase dramatically in recent years without incident. As I point out in chapter 25, there are a lot of imbalances, especially our potential federal deficit, to worry about in the years ahead. I would place the U.S. current account far down the list.

---

*Nonfinancial debt includes the debt of households, businesses, and government but excludes the debt of banks and other financial intermediaries.

At the root of the concerns about the U.S. current account deficit is the fact that by 2006, the financing of that deficit—that is, the inflow of money from overseas—siphoned off more than three-fifths of *all* the cross-border savings of the sixty-seven countries that ran current account surpluses in that year.* Developing countries, which accounted for half of those surpluses, were apparently unable to find sufficiently profitable investments at home that overcame market and political risk. Americans a decade ago likely could not have run up a nearly $800 billion annual current account deficit for the simple reason that we could not have attracted the foreign savings to finance it. In 1995, for example, cross-border savings were less than $350 billion.

Analysts agree that it is often useful to think of a country's current account balance in terms of its accounting equivalent: a country's domestic savings (that is, savings within a country by households, businesses, and governments) less its domestic investment (mainly productive capital assets and homes).† But there the agreement ends.

A country's current account balance and the difference between a country's domestic saving and domestic expenditure on investment will by construction, in a final accounting, always be equal.‡ Those who make decisions to save, however, are not the same as those who make decisions to invest. In fact, if we were to add up the total dollar amount of planned savings and the amount of planned investment for any particular period, they would almost never be equal. They come to equality only after plans are forced to change as trade, income, and asset flows are wrenched into alignment by shifts in exchange rates, prices, interest rates, and therefore levels of economic activity. As with all such market reconciliations, the adjustments of all the variables occur simultaneously. It is the equivalent of a solution to a set of simultaneous equations. The world's checkbook must always balance.

The causes of the outsized U.S. current account deficit of recent years are so interactive that it is difficult to disentangle them. For example, a rise in

---

*Cross-border savings are the sum of the balances of those countries that have surpluses.
†In general, national income accounting establishes that the gap between domestic saving and domestic investment is equivalent to net foreign saving; net foreign saving is a close approximation of the current account balance.
‡There are some technical differences, but they are not important.

household saving, *other things equal*, would lower a country's current account deficit. But other things are never equal. A rise in household saving implies a fall in household spending—and perhaps, as a consequence, a decline in corporate saving as profits decline. And the associated fall in revenues from taxes on profits would lower government saving, and on and on. Since all the components of saving and investment are intertwined, causal relationships are obscure.

Most foreigners and many U.S. analysts point to the burgeoning U.S. budget deficit as the primary cause of our current account imbalance. But over the past decade the fiscal balance has at times veered in directions opposite from the direction of the current account deficit. As our budget was building surpluses between 1998 and 2001, for example, our current account deficit continued to rise.

Some argue that the heavy purchases of U.S. Treasury obligations by other countries' monetary authorities, first Japan and then China, to suppress their exchange rates have elevated the dollar's foreign-exchange value and thereby played a role in the huge increase in U.S. imports (from 13 percent of U.S. GDP in early 2002 to almost 18 percent in late 2006). There is doubtless some truth in that, but the impact of official efforts to manipulate exchange rates, in my experience, is often exaggerated.* Vastly more significant is the U.S. dollar's status as the world's foremost reserve currency, which has so far fostered the financing of our external deficit. Many observers, however, consider this a vulnerability as well—foreign

---

*I have little doubt that China's monetary authorities' purchase of hundreds of billions of dollars to suppress its exchange rate has been successful. The Chinese financial system is still sufficiently primitive that market-generated offsets to those purchases are few. But apparently this is not the case with Japan. There is little evidence that Japan's purchase of hundreds of billions of dollars to suppress the yen has had much effect. Japan is part of a very sophisticated international financial system that can absorb huge quantities of securities with only marginal effects on interest rates and exchange rates. For example, billions of dollars of U.S. Treasury securities can be swapped for equivalent sums in high-grade bonds for a modest cost in terms of basis points. In other words, large accumulations or liquidations of U.S. treasuries can be made with only modest effects on interest rates. The same holds true for exchange rates. The Japanese monetary authorities purchased $20 billion in a single day a number of years ago, without evidence of a significant impact on the yen's exchange rate. Months later, not being adequately aware of the political sensitivity of such operations, I mentioned the ineffectual purchase publicly. My Japanese friends were not amused. Again, in March 2004, the Japanese abruptly ended a long period of very aggressive intervention against the yen. The exchange rate barely responded.

monetary authorities might close out their dollar positions suddenly and en masse by converting reserves to, say, euros or yen. I will address this concern in chapter 25.

The most compelling explanation for the historic rise in the U.S. current account deficit is that it stems from a broad set of forces. This does not have the attraction of a single, "smoking-gun" explanation such as our federal budget deficit, but it is more consonant with the reality of international finance. The rise appears to have coincided with a pronounced new phase of globalization. The key contributors, as I see it, have been a major decline in what economists call "home bias" and a significant acceleration in U.S. productivity growth.

Home bias is the parochial tendency of investors to invest their savings in their home country, even though this means passing up more profitable foreign opportunities. When people are familiar with an investment environment, they perceive less risk than they do for objectively comparable investments in distant, less familiar environs. A decline in home bias is reflected in savers increasingly reaching across national borders to invest in foreign assets. Such a shift causes a rise in current account surpluses of some countries and an offsetting rise in deficits of others. For the world as a whole, of course, exports must equal imports, and the world consolidated current account balance is always zero.

Home bias was very much in evidence globally for the half century following World War II. Domestic saving was directed almost wholly toward domestic investment, that is, plant, equipment, inventories, and housing within investors' sovereign borders. In a world with exceptionally strong home bias, external imbalances were small.

However, starting in the 1990s, home bias began to decline perceptibly, the consequence of a dismantling of restrictions on cross-border capital flows that more or less coincided with the boost to competitive capitalism from the demise of central planning. Private ownership and cross-border investment rose significantly. Moreover, the advance of information and communication technologies has effectively shrunk the time and distance that separate markets around the world. In short, vast improvements in technology and governance have expanded investors' geographic horizons, rendering foreign investment less risky than it appeared in earlier decades.

The increasing evidence of the protection of foreigners' property rights with the fall of central planning has decreased risk still further.

Accordingly, the weighted correlation between national saving rates and domestic investment rates for countries or regions representing virtually all of the world's gross domestic product, a measure of the degree of home bias, declined from a coefficient of around 0.95 in 1992, where it had hovered since 1970, to an estimated 0.74 in 2005. (If in every country saving equaled investment—that is, if there were 100 percent home bias—the correlation coefficient would be 1.0. On the other hand, if there were no home bias, and the amount of domestic saving bore no relationship to the amount and location of investments, the coefficient would be 0.)*

Only in the past decade has expanding trade been associated with the emergence of ever-larger U.S. trade and current account deficits, matched by a corresponding widening of the aggregate external surpluses of many of our trading partners, most recently including China. By 2006, large current account surpluses had emerged: China ($239 billion), Japan ($170 billion), Germany ($146 billion), and Saudi Arabia ($96 billion), all record high surpluses. Deficits in addition to that of the United States ($857 billion) included those of Spain ($108 billion), the United Kingdom ($68 billion), and France ($46 billion). To get a sense of how wide the dispersion (the extent to which saving-minus-investment imbalances of individual countries diverge from zero) has become, I calculated the absolute sum of countries' current account imbalances (irrespective of sign) as a percentage of world GDP. That ratio hovered between 2 and 3 percent between 1980 and 1996. By 2006, it had risen to almost 6 percent.

Decreasing home bias is the major determinant of wider surpluses and deficits, but differences of risk-adjusted rates of return may have been a contributor as well.† And certainly *relative* risk-adjusted rates of return are

---

*Obviously, if domestic saving exactly equaled domestic investment for every country, all current accounts would be in balance, and there would be no dispersion of such balances. Thus, the existence of current account imbalances requires the correlation between domestic saving and domestic investment—which reflects the degree of home bias—to be less than 1.0.

†"Risk-adjusted" is a term economists use to recognize that risky investments, if investors are to be induced to make them, require a higher rate of return to compensate for potential losses. The risk adjustment is an estimate of how much of the return on an asset is merely that extra compensation.

a key factor in determining to which countries excess savings are directed for investment.

Since 1995, the greater rates of productivity growth in the United States (compared with still-subdued rates abroad) apparently produced correspondingly higher risk-adjusted expected rates of return that fostered a disproportionate rise in the global demand for U.S.-based assets. This goes a long way toward explaining why such a large percentage of cross-border savings has been directed to the United States.*

I expect that the disputes over the causes of the recent sharp rise in the U.S. current account deficit will continue. The far more important question, however, is whether the seemingly inevitable external adjustment will be benign or, as many fear, will entail an international financial crisis as the dollar crashes. As I noted, I am far more inclined toward the more benign outcome.

Of greatest concern is what happens when foreigners begin to resist further increasing the share in their investment portfolios of net claims against U.S. residents, which is implied in current trends in external balances. Current account deficits have been cumulating as an ever-rising net negative international investment position of U.S. residents (nearly $2.5 trillion at the end of 2005), with an attendant rise in servicing costs. This trend cannot persist indefinitely. At some point, even if rates of return on investments in the United States remain competitively high, foreign investors will balk at the growing concentration in their investment portfolios. The well-established principle of not putting all your eggs in one basket holds for global finance as well as for the private household. If and when foreigners' appetite for U.S. assets slackens, it will be reflected in lessened demand for U.S. currency and thus a lower foreign-exchange value of the dollar.† A lower dollar, of course, will discourage importers and encourage

---

*To facilitate comparisons, all nondollar currencies are converted to dollars on the basis of market exchange rates. Purchasing power parities (PPPs), the major alternative means of converting, are ill-suited for dealing with cross-border flows of saving and investment. For the world as a whole, saving must equal investment, irrespective of the currency of record. For the years 2003–2005, the absolute value of the statistical discrepancy between world saving and investment was $330 billion annually converting with PPPs, but only $66 billion employing market exchange rates.

†I am disregarding the fact that not all claims against U.S. residents are in dollars, and not all dollar claims, such as Eurodollars, are against U.S. residents. The overlap between claims in dollars and those against U.S. residents is sufficiently large that these differences can be ignored.

exporters. Thus, foreign resistance to financing the U.S. external deficit will in itself reduce the deficit. Diversification of the reserves of the world's monetary authorities, and, even more relevant, the international reserves of private investors, has consequences.

Analysts worry that in order to service rising U.S. net debt to foreigners, our trade deficit will eventually have to be sharply reduced (or returned to surplus) and/or foreigners' willingness to invest in U.S. assets will have to rise enough to supply the funds to meet the servicing requirements of U.S. debtors.* That is not yet a problem, because the rate of return on our more than $2 trillion of U.S. direct investments abroad was 11 percent in 2005, much higher than current interest rates paid to foreigners on U.S. debt. The result is that our debt service and dividend payments to foreigners are still ahead of our receipts from foreigners of such income. But with the inexorable net rise in debt (the equal of the current account deficit adjusted for capital gains and losses), much larger net income payments to foreigners loom.

The reason I suspect that the persistently large U.S. current account deficits through 2006 did not have seriously negative consequences for the U.S. economy is that the deficits are a manifestation, in large part, of an ever-expanding specialization and division of labor that is evolving in a wholly new high-tech global environment. Pulling together all the evidence—anecdotal, circumstantial, and statistical—strongly suggests, to me at least, that the record current account deficit of the United States is part of a broader set of rising deficits and offsetting surpluses reflecting transactions of U.S. economic entities—households, businesses, and governments—mostly within the borders of the United States. These deficits and surpluses have arguably been growing for decades, possibly generations. The long-term up-drift in this broader swath of deficits has been persistent, but

---

*I am often asked why this is a problem, given that nearly all U.S. assets are denominated in dollars. Won't foreigners accept payments in U.S. dollars? Yes, they usually will. But if trade creditors decide to hold the dollar payments, they will have increased their investments in U.S. assets. If, however, they sell the dollars to a third party (in exchange for their own currency), that third party would be investing in U.S. assets. If no one wants to hold more U.S. assets at current prices, the dollars must eventually be sold at a discount on the foreign-exchange market, exerting downward pressure on the exchange value of the dollar.

gradual. However, the component of that broad set that captures only the net foreign financing of the imbalances of the individual U.S. economic entities—our current account deficit—increased from negligible in the early 1990s to 6.5 percent of our GDP by 2006.

From my perspective, policymakers have been focusing too narrowly on foreign claims on U.S. residents rather than on all claims, both foreign and domestic, that influence economic behavior and can be a cause of systemic concern. Current account balances refer only to transactions that cross sovereign borders. Our tabulations are loosely rooted in the obsession of the mercantilists of the early eighteenth century to achieve a surplus in their balance of payments that brought gold, then the measure of the wealth of a nation, into the country.

Were we to measure financial net balances of much smaller geographic divisions, such as the individual American states or Canadian provinces (which we don't), or of much larger groupings of nations, such as South America or Asia, the trends in these measures and their seeming implications could be quite different from those extracted solely from the conventional sovereignty-delineated national measure: the current account balance.

The choice of the appropriate geographical unit for measurement should depend on what we are trying to find out. I presume that in most instances, at least in a policy setting, we seek to judge the degree of economic stress that could augur significantly adverse economic outcomes. Making the best judgment in that case would require data on financial balances at the level of detail at which economic decisions are made: individual households, businesses, and governments. That is where stress is experienced and hence is where actions and trends that may destabilize economies would originate.

When a household spends more than its income on consumption and investments such as a house*—that is, more cash going out than coming in—it is designated by economists as a financial deficit household. It is a net borrower, or liquidator, of financial assets. A household that saves

---

*Investments can, of course, be negative: for example, a sale of an existing house or inventory liquidation.

through accumulation of financial assets or through a reduction in debt is called a financial surplus household, reflecting its positive cash flow. Similar designations are applied to businesses and governments—federal, state, and local. When we consolidate these deficits and surpluses for all U.S. residents, we end up with a residual that consists of Americans' net new claims on, or net new debt to, foreigners—that is, our current account surplus or deficit.*

But before consolidation, the ratios of both financial surpluses and financial deficits of individual U.S. economic entities—households, businesses, and governments—relative to their incomes, on average, have been on the rise for decades, possibly even since the nineteenth century.† For most of that period, deficits of some U.S. resident economic entities were almost wholly matched by surpluses of the remaining economic entities. Our current account balances were accordingly small.‡ What is special about the past decade is that the decline in home bias, coupled with significant capital gains on homes and other assets, has fostered a large increase in U.S. residents' purchase of foreign-produced goods and services, willingly financed by foreign investors.

Aggregate net claims against foreigners only (our current account) is an incomplete statistical picture of the degree of potential economic stress. It may understate or overstate a pending problem for an economy as a whole. Indeed, if we lived in a world where sovereign or other borders were disregarded for transactions in goods, services, and assets, measures of stress of the most narrowly defined economic units would be unambiguously the most informative. Nation-defined current account balances have important special uses relating to exchange rates, but I suspect the measure is too often used to signify some more generic malaise. That is a mistake.

---

*Actually, there are a few small capital transfer reconciling entries needed to achieve the current account balance.

†This is true whether we use the income of individual entities or the nation's gross domestic income or its equivalent gross domestic product. There is no income loss in the consolidation of individual incomes into a national total.

‡One exception was America's post–Civil War current account deficits, largely reflecting foreign financing of the vast railroad network that accounted for much of U.S. economic activity through the end of the century.

The trade and financing imbalances have been growing within the borders of the United States for some time. They reflect increasing specialization of economic function, which goes back to at least the beginnings of the Industrial Revolution. Movement away from economic self-sufficiency of individuals and nations arose from the division of labor, a process that continually subdivides tasks, creating ever-deeper levels of specialization and skill and, as a consequence, improves productivity and standards of living. Such specialization fosters trade among the nation's economic entities and, as it did even during the earliest days of commerce, with our international trading partners.

Over time, ever-growing proportions of U.S. households, nonfinancial businesses, and governments, both national and local, have funded their capital investments from sources other than their own household income, corporations' internal funds, or government taxes. In early America, almost all of that financing originated with U.S. financial institutions or other U.S. entities. The debt of U.S. residents to foreigners was small. The growing (and risk-prone) tendency to borrow in anticipation of future income by a significant proportion of Americans is reflected in a persistent rise in both household and corporate assets and liabilities relative to income.

A detailed calculation by Federal Reserve Board staff employing data from more than five thousand nonfinancial U.S. corporations for the years 1983 to 2004 found that growth in the sum of deficits of those corporations where capital expenditures exceeded cash flow persistently outpaced the growth in corporate value-added. The sum of surpluses and deficits, disregarding sign, as a ratio to a proxy for corporate value-added exhibits an average annual increase of 3.5 percent per year.* Data on the dispersion of the financial deficits of U.S. economic entities aside from nonfinancial corporations are sparse. A separate and less satisfactory calculation of only partly consolidated financial balances of individual economic entities relative to nominal GDP exhibits a rise over the past half century in the ab-

---

*The surpluses (and deficits) are measured as income before extraordinary items, plus depreciation, minus capital expenditures. The proxy for corporate value-added is gross margin, or sales less cost of goods sold.

solute sum of surpluses and deficits that is 1.25 percentage points per year faster than the rise of nominal GDP.*

The increase in the dispersion of the imbalances of the economic entities within U.S. national borders appears to have flattened somewhat over the past decade, according to calculations using data from the partly consolidated financial balances. Since the current account deficit accelerated during those years, it is plausible to assume that the overall process of dispersion of imbalances of U.S. economic entities continued but with an increasing proportion of deficits of U.S. households, businesses, and governments being financed from foreign rather than domestic sources. This is certainly obvious in the financing of our federal budget deficit and of business capital expenditures.† In short, the expansion of our current account deficit during the past decade arguably reflects the shift in trade and financing from within the borders of the United States to cross-border trade and finance.

Thus, the story of the erosion of our current account balance is a story of domestic financial imbalances that spilled out across sovereign borders in the early 1990s, at which point they were measured as rapidly rising cur-

---

*The measure estimates saving less investment imbalances among the seven consolidated nonfinancial sectors recorded in U.S. macroeconomic statistics: households, corporations, nonfarm noncorporate business, farms, state and local governments, the federal government, and the rest of the world. I include the "rest of the world" sector because it measures surpluses or deficits of U.S. residents even though they reflect the accumulation of net claims on, or of obligations to, foreigners. The other six sectors reflect net claims on, or obligations to, domestic residents only.

We do have considerable data on the consequences of surpluses and deficits: levels of unconsolidated debt and assets. The tie, of course, would be exact only if some economic entities always ran a deficit and the remainder always ran a surplus. Then, cumulating the deficits would yield the change in unconsolidated debt outstanding and cumulating the surpluses would yield the change in assets. If that were true, we could infer the degree of dispersion from estimates of unconsolidated assets and liabilities. Indeed, during the past half century, with the exception of the unusual period 1986–91, when the collapse of the savings-and-loan industry distorted the debt figures, the rate of change in both assets and liabilities relative to nominal GDP does rise. That in itself is not proof of rising dispersion, but it is merely another statistic that is consistent with my presumption of a rise in dispersion that over the long run has exceeded the rise in nominal GDP.

†Between 1995 and 2006, the proportion of nonfinancial corporate liabilities owed to foreigners rose markedly as a percentage of total nonfinancial corporate liabilities. The proportion of U.S. Treasury obligations owed to foreigners rose from 23 percent to 44 percent over those years. Foreign lending to U.S. households has always been negligible.

rent account deficits. Any balance that starts with a surplus (as it did in 1991) and becomes a deficit that rises rapidly is always a cause of concern, and almost inevitably becomes a political issue. But unless it matters greatly, for example, whether a U.S. resident corporation finances its capital outlays from foreign rather than domestic sources, the most relevant measure of imbalance should combine both domestic and foreign funding. The stress on U.S. economic entities has arguably increased little with the shift in the source of their financing. The rise in the ratio of imbalances (both foreign and domestic) to GDP is a much more modest and less scary trend than that exhibited by its foreign component (the current account) alone.

Many U.S. businesses, for example, previously purchased components from domestic suppliers but have switched in recent years to foreign suppliers. These companies generally view domestic and foreign suppliers as competitive in the same way that they view domestic suppliers as competing with each other. Moving from a domestic to a foreign source affects international balance-of-payments bookkeeping but arguably not macroeconomic stress. To be sure, firms and workers that lose sales will be adversely affected, at least until they can be reemployed in more competitive uses. But that is no different from the fallout from domestic competition. The one significant difference in a shift to cross-border suppliers is the effects of exchange rates during the adjustment process and beyond. From the perspective of individual stress, however, those effects are similar to those of a change in price of a key purchased component.

Additional evidence that surpluses and deficits of resident economic entities of the United States have indeed been rising relative to incomes over the past century is found in the increase in assets of financial intermediaries relative to nonfinancial assets and to nominal GDP. It is these financial institutions that have largely accepted deposits and made loans to match the financial surpluses and deficits of U.S. residents. Households have deposited the income they did not spend in commercial banks and thrift institutions, for example. The lending of those deposits enabled others to finance investments in homes and capital equipment and plant. Consequently, the size of these institutions can act as an alternative proxy for such surpluses and deficits. Indeed, one can surmise that it has been the need to intermediate these expanding surpluses and deficits that has, over the generations, driven the development of our formidable financial institutions.

Since 1946, the assets of U.S. financial intermediaries, even excluding the outsized growth in mortgage pools, have risen 1.8 percent per year relative to nominal GDP. From 1896 (the earliest date of comprehensive data on bank assets) to 1941, assets of banks, by far the dominant financial intermediaries in those years, rose 0.6 percent per year relative to GDP.

Implicit in a widening dispersion of financial surpluses and deficits of individual economic entities is the expectation of increasing cumulative deficits for some and, hence, a possible accelerating rise in debt as a share of income or its equivalent, GDP.* From 1900 to 1939, nonfinancial private debt in the United States rose almost 1 percent faster per year on average than nominal GDP. World War II and its aftermath inflated away the real burden of debt for a while; the debt-to-GDP ratio accordingly declined. The up-drift in the ratio, however, resumed shortly thereafter: from 1956 to 1996, nonfinancial business debt rose 1.8 percent faster at an annual rate than gross business product, and from 1996 to 2006, 1.2 percent faster.†

A rising debt-to-income ratio for households, or of total nonfinancial debt to GDP, is not, in itself, a measure of stress. It is largely a reflection of dispersion of a growing financial imbalance of economic entities that in turn reflects the irreversible up-drift in division of labor and specialization. Both nonfinancial-sector assets and debt have risen faster than income over the past half century. But debt *is* rising faster than assets; that is, debt leverage has been rising. Household debt as a percentage of assets, for example, reached 19.3 percent by the end of 2006, compared with 7.6 percent in 1952. Nonfinancial corporate liabilities as a percentage of assets rose from 28 percent in 1952 to 54 percent by 1993, but retreated to 43 percent by

---

*Cumulative deficits of individual economic entities will increase net debt—that is, gross debt less financial assets. In the large majority of instances, gross debt will rise with net debt.
†The trend toward intracountry dispersion of financial imbalances is likely occurring not only in the United States but in other countries as well. The existence of such a trend is suggested by the rise in unconsolidated nonfinancial debt of the major industrial economies, excluding the United States, over the past three decades, which has exceeded the growth of GDP by 1.6 percentage points annually.

the end of 2006, as corporations embarked on a major program to improve their balance sheets.

It is difficult to judge how problematic this long-term increase in leverage is. Since risk aversion is innate and unchanging, the willingness to take on increased leverage over the generations likely reflects an improved financial flexibility that enables leverage to increase without increased risk, at least up to a point. Bankers in the immediate post–Civil War years perceived the necessity to back two-fifths of their assets with equity. Less was too risky. Today's bankers are comfortable with a tenth. Nonetheless, bankruptcy is less prevalent today than 140 years ago. The same trends hold for households and businesses. Rising leverage appears to be the result of massive improvements in technology and infrastructure, not significantly more risk-inclined humans. Obviously, a surge of debt leverage above what the newer technologies can support invites crises. I am not sure where the tipping point is. Moreover, that late-1950s experience with consumer debt burdens has made me reluctant to underestimate the ability of most households and companies to manage their financial affairs.

It is tempting to conclude that the U.S. current account deficit is essentially a by-product of long-term forces, and is thus largely benign. After all, we do seem to have been able to finance it with relative ease in recent years. But do the apparent continued increases in the deficits of U.S. individual households and nonfinancial businesses themselves reflect growing economic strain? And does it matter whether those deficits are being financed from domestic or foreign sources? If economic decisions were made without regard to currency or cross-border risks, then one could argue that current account imbalances would be of no particular economic significance, and the accumulation of debt to foreigners would have few implications beyond the solvency of the debtors themselves. Whether the debt of U.S. entities was owed to domestic or foreign lenders would be of little import.

But national borders do matter, at least to some extent. Debt service payments on foreign loans ultimately must be funded from exports of tradable goods and services, or from capital inflows, whereas domestic debt has a broader base from which it can be serviced. For a business, cross-border transactions can be complicated by a volatile exchange rate, but generally this is a normal business risk. It is true that the market adjustment process seems to be less effective or transparent across borders than within national borders. Prices of identical goods at nearby locations, but across borders, for example, have been shown to differ significantly even when denominated in the same currency.* Thus, cross-border current account imbalances may impart a degree of economic stress that is likely greater than that stemming from domestic imbalances only. Cross-border legal and currency risks are important additions to normal domestic risks. But how significant are the differences?

Globalization is changing many of our economic guideposts. It is probably reasonable to assume that the worldwide dispersion of the financial balances of unconsolidated economic entities as a ratio to world nominal GDP noted earlier will continue to rise as increasing specialization and the division of labor spread globally. Whether the dispersion of world current account balances continues to increase as well is more of an open question. Such an increase would imply a further decline in home bias. But in a world of nation-states, home bias can decline only so far. It must eventually stabilize, as indeed it may already have.† In that event the U.S. current account deficit would likely move toward balance.

In the interim, whatever the significance and possible negative implications of the current account deficit, maintaining economic flexibility, as I have stressed, may be the most effective way to counter such risks. The piling up of dollar claims against U.S. residents is already leading to concerns about "concentration risk"—the too-many-eggs-in-one-basket worry that could prompt foreign holders to exchange dollars for other currencies, even when the dollar investments yield more. Although foreign investors

---

*The persistent divergence subsequent to the creation of the euro of many prices of identical goods among member countries of the euro area is analyzed in John H. Rogers (2002). For the case of U.S. and Canadian prices, see Charles Engel and John H. Rogers (1996).

†The correlation coefficient measures of home bias have flattened out since 2000. So have the measures of dispersion. This is consistent with the United States' accounting for a rising share of deficits.

have not yet significantly slowed their financing of U.S. capital investments, since early 2002 the value of the dollar relative to other currencies has declined, as has the share of dollar assets in some measures of global cross-border portfolios.*

If the current disturbing drift toward protectionism is contained and markets remain sufficiently flexible, changing terms of trade, interest rates, asset prices, and exchange rates should cause U.S. saving to rise relative to domestic investment. This would reduce the need for foreign financing and reverse the trend of the past decade toward increasing reliance on funds from abroad. If, however, the pernicious drift toward fiscal irresponsibility in the United States and elsewhere is not arrested and is compounded by a protectionist reversal of globalization, the process of adjusting the current account deficit could be quite painful for the United States and our trading partners.

---

*Of the more than $40 trillion equivalent of cross-border banking and international bond claims reported by the private sector to the Bank for International Settlements for the end of the third quarter of 2006, 43 percent were in dollars and 39 percent were in euros. Monetary authorities have been somewhat more inclined to hold dollar obligations: at the end of the third quarter of 2006, of the $4.7 trillion equivalent held as foreign-exchange reserves, approximately two-thirds were held in dollars and approximately one-quarter in euros.

GLOBALIZATION AND REGULATION

By all contemporaneous accounts, the world prior to 1914 seemed to be moving irreversibly toward higher levels of civility and civilization; human society seemed perfectible. The nineteenth century had brought an end to the wretched slave trade. Dehumanizing violence seemed on the decline. Aside from America's Civil War in the 1860s and the brief Franco-Prussian War of 1870–71, there had been no war engaging large parts of the "civilized" world since the Napoleonic era. The pace of global invention had advanced throughout the nineteenth century, bringing railroads, the telephone, the electric light, cinema, the motor car, and household conveniences too numerous to mention. Medical science, improved nutrition, and the mass distribution of potable water had elevated life expectancy in what we call the developed world from thirty-six years in 1820 to more than fifty by 1914. The sense of the irreversibility of such progress was universal.

World War I was more devastating to civility and civilization than the physically far more destructive World War II: the earlier conflict destroyed an idea. I cannot erase the thought of those pre–World War I years, when the future of mankind appeared unencumbered and without limit.* Today our outlook is starkly different from a century ago but perhaps a bit more consonant with reality. Will terror, global warming, or resurgent populism do to the current era of life-advancing globalization what World War I did to the previous one? No one can be confident of the answer. But in approaching the issue, it is worth probing the roots and institutions of post–World War II economics that have raised the standards of living of virtually all the inhabitants of this globe and helped restore some of humanity's hopes.

Individual economies grow and prosper as their inhabitants learn to specialize and engage in the division of labor. So it is on a global scale. Globalization—the deepening of specialization and the extension of the division of labor beyond national borders—is patently a key to understanding much of our recent economic history. A growing capacity to conduct transactions and take risks throughout the world is creating a truly global economy. Production has become more and more international. Much of what is assembled in final salable form in one country increasingly consists of components from many continents. Being able to seek out the most competitive sources of labor and material inputs worldwide rather than just nationwide not only reduces costs and price inflation but also raises the ratio of the value of outputs to inputs—the broadest measure of productivity and a useful proxy for standards of living. On average, standards of living have risen markedly. Hundreds of millions of people in developing countries have been elevated from subsistence poverty. Other hundreds of millions are now experiencing a level of affluence that people born in developed nations have experienced all their lives.

On the other hand, increased concentrations of income that have

---

*I still have a book from my student days, *Economics and the Public Welfare,* in which retired economist Benjamin Anderson evoked the idealism and optimism of that lost era in a way I've never forgotten: "Those who have an adult's recollection and an adult's understanding of the world which preceded the first World War look back upon it with a great nostalgia. There was a sense of security then which has never since existed. Progress was generally taken for granted. . . . Decade after decade had seen increasing political freedom, the progressive spread of democratic institutions, the steady lifting of the standard of life for the masses of men. . . . In financial matters the good faith of governments and central banks was taken for granted. Governments and central banks were not always able to keep their promises, but when this happened they were ashamed, and they took measures to make the promises good as far as they could."

emerged under globalization have rekindled the battle between the cultures of the welfare state and of capitalism—a battle some thought had ended once and for all with the disgrace of central planning. Hovering over us as well is the prospect of terrorism that would threaten the rule of law and hence prosperity. A worldwide debate is under way on the future of globalization and capitalism, and its resolution will define the world marketplace and the way we live for decades to come.

History warns us that globalization is reversible. We can lose many of the historic gains of the past quarter century. The barriers to trade and commerce that came down following World War II can be resurrected, but surely not without consequences similar to those that followed the stock-market crash of 1929.

I have two grave concerns about our ability to preserve the momentum of the world's recent material progress. First is the emergence of increasing concentrations of income, which is a threat to the comity and stability of democratic societies. Such inequality may, I fear, spark a politically expedient but economically destructive backlash. The second is the impact of the inevitable slowdown in the process of globalization itself. This could reduce world growth and diminish the broad sanction for capitalism that evolved out of the demise of the Soviet Union. People quickly adjust to higher standards of living, and if progress slows, they feel deprived and seek new explanations or new leadership. Ironically, capitalism now seems to be held in greater favor in the many parts of the developing world where growth is rapid—China, part of India, and much of Eastern Europe—than where it originated, in slower-growing Western Europe.

A "fully globalized" world is one in which unfettered production, trade, and finance are driven by profit seeking and risk taking that are wholly indifferent to distance and national borders. That state will never be achieved. People's inherent aversion to risk, and the home bias that is a manifestation of that aversion, mean that globalization has limits. Trade liberalization in recent decades has brought about a major lowering of barriers to movement in goods, services, and capital flows. But further progress will come with increasing difficulty, as the stalemate in the Doha round of trade negotiations demonstrated.

Because so much of our recent experience has little precedent, it is difficult to determine how long today's globalization dynamic will take to play out. And even then we have to be careful not to fall into the trap of equating the leveling-off of globalization with the exhaustion of opportunities for new investment. The closing of the American frontier at the end of the nineteenth century, for example, did not signal, as many feared, the onset of economic stagnation.

Post–World War II economic recovery was fostered initially by the widespread recognition of economists and political leaders that the surge of protectionism following World War I had been a primary contributor to the depth of the Great Depression. As a consequence, policymakers began systematically taking down trade barriers and, much later, barriers to financial flows. Before the fall of the Soviet Union, globalization was spurred further when the inflation-ridden 1970s provoked a rethinking of the heavy-handed economic policies and regulations that grew out of the Depression years.

Because of deregulation, increased innovation,* and lower barriers to trade and investment, cross-border trade in recent decades has been expanding at a pace far faster than GDP, implying a comparable rise, on average, in the ratio of imports to GDP worldwide. As a consequence, most economies are being increasingly exposed to the rigors and stress of international competition, which, while little different from the stress of domestic competition, appear less subject to control. The job insecurity engendered in developed economies by burgeoning imports is taking its toll on wage increases—fear of job loss has significantly muted employees' demands. Thus, imports, which of necessity are competitively priced, have been restraining inflationary pressures.

There were outsized gains in the volume of international trade in the first decades after World War II, but each country's exports and imports largely grew in lockstep. Significant and persistent trade imbalances were

---

*The dramatic decline in communication costs, as fiber optics spanned the globe, and falling transport costs everywhere have been additional important spurs to cross-border trade.

rare until the mid-1990s. It was only then that the globalization of capital markets began to develop, lowering the cost of financing and thereby augmenting the world stock of real capital, a key driver of productivity growth. Many savers, previously inclined, or constrained, to invest within their own sovereign borders, began reaching abroad to engage a broader choice of newly available investment opportunities. Given a wider variety of funding sources from which to choose, the average cost of capital to enterprises declined. The yield on the U.S. Treasury ten-year note, long the worldwide benchmark for interest rates, has been on a declining trend since 1981. It shrank by half by the time the Berlin Wall fell and by half again to its low in mid-2003.

The resulting advance of global financial markets has markedly improved the efficiency with which the world's savings are invested, a vital indirect contributor to world productivity growth.* As I saw it, from 1995 forward, the largely unregulated global markets, with some notable exceptions, appeared to be moving smoothly from one state of equilibrium to another. Adam Smith's invisible hand was at work on a global scale. But what does that invisible hand do? Why do we experience extended periods of stable or rising employment and output and only gradually changing exchange rates, prices, wages, and interest rates? Are we fools to trust such stability when we see it in the markets? Or, as a newly anointed finance minister once asked, "How can we control the inherent chaos of unregulated international trade and finance without significant governmental intervention?" Given the trillions of dollars of daily cross-border transactions, few of which are publicly recorded, indeed how can anyone be sure that an unregulated global system will work? Yet it does, day in and day out. Systemic breakdowns occur, of course, but they are surprisingly rare. Confidence that the global economy works the way it is supposed to work requires insight into the role of balancing forces. (Those forces regrettably seem more evident to economists than to the lawyers and politicians who do the regulating.)

Today's global "chaos," to use the misapprehension of my finance min-

---

*Even today, a significant fraction of world savings is wasted in the sense that it is financing largely unproductive capital investment, especially in the public sector.

ister friend, is without historical precedent. Not even in the "golden days" of more or less total international laissez-faire prior to the First World War did global finance play so large a role. As I've noted, the volume of international trade has been rising far more rapidly than real world GDP since the end of World War II. The expansion reflects the opening up of international markets as well as major gains in communication capabilities that inspired the *Economist* a few years ago to proclaim "the death of distance." In order to facilitate the financing, insuring, and timeliness of all that trade, the volume of cross-border transactions in financial instruments has had to rise even faster than the trade itself. Wholly new forms of finance had to be invented or developed—credit derivatives, asset-backed securities, oil futures, and the like all make the world's trading system function far more efficiently.

In many respects, the apparent stability of our global trade and financial system is a reaffirmation of the simple, time-tested principle promulgated by Adam Smith in 1776: Individuals trading freely with one another following their own self-interest leads to a growing, stable economy. The textbook model of market perfection works if its fundamental premises are observed: People must be free to act in their self-interest, unencumbered by external shocks or economic policy. The inevitable mistakes and euphorias of participants in the global marketplace and the inefficiencies spawned by those missteps produce economic imbalances, large and small. Yet even in crisis, economies seem inevitably to right themselves (though the process sometimes takes considerable time).

Crisis, at least for a while, destabilizes the relationships that characterize normal, functioning markets. It creates opportunities to reap abnormally high profits in the buying or selling of some goods, services, and assets. The scramble by market participants to seize those opportunities presses prices, exchange rates, and interest rates back to market-appropriate levels and thereby eliminates both the abnormal profit margins and the inefficiencies that create them. In other words, markets, fully free to reflect the value preferences of the world's consumers, will tend to equalize risk-adjusted rates of profit across the globe. Profits above such levels are evidence that consumers' preferences are being shortchanged. Too low a risk-adjusted rate of return is often evidence of a waste of productive resources, such as plant and equipment. Only when abrupt shifts in human exuberance or fears overwhelm the market-adjustment process do most imbalances become visible to all. But by then, they are all too visible.

The rapid pace of globalization of trade is being more than matched by an expanding degree of globalization of finance. An effective global financial system is one that guides the world's saving toward funding those capital investments that will produce most efficiently the goods and services that consumers most value. The United States, as foreigners are quick to point out, saves too little. Our national saving rate—a scant 13.7 percent of GDP in 2006—made the United States, by far, the developed country that saved the least. Even including the foreign saving that is invested in our domestic economy, overall investment in the United States, at 20.0 percent of GDP, was the third lowest among the G7 large industrial countries. But because we deploy our meager savings very efficiently and waste little, we have developed a capital stock that has produced the highest rate of productivity growth among the G7 nations over most of the past decade.

Implicit in the price of every good and service is a payment for financial services associated with the production, distribution, and marketing of the good or service. That payment has risen materially as a share of price and is the source of the rapidly increasing incomes of people with financial skills. The value of these services shows up most prominently in the United States, where, as I noted previously, the share of GDP flowing to financial institutions, including insurance, has risen dramatically in recent decades.*

Information systems that supply unprecedented detail on the state of financial markets support the ability of financial institutions to rapidly identify abnormal or niche profit opportunities—that is, those whose risk-adjusted rates of return are above normal. Abnormal returns in an essentially unregulated market generally reflect inefficiencies in the flow of the

---

*Much, but by no means all, of the increased U.S. value-added accruing from financial services ends up in New York City, the home of the New York Stock Exchange and many of the world's major financial institutions. But it also is spread across the entire United States, where a fifth of world GDP originates and must be financed. London, of course, is a growing rival to New York as an international financial center (by most measures it exceeds New York in cross-border finance), but almost all of Britain's financial activity originates in London. The financial needs of the rest of Britain are, in comparison with those of the United States, relatively small.

world's saving into capital investment. Heavy purchases of those niche assets restore their pricing to "normal." Although certainly not the objective of profit-seeking market participants, the resulting price adjustments, to paraphrase Adam Smith, benefit the world's consumers.

High financial profits have attracted a significant array of skilled people and institutions. Most prominent is the reinvigoration of the hedge fund industry. What I remember as a sleepy fringe of finance half a century ago has morphed into a vibrant trillion-dollar industry dominated by U.S. firms. Hedge funds and private equity funds appear to represent the finance of the future. But not just yet. The exceptionally high values the market (that is, consumers, indirectly) placed on financial services after the mid-1990s induced many junior partners of investment banking firms to create hedge fund boutiques. As a consequence, the hedge fund market became temporarily surfeited in 2006. Funds were forced into liquidation as too many new entrants tried to harvest the niche profits they saw their predecessors pick with outstanding success. But what was picked is no longer there; the easy money is mostly gone, and many of those eager would-be hedge fund tycoons saw their large new net worths fall sharply. Few on the outside have shed tears over their plight.

Even so, hedge fund investment strategies continue to be instrumental in eliminating abnormal market spreads and presumably much market inefficiency. Indeed, hedge funds have become critical players in world capital markets. They are said to account for a significant share of the volume on the New York Stock Exchange, and more generally supply much of the liquidity in otherwise stagnant markets. They are essentially free of government regulation, and I hope they will remain so. Imposing a blanket of costly regulation will succeed only in stifling the enthusiasm for seeking niche profits. Hedge funds would disappear or end up as undistinguished, nondescript investment vehicles, and the world's economies would be the worse for it.

The marketplace itself regulates hedge funds today through what's known as counterparty surveillance. In other words, constraints are imposed on hedge funds by their high-income investors and the banks and other institutions that lend them money. Protective of their own shareholders, these lenders have incentives to monitor hedge fund investment strategies very closely. As first a bank director (at JPMorgan), and then a bank regulator for eighteen years, I was acutely aware of how much better situated and staffed banks were to understand what other banks and hedge funds were doing as compared with the "by-the-book" regulation done by government financial regulatory agencies. As good as some bank examiners are in promoting sound banking practice, they have little chance of uncovering most fraud or embezzlement without the aid of a whistle-blower.

A major failure of private counterparty surveillance was the near-collapse of Long Term Capital Management, the 1998 financial train wreck described in chapter 9. LTCM's founders, who included two Nobel Prize winners, were held in such awe that they could, and did, refuse to offer collateral to their lenders—a fatal concession on the lenders' part. Before long, LTCM ran out of opportunities to earn niche profits, as imitators followed the firm's lead and glutted the market. Instead of returning all (not just some) capital to shareholders and declaring their mission complete, LTCM's principals turned into gamblers, making large bets that had little to do with their original business plan. In 1998, LTCM lost its shirt.

The episode shook the market. But it's indicative of the development of this sector, and of the financial system generally, that when another notable U.S. hedge fund, Amaranth, collapsed in 2006 with a loss of more than $6 billion, the world's financial system registered scarcely a tremor.

A recent financial innovation of major importance has been the credit default swap. The CDS, as it is called, is a derivative that transfers the credit risk, usually of a debt instrument, to a third party, at a price. Being able to profit from the loan transaction but transfer credit risk is a boon to banks and other financial intermediaries, which, in order to make an adequate rate of return on equity, have to heavily leverage their balance sheets by accepting deposit obligations and/or incurring debt. Most of the time, such institutions lend money and prosper. But in periods of adversity, they typically run into bad-debt problems, which in the past had forced them to sharply curtail lending. This in turn undermined economic activity more generally.

A market vehicle for transferring risk away from these highly leveraged loan originators can be critical for economic stability, especially in a global environment. In response to this need, the CDS was invented and took the market by storm. The Bank for International Settlements tabulated a worldwide notional value of more than $20 trillion equivalent in credit default swaps in mid-2006, up from $6 trillion at the end of 2004. The buffering power of these instruments was vividly demonstrated between 1998 and 2001, when CDSs were used to spread the risk of $1 trillion in loans to rapidly expanding telecommunications networks. Though a large proportion of these ventures defaulted in the tech bust, not a single major lending institution ran into trouble as a consequence. The losses were ultimately borne by highly capitalized institutions—insurers, pension funds, and the like—that had been the major suppliers of the credit default protection. They were well able to absorb the hit. Thus there was no repetition of the cascading defaults of an earlier era.

Regrettably, every time a hedge fund's problems make the news, political pressure to regulate the industry mounts. Hedge funds are both risk takers and very large, the thinking goes—doesn't that prove they are dangerous? Shouldn't the government rein them in? Leaving aside the undermining of market liquidity that such actions could induce, the benefit of more government regulation eludes me. Hedge funds change their holdings so rapidly that last night's balance sheet is probably of little use by 11 a.m.—so regulators would have to scrutinize the funds practically minute by minute. Any governmental restrictions on fund investment behavior (that's what regulation does) would curtail the risk taking that is integral to the contributions of hedge funds to the global economy, and especially to the economy of the United States. Why do we wish to inhibit the pollinating bees of Wall Street?

I say this having served as a regulator myself for eighteen years. When I accepted President Reagan's nomination to become chairman of the Fed, what drew me was the challenge of applying what I had learned about the economy and monetary policy over nearly four decades. Yet I knew that the Federal Reserve was also a major bank regulator and the overseer of America's payments systems. Avid defender though I was of letting markets function unencumbered, I knew that as chairman I would also be responsible for the Fed's vast regulatory apparatus. Could I reconcile that duty with my beliefs?

In fact, I had crossed that Rubicon long before, during my stint as chairman of President Ford's Council of Economic Advisors. Although the primary job of the CEA was to shoot down harebrained fiscal policy schemes, I did on occasion accept increased regulation—when it appeared to be the least bad of the options politically available to the administration. As Fed chairman, I decided, my personal views on regulation would have to be set aside. After all, I would take an oath of office that would commit me to uphold the Constitution of the United States and those laws whose enforcement falls under the purview of the Federal Reserve. Since I was an outlier in my libertarian opposition to most regulation, I planned to be largely passive in such matters and allow other Federal Reserve governors to take the lead.

Taking office, I was in for a pleasant surprise. I had known from my contact with Fed staff members, during the Ford administration especially, how extraordinarily qualified they were. What I had not known about was the staff's free-market orientation, which I now discovered characterized even the Division of Bank Supervision and Regulation. (Its chief, Bill Taylor, was a likable, thoroughly professional regulator. President Bush, the father, later appointed him to head the Federal Deposit Insurance Corporation, and his premature death in 1992 was a great blow to his colleagues and the nation.) So while the staff recommendations at the Federal Reserve Board were directed to implementing congressional mandates, they were always formulated with a view toward fostering competition and letting markets work. There was less emphasis on "thou shalt not" and more on management accountability and disclosure that would enable markets to function more effectively. The staff also fully recognized the power of counterparty surveillance as the first line of protection against overextended or inappropriate credit.

This view of regulation was no doubt influenced by the economists in the institution and on the Board. They were generally sensitive to the need to buttress the competitive market forces that the financial safety net of the United States tends to impair. This safety net—which includes such safeguards as deposit insurance, bank access to the Fed's discount facilities, and access to the Fed's vast electronic payments system—reduces the importance of reputation as a constraint on excessive debt creation. Nonetheless, managers' efforts to protect their reputations are important in all businesses but especially so in banking, where reputation is key to the overall soundness of a bank's operations. If a bank's loan portfolio or its employees are suspect, depositors disappear, often very quickly. But when the deposits are insured in some way, a run is less likely.

Studying the damage caused by Depression-era bank runs had led me to conclude that, on balance, deposit insurance is a positive.* Nonetheless, the presence of a government financial safety net undoubtedly fosters "moral hazard," the term used in the insurance business to describe why customers take actions they would not so readily consider were they not insured against the adverse consequences of their behavior. Regulations on lending and deposit taking hence must be carefully designed to minimize the moral hazard they inevitably create. Democracy requires trade-offs.

I was delighted that being a regulator was not the burden I had feared. Of the hundreds of Board votes on regulation during my tenure, I found myself in the minority just once. (I argued that a consumer law requiring disclosure of an interest rate relied on a method of calculation that was faulty—scarcely a major point of philosophical debate.) While I never shared the fervor of some for discussing the appropriate wording of a rule, I settled down to a comfortable role in which I asserted myself only on issues that I saw as important to the functioning of the Federal Reserve or to the financial system as a whole.

Over the years I learned a great deal about what kind of regulation produces the least interference. Three rules of thumb:

1. Regulation approved in a crisis must subsequently be fine-tuned. The Sarbanes-Oxley Act, rushed through Congress in the wake of the Enron and WorldCom bankruptcies and mandating greater financial disclosure by corporations, is today's prime candidate for revision.

---

*I had always thought the payment system should be wholly private, but I found that Fedwire, the electronic funds-transfer system operated by the Federal Reserve, does offer something no private bank can: riskless final settlements. The Fed's discount window serves as a lender of last resort, a function the private sector cannot provide without impairing a bank shareholder's value.

2. Sometimes several regulators are better than one. The solitary regulator becomes risk averse; he or she tries to guard against all imaginable negative outcomes, creating a crushing compliance burden. In the financial industries, where the Fed shares regulatory jurisdiction with the Comptroller of the Currency, the Securities and Exchange Commission, and other authorities, we tended to keep one another in check.

3. Regulations outlive their usefulness and should be renewed periodically. I learned this lesson watching Virgil Mattingly, the longtime chief of the Federal Reserve Board's legal staff. He took very seriously the statutory requirement to review each Federal Reserve regulation every five years; any regulation that was judged to be obsolete was unceremoniously scrapped.

An area in which more rather than less government involvement is needed, in my judgment, is the rooting out of fraud. It is the bane of any market system.* Indeed, Washington would do well to divert resources from creating new regulations to greatly stepping up the enforcement of anti-fraud and anti-racketeering laws.

It is not uncommon to see legislators and regulators rush to promulgate new laws and rules in response to market breakdowns, and the mistakes that result often take decades to correct. I had long argued that the Glass-Steagall Act, which in 1933 separated the business of securities underwriting from commercial banking, was based on faulty history. Testimony before Congress in 1933 was filled with anecdotes that gave the impression that inappropriate use by banks of their securities affiliates was undermining overall soundness. Only after World War II, when computers made it possible to evaluate the banking system as a whole, did it become evident that banks *with* securities affiliates had weathered the 1930s crisis better than those without affiliates. A few months before I took up my duties at the Fed, the Board introduced a proposal that would again allow banks to sell securities through affiliates, under very restrictive conditions. The Board

---

*Fraud is a destroyer of the market process itself because market participants need to rely on the veracity of other market participants.

continued to encourage easing of the restrictions, and I testified many times for legislative change. It took until 1999 for Glass-Steagall to be repealed by the Gramm-Leach-Bliley Act. Fortunately, Gramm-Leach-Bliley, which restored sorely needed flexibility to the financial industries, is no aberration. Awareness of the detrimental effects of excessive regulation and the need for economic adaptability has advanced substantially in recent years. We dare not go back.

Globalization, the extension of capitalism to world markets, like capitalism itself, is the object of intense criticism from those who see only the destructive side of creative destruction. Yet all credible evidence indicates that the benefits of globalization far exceed its costs, even beyond the realm of economics. For example, economist Barry Eichengreen and political scientist David Leblang, in a paper delivered in late 2006, found "evidence [during the 130-year span from 1870 to 2000] of positive relationships running in both directions between globalization and democracy." They found "that trade openness promotes democracy. . . . The impact of financial openness on democracy [is] not as strong but still point[s] in the same direction [and] . . . democracies are more likely to remove capital controls."

Accordingly, we should focus on addressing and assuaging the fears induced by the dark side of creative destruction rather than imposing limits on the economic edifice on which worldwide prosperity depends. Innovation is as important to our global financial marketplace as it is to technology, consumer products, or health care. As globalization expands and ultimately begins to slow, our financial system will need to retain its flexibility. Protectionism, whatever its guise, whether political or economic, whether it affects trade or finance, is a prescription for economic stagnation and political authoritarianism. We can do better than that. Indeed, we must.

TWENTY

THE "CONUNDRUM"

W hat is going on?" I complained in June 2004 to Vincent Rein- hart, director of the Division of Monetary Affairs at the Fed- eral Reserve Board. I was perturbed because we had increased the federal funds rate, and not only had yields on ten-year treasury notes failed to rise, they'd actually declined. It was a pattern we were accustomed to seeing only late in a credit-tightening cycle, when long-term interest rates began to fully reflect the lowered inflationary expectations that were the consequence of the Fed tightening.* Seeing yields decline at the begin- ning of a tightening cycle was extremely unusual.

This tightening cycle had barely even begun. I'd signaled its commence- ment less than two months earlier, when in testimony before the Joint Eco- nomic Committee of Congress I'd delivered a clear signal of the Fed's intention to raise rates: "The federal funds rate must rise at some point to prevent pressures on price inflation from eventually emerging. . . . The Fed- eral Reserve recognizes that sustained prosperity requires the maintenance

---

*More typical was the pattern of long-term interest rates in 1994, for example. In February and the ensuing months, we raised the federal funds rate a total of 175 basis points with the aim of defusing an incipient rise in inflation expectations. The yield on the treasury long-term note rose. Only at the end of 1994, after we raised the federal funds rate an additional 75 basis points, did the yield decline.

of price stability and will act, as necessary, to ensure that outcome." Our hope was to raise mortgage rates to levels that would defuse the boom in housing, which by then was producing an unwelcome froth.

The response from the market was immediate. Anticipating the increase in bond yields usually associated with an initial rise in the federal funds rate, market participants built large short positions in long-term debt instruments. Yields on ten-year treasury notes rose about 1 percentage point during the next several weeks. Our tightening program seemed to be right on track. But by June, market pressures seemingly coming out of nowhere drove long-term rates back down. Thinking we must be witnessing an aberration, I was both perplexed and intrigued.

Unexplainable market episodes are something Fed policymakers have to deal with all the time. One many an occasion I have been able to ferret out the causes of some pecularity in market pricing after a month or two of watching the anomaly play out. On other occasions, the aberration has remained a mystery. Price changes, of course, result from a shift in balance between supply and demand. But analysts can observe only the price consequences of the shift. Short of psychoanalyzing all market participants to determine what led them to act as they did, we may never be able to explain certain episodes. The stock-market crash of October 1987 is one such instance. To this day, there are competing hypotheses about what set off that record one-day plunge. The explanations range from strained relations with Germany to high interest rates. We certainly experienced the fact that there were more sellers than buyers. But nobody really knows why.

I did not come up with an explanation for the 2004 episode, and I decided that it must be just another odd passing event not to be repeated. I was mistaken. In February and March of 2005, the anomaly cropped up again. Reacting to continued Fed tightening, long-term rates again began to rise, but just as in 2004, market forces came into play to render those increases short-lived.

What were those market forces? They were surely global, because the declines in long-term interest rates during that period were at least as pronounced in major foreign financial markets as they were in the United States. Globalization, of course, had been a prominent disinflationary force since the mid-1980s. I was still intrigued by the vast pattern of change that I'd sketched out for my colleagues on the FOMC in December 1995, telling them, "It is very difficult to find inflationary forces anywhere in the world. Something different is going on." At that point, I couldn't yet prove it, but I explained what I thought was the answer:

> You may recall that earlier this year I raised the issue of the extraordinary impact of accelerating technologies, largely silicon-based technologies, on the turnover of capital stock, the fairly dramatic decline in the average age of the stock, and the creation as a consequence of a high degree of insecurity for those individuals in the labor markets who have to deal with continually changing technological apparatus. One example that I think brings this development close to home, even though it is an unrealistic example, is how secretaries would feel if the location of the keys on their typewriters were changed every two years. We are in effect doing that to the overall workforce. To my mind, this increasingly explains why wage patterns have been as restrained as they have been. One extraordinary piece of recent evidence is an unprecedented number of labor contracts with five- or six-year maturities. We never had a labor contract of more than three years' duration in the last 30 to 40 years. . . . The underlying technology changes that support this hypothesis appear only once every century, or 50 years. . . . In addition . . . the downsizing of products as a consequence of computer chip technologies has created . . . a significant decline in implicit transportation costs. We are producing very small products that are cheaper to move. . . . [Equally important] is the dramatic effect of telecommunications technology in reducing the cost of communications. . . . As the downsized products have spread and the cost of communications has fallen, the globe has become increasingly smaller. . . . We are now seeing . . . the proliferation of outsourcing . . . ever increasingly around the globe. What one would expect to see as this occurs—and indeed it is happening—is the combination of rising capital efficiency and falling nominal unit labor costs. . . . This is a new phenomenon, and it

raises interesting questions as to whether in fact there is something more profoundly important going on [for] the longer run.

We could not be sure of the appropriate assessment of our changing world for probably five to ten years, I told them, but the passage of time only brought the phenomenon of worldwide disinflation into sharper relief. With the new millennium, signs of it became increasingly evident, even among developing countries whose histories were rife with inflationary episodes. Mexico in 2003 was proudly able to market a first-time-ever twenty-year peso-denominated bond, only eight years after the nation faced a severe liquidity crisis in which the government could not find buyers for even short-term dollar-denominated debt and required a U.S.-led bailout. Admittedly, Mexico had taken a number of important steps to get its fiscal and monetary house in order following its 1995 near default. But there was nothing in those steps to suggest that it would quickly gain the ability to sell a relatively low-yield twenty-year peso-denominated bond. Mexico's checkered macroeconomic history had hitherto required long-term debt issues to be denominated in foreign currencies in order to attract investors.

Mexico was not an isolated case. Governments of other developing countries were increasingly issuing long-term debt in their own currencies at interest rates that developed countries would gladly have welcomed only a decade earlier. And I've noted, Brazil, contrary to previous experience, had been able to absorb a 40 percent devaluation of its currency in 2002, with only short-term and relatively modest inflationary consequences.

Inflation had been subdued virtually across the globe. Inflation expectations, reflected in long-term debt yields, plunged. The yields on developing nations' debt shrank to unprecedented lows. Double- and sometimes triple-digit annual inflation rates, historically a hallmark of developing economies, had, with a few exceptions, disappeared. Episodes of hyperinflation became extremely rare.* Developing countries averaged an annual increase of 50 percent in consumer prices between 1989 and 1998. By 2006, consumer price inflation had fallen to less than 5 percent.

---

*Zimbabwe, which has mangled its economy, has been the principal exception.

But even though globalization had reduced long-term interest rates, in the summer of 2004 we had no reason to expect that a Fed tightening would not carry long-term rates up with it. We anticipated that we would just be starting from a lower long-term rate than was customary in the past. The unprecedented response to the Federal Reserve's monetary tightening that year suggested that in addition to globalization, profoundly important forces had developed whose full significance was only now emerging. I was stumped. I called the historically unprecedented state of affairs a "conundrum." My puzzlement was not assuaged by the numerous bottles of Conundrum-label wine arriving at my office. I don't recall the vintage.

A little-noticed event in Europe offered the first clue to unraveling the new puzzle. Siemens, one of Germany's formidable exporters, had informed its union, IG Metall, in 2004 that unless the union agreed to a pay cut of more than 12 percent at two plants, Siemens would contemplate relocating the facilities to Eastern Europe. Boxed in, IG Metall acquiesced, and the exodus of Siemens's plants to the newly freed economies of Eastern Europe was stayed.* This event struck a chord for me because I had seen reports of similar confrontations earlier. It led me to review the pattern of wage increases in Germany. Employers had long been complaining that high wages were making them uncompetitive, even though average hourly compensation had not been rising very fast—at an annual rate of 2.3 percent between 1995 and 2002. Their message was obviously now finally getting through. Starting in late 2002, hourly labor cost growth was abruptly cut to half that rate, and it stayed very slow through the end of 2006.

Siemens and the rest of German industry, assisted by reforms allowing wider use of so-called temporary workers, were able to damp German wages, costs, and hence prices. Inflation expectations declined with the decline in the recorded rate of inflation. IG Metall's loss of bargaining power, of course, was wholly the result of forces outside German borders—the entrance on the competitive scene of at least 150 million low-priced, well-educated workers, released from the grip of the Soviet empire's centrally planned economic system.

---

*In September 2006, Volkswagen negotiated a similar agreement to lower average hourly earnings in exchange for securing jobs threatened by plant relocation.

The end of the cold war—the stand-down from the brink of war by the world's two nuclear superpowers—has little to challenge it as the second half of the century's most significant geopolitical event. The economic significance of the demise of the Soviet Union has been awesome in its own right, as I noted in chapter 6. The fall of the Berlin Wall exposed a state of economic ruin so devastating that central planning, earlier applauded as a "scientific" substitute for the "chaos" of the marketplace, fell into terminal disrepute. There was no eulogy or economic postmortem. It just disappeared, without a whimper, from political and economic discourse. As a consequence, Communist China, which had discovered the practical virtues of markets a decade earlier, accelerated its march toward free-market capitalism without, of course, ever acknowledging that that was what it was doing. India began to awaken from the bureaucratic socialism of former prime minister Jawaharlal Nehru. And any notions emerging economies might have had of implementing or expanding economy-wide forms of central planning were quietly shelved.

Soon well over a billion workers, many well educated, all low paid, began to gravitate to the world competitive marketplace from economies that had been almost wholly or in part centrally planned and insulated from global competition. The IMF estimates that in 2005 more than 800 million members of the world's labor force were engaged in export-oriented and therefore competitive markets, an increase of 500 million since the fall of the Berlin Wall in 1989 and 600 million since 1980, with East Asia accounting for half of the increase. Lesser numbers in Eastern Europe moved from behind the "protections" of centrally planned regimes to domestic competitive markets. Many hundreds of millions of people, mainly in China and India, have yet to make the transition.

This movement of workers into the marketplace reduced world wages, inflation, inflation expectations, and interest rates, and accordingly significantly contributed to rising world economic growth. Even though the aggregate payroll of the newly repositioned workforce was only a fraction of that of developed nations, the impact was pronounced. Not only did low-priced imports displace production and hence workers in developed countries, but the competitive effect of the displaced workers seeking new jobs suppressed the wages of workers not directly in the line of fire of low-priced imports. In addition, migration from Eastern to Western Europe of low-priced workers exposed part of the homegrown workforces of Western Europe to enhanced wage competition. Finally, exports from previously centrally planned economies competitively suppressed export prices of all economies.

Had these billion-plus low-cost workers arrived in world labor markets en masse overnight, I do not doubt that chaos would have ensued. The Soviet-dominated economies of Eastern Europe made the transition in a decade, but scarcely smoothly. However, they represented only a fraction of the potential tectonic shift. Most dominant by far has been China, where labor force data, to the extent they can be relied upon, suggest a slow, but gradually accelerating, government-controlled shift of the workforce of the rural provinces to the dynamic market-dominated regions of the Pearl River delta and other export-oriented areas. Vast numbers of Chinese workers left agriculture-related pursuits for manufacturing and service jobs in urban areas. Privately controlled businesses rose to claim a significant share of China's near 800-million-person workforce. By 2006, agriculture was down to little more than two-fifths of total employment. Chinese manufacturing employment has held steady in recent years despite massive workforce reductions in state-owned enterprises. The largest gains in employment over the last decade have been in services.

Importantly, it is the pace, the rate of change, of movement from centrally planned employment to competitive markets that determines the degree of disinflationary pressure on developed nations' wage costs and hence prices. Because of the indirect effects of competitive imports and immigration, the addition of *new* low-priced workers affects the whole structure of labor costs in developed countries. The greater the rate of worker additions to the competitive market, the greater the downward pressure on developed countries' wage costs and prices. The initial overall impact was perhaps a reduction of only a couple of percentage points of annual wage growth at best. That major systemic effects could stem from such an apparently modest initial impact may seem like a man lifting a ton of steel. But if he has a lever, he can. The trajectory of growth has been altered, engendering a circle of lessened wage costs leading to lesser inflation expectations, which in turn further depress wage growth and put a brake on price increases.

China is by far the dominant contributor to the trend. Over the past quarter century, the rising rate of worker migration to the export-oriented coastal provinces imparted an ever-increasing degree of wage (and price) disinflation to the developed economies. But this also suggests that once the shift of erstwhile centrally planned workers, desirous and capable of competing in world markets, is complete, the downward pressure on developed countries' wage rates and prices, at least from this global source, will cease. In 2000, half of China's workforce was still employed in primary industry (mostly in agriculture). South Korea had reached that level in 1970 on the way down. Today, primary-industry employment in China is roughly 45 percent, and in South Korea it is under 8 percent. If China were to follow South Korea's historic path over the next quarter century, its *rate* of internal migration (which is still rising) would not peak for another several years. But the quality of the data, both South Korea's in earlier years and China's today, limits the clarity with which we can gauge changing rates of migration. Moreover, given the differences between today's China and the South Korea of a quarter century earlier with respect to size, political orientation, and economic policies, analogies can be only suggestive.

The critical time for the world economic outlook and for policymakers will not be when the shifting of workers comes to an end, but when its rate of increase starts to slow. We know it must slow, since, at some point, however distant, the transition to competitive markets will be complete. As the rate of worker flows peaks, the disinflationary effects will start to lift and higher inflation pressures will emerge. That turning point may well be several years in the future, as the Korean analogy suggests. But early evidence that such a process is under way would enlist the increasingly anticipatory aspects of global finance to bring the market-turning date forward, possibly to three years or less.

While the marked reduction in inflation and inflation expectations after the fall of the Berlin Wall lowered inflation premiums embodied in long-term debt issues worldwide, its effect on real interest rates has been limited to the lowered risk premiums resulting from the reduced market volatility that lower inflation fosters. The rest of the decline in real interest rates appears to be the result of a significant increase in the world's average effective propensity to save relative to its propensity to invest those savings in productive assets. Excess potential savings flooded global financial markets, driving real interest rates lower. But this too appears to be the consequence of the post-Soviet shift to competitive markets among developing countries and their resulting surge in growth.

Global investments in plant, equipment, inventories, and homes must always be equal to global savings—the net means of financing these investments. Every asset must have an owner. The market value of "paper" claims against newly created capital assets must equal the market value of those assets. In a sense, the world's checkbook must balance. Savings, in the end, must equal investment for the world as a whole. But businesses and households plan their investments before they can know which savers in the world will ultimately finance them. And the world's savers plan their savings before they know what investments they will finance. Accordingly, the intended investment for any period almost never equals intended saving.

When both investors and savers try to achieve their intentions in the marketplace, any imbalance forces real interest rates to change until actual investment and actual savings are brought into equality. If intended investment exceeds intended savings, real interest rates will rise enough to dissuade investors from investing and/or persuade savers to save more. If intended savings exceeds intended investment, real interest rates will fall. Outside the textbooks, this process is not sequential but concurrent and instantaneous. We never observe actual global investment as different from actual global savings.

Despite their lower incomes, households and businesses in developing countries save greater shares of their income than do households and businesses in developed countries. Developed countries have vast financial networks that lend to consumers and businesses, most often backed by collateral, enabling a significant fraction to spend beyond their current incomes. Far fewer such financial networks exist in developing nations to entice people to spend beyond their incomes. Moreover, most developing nations are still so close to bare subsistence that households need to insure against future contingencies. They seek a buffer against feared destitution, and since few of these countries have government safety nets adequate to protect against adversity, the only way for the households to do so is to set money aside. People are forced to save for a rainy day and retirement.*

As reported to the IMF, savings as a percentage of nominal GDP for advanced economies (that is, developed nations) during the 1980s and 1990s tended to hover in the vicinity of 21 to 22 percent. Developing countries averaged 23 to 24 percent over those decades. But starting in 2000, the developing world's embrace of competitive markets and capitalist practices finally began to pay off. Foreign direct investment to employ a low-paid domestic workforce encouraged by increasingly credible property rights began to accelerate export-led growth.†

During the past five years, developing-country growth has been twice that of developed countries. Their savings rates, led by China, rose from 24 percent in 2001 to 32 percent in 2006 as consumption in these culturally conservative societies lagged, and investment fell far short of the rise in saving. Saving rates in the developed world have slipped below 20 percent since 2002. World investment has risen very modestly as a percentage of GDP, almost wholly in developing countries.‡ Oil-exporting countries chose to spend only a modest share of their increased revenues on new oil-productive capacity.

Economists, of course, can measure savings, but since saving intentions are rarely recorded anywhere, estimates of intentions are little better than an informed guess. However, it is not unreasonable to surmise that world intended savings has exceeded intended investment in recent years, as evidenced by the worldwide decline in real long-term interest rates—that is,

---

*One of my earliest statistical analyses for the National Industrial Conference Board, more than a half century ago, showed that American farmers, despite lower average incomes, saved a larger share of their income than did city dwellers. Urban incomes were not subject to the vagaries of weather that afflicted almost all farm families in those days. Note that back then, farmers' peer groups were other farmers and hence urban spending patterns had not fully infiltrated the farm community.

†Foreign direct investment in China, as I've noted, rose gradually from 1980 to 1990, but then rose seventeenfold by 2006, as the evidence that market capitalism was the most effective force for prosperity became widespread. Whether rightly or wrongly, foreign investors must have believed that lesson had been absorbed by Chinese governing authorities and was being implemented in their sometimes ambiguous rule of law.

‡A minor problem in doing such an evaluation is that recorded world savings and investment are separated by a statistical discrepancy.

those adjusted for inflation expectations. Even with no change in intended savings behavior by anyone, the growing share of world incomes accruing to developing economies with chronically higher savings rates would move intended world savings persistently higher year after year. And that trend would continue as long as developing economy growth rates exceeded those of developed economies, as they have since 2000. Ordinarily, when real interest rates fall, economists have difficulty determining whether it was a rise in intended savings or a fall in intended investment that was the proximate cause. But the surge in developing country savings, only half of which was invested in the developing world, suggests strongly that it was the spillover of developing country savings that drove real interest rates lower. Since actual recorded developed-country investment rose only modestly (driven by lower rates), *intended* investment in the developed world must have been stable, or close to it, as a share of GDP. In fact, as I note in chapter 25, intended investment in the United States has been lagging in recent years, judging from the larger share of internal corporate cash flow that has been returned to shareholders, presumably for lack of new investment opportunities. These data are consistent with the notion that this decade's decline in long-term interest rates, both nominal and real, is mainly the effect of geopolitical forces rather than that of the normal play of market forces.

If developing countries continue to grow at a rapid rate and financial networks expand to lend more readily to the increasing number of citizens with rising discretionary incomes, developing-country savings rates are bound to fall, at least back to 1980s and 1990s levels. The inbred human desire to keep up with the Joneses is already manifest in the nascent consumer markets of the developing world. Increases in consumption would tend to remove the downward pressure of excess savings on real interest rates.* But that would likely occur even if the rate of growth of developing country incomes should slow. In all economies, spending rarely keeps up with unexpected surges in income; hence savings rates rise. As income growth slows back to trend, savings rates tend to fall.

So, as erstwhile centrally planned workforces complete their transition to competitive markets, and as developing countries' increasingly sophisti-

---

*Provided, of course, that intended investment as a share of GDP does not fall in tandem.

cated financial systems facilitate the inbred propensity toward higher consumption and less saving, inflation, inflation premiums, and interest rates will gradually lose their disinflation buffer of the past decade. I will address the timing of these events in the final chapter.

The ability of developing economies to continue to grow faster than developed economies will fade unless developing nations can supplement their borrowed technology with new insights and innovations from their scientists and high-tech engineers. New ones are currently being schooled in China, India, and elsewhere in the technologies of the past century developed in the West. Some could reasonably be expected to move beyond the technological levels of developed economies. But more important to economic growth—and perhaps even a necessary condition for the technology of China, India, or Russia to move beyond that of, say, the United States—is political certainty.

How much has America's political system—its protection of individual rights, especially property rights, and its relatively low degree of regulation and low incidence of corruption—contributed to the gap between standards of living of U.S. residents and those of developing countries? I suspect a great deal. However, although we may have world-class universities, our primary and secondary education system, as I note in chapter 21, is deeply deficient in providing homegrown talent to operate our increasingly complex infrastructure, which pours out levels of goods and services that no country has been able to match.

Citizens of developing countries unable to find adequate risk-adjusted rates of return at home invest in the United States, where, for more than two centuries, property rights of all—U.S. citizens and foreigners—have received firm and equal protection under the law. Few developing countries protect the property rights of even their own citizens as we do the property rights of foreigners. When I say "risk-adjusted" rates of return, I'm referring to the degree of risk in developing countries, and in a number of developed countries as well, of outright confiscation of investments or its equivalent in the form of deadening regulation, capricious taxation, spotty enforcement of laws, or rampant corruption.

The point I wish to emphasize is that any proper measure of the degree of property rights in a country must encompass such factors as regulation and arbitrariness in the enforcement of laws. Corruption, in addition, drives up the cost of ownership. Most developing countries rate poorly on all these counts. In fact, a major reason they remain "developing" and find it difficult to graduate to "developed" is their low scores on property-rights enforcement. The United States ranks high. Its "political risk premiums" are among the lowest in the world.*

I can readily imagine the technology knowledge gap between developed and developing economies narrowing significantly. However, I find it difficult to foresee so marked a short-term change in China's authoritarianism, India's smothering bureaucracy, or Russia's erratic enforcement of property rights. In fact, investor perception of such political risk changes so slowly that it would likely be years following any fundamental and credible changes before such risks were largely excised from economic decision making.

I have always thought that measured inflation at a rate as low as 1 percent cannot be sustained in an economy using a fiat currency in a competitively democratic society with any remnant of populism (is any country immune?).† Such a currency, by its very nature, has as the only constraint on its supply the actions of the central bank, and cannot be entirely insulated from political influences. The U.S. inflations of 1946, 1950, and the late 1970s remain too vivid in my memory. (I had that view challenged in 2003 by the Japanese deflation, though, in the end, deflation did not take hold in the United States.) If a typical inflation rate of a democratically mandated fiat currency is north of 1 to 2 percent, what force could keep inflation below that mark as the two major disinflationary forces that I have discussed in this chapter recede? The most obvious answer is monetary policy. There will come a point at which central bankers, as I note in chapter 25, will be pressed once again to contain inflationary pressures.

Central bankers over the past several decades have absorbed an important principle: Price stability is the path to maximum sustainable economic

---

*However, America's reputation has been somewhat diminished by the thwarting of high-profile foreign acquisitions—of Unocal, by a Chinese company, in 2005, and of a company that managed U.S. ports, by Dubai Ports World, in 2006.

†Given the upward bias of measured prices, a 1 percent reported rate of price increase probably represents an economy with price stability.

growth. Many economists in fact credit central bank monetary policy as the key factor in the last decade's reduction in inflation worldwide. I would like to believe that. I do not deny that we adjusted policy to be consonant with global disinflationary trends as they emerged. But I very much doubt that either policy actions or central bank anti-inflationary credibility played the leading role in the fall of long-term interest rates in the past one to two decades. That decline (and the conundrum) can be accounted for by forces other than monetary policy. In fact, during my experience since the mid-1990s with the interaction between the policies of the world's central banks and the financial markets, I was struck by how relatively easy it was to bring inflation down. The inflationary pressures of which I was so acutely aware in the late 1980s were largely absent or, more accurately, dormant. The "conundrum" exposed this point.

To judge success in containing inflation, central banks look to changes in inflation expectations implicit in nominal long-term interest rates. Success is evident when long-term rates slip in the face of aggressive monetary tightening. But as I recall, during most of our initiatives to confront rising inflation pressures, aggressive tightening was unnecessary. Even a slight "tap on the brake" induced long-term rates to decline. It seemed too easy, a far cry from the monetary-policy crises of the 1970s. The ten-year treasury note yielded 8.7 percent on the day I was sworn in as Fed chairman and rose to 10.2 percent by Black Monday. The yield on the ten-year note then proceeded to fall for the next sixteen years, seemingly irrespective of the Fed's policy stance. I often wondered how much we would need to raise the federal funds rate to move the ten-year note higher for a sustained period. Countering huge global financial flows would have been a formidable task so long as international forces drove inflation expectations and real long-term interest rates lower and pressed stock and real estate prices higher. The forces driving the ten-year note appeared increasingly global. The best policy under such circumstances is to go with the flow—to calibrate monetary policy so that it is consistent with global forces. We did that. During the global financial transformations that confronted the Fed when I was chairman, our strategy was effective in that we understood what policies were most consistent with the stability of American financial markets. I doubt that we had the resources to counter the downward pressures on real long-term interest rates, which were becoming increasingly global. Certainly Japan did not.

The pervasive body of recent experience showing how effectively stable prices contribute to economic growth and standards of living will be a major incentive for world central bankers to contain inflationary pressures in the future. As I put it at a congressional hearing a few years ago, monetary policy should make even a fiat money economy behave "as though anchored by gold." Is it possible that the world has permanently learned the benefits of stable prices for economic growth and standards of living and will maintain policies that sustain them? I will address this question in chapter 25.

TWENTY-ONE

EDUCATION AND INCOME INEQUALITY

D espite an impressive five years of above-average economic growth that drove the unemployment rate well below 5 percent, a majority of Americans in 2006 reported significant dissatisfaction with the state of the economy. There has been a sense in middle-income America that in recent years prosperity's economic rewards have not been distributed fairly. And indeed, though "fairness" is in the eye of the beholder, it is true that income concentration has been rising since 1980.* The mood of a significant proportion of those answering pollsters' questions is disturbingly sour. The danger is that populist politicians, catering to such a mood, can marshal unexpected majorities in the Congress for short-sighted, counterproductive actions that could turn a state of bad feelings into a truly serious economic crisis.

Overshadowing the current anxiety is a problem of longer standing: many people's day-by-day experiences in the job market seem to contra-

---

*The standard measure of concentration of household income, for example, the "Gini coefficient," rose steadily between 1980 and 2005 from .403 to .469. Polls give each respondent equal weight, and there are far more lower- and middle-income earners who are doing poorly than upper-income earners who are doing well.

dict the well-documented evidence that competitive markets over the decades have elevated standards of living for the vast majority of Americans and much of the rest of the world. Too many perceive the increasingly competitive markets that are the hallmark of today's high-tech globalized economy as continually destroying jobs, and those losses are all too visible. Large layoffs are publicized in the media. Reductions in job slots in America's factories and offices appear unending.

It is thus not surprising that competition is often seen as a threat to job security. It is not perceived as a creator of higher wages either, although in the end it always has been and inevitably will be now as well. In the decades since World War II, real wages have risen as competitive markets have moved the capital and workers employed in obsolescent, low-productivity facilities to the new, more technology-intensive and thus more productive means in turning out the nation's GDP. Consequently, as the economic pie became larger, rewards to both capital and labor increased, and competitive forces have tended to keep shares of national income accruing to employee compensation and profits relatively trendless over the decades. The profit share tends to rise and the employee share to decline in the initial stages of a business cycle, and to reverse thereafter. And in fact if we look at the last decade or two, we can see that the net result is that the distribution of shares of national income between capital and labor has not been much different from their distribution in the past half century. This means that trends in real compensation per hour have tracked output per hour (that is, productivity) closely since the end of World War II,* which in turn implies that the distribution between labor compensation on the one hand and profits of the gains from productivity improvements on the other has been stable.

All this says little, however, about the distribution of labor compensation itself, which includes the income of factory workers, other nonsupervisory workers, and corporate executives, among others. It is not particularly

---

*If real labor income is a fixed share of real national income or GDP, then $L = a \cdot Y$, where $L =$ real labor income and $Y =$ real GDP, with a being labor's share of GDP. $L = w \cdot h$ where w is the real wage and h is the number of hours worked. Since $w \cdot h = a \cdot Y$, then $w = a \cdot (Y/h)$, where $(Y/h) =$ real output per hour. Thus, if over the long run labor share is fixed, the real wage must be proportional to output per hour.

comforting to a worker on the factory floor when his or her wage goes up minimally while the company's CEO gets a multimillion-dollar bonus. The distribution of labor compensation is driven by a different set of competitive forces that govern the supply and demand for relative skills. For the past decade, I have been tracking average hourly wages and salaries for the four-fifths of our nonfarm workforce who are production or nonsupervisory workers relative to the fifth who are "supervisory" employees, including skilled professionals and managers. In the spring of 2007, the supervisory workforce had average hourly salaries of approximately $59 per hour, compared with $17 per hour for the nonsupervisory employees. That means that one-fifth of the total number of employed Americans earned 46 percent of total wages and salaries. In 1997, that percentage was 41 percent.* The rise has been persistent over the decade. Average hourly earnings of production workers went up 3.4 percent annually, while supervisory workers' hourly earnings rose 5.6 percent.

Americans have generally been comfortable with high incomes from efforts that demonstrably contribute to the economic well-being of the nation and are thus clearly "earned." Although the notion of what is "earned" and "not earned" is open to interpretation, people do not seem shy about drawing conclusions. In recent years, for example, the American electorate and their representatives in Washington have been decidedly less tolerant of the dramatic rise in corporate executive compensation, an issue I will address in chapter 23.

The complex set of market forces by which the nation's output is distributed as income to the various creators of GDP is barely visible to the average American. It does no good to argue that unrestrained competition leaves a society *on average* better off, when, in recent years, workers see their bosses gaining large bonuses as they themselves get tepid wage increases. People have to experience competition's advantages firsthand. If they do not, some will turn to populist leaders who promise, for example,

---

*The numbers are estimated matching Bureau of Labor Statistics data on payroll employment (supervisory versus nonsupervisory), average hourly earnings of nonsupervisory workers, and total wages and salaries including bonuses and exercise of stock option grants estimated by the Department of Commerce from quarterly reports submitted to the Department of Labor by almost all employers.

to erect tariff walls. Such protectionism is perceived, erroneously, as securing high-paying jobs in steel, autos, textiles, and chemicals—the icons of America's *past* economic might. But twenty-first-century consumers are less disposed to the products of those industries than were their parents; the U.S. domestic economy, by implication, will no longer support the relative wages and job levels contracted in those industries during negotiations of an earlier period. Accordingly, steel and textile industry employment is off sharply from the peaks of the 1950s and 1960s. The declines will likely continue.

The loss of traditional manufacturing jobs in the United States is often considered a worrisome hollowing out of the economy. It is not. On the contrary, the shift of manufacturing jobs in steel, autos, and textiles, for example, to their more modern equivalents in computers, telecommunications, and information technology is a plus, not a minus, to the American standard of living. Traditional manufacturing companies are no longer the symbol of cutting-edge technologies; their roots lie deep in the nineteenth century or earlier. The world's consumers have increasingly been drawn to products embodying new ideas—cell phones over bicycles, for example. Global trade gives us access to a full range of products without requiring us to manufacture all of them domestically.

Were we to bow to the wishes of the economically uninformed and erect barriers to foreign trade, the pace of competition would surely slow, and tensions, I suppose, might at first appear to ease. After all, Richard Nixon's wage and price controls were highly popular when they were imposed in August 1971. The euphoria dissipated quickly as shortages began to appear. It is likely that such a scenario of growing discontent would be repeated were tariff walls raised. The American standard of living would soon begin to stagnate, and even decline, as a consequence of rising prices, deteriorating product choice, and, perhaps most visibly, our trading partners retaliating by shutting out our job-creating exports.

Manufacturing jobs can no longer be highly paid, since it is consumers who at the end of the day pay the wages of factory workers. And they have balked. They prefer Wal-Mart prices. Those prices, reflecting Chinese low wages, are inconsistent with a funding of high-wage traditional U.S. factories. Forcing U.S. consumers to pay above-market prices to support factory salaries eventually would run into severe resistance. But by then, the American standard of living would have fallen. The Peterson Institute of International Economics estimates that the cumulative effect of globalization since the end of World War II has added 10 percent to the level of the GDP of the United States. Shutting our doors to trade would bring the American standard of living down by that percentage. By comparison, the hugely painful retrenchment in real GDP from the third quarter of 1981 to the third quarter of 1982 was only 1.4 percent. Those who say it is better that fewer people experience the stress of globalization even if it means that some people are less wealthy are creating a false choice. Once walled off, a country loses its competitive verve and begins to stagnate, and stagnation leads to even more intense pain for more people.

If these dire outcomes are unacceptable, as I trust they are, what can be done to counter the distorted perception of how jobs are gained and lost and how incomes are generated? And how can we redress the reality of the continuing advance of income inequality? Both are, among other considerations, undermining support for competitive markets. As I have noted many times, competitive markets and, by extension, globalization and capitalism cannot be sustained without the support of a large proportion of society. The rule of law under which capitalist economic institutions function must be perceived as "fair" if these institutions are to continue to receive broad support. The only way to temper the bias against an economy that entails the timely repositioning of labor is to continue to support market incentives that create jobs and to find productive ways to ease the pain of job losers. That problem is not new. The growing inequality of income, however, *is* new, and it requires analysis as to its roots, and policy action where appropriate.

The Beatles did well in Britain, but they did *spectacularly* well when they gained access to the world market and reaped the benefits of vast audiences and record sales far beyond what was available to them at home. Nobody complained about globalization. Nor has anyone complained about Roger Federer's good fortune. His tennis skills would have earned him little if he had been confined to his native Switzerland. Businesses, of course, also gain large advantages when they become able to reach beyond their sovereign borders, advantages that they pass on, in part, to domestic customers through lower prices and, in part, to their shareholders. As economists would say, their marginal cost of going global is a very small fraction of their added worldwide revenues. Cross-border trade assists in recovering domestic sunk fixed costs, especially research and development. Boeing and Airbus, for example, would not have developed so many different types of aircraft if their markets were limited to sales in their own countries.

Until quite recently, judging from the numerous rounds of successful trade negotiations, globalization has been generally accepted. There is little doubt, however, that, driven by rapidly expanding innovation and competition, globalization has been a major contributor to the increasing concentration of income virtually everywhere. In the past couple of decades, innovation, especially Internet-related, has been moving faster than we can educate ourselves to apply advancing technologies. Thus, the shortfall of the supply of advanced skills relative to the demand for them is pressing the wages of skilled workers higher relative to the wages of the less skilled. There is no compelling reason why the pace of innovative ideas, which often come in bunches, should be immediately matched by a supply of skilled workers to implement them. The insights that advance cutting-edge technologies emerge from a very small part of that workforce.

As globalization increased the skilled wage premium, technological innovation was also taking a toll on lesser-skilled workers. The demand for moderately skilled workers declined as repetitive jobs were gradually displaced by computer programs. I recall architectural and engineering firms with acres of people drawing detailed designs for the newest building complex or jet aircraft. Those jobs are all gone—programmed out of existence. Lower-income workers, mainly in services not subject to global competition, have fared somewhat better. Fears of Americans that immigration is undercutting their wage levels have yet to be confirmed by hard evidence. In general, lower-income U.S. workers did poorly in the 1980s but have fared somewhat better in recent years.

During the past quarter century, as incomes at the middle and lower levels of the U.S. income distribution lagged, those of the most affluent rose rapidly. Americans have seen this before. The last time income in the United States was concentrated in the hands of such a relatively few people was a brief period in the late 1920s and, I suspect more durably, in the years preceding World War I. Owing to the rapid development of the United States as a national market in the latter part of the nineteenth century, income had become highly concentrated by the early years of the twentieth century, as the Rockefellers, Fords, Morgans, and Carnegies were able to reach beyond their local fiefdoms to leverage their incomes by many multiples. The newly rich were a much larger group than the prominent few families that so engaged the society pages at the turn of the century. The striking income disparities of the early twentieth century, however, were driven by a substantially larger concentration of wealth than exists today. Much of the income concentration of those days reflected interest, dividends, and capital gains from that wealth, rather than wage and salary differentials.*

In contrast, the income concentration of today owes more to the generation of high incomes from work spurred by the imbalance between the demand for skilled workers and their available supply. Nonetheless, the trends are troublesome. Corporate managers persistently identify the lack of skilled workers as one of today's greatest ongoing problems and are willing to bid up pay packages to acquire them.

Technological advance is rarely smooth. It can take years for labor markets to adjust to a surge in such demand. They do so by bidding up skilled-worker pay scales, which attracts workers from abroad and encourages resident workers to acquire more schooling or otherwise gain greater skills. But the response takes time, and access to skilled foreigners is constrained. In the interim, the rise in skilled-worker wage levels, unmatched by a proportionate rise for those with lesser skills, concentrates income in the upper brackets. By and large, aside from many protectionist initiatives, globalization's contribution to increasing inequality has not drawn heavy opposition—at least not yet. The difficulties encountered in the most re-

---

*Data on wealth distribution in the late nineteenth century are sparse, but the large prevalence of property income confirms the vast anecdotal evidence of those years. The decline in the concentration of income in the 1930s and through World War II owed to weakened asset values and capital losses, the hypertight labor markets of World War II, and the wage and price controls that inhibited supply and demand from functioning. Parenthetically, one consequence of those controls was the emergence of company-supplied medical insurance as a means to attract workers whose wages were frozen. The consequences of that system are all too evident to today's U.S. manufacturers.

cent multilateral effort (the Doha round of trade negotiation) to further ease restrictions on international trade, however, have raised political red flags against a further spread of globalization.

To a greater or lesser extent, most developed countries have experienced the impact of technology and globalization much as the United States has. Yet, although they confront increasing income concentration, the impact to date appears to be significantly milder than what we are experiencing in the United States. The United States is clearly an outlier among the global trading partners, and that calls for a broader explanation of the causes of U.S. income inequality. Part of the explanation is the more elaborate welfare systems, especially in Europe, that are engaged in far more extensive programs to redistribute income than has been deemed acceptable in the United States. But this is not new. Such disparities existed well before 1980, when income inequality began to become a global problem.

A very likely significant part of the explanation for recent developments appears to be the dysfunction of elementary and secondary education in the United States. A study conducted first in 1995 by the Lynch School of Education at Boston College revealed that although our fourth-grade students on an international comparison scale were above average in both math and science, by the time they reached their last year of high school they had fallen well below the international average. The leading nations included Singapore, Hong Kong, Sweden, and the Netherlands.* Follow-up studies in 1999 and 2003 indicated only modest U.S. relative improvement. This education disaster cannot be pinned on the quality of our children. Our students were average, or above, at age nine or ten. What do we do to them in the next seven or eight years that they test so poorly relative to their peers in other countries? What do we do to their learning process that requires business recruiters to dismiss vast numbers of "educated" applicants for modestly skilled jobs because they cannot write coherent sentences or add a column of numbers accurately?

It is not surprising that, as a consequence, too many of our students languish at too low a level of skill upon graduation, adding to the supply of

---

*The study and its follow-ups are available at the International Study Center's Web site, http://timss.bc.edu.

lesser-skilled labor in the face of an apparently declining demand. One can only wonder how our labor markets would behave if our students could match the accomplishments of their counterparts in Singapore.* These education-driven mismatches of skills coupled with the forces of globalization and innovation appear to explain much, if not most, of the failure of real wages at the middle and bottom of our income distribution to rise measurably during the past quarter century. The decline in the ability of labor unions to hold wages above the market has probably had some effect on middle-class incomes, but it cannot be a significant factor in the greater incidence of *increased* concentration of income in the United States relative to our trading partners, since globalization has weakened the bargaining power of unions worldwide.

The key policy levers to address the problem of increasing inequality, as I see it, are thus primarily education and immigration. Markets are already working in that direction. We need to quicken the process. Specifically, we need to harness better the forces of competition that have shaped the development of education in the United States, and we need to make immigration easier for highly skilled individuals. I'll return to these points below.

For three decades following World War II, in the face of advancing technologies and globalization, we managed to hold the distribution of income stable. How did we do it, and what lessons from that experience will help craft policies that can rein in the growth of income inequality and possibly reverse it?

The skill composition of our workforce at the end of World War II meshed reasonably well with the needs of our even-then-complex capital facilities. As a result, wage-skill differentials were stable, and percentage changes in wage rates were broadly the same for all job grades. The significant addition of college graduates to the labor force, in part the result of schooling financed by the GI Bill, was sufficient to contain wage increases for the highly skilled. Real wages of the lesser skilled also rose, in part as a result of effective high school education and the many skills learned during

---

*Ironically, many educators in Singapore marvel at the entrepreneurial skills of American youth.

the war. In short, technical proficiencies across all job levels appeared to rise about in line with the needs of our ever-more-complex infrastructure, stabilizing the income distribution in the United States for three decades. While the GI Bill and on-the-job training in the World War II military were not, of course, initially market-driven, they helped to meet the needs of a changing labor market.

By 1980, however, a persistent rise in income inequality began to take hold.* High-wage, middle-class factory jobs in the United States have been under pressure from technology and imports since they peaked at nearly twenty million in mid-1979. But in recent years, fear of outsourcing of service trades not previously subject to international competition has added to job insecurity. That insecurity, fostered by global competition, was new for many middle-income Americans, who increasingly became willing to forgo pay raises for job-tenure guarantees.

Our institutions of education have responded to the skill mismatch that became evident a quarter century ago, but only in part. When I was young (the 1940s), education was seen as preparation for a lifetime of work. Everyone viewed formal education as what you did in your early years. Either you ended your studies after high school or you went on to college and beyond. Whatever your final degree, educationally, you were set for life. A teenager with a high school diploma would follow his father into the local steel mill, or, if a college graduate, he would seek a job as an assistant to an executive in a large corporation. Steel mill jobs were high paying, and most people who took them expected to spend the whole of their working lives at the mill. The young male corporate assistants aspired to replace their bosses someday. Young women by and large took jobs as secretaries or teachers upon graduation, pending marriage and family. In 1940, only 30 percent of women between ages twenty-five and fifty-four were employed or seeking jobs. (Today the number is more than 75 percent.)

But as competition spurred creative destruction, the pace of job turnover quickened and the visions of a lifetime with a single employer faded.

---

*Interestingly, despite the marked increase in income concentration over the past quarter century, there is little evidence that the distribution of wealth in the United States has materially changed.

It became clear as the twentieth century drew to a close that high school or college graduates were likely to hold many different jobs through their working lives and even engage in more than one profession. In response, formal education gradually became a lifetime endeavor, and markets responded.

The first evidence of this was the dramatic increase in enrollment in community colleges. After years of being viewed as the backwater of American education, these institutions are now in the vanguard. Student enrollment in two-year colleges rose from 2.1 million in 1969 to 6.5 million in 2004. Almost a third of the students are aged thirty or older. These institutions specialize in teaching practical skills that are immediately applicable in the workplace, and have been especially helpful in retraining people who have lost their jobs for new opportunities. Some typical curricula: electronics maintenance, collision repair technology, nursing, massage therapy, and computer information security. These middle-income occupations require substantially more skills than were required of middle-income workers when I entered the labor force in the late 1940s.

A rising proportion of the population is also taking advantage of work-related instruction. The "corporate university" is rapidly becoming a permanent fixture in adult job-specific learning. Many corporations dissatisfied with the quality of new hires supplement their education and capabilities, equipping them to compete successfully in world markets. General Motors has an extensive "university" system with sixteen functional colleges. McDonald's educates more than five thousand employees a year at its aptly named Hamburger University.

Such responses to market needs are not new to American education, however; they have always been at its core. At the turn of the last century, technological advances required workers with a higher level of cognitive skills than was required for the dominant rural economy of previous decades—for instance, the ability to read manuals, to interpret blueprints, or to understand mathematical formulas. Youth were drawn from rural areas, where opportunities were limited, into more productive occupations in business and an advancing manufacturing sector. Our educational system responded: in the 1920s and 1930s, high school enrollment in this country expanded rapidly. It became the job of these institutions to prepare students for work life. In the context of the demands of the economy at that time, a high school diploma represented the training needed to be successful in most aspects of American enterprise. The economic returns in the job market from having a high school diploma rose, and as a result, high school enrollment rates climbed. By the time the United States entered World War II, the median level of education for a seventeen-year-old was a high school diploma—an accomplishment that set the United States apart from other countries.

New demands created by economic progress also importantly influenced the evolution of our system of higher education. Although many states had established land-grant schools earlier,* their support strengthened in the late nineteenth century as states whose economies specialized in agriculture and mining sought to take advantage of new scientific methods of production.

Early in the twentieth century, the content of education at an American college had evolved from a classically based curriculum to one combining the sciences, empirical studies, and modern liberal arts. Universities responded to the need for the application of science—particularly chemistry and physics—to the manufacture of steel, rubber, chemicals, drugs, petroleum, and other goods requiring the newer production technologies.

America's reputation as a world leader in higher education is grounded in the ability of these versatile institutions, taken together, to serve the practical needs of an economy and, more important, to unleash the creative thinking that moves it forward. It is the recognition of these values that has attracted such a large segment of the world student population to our institutions of higher learning. But while our universities and especially our community colleges have responded impressively, in recent decades our elementary and secondary schools have not.

In the foregoing, I have voiced concern about the state of our elementary and secondary education while lauding the world-class university system we have built over the generations. It should be clear, however, that unless the former can be brought up to world class, the latter will either

---

*Beginning in 1862, the federal government granted land (later, funding) to the states for the creation of educational institutions to teach engineering, agriculture, and military tactics. Cornell, Texas A&M, the University of California at Berkeley, and Penn State are among more than one hundred institutions founded under the land-grant program.

have to depend on foreign students or sink into mediocrity. The average age of our scientists and engineers is increasing, according to the National Science Foundation, and large numbers will retire in a very few years, lowering the supply of skilled workers relative to the growing requirements of an ever-more-complex capital stock. If we cannot replace these skilled workers, the pressure for a rising skilled-unskilled wage differential will grow, since no comparable shortage of lesser-skilled workers appears on the horizon.

One of the skills too many high school graduates lack is proficiency in math. It is that skill more than any other that is required to achieve skilled-job status. I do not pretend to be conversant with the details of U.S. education in the twenty-first century. Yet people whose scholarship I respect, and who are in a position to know, complain that the math teachers of my childhood have been replaced with teachers with degrees in education but much too often with no math or science degree or competence in the subject matter. In 2000, for example, nearly two-fifths of public secondary school math teachers did not have a major or minor in math, math education, or a related field. Lou Gerstner, former chairman of IBM and founder of the Teaching Commission, noted in an essay for the *Christian Science Monitor* (December 13, 2004): "The heart of the problem is the arcane way we recruit and prepare teachers, along with the lockstep single salary schedule" for all teachers, irrespective of their subject specialty, "no matter how desperately society may need a certain skill set and no matter how well a teacher performs in the classroom. That's senseless, yet it's still the norm in the teaching profession."

Different pay scales for high school teachers in different disciplines may go against the ethos of teaching. Perhaps money should not be an incentive. But it is. There are doubtless math teachers in our high schools who are sufficiently dedicated to forgo the much higher incomes they could earn in other jobs. But they must be few, for as Gerstner also points out, "according to a 2000 study of the largest urban school districts, nearly 95 percent reported an immediate demand for math teachers—a quantity problem on top of the quality problem we clearly already have."

It is becoming increasingly clear that a flat pay scale when demand is far from flat is a form of price fixing that undermines the ability to attract qualified math teachers. Since the financial opportunities for experts in math or science outside of teaching are vast, and for English literature teachers outside of teaching, limited, math teachers are likely to be a cut below the average teaching professional at the same pay grade. Teaching math is likely being left to those who are unable to claim the more lucrative jobs. That is far less true of English literature or history teachers.

Moreover, retirees or well-educated parents of students who volunteer to teach, part-time, courses such as math in which they have some proficiency are turned down because they lack a degree in education. To the extent that such practices are widespread, they are bureaucratic impediments to the functioning of market forces in education. Fortunately, proposals to remedy this dysfunctional state of affairs are gaining traction.

For example, James Simons, a distinguished mathematician who applied his skills to build one of Wall Street's most successful hedge funds, in 2004 turned his efforts toward enhancing the teaching of high school math. His Math for America has developed a high-stipend fellowship program to recruit and train high school math teachers. Senator Chuck Schumer of New York in 2006 embraced, and offered legislation to advance, this initiative.

Enhancing elementary and secondary school sensitivity to market forces should help restore the balance between the demand for and supply of skilled workers in the United States. I do not know whether vouchers, which bring an element of competition to public schools, are the final answer. But I suspect that Rose and Milton Friedman, devoting the end of their distinguished careers to advancing the policy, were on the right track. (I do not recall either ever being off track.)

Another step toward enhancing competition is an interesting paper written for the Hamilton Project (a Robert Rubin creation) at the Brookings Institution. The authors note that certification of teachers (which generally requires a degree in education) has little to do with whether a teacher is effective. They recommend opening up teaching to others who are qualified— including those who have a four-year undergraduate degree but not the formal requirements for certification. They estimate that removing the barrier of certification would encourage recent college graduates and older professionals to try a teaching career. In addition, they recommend tracking teacher and student performance and making the achievement of tenure more difficult. They simulated these recommendations through a model based on the performance of 150,000 Los Angeles students from 2000 to 2003. The authors conclude that if the school system screened out the least qualified quarter of teachers, student test scores would be raised by as much as 14 percentile points by graduation. These are very large changes, and, even if only fractionally achievable, such improvement in academic performance could go a long way to remedying the international inferiority of young American students.

A recognition of how poor our mathematics education had become and perhaps some reason for hope was the report in September 2006 by the National Council of Teachers of Mathematics, reversing its ill-chosen advisory of 1989. The earlier report recommended a curriculum that dropped emphasis on basic math skills (multiplication, division, square roots, and so on) and pressed students to seek more free-flowing solutions and to study a range of special math topics. I always wondered how you can learn math unless you have a thorough grounding in the basics and concentrate on a very few subjects at a time. Asking children to use their imagination before they know what they are imagining about seemed vacuous to me. It was.

Another education imperative goes beyond fostering market forces in schools. I recognize that left to their own devices, market incentives will not reach the education of those children "left behind" (to borrow a term from current U.S. education legislation). The cost of educational egalitarianism is doubtless high and may be difficult to justify in terms of economic efficiency and short-term productivity. Some students can achieve a given level of education far more easily, and therefore at far less cost, than others. Yet there is danger to a democratic society in leaving some children out of sync with its institutions. Such neglect contributes to exaggerated income concentration, and could conceivably be far more costly to the sustaining of capitalism and globalization in the long run. The value judgments involved in making such choices reach beyond the imperatives of the marketplace.

Unless our resident population, with the assistance of our schools, can supply the level of skills we need, which to date they have not, as our skilled baby boomers retire we will require a significant increase in the number of skilled workers migrating to the United States. As Bill Gates, the chairman of Microsoft, succinctly testified before Congress in March 2007, "America will find it infinitely more difficult to maintain its technological leadership if it shuts out the very people who are most able to help us compete." He added that we are "driving away the world's best and brightest precisely when we need them most."

Much of our skill shortage can be resolved with education reform. But at best, that will take years. The world is moving too fast for political and bureaucratic dawdling. We need to address quickly a double U.S. disability: the increasing income concentration and the increasing cost of staffing our highly complex capital stock. Both could be "cured" by opening up the United States to the world's very large and growing pool of skilled workers. Our skilled jobs are the highest paid in the world. Accordingly, were we to allow open migration of skilled workers to this country, there would soon be a lower wage premium of skilled over lesser skilled and an end to our shortages of skilled workers.* The shortages occur because we are inhibiting world competitive labor markets from functioning. Administrative exclusionary rules have been substituted for the pricing mechanism. In the process, we have created in this country a privileged, native-born elite of skilled workers whose incomes are being supported at noncompetitively high levels by immigration quotas on skilled professionals. Eliminating such restrictions would, at the stroke of a pen, reduce much income inequality and address the problem of a potentially noncompetitive capital stock.

The politics of immigration policy, of course, is influenced by far more than economics. Immigration policy confronts the considerably more difficult issue of the desire of the population to maintain the cultural roots that tie the society together and foster voluntary exchange to mutual advantage. The United States has always been able eventually to absorb waves of immigration and maintain the individual rights and freedoms bestowed by

---

*The rise in the income spread between skilled and less-skilled workers worldwide suggests that the shortage of skills is a global problem. Because international migration is so inhibited, the "price" for skills does not converge globally. It is clearly more of a problem in the United States than elsewhere. Hence, opening skilled immigration into the United States would put upward pressure on wages of non-U.S. skilled workers and increase income concentration by a modest amount; it would also lower the U.S. skilled wage level.

our Founding Fathers. But the transitions were always more difficult than hindsight makes them appear. If we are to continue to engage the world and improve our standard of living, we will have to either markedly improve our elementary and secondary education or lower our barriers to skilled immigrants. In fact, implementing both measures would confer important economic benefits.

Public policy is a series of choices. We can build exclusionary walls around the United States to keep out the goods, services, and people that compete with domestic producers and workers. The result would be a loss of competitive spark, leading to a stagnant and weakened economy. Our standard of living would fall and societal discontent would fester and rise, as the once-vaunted superpower fell from its position of world leadership.

Alternatively, we can engage the increasingly competitive high-tech world, address our domestic school system's failure to supply a level of newly skilled workers sufficient to quell our disturbing increase in income inequality, and further open our borders to the world's growing skilled-worker pool.

No alternative offers a rising American standard of living without the challenge and stress of borders open to goods and people. Choice is what public policy is all about. And with choice come both benefits and costs. To achieve the benefits, we need to accept the costs.

TWENTY-TWO

THE WORLD RETIRES. BUT CAN IT AFFORD TO?

Almost all of the developed world is at the edge of a demographic abyss for which there is no precedent: a huge cohort of workers, the baby-boom generation, is about to move from productive work to retirement. There are too few younger workers to replace them, and the shortfall among skilled workers is even worse. The leading edge of change is particularly evident in Germany, where, despite high unemployment, severe shortages of skilled workers are mounting. A German job recruitment executive told the *Financial Times* (November 28, 2006): "The battle for workers has already begun, and given the demographic trends in Germany and in parts of southern and eastern Europe, it is about to get a lot worse."

This tectonic shift is truly a twenty-first-century problem. Retirement is a relatively new phenomenon in human history; average life expectancy a century ago for much of the developed world was only forty-six years. Relatively few people survived long enough to experience retirement.

The ratio of the dependent elderly to the working-age population has been rising in the industrialized world for at least 150 years. The pace of increase slowed markedly with the birth of the baby-boom generation after

World War II. But dependency of the elderly will almost certainly rise more rapidly as that generation reaches retirement age. The acceleration will be particularly dramatic in Japan and Europe. In Japan, the population share of those at least sixty-five years of age climbed from 13 to 21 percent in the past decade, and United Nations demographers expect it to reach 31 percent by 2030. The Japanese working-age population is already declining and is projected to fall from eighty-four million in 2007 to sixty-nine million by 2030. Europe's working-age population is also anticipated to recede, though less than Japan's.

The changes projected for the United States are not as severe, but nonetheless present daunting challenges. Over the next quarter century, the annual growth rate of the working-age population in the United States is anticipated to slow, from 1 percent today to about 0.3 percent by 2030. At the same time, the percentage of the population that is over sixty-five will rise markedly. Though the overall population is expected to continue to age, much of the aging of the labor force has already occurred with the aging of the baby-boom generation. Once the baby boomers begin to retire, the mean age of the U.S. labor force is expected to stabilize.

These anticipated changes in the age structure of our population and workforce result largely from the decline in fertility that followed the postwar birth surge. After peaking in 1957 at 3.7 births over a woman's lifetime, the fertility rate in the United States fell to 1.8 by the mid-1970s; since 1990 it has stabilized at slightly less than 2.1, the so-called replacement rate, or the level required to hold the population constant in the absence of immigration or changes in longevity.* The decrease in the number of children per family since the baby boom has inevitably led to a projected increase in the ratio of elderly to those of working age.

Continued immigration, however, will mitigate the impact of a falling birth rate, and population growth will be sustained as well by increases in life expectancy. In 1950, an American man sixty-five years of age could expect, on average, to live until age seventy-eight, whereas now he can ex-

---

*The fertility rate used here is the total fertility rate. It is measured as the average number of children who would be born to a woman in her lifetime if she were to experience the birth rates by age observed in any given year.

pect to live to eighty-two. And if current trends continue, by 2030 he can expect to live to eighty-three. Women's life expectancy is rising similarly, from eighty in 1950 to roughly eighty-four today, and eighty-five by 2030, according to the Social Security Board of Trustees in 2007.*

Americans not only are living longer, but we are also generally living healthier. Rates of disability for the elderly have been declining, reflecting improvements in all phases of medicine, as well as the changing character of work. It is becoming less physically strenuous and more demanding intellectually, continuing a century-long trend toward a more conceptual and less physical economic output. In 1900, for example, only one out of every ten workers was in a professional, technical, or managerial occupation. By 1970, that proportion had doubled, and today those types of jobs account for about one-third of our workforce. An inevitable consequence, then, of the aging of America will be that more of our elderly population will have both the ability and the incentive to work later and later into old age.

Workers in their sixties have accumulated many years of valuable experience, so extending labor force participation by just a few years could have a sizable impact on economic output. But there is no getting around it: almost all of the baby-boom generation will have retired by 2030. And their retirement will be unmatched in length by any previous generation. Will those "golden years" be truly golden? How will the more slowly growing U.S. workforce that will follow the baby boomers produce goods and services for themselves and their families as well as for a retired population whose size is without precedent?

The hard facts of demography will have a profoundly wrenching effect on the balance of world economic power. Aging is not an immediate issue for less-developed nations, with the exception of China, which has suppressed its birth rate through central planning—the government's one-child policy. The United Nations projects that the share of world population residing in what are today's developed nations will fall to 15.2 percent by 2030 from 18.3 percent today. How developed nations cope in the face of

---

*The trustees for Social Security and Medicare include the secretaries of the treasury and labor and two public trustees appointed by the president.

such a shift may go a long way toward either assuaging or intensifying changes in the world's economic balance of power. Critical to the outcome is whether developed nations, confronted with loss of power and prestige, become inward looking and erect barriers to trade with a burgeoning developing world. How governments finesse the transfer of real resources from the shrinking shares of their populations who make up their productive workforce to a growing retirement population is likely to be a defining question of the next quarter century. For democratic societies, the politics will be particularly daunting, as an increasing share of the electorate will be benefit-recipient retirees.

The economics of retirement is straightforward: enough resources must be set aside over a lifetime of work to fund consumption during retirement. The bottom line in the success of all retirement systems is the availability of *real* resources at retirement. The financial arrangements associated with retirement facilitate the diversion of resources that make possible the consumption of goods and services after retirement, but they do not *produce* those goods and services. In the United States, Congress may pass, and the president may sign, legislation that, for example, provides an entitlement, upon retirement, to a specified level of health care. But who assures that the hospitals, pharmaceutical companies, physicians, nurses, and medical infrastructure generally will be in place to convert a paper promise into valuable future medical services?

A simple test for any retirement system is whether it can assure the availability of promised real resources to retirees without overly burdening the working-age population. By that measure, America may be on a collision course with reality. The oldest baby boomers become eligible for Social Security in 2008. By 2030, according to UN projections, people sixty-five years of age and older will account for more than 23 percent of the adult population, compared with 16 percent today. This huge population shift will expose all our financial retirement systems to severe stress and will require adjustments for which there are no historical precedents. The fact that a greater share of the dependents will be elderly rather than children will put an additional burden on society's resources, as the elderly, per capita, consume a relatively large share of resources, while children consume relatively little.

After receding for years, labor force participation among older Americans has edged somewhat higher recently owing to rising pressures on retirement incomes and a growing scarcity of experienced labor.* As I noted earlier, it will no doubt continue to rise. Nonetheless, the most effective way to boost future standards of living, and thereby accommodate the aspirations of *both* workers and retirees, is to increase the nation's saving and the productiveness of its uses.† We need significant additional saving in the decades ahead if we are to finance the construction of capital facilities—for example, cutting-edge high-tech plant and equipment—that will produce the additional real resources to ensure that the promised retirement benefits for the baby boomers will be redeemable in real terms. And we need to do this without having to severely raise burdens on tomorrow's workers.

However, by almost any measure, the additional saving required to take care of the surge in retirees is sufficiently large to raise serious questions about whether the federal government will be able to meet the retirement commitments already made.

The trustees of the Social Security system calculate that it would take either an *immediate* increase in the payroll tax from its current 12.4 percent to 14.4 percent, an immediate across-the-board cut in benefits of 13 percent, or some combination of the two to close the funding shortfall over the next seventy-five years. Postponing or phasing in the adjustments would require higher taxes or lower benefits later. And because of the large deficits projected beyond the seventy-five-year horizon, "seventy-five-year solvency," the somewhat arbitrary standard for social insurance, will require further adjustments later. While the projected shortfall is problematic, it doesn't, by itself, create insurmountable fiscal or economic difficulties. Most important, projections of Social Security benefits are relatively reliable. This is because the demographics of the retiree population are among

---

*Despite the growing feasibility of work at older ages, Americans have been retiring younger and younger. In 1940, for example, the median age of retirement for men was sixty-nine; by 2005, the median age was about sixty-two.

†Additionally, we could borrow from abroad, which should build up the U.S. physical capital stock. In so doing, however, we would also build up a liability to foreigners that we would have to finance in the future; that is, less of our future GDP would be available for consumption by U.S. residents.

economists' most accurate forecasts, and because Social Security is a defined-benefit program, so payments per beneficiary are reasonably predictable in advance.

Medicare, by contrast, poses a much bigger problem. The trustees forecast a seventy-five-year funding shortfall for Part A of Medicare, the Hospital Insurance Fund, which could be closed with an immediate increase of 3.5 percentage points on top of the current 2.9 percent levy on taxable payroll (to a total of 6.4 percent), or an immediate halving of benefits or some combination of the two. But that's not the end of it. The costs of Part B of Medicare, which pays doctors' bills and other outpatient expenses, and the new Part D, which pays for access to prescription drug coverage, are both projected to rise rapidly. But they are mandated to be met by general tax revenues, rather than by payroll taxes. Although not as visible as hospital insurance taxes, the claims on general tax revenues of future Parts B and D benefits are of the same order of magnitude as those of Part A.

The public trustees, coming at future Medicare costs from a different perspective, commented in 2006 that "if the Trustees' projections prove a reliable guide to the next few decades, absent an increase in earmarked sources of revenue for the program, in just 15 years payment of currently scheduled Medicare benefits would require General Fund transfers equal to 25 percent of Federal income tax revenues . . . —more than triple their 2005 fiscal burden—and less than 10 years later the General Fund transfer would equal nearly 40 percent of Federal income tax revenues." But even such numbers do not necessarily capture the full dimension of the problem, because projections of Medicare benefits are highly uncertain.

Health spending has been growing faster than the economy for many years, a growth fueled, in large part, by advances in technology. We know very little about how rapidly medical technology will evolve or how those innovations will translate into future spending. Technological innovations can greatly improve the quality of medical care and can, in some instances, reduce the costs of treatment and surely the costs of hospital administration. But because technology expands the set of treatment possibilities, it also has the potential to add to overall spending—in some cases by a great deal.

As encrypted private health records become sufficiently widespread, researchers will for the first time be able effectively to evaluate treatments and outcomes for a broad spectrum of diseases. I assume a standard for national best practices will emerge as a result. Eventually, public ratings of hospitals and physicians will come too; market competition can be expected to follow. Yet none of this is likely to happen very fast. Medical practice hinges on what traditionally has been a very private relationship between physician and patient, and both are reluctant to risk a breach in privacy.

Medical practice in the United States has evolved quite differently from region to region. I presume that nationwide best practices, by eliminating the worst treatments and practitioners, will enhance average outcomes. But it is by no means clear whether a nationwide awareness of and demand for best practices would increase or decrease medical expenditures. We need to keep in mind that the uncertainties—especially our inability to identify that upper bound of future demands for medical care—warrant significant restraint in policymaking. The critical reason to proceed cautiously is that new programs quickly develop constituencies willing to resist any curtailment fiercely. As a consequence, our ability to rein in deficit-expanding initiatives, should they later prove to have been excessive or misguided, is quite limited.

Policymakers should err on the side of prudence when considering new budget entitlement initiatives. Programs can always be expanded in the future should the resources for them become available, but they cannot easily be cut back if resources later fall short of commitments. This is why I believe that moving forward with an unfunded prescription drug program in 2003, before the problems of the severely underfunded and out-of-balance Medicare program as a whole were addressed, was a mistake, perhaps a very large one.*

Having participated in a number of studies that simulated future Medicare costs and benefits, I am struck by the breadth of the range of possible outcomes for, say, the year 2030. As I noted, the range of possibilities for

---

*Fortunately (and unusually), the cost of Medicare Part D, the prescription drug program, has to date come in below initial projections. Possibly the program has fostered the competition it was structured to create. However, it is still an unfunded, and large, growing expense.

Social Security is quite narrow. Demographers, of course, have the same good handle on the number of future Medicare beneficiaries. But average cost per beneficiary *under current law* depends not only on future technologies but also on patient choices and a whole series of other variables.

The forecasting complexity is such that the trustees have had to fall back on a simple algorithm—a projected rate of growth of benefits per Medicare recipient relative to the projected rate of growth of per capita GDP. Growth in real Medicare outlays per beneficiary has averaged approximately 4 percent a year over the past decade, about 2 percentage points higher than growth in real per capita GDP. The public trustees go on to note, "It seems reasonable to assume (per capita) health care and Medicare expenditure growth will gradually slow to the rate of growth of GDP—because there is presumably some upper limit to what share of their growing incomes Americans will want to devote to health care." That may in fact turn out to be true.

But, as anyone who knows the ways of Washington must realize, such an assumption also involves quite a spectacular leap. It implies a degree of restraint that is not written into current law. It assumes a fiscal victory in a political battle that has yet to be fought. As the public trustees themselves observe, "No such slowdown has materialized over the past half-century." Thus, the projected tax burden of mounting Medicare spending presumably would be even larger if based strictly on current entitlement law and current trends in health care spending.

There is a great deal of work to be done to set Medicare right. It should be apparent that to cover future Social Security and Medicare funding shortfalls wholly by raising taxes is economically infeasible. Doing so would imply unprecedented peacetime tax rates. At some point, tax rate increases become self-defeating: by absorbing purchasing power and reducing work and investment incentives, they reduce the economy's growth rate. Hence, the growth of the tax base slows and the projected additional tax revenues fail to materialize fully.

We are left with a most daunting reality: resolving the funding shortfall for federal social insurance is going to require benefit cuts. Government has a moral obligation to make these cuts sooner rather than later, to afford future retirees as much time as possible to adjust their plans for work, saving, and retirement spending. Failure to give Americans adequate warning that the retirement income upon which they have planned will be reduced could threaten major disruptions in people's lives.

Once the level of benefits that Social Security and Medicare can reasonably promise is determined, how can public policy ensure that the real resources will become available to fulfill those promises? Focusing on financial solvency within the Social Security and Medicare systems without regard to the broader macroeconomic picture does not ensure that the resources will be there. Without additional net saving, the real resources required to produce future benefits will not be produced. Thus, in addressing the imbalances of Social Security and Medicare, we need to ensure that measures taken now to finance future benefit commitments represent real additions to national saving and the productive assets they fund.

We need, in effect, to make real the phantom "lockboxes" of a few years back, which were supposed to contain the cash to fund future Social Security benefits. The lockboxes were so real to many Americans that former Speaker of the House Tom Foley tells the story of his mother's berating him for trying to disabuse her of that belief. "Mr. Foley," she said, "I hope you will not be offended at how surprised and shocked I am to find that the majority leader of the House of Representatives knows nothing about Social Security." At that time, the lockbox proposals would have required not only putting the social insurance trust funds (currently in surplus) off budget for accounting purposes, but also having Congress mandate that the remainder of the budget be balanced. For a brief period in the flush fiscal-surplus years at the turn of the millennium, a bipartisan commitment emerged to do just that. But, regrettably, the commitment collapsed when it became apparent that, in light of a less favorable economic environment, maintaining balance in the budget excluding Social Security and Medicare would require significantly lower spending or higher taxes.

Failure to address the imbalances between promises to future retirees and the economy's ability to meet those promises could have severe consequences for individual retirees and the economy as a whole. In the end, I expect the Medicare funding imbalance to be resolved by rescinding the benefits of the more affluent.* The frenzy of politics and the so-far-intractable continued increase in income inequality, in my judgment, leaves no other credible political alternative. Restored balance could occur through the development of private accounts (which I support) or through legislation requiring Medicare to be means-tested (as is Medicaid). Rationing is the only other realistic possibility, and that has little support in the United States. Most future Medicare benefits will surely be concentrated in the middle- and lower-income groups. Medical service for upper-income recipients will have to be funded by unsubsidized private medical insurance or out of pocket, probably in the form of copayments approaching 100 percent. Many will recoil from the concept of Medicare as welfare, as means-tested programs tend to be seen, but the arithmetic of twenty-first-century demographics in a highly competitive global economy necessitates it.

While I favor a liberal immigration policy, I do not do so as a means of increasing the working population in order to raise social insurance taxes to help address the Social Security/Medicare funding shortfall. Nor, for reasons I will discuss later, can we count on a fortuitous increase in productivity; the long-term ceiling for increases in output per hour in the United States appears to be 3 percent a year, with 2 percent being the most likely outcome. In brief, we likely won't have enough people working, nor will we likely have a sufficient increase in the amount each worker on average can produce, to cover the enormous shortfall from entitlements under current law. It may not even be close.

With so many unknowns, I fear that given our demographics and the limited upside potential of productivity growth, we may already have committed to a higher level of real medical resources for baby-boomer retirees than our government can realistically deliver. As previously noted, Congress can enact an entitlement, but that in itself does not produce the economic resources required to provide the hospitals, physicians, nurses, and

---

*How much a cut in benefits would reduce outlays on medical services is uncertain. Several years ago, I requested the Federal Reserve Board staff to simulate the level of medical service outlays through 2004, assuming that Medicare and Medicaid entitlements had never been enacted. The staff concluded that outlays would have been only modestly lower. Market efficiencies, however, could have been quite considerable.

pharmaceutical companies that will be essential in 2030 to meet the letter of current law. The size in 2030 of the transfer of real resources from worker-producers to retirees may be too large for the former to accept. The claims on the nation's output, because of an unfunded expansion of entitlements, may far exceed the output produced by a workforce only marginally larger than exists today. In short, the promises may have to be broken, or, perhaps better said, they may have to be "clarified."

The significant uncertainties about the availability of future real resources are reflected in uncertainties in retiree income replacement rates. Given today's expected yawning gap between retirement needs and even current large entitlement promises, private pension and insurance benefits are going to have to play an increasingly greater role. At the end of 2006, private pension funds in the United States had $5.6 trillion in assets: $2.3 trillion in the traditional defined-benefit programs and $3.3 trillion in defined-contribution plans, largely 401(k)s.* Private pension and profit-sharing funds paid out $344 billion in benefits in 2005.† By comparison, Social Security and Medicare paid out $845 billion. The former is bound to catch up with the latter as American workers and their employers take the steps necessary to meet workers' retirement income goals.

But that is years out. Now, defined-benefit pensions are in trouble. Those plans can flourish in periods of relatively short life expectancy after retirement and a rapidly growing population. The unprecedented size of the baby-boom generation and its projected longevity have dramatically reduced the advantages of defined-benefit plans. Significant pension obligations have already been defaulted to the Pension Benefit Guaranty Corporation.

The legal obligation to pay benefits in a defined-benefit plan of course rests with the employer: the pension fund is there for backup. But since certain levels of funding are mandated by law, corporations view their defined-benefit pension fund as a profit opportunity—the greater the pension fund's investment revenues, the less additional cash the sponsoring corporation is

---

*In addition, $3.7 trillion was held in individual retirement accounts (IRAs).
†Group health insurance paid out an additional $581 billion but predominantly to those under sixty-five years of age.

required to put into the fund. And the less the cash infusion, the less the current cost of labor, and the greater the profits. Consequently, the corporation is driven to find ways to reduce payments into the fund.

Since corporations know with reasonable certainty who will retire, when, and with what promised benefits for years into the future, isn't the cost a simple calculation? Not quite. The expected cost to a company of a defined-benefit plan depends in part on the status of pension benefits in the event of bankruptcy. For example, where pension benefits by contract have first claim on corporate resources in the event of default, the calculation of benefit cost is unambiguous. In such circumstances the corporation might choose to set up a pension fund of riskless U.S. Treasury securities whose maturities match the timing of the benefit payments. Benefits would be generated by the principal and accumulated interest of a U.S. Treasury security maturing in the year the benefits are required to be paid. In practice, corporations try every which way to get around so simple a program because it is the most costly. Corporate equity, real estate, junk bonds, and even AAA corporate bonds yield a greater return than treasuries. But all have risk of default, and in the event of default, the sponsoring corporation would have to use its other assets or not pay its pension obligations.

The debate as to what rate of return a pension fund should seek, and therefore how much risk it can accept, depends, in the end, on how certain the corporation wants to be of paying its promised benefits. The greater the risk to pension assets, the greater the profit margin of the investment.

Financial theory would seem to make the achievement of higher returns illusory. If the markets are pricing risk correctly, the pension fund's rate of return should be indifferent to the degree of risk in the portfolio, since higher rates of return compensate for the losses of risky securities, which often become worthless. But what is true in theory doesn't always work out in practice. (Or, more appropriately, you need a new theory.) Pension managers will tell you that the actual, realized rates of return over the long run for equities are above the so-called average risk-adjusted rates of return for the U.S. economy as a whole. Rates of return since the nineteenth century confirm that diversified holdings of stocks over decades-long holding periods have invariably yielded above-average real rates of return. As I've noted, this is probably the result of an innate human aversion to risk. Anyone willing to stomach the stress of irrevocable long-term commitments to stocks gains a higher return. Thus, defined-benefit pension funds that are able to hold investments untouched for decades often keep a majority of their assets in equities. To lower the cost to the corporation, defined-benefit pension funds take risks, including the risks of short-run fluctuations in the prices of their equities and other assets. And those risks, largely through heavy investments in equities, have consequences, both good and bad.

When stock prices are rising, capital gains in effect pay for a significant part of the corporation's contribution to its defined-benefit program. Since cash contributions are lower, reported profits, accordingly, are higher. Conversely, when stock prices fall, as they did from 2000 to 2002, a large number of pension plans became underfunded.

There is no getting around the fact that portfolio risks jeopardize retiree benefits. Many corporations with very large unfunded pension liabilities in recent years, such as steel companies and airlines, have chosen bankruptcy and turned their pension obligations over to the Pension Benefit Guaranty Corporation—that is, largely to the American taxpayer. Fortunately, the Pension Protection Act of 2006 significantly reduced taxpayers' exposure to private pension shortfalls, but it has by no means eliminated them.

All defined-benefit pension funds yield a rate of return that is variable and, especially in the short run, unpredictable. But the corporation has a legal obligation to pay a "defined" fixed benefit. This requires a third party (almost always the sponsoring corporation itself) to swap the variable revenues of a defined-benefit plan portfolio into the fixed payments required by contract. In recent years, the cost of that swap has grown. Partly as a consequence, many corporations have adopted defined-contribution pension plans. The share of total pension fund assets held under defined-benefit plans declined from 65 percent in 1985 to 41 percent at the end of 2006.

The trend shows no signs of abating. Corporate sponsors of defined-contribution plans will likely become more focused on the forms of investments their employees can make and even on some rules on how quickly, following retirement, such funds can be disbursed. I anticipate that defined-contribution plans will also gradually displace part of Social Security as the latter's financing capabilities fall with the ratio of workers to retired beneficiaries over time. As the magnitude and implications of the retirement burden gradually become evident to potential retirees, an increasingly healthy elderly population is very likely to find it necessary to postpone retirement. But of greater relevance, the transfer of *real* resources from workers to retirees will of necessity be increasingly financed by 401(k) plans, private insurance, and many as yet unidentified new financing vehicles.

In the United States, most higher-income baby boomers have wealth and sources of income that should prove more than adequate to fund retirement. Middle- and lower-income boomers will find financing more problematic. Endeavoring to maintain today's pay-as-you-go government-backed social insurance programs, whose arithmetic requires high ratios of workers to retirees, is going to prove increasingly burdensome and unacceptable. By default, the only viable option almost surely will turn out to be some form of private financing. I've posed a question in the title of this chapter: "The World Retires. But Can It Afford To?" The answer is: It will find ways. The world has no choice. Demography is destiny.

TWENTY-THREE

CORPORATE GOVERNANCE

D o I have to accept the Enron Prize?" I asked in November 2001 of my old friend and mentor Jim Baker. "It's part of the Baker Institute program at which you are speaking," he replied. I had not been aware that an award was being given at the dinner. Enron's stock was collapsing and within three weeks the company would be in default. That November, "prize" hardly seemed the appropriate term. But I owed Jim Baker a great deal, so, provided there was no official presentation or money involved, I agreed to accept the award.

Enron had puzzled me ever since I'd heard Jeffrey Skilling, its soon-to-be CEO, give a presentation at a meeting of the board of the Federal Reserve Bank of Dallas in December 2000. He went through a very sophisticated explanation of how this high-flying twenty-first-century company operated. It was impressive. But I came away with nagging questions: What did Enron produce? How did it make money? I understood the company's clever derivative and hedging strategies, but what profit stream was being hedged?

Enron's demise, according to Skilling after the fact, was precipitated by a collapse in confidence in the firm, which destroyed its ability to borrow. That didn't seem quite right to me. I presumed that if a major steel company experienced a collapse of confidence, its steel furnaces would still have some value. Impalpable Enron, however, went up in a puff of smoke, leaving little trace except the anger of its employees and shareholders. I had never seen a major U.S. company fall from icon to pariah to virtual nonexistence so quickly.

The Enron debacle and the scandal surrounding the collapse of WorldCom the following summer were particularly worrisome to me. In the quarter century prior to my joining the Fed, I'd served on fifteen publicly listed corporate boards (not all concurrently, of course) and had become quite familiar with the levers of power in those companies. I had also become increasingly aware of the disconnect between how American corporations were governed and how that governance was perceived by the public and our political leaders. The public, already suspicious of business ethics (if it doesn't consider the term an outright oxymoron), was not, I feared, prepared to accept revelations undercutting widely held beliefs about the way corporations were governed. Much of the corporate governance practices of myth have long since been displaced by the imperatives of a modern economy.

Throughout the nineteenth and early twentieth centuries, shareholders, in many instances controlling shareholders, actively participated in governing U.S. corporations. They appointed the board of directors, who in turn hired the CEO and other officers and, in general, controlled the strategies of the company. Corporate governance had the trappings of democratic representative government. But ownership diffused over the following generations, and the managerial and entrepreneurial skills of company founders were not always inherited by their offspring. As financial institutions evolved over the twentieth century, shareholding became a matter of investment, not active ownership. If a shareholder did not like the way a company was managed, he sold his stock. Only rarely was the management of reasonably profitable corporations challenged. Imperceptibly corporate governance moved from shareholder control to control by the CEO. Aside from the outspoken concern of a few academics, the change occurred quietly and largely by default.

As shareholders became ever less engaged, the CEOs began to recommend slates of directors to shareholders, who were soon rubber-stamping them. Periodically this paradigm went astray when a company or its management got into trouble. But such episodes were relatively rare. Democratic corporate governance had morphed into a type of authoritarianism. The CEO would enter the boardroom, explain the corporation's new capital investment program, and turn to his chief financial officer for corroboration. Then, without meaningful deliberation, the board would approve the project. The CEO of a profitable corporation today is given vast powers by the board of directors he essentially appoints.

Over the decades government agencies and various interest groups have pressed large institutional investors, especially pension funds, to vote their shares in a manner that would resurrect the "corporate democracy" of earlier decades. But these institutions argue that their responsibility to their pensioners is to invest profitably, and that their expertise is in judging financial market value, not in the alien practice of corporate management. Some public pension funds have become more engaged, but their activities are marginal. Market forces are driving private equity funds to become increasingly committed to overseeing the management of the properties they own, but while the trend is rapidly growing, these funds remain a very small segment of corporate governance. Market forces are also driving mergers and acquisitions, processes in which managements rarely survive unscathed. So-called hostile takeovers may be seen as pure corporate democracy once we recognize that the only "hostility" is between a set of new shareholders and the company's entrenched management; the existing shareholders are voluntarily selling their stock, and in most instances are eager to do so and presumably delighted with the price they get.

It should not come as a surprise that, as with authoritarianism everywhere, the lack of adequate accountability in corporate management has spawned abuse. It was pretty clear during my quarter century on corporate boards that petty abuse was widespread, and on occasion the abuse rose above the petty.

Accordingly, I am not surprised that the outsize CEO compensation packages of recent years have raised public concerns of unseemliness. Most nettling has been the dramatic rise in the ratio of CEO compensation relative to gains in average employee salary. Directors who determine executive salaries argue in response that key decisions by CEOs leverage vast amounts of market value. In global markets, the difference between a right move and an almost right move might represent hundreds of millions of dollars, whereas a generation ago, when the playing field was much smaller, the difference would have been in the tens of millions. Boards reflecting this view feel pressed by competition to seek the "very best" CEO and are obviously willing to pay what it takes to acquire the "stars."

A CEO's compensation has, on average, been tied closely to the market value of his or her firm. The average market capitalization of an S&P 500 corporation rose from less than $2 billion in 1980 to $26 billion in 2006. The average market value of the ten largest S&P 500 companies in 2006 was $260 billion. CEO compensation at such large U.S. corporations reportedly rose by 10 percent annually between 1993 and 2006,* triple the 3.1 percent annual increase of earnings of private-company production or nonsupervisory workers. In short, virtually all of the gap between CEO and worker pay reflects increasing corporate value driven by market forces. But that is CEO compensation *on average*. Hidden in the average are a large number of outliers. I suspect much of the visibly egregious "unearned" CEO compensation results from the need to set executive salaries in advance of performance. Even the most perceptive boards make regrettable choices some of the time, and those mistakes show up as hefty compensation paid for demonstrably inferior outcomes.

In my experience, another significant factor in excess CEO compensation occurs as a result of a general rise in stock prices, over which the average CEO has no control. A company's share price, and hence the value of related options, is heavily influenced by economy-wide forces—by changes in interest rates, inflation, and myriad other factors wholly unrelated to the success or failure of a particular corporate strategy. There have been more than a few dismaying examples of CEOs who nearly drove their companies to the wall and presided over significant declines in the prices of their stocks *relative* to those of competitors and the stock market overall. The

---

*There are arguably other factors in play. But global competition cannot be a major contributor because executive salaries in Europe and Japan have not gone up nearly as much as those in the United States. The argument that corporate boards are made up of cronies may explain the level of corporate compensation but not its accelerated pace in recent years. Corporate cronyism, if anything, was greater in years past.

CEOs nonetheless reaped large rewards because the strong performance of the stock market as a whole pulled up the prices of the forlorn companies' stocks.*

Using stock or options to compensate top executives should require that rewards reflect the success or failure of management's decisions. Grants of stock or options in lieu of cash could be used more effectively by tying such grants to measures of the firm's performance relative to a carefully chosen group of competitors over time. Some corporations do tie the value of stock and option grants to relative performance, but most do not.†

If the gap in CEO compensation relative to that of company workers, which reached its widest point in 2000, resumes its increase, I hope shareholders will look beyond their focus on investment returns and pay attention to CEO compensation. If compensation is inappropriate, it is their pockets that are being picked. There is no role here for government wage control. Taxpayer funds are not involved.

I was aware of the tendency toward "excess" compensation a generation ago. I recall a discussion of the salaries of the senior officers of Mobil Corporation at a compensation-committee meeting in the early 1980s. Management had hired Graef "Bud" Crystal, a well-known executive compensation consultant, to "assist" the committee in determining appropriate salary levels.‡ He put up a series of charts showing that the salaries of Mobil's top officers were only average relative to their corporate peers'. Obviously, Crystal asserted, Mobil would want its executive salaries to be above average. That prompted my fellow director, American Express CEO Howard Clark, to ask with a twinkle in his eye, "Bud, do you recommend that all corporate executives' pay be above the corporate executive pay average?" I chimed in, suggesting that Bud's regression analysis of competitive executive compensation was flawed. In the end, the top Mobil executives

---

*An individual company's stock value competes with all others for the portfolio choice of investors. Therefore, if one or more companies do well and their stock prices rise, the stock prices of less well-performing companies appear more attractive, *relatively*. This is why price movements of wholly unrelated stocks exhibit significant correlations.

†Stock options are subject to seemingly continuing abuse, as the predating-of-options scandal of the fall of 2006 demonstrated.

‡In a reversal in later years, Crystal became a critic of the process of determining corporate compensation.

got much but probably not all of what they had contemplated when they sicced Bud on the committee.

But even with increasing conformity and comity in CEO-appointed boards during most of the twentieth century, dissonance did arise on occasion to alter the direction of a company toward a better use of its resources. Shortly before I left for the Fed, I joined the majority of Alcoa directors in a rebellion against CEO Charles Parry, who was pressing the board to elevate chief operating officer C. Fred Fetterolf to succeed him upon retirement. There was no question of Fetterolf's superb understanding of the internal technical aspects of the company, but a number of us outside directors thought he lacked the broad global perspective that Alcoa was going to need in the following decade. The dissidents, led by W. H. Krome George, a former Alcoa chairman, and including me, Paul Miller of First Boston, Paul O'Neill, president of International Paper, and others, met one evening at the Links Club in New York and concluded that we had to counter Charlie's choice of Fred with an alternative. We surveyed the table and settled on O'Neill, my old friend and collaborator in the Ford administration. Support from most of the rest of the board and a little arm-twisting of Paul launched him on a very successful career as Alcoa's chairman until George W. Bush prevailed on him to become secretary of the treasury in 2001.*

Over my quarter century as an active board member, I observed that, among large corporations, the CEO, who chose directors, generally sought demonstrably qualified people, often CEOs of other corporations. However, I could not always tell if high-level boards were chosen for their knowledge and advice or if the CEO needed to give the appearance of plurality to what was in reality an authoritarian corporate regime. Likely, it was both.

Despite its all too obvious shortcomings, U.S. corporate governance over the past century must have had something to recommend it. For were it otherwise, the U.S. economy could hardly have risen to its current state of world economic leadership. There can be no doubt that American corporate business has been highly productive and profitable. It has been at the cutting edge of much of the past century's technology. This, along with my observations of a quarter century of board experience, has led me to

---

*In any event, Paul O'Neill was about to retire and turn over the reins to Alain Belda.

conclude, however reluctantly, that if owners are no longer the managers, CEO control and the authoritarianism it breeds are probably the only way to run an enterprise successfully. There do not appear to be credible alternatives to placing the power of governance in the hands of the CEO and trusting that even his handpicked directors will hold him to task, or, if they prove unable or unwilling, that corporate raiders will take over and revamp management.

When the scandals broke, first at Enron, then at WorldCom, I was a little relieved that the authoritarian nature of modern corporate governance did not become an issue, although there was a great deal of justified concern about the corporate abuses that authoritarianism fostered. Accounting fraud took center stage. What everyone was about to learn was that modern corporate accounting is largely based on a series of forecasts that do not necessarily have to reflect a company's history. This means that a significant part of corporate reporting involves wide discretion and, too often, is susceptible to abuse. For example, the calculated pension liability and consequent charges against income require a number of uncertain projections, which offer a wide range of potential pension costs, all reasonably defendable. A bank that receives a monthly mortgage payment cannot know for certain until the loan is repaid in full or defaults whether a given payment from the borrower constitutes interest or a return of principal. Depreciation charges to reflect the decline in economic value of fixed assets are understandably subject to broad discretion, depending on how rapidly facilities are expected to be made obsolete by technological advance. No wonder many corporate managements, running into competitive difficulties, tended to favorably bias their results to the edge of outright fraud. Some clearly went over the line. But accounting discretion can cover up only so much. The roof eventually had to fall in. And it did.

In the aftermath of the Enron and WorldCom scandals, the power of the corporate CEO has been diminished and that of the board of directors and shareholders enhanced. As the scandals unfolded, the tone of board meetings changed. When the CEO entered a board meeting in 2002, the joke went, he wondered if the first item on the agenda would be a request for his resignation. The dark humor darkened further. Another saying of that year was that the average CEO spent half his time with his general counsel, discussing how to keep them both out of jail. Exaggeration? Of course. But dark humor is too often very close to reality. Everyone agreed that the CEO was spending less time productively expanding the business.

Enron and WorldCom officers' theft of shareholders' assets created a political firestorm. An anticorporate populism had been lurking under the surface of American politics at least since the age of the Robber Barons of the latter part of the nineteenth century. Hastily deliberated and overwhelmingly approved, the Sarbanes-Oxley Act became law in 2002. To my surprise, it included useful reforms. One requires the CEO to attest that, in his or her judgment, the company's accounts truly reflect the value of the firm. Never mind generally accepted accounting principles (GAAP) and Financial Accounting Standards Board (FASB) rules; forget IRS and SEC legalisms; the question to the CEO is: Do your company's books, to the best of *your* knowledge, accurately reflect the corporation's underlying financial state?

This requirement also resolved for me the very thorny issue of whether the principles-based international accounting standards or the rules-based U.S. FASB and GAAP standards were a more effective way for a company to convey its corporate results. The Sarbanes-Oxley sign-off requirement for chief executives and chief financial officers bypassed the complexity of such judgments. It placed the responsibility of interpretation of financial results where it belongs. If the CEO was given the legal discretion to choose the accounting system and held accountable for the results, the shareholders would be best served.

But it has become clear, especially in retrospect, that by increasing the regulatory burden, Sarbanes-Oxley has decreased U.S. competitive flexibility. Section 404 has proved particularly cumbersome—it requires certain accounting best practices to be enforced by the companies' auditors, who in turn are overseen by a new agency, the Public Company Accounting Oversight Board (PCAOB). The acronym was soon pronounced "peek-a-boo," connoting clandestine surveillance. The new agency was not amused.

Today, after several years of implementation, few in the business community would argue that the cost and effort of implementing Section 404, not to mention the diversion of corporate management from business-expanding initiatives, have created a net plus for either their company or the U.S. economy as a whole. Overall, Sarbanes-Oxley is proving unnecessarily burdensome, but just as important, it is premised on certain myths about what level of governance is achievable.

Sarbanes-Oxley has highlighted the role of a company's audit committee and required that its chairman have professional qualifications. The implication is that this souped-up committee will have the ability to ferret out corporate wrongdoing, especially fraud, and present to shareholders a more accurate financial statement than was done in the past. In my more than eighteen years as a bank regulator, I recall very few instances of a bank regulator unearthing fraud or embezzlement through the examination process, souped-up or otherwise. While admittedly bank supervision isn't looking for criminal activity, the Fed's bank examiners nonetheless twice gave high grades to a Japanese bank branch in New York that for years had harbored a large ongoing embezzlement. A whistle-blower finally exposed the crimes. Indeed, very few regulators of my acquaintance can give me examples of fraud and embezzlement unearthed by anyone *other* than a whistle-blower. I readily grant that pre–Sarbanes-Oxley audit committees were not great discoverers of executive wrongdoing. But in truth, there is no way for an audit committee, new or old, to uncover wrongdoing short of deploying a vast army of investigators who would smother the firm with costly oversight that would likely stifle corporate risk taking and ultimately threaten the viability of the company.

Other Sarbanes-Oxley provisions extol the "independent" director. Somehow, it is argued, competing voices will keep management honest. In practice, directors who are independent of management tend to have very little experience in the business they have been appointed to oversee. They are not likely to know what type of chicanery is possible. I always thought President Roosevelt had it right when asked how he could appoint Joseph P. Kennedy, a Wall Street speculator (and father of JFK), as the first chairman of the Securities and Exchange Commission. Wasn't it the classic case of the fox guarding the henhouse? Roosevelt replied, "Set a thief to catch a thief."

A corporation can have only one strategy. Competing "independent" voices with wholly different agendas undermine the effectiveness of the CEO and the rest of the corporate board. I have served on boards with dissident directors. Only business that was legally required at board meetings got done. Missing from those meetings was the useful exchange of ideas that inform the corporate strategies of the CEO. With dissident directors—such as those who represent potential investors seeking to take over a company—human nature being what it is, most interchange between CEO-supporting directors and incumbent corporate management occurs outside the boardroom.

I do not wish to cast aspersions on the corporate takeover. On the contrary, it is a key facilitator of creative destruction, and doubtless the most effective remaining means by which shareholder voices can mold a corporation. But while change in management is often necessary, you cannot effectively run a corporation with differing authoritative voices espousing opposing corporate goals. It has to be one or the other. If the board is riven with conflicting interests, corporate governance will suffer. If directors cannot agree with the CEO's strategy, they should replace him. Corporate dissonance, of course, is unavoidable in periods of transition. But it is not a value to be pursued for its own sake. A cacophony produces only red ink.

The notion of enlisting representatives of a corporation's various stakeholders on the board—unions, community representatives, customers, suppliers, and so forth—has a nice democratic ring to it. But it is ill-advised and I strongly suspect it will not work. Today's highly competitive world needs each corporation to execute plans from a single coach, as it were. A vote by the whole team on each big play is a recipe for defeat. I assume that eventually some of the more abrasive edges of Sarbanes-Oxley, especially Section 404, will be honed down.

As good as American corporate governance, with all its warts, has proved to be over the decades, adjustments to the ever-changing global environment have exposed gaps that require attention. Accurate accounting is central to the functioning of free-market capitalism. If the signals engendering allocation of a nation's resources are distorted, the markets will be less effective in fostering rising standards of living. Capitalism expands wealth primarily through creative destruction—the process by which the cash flow from obsolescent, low-return capital coupled with new savings is invested in high-return, cutting-edge technologies. But for that process to function, markets need reliable data to gauge the return on assets.

Stock-option expensing is a case in point. In 2002, I joined the battle over this arcane, but critical, aspect of the dot-com boom of the 1990s. My good friend Warren Buffett, no neophyte in corporate evaluation, had joined the fray earlier. High-tech corporations in particular were engaged in a massive shift from paying wages, which subtracted from net income, to granting stock options, which at that time did not. This made a large difference in the results of some companies. In 2005, for example, Intel reported a net profit of $8.7 billion; by Intel's own reckoning, if the cost of options had been factored in, that figure would have been $1.3 billion smaller. I argued that options, which attracted skilled people—real resources—to a corporation, were, in principle, indistinguishable from cash wages or other forms of payment.

Accurate profit evaluation requires accurate cost accounting. Labor costs need to be recorded correctly or corporate management will be misled as to whether a corporate strategy is paying off. Whether it is paid as cash, an option grant, or access to the executive dining room should be of no consequence. The corporation needs to know the market value of the newly hired employee. The employee, by accepting a compensation package (including options), is effectively setting his market wage. And that market wage conveys the price of the labor resources required to produce a profit.

In an economy as large, diverse, and complex as ours, the accurate measurement of corporate performance is essential if our nation's resources are to be directed to their most efficient uses. Accurate input costs are essential for determining whether the corporation earns a profit from its current activities. Changes in balance-sheet valuations based on uncertain forecasts have become an increasingly important element in determining whether a particular corporate strategy has been successful. The basic principle of measuring profit as the value of output less the value of input is not altered by the complexity of measurement.

To assume that option grants are not an expense is to assume that the real resources that contributed to the creation of the value of the output were free. Surely the shareholders who granted options to employees do not consider the potential dilution of their share in the market capitalization of the corporation as having no cost to them.

Options are important to the venture-capital industry, and many in high-tech industries argued strenuously against making any changes to then-current practices. They maintained that the use of options is an exceptionally valuable compensation mechanism (correct); that recognizing an expense associated with these grants would reduce the use of options,* harming high-tech companies (possibly); that the effect of options on "fully diluted earnings per share" is already recognized (irrelevant);† and that we cannot measure the costs of options with sufficient accuracy to justify their recognition on financial statements (wrong).‡

This seemingly arcane accounting matter is, in fact, critically important for the accurate representation of corporate performance. Some thought not having to expense option grants was a major aid in raising capital to finance the rapid exploitation of advanced technologies. While the vital contribution of new technology to the growth of our economy is evident to all, not all new ideas create value on net. Not all new ideas should be financed. During the dot-com boom, substantial capital was wasted on enterprises whose prospects appeared more promising than they turned out to be. Waste is an inevitable by-product of the risk taking that generates the growth in our economy. However, the amount of waste becomes unnecessarily large when the earnings reports that help investors allocate investment are inaccurate.

Stock-option grants, properly constructed, can be highly effective in aligning the interests of corporate officers with those of shareholders. Regrettably, many of the particular grants were constructed to be self-serving. I guess I shouldn't have been surprised when high-tech industry lobbying phalanxes found their way to the Fed. I had several visits from groups of CEOs, often led by the canny Craig Barrett of Intel. The visiting CEOs had not counted on my quarter century of experience as a corporate director. I

---

*This would be true if the option recipient had been fooled as to the company's true profit performance.
†This adjustment corrects only the denominator (the number of shares) of the earnings-per-share ratio. It is the estimation of the numerator (earnings) that the accounting dispute is all about. Option grants do have the potential of increasing the number of shares outstanding and accordingly, decreasing earnings per share.
‡The means of estimating option expense is approximate. But so is a good deal of all other earnings estimation. Moreover, unless options are expensed, every corporation already implicitly reports an estimate of option expense on its income statement. That number for most companies, of course, is exactly zero. Were option grants truly without value or cost to the firm?

enjoyed countering their arguments. I often was tempted to ask Craig, whom I had gotten to respect and like, or any of the lobbyists for one cause or another who arrived on my doorstep: "If I could convince you that your arguments are wrong, would you be allowed, in your current employment, to change your view?" I never asked. It wasn't necessary. I was in the same position in 1994 when I engaged China's then premier Li Peng in a debate on capitalism versus communism (see chapter 14).

The argument in favor of expensing options eventually prevailed. In December 2004, the FASB changed its rules to require expensing of stock-option grants starting in 2005. The new rules went into place only after nearly being blocked by Congress, responding to the arguments of high-tech entrepreneurs.

Even before the scandals of 2002, there was much political angst about the rise in executive compensation in comparison to the pay of the average production worker. As I explain in chapter 25, the inexorable growth in the proportion of our GDP that is conceptual, especially technological, has increased the value of intellectual power relative to the value of human brawn many times over many generations. I am old enough to remember when physical prowess on the job was the source of legend and reverence. A large statue of Paul Bunyan, the mythical logger, still oversees the northern Minnesota lake country. Stevedores of a century ago were extolled for their brute strength. Today, the activities once carried out by stevedores are often run by young women at a computer console.

Relative compensation in our society is market determined, and reflects the value preferences of all participants in our economy. Is there a better arbiter? An equally consistent, but never successfully applied, standard is that all workers should share equally in the results of their collective efforts. By that ethos, all wage disparities are unjust. But averring that a certain set of income disparities is too large or too small requires a standard by which to judge. "Too large" accepts the premise that inequality at *some* level is justified. Why shouldn't it be lower? Or higher, for that matter?

I argue in chapter 21 that income disparities are politically destabilizing to society. But a cure that involves government wage controls, as opposed, for example, to helping lower-wage workers acquire more valuable skills, is too often worse than the disease. Even given the flawed aspects of corporate governance, executive salaries are ultimately and, one must assume, voluntarily assented to by the company's shareholders. As I noted earlier, there should be no role for government in this transaction. Wage control, like price control, invariably leads to grave unexpected distortions.

Given the shareholder-management divide, the autocratic-CEO paradigm appears to be the only arrangement that allows for the effective functioning of a corporation. We cannot get around the authoritarian imperative of today's corporate structure. But we can make sure nonperforming CEOs are removed, if not by current shareholders, then by making takeovers easier. A step in that direction would be to ease the rules of access to shareholder lists, currently largely controlled by incumbent management. Shareholders who seek anonymity can be protected by listing in street names.* Mergers, acquisitions, and spin-offs are a vital part of competition and creative destruction. The emergence of private equity funds appears to be a market response to the unwillingness of pension funds and other large institutional investors to engage in the owner oversight of corporate management that was a hallmark of earlier generations. Private equity funds investing in undervalued assets, and thereby achieving above-average rates of return on capital, furnish evidence that the capital had not been allocated appropriately in our economy. Shifting those assets to investors who manage them appropriately contributes to economic growth. Enhanced shareholder control would no doubt limit management's self-serving "golden parachutes," outsized bonuses, backdating of options, and post-employment perks now provided at the shareholders' expense.

Ultimate control of American corporations by their shareholders is essential to our market capitalist system. In corporations, as in most other human institutions, delegation of authority leads to a degree of authoritarianism. The proper balancing of effective control in governing corporations will never be wholly without controversy.

---

*"Street name" is the expression used when securities are held in the name of a broker or other nominee, rather than that of the shareholder.

THE LONG-TERM
ENERGY SQUEEZE

When hurricanes Katrina and Rita slammed into the soft underbelly of America's vast Texas-Louisiana oil complex in the summer of 2005, they tore a large hole in world supply. Prices of gasoline, diesel fuel, and home heating oil soared.

It had been an accident waiting to happen. Oil prices had been edging higher since 2002, as increases in global oil consumption progressively absorbed most of the remainder of the world's buffer of excess capacity, which had reached ten million barrels a day in 1986. In years past, that buffer had been adequate to absorb shocks even on the scale of Katrina and Rita without any worrisome impact on prices. By 2005, however, the world oil balance had become so precarious that even an unexpected maintenance shutdown in some East Coast refineries early in the year had been enough to drive prices higher.

Despite periodic predictions that the world was running out of oil, verified recoverable petroleum reserves belowground grew in line with oil consumption between 1986 and 2006. This was due largely to the development of technologies that increased the amount of oil that could be recovered from existing reservoirs. But the world's oil producers were far less successful in actually building the capacity to extract that oil from its deep caverns and to process it. Drilling and well completions fell behind as countries with large available reserves, mainly members of the Organization of Petroleum Exporting Countries (OPEC), failed to reinvest enough in wells and crude-oil processing infrastructure to meet rising demand.* Thus, while both world oil consumption and world oil reserves between 1986 and 2006 rose by 1.6 percent per year on average, crude-oil production capacity grew at a rate of only 0.8 percent.

Why didn't oil companies reinvest more of their sharply rising revenues? All OPEC oil reserves are owned or controlled by state monopolies. Their revenues are the principal source for financing the needs of rapidly growing populations. Energy investments must compete with many other priorities, including programs in some of the countries to diversify away from oil and gas. Private-sector oil and gas companies, in contrast to the national oil companies, have plowed a much larger share of cash flow into energy investments in recent years. But with the oil reserves of developed countries heavily depleted by more than a century of extraction, the payoff in increased oil reserves in that far less fruitful environment has been a small fraction of the return available to OPEC's national oil companies. More important, private-sector international oil companies are increasingly being blocked from access to OPEC's reserves.† The era when these companies had a virtual monopoly on technological expertise is long gone. They no longer have as much to offer in exchange for access to the Middle East's petroleum riches.

Half a century ago, the Seven Sisters—Standard Oil of New Jersey, Royal Dutch Shell, Texaco, and other giants—presided over world oil. Today the private international oil companies are a mere shadow of their past glory. Of course, their profits have surged as the prices of their large oil in

---

*According to the International Energy Agency, world outlays on exploration and development doubled between 2000 and 2005, but with costs rising in excess of 10 percent per year, the rise in real terms was less than 4 percent a year. That was not enough to convert oil reserves into adequate growth in crude-oil production capacity.

†Foreign companies are wholly prohibited from investing in the oil and gas reserves of Saudi Arabia, Kuwait, and Mexico. De facto prohibitions against foreign access are spreading to most countries with national oil companies.

ventories and assets have mounted.* But their opportunities to invest profitably in exploration and development are modest. And with access to the OPEC reservoirs curtailed, the international companies have few alternatives but to return much of their cash flows to shareholders through stock buybacks and dividends.

With the exception of Saudi Aramco, none of the OPEC national oil monopolies has professed a desire to contain oil-price increases by expanding crude-oil capacity. On the contrary, they seem most concerned that excess capacity will bring down prices and the huge revenues on which they have come to depend for domestic political purposes. When I met with Ali al-Naimi, the urbane Saudi oil minister, in May 2005, even he was clearly uncomfortable with measures the United States was proposing to restrain oil consumption and, by extension, OPEC oil revenues. Al-Naimi's country's clout is based on its 260 billion–plus barrels of proved reserves, and its considerable potential beyond that. He is acutely aware that if oil prices rise too high, consumption could be permanently lowered as major world consumers shift their emphasis to petroleum conservation. Most oil consumption is determined by the oil-consuming propensities of motor vehicle fleets, factories, and homes. While this infrastructure cannot be altered overnight, it can and does change. The Saudis learned that lesson in the 1970s. The growth of consumption slowed radically in the years following the oil-price shocks, and never fully recovered even as prices fell. What happened then could happen again. Today the United States consumes a fourth of world oil; if we lowered our growth path of consumption, and especially if others followed suit, Saudi Arabia's world prominence would surely diminish.

Ever since President Franklin D. Roosevelt met King Ibn Saud aboard the USS *Quincy* in February 1945, the U.S.-Saudi relationship has been close. It was an American oil company, Standard Oil of California (later Chevron), that had discovered oil in the Saudi sands in March 1938, under a concession granted in 1933. And it was a consortium of American oil companies that formed the Arabian American Oil Company (Aramco) to develop those resources. The ties were firm between what became by 1992

---

*Last-in, first-out accounting reduces but does not eliminate such spikes in profits.

the world's largest oil producer and the United States (always the world's largest consumer). The relationship even survived Saudi Arabia's national-ization of Aramco in 1976.* As a Mobil Corporation director from 1977 to 1987, I was acutely aware of America's continuing connection to Saudi Arabia. Prior to 1976, Mobil's dividends from its 10 percent share of Ar-amco were a major component of Mobil's earnings, and access to Saudi crude oil in subsequent years played a prominent part in the company's operations. Saudi Aramco has been investing a significant part of its in-creased oil revenues of the past five years in capacity expansion, though still a far smaller proportion than the oil companies of the United States, the United Kingdom, Canada, Norway, and even Russia.

OPEC's reluctance to expand capacity has dramatically affected the petroleum market. The buffer between supply and demand has narrowed to the point where it is unable to absorb, without price consequences, shut-downs of even a small part of the world's production. Growing threats of violence to oil fields, pipelines, storage facilities, and refineries, especially in the Middle East and Nigeria, threaten this fragile balance. The February 2006 terrorist attack on Abqaiq, Saudi Arabia's vast seven-million-barrel-a-day crude-oil processing facility, failed, but not by much. By some accounts the attackers penetrated the first line of defense. Had they succeeded, the resultant oil price surge would have severely unsettled world financial mar-kets and, depending on the extent of the oil facility shutdown, could have brought much of world economic expansion to a halt, or worse. More re-cently, fears escalated that if Iran felt itself to be sufficiently threatened or provoked, it might block the Persian Gulf's Strait of Hormuz, the shipping artery for a fifth of the world's crude oil.

Fortunately, the action of the market has created a new kind of buffer. Developed-world oil producers, consumers, and, more recently, investors brought aboveground inventories of oil to record levels. For most of the history of oil, only those who could physically store large quantities of oil had the ability to trade. Inventories were held largely for precautionary purposes, particularly against unanticipated cutbacks in production any-

*Saudi Arabia gained a 60 percent control of Aramco in 1974 before it was fully nationalized.

where in the world. But important advances in finance have opened the way for a far greater number of players to take part in the oil markets and hence in oil price determination. Thus, when in 2004 it became apparent that the world's petroleum industry was not investing enough to expand crude-oil production capacity to meet rising demand, auguring still-higher prices, hedge funds and other investors seeking long-term investments in oil began bidding up its price. This went on until they had induced owners of inventories to sell some of them. Investors accumulated substantial net long positions in crude-oil futures, largely in the over-the-counter market. When all offsetting claims are considered, the sellers of those contracts promising future delivery to investors were of necessity owners of the billions of barrels of private inventories of oil held throughout the world.

Sales of oil to investors through futures contracts left many oil companies unhedged and exposed to surges in demand. They quickly sought to replace the newly encumbered inventories. Their increased inventory demand was superimposed on rising consumption demands, pressing oil production and prices still higher. The consequence has been an accumulation of inventories that reflects both the traditional precautionary holdings of industry and the additional quantities held in "escrow" by industry to fulfill obligations to investors under the terms of futures contracts. In other words, some of the oil in the world's storage tanks and pipelines is spoken for by investors. The extent of the rapid buildup in participation by financial institutions in claims on real barrels of oil is reflected in the nearly sixfold rise from December 2004 to June 2006 in the notional value of commodity derivatives, mainly oil, reported to the Bank for International Settlements.

The investors and speculators who are the new participants in the world's more than $2-trillion-a-year oil market are contributing to and hastening an adjustment process that has become urgent with the virtual elimination of an adequate world supply buffer. Demand from the investment community caused oil prices to rise sooner than they would have otherwise, spurring investors to assist in the accumulation of record oil inventories, adding to the thin buffer between oil supply and demand. That is, the addition of investors to the oil market did not increase the supply of oil in the world, but their activities speeded the necessary price adjustment that moved some crude oil from OPEC reserves to the aboveground inventories of the developed world. This promoted greater oil security, which, I presume, will reduce price pressures over the long run.

This speeded-up adjustment process and the soaring gasoline prices that accompanied it sparked a lot of controversy, of course. As crude oil reached an all-time high of $75 a barrel, some critics asserted that speculators and the oil industry were engaged in a vast price-gouging scheme. Recent American history is replete with oil price spikes, leading to accusations of oil company conspiracies, triggering congressional investigations. When the investigation fails to uncover collusion, the report is quietly shelved. Conspiracies are exciting, and the price shifts certainly have been significant, not to mention painful for some consumers. But the reality is much more mundane: we were again seeing market forces effectively at work.

Consider: had prices not risen owing to the anticipatory buying by investors, oil consumption would have increased at a faster pace, bringing forward the time when demand would smack into the supply ceiling. At that point, world consumers would rapidly run through their inventories, and prices would rocket sharply higher, with severe consequences for world economic stability. Instead, in response to higher prices induced by investor demand, producers have increased production measurably, and some consumption has been discouraged. Even though crude-oil production capacity remains inadequate, it too rose in response to higher prices. The bottom line is that without the buildup of inventories owing to speculation, the world would surely have eventually experienced a far more precipitate and severe oil shock than actually occurred.

If we still had the ten million barrels a day of spare capacity that existed two decades ago, neither surges in demand nor temporary shutdowns of output from violence, hurricanes, or unscheduled maintenance would have much, if any, impact on price. None of the tight balance between supply and demand is due to any shortage of oil in the ground. The problem is that aside from Saudi Aramco, those who would like to invest (private-sector international oil companies) cannot find profitable investments, and those who can invest (national oil companies) choose not to.

Many members of OPEC have announced short-term production expansion plans in response to higher oil prices. But how firm such plans are is difficult to judge. Opportunities to expand oil production elsewhere are limited to a few regions, notably the former Soviet Union. But even there, investment has slowed in the wake of the renewed consolidation of Russia's oil industry under the control of the Kremlin.

Besides feared shortfalls in crude-oil production capacity, the adequacy of world refining capacity has become worrisome as well. World refinery capacity increased at an annual rate of only 0.9 percent between 1986 and 2006, in line with crude-oil capacity's inadequate growth of 0.8 percent. Indeed, over the past decade, crude-oil production and refinery inputs have increased faster than refining capacity. World refinery output has recently risen almost to the limit of effective refining capacity. Should refining capacity fall below crude-oil production capacity, lack of refining capacity could become the binding constraint on growth in oil use—with minor exceptions, petroleum must be refined before it can be consumed. This may already be happening for certain grades of oil, given the growing mismatch between the heavier and more sulfurous (or "sour") composition of world crude-oil production and the rising world demand for lighter, "sweeter" petroleum products. (Heavier oil now accounts for more than two-thirds of world output.) We cannot change the quality of the oil that comes out of the ground; there is thus a special need to add adequate coking and desulfurization refinery capacity to convert the average gravity and sulfur content of much of the world's indigenous crude oil to the lighter and sweeter oil needed for product markets, particularly transportation fuels that must meet ever more stringent environmental requirements.

Yet the expansion and modernization of refineries are lagging. For example, no refinery has been built from scratch in the United States since 1976. While several are now on the drawing board, a major problem is the uncertainty of potential future environmental standards—because a typical new refinery represents a thirty-year financial commitment, such uncertainty renders refinery investments particularly risky. To encourage adequate refining capacity in the United States, we will probably need to either grandfather existing environmental regulations for new refinery capacity additions or lock in a schedule of future requirements. That would eliminate a large unknown and help move construction forward.

The consequence of lagging refinery modernization has been reflected in a significant price spread between the higher-priced light sweet crudes such as Brent, which are easier to refine, and the heavier crudes such as Maya. Moreover, refining-capacity pressures have opened up refining-market profit margins, which have added to the prices of gasoline and other refined products.

How did we arrive at a state of affairs in which the balance of supply and demand is so fragile that weather, not to mention individual acts of sabotage or local insurrection, could have a significant impact on world energy supplies and hence on world economic expansion?

During the oil industry's first great wave of growth, in the closing years of the nineteenth century, producers judged that price stability was going to be essential to the continued expansion of the market. The necessary pricing power was in the hands of the Americans, especially John D. Rockefeller. He achieved some success in stabilizing prices around the turn of the century by gaining control of nine-tenths of U.S. refining capacity. Even after the U.S. Supreme Court broke up Rockefeller's Standard Oil trust in 1911, pricing power remained with the United States—first with the U.S. oil companies and later with the Texas Railroad Commission. For decades, the commissioners would raise limits on output to suppress price spikes and cut permissible output to prevent sharp price declines.*

Indeed, as late as 1952, crude-oil production in the United States (44 percent of it in Texas) still accounted for more than half of the world total. In 1951, excess Texas crude was supplied to the market to contain the impact on oil prices of the aborted nationalization by Mohammed Mossadeq of Iranian oil. Excess American oil was again released to the market to counter the price pressures induced by the Suez crisis of 1956 and the Six-Day War of 1967.

American oil's historical role, however, ended in 1971, when rising

---

*It is one of those peculiarities of history that a railroad commission would turn out to be the arbiter of the balance of world oil supply and demand. Although originally empowered to regulate Texas railroads, it later was used as a vehicle to prorate crude-oil liftings.

world demand finally absorbed the excess crude-oil capacity of the United States. At that point, U.S. energy independence came to an end. The locus of pricing power shifted abruptly, at first to a few large Middle Eastern producers and ultimately to globalized market forces broader than they, or anyone, can contain.

To capitalize on their newly acquired pricing power, many producing nations in the early 1970s, especially in the Middle East, nationalized their oil companies. The magnitude of that power, however, was not fully evident until the oil embargo of 1973. During that period, posted crude-oil prices at Ras Tanura, Saudi Arabia, rose to more than $11 per barrel, far above the $1.80 that had been charged from 1961 to 1970. The further surge in oil prices that accompanied the Iranian Revolution in 1979 eventually pushed prices to $39 per barrel by February 1981—$77 per barrel in 2006 prices. The price peak of 2006 matched the previous record of 1981, after adjusting for inflation.

The higher prices of the 1970s abruptly ended an extraordinary period of growth of U.S. and world consumption of petroleum, which until then far exceeded the growth of GDP. That increased "intensity" of oil use was a hallmark of the decades following World War II. In retrospect, it can be seen that the surge in oil product prices between 1972 and 1981 nearly halted the growth of world consumption. Indeed, by 1986 a global glut drove crude prices down to $11 a barrel. Oil consumption, given time, has turned out to be far more price sensitive than almost anyone had imagined. Following the price escalation of the 1970s, world oil consumption per real-dollar equivalent of global GDP declined by more than one-third. In the United States, between 1945 and 1973, consumption of petroleum products had risen at a startling average annual rate of 4.5 percent, well in excess of the growth of our real GDP. In contrast, between 1973 and 2006, U.S. consumption grew, on average, by only 0.5 percent per year, far short of the rise in real GDP. In consequence, the ratio of U.S. oil consumption to GDP fell by half.

Much of the decline in the ratio of oil consumption to GDP resulted from growth in the proportion of U.S. GDP composed of service, high-tech, and other less oil-intensive industries. The remainder of the decline has been due to improved energy conservation: greater home insulation, better gasoline mileage, and streamlined production processes. Much of that displacement was achieved by 1985. Progress in reducing oil intensity has continued since then, but more slowly. For example, after the initial surge in the fuel efficiencies of our light motor vehicles during the 1980s, reflecting the earlier run-up in oil prices, improvements slowed to a trickle.

The more modest rate of decline in oil intensity of the U.S. economy after 1985 should not be surprising, given the generally lower level of real oil prices that prevailed through much of that period. Longer-term U.S. demand elasticities (that is, demand's sensitivity to price change) have proved noticeably higher over the past three decades than those evident through the 1960s.

The ratio of intensity of use since 1973 also fell by half in the euro area, and by even more than half in Britain and Japan, where intensity is currently below that of the United States. By comparison, oil use in the developing world is too often wasteful by comparison; there the ratios of oil consumption to GDP average well above those of the developed countries. Intensity has not measurably decreased in recent years with the exception of some declines in Mexico and Brazil and possibly China.

Although the production quotas of OPEC have been a significant factor in price determination for the past third of a century, the story since 1973 has been as much about the power of markets as it has been about power over markets. The Arab oil embargo that followed the Arab-Israeli war of 1973 led many observers, me included, to fear that the gap between supply and demand could become so large that rationing would be the only politically acceptable solution to petroleum shortages.* Yet the resolution of the supply/demand imbalance did not occur that way. Instead, the pressure of high prices prompted consumers to change their behavior, and the intensity of oil use declined. (In the United States, of course, mandated fuel-efficiency standards for cars and light trucks induced the slower growth of gasoline demand. I, and a number of my colleagues at the Council of

---

*Having observed that rapid gains in U.S. consumption before 1973 seemed insensitive to price change, I feared the oil price rise required to bring demand down to the levels of output implied by a long embargo would not be politically acceptable. After all, President Nixon imposed wage and price controls in 1971 to quell anxiety about inflation.

Economic Advisors, believed, however, that even without government-enforced standards, market forces would have led to increased fuel efficiency. Indeed, the number of small, fuel-efficient Japanese cars that were imported into U.S. markets rose throughout the 1970s as the price of oil moved higher.)

This effect was quite dramatic. For example, based on then-recent trends in petroleum use, the U.S. Department of Energy projected in 1979 that world oil prices would reach nearly $60 per barrel by 1995—the equivalent of more than $150 in 2006 prices. The failure of oil prices to rise as projected is a testament to the power of markets and the new technologies they fostered.

Since oil use is less than two-thirds as important an input into world GDP as it was three decades ago, the effect of the oil price surge on the world economy during the first half of 2006, though noticeable, proved significantly less consequential to economic growth and inflation than the surges in the 1970s. Throughout 2006, it was difficult to find serious evidence of any erosion in world economic activity as a consequence of sharply higher oil prices. Indeed, we have just experienced one of the strongest global economic expansions since the end of World War II. The United States, especially, was able to absorb the implicit tax of rising oil prices through 2006.

Nonetheless, holders of private inventories of oil, both industry and investors, apparently foresee little likelihood of a change in petroleum supply/demand fundamentals sufficient to alter long-term concerns. This does not mean that oil prices will necessarily move higher. If the market is efficient, then all knowledge affecting the prospective future supply/demand balance ought already to be reflected in the spot prices of crude oil.* Many analysts saw spot prices of early 2007 embodying a large "terror-

---

*Spot prices in principle embody the market participants' knowledge not only of the forces setting spot prices but also of those setting futures prices. In fact, when the market participants perceive a forthcoming very large rise in price, long-term futures prices will rise and pull up the spot price with them. If the spot price is below longer-term futures by more than the carrying cost of inventories, speculators can buy spot oil, sell the distant futures, store the spot oil, pay interest on the money borrowed to hold the oil, and, at the expiration of the contract, deliver the oil and pocket the profit. This arbitrage will go on until the spot price is brought up to the distant future price less carrying costs of inventory.

ist" risk premium. (Middle East peace would doubtless initiate a sharp drop in oil prices.) To move crude-oil prices would require a change, or the threat of a change, to the prospective supply/demand balance. History tells us that will happen—that the balance will shift often and in either direction. Technology cannot prevent that. But it can assuage the cost and price impacts that such tight markets foster.

The hit-or-miss exploration and development of oil and gas during the petroleum industry's early years have given way to a more systematic approach. Dramatic changes in technology in recent years have made existing oil reserves stretch further while keeping the costs of oil production lower than they otherwise would be. Seismic imaging and advanced drilling techniques are facilitating the discovery of promising deepwater reservoirs, especially in the Gulf of Mexico, and making possible the continued development of mature onshore fields. Accordingly, one might expect that the cost of developing new fields would have declined. But development-cost reductions have been overwhelmed by shortages and higher prices of drilling rigs, as well as escalating wages of skilled oil workers.* Technology has not been able fully to counter those factors.

Much of the innovation in oil development outside OPEC has been directed at overcoming increasingly inhospitable and costly exploratory environments, the consequence of more than a century of draining the more immediately accessible sources of crude oil. Still, consistent with declining long-term marginal costs of extraction, distant futures prices for crude oil moved lower, on net, during the 1990s. Prices of the most-distant (seven-year) futures fell from a bit more than $20 per barrel before the first Gulf War to less than $18 a barrel on average in 1999. Between 1991 and 2000, although spot prices ranged between $11 and $35 per barrel, distant futures exhibited little variation. It appeared for a while that we had reached the long-term price-stability nirvana that oil companies have sought since

---

*The long period (1986–99) of subdued oil prices lessened the need for and the attraction of oil industry jobs. The number of employees engaged in oil and gas extraction fell from a peak of 271,000 in July 1982 to 118,000 by the end of 2003. Employment recovered markedly through 2007. Labor supply has not caught up to demand; thus, since the fall of 2004, average hourly earnings of oil industry workers have risen far faster than those of the nation as a whole.

the days of John D. Rockefeller. But it was not to be. Long-term price stability has, of course, eroded noticeably since 2000. Distant futures prices have risen sharply. In June 2007, prices for delivery in 2013 of light sweet crude exceeded $70 per barrel. This surge arguably reflects the growing presumption that increases in crude-oil capacity outside OPEC will no longer be adequate to serve rising world demand, especially from emerging Asia. Additionally, the longer-term crude price has presumably been driven up since 2000 by renewed fears of supply disruptions in the Middle East and elsewhere.

Because of the geographic concentration of proved reserves (three-fifths in the Middle East, three-fourths in OPEC), much of the investment in crude-oil productive capacity required to meet future demand, without prices rising unduly, will need to be undertaken by national oil companies in OPEC and other developing economies. Meanwhile, productive capacity does continue to expand, albeit gradually, and exploration and development activities are ongoing, even in developed industrial countries. Conversion of the vast Athabasca oil sands reserves in Canada to actual productive capacity, while slow, has made this unconventional source of oil competitive at recent market prices. However, despite improved technology and high prices, proved reserves in the developed countries are being depleted because additions to these reserves have not kept pace with oil extraction.

Before I borrow the oracle's crystal ball to peer into the future of petroleum, we must survey the rest of the energy complex with which oil is inextricably intertwined.

Compared with oil, the natural-gas industry is relatively new. Through much of the early history of petroleum exploration, drillers could not tell whether a successful hit would turn up valuable crude oil or natural gas, which was wastefully "flared," or burned off, for lack of transport facilities. But after many of the transportation hurdles had been surmounted, gas production for market surged more than sixfold between 1940 and 1970. In recent decades, natural gas has blossomed into a major source of energy, reflecting its myriad new uses in industry and as a clean-burning source of electric power. In 2005, natural gas supplied nearly three-fifths as much energy as oil. In contrast to oil, the natural gas consumed in the United States is almost solely produced in the United States and Canada, from which in 2006 the United States imported a fifth of its twenty-two trillion cubic feet of consumption. The reason for the emphasis on domestic production is that natural gas is still much harder to handle than oil. It is difficult to transport in its gaseous form through pipelines and is particularly challenging in its cryogenic form when transported as liquefied natural gas (LNG). It is also difficult to store: in gaseous form, it requires deep salt caverns.

At times, in recent years, supply has not kept pace with the growth of demand. Indeed, the inventories of natural gas held in storage caverns were drawn down to record lows during the winter of 2003. As a consequence, spot prices of gas spiked. The very technologies that have improved our oil and gas drilling success rates have also enabled us to drain newly discovered gas reservoirs at an increasingly rapid pace. Data for Texas, for example, show that since 2000, output from new wells declined by more than 60 percent after one year of operation. That compares with roughly 25 percent in the early 1980s. As a result, merely to hold net marketed gas production stable, new discoveries and the drilling activity associated with them have had to rise.

The combination of demand for gas in our power plants—where its use tends to be less damaging to the environment than the burning of coal or oil—and continued demand from households, commercial establishments, and industry has put significant pressure on the natural-gas reserve base. Until recently, virtually all new electric power facilities on the drawing board had been gas-fired or "dual-fired," able to burn gas or oil. To meet higher anticipated needs, the always-present tension between energy requirements and environmental concerns will doubtless grow in the years ahead.

U.S. natural-gas prices, even seasonally adjusted, have historically displayed far greater volatility than prices of crude oil. Doubtless this reflects, in part, the relatively primitive state of global trade in natural gas—oil's broader and more diverse market tends to damp down wild swings in price. Over the past few years, despite markedly higher U.S. drilling activity, the U.S. natural-gas industry has been unable to expand production noticeably, and we have also been unable to increase imports from Canada.* Significant pressure on prices has ensued.

North America's still-limited capability to import LNG has effectively restricted our access to abundant gas supplies elsewhere in the world. Because of that limitation (in 2006, LNG supplied only 2 percent of U.S. consumption†), we have been unable to continue to compete effectively in such industries as ammonia and fertilizer when natural-gas prices spike in the United States and not in other countries. The difficulties associated with inadequate domestic supplies will eventually be resolved as consumers and producers react to the signals provided by market prices. Indeed, the process is already under way. Moreover, as a result of substantial cost reductions for liquefaction and transportation of LNG, significant global trade in natural gas is emerging—a very promising development.

At the liquefaction end of the process, new investments are in the works across the globe, especially in Qatar, Australia, and Nigeria. Enormous tankers to transport LNG are being constructed, even without commitments from specific long-term delivery contracts. The increasing availability of LNG around the world should lead to much greater flexibility and efficiency in the allocation of natural-gas resources. According to tabulations by BP, worldwide imports of all natural gas in 2006 were only 26 percent of world consumption, compared with 63 percent for oil. LNG accounted for 7 percent of world natural-gas consumption. Clearly, the gas industry has a long way to go before trading on a world market will be able to supply unexpected needs through a quick diversion of product from one country to another, thereby checking big swings in prices. In the end, such international price damping for natural gas will require a yet-to-be-developed broad spot market in LNG. Today almost all waterborne natural-gas trade is still under longer-term contracts. Spot cargoes are currently modest in size but growing. An effective spot market will require a robust futures market for delivery of LNG, with certified storage locations around the world for contract deliv-

---

*Canada's expansion of the Athabasca oil sand deposits and the energy inputs needed for that expansion have soaked up a good deal of the Canadian gas supply.
†In 2006, two-thirds of our LNG imports came from Trinidad, our major long-term supplier.

ery adjusted for transport costs. Spot cargoes can be traded and delivered under contract, and LNG futures markets will eventually arbitrage against current piped-gas markets in the United States and the United Kingdom. Such a market is still a long way off, but it will be required if natural gas is to gain the same supply flexibility that exists in petroleum products. For example, following Katrina, the void in U.S. markets for gasoline was quickly filled with spot shipments from Europe.

The larger question, of course, is what increased world trade in LNG and expanded capacity for U.S. imports of LNG will do to natural-gas prices in the United States. Prices of LNG for imports under long-term contracts follow the Henry Hub spot price in America without its alternating price spikes and dives.* With a global spot market in LNG, prices would be more volatile than these long-term contract prices, but I suspect far less volatile than the prices at Henry Hub.

In addition to increased supplies from abroad, North America still has numerous unexploited sources of gas. Major quantities of recoverable gas reserves are located in Alaska and the northern territories of Canada, and reserves of coal-bed methane and so-called tight sands gas in the Mountain States are significant. Gas-to-liquids technology offers major future benefits through the conversion of natural gas into liquid transportation fuels. But for now, rapid advancement of this technology is being delayed by the sharp rise in all energy project construction costs, and by difficulties in scaling up pilot plants to industrial size.

In the more distant future, perhaps a generation or more ahead, lies the potential to develop productive capacity from natural-gas hydrates. Located in marine sediments and the Arctic, these icelike structures store immense quantities of methane. Although the size of these potential resources is not well measured, estimates from the U.S. Geological Survey indicate that the United States alone may possess two hundred quadrillion cubic feet of natural gas in the form of hydrates. To put this figure in perspective,

---

*Henry Hub is the Louisiana location on the natural-gas pipeline that is used as a reference point for pricing gas.

the world's proved reserves of natural gas are on the order of six quadrillion cubic feet.

Long-term shortages of gas and oil have inevitably stimulated renewed interest in the expansion of coal, nuclear power, and renewable energy sources, the most prominent of which are hydroelectric power from dams and the energy generated through the recycling of waste and by-products from industry and agriculture. Solar and wind power have proved economical in small-scale and specialized uses, but together account for only a tiny fraction of energy use.

The United States has large reserves of coal, primarily dedicated to electric power generation. But the burning of coal in power plants has been restrained by concerns about global warming and other environmental damage. Technology has already alleviated some of these concerns, and given the limited range of alternatives, coal is likely to remain a major fallback in the energy future of the United States.

Nuclear energy is an obvious alternative to coal in electric power generation. Though low prices for competing fuels and concerns about safety have been a drag on the nuclear industry for years, nuclear plants do not emit greenhouse gas. Nuclear's share of electricity production in the United States increased from less than 5 percent in 1973 to 20 percent about a decade ago, a level it has since maintained. Given steps that have been taken over the years to make nuclear energy safer and the obvious environmental advantages it offers in reducing CO_2 emissions, there is no longer a persuasive case against increasing nuclear generation at the expense of coal.

The major challenge will be to find an acceptable way to store spent fuel and radioactive waste. Nuclear power induces fears beyond any rational calculation. To be sure, there are the frightening stories of Soviet nuclear facilities constructed with little regard for safety. The inhabitants of secret cities not on the map of the USSR were exposed to nuclear radiation in their water and air for decades. Nuclear power is not safe without a significant protective infrastructure. But then, neither is drinking water. The safeguards at nuclear power plants in the United States are such that the public has never suffered a radiation-induced death or serious injury owing to a breakdown. The closest call, of course, was Three Mile Island, which caused a great scare in 1979. But after extensive study, no evidence of increased thyroid cancer was found, and seventeen years after the event, a U.S. district court rejected such claims and was upheld by the U.S. Third Court of Appeals. The *political* verdict, however, was: guilty.

Nuclear power is a major means to combat global warming. Its use should be avoided only if it constitutes a threat to life expectancy that outweighs the gains it can give to us. By that criterion, I believe we significantly underuse nuclear power.

There can be very little doubt that global warming is real and man-made. We may have to rename Glacier National Park when its glaciers disappear, in what now looks to be 2030, according to park scientists. Yet as an economist, I have grave doubts that international agreements imposing a globalized so-called cap-and-trade system on CO_2 emissions will prove feasible. Almost all economists applaud the trade aspect. Paying for permission to pollute would eliminate a lot of CO_2 emissions that are associated with low-value-added economic activity. But the critical element of cap and trade is the overall cap a country is allowed. In principle, a country can set a cap on total CO_2 emissions. It can auction off or give away "permissions" adding up to this predetermined limit. Companies that emit less CO_2 than their quota can sell the unused permits in the open market. Those that need to engage in CO_2-emitting activities that cause them to breach their quota can purchase the needed additional permits in the market.

The effectiveness of any cap-and-trade scheme, however, depends on the size of the cap. That is its Achilles' heel. For example, the European Union appeared to have successfully implemented such a program in 2005, only to find that its cap was too high, meaning it didn't save very much in total emissions. The European Commission reported in May 2006 that the EU's original fifteen members would cut emissions by 2010 by only 0.6 percent compared with 1990 levels. The Kyoto Protocol target is 8 percent by 2012. When that fact emerged, the price of permits fell by two-thirds. The system inconvenienced very few.

There is no effective way to meaningfully reduce emissions without negatively impacting a large part of an economy. Net, it is a tax. If the cap is low enough to make a meaningful inroad into CO_2 emissions, permits will become expensive and large numbers of companies will experience cost increases that make them less competitive. Jobs will be lost and real incomes of workers constrained. Can a national parliament vote to impose costs on constituents when the benefits of its actions are spread across the globe, wholly independently of where the CO_2 savings come from?

More generally, can a democratic government stand against an accusation that whatever savings in CO_2 emissions are pressed on its constituents, they are likely to be more than wiped out by increased emissions coming from developing countries that were not included in the agreement reached in Kyoto in 1997? And can developing countries be asked to forgo creating the carbon emissions associated with economic development? Should access to "free" pollution permits be shut off only after a large number of countries have become developed? I doubt very much that a Kyoto-type accord will bring world agreement on some form of penalty for the emission of greenhouse gases. Spewing CO_2 into the atmosphere is as much a violation of property rights as my dumping refuse into my neighbor's yard. But protecting such rights and assessing the costs of an infringement are exceptionally difficult because monitoring the cost is not feasible. Our recent difficult history with international agreements requiring broad acceptance, whether in the World Trade Organization, the United Nations, or any other world forum, makes me pessimistic. Cap-and-trade systems or carbon taxes are likely to be popular only until real people lose real jobs as their consequence.

Ideally, of course, carbon emissions should be delinked from production technologically *before* cap-and-trade regimes are put in place, rendering the latter unnecessary. Forcing delinkage, which is what caps do, rarely yields an optimum allocation of resources, as the world's experiences with central planning have amply demonstrated. Forced cutbacks in output will doubtless create a political response to curb imports. That process leads to a gradual reversal of the gains of postwar liberalization. A carbon tax might not be job-destroying if it were uniform across the globe, but I am skeptical that such uniformity is even remotely feasible. Unless we find technologies to delink emissions from output, emissions can be suppressed only through lower production and employment. If we do find those technologies, emissions will fall without a cap-and-trade regime. An effective cap-and-trade regime might be expected to create price incentives for developing new technology, but the development process would likely be too protracted for political comfort. There are no simple or costless solutions to this vexing problem.

I fear that a more likely response to global warming will be to quibble until the dangers it poses to national economies become more apparent—until, for example, countries are forced to build dikes around vulnerable cities to stave off rising sea levels and floods. (The Dutch have succeeded with dikes for centuries; the Venetians have been less successful.) Remediation is far more likely than prevention to garner adequate political and popular support. It has the advantage that the costs are borne by the same populace that achieves the benefits. But if there is more to global warming than flooding (for example, adverse weather), that solution will fall short.

The preceding analysis leads us to another hard truth: We are unlikely to wean ourselves fully from traditional petroleum for as long as it lasts. The call for "energy independence" by President Nixon in 1973 was political grandstanding, as were similar declarations by subsequent presidents. The only meaningful definition of energy independence is world price leadership based on the availability of extensive, unexploited reserves in the ground or the type of shut-in excess crude oil that the Texas Railroad Commission controlled. Petroleum independence from a national-security perspective, which the United States enjoyed until 1971, is long gone.

How many years will the oil last? Supplies will shrink well before the end of this century, most experts now say. Of course, pundits have been forecasting the peak and decline of the production of petroleum since shortly after Colonel Drake struck oil in 1859 in Titusville, Pennsylvania. Few doubt that oil will eventually run out. The reservoirs are finite, as is their number. Crude-oil production peaked in the United States' lower forty-eight states in 1970, in Alaska in 1988, and in the North Sea in 1999, and output of Mexico's vast Cantarell field apparently topped out in 2005. Ultimately, all reservoirs will peak, and few large new ones are likely to be found in the now thoroughly drill-pocked developed world. There is some promise in deepwater exploration and development, but such endeavors are costly. Despite vast investments in exploration and development, proved reserves in the nations composing the Organization for Economic Cooperation and Development have fallen from 113 billion barrels in 1997 to 80 billion barrels in 2006, according to BP, a most useful source of such data. The most recent major discoveries were in Alaska in December 1967, the North Sea in November 1969, and Cantarell in 1971.

Despite all this, calculating the day when conventional world petroleum will reach peak output is not simple, because technology has continually increased recoveries from reservoirs and stretched out projections of when they will finally run dry. The "central-tendency scenarios" of the U.S. Department of Energy now project midcentury as the point when petroleum production will peak worldwide.

Well before the geology of oil reservoir depletion takes hold, however, market forces and consequent price pressures are likely to displace much of current petroleum use in the United States. If history is any guide, oil will be overtaken by less costly alternatives well before conventional oil reserves run out. Indeed, oil displaced coal despite still-vast untapped reserves of coal, and coal displaced wood before our forestlands were denuded. Forecasting oil's supply/demand balance by midcentury, or any other date, is a daunting challenge, but such forecasting is nonetheless a useful exercise as a first approximation of our energy future.

The experience of the past fifty years—and indeed much longer than that—affirms that market forces will play a key role in conserving scarce energy resources, directing those resources to their most highly valued uses. Market-driven improvements in technology and shifts in the structure of economic activity are reducing the intensity of the world's oil use, and recent oil price increases will presumably hasten the displacement of oil-intensive production facilities. Leaving aside the actions of the Texas Railroad Commission, the impact of activist policies since the end of World War II has been minor, and usually overridden by market forces. The imposition of gasoline rationing in 1973 in the United States merely created embarrassingly long lines at American gasoline service stations. Although long-term projections inevitably balance petroleum supply with demand at a level considerably higher than today's nearly eighty-five million barrels a day, too many things can be wrong in such projections, and the markets sense that.* (Oil pundits, I fear, often do not give Murphy's Law the credence it deserves.)

In the United States, hybrids that run on both electricity and gasoline are rapidly gaining share of the light-motor-vehicle market. Over the horizon are plug-in electric vehicles, now in an exploratory stage. I recently had an occasion to drive one. My only complaint was that stepping on the accelerator produced a surge forward accompanied by an eerie and disturbing silence. I predict that the bestselling models will have an audio system that simulates the sound of a gasoline engine revving up. People want the comfort of the expected.

Today, plug-in hybrids or electrics have a niche market. If world turmoil expands, and with it oil prices, plug-ins are going to look quite attractive. If we charged them off an electrical grid that obtained its power from nuclear generation, we would, in addition, remove more CO_2 from the atmosphere than we could by any other feasible change in the way we live today. The Department of Energy estimates that without any additional generating capacity, 84 percent of the 220 million light vehicles on our highways now, if they were plug-in hybrids, could be charged overnight, when electricity load factors are quite low. Modest additions to capacity could accommodate the rest.

As I noted earlier, the ratio of world oil consumption to real GDP, the most general measure of oil use intensity, peaked in 1973 and has progressed steadily downward to the current level of less than two-thirds of

---

*Data on worldwide production and hence consumption are sketchy. The OECD compiles reasonably good data of industrial countries' production, consumption, and inventories of oil. But OECD production makes up only a fourth of world output. Production data for most OPEC members are state secrets. Estimates are made by spotters who count the number and capacity of tankers leaving ports of export. They observe the vessels' draft in order to estimate tons on board. By finding out (in part from recipients of the exports) how much the exporters' oil typically weighs per barrel, the observers are able to convert these tonnage estimates to barrels. Domestic consumption estimates are added to exports net of imports to calculate production.

Even though such estimates are rough, the International Energy Agency's compiled data do describe the general state of world oil balances. Half of refinery capacity resides in and is accurately measured by the OECD. Much of the rest is either reported or reasonably estimated. The ultimate reconciliation is whether world crude-oil production, after adjusting for crude-oil inventories, matches estimates of crude-oil inputs into refineries. The discrepancies are smaller than I would have guessed.

where it was in 1973. However, developing nations have far higher oil use per dollar of GDP than developed countries: China and India have twice that of the United States; Brazil and Mexico, half again higher than the United States. Thus, even though I expect oil intensity to fall for most if not all countries, the large shift of shares of the world's GDP from developed to developing nations (with higher oil intensity) implies markedly less of a decline in world average intensity than that of the individual countries viewed separately.

Two powerful economic forces drive the shift in world GDP shares toward the developing world. The first is demographic—the great mass of the world's younger workers live in developing nations. The second is productivity growth fostered by the shift to free-market capitalism. As I note in the concluding chapter of this book, developed nations, by definition at the cutting edge of technology, need new innovative insights to boost productivity. Developing nations generally can upgrade just by adopting existing technologies. Taking all this into account, the International Energy Agency (IEA) estimates world petroleum consumption growth at 1.3 percent per year on average between 2005 and 2030. The U.S. Energy Information Administration (EIA) projects 1.4 percent.

There is certainly enough oil in the ground to meet a rise in world oil demand from 84 million barrels per day in 2005 to 116 million barrels per day in 2030, the IEA's projection. But will OPEC members, penciled in by the IEA to supply nearly half of the increase, be willing to do so? It is possible. Their populations are growing rapidly, generating an ever-growing need for cash in government budgets and thus increased oil revenues. And it is perfectly plausible that the Iraq insurgency will end and that Iraq will generate more than 5 million barrels a day from its vast untapped reserves, as the EIA projects (up from 2 million barrels per day in 2006). But too many things have to go right to achieve the IEA's and EIA's benign vision of 2030—a balancing of world oil supply and demand with real oil prices only modestly higher. I cannot forget how wildly wrong the U.S. Department of Energy was in its 1979 forecast of $150-a-barrel oil in 1995 (in 2006 prices).*

---

*The DOE's basic miss was to underestimate the long-term price elasticity for oil. It is price elasticity that determines the price change needed to converge supply and demand. Obviously,

To achieve the twin goals of enhanced national security and curtailed global warming, the growth rate of U.S. petroleum consumption must flatten, and eventually consumption must decline outright. The big opportunity for displacement is on America's highways, where one out of every seven barrels of petroleum consumed *worldwide* is burned: 9.5 million barrels per day in gasoline and 2.5 million barrels per day in highway diesel in 2005. The latter is consumed by the nation's eight million heavy trucks, which average less than seven miles to the gallon. By themselves, those heavy trucks consume as much petroleum as all of Germany. Only China and Japan, and of course the United States, consume substantially more.

In looking to the future, we are not likely to find the answer to the question "What does OPEC need to do?" as useful as the answer to the question "What are they *likely* to do?" Attempts to answer "What needs to be done?" have a decidedly mixed historical record of accomplishment. I would thus be more inclined to accept the IEA "contingency forecast," which assumes that OPEC will lag in expanding its crude-oil capacity. The consequence, according to the IEA, will be an average world price of $130 per barrel ($74 in 2005 prices) versus about $50 in 2005. Oil demand in 2030 in this scenario remains surprisingly strong—it is still 109 million barrels per day, up from 84 million in 2005. (The IEA "reference case," in which OPEC is assumed not to lag, foresees 116 million barrels per day.) This is not a shock scenario, and there are lots of scenarios that anticipate far worse.

I trust that at the end of the day we will allow markets to guide our preferences in reducing petroleum consumption. Our experience with oil rationing, as I noted earlier, has been poor.* Another way to curb consumption would be a gasoline tax of, say, $3 or more per gallon, phased in over five or ten years with the resulting revenue used to lower income or other taxes. I come very reluctantly to taxes as an alternative way to accomplish what competitive markets could do. But while oil markets are highly competitive in the developed world, the market approach is clearly vulnerable

---

the lesser the price elasticity, the more prices have to change to balance projected supplies and demands.

*Rationing did seem to work in the United States during World War II, but even then, black markets were extensive.

in a world where a single act of terrorism can shut down massive chunks of oil production and cripple the global economy. There is no insurance, or hedging strategy, that can defend against that. We often forget that to function effectively, a competitive market must be voluntary and free of significant threats of violence, and that trade must be unencumbered. Remember, markets are not ends in themselves. They are constructs to assist populations in achieving the optimum allocation of resources.

We need significantly higher gasoline prices to wean us off gasoline-powered motor vehicles. The geopolitical price premium is apparently not large enough to do that unassisted. The expectation of higher gasoline prices through taxes (or an oil-supply squeeze) would galvanize large technical breakthroughs in the production of ethanol. Corn ethanol, though valuable, can play only a limited role, because its ability to displace gasoline is modest at best. One bushel of corn yields only 7.2 gallons of ethanol, which means that all 11 billion bushels of corn that the United States produced in 2006 would have yielded only 5.2 million barrels of ethanol a day, the energy equivalent of 3.9 million barrels a day of gasoline, or only a third of U.S. highway use, and less than a fifth of the 21 million barrels a day Americans consumed in 2006. And, of course, if all corn were devoted to ethanol, our pigs would starve. Cellulosic ethanol derived from switchgrass or agricultural waste seems to hold greater promise. A joint study by the U.S. Department of Agriculture and Department of Energy credibly estimates that fuels derived from plant matter, or biomass, have "the potential of sustainably supplying much more than one-third of the nation's current petroleum consumption." Other countries' use of biodiesel fuel, which is derived from vegetable oils and other sources, can add to the displacement of OPEC petroleum.

Alternatively, if ethanol fails and if gasoline prices are high enough, plug-in hybrids will significantly displace petroleum consumption over time. Battery technology is making gradual progress; there is already ample electric power being generated to supply plug-ins, particularly if power companies move more toward peak-load pricing. If we can shed our fear of nuclear power, the concern that plug-in hybrids will ultimately be powered from conventional electric utilities burning polluting coal will be resolved.

Conventional hybrid cars, cars running on cellulosic ethanol, and plug-ins could displace a major part of the petroleum burned on U.S. highways. Wider use of more efficient diesel engines could induce further significant displacement of petroleum. But to speed such displacement would require either a vast increase in supplies of cellulosic ethanol or very expensive gasoline. Taxes can ensure the latter. I consider the argument that gasoline tax hikes are politically infeasible irrelevant. Sometimes the duty of political leadership is to convince constituencies that they are just plain wrong. Leaders who do not do that are followers.

A gasoline tax would not impose a very large burden, especially if phased in over a number of years. U.S. household motor fuel outlays, at 3 percent of disposable income in early 2007, are where they were from 1953 to 1973 and far below the 4.5 percent experienced during the crisis of 1980. Even at heights of $3-plus per gallon in July 2006, motor fuel consumed only 3.8 percent of disposable personal income. Yet Americans are very sensitive to gasoline prices. We complain when they rise. Americans nonetheless continue to drive as much as before. In the face of gasoline price spikes, they reduce mileage driven only for a short while. The average number of miles driven per licensed driver has continued to drift upward: from 10,500 miles per driver in 1980 to 14,800 miles in 2006, an increase of 1.3 percent per year. With higher prices, since 2002 the increase has slowed to 0.2 percent per year. Drivers consume less gasoline only because they eventually buy more fuel-efficient cars.

It should be obvious that as long as the United States is beholden to potentially unfriendly sources of oil and gas, we are vulnerable to economic crises over which we have little control. Petroleum is so embedded in today's economic world that an abrupt severance of supply could disrupt our economy and those of other countries. U.S. national security will eventually require that we see petroleum as an energy source of choice, not necessity.

The burgeoning global economy devours vast amounts of energy. Despite the dramatic fall in the amount of oil, and more generally energy, consumed per dollar of world output, all credible longer-term forecasts conclude that to continue on the path of world growth over the next quarter century at rates commensurate with those of the past quarter century will require between one-fourth and two-fifths more oil than we use today.

Most of this oil will have to come from politically volatile regions because, as we have seen, that is where most of the readily extractable oil resides.

What do governments whose economies and citizens have become heavily dependent on imports of oil do when the flow becomes unreliable? The intense attention of the developed world to Middle Eastern political affairs has always been critically tied to oil security. The reaction to, and reversal of, Mossadeq's nationalization of Anglo-Iranian Oil in 1951 and the aborted effort of Britain and France to reverse Nasser's takeover of the key Suez Canal link for oil flows to Europe in 1956 are but two prominent historical examples. And whatever their publicized angst over Saddam Hussein's "weapons of mass destruction," American and British authorities were also concerned about violence in an area that harbors a resource indispensable for the functioning of the world economy.

I am saddened that it is politically inconvenient to acknowledge what everyone knows: the Iraq war is largely about oil. Thus, projections of world oil supply and demand that do not note the highly precarious environment of the Middle East are avoiding the eight-hundred-pound gorilla that could bring world economic growth to a halt. I do not pretend to know how or whether the turmoil in the Middle East will be resolved. I do know that the future of the Middle East is a most important consideration in any long-term energy forecast. Even though oil-use intensity has been significantly reduced, the role of oil is still such that an oil crisis can wreak heavy damage on the world economy. Until industrial economies disengage themselves from, as President George W. Bush put it, "our addiction to oil," the stability of the industrial economies and hence the global economy will remain at risk.

TWENTY-FIVE

THE DELPHIC FUTURE

P eople have always been enthralled by the notion that it is possible to peer into the future. Ancient Greek generals sought audiences with the oracle at Delphi to guide their military adventures. Fortune-tellers thrive to this day. Modern Wall Street employs phalanxes of very smart people to read what the entrails of market performance say about future stock prices.

To what extent *can* we anticipate what lies ahead? Inbred within all of us is the capacity to weigh probabilities, a gift that helps to guide our actions in everything from the mundane to matters of life and death. These judgments are not always right, but they have manifestly been good enough to enable humans to survive and multiply. Modern economic policymakers formalize such decision making in mathematical terms, but humans were judging probabilities long before we invented the math to explain them.

Fortunately for policymakers, there is a degree of historical continuity in the way democratic societies and market economies function. This enables us to reach back into the past to infer inherently persistent stabilities that, while not having the certainty we attach to physical laws, nonetheless offer a window on the future that is more certain than the random outcome of a coin toss. There is indeed much that we can infer about the U.S. economy and the world at large in the decades ahead, especially if we adopt Winston Churchill's insight: "The further backward you look, the further forward you can see."

Most legal and economic institutions change slowly enough to facilitate anticipating future outcomes with some reasonable degree of probability. Nonetheless, a large body of academic literature exists that questions how successfully people can forecast financial outcomes. Proponents of "efficient-market theory" have famously argued that all publicly available information that would induce a stock-price change is efficiently factored by the market into the current price of the stock. Hence, unless an investor has special or inside knowledge not available to the market at large, he or she cannot anticipate price changes. As evidence, they point to the well-known inability of managed equity mutual funds to outperform the S&P 500 consistently. The evidence that some investors do consistently beat the market year after year is not surprising. It's just what one would expect. Even if investment results are purely a matter of chance, a small number of investors will do exceptionally well—as well as the lucky coin tosser who turns up heads ten straight times. The probability of ten consecutive heads is 0.1 percent; thus, when you have millions of coin tossers, or investors, in the end there will be thousands of very successful practitioners of coin tossing, or stock picking.

Yet the theory of efficient markets cannot explain stock-market crashes. How does one make sense of the unprecedented drop (involving the loss of more than a fifth of the total value of the Dow Jones Industrial Average) on October 19, 1987? As a newly anointed Fed chairman, I was watching the markets very closely. What new piece of information surfaced between the market's close at the end of the previous trading day and its close on October 19? I am aware of none. As prices careened downward all that day, human nature, in the form of unreasoning fear, took hold, and investors sought relief from pain by unloading their positions regardless of whether it made financial sense. No financial information was driving those prices. The fear of continued loss of wealth had simply become unbearable.* And while the economy and corporate profits subsequently advanced, it took nearly two years for the Dow to recover fully.

When markets are behaving rationally, as they do almost all the time, they appear to engage in a "random walk": the past gives no better indication than a coin flip of the future direction of the price of a stock. But sometimes that walk is interrupted by a stampede. When gripped by fear, people rush to disengage from commitments, and stocks will plunge. And when people are driven by euphoria, they will drive up prices to nonsensical levels.

So the key question remains, as I summarized it in a 1996 reflection I shall never live down, "How do we know when irrational exuberance has unduly escalated asset values, which then become subject to unexpected and prolonged contractions?" It is often suggested that the richest investors are those best at gauging shifts in human psychology rather than at forecasting earnings per share of ExxonMobil. A whole school of stock-market psychologists has arisen around this thesis. They call themselves Contrarians. They trade on the view that irrational exuberance eventually ends up in falling stock prices, as shares get bid up for no plausible reason, and then, when that becomes evident, fear grips the market and prices unravel. Contrarians pride themselves on trading against crowd psychology. Since stock prices are cyclical, some do succeed by trading contrary to the crowd. But you rarely hear about those who try this approach and lose their shirts. I also never hear much from coin tossers who lose.

Perhaps someday investors will be able to gauge when markets veer from the rational and turn irrational. But I doubt it. Inbred human propensities to swing from euphoria to fear and back again seem permanent: generations of experience do not appear to have tempered those propensities. I would think that we learn from experience, and, in one sense, we do. I, for example, when asked what worrisome imbalances and problems lie over the forecast horizon, invariably respond that financial crises that are foreseeable by market participants rarely happen. If a stock-market bulge is perceived to be the precursor of a crash, speculators and investors will try to sell out earlier. That defuses the nascent bubble and a crash is avoided. The sudden eruptions of

---

*I find the oft-quoted explanation that it was program trading unconvincing. As prices tumbled, sellers could have turned off the program-trading switch.

fear or euphoria are phenomena that nobody anticipates. The horrendous decline in stocks on "Black Monday" came out of the dark.

Successful investing is difficult. Some of history's most successful investors, such as my friend Warren Buffett, were early to understand the now well-documented anomaly that the rate of return on stocks, even adjusted for risk, exceeds that on less-risky bonds and other debt instruments, provided one is willing to buy and *hold* equities for the very long run. "My favorite holding period is forever," said Buffett in an interview. The market pays a premium to those willing to endure the angst of watching their net worth fluctuate beyond what Wall Streeters call the "sleeping point."

The lessons of stock-market investing apply to the forecasting of whole economies. Because markets tend to steady themselves, a market economy turns out to be more stable and forecastable over the long run than in the short run—assuming, of course, that the society and institutions upon which it rests remain stable. Long-term economic forecasting is grounded in two sets of historically stable data: (1) population, which is the most forecastable statistic with which economists deal, and (2) productivity growth, the consequence of the incremental buildup of knowledge and the source of sustainable growth. Since knowledge is never lost, productivity will always rise.*

What, then, can we reasonably project for the U.S. economy for, say, the year 2030? Little, unless we first specify certain assumptions. I need affirmative answers to the following questions to get started. Will the rule of law still be firm in 2030? Will we still adhere to the principle of globalized free markets, with protectionism held in check? (By protectionism, I mean not just barriers to international trade and finance but governmental restrictions against competition in domestic markets as well.) Will we have fixed our dysfunctional elementary and secondary school systems? Will the consequences of global warming emerge slowly enough so as not to significantly affect U.S. economic activity by 2030? And finally, will we have kept terrorist attacks in the United States at bay? Unsaid are those possibilities, such as a wider war or a pandemic, that could upset any forecast. This is a rather long list of preconditions, but unless I can assume them, it is futile to venture very far over the horizon.

---

*Output per hour, the conventional proxy for productivity, can and does decline at times.

In my experience, the most important is the nature of our rule of law. I do not believe most Americans are aware of how critical the Constitution of the United States has been, and will continue to be, to the prosperity of our nation. To have had, for more than two centuries, unrivaled protection of individual rights, and especially property rights, for all participants in our economy, both native-born and immigrant, is a profoundly important contributor to our adventuresomeness and prosperity. To be largely free of fear of a secret police arbitrarily hauling us off for interrogation for "crimes" we never knew existed is something not to be taken for granted. Nor is freedom from the threat of arbitrary confiscation of a business to which we have devoted much of our life. The principle of individual freedom touches a deep cultural chord in Americans: the belief embodied in our Constitution of the basic equality of all citizens before the law. Reality has not always matched this ideal, and discrimination against African Americans in particular forces us periodically to revisit the early constitutional debates about slavery and its violent resolution in the Civil War; we've come a long way, but we have a distance yet to travel.

America's unrivaled protection of property rights has long attracted foreign investment to our shores. Some investors come in order to participate in a vibrant, open economy; others simply view the United States as a safe haven for their savings that is not available in their home country. As I shall explain, the ability of the American legal system to extend those cherished property rights to an economy predominantly driven by intellectual property will be a major challenge. And, of course, most detrimental of all to our standard of living would be a reemergence of protectionism and other policies that seek stability by preventing the change that is necessary for growth. Economic reregulation would be a distinct step backward in our quest for a prosperous future.

The impact that fixing our school system would have on our future levels of economic activity may not be easy to measure, but unless we do so and begin to reverse a quarter century of increases in income inequality, the cultural ties that bind our society could become undone. Disaffection, breakdowns of authority, even large-scale violence could ensue, jeopardizing the civility on which growing economies depend.

The timing of global warming's impact is even harder to foretell. Today's scientific consensus focuses on effects that are likely to emerge in the second half of this century—a millisecond in climatological time but beyond our forecast period. There is as yet little we can anticipate for the years immediately ahead. Nonetheless, I would expect the markets to respond even before the answers become clear—already insurers are rethinking storm and flood coverage, for example. The prospect of climate change is affecting energy markets as well.

Finally, there is the risk of a renewal of terrorist attacks. When engulfed in fear, people disengage from the normal daily market interaction that is an integral part of an economy based on the division of labor and specialization. The terrorism of 9/11 was a defining moment that underscored the critical value of our highly flexible, largely unregulated economy, which weathered the shock with minimal longer-run consequences. We could probably absorb terrorist attacks like those being experienced today in the Middle East and Europe. But larger-scale attacks* or more widespread warfare would surely be destabilizing.

I have been encouraged by the ability of market economies to persevere through violence and the threats of violence. World Bank data indicate that Israel has managed to create a per capita national income at nearly half the level of that of the United States and roughly equal to per capita incomes recorded in Greece and Portugal.† Lebanon's GDP for 2006, despite the confrontation between Hezbollah and the Israeli military, was down only 4 percent. Even Iraq has managed to maintain a semblance of a functioning economy through all its turmoil of recent years.

The long list of caveats does not inordinately tie our forecasting hands. After all, such a list has always existed in one form or another, and yet the record of *long-term* forecasting of the U.S. economy overall in my experience has been reasonably impressive.

So given the presumed base of global, flexible markets protected by the rule of law, what can we project as our most likely future? What is the most likely level of overall activity we can expect in our arbitrarily chosen 2030 forecast year? We can project real GDP as long as we have projections of

---

*A nuclear detonation on U.S. soil, I fear, could temporarily unhinge our economy.
†U.S. aid accounts for only a small part of Israel's economy.

hours worked and productivity, proxied by real GDP per hour. We know with some degree of certainty the size of our population age sixteen and over in 2030. Most of them have already been born. The proportion of the population, especially the part under sixty-five years of age, that participates in our labor force is high and reasonably stable. Our population older than sixty-five years is expected to almost double by 2030, and the current 15 percent participation rate for that part of the labor force will rise as well, thus adding a more than usual number of elderly workers by 2030. The size of immigration within the politically and culturally feasible range of possibilities does not matter much to the overall labor force forecast. Our next step is to set the proportion of the total labor force that will likely be employed in 2030 (or in a contiguous year if 2030 happens to be a year of recession). Given our assumptions and the economy's historical record, it is difficult to imagine the employment rate of the civilian labor force being outside the rather narrow range of 90 to 96 percent (that is, an unemployment rate between 4 and 10 percent). America's fifty-year average is more than 94 percent, with nonrecession years (the assumption for 2030) near 95 percent. Combining labor force participation rates, population projections, a near 5 percent unemployment rate, and a stable workweek yields an annual growth rate in hours worked in the United States through 2030 of 0.5 percent.[*]

The most encouraging aspect of productivity growth is how remarkably stable it has been for the last century and more. Over much of that period, a substantial boost in U.S. productivity reflected the shift of workers from farms to urban factories and service establishments.[†] But gains in national productivity owing to farmworkers moving into higher-productivity nonfarm jobs are essentially over. Less than 2 percent of the U.S. workforce remains on farms, and that number is not likely to change much. Thus, future national productivity growth will closely mirror the growth in nonfarm productivity. Output per hour is the best measure we have of that growth.

---

[*]After a long decline from sixty-hour workweeks a couple of centuries ago, factory average weekly hours settled at forty just after World War II and have held steady ever since. The shift of the employment share to the service sector (where the workweek is shorter) has been reflected in a slight overall decline in the weekly average.

[†]Even to this day output per hour on farms is less than in nonfarm regions, despite the remarkable gains in crop and livestock yields achieved since the end of World War II.

All gains in efficiency are the result of new ideas in the way people organize their physical reality. To be sure, twenty-first-century human beings are physically taller and stronger than earlier generations, thanks to improved nutrition and health. But that has added very little to our ability to produce. Over the generations it has been new ideas embodied in newly built plant and equipment that better leverage and multiply human effort. From the development of the textile loom two centuries ago to today's Internet, output per hour has increased fiftyfold.

Statisticians usually attribute the growth in output per hour to three primary economic "causes": the quantity of physical plant and equipment, which they call "capital deepening"; the quality of labor input, which is a reflection of education; and the otherwise unexplained, which they infer results from organizational restructuring and new insights in how to generate the nation's output. In all categories, productivity growth results from ideas translated into valued goods and services. The quality of raw materials used in the production process adds only modestly.

If we smooth through the raw data on output per hour, a remarkably stable pattern of growth emerges, going back to 1870. Annual growth of nonfarm business output per hour has averaged close to 2.2 percent since then. Even without adjusting for the business cycle, wars, and other crises, the range of overlapping consecutive fifteen-year averages of the annual increase in output per hour stays consistently between 1 and 3 percent.* I suspect that a good deal of even that modest volatility is statistical "noise," random aberrations resulting from the uncertain quality of the data, especially for the years preceding World War II.

There is little doubt, however, that the burst of U.S. nonfarm productivity growth from 1995 to 2002 has given way to a lessened pace of growth. Output per hour, for example, after the large surge in growth peaked at 4 percent (a four-quarter rate of change) and above in 2002 and 2003, slipped to a 1 percent rate by the first quarter of 2007. Profitable opportunities for further advance appear to have temporarily dwindled, as

---

*Growth rates slowed following the sharp increase in energy costs in the 1970s and presumably because of it. The technology boom of the past decade has accelerated growth in output per hour, restoring it to its long-term trend.

has often occurred in the past. Innovative expansion seems to come in waves. New products and new companies were major factors in the surge of new issues of stock between 1997 and 2000, and the apparent fall-off in applications of innovation since then has been reflected in the decline in stock issuance. The slowdown in innovation is particularly evident in the dramatic swing in corporations' use of their internal cash flow (the result of earlier gains in the application of new technologies) from fixed investment to buybacks of company common stock and cash disbursed to shareholders in the process of implementing mergers and acquisitions. Such return of cash to shareholders of nonfinancial corporations rose from $180 billion in 2003 to more than $700 billion in 2006. Fixed investment, on the other hand, rose only from $748 billion in 2003 to $967 billion in 2006. A corporation returns equity capital to shareholders when it cannot find opportunities for prospective risk-adjusted rates of return superior to the rate of return that the corporation obtains from existing assets. Large cash disbursements to shareholders are usually a signal of lowered prospective rates of return on fixed investments available to the corporation, the likely result of a slowed pace of profitable new applications of innovation.*

Similar signals are reflected in price trends in high-tech equipment, which had been the driving force in rising overall nonfarm productivity growth between 1998 and 2002. At the Federal Reserve, we monitored those price trends as one proxy of the rate of growth of productivity in the high-tech equipment sector itself, a significant part of recent overall productivity gains. Falling prices are generally possible over protracted periods only if unit labor costs are falling in tandem, a trend that is not likely unless productivity is rising fast. And thus the rate of productivity advance should be reflected, and readily observable, in the rate of decline in price. Prices of information-processing equipment and software, for example, fell by more than 4 percent in 2002, but by less than 1 percent at an annual rate by the first quarter of 2007. Prices of information-processing equipment (and software) have fallen every quarter since 1991. But declines were especially

---

*The withdrawal of shareholder capital from corporations with less promising investment opportunities for investment in companies with cutting-edge technologies is an important example of the financing of creative destruction.

rapid during periods of surging innovation, like 1998, when prospective PC buyers often hesitated because prices were dropping rapidly; waiting afforded the opportunity to obtain a cheaper and better PC. The recent slowing of high-tech price decline is thus further confirmation of a decline in the availability of new, cutting-edge technological applications that can be exploited to increase the rate of growth of overall productivity.

As this book goes to press (June 2007), evidence of a rebound in measured productivity growth or the rate of price decline for high-tech equipment is lacking. But history tells us that such a turn will take place. It always has.

Our historical experience strongly suggests that as long as the United States remains at technology's cutting edge, annual productivity growth over the long run should range between 0 and 3 percent. As I've noted, since 1870, growth in nonfarm business output per hour has averaged slightly more than 2 percent per year, which implies that real GDP per hour has risen slightly less.* The near century and a half of data encompasses periods of war, crises, protectionism, inflation, and unemployment. I do not believe it is too great a stretch to assume that the same fundamental forces that governed the United States over the past two centuries will govern this country between now and 2030. That 2 percent is probably not a bad approximation of how fast, on average, humans can advance the frontier of innovation, and it seems our best forecast for the next quarter century.

But why not higher—say, 4 percent per year or more? After all, in much of the developing world, annual output per hour has been averaging growth of far more than 2 percent. But those nations have been able to "borrow" the proved technologies of the developed world and have not themselves had to undertake the slow step-by-step effort to advance cutting-edge technologies.

U.S. productivity in 2005 was 2.8 times higher than in 1955. That is because we knew so much more in 2005 than a half century earlier about how our physical world operates. Every year, millions of innovations incrementally improved overall productivity. This process has become particularly

---

*Much of the GDP excluding nonfarm business is measured by input, not output, and therefore is implicitly assumed to have no productivity growth.

It is conceivable that by 2030 economists will have devised a new means of measuring an economy's productivity directly, rather than through its proxy, output per hour.

evident since the discovery of the exceptional electrical properties of silicon semiconductors following World War II. Gordon Moore, a founder of Intel, suggested in 1965 that the complexity of an integrated circuit, with respect to cost, doubled every year.* He proved prophetic. The persistent downsizing of all electronic applications has enabled the large, bulky walkie-talkies of World War II to morph into today's tiny cell phones, and the boxy original television tubes and computer display screens to go flat. All machinery output, from textile looms and motor vehicles to the routers and servers of the Internet, embodies progressively smaller microprocessors. We have turned light waves into lasers that, when joined with digital technology, dramatically improved data and voice communication and helped create a whole new world of information. It enabled business to adopt just-in-time inventorying, to lower scrap rates, and to reduce the need for backup employment to ensure against production and supply snafus.

Yet why hasn't productivity growth been even faster? Couldn't what we knew in 2005 have been figured out by, say, 1980, thereby doubling the rate of productivity gains (and increases in standard of living) between 1955 and 1980? The simple answer is that human beings are not smart enough. Our history suggests that the ceiling on the productivity growth of an economy over the long term at the cutting edge of technology is at the most 3 percent per year. It takes time to apply new ideas and often decades before those ideas show up in productivity levels. Paul David, a professor of economic history at Stanford, wrote a seminal article in 1989 that addressed the puzzle of why, in the famous words of Nobel laureate economist and then–MIT professor Robert Solow, computers were "everywhere but in the productivity statistics."

It was David's article that heightened my interest in long-term productivity trends. He pointed out that it often took decades for a new invention to be diffused sufficiently widely to affect the levels of productivity. As an

---

*Ten years later, in 1975, Moore revisited his analysis and reported, "I had no idea this was going to be an accurate prediction, but amazingly enough instead of ten doubling[s], we got nine over the ten years." He added that he thought the rate of doubling from then on would slow to a still-amazing once every two years. Moore's basic insight has now held true for more than four decades.

example, he offered the U.S. experience of the gradual displacement of the steam engine with the electric motor.

Following Thomas Edison's spectacular illumination of lower Manhattan in 1882, it took some four decades for even half of the nation's factories to be electrified. Electric power did not fully exhibit its superiority over steam power until a whole generation of multistory factories was displaced after World War I. David explains vividly what caused the delay. The best factories of the day were poorly designed to take advantage of the new technology. They ran on so-called group drives, elaborate arrangements of pulleys and shafts that transferred power from a central source—a steam engine or water turbine—to machines throughout the plant. To avoid power losses and break-downs, the lengths of the shared drive shafts had to be limited. This was best achieved when factories rose vertically, with one or more shafts per floor, each driving a group of machines.*

Simply substituting large electric motors to power the existing drive shafts, even when feasible, did not improve productivity very much. Factory owners realized that electricity's revolutionary potential would require far more dramatic change: power delivered by wire made central power sources, group drives, and the very buildings that housed them obsolete. Because electricity opened the way to equipping each production machine with its own small, efficient motor, sprawling single-story plants came into vogue. In them, machinery could readily be arranged and rearranged for greatest efficiency, and materials could be moved about with ease. But abandoning city factories and moving to the wider spaces of the countryside was a slow, capital-intensive process. That was why, David explains, electrifying America's factories took dozens of years. But eventually millions of acres of one-story plants embedding electric-motor-driven power dotted America's Midwest industrial belt, and growth in output per hour finally began to accelerate.

The low-inflation, low-interest-rate period of the early 1960s, as best I can judge, was owing to the application for commercial use of World War II military technology, as well as the large backlog of invention built up during

---

*I recall visiting in the 1960s a tall and narrow stamping plant built at the turn of the century. I was struck by its unusual shape. But it was only decades later that I learned that I had entered one of the last surviving relics of a certain aspect of America's industrial history.

the 1930s.* Decades later, the delayed emergence of accelerating productivity repeated itself: computers (and the Internet) are now everywhere, *including the productivity statistics.*†

Which brings us to our bottom line. Coupled with the projected 0.5 percent annual increase in hours worked between 2005 and 2030 that follows from the demographic assumptions cited earlier, a slightly less than 2 percent annual average growth in GDP per hour implies a real GDP growth rate of slightly less than 2.5 percent per year, on average, between now and 2030. That compares with 3.1 percent per year, on average, over the past quarter century, when labor force growth was considerably faster.

A rriving at a credible forecast for the level of real GDP for 2030 is a start, but it doesn't tell us much about the nature of the dynamic that will be driving U.S. economic activity a quarter century in the future, or about the quality of our lives. For superimposed on these powerful trends will be the consequences of an inevitable completion of major aspects of globalization.

At some point, globalization's vast economic migration—the epoch-making shift of fully half of the world's three-billion-person labor force from behind the walls of economies that were centrally planned, in part or in whole, to competitive world markets—will be complete, or as complete as it can possibly get.

---

*Low inflation reflected flat nonfarm business unit labor cost, the result of solid growth in productivity, which in turn was the result of increased investment in, but especially the delayed application of, the earlier technologies. Professor David demonstrated the extraordinary lag from technological advance to its consequence in rapidly rising total factor productivity, a measure of applied technology and other insights. That disinflationary episode lasted only a few years, coming to an end with the Vietnam military buildup. A much larger continuing disinflation was to come as a consequence of the end of the cold war.
†Recent decades' productivity growth derives largely from the continuous improvement and filling out of networks of interrelated technologies. Innovation renders parts of existing networks obsolete, as new technologies sprout up to replace them. Efficiency and productivity improve. But at any point in the process, only part of what is technologically known has had time to be applied. Purchasing managers year after year consistently identify only half their facilities as embodying state-of-the-art technology. There is always a lot of existing network construction in progress, implying that a higher level of productivity will emerge upon its completion. Whether those uncompleted networks fill out, for example, over two years or four years significantly affects the *rate of growth* of productivity.

The continuing *acceleration* of the flow of workers to competitive markets during the past decade has been a potent disinflationary force. That acceleration has depressed wage growth and held down inflation virtually uniformly across the globe. Leaving aside Venezuela, Argentina, Iran, and Zimbabwe, inflation during 2006 in all developed and major developing nations was clustered between 0 and 7 percent.* Similarly narrow ranges describe long-term interest rates. Such globally subdued price and interest-rate pressures are exceptionally rare in my experience.

For the former centrally planned economies of Eastern Europe, the transition is already largely complete. But that is not the case in China, by far the largest player in the transition. There the movement of workforces from the rural provinces to the highly competitive factories of the Pearl River delta has been gradual and controlled. Of China's nearly 800-million-person labor force, approximately half are now resident in urban areas most subject to competitive forces.†

The rate of flow of workers to competitive labor markets will eventually slow, and as a result, disinflationary pressures should start to lift. China's wage-rate growth should mount, as should its rate of inflation. The first signs are likely to be a rise of export prices, best measured by the prices of Chinese goods imported into the United States.‡ Falling import prices from China have had a powerful ripple effect. They have suppressed the prices of competing U.S.-made goods and contained the wages of the workers who produce them—as well as the wages of any who compete against the workers who produce the goods that vie with the Chinese imports.§ Accordingly,

---

*These rates are as measured by the consumer price index.

†In India, while call centers and a burgeoning high-tech industry garner headlines, the vast bulk of employment remains rural. I expect the rate of migration from the rural areas to cities that produce exportable goods and services to rise, but the numbers do not yet seem large.

‡Export prices reported by China, which have been rising, appear to reflect a significant change in the composition of exports toward higher-pried goods. U.S. import price indexes have fixed quantity weights.

§This process is highly leveraged for imports that compete with domestically produced goods, and especially so for those imports that have substantially different labor costs. If an importer offers a 10 percent discount from prevailing market prices, failure to follow implies a consequent loss of market share. If I am a domestic producer with a modest share of the market, the loss of share could be devastating if I hold prices firm and all other domestic producers meet the importer's price. The risks of such an outcome are often too high to contemplate. Thus,

an easing of disinflationary pressures should foster a pickup of price inflation and wage growth in the United States. It should be noted that import prices from China rose markedly in spring 2007 for the first time in years.

The burden of managing this shift will fall on the Federal Reserve. The final arbiter of inflation is monetary policy. How significant—and how corrosive—these price pressures will become for the American economy will depend in large part on the Fed's ability to respond. When the under-lying disinflationary pressures and excess world saving propensities begin to ease—or what amounts to the same thing, when inflationary pressures and real long-term interest rates rise—the degree of monetary restraint required to contain any given rate of inflation will increase.

How the Federal Reserve responds to a reemergence of inflation and expected falling world saving propensities will have a profound effect not only on how the U.S. economy of 2030 turns out but also, by extension, on our trading partners worldwide. The Federal Reserve's pre-1979 track re-cord in heading off inflationary pressures, as Milton Friedman often pointed out, was not a distinguished one. In part, that earlier history was a conse-quence of poor forecasting and analysis, but it also reflected pressures from populist politicians inherently biased toward lower interest rates. (Friedman was less critical of the Fed's post-1979 performance.) During my eighteen-and-a-half-year tenure, I cannot remember many calls from presidents or Capitol Hill for the Fed to *raise* interest rates. In fact, I believe there was none. As recently as August 1991, Senator Paul Sarbanes, in response to what he considered intolerably high interest rates, sought to remove voting authority on the FOMC from what he perceived were the "inherently hawkish" presidents of the Federal Reserve banks.* Interest rates declined with the 1991 recession, and the proposal was shelved.

I regret to say that Federal Reserve independence is not set in stone. FOMC discretion is granted by statute and can be withdrawn by statute. I fear that my successors on the FOMC, as they strive to maintain price sta-

---

small amounts of imports have often had the effect of bringing prices down for a whole domes-tic U.S. market.

*Historical tabulations had indicated the bank presidents were more inclined to tighten than were Board members. And the bank presidents are not confirmed by the Senate; Federal Re-serve governors are.

bility in the coming quarter century, will run into populist resistance from Congress, if not from the White House. As Fed chairman, I was largely spared such pressures because long-term interest rates, especially mortgage interest rates, declined persistently throughout my tenure.

It is possible that Congress has observed the remarkable prosperity that emerged in the United States and elsewhere as a consequence of low inflation and has learned from this happy circumstance. But I fear that containing inflation through higher interest rates will be as unpopular in the future as it was when Paul Volcker did it more than twenty-five years ago. "You're high on the hit parade for lynching," Senator Mark Andrews told Volcker bluntly in October 1981; Senator Dennis DeConcini complained in 1983 that Volcker had "almost single-handedly caused one of the worst economic crises" in American history. In December 1982, more ominously, *BusinessWeek* reported, "There are a number of bills in the hopper that would severely limit the Fed's vaunted independence by giving Capitol Hill and the Administration a more direct voice in making monetary policy." When it became apparent that the Fed was on the right course, such criticism disappeared virtually overnight—but sadly, so did the collective memory that there had been such shortsighted and counterproductive criticism. Unless politicians remember that events proved such criticism of Fed policy to have been wrong, how does understanding of monetary policy by our political leadership advance? A key question regarding the future is the political environment that the Fed will have to confront in its quest to preserve the low inflation rates of the past quarter century.

This brings us back to globalization. If my suppositions about the nature of the current grip of disinflationary pressure are anywhere near accurate, then wages and prices are being suppressed by a massive shift of low-cost labor, which, by its nature, must come to an end. A lessening in the degree of disinflation suggested by the upturn in prices of U.S. imports from China in spring 2007 and the firming of real long-term interest rates as this book goes to the press raise the possibility that the turn may be upon us sooner rather than later. So at some point in the next few years, unless contained, inflation will return to a higher long-term rate.

But what is that rate? Price levels, as economic historians can best estimate them, did not materially change in the United States or much of Europe between the eighteenth century and World War II. Prices were defined in terms of gold or other precious metals, and paper money was supposed to be convertible into precious metals on demand at a fixed price. While cyclically variable, prices of goods and services exhibited no persistent trend. During wars, governments might print money not convertible into gold or silver, and prices consequently temporarily spiked. Hence the phrase during our Revolutionary War of "not worth a continental," the name of the wartime currency. During our Civil War, the "greenbacks" met a similar fate. Fiat money—paper money created by government decree—was in deep disrepute.

In those years, governments were perceived as unable to affect the business cycle, and few tried. Inflation expectations, as we understand them today, were nil. Money was backed by gold or silver, and price levels over the long run rose or fell owing largely to changes in the supply of gold or silver. The inflation rate over the long run was essentially zero. Moreover, there is ample evidence that interest rates (effectively on borrowed gold) in centuries past were not significantly different from those of the early twentieth century.* All this suggests that for centuries, inflation was quiescent, and therefore so were inflation premiums.

The monetary landscape in the United States changed beginning in the late nineteenth century, when stagnant prices for agricultural produce fostered the free silver movement, which advocated the coinage of silver in a way that would have inflated overall prices. There was deep popular concern over the straitjacket the gold standard placed on prices, most famously expressed in William Jennings Bryan's "Cross of Gold" speech in 1896.

The monetary orthodoxy that defined the gold standard was beginning to crack. Fabian socialism in Britain and later the La Follette Progressive movement in the United States were reordering the priorities of democratic governments. Prices spiked in World War I and fell sharply in its aftermath. But pre-1914 levels were never fully reestablished. Central banks had

---

*British "consols," which were the nineteenth-century equivalent of today's U.S. long-term treasuries, yielded a steady rate of approximately 3 percent from 1840 until World War I. For interesting background, see Sidney Homer and Richard Sylla's *A History of Interest Rates*.

found ways to circumvent gold standard rules. And after the Great Depression of the 1930s, the gold standard was effectively abandoned virtually worldwide.

I have always harbored a nostalgia for the gold standard's inherent price stability—a stable currency was its primary goal. But I've long since acquiesced in the fact that the gold standard does not readily accommodate the widely accepted current view of the appropriate functions of government—in particular the need for government to provide a social safety net. The propensity of Congress to create benefits for constituents without specifying the means by which they are to be funded has led to deficit spending in every fiscal year since 1970, with the exception of the surpluses of 1998 to 2001 generated by the stock-market boom. The shifting of real resources required to perform such functions has imparted a bias toward inflation. In the political arena, the pressure to make low-interest-rate credit generally available and to use fiscal measures to boost employment and avoid the unpleasantness of downward adjustments in nominal wages and prices has become nearly impossible to resist. For the most part, the American people have tolerated the inflation bias as an acceptable cost of the modern welfare state. There is no support for the gold standard today, and I see no likelihood of its return.

Price levels rose sharply during World War II, and although the rate of inflation slowed at the end of the war, it never turned sufficiently negative to restore anything close to the price levels of 1939. The rate of inflation has varied ever since, yet for almost every year during the past seven decades, the rate has been positive, meaning the *level* of prices has continued to rise. In 2006, consumer prices in the United States were almost fifteen times higher than they were in 1939. In fact, the price patterns have much in common with evidence of global warming in recent decades. Both accelerations bear the imprint of human intervention.

We know that the average inflation rate under the gold and earlier commodity standards was essentially zero. At the height of the gold standard between 1870 and 1913, just prior to World War I, the cost of living in the United States, as calculated by the Federal Reserve Bank of New York, rose by a scant 0.2 percent per annum on average. From 1939 to 1989, the year of the fall of the Berlin Wall and before the onset of the post–cold war wage-price disinflation, the CPI rose ninefold, or 4.5 percent per year.* This reflects the fact that there is no inherent anchor in a fiat-money regime. What constitutes its "normal" inflation rate is a function solely of a country's culture and history. In the United States, modest amounts of inflation are politically tolerated, but inflation rates close to double digits create a political storm. Indeed, Richard Nixon felt the political need to impose wage and price controls in 1971 even though the inflation rate was below 5 percent. Thus, while political considerations mean that the gold standard can be ruled out as a way to suppress a forthcoming rise in inflationary pressures, ironically, politics driven by an irate populace just might accomplish the same purpose. But that is unlikely before inflation moves above 5 percent at least. The 4.5 percent inflation rate, on average, for the half century following the abandonment of the gold standard is not necessarily the norm for the future. Nonetheless, it is probably not a bad first approximation of what we will face.

An inflation rate of 4 to 5 percent is not to be taken lightly—no one will be happy to see his or her saved dollars lose half their purchasing power in fifteen years or so. And while it is true that such a rate has not proved economically destabilizing in the past, an inflation projection in that range assumes a generally benign impact of retirement of the baby boomers, at least through the year 2030. As we have seen, today's relative fiscal quiescence masks a pending tsunami. It will hit as a significant proportion of the nation's highly productive population retires to become recipients of our federal pay-as-you-go health and retirement system, rather than contributors to it. Over time, unless this is addressed, it could add massively to the demand for economic resources and heighten inflationary pressures.

Thus, without a change of policy, a higher rate of inflation can be anticipated in the United States. I know that the Federal Reserve, left alone, has the capacity and perseverance to effectively contain the inflation pressures I foresee. Yet to keep the inflation rate down to a gold standard level

---

*Included in this period was the seemingly anomalous low-inflation, low-interest-rate period of the early 1960s, which had many of the characteristics of today's global disinflation. As I noted earlier, its cause was in a way similar to the aftermath of the cold war, in that it was noneconomic: the delayed application for commercial use of gains in military technology during World War II and the large backlog of invention built up during the 1930s.

of under 1 percent, or even a less draconian 1 to 2 percent range, the Fed, given my scenario, would have to constrain monetary expansion so drastically that it could temporarily drive up interest rates into the double-digit range not seen since the days of Paul Volcker. Whether the Fed will be allowed to apply the hard-earned monetary policy lessons of the past four decades is a critical unknown. But the dysfunctional state of American politics does not give me great confidence in the short run. We could instead see a return of populist, anti-Fed rhetoric, which has lain dormant since 1991.

My fear is that as Washington strives to make good on the implicit promises made in the social contract that characterizes contemporary America, CPI inflation rates by 2030 will be some 4½ percent or higher. The "higher" is meant to reflect whatever inflation premium might arise as a consequence of the inadequate funding for health and retirement benefits for baby boomers. In the end, I see a positive fiscal outcome, as I note in chapter 22. But I suspect it is likely that to restore policy sanity we will first have to trudge through economic and political minefields before we act decisively. I am reminded of Winston Churchill's perception of Americans, who "can always be counted on to do the right thing—after they have exhausted all other possibilities." The trip through the minefields is a major source of risk for my forecast, and it could be manifested in higher paths for interest rates and inflation.

An elevated inflation rate, if allowed to develop, will create a different financial environment than currently prevails. In part, this is because its emergence is likely to parallel a decline in the developing world's currently above-normal propensity to save. As noted earlier, developing-country savings rates have historically averaged only a few percentage points higher than those of developed countries. But owing to the combination of a surging China, with its historically high savings rate,* and OPEC's recent huge accumulation of liquid assets,† savings rates in developing countries ballooned to 32 percent in 2006, while the rates in developed countries averaged less than 20 percent.

---

*China's savings rate is the result both of low government provisions for health and retirement and of soaring business savings.

†Oil-exporting nations reported $349 billion in foreign exchange at the end of 2006, compared with only $140 billion at the end of 2002.

As China continues its trek toward Western consumerism, its savings rate will fall. And though oil prices are more likely than not to go higher, any increase in OPEC's savings rates is likely to be far less than has occurred since 2001. Implicit in such a scenario is a consequent removal of an excess of saving intentions over investment intentions and, therefore, the lifting of that important factor that has helped suppress real interest rates since early this decade. Moreover, having largely bestowed its benefits, globalization will slow its pace. The recent frenetic pace of world economic growth will decline. The World Bank estimates that annual global GDP growth at market exchange rates will slow to 3 percent over the next quarter century. Global GDP grew at a 3.7 percent annual rate between 2003 and 2006.

The dispersion of current account balances, a function of the pace of the globalized division of labor and specialization, should also slow. The U.S. current account is thus likely to shrink, though aggregate world imbalances may not. Other countries could eventually replace the United States as the major absorber of cross-border saving flows.

With real interest rates and expected inflation likely to rise on average over the next quarter century, so would nominal long-term rates. The order of magnitude of interest rate change is difficult to pin down because of the uncertainties that a quarter century can bring. But for illustrative purposes, if real rates on ten-year U.S. Treasury notes were to rise by 1 percentage point from today's 2.5 percent (owing to a fall in global saving intentions) and if fiat-money inflation expectations added the 4.5 percentage points it has implied in the past, that would create a nominal yield for the ten-year note of 8 percent. Again, this excludes whatever premium is required to fund the obligations to baby-boomer retirees. But we can take this level as illustrative: sometime before 2030 the world is likely to be trading ten-year U.S. treasuries at a rate of at least 8 percent. This level is only a baseline—an oil crisis, a major terrorist attack, or an impasse in the U.S. Congress over future budget problems could send long-term rates significantly higher for brief periods.

There are other threats to the long-term financial stability of the United States and the rest of the world besides a rise in riskless interest rates. A hallmark of the past two decades has been a persistent fall in risk premiums. It is difficult to discern whether investors believe underlying risks have diminished and hence they do not require the yield premiums over riskless trea-suries that were prevalent in the past, or whether it is a need for additional interest income that is pushing them to reach for higher-yielding debt in-struments. Spreads over U.S. treasuries of CCC-rated corporate bonds (so-called junk bonds) in mid-2007 were mind-bogglingly low. For example, this spread declined from 23 percentage points amid a plethora of junk bond defaults at the end of the recession in October 2002 to little more than 4 percentage points in June 2007, despite a large rise in issuance of CCC bonds. Spreads of emerging-market bond yields over those of U.S. treasuries have declined from 10 percentage points in 2002 to less than 1½ percent-age points in June 2007. This compression of risk premiums is global. I am uncertain whether in periods of euphoria people reach for an amount of risk that is at the outer limits of human tolerance, irrespective of the insti-tutional environment in which they live. The prevailing financial infra-structure perhaps merely leverages this risk tolerance. For decades prior to the Civil War, banks had to hold capital well in excess of 40 percent to se-cure their notes and deposits. By 1900, national banks' capital cover was down to 20 percent of assets, to 12 percent by 1925, and below 10 percent in recent years. But owing to financial flexibility and far greater sources of liquidity, the fundamental risk borne by the individual banks, and pre-sumably investors generally, may not have changed much over that time period.

It may not matter. As I noted in my farewell remarks to the Federal Re-serve Bank of Kansas City's Jackson Hole Symposium in August 2005, "History has not dealt kindly with the aftermath of protracted periods of low risk premiums."

At a minimum, as riskless interest rates rise and risk premiums are purged of the unsustainable optimism they now embody, prices of income-earning assets will surely grow far more slowly than during the past six years. As a consequence of the decline in long-term nominal and real inter-est rates since 1981, asset prices worldwide have risen faster than nominal world GDP in every year, with the exceptions of 1987 and 2001–2 (the years of the dot-com bubble collapse). This surge in the value of stocks, real estate deeds, and other claims on income-earning assets—that is, direct and indirect claims on assets, whether physical or intellectual—is what I designate an increase in liquidity. These paper claims represent purchasing power that can quite readily be used to buy a car, say, or a company.

The market value of stock and the liabilities of nonfinancial corporations and governments is the source of investments and hence the creation of liabilities by banks and other financial institutions. This process of financial intermediation is a major cause of the overwhelming sense of liquidity that has suffused financial markets for a quarter century. If interest rates start to rise and asset prices broadly fall, "excess" liquidity will dry up, possibly fairly quickly. Remember, the market value of an income-earning security is its *expected* future income leavened by a discount factor that changes according to euphoria and fear as well as more rational assessments of the future. It is those judgments that determine the value of stock and other income-earning assets. It is those judgments that determine how much wealth a society has. Large manufacturing plants, office towers, even homes, have value only to the extent that market participants value their future use. If the world were to come to an end in an hour, all symbols of wealth would be judged worthless. Something far short of doomsday—say, a dollop more of uncertainty added to the mix of our future outcomes—and market participants will lower their bids and will value real assets less. Nothing has to be happening outside our heads. Value is what people perceive it to be. Hence liquidity can come or go with the appearance of a new idea or fear.

A related concern in financial markets is the large and continuing accumulation of U.S. Treasury securities by foreign central banks, mainly in Asia. Market participants fear an impact on dollar interest and exchange rates if and when those central banks stop purchasing U.S. securities or, worse, try to sell off large blocks of holdings. The accumulations are largely the result of endeavors mainly by China and Japan to suppress their exchange rates to foster exports and economic growth. Between the end of 2001 and March 2007, China and Japan combined accumulated $1.5 trillion of foreign exchange, of which four-fifths appears to be in dollar claims—that is, holdings of U.S. Treasury and agency securities and other short-term claims, including Eurodollars.*

---

*China has embarked on an announced program to diversify part of its huge foreign-exchange reserves (1.2 trillion in dollars and the dollar equivalent of nondollar assets).

Should the rate of accumulation slow or turn to liquidation, there will surely be some downward pressure on the U.S. dollar exchange rate and upward pressure on U.S. long-term interest rates. But the foreign-exchange markets for the major currencies have become so liquid that the currency transactions required to implement large international transfers of U.S. dollar deposits can be accomplished with only modest disturbance to markets. For interest rates, the extent of a rise is likely to be less than many analysts fear, certainly less than a percentage point and conceivably much less. Liquidation of U.S. Treasury securities by central banks (or any other market participant) does not change the total amount outstanding of U.S. Treasury debt. Nor does the outstanding amount of securities or other assets that the central banks purchase with the proceeds of their sales. Such transactions are swaps, which affect the spread between two securities but need not affect the overall level of interest rates. It is similar to an exchange of currencies.*

The impact on interest rate spreads of a swap involving a large block of U.S. treasuries by a central bank (or anyone else) depends on the size of the portfolios of the world's other investors, and, importantly, the proportions of those investments that are close substitutes of treasuries with respect to maturity, the currency of denomination, liquidity, and credit risk. Holders of close substitutes such as AAA corporate bonds and mortgage-backed securities can be induced to swap for treasuries without undue disturbance to markets.

The international financial market has become so large and liquid† that sales of tens of billions of U.S. treasuries, perhaps hundreds of billions, can be transacted without crisis-causing shocks to markets. We have had much evidence of the market's capability to absorb major transfers of U.S. treasuries in recent years. For example, Japanese monetary authorities, after having accumulated nearly $40 billion a month of foreign exchange, pre-

---

*Such swaps are quite different from the liquidation of equities whose values are falling because the discounted expectations of future earnings are falling. In that case, the overall value of equities declines. There is no offset. It is not a swap.

†Aggregate holdings of foreign exchange by central banks and world private-sector portfolios of foreign cross-border liquid assets approached $50 trillion in early 2007, according to the BIS and IMF. Domestic nonfinancial corporate liabilities are also available as substitutes for U.S. treasuries, probably at modest price concessions. Such liabilities net of foreign holdings of the United States and Japan alone amounted to $33 trillion at the end of 2006.

dominantly in U.S. treasuries, between the summer of 2003 and early 2004, abruptly ended that practice in March 2004. Yet it is difficult to find significant traces of that abrupt change in either the prices of the U.S. Treasury ten-year note or the dollar-yen exchange rate. Earlier, Japanese authorities purchased $20 billion of U.S. treasuries *in one day,* with little result.

While it is conceivable that as part of a financial crisis brewing for other reasons, major liquidations in holdings of U.S. treasuries by foreign central banks could cause havoc, I see even that as a stretch.

But that is not the end of financial fears. Along with the dramatic rise in liquidity since the early 1980s has come the development of technologies that have enabled financial markets to revolutionize the spreading of risk, as we have seen. Three or four decades ago, markets could deal only with plain vanilla stocks and bonds. Financial derivatives were simple and few. But with the advent of the ability to do around-the-clock business real-time in today's linked worldwide markets, derivatives, collateralized debt obligations, and other complex products have arisen that can distribute risk across financial products, geography, and time. Although the New York Stock Exchange has become a lesser presence in world finance, its trading volume has risen from several million shares a day in the 1950s to nearly two billion shares a day in recent years. Yet, with the exceptions of financial spasms such as the stock market crash in October 1987 and the crippling crises of 1997–98, markets seem to adjust smoothly from one hour to the next, one day to the next, as if guided by an "international invisible hand," if I may paraphrase Adam Smith. What is happening is that millions of traders worldwide are seeking to buy undervalued assets and sell those that appear overpriced. It is a process that continually improves the efficiency of directing scarce savings to their most productive investment. This process, far from its characterization by populist critics as blind speculation, is a major contributor to a nation's growth in productivity and its standard of living. Nonetheless, the never-ending jockeying for advantage among traders is continuously rebalancing supply and demand at a pace that is too fast for human comprehension. The trades, of necessity, are thus becoming increasingly computerized, and traditional "outcry" trading on the floors of stock and commodity exchanges is rapidly being replaced by computer algorithms. As information costs drop, the nature of the U.S.

economy will change. With investment banks, hedge funds, and private equity funds all seeking niche or above risk-adjusted rates of return, the distinctions between these institutions will gradually blur. So will the defining line between nonfinancial businesses and commercial banks, as the distinction between what constitutes finance and commerce largely disappears.

Markets have become too huge, complex, and fast-moving to be subject to twentieth-century supervision and regulation. No wonder this globalized financial behemoth stretches beyond the full comprehension of even the most sophisticated market participants. Financial regulators are required to oversee a system far more complex than what existed when the regulations still governing financial markets were originally written. Today, oversight of these transactions is essentially by means of individual-market-participant counterparty surveillance. Each lender, to protect its shareholders, keeps a tab on its customers' investment positions. Regulators can still pretend to provide oversight, but their capabilities are much diminished and declining.

For over eighteen years, my Board colleagues and I presided over much of this process at the Fed. Only belatedly did I, and I suspect many of my colleagues, come to realize that the power to regulate administratively was fading. We increasingly judged that we would have to rely on counterparty surveillance to do the heavy lifting. Since markets have become too complex for effective human intervention, the most promising anticrisis policies are those that maintain maximum market flexibility—freedom of action for key market participants such as hedge funds, private equity funds, and investment banks. The elimination of financial market inefficiencies enables liquid free markets to address imbalances. The purpose of hedge funds and others is to make money, but their actions extirpate inefficiencies and imbalances, and thereby reduce the waste of scarce savings. These institutions thereby contribute to higher levels of productivity and overall standards of living.

Many critics find this reliance on the invisible hand to be unsettling. As a precaution and backup, they wonder, should not the world's senior financial officers, such as the finance ministers and central bankers of major nations, seek to regulate this huge new global presence? Even if global regulation can't do much good, at least, it is argued, it cannot do any harm. But in fact it can. Regulation, by its nature, inhibits freedom of market action, and that freedom to act expeditiously is what rebalances markets.

Undermine this freedom and the whole market-balancing process is put at risk. We never, of course, know all the many millions of transactions that occur every day. Neither does a U.S. Air Force B-2 pilot know, *or need to know*, the millions of automatic split-second computer-based adjustments that keep his aircraft in the air.

In today's world, I fail to see how adding more government regulation can help. Collecting data on hedge fund balance sheets, for example, would be futile, since the data would probably be obsolete before the ink dried. Should we set up a global reporting system of the positions of hedge and private equity funds to see if there are any dangerous concentrations that could indicate potential financial implosions? I have been dealing with financial market reports for almost six decades. I would not be able to judge from such reports whether concentrations of positions reflected markets in the process of doing what they are supposed to do—remove imbalances from the system—or whether some dangerous trading was emerging. I would truly be surprised if *anyone* could.

To be sure, the "invisible hand" presupposes that market participants act in their self-interest, and there are occasions when they do take demonstrably stupid risks. For example, I was shaken by the recent revelation that dealers in credit default swaps were being dangerously lax in keeping detailed records of the legal commitments that stemmed from their over-the-counter transactions. In the event of a significant price change, disputes over contract language could produce a real but unnecessary crisis.* This episode was a problem not of market price risk but of operational risk— that is, the risks associated with a breakdown in the infrastructure that enables markets to function.

Superimposed on the longer-term forces I've discussed, it is important to remember, is the business cycle. It is not dead, even though it has been muted for the past two decades. There is little doubt that the emergence of just-in-time inventory programs and increasing service output has markedly diminished the amplitude of fluctuations in GDP. But human nature does not change. History is replete with waves of self-reinforcing enthu-

---

*Fortunately, with the assistance of the Federal Reserve Bank of New York, this particular problem is on its way to being solved.

siasm and despair, innate human characteristics not subject to a learning curve. Those waves are mirrored in the business cycle.

Taken together, the financial problems confronting the next quarter century do not make a pretty picture. Yet we have lived through far worse. None of them will permanently undermine our institutions, or even likely topple the U.S. economy from its place of world leadership. Indeed there are currently a number of feared financial imbalances that are likely to be resolved with far less impact on U.S. economic activity than is generally supposed. I indicated in chapter 18 that the unwinding of our current account deficit is not likely to have a major impact on economic activity or employment. The fear that a liquidation of much of China's and Japan's huge foreign-exchange reserves will drive U.S. interest rates sharply higher and dollar exchange rates lower is also exaggerated.

There is little we can do to avoid the easing of global disinflationary forces. I view that as a return to fiat-money normalcy, not a new aberration. What is more, we have it within our power to sharply mitigate some of the more dire features of the scenario I have outlined above. First, the president and Congress must not interfere with the Federal Open Market Committee's efforts to contain the inevitable inflationary pressures that will eventually emerge (the members will need no encouragement). Monetary policy can simulate the gold standard's stable prices. Episodes of higher interest rates will be required. But the Volcker Fed demonstrated that it can be done.

Second, the president and Congress must make certain that the economic and financial flexibility that enabled the U.S. economy to absorb the shock of 9/11 is not impaired. Markets should remain free to function without the administrative constraints—particularly those on wages, prices, and interest rates—that have disabled them in the past. This is especially important in a world of massive movements of funds, huge trading volumes, and markets rendered inevitably opaque by their increasing complexity. Economic and financial shocks will occur: human nature, with its fears and its foibles, remains a wild card. The resulting shocks will, as always, be difficult to anticipate, so the ability to absorb them is a paramount requirement for stability of output and employment.

Hands-on supervision and regulation—the twentieth-century financial model—is being swamped by the volume and complexity of twenty-first-century finance. Only in areas of operational risk and business and consumer fraud do the principles of twentieth-century regulation remain intact. Much regulation will continue to be aimed at ensuring that rapid-fire, risk-laden dealings are financed by wealthy professional investors, not by the general public. Efforts to monitor and influence market behavior that is proceeding at Mach speeds will fail. Public-sector surveillance is no longer up to the task. The armies of examiners that would be needed to maintain surveillance on today's global transactions would by their actions undermine the financial flexibility so essential to our future. We have no sensible choice other than to let markets work. Market failure is the rare exception, and its consequences can be assuaged by a flexible economic and financial system.

However we get to 2030, the U.S. economy should end up much larger, absent unexpectedly long crises—three-fourths larger in real terms than that in which we operate today. What's more, its output will be far more conceptual in nature. The long-standing trend away from value produced by manual labor and natural resources and toward the intangible value-added we associate with the digital economy can be expected to continue. Today it takes a lot less physical material to produce a unit of output than it did in generations past. Indeed, the physical amount of materials and fuels either consumed in the production of output or embodied in the output has increased very modestly over the past half century. The output of our economy is not quite literally *lighter,* but it is close.

Thin fiber-optic cable, for instance, has replaced huge tonnages of copper wire. New architectural, engineering, and materials technologies have enabled the construction of buildings enclosing the same space with far less physical material than was required fifty or one hundred years ago. Mobile phones have not only downsized but also morphed into multipurpose communication devices. The movement over the decades toward production of services that require little physical input has also been a major contributor to the marked rise in the ratio of constant dollars of GDP to tons of input.

If you compare the dollar value of the gross domestic product—that is, the market value of all goods and services produced—of 2006 with the GDP of 1946, after adjusting for inflation, the GDP of the country over which George W. Bush presides is seven times larger than Harry Truman's. The weight of the inputs of materials required to produce the 2006 output, however, is only modestly greater than was required to produce the 1946 output. This means that almost all of the real-value-added increases in our output reflect the embodiment of ideas.

The dramatic shift during the past half century toward the less tangible and more conceptual—the amount of weight the economy has lost, as it were—stems from several causes. The challenge of accumulating physical goods in an ever more crowded geographical environment has clearly resulted in pressures to economize on size and space. Similarly, the prospect of increasing costs of discovering, developing, and processing ever-larger quantities of physical resources in less amenable terrain has raised marginal costs and shifted producers toward downsized alternatives. Moreover, as the technological frontier has moved forward and pressed for information processing to speed up, the laws of physics have required microchips to become ever more compact.

The new downsized economy operates differently from its predecessors. In the typical case of a manufactured good, the incremental cost of increasing output by one unit ultimately rises as production expands. In the realm of conceptual output, however, production is often characterized by constant, and often negligible, marginal cost. Though the setup cost of creating an online medical dictionary, for instance, may be huge, the cost of reproduction and distribution may be near zero if the means of distribution is the Internet. The emergence of an electronic platform for the transmission of ideas at negligible marginal cost is doubtless an important factor explaining the most recent increased conceptualization of the GDP. The demand for conceptual products is clearly impeded to a much lesser degree by rising marginal cost and, hence, price, than is the demand for physical products.

The high cost of developing software and the negligible production and, if online, distribution costs tend to suggest a natural monopoly—a good or service that is supplied most efficiently by one firm. A stock exchange is an obvious example. It is most efficient to have all the trading of a stock concentrated in one market. Bid-asked spreads narrow and transaction costs decline. In the 1930s, Alcoa was the sole U.S. producer of raw aluminum. It kept its monopoly by passing on, in ever-lower prices, almost all its increases in efficiency. Potential competitors could not envision an acceptable rate of return if they had to match Alcoa's low prices.*

Today's version of that aspiring natural monopoly is Microsoft, with its remarkable dominance in personal computer operating systems. Getting into a market early with the capability to define a new industry's template fends off potential competitors. Creating and cultivating this lock-in effect is thus a prime business strategy in our new digital world. Despite this advantage, Microsoft's natural monopoly has proved far from absolute. The dominance of its Windows operating system has been eroded by competition from Apple and open-source Linux. Natural monopolies, in the end, are displaced by technological breakthroughs and new paradigms.

Strategies come and go, but the ultimate competitive goal remains: gaining the maximum rate of return, adjusted for risk. Competition effectively works, whatever the strategy, provided free and open markets prevail. Antitrust policy, never in my judgment an effective procompetition tool, is going to find its twentieth-century standards far out of date for the new digital age, in which an innovation can turn an eight-hundred-pound gorilla into a baby chimpanzee overnight.[†]

The trend toward conceptual products is irreversibly increasing the emphasis on intellectual property and its protection—a second area of the law that is likely to be challenged. The president's Council of Economic Advisors in early 2006 cited output by industries "highly dependent on patent . . . and copyright protection," such as pharmaceuticals, informa-

---

*It is often said that many companies do lower prices in an attempt to drive competitors out of business. But unless their costs are persistently lower than competitors', this is a losing strategy. To raise prices after potential competitors retire from the market is decidedly short-sighted. Despite claims that it is a common practice, I have seen very little of it in my six decades observing business. It is an effective way to lose customers.

†Antitrust policy in the United States was born in the nineteenth century and evolved in twentieth-century law in reaction to allegations of price fixing and other transgressions contrary to then current views of how markets should work. I have always thought the competitive model employed by the courts to judge infractions was not one that maximized economic efficiency. I fear that applying that twentieth-century model to markets of the twenty-first century will be even more counterproductive. Freeing up markets by withdrawing subsidies and anticompetition regulation, in my judgment, has always been the most effective antimonopoly policy.

tion technology, software, and communications, as accounting for almost a fifth of U.S. economic activity in 2003. The council also estimated that a third of market value of publicly traded U.S. corporations in September 2005 ($15 trillion) was attributable to intellectual property; of that third, software and other copyright-protected materials represented nearly two-fifths, patents a third, and trade secrets the remainder. It is almost certainly the case that intellectual property's share of stock-market value is much larger than its share of economic activity. Industries with disproportionately large shares of intellectual property are also the most rapidly growing industries in the U.S. economy. I see no obstacle to intellectual property's share of GDP rising into 2030.*

Before World War I, markets in the United States were essentially uninhibited by government regulations, but were supported by rights to property, which in those years largely meant physical property. Intellectual property—patents, copyrights, and trademarks—represented a far less important aspect of the economy. One of the most significant inventions of the nineteenth century was the cotton gin: perhaps it was a sign of the times that the cotton gin design was never effectively protected.

Only in recent decades, as the economic product of the United States has become so predominantly conceptual, have issues related to the protection of intellectual property rights come to be seen as significant sources of legal and business uncertainty. In part, this uncertainty derives from the fact that intellectual property is importantly different from physical property. Because physical assets have a material existence, they are more capable of being defended by police or private security forces. By contrast, intellectual property can be stolen by an act as simple as publishing an idea without the permission of the originator. Significantly, one individual's use of an idea does not make that idea unavailable to others for their own simultaneous use.

Even more to the point, new ideas—the building blocks of intellectual

---

*The major loser of GDP share by 2030 is likely to be U.S. manufacturing (excluding high tech). Moreover, continued productivity growth will further shrink the number of jobs in manufacturing

property—almost invariably build on old ideas in ways that are difficult or impossible to trace. From an economic perspective, this provides a rationale for making calculus, developed initially by Newton and Leibniz, freely available, despite the fact that the insights of calculus have immeasurably increased wealth over the generations. Should the law have protected Newton's and Leibniz's claims in the same way that we do those of owners of land? Or should the law allow their insights to be more freely available to those who would build on them, with the aim of maximizing the wealth of the society as a whole? Are all property rights inalienable, or must they conform to the reality that conditions them?

These questions bedevil economists and jurists, for they touch on fundamental principles governing the organization of a modern economy and, hence, its society. Whether we protect intellectual property as an inalienable right or as a privilege vouchsafed by the sovereign state, such protection inevitably entails making choices that have crucial implications for the balance we strike between the interests of those who innovate and those who would benefit from innovation.

My libertarianism draws me to the initial conclusion that if somebody creates an idea, he or she has the right of ownership. Yet the creator of an idea automatically has its use. So the question is: should others be restricted from using the idea? It is at least conceivable that if the right to exclusive use of ideas cumulated through enough generations, some far future newly born generation would find all ideas necessary for survival already legally spoken for, and off-limits without the permission of those holding the rights to the ideas. Clearly the protection of one person's right cannot be at the expense of another's right to life (as it would be in such an instance), or the magnificent edifice of individual rights would harbor an internal contradiction. While far-fetched, this scenario nonetheless demonstrates that if state protection of *some* intellectual creations possibly violates others' rights and hence should be invalid, then some intellectual creations cannot be protected. Once a general principle is breached, where does it end? In practice, of course, only a very small segment of intellectual creation has been chosen for protection under the legal constructs of patents, copyrights, and trademarks.

In the case of physical property, we take it for granted that the ownership right should have the potential of persisting as long as the physical object itself.* In the case of an idea, however, we have chosen to strike a different balance in recognition of the chaos that could follow from having to trace back all the insights implicit in one's current undertaking and pay a royalty to the originator of each one. Rather than adopting that obviously unworkable approach, Americans have chosen instead to follow the lead of British common law and place time limits on intellectual property rights.

But are we striking the right balance? Most participants in the intellectual property debate apply a pragmatic standard: Are the protections sufficiently broad to encourage innovation but not so broad as to shut down follow-on innovations? Are such protections so vague that they produce uncertainties that raise risk premiums and the cost of capital?

Almost four decades ago, a young Stephen Breyer summed up the dilemma by quoting *Hamlet*. Writing in the *Harvard Law Review*, the future Supreme Court justice noted,

> It is difficult to do other than take an ambivalent position on the question of whether current copyright protection—considered as a whole—is justified. One might compare this position with that of Professor Machlup, who, after studying the patent system, concluded, "None of the empirical evidence at our disposal and none of the theoretical arguments presented either confirms or confutes the belief that the patent system has promoted the progress of the technical arts and the productivity of the economy." The position suggests that the case for copyright in books rests not upon proven need, but rather upon uncertainty as to what would happen if protection were removed. One may suspect that the risk of harm is small, but the world without copyright is nonetheless an "undiscover'd country" which "puzzles the will, / And makes us rather bear those ills we have / Than fly to others that we know not of."

---

*In practice, British common law allows the bestowing of property to living people but not to future generations, which could in effect tie up property in perpetuity.

How appropriate is our current system—developed for a world in which physical assets predominated—for an economy in which value increasingly is embodied in ideas rather than tangible capital? Arguably, the single most important economic decision our lawmakers and courts will face in the next twenty-five years is to clarify the rules of intellectual property.

In summary, what can we glean from this attempt to peer into the future? Setting aside the wild cards on which no one has much of a handle—a nuclear detonation on U.S. soil, a flu pandemic, a dramatic revival of protectionism, or a failure to agree on a noninflationary solution to Medicare's fiscal imbalance are just some examples—the United States in 2030 is likely to be characterized by:

1. A real GDP three-fourths higher than that of 2006
2. A continuation of the conceptualization of U.S. GDP and the increased prominence of intellectual property rights legislation and litigation
3. A Federal Reserve System that will be confronted with the challenge of inflation pressures and populist politics that have been relatively quiescent in recent years

If the Fed is prevented from constraining inflationary forces, we could be faced with:

4. A core inflation rate markedly above the 2.2 percent of 2006
5. A ten-year treasury note flirting with a double-digit yield sometime before 2030, compared with under 5 percent in 2006
6. Risk spreads and equity premiums significantly larger than in 2006, and
7. Therefore, yields on stocks greater than in 2006 (the result of a projected quarter century of subdued asset price increases through 2030), and, consonant with that, lower ratios of real estate capitalization

Turning to the outlook for the rest of the world, the United Kingdom has had a remarkable renaissance since Margaret Thatcher's decisive freeing up of market competition in Britain starting in the 1980s. The success was dramatic, and to its credit, "New Labour" under the leadership of Tony Blair and Gordon Brown embraced the new freedoms, tempering their party's historical Fabian socialist ethos with a fresh emphasis on opportunity. Britain has welcomed foreign investment and takeovers of British corporate icons. The current government recognized that aside from issues of national security and pride, the nationality of British corporate shareholders has little impact on the standard of living of the average citizen.

Today London is arguably the world's leader in cross-border finance, though New York, by financing much of the vast economy of the United States, remains the financial capital of the world. London's restoration of its nineteenth-century dominance of international markets began in 1986 with the "Big Bang" that significantly deregulated British finance, and there has been no turning back. Inventive technologies have dramatically improved the effectiveness with which global savings have been employed to finance global investment in plant and equipment. That improved productivity of capital has engendered increased incomes for financial expertise, and UK finance has prospered. The large tax revenues that have emerged have been used by the Labour government to counter the income inequality that is an inevitable by-product of increasing technologically oriented financial competition.

The per capita GDP of the United Kingdom has recently outdistanced those of Germany and France. Britain's demographics are not so dire as those of the Continent, though its education of its children has many of the shortcomings of the American system. If Britain continues its new openness (a highly reasonable expectation), it should do well in the world of 2030.

Continental Europe's outlook will remain unclear until it concludes it cannot maintain a pay-as-you-go welfare state that requires a growing population to finance it. With its birth rate well below its natural replacement rate and few forecasters anticipating a recovery, continental Europe's workforce, unless heavily augmented with new immigrant workers, is set to decline, and its elderly dependency ratio to rise. Europe's appetite for increased immigration, however, seems limited. To counter all this, Europe's productivity growth rate would have to accelerate to a pace that to date has seemed out of reach. Recognizing this problem, the European Council in 2000 advanced an ambitious program, the Lisbon Agenda, to bring the continent's state of technology to world leadership. But the program languished and has since been put on hold. Without an increase in productivity growth, it is difficult to see how Europe can maintain the dominant role it has played in the world economy since the end of World War II. But the emergence of new leaders in France, Germany, and Great Britain may be a signal that Europe will strengthen its commitment to the goals of Lisbon. The seeming convergence of many of the economic perspectives of Nicolas Sarkozy, Angela Merkel, and Gordon Brown makes a European resurgence appear more likely.

Japan's demographic future, if anything, appears even less promising than that of Europe. Japan is strongly resisting immigration, except by those of Japanese ancestry. Its level of technology is already world-class, so its upside potential for productivity growth is presumably as limited as that of the United States. Many forecasters see Japan losing its status as the world's second-largest economy (valued at market exchange rates) sometime before 2030. The Japanese are not likely to find that outcome to their preference and may well take steps to counter it. In any event, Japan will remain wealthy, a formidable force in both technology and finance.

Russia has vast natural resources, but it is plagued by a declining population, and as I noted in chapter 16, the nonenergy sections of its economy are at risk from the effects of the Dutch disease. Its encouraging embrace of the rule of law and respect for property rights has given way under Vladimir Putin to selective enforcement of the law based on nationalist expediency, a negation of the very basis of the rule of law. Because of its energy resources, Russia will remain a formidable player on the global economic scene. But unless it fully restores the rule of law, the nation is unlikely to create a world-class economy. As long as Russia's energy resources remain abundant and their prices high, per capita GDP will likely continue to rise. But Russia's per capita GDP is less than a third (measured by purchasing power parity) of that of the United States, and thus Russia has a long way to go before it joins the club of developed nations.

India has great potential if it can end its embrace of the Fabian social-ism that it inherited from Britain. It has done so for its export-oriented, world-class high-tech services. But this kernel of modernity is only a small part of the sprawling economy of India. Even as tourism-associated service industries prosper, fully three-fifths of India's workforce toil in unproduc-tive agriculture. While India is an admirable democracy—the largest in the world—its economy, despite important reforms since 1990, remains heav-ily bureaucratic. Its economic growth rate in recent years is among the highest in the world, but that is off a very low base. Indeed, India's per cap-ita GDP four decades ago was equal to that of China, but is now less than half of China's and still losing ground. It is conceivable that India can un-dergo as radical a reform as China and become world-prominent. But at this writing, its politics appear to be leading India in a discouraging direction. Fortunately, though India's twenty-first-century service enclave is small, its glitter is just too evident to dismiss. Ideas do matter. And the nation is bound to be attracted by twenty-first-century ideas as well as twenty-first-century technology. India may find it useful to follow the British, whose evolution seems to have melded the free-market notions of the Enlighten-ment with the sensibilities of the Fabians.

Among the challengers to America's world economic leadership, that leaves populous China as the major competitor in 2030. China was more prosperous than Europe in the thirteenth century. It lost its way for many centuries, only to embark on a remarkable renaissance as it transformed itself on a vast scale virtually overnight. China's embrace of free-market compe-tition, first in agriculture, then in industry, and finally in opening itself to international trade and finance, has placed this ancient society on the path to greater political freedom. No matter what official rhetoric may be, the tangible lessening of power from one generation of leaders to the next gives hope that a more democratic China will displace the authoritarian Com-munist Party. While some authoritarian states have for a time successfully adopted competitive market policies, over the longer term the correlation between democracy and open trade is too stark to ignore.

I do not pretend to be able to foresee with certainty whether China will remain on its current path toward greater political freedom and in-creasing prominence as a world economic power, or whether, to retain the political control it is losing day by day to market forces, the Communist Party will seek to reestablish the economic rigidity that prevailed prior to Deng Xiaoping's bold reforms. Much of how the world will look in 2030 rests on this outcome. If China continues to press ahead toward free-market capitalism, it will surely propel the world to new levels of prosperity.

Even as nations as mighty as the United States and China vie for economic supremacy in that new world, they may find themselves partially bending to a force more powerful still: full-blown market globalization. The control of governments over the daily lives of their citizens has dramatically waned as market capitalism has expanded. Gradually, without fanfare, the voluntary promptings of individuals in the marketplace have displaced many of the powers of the state.* Much regulation promulgating limits to commercial transactions has quietly been dismantled in favor of capitalism's market self-regulation. The underlying principle is simple: You cannot have both the markets and a government edict setting the price of copper, for example. One displaces the other. The deregulation of the U.S. economy starting in the 1970s, Britain's freeing of enterprise under Thatcher, Europe's partial efforts in 2000 to start building a world-class competitive market, the embrace of markets by most of the former Soviet bloc, India's struggle to disengage from its stifling bureaucracy, and, of course, China's remarkable resurgence—all have reduced governments' administrative sway over their economies, and hence their societies.

I have learned to view economic outcomes over the long run as being determined largely, but not wholly, by the innate characteristics of people working through the institutions we build to govern the division of labor. The original idea of people's specializing to their mutual benefit is buried too far back in antiquity to identify its source, but such practices inspired John Locke and others of the Enlightenment to articulate notions of inalienable rights as the basis of the rule of law to govern societies. From that hotbed of liberated thought came the insights of Adam Smith and his colleagues, who discovered the basic principles of human behavior that still govern the workings of the productive forces of the marketplace.

---

*A significant segment of postwar government *political* control has been implemented through economic measures.

The last decade of unprecedented economic growth in much of both the developed and the developing world is the ultimate proof of the dysfunction of a more than seventy-year-long economic experiment. The Soviet bloc's stunning collapse led to or accelerated the abandonment of central planning throughout the world, with China and India in the vanguard. The evidence of increasing property rights, and the rule of law more generally, leading to increasing levels of material well-being is extraordinarily persuasive. Formal statistical proof is inhibited by the difficulty of measuring quantitatively subtle changes in the rule of law. But the qualitative evidence is hard to deny. The widespread dismantling of much of the apparatus of state control and its replacement with market-based institutions appears invariably to improve economic performance. Over the past six decades, such improvement has been striking in China, India, Russia, West Germany, and Eastern Europe, to name only the major examples. In fact, the instances in which expansion of free markets, property rights, and the rule of law didn't contribute to economic well-being, and instances where increased central planning enhanced economic well-being, are few. Nonetheless, the rule of law is only a necessary condition, not a sufficient one, for sustained prosperity. Culture, education, and geography each may play a crucial role.

Why is this relationship between the rule of law and material well-being seemingly so immutable? In my experience, it is rooted in a key aspect of human nature. In life, unless we take action, we perish. But action risks unforeseen consequences. The extent to which people are willing to take risks depends on the rewards they think they may gain. Effective property and individual rights in general decrease uncertainty and open a wider scope for risk taking and the actions that can produce material well-being. Inaction produces nothing.

Rational risk taking is indispensable to material progress. When it is impaired or nonexistent, only the most necessary actions are taken. Economic output is minimal, driven not by the calculated willingness to take risks but often as a result of state coercion. The evidence of human history strongly suggests that positive incentives are far more effective than fear and force. The alternative to individual property rights is collective ownership, which has failed time and time again to produce a civil and prosperous society. It did not work for Robert Owen's optimistically named New Harmony in

1826, or for Lenin and Stalin's communism, or for Mao's Cultural Revolution. It is not working today in North Korea or Cuba.

The evidence, as best I can read it, suggests that for any given culture and level of education, the greater the freedom to compete and the stronger the rule of law, the greater the material wealth produced.* But, regrettably, the greater the degree of competition—and, consequently, the more rapid the onset of obsolescence of existing capital facilities and the skills of the workers who staff them—the greater the degree of stress and anxiety experienced by market participants. Many successful companies in Silicon Valley, arguably the poster child of induced obsolescence, have had to reinvent large segments of their businesses every couple of years.

Confronted with the angst of the baneful side of creative destruction, virtually all of the developed world and an ever-increasing part of the developing world have elected to accept a lesser degree of material well-being in exchange for a reduction of competitive stress.

In the United States, Republicans and Democrats have long shared a general consensus in support of Social Security, Medicare, and other programs that emerged from Roosevelt's New Deal and Lyndon Johnson's Great Society, even though there is much disagreement about the details. Virtually all aspects of our existing social safety net would be reauthorized by large majorities of Congress, were they subject to renewal. I do not doubt that, with time and changing economic circumstances, the consensus will evolve, but probably within relatively narrow bounds.

Social safety nets exist virtually everywhere, to a greater or lesser extent. By their nature, they inhibit the full exercise of laissez-faire, mainly through labor laws and income redistribution programs. But it has become evident that in a globally competitive world, there are limits to the size and nature of social safety nets that markets can tolerate without severely negative economic consequences. Continental Europe, for example, is currently struggling to find an acceptable way to scale back retirement benefits and worker protections against job loss.

---

*I am also coming around to the conclusion that the success of five- and ten-year economic forecasts is as much dependent on a forecast of the degree of the rule of law as on our most sophisticated econometrics.

As awesomely productive as market capitalism has proved to be, its Achilles' heel is a growing perception that its rewards, increasingly skewed to the skilled, are not distributed justly. Market capitalism on a global scale continues to require ever-greater skills as one new technology builds on another. Given that raw human intelligence is probably no greater today than in ancient Greece, our advancement will depend on additions to the vast heritage of human knowledge accumulated over the generations.

A dysfunctional U.S. elementary and secondary education system has failed to prepare our students sufficiently rapidly to prevent a shortage of skilled workers and a surfeit of lesser-skilled ones, expanding the pay gap between the two groups. Unless America's education system can raise skill levels as quickly as technology requires, skilled workers will continue to earn greater wage increases, leading to ever more disturbing extremes of income concentration. As I've noted, education reform will take years, and we need to address increasing income inequality now. Increasing taxes on the rich, a seemingly simple remedy, is likely to prove counterproductive to economic growth. We can immediately both damp skilled-worker income and enhance the skill level of our workforce by opening our borders to large numbers of immigrants with the vital skills our economy needs. On the success of these seemingly quite doable reforms involving education and immigration will likely rest popular acceptance of capitalist practice in the United States for years to come.

It is not an accident that human beings persevere and advance in the face of adversity. Adaptation is in our nature, a fact that leads me to be deeply optimistic about our future. Seers from the oracle of Delphi to today's Wall Street futurists have sought to ride this long-term positive trend that human nature directs. The Enlightenment's legacy of individual rights and economic freedom has unleashed billions of people to pursue the imperatives of their nature—to work toward better lives for themselves and their families. Progress is not automatic, however; it will demand future adaptations as yet unimaginable. But the frontier of hope that we all innately pursue will never close.

ACKNOWLEDGMENTS

When I left the Federal Reserve in January 2006, I knew I would miss working with the best team of economists in the world. The transition into private life was eased—and made much more exciting—by the new team that coalesced around the creation of this book.

Some of the more important contributors to this effort are former Fed colleagues. Michelle Smith, Pat Parkinson, Bob Agnew, Karen Johnson, Louise Roseman, Virgil Mattingly, Dave Stockton, Charles Siegman, Joyce Zickler, Nellie Liang, Louise Sheiner, Jim Kennedy, and Tom Connors each filled in gaps in my recollection and provided insights that helped move the writing along. Ted Truman was generous with his time and shared notes and photos from our many trips abroad together. Don Kohn offered valuable reactions to and criticisms of portions of the manuscript.

Lynn Fox, for several years the Fed's communications chief, proved a resourceful researcher, a font of stories and ideas, and an adroit editor of some of the early drafts. David Howard, a former deputy director of the Fed's Division of International Finance and like me a recently minted retiree, brought to bear his expertise to backstop me on a number of key technical discussions; he is both a sharp-eyed critic and a tough debater.

Friends and professional acquaintances took the time to provide essential insights, anecdotes, and information. Martin Anderson shared memories about the Nixon and Reagan years. Justice Stephen Breyer helped sharpen my thinking on intellectual property and other matters of law. Ambassador James Matlock provided recollections of Gorbachev's Soviet Union. With UK prime minister Gordon Brown, I have enjoyed wide-ranging discussions on globalization and the British (and Scottish) Enlightenment. Former president Bill Clinton provided insights into his thinking on economic policy issues; former White House adviser Gene Sperling helped fill in my understanding of the Clinton years.

My especial thanks to Bob Rubin, former secretary of the treasury, who was very forthcoming with his recollections of events we shared. His deputy and eventual successor, Larry Summers, helped our joint understanding of the evolving complexity of globalization during the Clinton presidency and since.

Bob Woodward provided transcripts of extensive interviews with me conducted during my tenure at the Fed—a gesture that showed not only generosity but also sympathy for a novice author. Daniel Yergin's excellent *The Commanding Heights* (coauthored with Joseph Stanislaw) refreshed my memory of many events in which I participated or witnessed. Michael Beschloss read the entire manuscript in draft; his thoughtful insights and adroit editorial suggestions made me appreciate why his own books are so good.

Fact checking and research were the domain of Joan Levinstein and Jane Cavolina, with contributions by Lisa Bergson and Vicky Sufian; Mia Diehl expertly orchestrated our photo research.

This project would have gotten nowhere without Katie Byers, Lisa Panasiti, and Maddy Estrada—my highly organized and highly patient assistants. I marveled at Katie's rapid, error-free transcription of my barely decipherable handwritten prose, often water-soaked. This book came into existence several times over under her fingertips.

I could not have chosen a better editor for this book than The Penguin Press's Scott Moyers. He is a wizard of organization and remarkably knowledgeable over a wide range of subjects. Throughout many months of writing, Scott was encouraging, judicious, thoughtful, and deft; in the bargain, he is the son of former Federal Reserve Board employees. Scott's able assistant, Laura Stickney, managed to keep the disparate members of the book team focused on our common goal—no easy feat. The Penguin Press's president and publisher, Ann Godoff, supported the project with wonderful enthusiasm. The production team—Bruce Giffords, Darren Haggar, Adam Goldberger, and Amanda Dewey—shepherded this volume into print with skill and patience.

My constant guide in the mysterious realm of book writing and publishing has been Bob Barnett. As is true of many books centered on Washington, *The Age of Turbulence* would not have happened as easily without his help.

Peter Petre has been my collaborator in the writing. He taught me the age-old art of narrating in the first person. I had always viewed myself as an observer of events, never as part of them. The transition was a struggle and Peter was patient. He was my window to the reader, with whom he has had vast experience during two decades as a *Fortune* writer and editor. He took special care in getting the autobiographical sections to come alive.

Very few first-time authors can boast of having a muse who is a beautiful, brilliant journalist and an accomplished author herself. I can. Andrea Mitchell, my wife, is my number one ally and closest friend. On this project, she has been my astute counselor and most discerning reader, and her suggestions have helped shape the book. She is, and always will be, my inspiration.

But the final read and draft were mine. There are errors in this book. I do not know where they are. If I did, they wouldn't be there. But with close to two hundred thousand words, my probabilistic mind tells me some are wrong. My apologies in advance.

A NOTE ON SOURCES

The discussions of economics and economic policy in *The Age of Turbulence* rely on data drawn almost entirely from publicly available sources: Web sites and publications of government statistical agencies, industry groups, and professional associations. U.S. government sources include the Bureau of Economic Analysis and the Census Bureau, both of the Department of Commerce; the Bureau of Labor Statistics and other units of the Department of Labor; the Congressional Budget Office; the Office of Management and Budget; the Office of the Comptroller of the Currency; the Social Security Administration; the Federal Deposit Insurance Corporation; the Office of Federal Housing Enterprise Oversight; and, of course, the Board of Governors of the Federal Reserve. International sources include the International Monetary Fund, the World Bank, the Bank for International Settlements, the Organization for Economic Cooperation and Development, and the statistical agencies of other governments, such as China's National Bureau of Statistics and Germany's Federal Statistical Office, as well as central banks.

Professionals at dozens of organizations, associations, and companies responded helpfully to requests for information and data: the Aluminum Association, the American Iron and Steel Institute, the American Presidency Project, the American Water Works Association, the Association of American Railroads, the Can Manufacturers Institute, the Center for the Study of the American Electorate, the Conference Board, the European Bank for Reconstruction and Development, Exxon Mobil Corporation, the Food Marketing Institute, George Washington High School, Global Insight, the Heritage Foundation, JPMorgan Chase, the Juilliard School, the National Bureau of Economic Research, the National Cotton Council of America, the NYU Leonard N. Stern School of Business, the Securities Industry and Financial Markets Association, Standard & Poor's, the U.S. Senate Historical Office, the U.S. Senate Library, Watson Wyatt, and Wilshire Associates. The Web sites of CNET, Gary S. Swindell, Intel, *Wired*, and WTRG Economics were also useful.

The autobiographical sections of *The Age of Turbulence* draw on a wide variety of sources, both contemporary and historical, published and unpublished, as well as discussions with acquaintances and friends whose names may be found in the acknowledgments.

Oral historians Erwin C. Hargrove and Samuel A. Morley interviewed me at length in 1978 about my initial years of public service as chairman of the Council of Economic Advisors; in writing chapter 3 ("Economics Meets Politics"), I used the unpublished transcript of that interview, as well as the edited version that appeared in their book. I also drew upon my notes for speeches and meetings during my decades as a private consultant, and upon articles and essays I wrote for publication during those years. My scripts for the Public Broadcasting System's *Nightly Business Report*, on which I appeared regularly in the 1980s, were another useful source.

Chapter 3 and chapter 4 ("Private Citizen") are also informed by congressional testimony I gave as chairman of the CEA, as well as by testimony I gave as chairman of the National Commission on Social Security Reform. The development of my thinking on economic and public policy may be traced in the transcripts of the hundreds of speeches and congressional testimonies I gave as chairman of the Federal Reserve Board. Speeches and testimony are available online via FRASER, the Federal Reserve Archival System for Economic Research (http://fraser.stlouisfed.org/historicaldocs), on the Federal Reserve Web site (www.federal reserve.gov/newsevents.htm), and by way of Freedom of Information Act requests from the Fed. I sometimes cite verbatim deliberations within the Fed; these are drawn from transcripts of Federal Open Market Committee meetings, which are available through 2001 on the Federal Reserve Web site. All quotations from congressional hearings are in the public record, which may be accessed via the Web site of the Government Printing Office (www.gpoaccess.gov/ chearings/index.html), the Library of Congress, and other avenues.

During my tenure at the Federal Reserve, I made it a practice not to appear on television and rarely did on-the-record interviews with journalists; however, I regularly gave background interviews. Chapters 5 through 11, which cover my career at the Fed, draw on many sessions over the years with Bob Woodward, transcripts of which he generously made available for this project. The transcripts were the basis for *Maestro*, his book about me and the Fed. The narrative in chapter 7 ("A Democrat's Agenda") of discussions with Paul O'Neill during his service as treasury secretary was helped by the accounts in *The Price of Loyalty*, the book on which he cooperated with journalist Ron Suskind. Similarly, my recollections of meetings and experiences with Bob Rubin and Larry Summers in chapters 8, 9, and 10 benefited from Secretary Rubin's memoir written with journalist Jacob Weisberg, *In an Uncertain World*.

My remembrances of the collapse of centralized planning and the growth of global capitalist markets (chapter 6, "The Fall of the Wall"; chapter 19, "Globalization and Regulation"; and elsewhere in this book) were enhanced by Daniel Yergin and Joseph Stanislaw's seminal *The Commanding Heights*; the corresponding Web site (www.pbs.org/commanding heights) features interviews with world leaders and economists that are sometimes quoted in these pages. Tom Friedman's *The World Is Flat* filled in a lot of gaps in my understanding of recent technological advances.

Interviews for this book were conducted with Bill Clinton, Stephen Breyer, Bob Rubin, Martin Anderson, Gene Sperling, Paul David, and others. This account is also informed by the work of my biographers. And the narrative throughout is influenced as well as inspired by the memoir of my wife, Andrea Mitchell, *Talking Back . . . to Presidents, Dictators, and Assorted Scoundrels*.

I have striven to minimize the inevitable errors of memory by drawing quotations, facts, and descriptive details from primary documents, contemporary news accounts (in particular from the *New York Times*, the *Financial Times*, the *Wall Street Journal*, the *Washington Post*, the BBC, the *Economist*, *Newsweek*, and *Time*), standard reference works, and archival and market-data services. *The Age of Turbulence* derives from six decades of accumulated knowledge; to name all my sources, if I could remember them, would probably require as many pages as the book itself. A select bibliography of books and articles follows.

BIBLIOGRAPHY

Allen, Frederick Lewis. *The Lords of Creation.* New York: Harper & Brothers, 1935.

Anderson, Benjamin M. *Economics and the Public Welfare: Financial and Economic History of the United States, 1914–1946.* New York: D. Van Nostrand, 1949.

Anderson, Martin. *Revolution.* San Diego: Harcourt Brace Jovanovich, 1988.

Baker, James A., III, with Steve Fiffer. *"Work hard, study . . . and keep out of politics!": Adventures and Lessons from an Unexpected Public Life.* New York: G. P. Putnam's Sons, 2006.

Beckner, Steven K. *Back from the Brink: The Greenspan Years.* New York: John Wiley & Sons, 1996.

Beman, Lewis. "The Chastening of the Washington Economists." *Fortune,* January 1976.

Bergsten, C. Fred, Bates Gill, Nicholas Lardy, and Derek Mitchell. *China: The Balance Sheet.* New York: Public Affairs (Perseus Books), 2006.

Breyer, Stephen. "The Uneasy Case for Copyright: A Study of Copyright in Books, Photocopies, and Computer Programs." *Harvard Law Review* 84, no. 2 (December 1970): 281–355.

Burck, Gilbert, and Sanford Parker. "The Coming Turn in Consumer Credit." *Fortune,* March 1956.

———. "The Danger in Mortgage Debt." *Fortune,* April 1956.

Burns, Arthur F., and Wesley C. Mitchell. *Measuring Business Cycles.* New York: National Bureau of Economic Research, 1946.

Cannon, Lou. *Reagan.* New York: G. P. Putnam's Sons, 1982.

Cardoso, Fernando Henrique, with Brian Winter. *The Accidental President of Brazil: A Memoir.* New York: Public Affairs, 2006.

Chernow, Ron. *Alexander Hamilton.* New York: Penguin Press, 2004.

———. *The House of Morgan: An American Banking Dynasty and the Rise of Modern Finance.* New York: Touchstone, 1990.

———. *Titan: The Life of John D. Rockefeller, Sr.* New York: Random House, 1998.

David, Paul A. "The Dynamo and the Computer: An Historical Perspective on the Modern Productivity Paradox." *American Economic Review* 80, no. 2 (May 1989): 355–61. See also David's longer paper: "Computer and Dynamo: The Modern Productivity Paradox in a Not-Too-Distant Mirror." *Center for Economic Policy Research* 172, Stanford University (July 1989).

Dornbusch, Rudiger, and Sebastian Edwards, eds. *The Macroeconomics of Populism in Latin America.* Chicago: University of Chicago Press, 1991.

Eichengreen, Barry, and David Leblang. "Democracy and Globalization." *Bank for International Settlements Working Papers* 219 (December 2006).

Engel, Charles, and John H. Rogers. "How Wide Is the Border?" *American Economic Review* 80 (1996): 1112–25.

Feldstein, Martin. "There's More to Growth Than China . . ." *Wall Street Journal,* February 16, 2006.

Ford, Gerald R. *A Time to Heal: The Autobiography of Gerald R. Ford.* New York: Harper & Row / Reader's Digest Association, 1979.

Friedman, Milton, and Rose D. Friedman. *Free to Choose: A Personal Statement.* New York: Harcourt Brace Jovanovich, 1980.

Friedman, Milton, and Anna (Jacobson) Schwartz. *A Monetary History of the United States, 1867–1960.* Princeton, N.J.: Princeton University Press, 1963.

Friedman, Thomas L. *The World Is Flat: A Brief History of the Twenty-first Century.* New York: Farrar, Straus & Giroux, 2005.

Garment, Leonard. *Crazy Rhythm: From Brooklyn and Jazz to Nixon's White House, Watergate, and Beyond.* New York: Times Books, 1997.

Gerstner, Louis V., Jr. "Math Teacher Pay Doesn't Add Up." *Christian Science Monitor,* December 13, 2004.

Goldman, Eric. *The Tragedy of Lyndon Johnson.* New York: Alfred A. Knopf, 1969.

Gorbachev, Mikhail. "Rosneft Will Reinforce Russian Reform." *Financial Times,* July 12, 2006.

Gordon, Robert, Thomas J. Kane, and Douglas O. Staiger. "Identifying Effective Teachers Using Performance on the Job." *The Hamilton Project Policy Brief* 2006-01. Washington, D.C.: Brookings Institution (April 2006).

Greenspan, Herbert. *Recovery Ahead! An Exposition of the Way We're Going Through 1936*. New York: H. R. Regan, 1935.

Hammond, Bray. *Banks and Politics in America: From the Revolution to the Civil War*. Princeton, N.J.: Princeton University Press, 1957.

Hargrove, Erwin, and Samuel Morley, eds. *The President and the Council of Economic Advisers: Interviews with CEA Chairmen*. Boulder, Colo.: Westview Press, 1984.

Heilbroner, Robert. *The Worldly Philosophers: The Lives, Times, and Ideas of the Great Economic Thinkers*. New York: Touchstone, 1999.

Heritage Foundation. "Index of Economic Freedom 2007." www.heritage.org/index/ (accessed March 24, 2007).

Homer, Sidney, and Richard Sylla. *A History of Interest Rates*. New Brunswick, N.J.: Rutgers University Press, 1991.

Hubbard, Glenn, with Eric Engen. "Federal Government Debt and Interest Rates." In *NBER Macroeconomics Annual 2004*. Cambridge, Mass.: MIT Press, 2005.

Ingersoll, Richard M. *Out of Field Teaching and the Limits of Teacher Policy: A Research Report*. Center for the Study of Teaching and Policy, University of Washington (September 2003).

Keynes, John Maynard. *Economic Consequences of the Peace*. New York: Harcourt, Brace and Howe, 1920. www.historical textarchive.com/books.php?op=viewbook &bookid=12 (accessed March 24, 2007).

———. *The General Theory of Employment, Interest and Money*. New York: Harcourt, Brace, 1936.

Klein, Joe. *The Natural: The Misunderstood Presidency of Bill Clinton*. New York: Coronet, 2002.

Lazear, Edward P. "Teacher Incentives." *Swedish Economic Policy Review* 10 (2003): 179–214.

Lefèvre, Edwin. *Reminiscences of a Stock Operator*. Hoboken, N.J.: John Wiley & Sons, 2005.

Locke, John. *The Second Treatise of Civil Government*. London: A. Millar, 1764. www .constitution.org/jl/2ndtreat.htm (accessed April 6, 2007).

Luce, Edward. *In Spite of the Gods: The Strange Rise of Modern India*. London: Little, Brown, 2006.

Maddison, Angus. "Measuring and Interpreting World Economic Performance 1500–2001." *Review of Income and Wealth* 51 (March 2005): 1–35.

———. "The Millennium: Poor Until 1820." *Wall Street Journal*, January 11, 1999.

———. *The World Economy: A Millennial Perspective*. Paris: Development Center of the Organization for Economic Cooperation and Development, 2001.

———. *The World Economy: Historical Statistics*. Paris: Development Center of the Organization for Economic Cooperation and Development, 2003.

McLean, Iain. "Adam Smith and the Modern Left." Lecture delivered at MZES/Facultaet Kolloquium, University of Mannheim, June 15, 2005. www.nuffield.ox.ac.uk/ Politics/papers/2005/mclean%20smith.pdf (accessed March 24, 2007).

Martin, Justin. *Greenspan: The Man Behind Money*. Cambridge, Mass.: Perseus, 2000.

Mitchell, Andrea. *Talking Back . . . to Presidents, Dictators, and Assorted Scoundrels*. New York: Penguin Books, 2007.

Ned Davis Research Inc. *Markets in Motion: A Financial Market History 1900–2004*. New York: John Wiley & Sons, 2005.

Ottaviano, Gianmarco I. P., and Giovanni Peri. "Rethinking the Effects of Immigration on Wages." *NBER Working Papers* 12497 (August 2006).

Perlack, Robert D., Lynn L. Wright, Anthony F. Turhollow, et al. *Biomass as Feedstock for a Bioenergy and Bioproducts Industry: The Technical Feasibility of a Billion-Ton Annual Supply*. Oak Ridge, Tenn.: Oak Ridge National Laboratory, 2005. http://feedstockreview .ornl.gov/pdf/billion%5Fton%5Fvision.pdf (accessed April 17, 2007).

Piketty, Thomas, and Emmanuel Saez. "Income Inequality in the United States, 1913–2002" (November 2004). http://elsa .berkeley.edu/~saez/ (accessed March 28, 2007).

Rand, Ayn. *Atlas Shrugged*. New York: Random House, 1957.

———. *The Fountainhead*. Indianapolis: Bobbs-Merrill, 1943.

Rand, Ayn, with Nathaniel Branden, Alan Greenspan, and Robert Hessen. *Capitalism: The Unknown Ideal*. New York: New American Library, 1966.

Reeves, Richard. *President Reagan: The Tri-*

umph of Imagination. New York: Simon & Schuster, 2005.

Rogers, John H. "Monetary Union, Price Level Convergence, and Inflation: How Close Is Europe to the United States?" *Board of Governors of the Federal Reserve System, International Finance Discussion Paper 740* (2002).

Rubin, Robert E., and Jacob Weisberg. *In an Uncertain World: Tough Choices from Wall Street to Washington.* New York: Random House, 2003.

Sala-i-Martin, Xavier. "The World Distribution of Income (Estimated from Individual Country Distributions)." *NBER Working Papers* 8933 (2002).

Schumpeter, Joseph Alois. *Capitalism, Socialism and Democracy.* New York: Harper & Row, 1975.

Sen, Amartya. "Democracy as a Universal Value." *Journal of Democracy* 10, no. 3 (1999): 3–17.

Siegel, Jeremy J. *Stocks for the Long Run: The Definitive Guide to Financial Market Returns and Long-Term Investment Strategies.* New York: McGraw-Hill, 2002.

Smith, Adam. *An Inquiry into the Nature and Causes of the Wealth of Nations.* 5th ed. London: Methuen & Co., 1904. http://www.econlib.org/library/Smith/smWN.html (accessed March 24, 2007).

———. *Lectures on Jurisprudence.* Vol. 5 of *Glasgow Edition of the Works and Correspondence of Adam Smith.* Indianapolis: Liberty Fund, 1982. http://oll.libertyfund.org/ToC/0141-06.php (accessed March 24, 2007).

———. *The Theory of Moral Sentiments.* New York: Oxford University Press, 1976.

Strouse, Jean. *Morgan: American Financier.* New York: Random House, 1999.

Suskind, Ron. *The Price of Loyalty: George W. Bush, the White House, and the Education of Paul O'Neill.* New York: Simon & Schuster, 2004.

United States. *Historical Statistics of the United States: Colonial Times to 1970.* Washington, D.C.: U.S. Department of Commerce, Bureau of the Census, 1975.

———. *The Report of the President's Commission on an All-Volunteer Armed Force.* New York: Macmillan, 1970.

Useem, Jerry. "'The Devil's Excrement.'" *Fortune,* February 3, 2003.

Volcker, Paul, and Toyoo Gyohten. *Changing Fortunes: The World's Money and the Threat to American Leadership.* New York: Times Books, 1992.

Woodward, Bob. *The Agenda: Inside the Clinton White House.* New York: Simon & Schuster, 1994.

———. *Maestro: Greenspan's Fed and the American Boom.* New York: Simon & Schuster, 2005.

———. *State of Denial.* New York: Simon & Schuster, 2006.

Yergin, Daniel. *The Prize: The Epic Quest for Oil, Money, and Power.* New York: Simon & Schuster, 1991.

Yergin, Daniel, and Joseph Stanislaw. *The Commanding Heights: The Battle Between Government and the Marketplace That Is Remaking the Modern World.* New York: Simon & Schuster, 1998.